CAUGHT

CAUGHT

The Prison State and
the Lockdown of American Politics

Marie Gottschalk

Princeton University Press
Princeton and Oxford

Library of Congress Cataloging-in-Publication Data

Gottschalk, Marie.
Caught : the prison state and the lockdown of American politics / Marie Gottschalk.
pages cm

Summary: "The huge prison buildup of the past four decades has few defenders today, yet reforms to reduce the number of people in U.S. jails and prisons have been remarkably modest. Meanwhile, a carceral state has sprouted in the shadows of mass imprisonment, extending its reach far beyond the prison gate. It includes not only the country's vast archipelago of jails and prisons but also the growing range of penal punishments and controls that lie in the never-never land between prison and full citizenship, from probation and parole to immigrant detention, felon disenfranchisement, and extensive lifetime restrictions on sex offenders. As it sunders families and communities and reworks conceptions of democracy, rights, and citizenship, this ever-widening carceral state poses a formidable political and social challenge. In this book, Marie Gottschalk examines why the carceral state, with its growing number of outcasts, remains so tenacious in the United States. She analyzes the shortcomings of the two dominant penal reform strategies—one focused on addressing racial disparities, the other on seeking bipartisan, race-neutral solutions centered on reentry, justice reinvestment, and reducing recidivism. In this bracing appraisal of the politics of penal reform, Gottschalk exposes the broader pathologies in American politics that are preventing the country from solving its most pressing problems, including the stranglehold that neoliberalism exerts on public policy. She concludes by sketching out a promising alternative path to begin dismantling the carceral state."—Provided by publisher.

Includes bibliographical references and index.

ISBN 978-0-691-16405-2 (hardback)

1. Prisons—United States. 2. Imprisonment—Government policy—United States. 3. Corrections—Political aspects—United States. 4. United States—Politics and government. I. Title.
HV9471.G667 2006
365'.973—dc23

2014012523

British Library Cataloging-in-Publication Data is available

This book has been composed in Minion Pro and ITC Avant Garde Gothic

Printed on acid-free paper. ∞

Printed in the United States of America

3 5 7 9 10 8 6 4 2

In loving memory of Jai Dev Kohli

I never saw a man who looked
With such a wistful eye
Upon that little tent of blue
Which prisoners call the sky,
And at every drifting cloud that went
With sails of silver by.

—OSCAR WILDE, *The Ballad of Reading Gaol*

Contents

Figures

Abbreviations

ABC	American Bail Coalition
ACA	American Correctional Association
ACLU	American Civil Liberties Union
AEDPA	Antiterrorism and Effective Death Penalty Act of 1996
AFSC	American Friends Service Committee
ALEC	American Legislative Exchange Council
APA	Administrative Procedure Act
ATF	Americans for Tax Reform
BOP	U.S. Federal Bureau of Prisons
CAFRA	Civil Asset Forfeiture Reform Act of 2000
CAP	Criminal Alien Program
CBC	Congressional Black Caucus
CBO	Congressional Budget Office
CCP	Community Corrections Partnership
CCA	Corrections Corporation of America
CCPOA	California Correctional Peace Officers Association
CDC, CDCR	California Department of Corrections and Rehabilitation
COPS	Community Oriented Policing Services
CORE	Congress of Racial Equality
CPT	Committee for the Prevention of Torture and Inhuman or Degrading Treatment or Punishment
CSG	Council of State Governments Justice Center
DEA	Drug Enforcement Administration
DHS	U.S. Department of Homeland Security
DIY	Do It Yourself
DOC	Department of Corrections
DOJ	U.S. Department of Justice
FBI	Federal Bureau of Investigation
FDOC	Florida Department of Corrections
FOP	Fugitive Operations Program
FOT	Fugitive Operations Team
FPI	Federal Prison Industries
GAO	U.S. Government Accountability Office
HOPE	Hawaii's Opportunity Probation with Enforcement
ICE	Immigration and Customs Enforcement
IIRIRA	Illegal Immigration Reform and Immigrant Responsibility Act of 1996
INS	Immigration and Naturalization Service

JLWOP	Juvenile Life in Prison Without the Possibility of Parole
LEAA	Law Enforcement Assistance Administration
LFO	Legal Financial Obligation
LRB	Lease Revenue Bond
LWOP	Life in Prison Without the Possibility of Parole
NAACP	National Association for the Advancement of Colored People
NAAUSA	National Association of Assistant United States Attorneys
NACDL	National Association of Criminal Defense Lawyers
NCIA	National Correctional Industries Association
PIECP	Prison Industries Enhancement Certification Program
PLRA	Prison Litigation Reform Act (1996)
PPACA	Patient Protection and Affordable Care Act (2010)
PREA	Prison Rape Elimination Act of 2003
REIT	Real Estate Investment Trust
SMART	Office of Sex Offender Sentencing, Monitoring, Apprehending, Registering, and Tracking
SORNA	Sex Offender Registration and Notification Act (2006)
SCLC	Southern Christian Leadership Conference
SNCC	Student Nonviolent Coordinating Committee
TCJS	Texas Commission on Jail Standards
TDCJ	Texas Department of Criminal Justice
USMS	U.S. Marshals Service
USSC	U.S. Sentencing Commission
VOTE	Voice of the Ex-Offender
VRA	Voting Rights Act of 1965

CAUGHT

Introduction

The Prison State and the
Lockdown of American Politics

To see what is in front of one's nose needs a constant struggle.
—GEORGE ORWELL

Fifteen years ago, mass imprisonment was largely an invisible issue in the United States. Since then, criticism of the country's extraordinary incarceration rate has become widespread across the political spectrum. The huge prison buildup of the past four decades has few ardent defenders today. But reforms to reduce the number of people in jail and prison have been remarkably modest so far.

Meanwhile, a tenacious carceral state has sprouted in the shadows of mass imprisonment and has been extending its reach far beyond the prison gate. It includes not only the country's vast archipelago of jails and prisons, but also the far-reaching and growing range of penal punishments and controls that lies in the never-never land between the prison gate and full citizenship. As it sunders families and communities and radically reworks conceptions of democracy, rights, and citizenship, the carceral state poses a formidable political and social challenge.

The reach of the carceral state today is truly breathtaking. It extends well beyond the estimated 2.2 million people sitting in jail or prison today in the United States.[1] It encompasses the more than eight million people—or in one in twenty-three adults—who are under some form of state control, including jail, prison, probation, parole, community sanctions, drug courts, immigrant detention, and other forms of government supervision.[2] It also includes the millions of people who are booked into jail each year—perhaps nearly seven million—and the estimated 7.5 percent of all adults who are felons or ex-felons.[3]

The carceral state directly shapes, and in some cases deforms, the lives of tens of millions of people who have never served a day in jail or prison or been arrested. An estimated eight million minors—or one in ten children—have had an incarcerated parent. Two million young children currently have a mother or father serving time in state or federal prison.[4] Millions of people reside in neighborhoods and communities that have been depopulated and upended as so many of their young men and women have been sent away to prison during what should be the prime of their lives. Hundreds of rural communities have chased after the illusion that constructing a prison or jail will jump-start their ailing economies.

The problem of the carceral state is no longer confined to the prison cell and prison yard and to poor urban communities and minority groups—if it ever was. The U.S. penal system has grown so extensive that it has begun to metastasize. It has altered how key governing institutions and public services and benefits operate—everything from elections to schools to public housing. The carceral state also has begun to distort essential demographic, political, and socioeconomic databases, leading to misleading findings about trends in vital areas such as economic growth, political participation, unemployment, poverty, and public health.

The carceral state has been radically remaking conceptions of citizenship as it creates a large and permanent group of political, economic, and social outcasts. It has been cleaving off wide swaths of people in the United States from the promise of the American Dream or "American Creed"—the faith that everyone has an inalienable right to freedom, justice, and equal opportunities to get ahead, and that everyone stands equal before the law.[5] The political consequences of this are potentially explosive because the American Dream arguably has been the country's central ideology, serving as a kind of societal glue holding otherwise disparate groups together.[6]

Millions have been condemned to "civil death," denied core civil liberties and social benefits because of a criminal conviction. An estimated six million people have been disenfranchised either temporarily or permanently because of a criminal conviction. This is about 2.5 percent of the total U.S. voting age population, or one in forty adults.[7] Millions of Americans have been denied public benefits like student loans, food stamps, and public housing because of their criminal records. Likewise, owing to a prior run-in with the law, many people are ineligible to receive state licenses for a range of occupations—from hairdressing to palm reading to nursing. Many incarcerated mothers and fathers are at risk of having their parental rights severed, sometimes after they have been behind bars for as little as fifteen months.[8]

For those seeking to dismantle the carceral state, the key challenge is not trying to determine what specific sentencing and other reforms would slash the number of people in jail and prison. The real challenge is figuring out how to create a political environment that is more receptive to such reforms and how to make the far-reaching consequences of the carceral state into a leading political and public policy issue.[9]

This book analyzes why the carceral state, with its growing number of outcasts, remains so tenacious in the United States. It examines the shortcomings of the dominant penal reform strategies and lays out an alternative path to dismantling the carceral state. In doing so, I use the problem of the carceral state as a lens to examine the wider pathologies that have captured American politics today and are preventing the country from solving its most pressing problems.

The Leading Penal Reform Strategies

The ways in which elites, interest groups, the media, and social movements define and frame an issue can powerfully influence not only public opinion but also public policy. Under certain circumstances, framing an issue in a new way can release tremendous new forces that transform the public debate.[10] Over the past decade or so, the growing opposition to mass incarceration has tended to gravitate toward two different poles, both of them inadequate in the face of these challenges.

One pole identifies racial disparities, racial discrimination, and institutional racism as the front lines in the challenge to the carceral state. Michelle Alexander's characterization of mass incarceration as "the new Jim Crow" exemplifies this view.[11] Alexander singles out the color-blind racism of the new Jim Crow, especially as manifested in the war on drugs, as the major driver of the carceral state. She contends that the new Jim Crow is in many ways a more challenging political foe than the in-your-face racism of the old Jim Crow.

The other pole seeks to find a winning nonpartisan path out of mass incarceration by downplaying its stark racial causes and racial consequences. The emphasis instead is on how the fiscal burden of the vast penal system is growing untenable. Here the imperative has been to find rational, cost-effective, evidence-based alternatives for some offenders, primarily drug and other nonviolent offenders, without jeopardizing public safety.

This is largely the stance of the Pew Center on the States, the Council of State Governments, and the U.S. Department of Justice. They have joined together to promote reentry programs and justice reinvestment schemes largely aimed at reducing the recidivism rates of ex-offenders. Thanks to their work, the three R's—reentry, justice reinvestment, and recidivism—dominate discussions of penal reform in Washington, DC and in many state capitals. This approach is compatible with the growing push to alter the public conversation about all sorts of social problems by adopting a "practical tone" that avoids discussions of hot-button issues like fairness between groups or the historical legacy of racism.[12]

The new Jim Crow and the fiscal imperative frames have made major contributions to our understanding of the carceral state and have pried open some important political space to challenge it. In particular, the contributions of Alexander's *The New Jim Crow* cannot be underestimated. No other book has been so vital in making the problem of the carceral state starkly visible to the wider public and in rallying members of disadvantaged communities and other groups to take on the project of dismantling it.

But these two frames also have some shortcomings. They have contributed to some public misperceptions about the relationship between crime and punishment and about who is being sent to prison and why. This has fostered some misguided penal reform efforts. Furthermore, these two frames are unlikely to germinate and sustain the broad political movement necessary to dramatically reduce the number of people in jail and prison or ameliorate the many ways in which the carceral state has deformed U.S. society and political institutions.

Race and the Carceral State

Race matters, and it matters profoundly in any discussion of how to dismantle the carceral state. But, as in the case of other major shifts in public policy and American political development, "the racial character of the contemporary system is more than just a legacy of our troubled past."[13] Racial and other disquieting disparities do not automatically flow from that troubled past. They are the product of politics—of how key politicians, other public figures, interest groups, the media, and social movements choose to draw from that past, reinvent that past, and discard pieces of the past as they adjust their political strategies to the political, social, and economic realities of the present. In the process, they create new institutional and political arrangements that inscribe the past in new ways onto the present. As Michelle Alexander so persuasively, eloquently, and mournfully demonstrates in *The New Jim Crow*, the emergence of color-blind racism in the post–civil rights era is one such adaptation that poses a major obstacle to dismantling the carceral state. But there are others.

Building on Alexander's work, I identify some other underlying political, economic, and social factors that spark and sustain such punitive policies not only for certain blacks, but also for certain whites, Latinos, immigrants, and members of other demographic groups. Bluntly stated, the United States would still have an incarceration crisis even if African Americans were sent to prison and jail at "only" the rate at which whites in the United States are currently locked up, as shown in figure 1.1 and elaborated in chapter 6.

A century ago, the massive disenfranchisement of blacks at the dawn of the Jim Crow era through the poll tax, literacy tests, and violent intimidation overshadowed the vast and simultaneous disenfranchisement of poor whites that undermined the growth of the Populist movement in the South. Likewise, the hyper-incarceration of black men today has overshadowed the growing incarceration rates of poor whites, Latinos, immigrants, and women. Many political and policy debates over the carceral state remain mired in viewing this as primarily a black-white issue. Even "Latino civil rights and advocacy organizations have yet to fully understand the devastating effects of a discriminatory criminal justice system on Latino life," explains one knowledgeable observer.[14]

The carceral state has disproportionately hurt African American men. But it also has been targeting a rising number of people from other historically disadvantaged groups. The United States, with just 5 percent of the world's population, incarcerates almost one-third of the 625,000 women and girls confined to jails and prisons worldwide.[15] In a major shift, Hispanics now constitute 35 percent of all federal prisoners, making them the largest ethnic or racial group in the federal prison system.[16] This is a consequence of the escalation in immigration raids and prosecutions for immigration violations, as well as the relative drop in federal prosecutions of certain other crimes, including gun trafficking, corruption, organized crime, and white-collar crime (see figure 10.2, p. 225). Since the 1990s, black-white disparities in incarceration have been falling. Some of this decline is

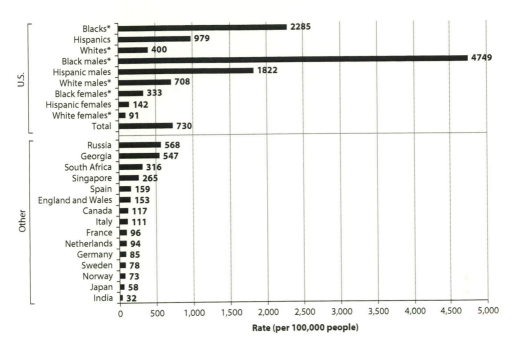

Figure 1.1. Incarceration Rates, Select Countries and Groups

* *Excludes people of Hispanic or Latino origin*
Sources: See p. 338, n. 16; Roy Walmsley, "World Prison Population List," 9th ed. (London: King's College, International Centre for Prison Studies, May 2011), http://www.kcl.ac.uk /depst/law/research/icps/downloads/wppl-8th_41.pdf (retrieved February 11, 2014).

likely the result of changes in the way the U.S. Department of Justice enumerates Hispanic inmates, but some of the decline appears to be real.[17] Poor whites, Hispanics, and women have been a booming growth area for the carceral state, as discussed in chapters 6 and 10. But so far these other groups and their advocates have not been central to the growing debate over penal reform.

Alexander identifies ostensibly color-blind drug laws and law enforcement policies as the main culprit in mass incarceration today. But drug offenders comprise only about 20 percent of offenders in state prisons, or about the same proportion as property offenders. People whose primary offense was a violent one comprise about half of all state inmates. Even if we could release all drug offenders today, without other major changes in U.S. laws and penal policies and practices, the United States would continue to be the world's warden, and a stint in prison or jail would continue to be a rite of passage for many African Americans. Although ending the war on drugs would not make a major dent in the overall prison population, it could reduce considerably the number of incarcerated women, especially African American women. Women, who have been the fastest growing segment of the prison population, are much more likely than male inmates to be serving time for a drug offense.[18] An end to the war on drugs would also likely have a major impact on the federal prison population, since drug offenders constitute about half of all federal inmates.[19]

As the war on crime has been winding down on some fronts, it has been ratcheting up on new ones. With changes in drug policies in some urban areas, the proportion of blacks swept up in the war on drugs has been declining, as discussed in chapter 6. But a new front in the war on drugs has opened up in rural, predominantly white areas that reportedly are facing the scourge of methamphetamine labs, prescription drug abuse, and heroin. Furthermore, since the 1990s, U.S. politicians and policy makers have been laying the institutional and political groundwork for a large-scale war against sex offenders, as discussed in chapter 9. The wider public has been a willing conscript in this new war, which has eerie parallels with the origins and development of the war on drugs four decades ago. The wave of draconian sex offender laws has struck hardest at older white men.

The carceral state also has expanded its capacity to apprehend, detain, punish, and deport immigrants, as elaborated in chapter 10. It has done so partly by retrofitting the hard-line politics, policies, and tactics that fueled the prison boom of the 1980s and 1990s and by creating new institutions that dissolve the distinction between law enforcement and immigration enforcement. The growing criminalization of immigration enforcement beginning in the 1980s and the rapid expansion of the immigrant detention system are creating a "crimmigration crisis."[20]

The historical evidence presented by Alexander and many others is overwhelming that racial animus and the quest to preserve white supremacy have been central factors in American political development, including the development of the U.S. criminal justice system.[21] But as the racial order continues to invent new ways to target blacks, it has generated punitive policies and practices that migrate to other dispossessed groups in the United States. In the words of James Q. Whitman, the U.S. penal system has a strong tendency to "level down." The much-heralded "liberal" features of American political culture ironically have helped to render the U.S. penal system harsher, more degrading, and less forgiving as it extends a brute egalitarianism across the board.[22]

The United States is exceptional not only because it locks up so many people but also because brutal, dehumanizing practices and conditions are endemic to many U.S. jails and prisons, whether they are predominantly black, predominantly white, or mostly multiracial and multiethnic. The wider public has a history of being largely indifferent to prison conditions "even when the victims were white men."[23] The massive increase in the number of inmates since the 1970s has overwhelmed the capacity of many correctional authorities "to safely and humanely house and administer them," as discussed in chapter 2.[24] Today we have what one critic calls "mass imprisonment on the cheap."[25] The majority of U.S. prisons and many jails "hold more people than they can deal with safely and effectively, creating a degree of disorder and tension almost certain to erupt in violence," a national blue-ribbon commission concluded in 2006.[26] Resource constraints alone do not explain why the prison buildup coincided with a new "mean season" in corrections.[27] As the "rehabilitative ideal" was cast out in the 1970s, more prisoners were depicted as brutal, hardened criminals who were neither deserving of nor capable of rehabilitation and redemption.[28]

Right on Crime?

Alexander and many other critics who focus on the racial disparities of the carceral state acknowledge that class, gender, ethnicity, and other factors complicate any discussion of race and mass incarceration but do not develop this point.[29] The intense focus on the racial dimension of the carceral state sometimes obscures the importance of other factors in determining who is punished and for what. In particular, it obscures how certain shifts in the wider political economy pose major impediments to the emergence of a successful broad-based political movement to dismantle the carceral state. Key economic factors discussed in this book include deep structural changes in the job market, growing income and other inequalities, the escalating political assault on the public sector and organized labor, and the economic decline of wide swaths of urban and rural America. A central theme is how the deep penetration of neoliberalism into nearly all aspects of U.S. public policy and politics is fostering economic and political inequalities and eroding democratic institutions.

The predominant economic frameworks employed in public discussions of the carceral state tend to fall into one of two other categories. On the one hand—usually the left hand—are believers in the prison-industrial complex. They contend that the carceral state is largely the consequence of vested economic interests that have captured and corrupted penal policy. For some of these critics, denunciation of the awesome power of the prison-industrial complex substitutes for careful analysis of the specific, complex, and shifting political, economic, and institutional factors that sustain the carceral state and that deeply complicate the politics of penal reform.[30]

On the other hand is the elite bipartisan coalition that has been congealing around the purported fiscal burden of mass imprisonment. The Great Recession has raised many expectations that the United States will begin closing many of its jails and prisons because it can no longer afford to keep so many people locked up. Publications and institutions spanning the political spectrum, from the libertarian *Reason* magazine and Cato Institute to the left-leaning *Nation* and *American Prospect*, have embraced framing the problem of the carceral state as primarily a dollars-and-cents issue that begs for a bipartisan solution.[31] They contend that the United States can do more to promote public safety and save money by reducing its reliance on prisons and by ending expensive, misguided criminal justice adventures like the war on drugs.

A group of brand-name conservatives, including Newt Gingrich, Grover Norquist, and Edwin Meese III, have joined Right on Crime, a national initiative led by the Texas Public Policy Foundation, one of the nation's leading state-based conservative think tanks.[32] This initiative aims to better align the conservative agenda on criminal justice reform with traditional conservative concerns about limited government, individual liberty, and free enterprise.[33] When it launched a new campaign against mass incarceration in spring 2011, the National Association for the Advancement of Colored People (NAACP), the country's foremost identity-based civil rights organization, prominently featured its alliance with the Right on Crime coalition. This prompted a spate of headlines proclaiming "NAACP Joins with Gingrich in Urging Prison Reform."[34]

Alliances like these have bolstered a wave of optimism that the country is finally ready to enact major reforms to reduce the incarceration rate. The penal optimists point to the slew of penal reforms enacted over the past decade or so. These include measures to expand the use of alternative sentences and drug courts, loosen restrictions on parole eligibility, reduce revocations of parole and probation for minor infractions, and dial down the war on drugs (most notably, by legalizing or decriminalizing marijuana possession and reducing mandatory minimums for other drug offenses).[35] They note that dozens of states have cut their corrections budgets in recent years, and many have closed or considered closing penal facilities to save money.[36] They also note that in 2009, the total number of inmates in state prisons dipped for the first time since 1972 and has continued to fall since then.

This optimism that we are at the beginning of the end of the carceral state because the fiscal costs have become too high to sustain is unwarranted for several reasons. Below the surface of the apparent left-right consensus on the fiscal imperative to reduce the number of people in prison or jail are enormous differences over key issues, including juvenile justice reform, indigent defense, executive clemency, the privatization of corrections, and the abuse of civil forfeiture laws, to name just a few.[37] Furthermore, while the total number of people in U.S. jails and prisons has largely stabilized since the onset of the Great Recession, no major contraction appears in sight. The U.S. incarceration rate of 730 per 100,000 is still the highest in the world and rivals the estimated rate that citizens of the Soviet Union were being sent to the gulags during the final years of Stalin's rule in the early 1950s (see figure 1.1).[38]

Between 2009 and 2012, the total inmate population in the United States fell by just 2.5 percent, or 56,500 people.[39] California, which has been under enormous political and legal pressure to reduce its prison population thanks to the 2011 *Brown v. Plata* decision, accounts for about 75 percent of this drop.[40] The number of inmates has continued to grow in about half of the states while declining slightly in the other half.[41] Meanwhile, the federal prison population has continued to gallop along at a brisk pace, as has the number of immigrants detained by the federal government. In 2011, the Department of Justice projected that by 2018 the federal prison population would grow by nearly 12 percent.[42]

It is unlikely that the fiscal and economic burden will single-handedly unhinge the carceral state, even in the wake of the wrenching economic upheavals and distress brought on by the 2008 financial crisis and the Great Recession. Indeed, these upheavals could spur yet another round of get-tough policies, as elaborated in chapter 2. Despite the prison-building boom, corrections costs remain a relatively small component of state expenditures. Although corrections has been one of the fastest growing items in state budgets, second only to Medicaid, it still lags far behind what states spend on other sectors. In fiscal 2010, state expenditures on corrections totaled $48.5 billion, or less than 3 percent of the nearly $2 trillion in total state expenditures. This is less than half of what states spend on highways.[43] Despite substantial increases over the last two decades in the budget for the federal Bureau of Prisons, its nearly $7 billion budget in fiscal 2013 was truly a drop in the bucket of total federal expenditures.

Most prison costs are fixed and are not easily cut. The only way to seriously reduce spending on corrections is to shut down penal facilities and lay off correctional staff. Faced with powerful interests that profit politically and economically from mass imprisonment, states (with a few notable exceptions like New York State) have been making largely symbolic cuts that do not significantly reduce the incarcerated population or save much money.[44] But they do render life in prison and life after prison leaner and meaner, as detailed in chapter 2. Homicides, assaults, and other acts of violence appear to be on the rise in federal penitentiaries and in some state prisons as staff positions go unfilled due to budget cuts.[45] Thirty-six of forty-four states surveyed in the wake of the Great Recession reported cuts in corrections staffing, and half said that they had eliminated or reduced programs for inmates. Several states reported that they had cut back on health services, and nearly a third reported that they had cut back on food services.[46]

Levying fees for meals, housing, and visits to the doctor on people serving time is becoming more common. Politicians in Des Moines, Iowa even considered charging inmates for toilet paper to save a couple of thousand dollars each year.[47] Some local jails have stopped providing underwear to inmates, who must now purchase it themselves from the facility's commissary or go without if they are too indigent. As Donald Leach, a former vice president of the American Jail Association, quipped, "Inmates don't have a constitutional right to underwear."[48] Or to tampons or sanitary napkins, which many female inmates must purchase on their own from the prison commissary or else fashion crude substitutes from toilet paper.

The budget deficit hysteria of the past few years has helped foster what some are calling a new war on the poor with the criminalization of poverty, as discussed in chapter 2.[49] Budget cuts are compromising the activities of the court system and legal services for the poor today. Justice delayed is increasingly justice denied as judges and courthouses go on furloughs, judgeships remain vacant to save money, and trials are postponed. As the number of people arrested and convicted and the severity of punishments escalated over the past four decades, legal aid budgets did not keep pace and in many cases actually declined. "[I]t is better to be rich and guilty than poor and innocent" in America today, lamented Stephen Bright of the Southern Center for Human Rights in summing up the sorry state of legal services for the poor.[50] In February 2012, Attorney General Eric Holder denounced the indigent defense crisis facing the United States.[51] A year later, the fiftieth anniversary of the landmark *Gideon v. Wainwright* decision upholding the right to counsel for indigent defendants was cause not for celebration but for widespread lament. As one observer noted on the anniversary, "[T]here is no meaningful right to counsel for Americans too poor to afford their own attorney."[52] The 2013 sequestration and other recent budget cuts have pushed legal services for the poor past the breaking point in many jurisdictions.[53]

As judicial budgets contract, judges have become exceptionally aggressive about collecting fines and fees. Poor people who cannot pay these off are being sent to jail, a practice of dubious constitutionality. The number of ordinances against the poor for actions such as vagrancy, panhandling, and sleeping on the pavement has been rising over the last decade. At the same time that poverty is being criminalized, states and the federal government have been slashing social services for the poor, which will likely result in more people ending up in prison.

Neoliberalism and the Carceral State

The fiscal imperative argument is inattentive to how the wider U.S. political economy shapes the contours of the carceral state and the political possibilities to dismantle it. Research that situates the U.S. carceral state in a comparative framework suggests that fundamental differences in how the polity and economy are organized explain vast differences in penal policy among industrialized countries. Nicola Lacey and others argue that countries with neoliberal, first-past-the-post electoral systems (notably the United States and Britain) create a reinforcing political and economic environment that fosters more punitive and exclusionary penal policies. Countries that have coordinated market economics and more consensual electoral systems with proportional representation (such as Germany) tend to be less punitive because they are more conducive to inclusionary and welfarist policies.[54]

Such macro-level analyses of political and economic differences to explain cross-national differences in penal policy are extremely revealing. But they come at the cost of more fine-grained understandings of the specific political, economic, and institutional factors that shape penal policy at a specific moment in a specific place. For all their considerable strengths, these bird's eye views are less helpful in explaining important swings in punishment in a single country over time or important variations in punitiveness and penal policy in a single country at a given moment. This is a problem particularly in the case of the United States, which has a federal system of government in which criminal justice policy is primarily forged at the state and local levels; each state operates its own prison system; and counties, not states, run most of the jails.

The construction of such an expansive and unforgiving carceral state in the United States is a national phenomenon that has left no state untouched. All fifty states have seen their incarceration rates explode since the 1970s. But the state-level variation in incarceration rates is still enormous, far greater than what exists across Western Europe. Rates range from a high of more than 1,600 per 100,000 people in Louisiana to a low of about 200 per 100,000 in Rhode Island (see figure 1.2). This great variation and the fact that crime control in the United States is primarily a local and state function, not a federal one, suggest that local, state, and perhaps regional factors might help explain U.S. penal policies. Trying to unravel why the carceral state has been more extensive, abusive, and degrading in some states than others is a growing and promising area of research. In order to understand the political possibilities for dismantling the carceral state, we need a more specific understanding of developments on the ground, especially how the neoliberal turn in public policy got filtered through specific electoral, party, and other institutional developments and arrangements at the local and state levels.

African Americans have been and remain central targets of the carceral state and without question have been disproportionately harmed by it. But more members of other groups are finding themselves economically and politically disenfranchised and socially marginalized as a new political and economic order takes hold and the carceral state expands its reach. A defining feature of that new order is the onslaught of neoliberalism since the 1970s, which has widened the gap between the political and economic haves and the political and economic have-nots.

The turn toward neoliberalism has been a growing area of political and scholarly interest. But as Loïc Wacquant notes, "[N]eoliberalism is an elusive and contested notion, a hybrid term awkwardly suspended between the lay idiom of political debate and the technical terminology of social science."[55] Neoliberalism is an ideology and package of policies that deify low taxes, macroeconomic stabilization (through low inflation and low public debt), financial and trade deregulation, privatization of public assets and services, and the retrenchment of the welfare state. The neoliberal agenda shuns Keynesianism, a comprehensive state-supported safety net, and strong labor unions. Neoliberalism has long rested on privatizing failure and denigrating the role of government to solve economic and social problems.[56]

Today, the neoliberal agenda rests on a powerful consensus among political elites of the two major political parties that the country's budget deficits are the preeminent domestic threats to its economic and political future. This unwarranted budget deficit hysteria—or what Nobel laureate Joseph Stiglitz calls "deficit fetishism"—has asphyxiated the political imagination, not just with respect to mass incarceration but also to many other pressing social and economic problems, such as the lack of universal health care and good public schools for all.[57] These developments have put a premium on pursuing short-term goals couched in budget deficit terms and emphasizing individualized and privatized solutions over government-led ones among the leadership of both parties.[58]

Neoliberalism is a defining global trend. However, it has taken root more quickly in some countries and jurisdictions than others and has captured some social and economic policies faster than others. The specific institutional and political context helps explain why. Wacquant focuses primarily on the imposition of

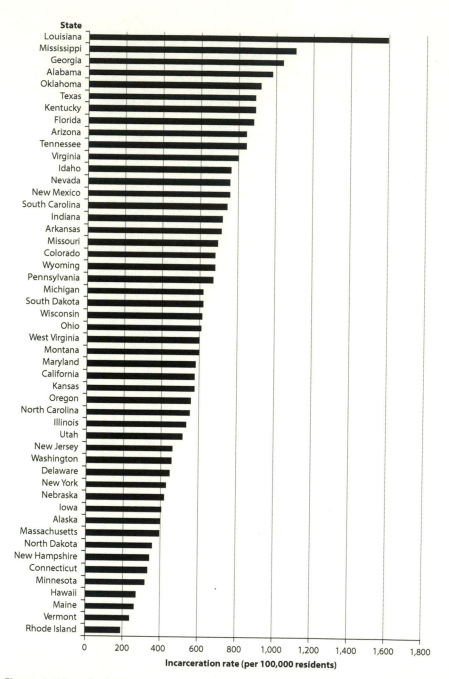

Figure 1.2. State by State Incarceration Rates, 2012

Source: The Sentencing Project, "Interactive Map: Total Corrections Population," http://
www.sentencingproject.org/map/map.cfm#map (retrieved March 13, 2014). Includes both
jail and prison populations. Data from earlier years used when 2012 data were not
available.

neoliberalism at the national and international levels. But neoliberalism operates at multiple levels of government and in multiple political spheres. In short, it is important to understand how neoliberalism operates "in the trenches."[59]

Wacquant argues that the penal policies that flow from neoliberalism have been "remarkably discriminating" as they have targeted the poor and disadvantaged while leaving the middle and upper classes "largely spared."[60] That may have been true in the early decades of the prison buildup, but it is no longer true today. The poor and members of other disadvantaged groups certainly continue to bear the brunt of U.S. penal policies. But the carceral state has grown so expansive that it now deeply penetrates wide swaths of political, economic, and social life in the United States. In their case study of welfare reform, Joe Soss, Richard C. Fording, and Sanford F. Schram show how neoliberalism "de-democratizes the citizenry in far-reaching ways."[61] This is even truer in the case of neoliberalism and the carceral state, as elaborated in chapter 11 and elsewhere in this book. In short, there are no longer six degrees of separation from the carceral state for many Americans.

Neoliberalism in theory and neoliberalism in practice are fraught with contradictions, as Bernard Harcourt demonstrates in his excavation of the deep philosophical and political origins of neoliberalism stretching back to the eighteenth century.[62] Neoliberalism's political vitality has long depended on political sleights of hand that keep those contradictions out of the public eye and out of the public debate. How else could such a massive and costly expansion of the penal system take place at a time when calls for shrinking the government and slashing taxes so dominated the political landscape (as discussed in chapter 3)? In the case of welfare reform, neoliberalism has failed abysmally on its own terms. It ushered in a promiscuous privatization that fostered corruption and fraud without reducing the poverty rate.[63]

As shown in the coming chapters, neoliberalism in penal policy is also failing on its own terms. The state has not retreated. A higher proportion of the population is under its direct control through prison, jail, probation, parole, and community service than at any time in U.S. history. Furthermore, the government's penal, welfare, social service, surveillance, governing, economic, and political functions have become deeply entangled in ways that are creating troubling gradations of citizenship and belonging. In addition, these functions are growing more enmeshed with the private sector, which is even less transparent and accountable than the public sector. Taken together, these developments are upending the lives of enormous swaths of people in the United States, most of whom have never spent a day in jail or prison. They mark the emergence of the carceral state and raise troubling questions about the vitality of U.S. democracy and the legitimacy of the new economic and political order.

Developments in penal policy cannot be understood separately from wider developments in economic and social policy. Wacquant contends that mass incarceration was a political response to contain real and perceived fears of urban disorder and unrest as the Fordist model of industrial production disintegrated and neoliberalism took hold.[64] But, as shown in chapter 7, the neoliberal punitive turn was not just a response to the economic and political disorders of the 1960s and 1970s. It was deeply conditioned by the political struggles in the 1940s and 1950s over law and order and civil rights. It also was deeply conditioned by the reconfigurations of black politics and the broader political terrain with the demise of the civil rights and Black Power movements.

Much of the work on neoliberalism is not attentive enough to the roles of race, gender, and ethnicity in shaping economic policies.[65] Likewise, much of the literature on race is inattentive to how the sinews of the political economy shape policy and politics. The U.S. version of neoliberalism is heavily race-inflected, Michael Dawson argues. As neoliberalism restructures the U.S. economy, it "has sharpened already existing class cleavages, further undermining the myth of a 'monolithic' black community, and by extension making even more difficult the task of building unified black political movements."[66] This helps explain why organized opposition to the carceral state from African Americans has been so muted or ineffective until recently, as elaborated in chapters 6 and 7.

Carceral Clawback

The construction of the carceral state was the result of a complex set of historical, institutional, and political developments. No single factor explains its rise, and no single factor will bring about its demise. Mounting fiscal pressures will not be enough on their own to spur communities, states, and the federal government to make deep and lasting cuts in their prison and jail populations. It was mistakenly assumed four decades ago that shared disillusionment on the right and the left with indeterminate sentences and prison rehabilitation programs would shrink the inmate population. Instead, it exploded. The "race to incarcerate" began in the 1970s at a time when states faced dire financial straits. It persisted over the next four decades despite wide fluctuations in the crime rate, public opinion, and the economy.[67]

Several factors help explain why "carceral clawback" is so tenacious.[68] Prisons are incredibly "resilient, flexible, and enabling institutions that can resist, incorporate, redefine, and absorb critical discourse."[69] Moreover, as the carceral state has grown, so has the political clout and political acumen of groups, institutions, and organizations with vested economic interests in maintaining the world's largest penal system. They include prison guards' unions, state departments of corrections, law enforcement groups, the private corrections industry, and the financial firms that devise bonds and other mechanisms to fund the carceral state. These vested interests were not necessarily the main catalysts for the emergence of the carceral state, but they represent major impediments to reducing the prison population today and reining in the carceral state, as elaborated in chapter 3.

Furthermore, opponents of the carceral state have been poorly positioned to challenge these vested interests. It is not just a question of gross disparities in political resources that disadvantages them. With their single-minded focus on mobilizing around a particular criminal justice issue, such as opposition to the death penalty, some advocacy groups have failed to see how their actions impinge on the broader politics of penal reform.[70] Another political challenge is that the development of the carceral state coincided with new patterns of racial inequality that have important implications for the politics of crime and punishment. Notably, these developments have greatly enhanced the public policing power of African American elites and partly explain their relative silence on the question of mass incarceration and the growth of the carceral state until recently. They also help explain why some leading identity-based civil rights and other organizations have been slow to mobilize against the carceral state, as discussed in chapters 6 and 7.

Many of the harshest critics of mass incarceration talk about the need to forge a broader social or political movement to bring down the carceral state. However, they generally have not inserted their analyses of the pathologies of the carceral state into a wider and more nuanced understanding of the main economic, political, and social currents shaping the United States today and thus the possibilities for penal reform. In short, "many progressives have failed to update their reform concerns and advocacy in light of twenty-first century realities."[71] One of those key realities is the tenacity of neoliberalism in American politics.

The broader political and economic environment helps determine whether politicians, other public figures, interest groups, and organizations lean more toward individual or structural explanations and solutions for major public problems. Individual explanations that stress personal responsibility have continued to trump structural ones in discussions of crime, punishment, and penal reform, thus reinforcing the neoliberal slant in penal policy. Several factors elaborated in this book help explain why. They include the emergence of color-blind racism in the wake of the civil rights movement, as Alexander argues; widening class, educational, and residential differences among blacks; important shifts in the electorate and in the political parties; and the organizational impediments to securing meaningful representation for the most disadvantaged groups in advocacy organizations dedicated to economic and social justice.

The obsessive pursuit of short-term goals in penal policy in service to budget deficit concerns has crowded out more ambitious goals. As politicians and policy makers pursue reentry and justice reinvestment schemes, they have left off the table any serious discussion of ameliorating the structural causes of high concentrations of crime and poverty in certain communities. Reducing the imprisonment rate in state and federal prisons to its historical norm of 120 to 130 inmates per 100,000 people—which would be about one-quarter of the current imprisonment rate—is off the table (see figure 1.3). So is a relatively more modest goal like cutting the incarceration rate for jails and prisons in half, to about 350 per 100,000. This would still be an extraordinarily high rate compared to the rates of other Western countries (see figure 1.1). But there is an even larger problem with this strategy, as discussed in chapters 4 and 5. The dogged pursuit of the three R's—that is, reentry, justice reinvestment, and reducing the recidivism rate—may actually be coming at the cost of fortifying both the carceral state and the sharp right turn in American politics over the long term. This is a sadly familiar historical pattern.

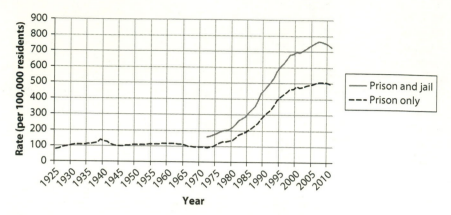

Figure 1.3. U.S. Imprisonment and Incarceration Rates, 1925–2011
Source: Courtesy of Bruce Western, analyses for Jeremy Travis, Bruce Western, and Steve Redburn, eds., *The Growth of Incarceration in the United States: Exploring Causes and Consequences* (Washington, DC: National Academies Press, 2014), 35, fig. 2.1 and 421–22, appendix B.

Many previous bursts of penal reform optimism ended up shifting penal policies in a more punitive direction.

Stumbling on the Road to Reform

Major shifts in public policy often have unintended negative consequences, and penal policy is no exception. The road to a just criminal justice system is littered with bursts of optimism that ended up yielding a sharp right turn in penal policy. More than half a century of political agitation finally brought about bans on the convict-leasing system throughout much of the South by the 1920s.[72] But the state-run chain gangs and penal farms that replaced the brutal and corrupt practice of leasing out convicts to the highest bidder, who often worked them to death's door to turn a profit, became enduring symbols of "southern backwardness, brutality, and racism."[73] As Robert Perkinson wryly observes, "Strange as it seems, the chain gang, in which thousands of prisoners, most of them black, were loaded onto cattle trucks and carted around the state to pound rocks and shovel dirt, was celebrated as a humanitarian advance."[74]

Moments of apparent left-right convergence on penal policy are fraught with possibility and peril. Growing disillusionment on the left and right with rehabilitation and judicial discretion in the 1970s provided a huge political opening for conservatives to move penal policy in a more punitive direction, partly because this disillusionment coincided with a spike in crime rates.[75] Indeterminate sentences and parole boards were cast out at the federal level and in many states. Tough mandatory and advisory sentencing guidelines, and harsh mandatory minimum, habitual offender, and determinate sentencing statutes replaced them. At the federal level, a highly politicized sentencing commission was established that leaned toward prosecutors and increasingly favored mandatory over advisory sentencing guidelines. Federal judges, who initially overwhelmingly opposed the guidelines, ended up slavishly following them in many cases.[76]

Like earlier bursts of penal reform, the three-R approach might actually entrench the carceral state even further over the long run. Discussions of justice reinvestment, recidivism, and reentry exemplify how the language and techniques of cost-benefit analysis have come to dominate mainstream conceptions of penal reform.[77] This is politically perilous for several reasons.

As discussed in chapters 4 and 5, evaluating each penal reform primarily by putting it on the evidence-based, cost-benefit scales to determine whether it reduces crime while saving public money reinforces the tight linkage in the public mind between punishment and crime. It is at odds with some of the most compelling research findings of the last decade or so about the relationship between punishment and crime. We have long known that crime rates move up and down quite independently of punishment practices. More recent research has helped pinpoint the precise relationship between incarceration rates and crime rates.[78] A 2014 National Research Council study concluded that the "increase in incarceration may have caused a decrease in crime, but the magnitude is highly uncertain and the results of most studies suggest it was unlikely to have been large."[79]

Recasting the problem of mass incarceration in econometric or cost-benefit language is problematic in many ways. It does little to challenge the excessively punitive rhetoric that has left such a pernicious mark on penal policy over the last half century. It also is no match for the considerable economic interests that are now deeply invested in the perpetuation of the carceral state. Furthermore, it constricts the political space to challenge penal policies and practices on social justice or human rights grounds. Among elite policy makers and the wider public, creating a safe, healthy, and humane penal system is generally not considered a credible and desirable public policy goal on its own. This goal has to be linked somehow to enhancing public safety and saving public money.

Encased in a shell of evidence-based research, the three-R approach is broadly seen as a way to wring politics out of penal reform. The aim is to devise penal reforms that attract overwhelming bipartisan consensus. But this goal comes at a high cost. It leaves largely unchallenged and unquestioned the political calculations and interests that built the carceral state in the first place. The narrow emphasis on evidence-based research related to recidivism fosters the impression that the birth of the carceral state was the result of bad or nonexistent research rather than bad politics or bad policy.

No wonder then that ending this vast public policy experiment with mass incarceration is not considered a worthy goal in and of itself. Calls to slash the U.S. incarceration rate to bring it more in line with its historic levels and with the incarceration rates of other Western countries are viewed as wildly utopian or dangerously radical. This is so despite the pile of evidence-based research that the relationship between punishment practices and public safety is a loose one at best.

Alarmed by the noxious consequences of the hyper-politicization of criminal justice policy-making since the 1970s, experts on crime and punishment generally have recoiled from paying serious attention to the ways in which the political context influences all aspects of crime and punishment.[80] But as David Bazelon, the chief judge of the U.S. Court of Appeals in Washington, DC, warned more than three decades ago, "[P]olitics is at the heart of American criminology."[81] Many experts in this area have sought refuge in producing state-of-the-art, ostensibly apolitical, evidence-based research centered largely on how to help government agencies or other groups reduce crime. Such a "narrowly instrumental focus appears to forget that in a liberal democracy it matters not only that crime is prevented and detected, but also *how* that happens."[82] Ian Loader and Richard Sparks rightfully beseech these experts to recognize that all aspects of crime and punishment are inherently political, for they are central to how we think about what constitutes a good and fair society.[83] In short, crime control strategies are profoundly political because they both reflect and direct the distribution of power in society.[84]

Framing solutions to the problem of the carceral state primarily in "neutral," scientific, and nonpartisan language ends up ceding important political ground, rendering reforms to dismantle the carceral state vulnerable to resurgent law-and-order rhetoric. Moreover, since "cost savings and lower reoffending rates are presented as ends in themselves—that are somehow separate from thornier matters of human rights, morality, or justice—what is to protect against practices that might be extremely harsh, but reduce overheads or recidivism?"[85]

The three-R approach to limited penal reform has been unfolding alongside a growing push to banish certain people, in some cases permanently, including lifers, immigrants, and people convicted of violent or sexual offenses, as discussed in chapters 8, 9, and 10. These simultaneous and seemingly contradictory gestures are really two sides of the same coin. Both approaches are manifestations of what some sociologists characterize as the "death of the social" with the rise of neoliberalism and globalization and the devolution of the government.[86] With the "death of the social," problems like crime, poverty, mass unemployment, and mass incarceration are no longer seen as having fundamental structural causes that can be ameliorated by policies and resources mobilized by the state. Rather, these problems are regarded "as either the product of chance or individual action."[87] State actors and state agencies are considered part of the problem rather than part of the solution. As such, any quest to develop visionary state-led social and economic policies that seek to address the growing inequalities in the United States is considered politically impolitic.

Instead, the focus is on devising micro-interventions at the local and community levels to change the behavior of individuals. The delegated engineers for these micro-interventions are private-sector, nonprofit, or state actors who are specialists in a very particular area—like substance abuse or anger management or résumé writing.[88] In short, we live in an oxymoronic age of DIY—that is, do-it-yourself—

social policies. Those individuals deemed unable or unwilling to change must be banished—either to the prison or to the prison beyond the prison. Why? Because even though local communities have been valorized as the primary sites of political, social, and economic sustenance, they also are regarded as fragile bulwarks in the face of all the turmoil and anxiety wrought by neoliberalism, globalization, and the coming of the white minority in U.S. politics.[89]

The current economic crisis certainly presents an opportunity to redirect U.S. penal policy that opponents of the prison boom should certainly exploit. But the recidivism-reinvestment-reentry model of penal reform is not likely to result in a major retrenchment of the carceral state. Since the pernicious politics that gave birth to the carceral state remain fundamentally unchallenged, another burst of punitive law-and-order policy-making remains an imminent threat. The country's current economic malaise does not provide much of a firewall against that. Indeed, for a variety of reasons, the economic plight of the United States today could actually be the catalyst for another burst of get-tough policies, as elaborated in chapter 2. Furthermore, staking the future of penal reform primarily on a dollars-and-cents logic is rendering life in U.S. prisons and jails even leaner and meaner as government officials and policy makers slash corrections budgets.

Framing the problem of mass imprisonment as largely a fiscal problem (i.e., we just cannot afford it anymore) will not sustain the political momentum needed over the long haul to slash the prison population and dismantle the carceral state. But the problems with the single-minded focus on the fiscal burden of mass imprisonment run deeper than that. The fiscal imperative argument is providing a huge political opening for the expansion of the private prison industry and for a possible return to one of the most ignominious chapters in U.S. penal history—the unbridled exploitation of penal labor for profit, as discussed in chapter 3. It has helped to bolster the conservative, neoliberal, austerity-first view of what is possible in American politics today. Furthermore, the fiscal approach to penal reform is wholly inadequate to tackle the wide range of problems associated with the emergence of a tenacious carceral state that is altering how key social and political institutions operate and perverting what it means to be a citizen in the United States, as discussed in chapter 11. It slights the compelling civil and human rights concerns that the carceral state raises as it removes wide swaths of historically disadvantaged groups from their neighborhoods, leaving behind devastated families and communities and troubling questions about the fairness and legitimacy of U.S. political institutions and the broader social order.

Chapter Summary

Chapter 2 analyzes why the financial meltdown and the Great Recession are not likely be catalysts for the beginning of the end of mass incarceration in the United States. It also analyzes why some of the current political and economic strains in the United States could trigger another round of get-tough policies. Chapter 3 shows how the new political economy of the carceral state is an impediment to reversing the prison boom. It examines financing gimmicks that have kept the true costs of the prison buildup concealed. It also analyzes important changes in the use of penal labor and in the privatization of corrections and criminal justice. Chapters 4 and 5 critique the three-R approach to penal reform with its emphasis on justice reinvestment, reentry, and reducing recidivism. Chapters 6 and 7 analyze the strengths and weaknesses of framing the problem of the carceral state as primarily a problem of racial disparities and of color-blind racism. Chapters 8, 9, and 10 analyze how the carceral state is continuing to extend its reach with the war on sex offenders, the war on immigrants, and the war on the "worst of the worst," including people serving life and other lengthy sentences. Chapter 11 scrutinizes how the carceral state is deforming key political and governing institutions at great cost to the vitality of democracy in the United States. The final chapter sketches out an alternative political and public policy path to begin razing the carceral state.

The Carceral State and American Politics

There really is no such thing as a politics of penal policy per se. The carceral state must be understood within the larger political, economic, and institutional context in which it is so deeply embedded. It is critical to examine not just the actions and preferences of critical political actors and policy makers with respect to penal policy, but also the objectives these actors pursue simultaneously in other key realms of politics and economics. It also is important to situate the problem of the carceral state within the main political and economic currents that shape American politics and the U.S. political economy today. Using such a broad lens brings penal policy into better focus. It reveals the competing and contradictory views and impulses of key political actors and policy makers that stand in the way of dismantling the carceral state. It also reveals the enormous obstacles to forging a powerful political movement that fundamentally challenges the carceral state and other gaping political and economic inequalities in the United States today.

The U.S. carceral state may be exceptional in its size and tenacity. But many of the political, economic, and social forces that sustain the carceral state and stand in the way of genuine penal reform are not. The tale of the carceral state is really one chapter in a longer story about the huge disconnect between the breathtaking problems that grip the United States and the unwillingness or inability of the political system to remedy them. Many of the pathologies that run through the carceral state also run through American politics today. They include the unwarranted reverence for nonpartisanship at all costs, the uncritical acceptance of neoliberalism in all aspects of public policy, the stranglehold that economic and financial interests exert on politics and policy-making, the growing political and economic disenfranchisement of wide swaths of the population, and the gross limitations of oppositional strategies formed primarily around identity-based politics.

Framing the problem of mass incarceration in highly economistic language has political ramifications that extend far beyond penal policy. Hitching the movement against mass incarceration to the purported fiscal burden of the carceral state helps reinforce the premise that eliminating government deficits and government debt should be the top national priority. Politicians and policy makers across the board have treated shrinking government budgets as a political given rather than as political terrain to be contested.[90] This has emboldened claims that excessive spending on social programs like Medicaid, Medicare, and Social Security is the primary source of the country's red ink, rather than the tax cuts for the wealthy enacted under President George W. Bush, the crushing costs of the "war on terror" and the wars in Iraq and Afghanistan, and the economic contraction sparked by the 2008 financial meltdown.[91]

The fiscal frame also obscures the deeper structural problems that vex the U.S. economy, including promiscuous globalization, excessive financialization and deregulation, and alarming economic inequalities that are hollowing out the U.S. economy and standard of living. What was once the conservative stance on what ails the U.S. economy has become the mainstream bipartisan position, as evidenced most pointedly by President Barack Obama's wholesale embrace of deficit politics in 2010 despite projections from the Congressional Budget Office (CBO) at the time that the annual deficit would fall to manageable levels once the economy revived.[92]

We've been down this road before. In the early 1980s, David Stockman, President Ronald Reagan's first budget director, admitted that the White House strategically wielded the budget deficit hysteria to slash and burn social programs, shrink the government's role in social welfare and other services, and further the cause of privatization.[93] Grover Norquist, one of the leaders of the Right on Crime initiative, is the nation's foremost anti-tax crusader and is widely known for bluntly stating that he aims to shrink government "down to the size where we can drown it in the bathtub."[94] Norquist's organization, Americans for Tax Reform (ATF), was behind the controversial Taxpayer Protection Pledge, which more than 95 percent of the Republicans in Congress had signed as of early 2013.[95]

ATF is a member of the American Legislative Exchange Council (ALEC), which has been a leading force for decades in pushing prison construction, privatization of the penal system, and punitive measures like "truth in sentencing" and "three strikes-and-you're-out" statutes, as elaborated in chapter 3. Recently, ALEC has been at the forefront of the assault on public-sector unions and public schools through the expansion of vouchers, charter schools, and online "virtual schools."[96] It also was the leading incubator of a spate of punitive legislation directed at immigrants, as elaborated in chapter 10. It has championed the controversial Stand Your Ground gun laws, which were at the center of the national firestorm over the February 2012 shooting death of seventeen-year-old Trayvon Martin in Florida.[97] ALEC was forced to disband its Public Safety and Election Task Force shortly after Martin's death, thanks to pressure from a boycott organized by the Occupy Wall Street movement and the Center for Media and Democracy that targeted its major corporate funders.[98]

Today the pillars of the U.S. social welfare state, including Medicare, Medicaid, Social Security, a vibrant labor movement, and adequately funded public schools, are vulnerable to direct assaults from the right and to kinder, gentler jabs from President Obama and some other leading Democrats.[99] In such a political environment, it is hard to imagine that calls for justice reinvestment couched in economistic and ostensibly nonpartisan language will actually result in reallocating the tens of billions spent annually on corrections to social and economic programs that reduce crime and improve the lives of people residing in high-crime communities.

Framing the carceral state primarily as an economic issue may yield some short-term benefits. But in the absence of more compelling arguments against the prison buildup, it becomes that much easier to revert to funding a vast carceral state, no questions asked, once the economy picks up.

A durable reform movement to weather the backlash that efforts to substantially reduce the incarceration rate will inevitably spark has yet to coalesce. The budgetary and other economic problems brought on by the financial meltdown and Great Recession do not spell the beginning of the end of mass incarceration and the carceral state in the United States. To borrow from Winston Churchill, "It is not even the beginning of the end. But it is, perhaps, the end of the beginning."[100]

Criminal justice is fundamentally a political problem, not a crime and punishment or a dollars-and-cents problem. A huge penal system is well on its way to becoming the new normal and a key governing institution in the United States. Like the vast military-industrial complex that quickly insinuated itself into the political and economic fabric in the postwar decades, the carceral state has become integral to the U.S. polity, economy, and society in ways that we have yet to fully acknowledge.

PART I

The Political Economy of Penal Reform

CHAPTER TWO

Show Me the Money

The Great Recession and the Great Confinement

Prison is insatiable. It devours everything in its path and
swallows whole anything that attempts to deter it. All these years
I have spent inside, I have observed just how effectively
the system crushes its opposition.[1]

—KENNETH E. HARTMAN

The 2008 financial meltdown provided an important political opening
to rethink the direction of U.S. penal policies. The economic crisis created
high expectations that the United States would begin slashing its prison and
jail population because it could no longer afford to keep so many people locked
up. As Attorney General Eric Holder told the American Bar Association in 2009,
the country's high incarceration rate is "unsustainable economically."[2] But mounting budgetary and fiscal pressures will not be enough on their own to spur cities,
counties, states, and the federal government to make deep and lasting cuts in their
incarceration rates and to address the far-reaching political, social, and economic
consequences of the carceral state.

The historical record is sobering on this point. The race to incarcerate began in
the 1970s at a time when the U.S. economy was mired in stagflation.[3] It persisted
over the next four decades despite wide fluctuations in the country's economic
health and crime rates. In the 1980s, when the prison population was one-quarter
of what it is today, a prominent advisory board, appointed by President Ronald
Reagan, raised concerns about the fiscal burden of prisons and about the escalating human toll of prison overcrowding.[4] But the U.S. Department of Justice
(DOJ) suppressed release of its final report, and nearly all one thousand copies of
it disappeared.[5]

A decade and a half later, during the 2001 recession, expectations again rose
that the prison boom would finally end as severe budget deficits would force states
to close facilities and lay off guards. At the time, fiscally conservative Republicans
previously known for being penal hard-liners championed a number of sentencing
and drug-law reforms.[6] But these changes did not make much of a dent in the U.S.
incarceration rate, which continued to march upward.

Likewise, the Great Recession has spurred excessive hopes that the United States is at the beginning of the end of mass incarceration because the fiscal costs are too high to sustain. These hopes are rooted in several misunderstandings about the political, economic, and institutional forces that built and sustain the carceral state and about certain broader currents in U.S. politics that are thrashing public policy. They rest on an exaggerated sense of the fiscal burden that corrections imposes on government budgets and of the money that could be saved by reducing the number of people in jail or prison, as elaborated in this chapter. Furthermore, if history tells us anything, the economic and political fallout from the financial meltdown and Great Recession could usher in a period of greater punitiveness, not less. If public anxiety escalates in the face of growing inequalities and persistent economic distress, law enforcement will likely be called upon to quell growing political dissent and protests, as discussed below.

Moreover, for some state actors, crime does pay, as shown in this chapter. Civil forfeiture laws provide police and law enforcement agencies with key sources of funding, much of which is publicly unaccountable. They are a major incentive to keep the war on drugs going. The huge prison population artificially suppresses the official unemployment rate. Penal Keynesianism props up a lumbering economy. Contracting out empty prison beds to the federal government or other states has become a lucrative business for states and counties that have reduced their own inmate populations.

The elite-level bipartisan political fixation on deficit reduction at all costs has provided a license for a race to the bottom as legislators and other state officials slash budgets for everything from education to health care to public transportation to corrections, as discussed in this chapter. Under pressure to cut corrections budgets, but confronted with powerful interests that profit politically and economically from keeping large numbers of people under state supervision, public officials have been making largely symbolic budget cuts. These cuts do little to reduce the incarcerated population—or save much money—but they do render life in prison and life after prison tougher for those who serve time. States, counties, and municipalities also have imposed onerous fees and monetary penalties on defendants, prisoners, probationers, and parolees, and slashed spending on health, education, social services, and other programs that help keep people out of prison.

The Blurry Bottom Line

The extent of the fiscal burden of the carceral state is widely misunderstood. Corrections has been one of the fastest growing segments of state budgets since the 1980s, second only to Medicaid.[7] However, even in the wake of the massive prison buildup, spending on corrections remains a relatively small component of state budgets. Between fiscal 1982 and fiscal 2010, spending on corrections fluctuated between 2 percent and 3 percent of total expenditures by state governments, lagging far behind total spending for education (which varied between 29 and 33 percent) and public welfare (22–25 percent).[8]

The only way to make major reductions in corrections budgets is to close penal facilities and reduce the correctional staff. Labor costs account for about three-quarters of the expense of operating a prison. Incremental releases of prisoners do not save much money because the marginal cost of housing and caring for each additional prisoner is far below the annual average operating cost per prisoner. In some cases, these marginal costs are comparable to what it costs to monitor an offender in one of the better community corrections or drug court programs rather than sending him or her to prison.[9]

Furthermore, transferring people out of the criminal justice system does not necessarily mean transferring them off the government tab. The moral and human rights arguments for compassionate release of elderly and infirm prisoners are compelling, but the fiscal ones are overstated. Prisons spend on average more than twice as much to incarcerate an elderly person than a younger one, or about $60,000 to $70,000 a year, because older inmates have greater health-care needs.[10] If these elderly inmates remain in prison, correctional budgets will bear most of the costs of caring for them. If they are released early, many of these costs will likely be shifted to Medicaid, Medicare, Social Security, and other public programs. Individual states would save some money because the federal government funds these programs wholly or in part, but some public entity would still be picking up much of the tab.[11]

The Culture of Control, Revisited

The 2008 financial collapse was the catalyst for an economic crisis that may herald a period of greater public punitiveness, not less. Spreading economic despair and poverty, the wave of foreclosures, persistent unemployment, and deep anxiety about the country's economic future may effectively fortify the "culture of control" that David Garland identified as the lifeblood of the prison boom launched nearly four decades ago. In Garland's account, societal angst stemming from deep structural changes in the U.S. economy and society in the immediate postwar decades ushered in a new culture of control premised on harsh punishment and extensive surveillance.[12] The widespread perception of the government's impotency to mitigate the economic upheavals of the 1970s also fostered the culture of control, according to Garland.

Washington's inability to tame the economic demons in the wake of the 2008 financial meltdown (and its alleged culpability in releasing those demons) has once again cast doubt on the efficacy, legitimacy, and raison d'être of the government. As states and the federal government struggle to restore economic health, the temptation for public officials to act out in impulsive and unreflective ways and to promote highly punitive measures for their immediate symbolic and expressive value is great.[13] Furthermore, there is a well-established "relationship between economic insecurity and scapegoating behavior."[14] Claims that immigrants are stealing jobs from citizens and pushing crime rates upward have more traction in a weak economy, justifying harsher attacks on them, as elaborated in chapter 10.

Public opinion surveys suggest that anxiety about the economy remains deep and persistent even though the public mood has picked up somewhat since the Great Recession was technically declared to be over in June 2009. People in the United States who consider themselves middle class have a very dim view of their futures.[15] Research suggests that men—especially white men—who expect their economic situation to deteriorate are considerably more punitive.[16] The recent surges in firearm purchases and in anti-government "patriot groups" are ominous indicators of growing public anxiety that have important implications for penal policy and law enforcement.[17] So are public controversies over Stand Your Ground gun laws and brazen displays of weapons in public venues like Starbucks and at public events, like the health-care reform town meetings in summer 2009. The not-too-subtle message appears to be that if the state is not prepared to protect the public, individuals are locked and loaded to do so.

Crime Rates, Economic Distress, and Public Anxieties

Deteriorating economic conditions do not necessarily propel crime rates upward—but the public often believes they do. And as the sociologist W. I. Thomas once remarked, if people define situations as real, they are real in their consequences. A vast and growing number of Americans believe that crime worsened due to the Great Recession. More adults than ever reported that crime in their community had increased, and that they expected that the poor economy would cause crime rates to escalate even further.[18] Most Americans are unaware that gun crime and other violent crime are markedly lower than they were two decades ago, and that crime rates have fallen to lows not seen since the early 1960s.[19]

Levels of fear of crime and concern about crime have consistently predicted public attitudes toward punitiveness. There is a deep-seated belief that crime rates rise during economic downturns and recede during recoveries, even though the evidence for this claim is mixed. For example, crime rose during the boom years of the 1960s; it fell during the Reagan recession of the early 1980s; rose during the recession of the late 1980s and early 1990s (thanks largely to the destabilization of established drug markets with the introduction of the crack trade); and then fell during the economic expansion of the 1990s. Certain crimes tend to rise in recessions and recede in good times, but this relationship is not ironclad. For example, there is a general consensus that child abuse and neglect usually escalate in economic downturns.[20]

Some evidence suggests that the crime rate for other offenses, notably robbery and assault, drops during tough economic times as people go out less, shop less, carry less money, and have less to spend on alcohol.[21] This may explain why crime spiked in the Roaring '20s but plummeted after the 1929 stock market crash. But it cannot account for the drop in property crime and violent crime in the United States and Europe during the 1990s, which some have attributed in large part to the economic expansion during that decade.

Analyses that use unemployment as a proxy for economic distress have not settled the question of whether rising unemployment causes spikes in crime.[22] Studies that use alternate measures of macroeconomic distress—such as trends in the per capita growth rate, consumer confidence, or wage growth—have identified a more nuanced relationship between economic distress and crime.[23] A key factor in driving crime rates up may not be unemployment per se but rather the deterioration in labor market conditions for young, unskilled men, particularly an erosion of their wages.[24] The crime rate may also be inversely related to changes in consumer confidence about the economy. When people feel less confident about their own financial situation and the economic future of the country, the crime rate rises.[25]

Studies of the United States and other advanced industrialized countries indicate that incarceration rates tend to increase with rising unemployment rates, regardless of whether the crime rate is rising or falling.[26] The hedge fund Pershing Square Capital Management, a major investor until recently in Corrections Corporation of America (CCA), made bullish projections for the private prison industry in the wake of the Great Recession. Pershing based these projections partly on the historic relationship between a faltering economy and an accelerated rate of growth in the prison population.[27]

There is no consensus about the underlying causal relationship between the unemployment rate and the incarceration rate. Some suggest that judges, prosecutors, legislators, the media, and the public support more punitive measures during hard times out of the often unfounded fear that crime inevitably rises as the economy falls. A related factor is likely the more generalized fear that the growing number of the dispossessed poses a threat not only to public safety but also to the wider social and economic order and therefore must be dealt with severely.[28] Furthermore, when the unemployment rate is higher, judges are more likely to encounter people who are unemployed. Sentencing research affirms that low-status unemployed defendants are more likely to receive stiffer sentences, even after controlling for offense characteristics and criminal history.[29]

The Criminalization of Dissent

Crime does not necessarily rise during periods of economic distress, but protests, strikes, and civil unrest often do as the unemployed, unions, the elderly, veterans, the poor, and the sliding middle class take to the streets. When that happens, government officials, politicians, and prominent commentators often conflate crime and social protest. Labeling demonstrations and other acts of protest as crimes is an age-old strategy to justify expansions of law enforcement and to delegitimize challenges to the prevailing political and economic order. As the Occupy Wall Street movement gained national traction in fall 2011, House Majority Leader Eric Cantor (R-VA) warned about the "growing mobs on Wall Street and in other cities across the country."[30] Likewise, leading politicians from across the political spectrum in Britain agreed with Prime Minister David Cameron's initial portrayal of the August 2011 urban unrest in Britain, which was sparked by the shooting death by police of a father of three in Tottenham, as "criminality, pure and simple."[31]

The imposing armories that dot American cities were built as part of the late-nineteenth-century response to the wide-scale urban unrest of the Gilded Age, including the infamous strike wave in 1877 and the 1886 Haymarket riot. Designed to intimidate the "dangerous classes," these massive structures were home to National Guard units that were thought to be more willing than local police to fire upon strikers.[32] Decades later, during the Great Depression, huge numbers of Americans took to the streets, fueling fears that the social and economic fabric of the United States was coming apart.[33] This political unrest triggered calls for greater policing powers to regain control as armed soldiers stood guard at government buildings in Washington.[34]

The Depression provided an opportunity to legitimize the expansion of a huge number of federal and state powers, ranging from government control of the economy to law enforcement. The profound social anxiety associated with massive economic distress made the public susceptible to calls from President Franklin D. Roosevelt and Federal Bureau of Investigations (FBI) director J. Edgar Hoover to get tough on criminals—whatever the cost—even as crime rates fell in the 1930s. The Depression was a wildly successful period for the FBI and other arms of law enforcement. The country's dire economic straits at the time did not preclude the government from investing heavily in prisons and other tough sanctions. Furthermore, public officials promoted prison construction and the expansion of law enforcement as public works programs that would boost the failing economy.[35]

Managing Marginalization

One notable feature of the 2008 financial meltdown and Great Recession is the relative political quiescence thus far in the face of rapid economic deterioration and far-reaching irresponsibility, trickery, and corruption on the part of the financial sector and its government patrons. We have yet to see many large street demonstrations, sit-ins, or other major acts of protest that fundamentally challenge the economic and political order, unlike during the Gilded Age, the Progressive era, the Great Depression, and the civil rights era. It may still be too early to tell whether the United States will ride out the sharpest economic downturn in eighty years with widespread anger resting alongside collective passivity.[36] It is still not clear whether the stirrings of the Tea Party and Occupy Wall Street movements, the massive 2011 protests against Governor Scott Walker (R-WI), and the wave of confrontations between police and protestors over foreclosures are the harbingers of a new era of widespread political unrest.[37]

With a few exceptions, U.S. cities have not experienced large-scale civil violence and civil unrest since the upheavals of the 1960s and 1970s.[38] As Michael Katz notes, this is so even though many of the conditions that sparked previous periods of urban unrest—including a tattered social safety net, persistent police brutality, and widespread poverty, unemployment, income inequality, and segregation—have not been remedied or have worsened.[39] Although high levels of criminal violence persist in certain urban neighborhoods, as discussed in chapter 12, widespread civil violence or civil unrest directed at the police and other symbols of the state has been largely absent.

Katz identifies several mechanisms that have been key to "managing marginalization" such that American cities "do not burn" very often. These include select incorporation of minorities, notably through public sector–related employment; intensive police surveillance and repression; superficial reforms "that respond to insurgent demands without devolving real power or redistributing significant resources"; the private sector's aggressive cultivation of a consumer identity among African Americans at the cost of their political identity; and the indirect control of minority urban leaders through the enormous powers that state legislatures exercise over urban areas.[40] These mechanisms to manage marginalization "set in motion a process of de-politicization that undercuts the capacity for collective action."[41]

The aggressive model of policing dissent that emerged more than a decade ago in response to the anti-globalization movement and 9/11 is a key factor in this urban quiescence.[42] It rests on confronting protesters with decisive force, including massive numbers of heavily armed, military-style police officers. Using tactics pioneered during the 1999 Seattle protests against the World Trade Organization, the 2003 protests in Miami during the Free Trade of Americas meetings, and the 2004 Republican National Convention in New York City, law enforcement officers routinely wield intrusive, preemptive, and aggressive tactics to quell protests. The 2011–12 Occupy Wall Street protests, which were remarkably modest and peaceful by historical standards and when compared to the recent wave of protests in Europe, nonetheless elicited an aggressive confrontational response from many police departments. They also elicited a political overreaction that sought to criminalize the demonstrators, which helps explain why the movement could not sustain its momentum.[43]

It remains an open question whether these mechanisms that keep the lid on civil unrest will continue to work in the face of escalating inequalities, the contraction of public-sector jobs, and reductions in spending on education, health care, and social services that cut to the bone. Furthermore, budget cutbacks have forced some cities to lay off huge numbers of firefighters and police officers, their first line of defense in managing marginalization and criminalizing dissent. Should large-scale civil unrest break out in the next few years, calls to bolster law enforcement will likely increase, as will efforts to portray these protests as criminal behavior that must be severely punished.

Penal Keynesianism

Most prison costs are fixed and are not easily cut. Since labor costs compose about three-quarters of corrections costs, the only way to save significant money is to close facilities and lay off guards and other correctional staff. But public officials who attempt to close penal facilities face fierce local resistance, even when they have promised not to eliminate anyone's job or release any offenders early.[44] In New York State, total prison expenditures increased markedly between 1999 and 2009 despite a major decline in the prison population during this period.[45] From 2006 through 2010, New Jersey reduced its prison population by nearly 9 percent thanks to increased use of parole and reductions in parole revocations for technical violations, but prison expenditures increased by more than 3 percent.[46]

Which penal facilities states decide to close is almost as important a policy and political question as whether they are closing facilities or not. In 2011 and 2012, Michigan announced plans to shutter the only two state prisons located in the city of Detroit, which accounts for about a third of the state's prison population. Many offenders from Detroit must now serve their sentences in remote prisons located hundreds of miles from home.[47]

Mass incarceration exerts a "Keynesian, stabilizing effect, to be sustained for economic reasons," especially during a downturn in the economy.[48] The huge incarcerated population in the United States artificially lowers the official unemployment rate for males by at least 2 percentage points, making the U.S. economy appear more successful than it actually is.[49] It also masks the huge and rising unemployment rates among young African American men. Many of these men are incarcerated and thus not included in standard measures of unemployment, as elaborated in chapter 11.

Furthermore, corrections and law enforcement have become major sources of employment in the aggregate, even if individual prisons do not necessarily buoy the local labor market. As Michael Cavadino and James Dignan explain, "In a perverse variation of Keynes's hypothetical cure for recession—get the state to hire large numbers of people to dig holes and then fill them in again—the USA has hired one lot of people to keep another lot locked up."[50] Local, state, and federal spending on corrections was upwards of $85 billion in 2012.[51] The country spends over $100 billion on police and over $50 billion on the judiciary.[52] By one calculation, one in four people employed in the United States is engaged in some type of guard labor, a fourfold increase from a century ago.[53] One in eight state employees works in corrections.[54] As of 2008, about three-quarters of a million people were directly employed by correctional institutions as guards, supervisors, and other support staff. Many more were employed in corrections through the multi-billion-dollar private corrections industry, "which constructs, finances, equips, and provides health care, education, food, rehabilitation, and other services to prisons and jails."[55] As a point of comparison, the entire workforce of the auto-manufacturing sector totaled 880,000 people in 2008.

Penal Keynesianism was a key consideration in the shape of and debate over the controversial American Recovery and Reinvestment Act of 2009. As the U.S. Congress began putting together this controversial economic stimulus package in late 2008, the U.S. Conference of Mayors promulgated a $5.5 billion public safety wish list. The mayors said they wanted to use the stimulus money to purchase all kinds of SWAT equipment, including helicopters, armored vehicles, and military grade rifles. Unmanned drones were an especially popular item.[56]

In its 2009 stimulus proposal, the Obama administration explicitly sought to fund projects that were "shovel ready." Thanks to the prison boom of the last four decades, many states now have the experience and capacity to build prisons fast. Some states and communities planned to use the stimulus money they received from Washington to expand or maintain their penal facilities. In fiscal 2010 and 2011, the federal stimulus package pumped more than $2 billion into the corrections budgets of forty-four states, according to a survey by the Vera Institute. This amounted to about 3 percent of their total spending on corrections for those two years. The impact of the federal stimulus bill on state corrections budgets was highly uneven. Alaska used no federal stimulus money for corrections, while federal stimulus money constituted nearly one-third of Alabama's corrections budget in fiscal 2010.[57]

The Recovery Act resuscitated two controversial law enforcement programs that Congress and the Bush administration had begun to phase out—the Community Oriented Policing Services, or COPS program, and the Byrne Justice Assistance Grants. The stimulus bill pumped $1 billion into COPS, which provides federal grants to local police forces and was one of the signature programs of the Clinton administration's draconian 1994 crime bill. COPS was created to reduce crime by promoting community policing tactics whereby police officers would walk (or bike) their beat and act more like members of the community than aggressive outside enforcers. But COPS also fostered more confrontational styles of policing by funding SWAT teams and encouraging the broader use of paramilitary tactics and equipment.[58]

Over the years, many Democrats have persistently defended COPS while many conservatives and Republicans have called for phasing it out. In the 2009 debate over the stimulus package, Senator Patrick Leahy (D-VT), chairman of the Judiciary Committee, promoted spending more on COPS because it would aid the economy "as fast, or faster than, other spending." In making the case for COPS, Leahy, police chiefs, and law enforcement organizations stoked public fears of rising crime during economic downturns.[59]

The stimulus package also threw a lifeline to the controversial Byrne program, which was established under the Anti-Drug Abuse Act of 1988 and became a cornerstone of the war on drugs. Over the years, Byrne money has supported a wide range of activities, including after-school, victims' assistance, and substance abuse programs. But the bulk of these grants has gone to fund law enforcement programs, most notably special drug enforcement units and anti-gang initiatives. The Byrne drug units, which are largely unaccountable to local police chiefs and sheriffs, proliferated across the country in spite of their contested efficacy.[60]

Though championed by police unions and other law enforcement organizations, the Byrne program has come under withering attack from the right and the left over the years, including critics at the Heritage Foundation, the National Taxpayers Union, the American Civil Liberties Union (ACLU), the National Black

Police Association, and the Drug Policy Alliance.[61] Byrne grants have encouraged law enforcement officials to focus on low-level drug arrests rather than pursuing big dealers because the funds are typically awarded based on the number of arrests—not the significance of the arrests.[62] The ACLU has documented numerous abuses by Byrne drug task forces. In the mid-1990s, a Byrne-funded drug unit was responsible for the debacle in Tulia, Texas, in which dozens of African Americans received lengthy sentences for drug dealing based on the uncorroborated testimony of a single undercover police officer who was white.[63]

In December 2007, Congress unexpectedly slashed Byrne grants by two-thirds to a record low allocation of $170 million.[64] State and local officials pushed hard to restore the Byrne grants in the stimulus package, promoting them as a key means to reduce crime and generate jobs.[65] The Recovery Act of 2009 included more than $2 billion in new Byrne funding (more than double the amount provided in any single year up until then) and an additional $600 million to increase state and local law enforcement across the country.[66] In fiscal 2013 and 2014, Democrats successfully fought back Republican efforts to zero out spending for the COPS and Byrne programs.[67]

In marshalling support for the jobs bill it introduced in fall 2011, the Obama administration once again invoked penal Keynesianism and law-and-order concerns. In his public appearances with police chiefs, Vice President Joe Biden emphasized how the American Jobs Act would put thousands of police and firefighters back on the street. The White House supported Biden's inflammatory claims that rape and murder rates would escalate if Congress failed to pass the jobs bill.[68]

Crime Does Pay

Crime continues to pay in other ways for public officials. Faced with tighter budgets, more public officials now view the courts, corrections, and law enforcement as revenue-generating opportunities. This has not only intensified the war on the poor in the United States but also the war on key civil rights protections of the U.S. Constitution. Law enforcement has an enormous financial stake in continuing the war on drugs, which has become a huge cash cow and in some instances a huge slush fund for police and prosecutors. This is thanks to civil forfeiture laws that permit law enforcement officers (usually the police) to seize property they "suspect" may be associated with criminal activity.[69] Criminal forfeiture requires that a person be convicted of an offense before his or her property may be confiscated. But in civil forfeiture cases, property owners do not even need to be charged with or convicted of a crime to lose cash, cars, homes, jewelry, or other property. Often the only way to get the property back is to go to court at one's own expense to prove that the property is "innocent." North Carolina is the only state that requires a criminal conviction before a person's property may be seized.[70]

As the war on drugs was gearing up in the 1970s and 1980s, state and local law enforcement agencies were granted enormous authority to keep for their own use most of the cash and other assets that they seized. Forfeitures were a way to wage costly new wars against crime and drugs at a time when political pressure was growing to slash public spending. In 1989, Attorney General Richard Thornburgh boasted, "It's now possible for a drug dealer to serve time in a forfeiture-financed prison after being arrested by agents driving a forfeiture-provided automobile while working on a forfeiture-funded sting operation."[71] Byrne-funded drug task forces in Texas would ignore vehicles heading north with drugs, preferring to concentrate their efforts on seizing drug money making its way back to suppliers in Mexico, a portion of which they would be able to keep under the asset forfeiture laws.[72]

Over the years, the scope of asset forfeiture laws expanded while procedural protections eroded.[73] Mere suspicion of illegal activity with a very low bar for probable cause has been enough to seize cash and property, including homes and cars, without a hearing or notice. Assets still may be subject to forfeiture even though neither the owner nor anyone else has been charged with a crime and even in cases where a defendant is ultimately found innocent. The barriers to successfully fighting forfeitures in the courts are high, especially for people who lack the means to hire an attorney and pay the court costs to get their property and cash back.[74]

Forfeitures have become a major source of revenue for law enforcement. It is hard to get a handle on the total amount brought in by forfeitures, partly because there is little public oversight or reporting about how police and prosecutors use civil forfeitures or spend the proceeds. The federal government reportedly seized $4.2 billion in assets in fiscal 2012, more than double the amount seized in 2011 and about four times the amount seized in 2006.[75] A "heavy veil of secrecy" cloaks "the details of most federal forfeiture cases, the vast majority of which were made based on investigations that are not disclosed in public records or even reviewed in federal court."[76]

"Forfeiture corridors" have become the new speed traps and are major cash cows for some communities.[77] Police officers in Tulsa, Oklahoma, brazenly drive around in a Cadillac Escalade stenciled with the words, "This used to be a drug dealer's car, now it's ours!"[78] In some Texas counties, civil forfeitures cover almost 40 percent of the police budgets.[79] Police officers in a Texas town that is a hotbed of forfeiture activity actually keep pre-signed, pre-notarized documents with them to record what property they are seizing.[80] An agitated drug-sniffing dog during a routine traffic stop is enough probable cause to seize property.[81]

In 2000, the U.S. Congress unanimously enacted the Civil Asset Forfeiture Reform Act (CAFRA) in the face of rising public concern that the overzealous enforcement of forfeiture laws was endangering individual property rights.[82] Several states enacted comparable reforms while other states enacted tougher measures. But many of these reforms have gaping loopholes.[83] After 9/11, civil forfeitures entered a new frontier. Law enforcement officials began taking advantage of a lesser known provision of the Patriot Act that seriously weakened several of CAFRA's protections for property owners subject to terror-related investigations, even those at a very preliminary stage.[84]

Pay-As-You-Go Criminal Justice System

As state funding tightens, legislators across the country have been pushing the courts, departments of corrections, and other criminal justice agencies to slash their budgets and generate more revenue. In the majority of felony and misdemeanor cases, courts and departments of corrections now routinely impose substantial fees and fines that supplement other criminal penalties. Police officers in St. Joseph, Missouri, even bill defendants for the $26 or so it costs to "Taser" them during an arrest.[85] States and counties view these legal financial obligations (LFOs) as critical sources of revenue. But they do not systematically collect evidence to determine whether or not their efforts actually make money.[86]

Levying fees on inmates for meals, lodging, visits to the doctor, and other items are becoming more common. In some cases, former prisoners and family members of juvenile offenders have been sent to prison because they could not pay off corrections fees.[87] Prison administrators also have been charging inmates more exorbitant prices for items they purchase from the commissary. They have been diverting the profits they reap from commissary sales to the state's general fund rather than using them, as they did in the past, to fund programs and services for prisoners.[88]

This pay-as-you-go push is undermining the integrity of the criminal justice system. For instance, judges in New Orleans's criminal court pressured their colleagues to levy more LFOs on defendants. Judges who collected less than their "fair share" received fewer operating funds.[89] A recent study by the nonpartisan Conference of State Court Administrators was titled "Courts Are Not Revenue Centers."[90] As judicial and corrections budgets contract, judges and departments of corrections in some jurisdictions have become exceptionally aggressive about collecting fines and fees.[91] These LFOs are typically levied with little regard for the defendant's ability to pay. Some jurisdictions in Florida permit "collection courts" to jail debtors even though they have no right to representation by a public defender.[92]

In some places, prosecutors are raising money by essentially turning their hot-check divisions into collection agencies for unscrupulous payday and other lenders.[93] District attorneys have permitted debt collection agencies to use their official government letterheads to threaten criminal action on unpaid debts. The companies seek to collect not only the debt but also high penalty fees, some of which are kicked back to the prosecutors.[94]

People with LFOs live "under constant threat of being sent back to jail or prison, solely because they cannot pay what has become an unmanageable legal debt."[95] They also must contend with impaired credit ratings and housing and employment prospects, sometimes for decades after they have served their sentences. Failure to pay these fees and fines can be cause to send someone to prison or jail, despite a series of U.S. Supreme Court decisions that banned or restricted the imprisonment of debtors.[96] Judges have creatively circumvented these decisions by, for example, claiming that the debtor had not been arrested for nonpayment but rather for contempt of court for failing to comply with a court order to pay. In some instances, people are serving more time in jail for failing to pay court costs than they served under their original sentence.[97]

"Honey Holes"

To ease their budget woes, states and municipalities have sought other ways besides civil forfeitures and LFOs to turn a profit from the criminal justice system. Louisiana has been a pioneer in devising for-profit public solutions for the problem of too many prisoners and too little money. In the early 1990s, Louisiana, which today has the country's highest incarceration rate (see figure 1.2, p. 12), was under a federal court order to alleviate prison overcrowding. But instead of releasing prisoners early or reducing its tough sentences, the state turned to local sheriffs to address its overcrowding problem. It agreed to pay the sheriffs of local parishes a fixed per diem for each state prisoner they agreed to house in local jails. The sheriffs could keep as profit any leftover money. Promises of a higher per diem rate and of a guaranteed occupancy rate prompted local sheriffs to go on a prison-building binge. Private prison firms and investors with close ties to government officials largely funded this binge. Today, more than half of the state's 40,000 inmates are housed in local prisons run by sheriffs or private for-profit companies.[98]

In many rural communities in Louisiana, the local prison is the sheriff's major revenue generator, second only to local sales tax revenues. Profits from the local prisons—or "honey holes," as they have been nicknamed—pay for everything from new squad cars to bulletproof vests. This quasi-public solution is a win-win situation for state and local budgets and a huge loss for inmates. An inmate housed at Louisiana's state penitentiary in Angola costs the state about $63 per day. But the state only pays $24 per diem to local sheriffs for each state prisoner they shelter—by far the lowest that any state spends on its prisoners. Local sheriff-run prisons in Louisiana are notorious for their abhorrent living conditions and the lack of educational, vocational, or rehabilitation programs.

Bed Brokering

In Louisiana and elsewhere, a brisk business of "bed brokering" or "bed renting" has developed as inmates are shuffled off to states and counties with empty cells. States and municipalities that have excess penal capacity—either because penal reforms have cut their inmate populations or because they over-invested in prison construction—have aggressively sought to fill their empty beds. Each day parish sheriffs in Louisiana work the phones and their networks to assure that the beds in their parish jails remain full with state prisoners. Private agencies have sprung up across the country to negotiate prison space on a flat fee per bed basis. The motto of Inmate Placement Services of Nashville is "a bed for every inmate and an inmate for every bed."[99] Corrections administrators are turning to services like JailBed Space.com, which provides a detailed, up-to-date, county-by-county breakdown on color-coded maps of where empty cells are available for rent nationwide.[100]

Michigan, hailed as a penal success story for trimming its prison population, has become a major importer of inmates from other states and has courted the federal government to fill its unused beds.

Although some states forbid sending their inmates to out-of-state facilities, many do not. Hawaii, which has only one state prison within its borders, routinely transfers many of its prisoners to privately run facilities on the mainland to serve out their sentences.[101] Locating inmates so far from their families and communities impedes their chances for successful reentry into society. It also "stretch[es] the chain of accountability beyond the breaking point."[102] Critics charge that these out-of-state transfers "are a strange throwback to corrections policies of two or three centuries ago, when felons were banished to penal colonies in Australia or the New World."[103] But in the 1983 *Olim v. Wakinekona* decision, the U.S. Supreme Court ruled that out-of-state transfers—even ones that involve long distances and an ocean crossing—are constitutional. Some states have even seriously considered a *maquiladora* solution to the problem of too many prisons and too little money and cell space. In 2003, Arizona legislators voted down a bill that would have required the state to seek proposals from private prison firms to construct and manage a prison that would house some of its inmates across the border in the Mexican state of Sonora, where labor and other costs are lower. Governor Arnold Schwarzenegger (R-CA) floated a similar proposal in 2010.[104]

The interstate commerce in prison-made goods, which is discussed in chapter 3, is more tightly regulated than the business of exporting and importing prisoners between states. States that export inmates often have no standing to regulate what happens in these distant facilities.[105] Some private prisons are filled to capacity with small numbers of inmates from numerous states. As such, individual states have neither the incentive nor the capacity to monitor prison conditions in these out-of-state facilities. Host states often adopt a hands-off approach, especially if the private prison does not house any of its own residents.[106] Out-of-state inmates "are supposed to be treated according to the laws and regulations granted by their home states—but rarely are."[107] These prisoners often have greater difficulty filing appeals or grievances because home state laws and prison regulation handbooks are rarely available.

The barreling growth of the federal prison population and of the number of immigrants detained by Immigration and Customs Enforcement (ICE) has been a major driver of the bed brokering business at the local and state levels. For cash-strapped states and municipalities, the federal government's inmates and detainees are tantalizing cash cows. Counties have sought to free up space in their local jails so they could begin housing federal prisoners and detainees, which are more lucrative. New Jersey transferred some of its inmates in state prisons to a string of poorly supervised, poorly regulated, and dangerous halfway houses run on the cheap by a private firm with close ties to Governor Chris Christie (R-NJ) and other state lawmakers. This allowed New Jersey to contract out beds in its state prisons to the federal government, which pays a high per diem rate to house federal inmates and immigrant detainees.[108]

Economically distressed towns, some of them struggling to meet bond payments for prisons that stand empty, have vied with one another to house the "enemy combatants" from Guantánamo, Cuba, that President Obama had promised to transfer to the mainland.[109] In December 2009, the administration announced it would be purchasing an unused state prison in Thomson, Illinois, to house the detainees. The White House predicted that this move would increase local earnings by $800 million to $1 billion and reduce the local unemployment rate by 2 percentage points.[110] In the face of strong congressional opposition, the administration backed down from its plans to transfer the Guantánamo detainees to this facility. But in October 2012, the administration announced it would purchase the facility to house other high-security inmates. Senator Richard Durbin (D-IL), who in summer 2012 conducted the Senate's first ever hearings on solitary confinement in the United States, hailed the federal government's purchase of the Thomson facility. He applauded the hundreds of construction jobs and more than one thousand permanent jobs the new federal prison purportedly would bring to the state.[111] Left unsaid was how many of Thomson's high-security prisoners would end up like the high-security prisoners in ADX Florence in Colorado—confined to their cells nearly round-the-clock for years on end without any human contact.

Leaner and Meaner

As the United States became the world's warden in the late twentieth century, it became increasingly desensitized not only to the huge numbers of people locked up but also to the degrading conditions of confinement that are endemic to U.S. prisons and jails. "Devolving standards of decency" characterized the punishment wave of the last four decades as retribution and incapacitation, not rehabilitation, became the primary justification for incarceration.[112] As the commitment to rehabilitation eroded, so did the "vague but still effective moral restraining edge that indirectly limited the amount of prison pain that could be openly delivered and would be publicly tolerated," explains Craig Haney, a national expert on prison conditions.[113]

The Great Recession has hastened this race to the bottom as budget cutters targeted so-called nonessential prison services such as educational, substance abuse, and vocational programs that help reduce recidivism and were already grossly underfunded. Dozens of states and the federal government have cut their operating costs per prisoner.[114] This development is particularly troubling in the U.S. case because a major theme of U.S. penal history is how degrading punishments have repeatedly trumped calls for human dignity.[115] Furthermore, independent oversight of U.S. prisons and jails is minimal or nonexistent compared to other Western countries. It is so minimal that Yelp, the popular website that consumers rely on for reviews of restaurants, hair stylists, and the like, has become one of the few outlets to publicly review conditions in U.S. prisons and jails.[116]

Just as states and municipalities vary enormously in per capita spending on education or health care, per capita spending on inmates varies greatly.[117] Indiana spends on average just over $14,000 per year per inmate—or less than half the national average. At the other end is New York State, which spends about $60,000 per year, or about twice the national average, and New York City, which spends $168,000 per year for each inmate in the city jail system.[118] Notably, three-quarters of the dozen states with the highest imprisonment rates rank among the bottom dozen in annual operating costs per state prison inmate.[119]

States that spend comparatively more on their inmates are under growing pressure from lawmakers to cut their expenses by eliminating programs, reducing services, shifting more costs to prisoners and their families, and adopting controversial measures from states and counties that run their corrections systems on the cheap. For example, a Texas legislator introduced a bill in 2011 to permit the establishment of tent cities to house inmates. The plan was inspired by the activities of Joe Arpaio, the controversial sheriff of Maricopa County, which includes Phoenix. Arpaio has become a reviled and revered national figure for his boasts about his low-cost un-air-conditioned tent city (where temperatures can rise to 120 degrees in the desert heat) and his other cost-saving, dignity-robbing, get-tough measures.[120]

Some lawmakers contend that their states need to address the budget crunch by cutting what they spend on each inmate rather than by releasing felons and closing prisons.[121] A California assemblyman from San Bernardino County dismissed a study that found that his county sends twice as many people to prison and consumes more state corrections money than Alameda County, which has a comparable crime rate. He argued that state officials should be creating partnerships with private prisons to cut costs rather than pressuring San Bernardino to reduce how many people it sends to prison. The legislator also said California should learn to be more like Texas, "which has the same amount of prisoners, and they do it with a third of the cost."[122]

On several key indicators—notably the incidence of riots, homicides, escapes, and suicides—U.S. prisons appear to be better run than they were prior to the onset of the prison buildup in the 1970s.[123] But in many other ways, they have become harsher and more punishing institutions thanks to cutbacks in programming and services and to the attacks on "luxuries" behind bars, such as television, that relieve some of the mind-numbing monotony of prison life.[124] Several state prison systems have even cut back from serving three to two meals a day on weekends and holidays.[125] State inmates in Ohio complained that many of them were going hungry because of the nearly twenty hours that elapsed between when they were fed dinner on Friday and when they received "brunch" on Saturday.[126] But as the Supreme Court ruled in *Rhodes v. Chapman* and reaffirmed a decade later in *Wilson v. Seiter*, the Constitution "does not mandate comfortable prisons."[127]

U.S. prisons and jails were in trouble long before the financial crisis of 2008 hit. The key features of the U.S. crisis in corrections include: severe overcrowding, "a lack of effective programming and treatment, the persistence of dangerous and deprived conditions of confinement, and the extensive use of forceful, extreme, and potentially damaging techniques of institutional control."[128] The wave of budget cuts since the onset of the Great Recession appears to have contributed to a further deterioration in the quality of life behind bars and in the quality of life in the disadvantaged communities many prisoners come from and return to after they are released.

It is difficult to assess how much the quality of life in U.S. prisons and jails has eroded with the onset of the Great Recession. This is due to many factors, including rising barriers to access for the media, researchers, and other outside observers, as discussed further in chapter 12. Prisons, jails, and criminal justice institutions are among the least transparent and democratically accountable institutions in the United States.[129] Prisoners' rights advocates say they regularly encounter prison administrators and criminal justice officials who refuse to produce public records in violation of state open record laws, charge excessive fees for public records, and routinely deny members of the public access to what are supposed to be public trials and open courtrooms. In one shocking case, prisoners' rights lawyers discovered a brazen effort by sheriffs in Alabama to hide how much they were skimming from food money allocated for detainees, many of whom were very skinny and very hungry.[130]

There are many other obstacles. They include the lack of sufficient independent monitoring and oversight mechanisms, no national reporting standards on safety, health, and abuse in U.S. correctional facilities, insufficient financial and other resources to support statistical databases, no mandatory federal reporting requirements for key indicators (such as the prevalence of assaults in prison), and quality control issues that vex the limited data that are available.[131] A 2009 National Research Council report even questioned the reliability of data collected by the U.S. Department of Justice's Bureau of Justice Statistics, the country's premier source of statistical information on the criminal justice system.[132]

For these reasons, it is difficult to get an accurate and complete picture of the extent of prison overcrowding, a key indicator of the quality of life in prisons. Prison overcrowding has numerous documented adverse effects on the mental and physical health of inmates, including an increased risk of suicide.[133] Some penal systems, including the federal Bureau of Prisons (BOP), have stopped releasing capacity figures calculated on the basis of how many prison beds a facility was originally designed to contain. Instead, they started measuring capacity based on how many beds can be squeezed into a facility. This revised yardstick was akin to claiming a three-bedroom home can actually accommodate twenty-five people if beds were placed in living rooms, laundry rooms, and storage spaces, explains a key attorney in the legal battles waged against the overcrowded California prison system.[134] In 1995, Connecticut enacted a law that declared capacity figures of state prisons fluid and therefore meaningless and subsequently stopped reporting capacity figures to the federal government.[135]

As of late 2011, at least half of all states were operating their prison systems at above their design capacity.[136] Some jurisdictions were operating facilities way above capacity—including California, which along with Alabama, was operating at nearly double its design capacity prior to the 2011 "realignment" sparked by the legal wrangling the *Brown v. Plata* case. As the federal prison population has grown, federal penitentiaries have become more overcrowded and understaffed. Depending on the security level, the federal prison system was operating at 38–52 percent on average above its rated capacity as of 2012.[137]

The quality of life can vary enormously between correctional facilities, even for prisons and jails at the same custody level. In short, "some prisons are more survivable than others."[138] This is due to differences in factors like the size of the prison population, the age and layout of the physical plant, staffing levels, staff training, the administration's leadership and philosophy, and average spending per inmate.[139] As one expert on correctional health care explains, "If you have seen one prison, you have seen one prison."[140]

Suicide and homicide rates for prisoners differ considerably between penal facilities.[141] After declining significantly between 2001 and 2007, the suicide rate for local jails has been steadily rising. This is likely as a consequence of cutbacks in spending on correctional and community mental health services and on psychiatric beds in mental health institutions, according to mental health experts.[142]

There has been a spate of reports recently about major riots and disturbances in severely overcrowded and mismanaged jails and state prisons.[143] Triple-celling in Georgia sparked a major inmate strike in late 2010.[144] Reports of riots sparked by poor or insufficient food are rising.[145]

For years, unions that represent correctional officers have complained of dangerous staffing and safety levels in state prisons because the number of staff members has not kept pace with the number of inmates.[146] One cannot be sure about trends in prison violence because many states do not systematically collect and report data pertaining to inmate-on-inmate assaults. In addition, there are no reliable national measures of nonlethal violence perpetrated by staff members against incarcerated men and women, despite concerns that use of excessive force is a problem in many jails and prisons.[147] Homicides, assaults, and other acts of violence appear to be on the rise in federal penitentiaries, after falling for years.[148] The inmate-to-staff ratio in federal prisons has escalated—from about 3.6 inmates per staff member in 1997 to about five to one in 2011, compared to a three-to-one ratio for the largest state prison systems. BOP studies have found that higher inmate-to-staff ratios are associated with higher levels of violence among inmates.[149] In 2010, a spokesperson for the federal BOP acknowledged that assaults on staff had become "more severe."[150]

In 2006, the blue ribbon Katzenbach commission concluded that the chronic idleness that afflicts U.S. penal institutions poses one of the greatest threats to safety in prisons.[151] Even prior to the Great Recession, many prisoners were not participating in jobs or educational or other programming.[152] Since then, inmates have had even more time on their hands as the Great Recession hastened many of the downward trends in prison programming and other services.[153] To address a budget shortfall in 2011, Texas legislators radically slashed education programs in state prisons.[154] In 2012–13, the Indiana legislature drastically curtailed one of the country's largest higher education programs for prisoners.[155] Florida offers barely any substance abuse treatment slots for its 100,000 state prisoners.[156] As of 2010, Oklahoma had no drug treatment programs in medium- or maximum-security facilities and had eliminated all sex offender treatment despite state statutes mandating such treatment.[157] When Louisiana abruptly closed Phelps Correctional Center in September 2012 to save money, it abruptly transferred 800 of its nearly 1,000 inmates to Angola state prison. This mass transfer pushed the population of the country's largest maximum-security prison to over 6,000 inmates for the first time in its century-long history.[158]

Lack of Oversight

The race to the bottom is especially perilous in the U.S. case because of the general absence of independent inspection and monitoring of correctional facilities by outside boards or organizations.[159] As the Katzenbach commission concluded in 2006, "Most correctional facilities are surrounded by more than physical walls; they are walled off from external monitoring and public scrutiny to a degree inconsistent with the responsibility of public institutions."[160]

The American Correctional Association has established a minimal set of standards for the accreditation of U.S. penal facilities, but only a tiny fraction of the country's jails and fewer than half of its prisons are accredited.[161] Furthermore, the ACA, which is heavily dependent on the corrections industry for its funding, can hardly be considered an independent watchdog. ACA standards are important in maintaining some level of accountability, but they are primarily procedural and formulaic. ACA visits are highly structured, with much advance warning. Inspectors focus primarily on ascertaining what the written procedures of an institution are, rather than observing whether those procedures are actually followed.[162]

In other Western countries, independent oversight of correctional facilities is standard practice.[163] Most European countries are party to the Committee for the Prevention of Torture and Inhuman or Degrading Treatment or Punishment (CPT), an intergovernmental body that has the authority to inspect and report on conditions in any prison of member nations. CPT observers are entitled to move about freely in all prisons and other places where people are confined against their will. They are permitted to speak privately with all prisoners and other detainees and to have access to any other information they need to determine whether the facilities are adhering to the European Prison Rules.[164]

Many European countries have established extensive, independent oversight mechanisms in addition to the courts to monitor prison conditions. But the judiciary has been the primary watchdog of U.S. jails and prisons. The start of the upward turn in the incarceration rate in the 1970s coincided with the high point in landmark court cases that established some minimal constitutional protections for housing, treating, and disciplining prisoners. After some initial victories, a backlash was in full force by the late 1980s. For more than three decades now, the courts and Congress have been doggedly stripping away these protections and greatly restricting prisoners' access to the courts to challenge the conditions of their confinement.

In the late 1990s, state and local governments began invoking provisions of the federal Prison Litigation Reform Act (PLRA) that permitted them to terminate ongoing judicial oversight of their penal facilities. Congress enacted the PLRA in 1995 with the express aim of getting the courts out of the business of monitoring U.S. jails and prisons and of greatly restricting inmates' access to the courts to challenge their conditions of confinement.[165] The PLRA has made it extremely difficult to hold state officials and prison administrators accountable for the unsafe and degrading conditions of their facilities and "has led to the shutdown of many prisoners rights projects across the United States."[166] As a consequence, putting one's health at serious risk has become a routine part of doing time in many U.S. penal facilities.

Inadequate and unsafe health care has been a leading issue for prison litigation. Health-care spending per capita on prisoners ranges widely, from $11,800 annually in California to $2,200 in Illinois, according to a survey of forty-four states.[167] Thanks to landmark litigation during the heyday of the prisoners' rights movement, inmates in the United States are the only group of people who have a constitutional right to medical care. But over the years "the federal courts have failed to provide an effective form of oversight of medical care in prisons, and no other form of serious oversight exists in the United States."[168] Medical and mental health care is grossly deficient and grossly underfunded in many U.S. prisons and jails.

Reductions in prison population levels will not automatically cure that problem. Michigan, for example, has been widely heralded for its exceptional success recently in reducing its inmate population and closing several penal facilities. But as one expert on the ongoing health-care crisis in Michigan prisons notes, "nothing about the current financial crisis offers grounds for optimism that Michigan will address the current lack of necessary medical care within its prisons."[169] Notably, the U.S. Supreme Court even suggested in the 1991 *Wilson v. Seiter* decision that consideration of fiscal costs could overrule Eighth Amendment claims that prison administrators were deliberately indifferent to an inmate's constitutional protections against cruel and unusual punishment.[170]

As the courts have retreated, states, municipalities, and the federal government generally have resisted establishing independent, adequately financed government bodies with real administrative teeth to monitor and rectify penal conditions and to report their findings to lawmakers and the general public. A comprehensive survey of the correctional oversight mechanisms in each of the fifty states concluded, "formal and comprehensive external oversight—in the form of inspections and routine monitoring of conditions—is truly rare in this country."[171] In 2008, the American Bar Association approved a resolution calling on all levels of government to establish public bodies tasked with regularly monitoring and publicly reporting on the conditions in the correctional and detention facilities in their jurisdiction.[172] But many states, counties, and municipalities continue to balk at imposing greater independent oversight and establishing enforceable standards in their prisons and jails. In 2004, California governor Arnold Schwarzenegger rejected the creation of an independent civilian oversight commission, a key recommendation of his handpicked panel headed by former governor George Deukmejian, a law-and-order conservative. The panel had concluded that the California Department of Corrections was "dysfunctional."[173]

For years, prisoners' rights groups in Texas have been calling for greater independent oversight of the penal system, including permitting unannounced visits to lockups to investigate inmate complaints, but to no avail.[174] The oversight problems are especially acute in county jails in Texas, which has no state standards for health care in these penal facilities. The Texas Commission on Jail Standards (TCJS), which is charged with ensuring that the state's county jails meet basic life and structural safety standards, only requires these facilities to have a medical plan to provide care for inmates.[175] The number of inmates in county jails in Texas who die of illness-related causes nearly rivals the number who die of such causes in the state's prisons—even though county jails usually house half as many inmates and keep them for shorter periods of time. In the 2012–14 biennial budget, Texas legislators cut the TCJS budget by nearly one-third.[176] As of late 2012, the commission had only four inspectors responsible for monitoring conditions in the 244 jails under its jurisdiction and for providing these facilities with technical and other assistance to comply with the standards.[177]

In 2004, TCJS inspectors discovered that the Dallas County jail, the nation's seventh-largest jail system, lacked sufficient smoke detectors and had an inadequate emergency ventilation system, which put inmates at serious risk.[178] It was major news when the jail finally began installing more smoke detectors four years later in June 2008 and finally passed a state inspection in August 2010 for the first time since 2003. To reach that point, "it took a federal lawsuit, over $100 million in improvements and seven years," during which time thousands of inmates were held in Dallas jails that repeatedly failed state inspections.[179]

Even in the face of widespread allegations of abusive conditions, the DOJ has been reluctant to investigate U.S. jails and prisons and to bring civil and criminal action when appropriate. In 2009, the Civil Rights Division of the Department of Justice released a scathing report on the "alarming" number of deaths at Houston's Harris County jail. The report also raised serious concerns about extreme overcrowding and excessive use of force at the jail.[180] Although conditions apparently have not improved significantly, the DOJ has yet to sue the Harris County jail, which also has one of the highest rates of reported sexual abuse of any jail in the country.[181] The DOJ has been slow to launch a major federal civil rights investigation of the Los Angeles county jail system despite numerous reports of pervasive abuse instigated by deputies, including assaults on scores of non-resisting inmates, some of whom were in wheelchairs.[182] In 2013 and 2014, the Justice Department released reports documenting grotesque abuses of mentally ill inmates at a county jail near Pensacola, Florida, and in Pennsylvania's state prisons.[183] The DOJ has been far more aggressive about investigating conditions in local jails and state prisons than in federal penitentiaries, which are under its direct auspices. In May 2013, the GAO issued a disturbing report on the escalating use of administrative segregation in the federal prison system without proper monitoring and safeguards.[184]

The War on the Poor

Mean-spirited cutbacks in corrections budgets and saddling offenders with more fees and other legal financial obligations are part of what some are calling a new war on the poor as poverty is increasingly criminalized.[185] That war is impairing not only the quality of life in U.S. prisons and jails but also the quality of life in the disadvantaged communities that most prisoners come from and return to.

The number of ordinances against the poor for acts of vagrancy, panhandling, and sleeping on the pavement has been rising. At the same time, public sympathy for the poor has been falling since the onset of the Great Recession.[186] "Zero tolerance" policing appears to have been ramped up as officers issue more tickets and make more arrests for minor infractions like jaywalking, littering, truancy, and carrying an open container of alcohol. As a consequence of the poor economy, more defendants are remaining in jail because they and their families cannot afford to post even minimal bonds.

Lawmakers in Washington, DC, and dozens of states have introduced measures of questionable constitutionality that would require drug tests for people receiving public benefits, such as unemployment assistance, welfare, food stamps, public housing, and job training.[187] Several states have enacted such measures, led by Florida, which in July 2011 began requiring adults to pass a drug test in order to be eligible for public assistance.[188] In December 2013, a federal judge ruled that Florida's mandatory drug tests for welfare applicants were unconstitutional.[189] About twenty states already prohibit unemployment assistance for anyone who loses a job due to drug use, and more than a dozen deny welfare benefits to anyone convicted of a drug felony.[190]

At the same time that poverty is increasingly criminalized, states and the federal government have been slashing social services for the poor as the carceral state has expanded at the expense of the welfare state.[191] This may result in more people ending up in prison. By a number of measures—expenditures, personnel, congressional hearings, and legislation—the law enforcement apparatus has been growing while social welfare provision has been contracting. The carceral state has become the primary regulator of the poor and a main conduit of social services for the poor and disadvantaged. Jails and prisons in the United States are now responsible for the largest number of mentally ill people in the country. People who are poor can often get better mental health treatment in jail than in the community. As mental health clinics have gone begging in many communities, urban jails have become the most comprehensive providers of mental health services.[192] Drug courts, domestic violence courts, and parole and probation officers not only monitor the behavior of offenders but also often provide key links to dwindling social services and employment and educational opportunities, as discussed in other chapters.

Some legislators and other public figures have been enthusiastically promoting the cost-savings potential of drug testing for public benefits. In doing so, they also have fostered the image of low-income people as lazy substance abusers who have no one to blame but themselves for their economic and other troubles. In remarks reminiscent of the infamous attacks on "welfare queens" during the Reagan era, Governors Rick Scott (R-FL), Tom Corbett (R-PA), and others have charged that people on public assistance are much more likely to abuse drugs than people who are not (despite studies showing that substance abuse is not substantially more prevalent among welfare recipients).[193] Seeking to explain his state's lagging job growth, Corbett unleashed a firestorm in 2013 when he said one of the main problems was that employers "can't find anyone who has passed a drug test."[194]

Conclusion

Lingering fiscal pressures in the wake of the 2008 financial collapse and economic crisis do not necessarily herald the beginning of the end of the carceral state. In fact, they could prompt a turn toward greater punitiveness, not less, as escalating political and economic anxieties spur more protests and other forms of civil dissent. Furthermore, for some state actors, crime does pay—and handsomely, thanks to the political and economic dividends of civil forfeitures, penal Keynesianism, and bed brokering. In addition, the Great Recession has exacerbated the quiet crisis in the U.S. penal system. Governing under the influence of deficit hysteria, state officials have been making cuts to their corrections and criminal justice budgets that do not save much money. But these cuts have further eroded the quality of life in U.S. jails and prisons. They also have impeded the reintegration of released prisoners back into society and denied many defendants a just and fair adjudication of their cases. At the same time, lawmakers have ramped up the war on the poor as poverty is increasingly criminalized.

Claims that a rollback of the carceral state is inevitable due to its crushing burden on state and local budgets assume that the fiscal costs of the carceral state are transparent and democratically accountable. But the prison buildup of the 1980s and '90s was made possible in part by keeping its real economic and budgetary costs hidden through fiscal sleights of hand, as discussed in the next chapter. Moreover, the prison boom created and empowered new political and economic interests that have a large stake in maintaining the carceral state. Prison guards' unions, private prison companies, public bond dealers, and the suppliers of everything from telephone services to Taser stun guns compose a "motley group of perversely motivated interests" that has coalesced "to sustain and profit from mass imprisonment."[195] They became masters at promoting prisons as economic saviors for distressed communities while keeping the real costs concealed. Furthermore, claims about the growing fiscal burden of the carceral state have provided a huge political opening for the privatization of prisons and the unbridled exploitation of penal labor, as discussed in the next chapter.

CHAPTER THREE

Squaring the Political Circle

The New Political Economy of the Carceral State

It is difficult to get a man to understand something when
his salary depends upon his not understanding it.
—UPTON SINCLAIR

The forces that launched the prison boom are not identical to the ones that sustain the carceral state today. The punitive turn was at the start primarily a political project, not an economic one. But the prison boom created powerful economic actors with close ties to the political sector who are deeply vested today in the carceral state. These include prison guards' unions, the private prison industry, segments of the financial sector, and other private-sector interests.

These groups have been deeply engaged in a project to reengineer the carceral state so that it can withstand calls for its retrenchment or dismantling. In the name of making prisons pay their own way, corporations have sought to loosen or eliminate long-standing restrictions on the exploitation of penal labor. The private prison industry has aggressively sought to privatize more pieces of the penal system by, among other things, buying prisons and jails outright from cash-strapped states and counties and then leasing the facilities back to them. The private sector also has sought to privatize the booming market for bail bonds, community corrections, and alternatives to incarceration. These private-sector interests and their close allies in the public sector represent major obstacles to dismantling the carceral state.

The pillars of the new political economy that began congealing in the 1970s cut through the carceral state. They help explain why the carceral state is so resilient despite its enormous human costs and the threat it poses to democratic institutions. These pillars include the ascendance of the financial sector in the U.S. economy and American politics, the emergence of a well-organized and well-endowed conservative movement with strong ties to the financial sector, the decimation of organized labor, and the hollowing out of parts of the state through privatization and deregulation.

In the 1970s and 1980s, states launched expensive prison-building sprees that entailed major expansions of the public sector at a time when the movement to slash taxes and shrink the government was burgeoning. Leading law-and-order conservatives, many of whom were closely associated with this broader conservative movement, faced a dilemma: how do you engineer a massive and expensive expansion of the penal system while at the same time spearheading a vehemently anti-tax, anti-government movement? In some cases, legislators simply plowed ahead with defunding social services and education to finance the prison boom in a virulently anti-tax environment because they faced little political opposition to doing so. But in many instances, as discussed below, they had to devise ways to square this political circle to keep the economic and other costs of the prison boom obscured from public scrutiny.[1]

Several factors help explain how they were able to accomplish this. The development of innovative financing mechanisms helped keep the true fiscal costs of the prison boom out of the public eye. Furthermore, politicians and government officials shrewdly emphasized how their prisons and jails were comparatively austere and efficient institutions. This deflected attention away from how their corrections budgets were growing by leaps and bounds. Moreover, as states established and modernized their departments of corrections, these state agencies became important independent political actors with vested interests in maintaining or expanding the carceral state.

This chapter begins with a brief analysis of several important factors in the origins and development of the prison buildup in the South and Southwest that help explain how law-and-order legislators and other public officials were able to square the political circle. It focuses on several key states, including California, Arizona, and Texas, that were cauldrons of both the new conservative movement and the turn toward more punitiveness. The chapter then examines how the prison buildup created powerful new political and economic interests that have deftly sought to maintain or expand the carceral state by eviscerating restrictions on the use of penal labor and by privatizing more pieces of the criminal justice system. The recent fiscal crisis has provided an enormous political opportunity to further these two goals, for which prominent conservatives have been steadily laying the political and legislative groundwork for decades with their relentless attacks on taxes and the public sector.

California: Off the Books

Proponents of the fiscal imperative argument discussed in chapters 1 and 2 contend that the United States will begin dismantling the carceral state because it can no longer afford such an expensive penal system in the face of a severely ailing economy and overstressed government budgets and taxpayers. Their argument rests on the assumption that the financial costs of the carceral state are transparent and democratically accountable. It also assumes that the costs of the carceral state are a universal burden. But in California and elsewhere, these costs were obscured from public view. Furthermore, they were a burden to some and a boon to others.

California, which was a trailblazer for the "rehabilitative ideal" in the 1940s and 1950s, became ground zero for the taxpayer revolt of the 1970s and 1980s. With passage of Proposition 13 in 1978, which capped property taxes and deprived municipal governments of key revenues, the state became a national beacon of the rising conservative movement. Although California faced growing opposition to tax increases and any expansion of the public sector, it built approximately two dozen prisons (at a cost of about $280 million to $350 million each) between 1984 and 2005.[2]

Over the years, the California Department of Corrections (CDC) has been extremely inept at managing what goes on inside its prisons (partly because of organized resistance from the state's powerful prison guards' union).[3] But the department has been highly capable when it comes to building more prisons. In California and many other states, the postwar establishment of statewide departments of corrections to oversee their penal facilities, which had been run largely as independent, patronage-ridden fiefdoms, was a critical development.[4] For the first time, states had the capacity to develop integrated penal systems, pursue large-scale prison construction schemes, and respond to national trends in penal policy.

In California and elsewhere, state departments of corrections became powerful, independent political actors in their own right as they centralized and modernized. These departments increased their capacity to shape political debates over penal policy, to thwart federal court interventions, and to pursue major prison-building programs.[5] As legislators sought to build up their penal capacity, they often enacted measures that exempted their departments of corrections from key oversight, budgeting, and financial rules that applied to other state agencies. The administrative procedure acts in more than half of the states explicitly exempt corrections regulations.[6]

In California, a joint legislative committee created in 1982 periodically held hearings that provided the CDC with a highly visible platform to promulgate dire projections about an imminent prison-overcrowding crisis and to promote a vast expansion in the state's penal system. A dramatic increase in the CDC's planning capacity allowed the agency, beginning in 1984, to produce alarmist five-year master plans.[7] These predictions, however dire, would not be enough to neutralize rising public reluctance to pay for more state services, especially prisons. Laboring in the shadow of Proposition 13, legislators and other state officials were increasingly doubtful that taxpayers would support new prison bond packages at the polls. With the help of the state's financial sector, California and other states turned to lease revenue bonds (LRBs) as a backdoor way to fund new prison construction. These bonds allowed legislators and corrections administrators to maneuver around growing anti-tax sentiment.

LRBs skirted states' balanced budget statutes and requirements that voters must ratify new government bond projects. They originally were designed to provide financing for projects that could generate streams of revenue to pay for themselves, such as toll roads, hospitals, parking facilities, and recreational projects. In a creative sleight of public financing, state treasurers together with law firms and investment bankers devised an innovative way for prisons to generate "revenue."[8] States or municipalities would establish an entity or agency to finance new prison construction by issuing lease revenue bonds. This entity or agency would then lease the prisons back to the state or municipality, which was responsible for funding the lease payments that service the bond debt. As *Forbes* explained, "Essentially, the state takes money from one pocket (the general fund appropriations to the prison system) and puts it into another pocket (the agency created for the facility), and then the agency distributes the money to the bondholders."[9] A 1999 report prepared for the Association of State Correctional Administrators advised how revenue bonds could be used to construct additional prisons without exceeding a state or local government's overall debt limit and without having to go before the voters to get approval for a general obligation bond.[10]

The courts generally have held that LRBs do not violate state constitutional mandates that voters approve all debt.[11] LRBs do not require voter approval because technically they do not have the state's "full faith and credit" behind them. But the bonds do imply that the state or local community that issues the bonds has a moral obligation to cover defaults. As such, any default puts at risk the credit rating of the state or municipality that issued the bonds and typically raises the costs of future borrowing.[12]

These revenue bonds became a popular way to finance new prison construction in California and elsewhere beginning in the mid-1980s. Prior to that, new prisons typically were funded either on a pay-as-you-go basis out of general revenue funds or by borrowing money through taxpayer-sanctioned bond referendums.[13] LRBs could be quickly organized and issued. By 1996, more than half of all new prison debt nationwide was in the form of LRBs, which tend to be more expensive to issue than straightforward state bond sales.[14]

The newfangled LRBs allowed the huge costs of the prison buildup and the budgetary trade-offs they necessitated to stay obscured from public view.[15] Thanks to the LRBs, the mechanisms to fund and construct prisons were opaque, fragmented, and not publicly accountable.[16] The full construction costs for new prisons were not enumerated in states' annual budgets but rather in less noticed government reports. LRBs "obscured both the near- and long-term costs of failing to make needed policy changes."[17]

For years, anti-prison activists have sought to spur a wider debate over this invisible issue by drawing public attention to how LRBs are "overpriced, fiscally unsound, and undemocratic."[18] Recently a few critics on the right have joined them. Some Tea Partiers have begun to stir over what they characterize as an "outrageous" financing mechanism to build jails and prisons that dupes voters.[19]

Given the chance for a straight up or down vote, many voters do not want to fund more prisons. Houston found that out in 2007 when voters rejected a bond referendum for a new jail. Six years later, voters approved a $70 million measure by a bare 50.1 percent to finance what was euphemistically named a "joint inmate processing center"—not a jail—on the ballot.[20]

The Carceral State and Economic Development

At the same time that state officials, with the help of the financial sector, were turning to LRBs to keep the real budgetary burden of the prison boom cloaked, public officials in California and elsewhere were promoting prison construction as a key tool of economic development, especially in rural areas.[21] The CDC's Prison Siting Office was extremely effective at persuading economically distressed communities in California that a new prison in their midst would provide an economic windfall. In the mid-1980s, the office began strategically targeting rural communities for new prison construction, figuring they would put up less political resistance than urban areas.[22]

We now know that prisons provide few economic benefits to local communities, notably the rural areas that have been the primary sites for new prison construction since the 1980s. Rural counties with prisons do not have lower unemployment rates or higher per capita incomes than rural counties without prisons. Many of the new jobs created by prisons go to people living outside the county where the prison is built. Prisons also fail to generate significant linkages to the local economy, because local businesses often are unable to provide the goods and services needed to operate penal facilities. Research suggests that prison construction might actually impede economic growth in rural areas, especially in counties that lag behind in the number of college graduates, and that prison towns have experienced a greater increase in unemployment and poverty.[23] Anti-prison activists have been using such findings to challenge popular claims that prisons bring economic development to rural communities.[24] But during economic hard times, this is a tougher case to make.

Well-organized consortiums of private companies that specialize in pitching speculative and risky prison projects have continued to troll communities desperate for jobs, especially in rural areas in the South and Southwest. They have used misleading or outright false feasibility studies to sell local public officials on the idea that a speculative jail or prison financed by lease revenue bonds will bring economic salvation.[25] In some cases, bribes of local officials have greased the way for penal facilities built on spec with long-term bonds. Many states and municipalities have been locked into paying for unneeded prison space because the promised inmate windfall never materialized.[26] The Internal Revenue Service has begun auditing some of these bond arrangements to see if they abused the rules for tax-exempt status.[27]

In the aftermath of the Great Recession, many towns and counties in the South and Southwest have been scrambling to avoid defaulting on these bonds by raising taxes and fees, laying off public employees, and slashing their budgets. As of 2011, more than half of all privately operated county jail beds in Texas were empty.[28] The 1,100-bed private county lockup in Anson, Texas, is derisively known as the Jail to

Nowhere because it remains empty. Local officials in Texas have been wrangling with state legislators over whether the state should bail them out for their speculative jail-building sprees.[29]

These disputes are related to a larger battle playing out across the country over who gets to stand first in line in bankruptcy court. With the onset of the Great Recession, more municipalities and counties have faced the prospect not just of defaulting on certain bonds, but also of actually having to declare bankruptcy. This has spurred a fierce fight over who gets preferential treatment in bankruptcy court—most famously in the tragic saga playing out in Detroit since the city declared bankruptcy in 2013. Some states have enacted laws and pursued policies that favor bondholders over public pensions and other obligations in bankruptcy cases.[30] In a decision with national repercussions, a federal judge ruled in December 2013 that Detroit's obligation to pay employee pensions in full was not inviolable.

Arizona: Cheap and Mean

LRBs and the economic windfall that prison construction purportedly brings to communities have been just two of the ways to divert the public gaze away from the true budgetary and other costs of the penal system. Another strategy has been to keep political attention focused on how state officials have struggled to operate "cheap and mean" facilities in the face of intrusive federal judges bent on mollycoddling felons by insisting on greater federal oversight of penal facilities. This helps explain how Arizona has been able to build and sustain a massive and expensive penal system while extolling fiscal conservatism and casting disdain on the public sector.

Fiscal frugality has long been the "guiding principle of all government endeavors in Arizona," the home state of Barry Goldwater, the standard-bearer of the resurgent conservative movement.[31] Until the late 1970s, Arizona doggedly resisted making a big investment in new penal facilities. Yet between 1971 and 2000, the state's incarceration rate increased nearly sevenfold and spending on corrections skyrocketed.[32] As the prison population grew, the state's DOC solidified its position "as one of the largest and most politically influential state agencies in Arizona."[33] During the recessions of the early 1990s and early 2000s, some public officials proposed promising reforms to save money by reducing the prison population. But those reforms were scuttled as penal policy veered off in a more punitive direction.

Mona Lynch portrays the punitive turn in Arizona as largely a top-down phenomenon prompted by a major political realignment. Until the 1950s, Arizona looked like a traditional one-party Southern state dominated by conservative Democrats. Beginning in the 1960s, the state became more politically competitive as right-leaning Republicans made serious electoral inroads, and pockets of progressive Democrats challenged the party's old guard, especially in urban areas. This new political competition set the stage for the hyper-politicization of penal policy. Lawmakers and state officials generally did not waver from their hard-line policies even in the face of reports from the DOC and elsewhere in the 1990s that the new punitive regime had had no measurable impact on the state's crime rate, and that plans for another round of get-tough policies would necessitate a massive increase in spending on corrections.[34]

As in the case of California, state officials and politicians in Arizona instigated the prison boom, but other groups mobilized subsequently to spur it on. Victims' rights groups and unionized prison guards were not key political actors in propelling Arizona's boom, unlike in California. Law enforcement officers, notably prosecutors and sheriffs who shrewdly used the media, played a central role in Arizona. As severe economic distress gripped the state in the early 1990s, they mobilized to defend and extend the harsh sentencing regime and thwarted proposals to reduce the state's prison population. As a result, the reform efforts of the early 1990s morphed into yet another round of get-tough legislation.[35]

Several factors helped neutralize or deflect concerns about how the huge size and growing expense of the penal system were at odds with Arizona's historical commitment to frugality and a limited public sector. Lawmakers required that all new prisons be constructed predominantly with inmate labor.[36] Administrators and state officials also stressed how the state's penal system was "cheap and mean." At every opportunity they underscored their frugality. "So even when *actual* spending was profligate . . . such expenditures were sold politically to the populace as both necessary and cost-efficient," explains Lynch.[37]

In their public statements and annual reports, state officials in Arizona celebrated cost-saving measures like reducing the use of heat and air-conditioning in prisons, leveling more fees on inmates and their families, purchasing "seconds" of damaged or old food from wholesalers, and cutting off the electricity on cell blocks during the day.[38] They even heralded the cost savings to be had by converting the gas chamber to accommodate administration of capital punishment by lethal injection.[39] State officials also stressed the exploitation of penal labor to save money, noting how penal farms were run almost entirely by inmate labor, and that all prison construction projects were required by law to use inmate labor.[40] In its annual reports, Arizona's DOC "prided itself on spending significantly less than the national average on inmates."[41] This deflected attention from the fact that, as of 1999, Arizona "ranked among the top three states in the nation in terms of the proportion of the state budget allocated to corrections."[42]

The emphasis on fiscal conservatism legitimized a new "race to the bottom" in Arizona's penal facilities. As spending for corrections skyrocketed in Arizona, state officials emphasized how they were toughening up life behind bars for inmates. They attacked the reputed "good life" in prison by requiring inmates to do a stint of hard labor during their confinement and by imposing new restrictions on clothes, grooming, personal items, visitors, and compassionate leave.[43] Alleged luxuries like television, weight-lifting equipment, access to the courts, and even suntan lotion for inmates working in the blazing Arizona desert sun came under attack. As in the case of California, Arizona's legislators moved to exempt the state's DOC from key rules that applied to other state agencies, including a requirement that the state give notice and hold public hearings on all major changes in rules and practices. This exemption "contributed to the acceleration of the flagrant punitiveness of Arizona prisons."[44]

Arizona became a leader not only in incarcerating its citizens but also in pioneering the widespread use of supermax prisons and humiliating and degrading punishments like chain gangs. Beginning in the mid-1990s, prison guards in Arizona routinely deployed pepper gas and Israeli foggers on inmates. In 1997, the director of corrections authorized the use of attack dogs in cell extractions. The dogs were trained to bite and hold on as the inmate was pulled from his cell by an animal attached to a 30-foot leash.[45]

In the late 1970s and early 1980s, Arizona scrambled to comply with federal consent decrees concerning prison overcrowding and other violations. But by the mid-1980s, leading state officials were staking out a more oppositional stance to prisoner lawsuits and federal oversight. The DOC and governor's office doggedly fought to dismantle the limited federal protections the courts had extended to prisoners beginning in the 1960s. The DOC openly defied earlier decrees in the name of budgetary constraints and aggressively sought to overturn court decisions extending prisoners' rights. Along with Texas and Florida, Arizona became a "trailblazer that ultimately reshaped the national landscape of prisoner litigation" by greatly restricting prisoner access to the federal courts and limiting federal judicial oversight.[46]

Arizona's 1996 U.S. Supreme Court victory in *Lewis v. Casey* further emboldened state officials.[47] The state began refusing to pay special master's fees in federal consent decrees and challenged them in the courts. It denied the U.S. Department of Justice access to state prisons to investigate numerous allegations of employee sexual misconduct involving prisoners.[48] In the mid-1990s, state officials in Arizona provided the legislative blueprint and crucial political momentum to propel the U.S. Congress to enact the Prison Litigation Reform Act (PLRA), which has greatly restricted inmates' access to the courts to challenge their conditions of confinement.[49]

State officials in Arizona demonized federal judges and other individuals and organizations that attempted to intervene in the operation of the penal system. They kept the public focus on states' rights issues and allegations of excessive federal intrusion. State officials raged that Arizona's prisons had become such a fiscal burden largely because of onerous and intrusive federal regulation and oversight of the state's penal system. They also blamed federal permissiveness to inmate lawsuits. Their withering attacks on Washington and the federal judiciary obscured the fact that the prison boom in Arizona had radically increased the power of the state government, the size of the public sector, and the fiscal burden of the penal system.

Texas: The Control Model

The prison boom was slower to take off in Texas than Arizona or California. It wasn't until the early 1990s that the Lone Star State's incarceration rate leapfrogged ahead of California's and that of the rest of the South.[50] In a familiar story, as Republicans made electoral inroads in the state in the 1980s and as old guard Democrats vied with pockets of progressive Democrats, the stage was set for the hyper-politicization of penal policy in a retributive, law-and-order direction. When Republican governor William P. Clements returned to office in 1987, he pushed for a major prison expansion. He sought the help of business leaders and law enforcement groups, notably the Texas District & County Attorneys Association (TDCAA) and the Criminal Justice Task Force, which the administration had established to coordinate efforts to pass an anti-crime and prison expansion package. Even though the dire state of the Texas economy dominated the 1986 election, Clements succeeded in securing a major general obligation bond for prison expansion that was bundled within a larger set of bonds. This jettisoned a long-standing commitment to pay-as-you-go fiscal management.

The ongoing legal reverberations of the 1980 *Ruíz v. Estelle* decision, which declared Texas's overcrowded and unhealthy prisons to be unconstitutional, provided Clements and other hard-liners with an opportunity to expand the state's penal system and to bureaucratize and professionalize its control model. Penal hard-liners faced little resistance because they operated in a political culture characterized by low levels of political participation. This included low voter turnout and the absence of statewide civic associations for African Americans, low-income people, and Mexican Americans—the groups most likely to be ensnared in the state's growing dragnet.[51]

Battered around in the courts for about two decades, *Ruíz v. Estelle* eventually brought about some important changes in the state's penal system. But indirectly it also "helped create an equally severe and infinitely larger prison system in its place."[52] Penal hard-liners eventually eviscerated many of the court-ordered reforms after wars of attrition played out in the legal arena. As for David Resendez Ruíz, the lead plaintiff in this landmark federal lawsuit, he was kept in solitary confinement in a cramped, dank, dungeon-like cell for decades after the lawsuit was settled. Just months before he died in 2005, he was moved to a prison hospital after being denied medical parole. As Robert Perkinson dryly notes, Ruíz fought the law, but the law ultimately won.[53]

To sum up, for decades now, lawmakers in California, Texas, Arizona, and elsewhere have readily finessed the potential political obstacles posed by massive increases in spending on corrections amidst periodic economic downturns and mounting calls for fiscal conservatism, government retrenchment, and no new taxes. Never very attached to the rehabilitative model to begin with, Texas and Arizona became forerunners of a leading alternative model of punishment premised on maximum control at minimum cost with little outside oversight. They became crucibles for get-tough innovations, including three-strikes laws, boot camps, the extensive use of solitary confinement, the revival of humiliating and degrading punishments like chain gangs, and an uncompromising defiance of federal intervention and oversight.

Penal Labor: Back to the Future?

Some leading conservatives have long contended that the fiscal burden of the carceral state was manageable as long as prisons were liberated to pay their own way.[54] The push to deregulate penal labor quickened with the onset of the Great Recession. More lawmakers began touting prison labor as a salve on their budget crises. During the Great Recession, Republican state senator Al Melvin championed inmate labor as *the* solution bar none for Arizona's budget woes.[55] Many government officials have applauded putting inmates to work doing tasks previously performed by public-sector workers—everything from hanging holiday decorations to breaking apart beaver dams to maintaining public buildings to collecting road kill along highways to manning call centers for state agencies.[56] Government officials embarking on new prison construction have emphasized how they are economizing by using the cheap sweat of incarcerated men to build new lockups.[57]

Across the country, lawmakers have been aggressively pushing to expand the use of penal labor through partnerships with private-sector firms. Some supporters of deregulating penal labor have championed these partnerships as a way to lure jobs lost to overseas competition back to the United States. Long before the Great Recession set in, former Reagan attorney general Ed Meese and others were championing prison labor as a way to reverse the exodus of U.S. jobs overseas to countries with lower wages and laxer environmental and labor protections.[58] A 1995 study for the National Institute of Justice touted inmate labor as a dependable and cost-effective alternative to investing in *maquiladoras* and other types of overseas production.[59] Government officials also have championed partnerships with the private sector as a way to offset labor shortages resulting from a dwindling supply of undocumented workers, especially in the agricultural sector.[60] In 2011, Governor Nathan Deal (R-GA) proposed sending unemployed probationers to toil in Georgia's fields as a solution for a labor shortage that farmers claimed was a consequence of the immigration crackdown. Critics blasted this proposal as a modern-day reinvention of the reviled convict-leasing system of a century ago.[61]

About half of all inmates in federal and state prisons, or about 800,000 people as of 2010, have some sort of work assignment, according to federal surveys. If we assume that about half of all people confined in jails also have some sort of work activity, which may be too generous an assumption, then about 1.1 million inmates were working in 2010.[62] Most prison work assignments are related to some aspect of running the penal facility, such as food service, building maintenance, and office administration. In the federal and state prison systems, public works assignments (such as park and road maintenance) are the second most common work assignment, followed by employment in prison industries that produce products for the government and private sector. In about one out of six prisons, inmates are engaged in agricultural activities. These prisons tend to be concentrated in the South and Southwest where most of the country's penal farms are located.[63]

The goal of turning prisons into moneymaking machines or at least ensuring that they pay their own way is not that far-fetched. The United States has a long history of exploiting inmate labor to make prisons and penal farms highly productive and lucrative. As George J. Beto, the director of the Texas Department of Corrections, told the American Correctional Association in 1970, "the tax-conscious constituent will demand it."[64] In the nineteenth century and well into the twentieth, many penal systems paid for themselves, thanks to the brutal convict-leasing system in the South and the "gruesomely exploitative" prison factories in the North and West.[65]

When the penitentiary took root in the early nineteenth century in the United States, supporters promoted it as a way to mend men's minds and turn them into law-abiding citizens of the new republic. But by 1866, a disillusioned U.S. prison chaplain was lamenting that the main objective of the penitentiary "has [been] to make *nails*, and not *men*."[66] With the invention of the penitentiary, many government officials—especially in the South—feared that their expensive new penal systems would become "vampire[s] upon the public treasury."[67] They sought to make their penal enterprises not just self-sustaining but also highly profitable.[68]

For more than half a century following the Civil War, controversies over the convict-leasing system were a defining feature of Southern politics.[69] Under the lease system, state authorities and prison officials hired out convicts to private contractors who exploited their labor under appalling conditions for a fixed sum. Guarded by overseers with guns and bloodhounds, leased-out convicts labored in "nurseries of death" under conditions that were in many ways more brutal than slave life on the antebellum plantation.[70] For many states, leasing out convicts was their single largest source of budget revenue.

Convict leasing was at the center of some of the most politically charged issues of the late nineteenth and early twentieth centuries in the South. By the mid-1920s, states throughout the South had enacted bans on leasing out convicts. State-run chain gangs and penal farms, which were modeled on the old slave plantation system, became the symbols of a more enlightened public notion of economic development and punishment in the Progressive era. The inhumane and cruel conditions on Southern penal farms and chain gangs went largely unchanged and unchallenged until the civil rights and the prisoners' rights movements targeted them in the 1960s and 1970s.[71]

In the North and West, controversies swirled around factories run by private companies inside prisons. By the Gilded Age, many penitentiaries in the North and West had been turned into industrial enterprises whose productivity and profitability were premised on meting out "highly rationalized forms of torture" to prisoners with few legal protections.[72] At key moments, inmates in Northern prisons succeeded in turning the "prison into a stage upon which to dramatize their grievances and publicly indict their captors."[73] Their strikes, riots, and other protest actions against contracted penal labor resonated with growing public concerns in the late nineteenth century about the new industrial economy. Public angst centered on how not just prisoners but also artisans and factory workers were being transformed into "industrial slaves" dominated by an amoral, instrumental, bottom-line rationality.[74] Growing opposition to the prison factory system was a major political issue in the nineteenth century and early twentieth century.[75]

Workingmen's organizations and the nascent labor movement forged powerful coalitions with penal reformers, politicians, and members of the clergy that ultimately succeeded in abolishing contract prison labor across the country after the New York State legislature took the first step in 1894. Government officials scrambled to replace contract labor with a workable state-use system of prison industries whereby inmates produced items to be used by government agencies.[76] But a broader political movement led by organized labor eventually turned the public tide against state-use prison industries and against deploying convict labor on public works projects. In the 1930s, Congress enacted several important pieces of legislation that largely preempted state legislation by greatly limiting the manufacture, distribution, and sale of prison-made products to the public and private interests.

These measures did not completely outlaw the use of prison labor. Rather, they "formalized and legitimized" its use. In 1934, the Federal Prison Industries (FPI), a government corporation charged with managing penal labor, was created.[77] In the postwar decades, the federal government and the states "were still able to force inmates to work for little or no pay, often under terrible conditions," as long as inmates were producing items for state use.[78] However, the limits on interstate commerce in inmate-made goods and other restrictions largely locked the private sector out of the convict labor business and thus set important bounds on how much the penal labor market could grow.[79]

Slaves of the State

Since the 1930s, the federal prison system has developed a phenomenal industrial capacity. During World War II, the FPI was a major military supplier as prison factories worked round-the-clock producing everything from bomb fins and casings to parachutes and cargo nets. Government officials, the press, and the public widely praised inmates for their patriotic contributions to the war effort.[80] As military contracts dried up after the war, FPI diversified its production to attract contracts with other government agencies. FPI's business with the military subsequently picked up again thanks to the Cold War, the Vietnam War, and the defense buildup under the Reagan administration. Today, Federal Prison Industries, which took the trade name UNICOR in 1977, is a major military supplier of everything from helmets to protective goggles to uniforms to cables for TOW and Patriot missiles.[81] In 2011, nearly half of UNICOR's $900 million in revenues came from military contracts, making it the country's fifty-sixth largest military contractor, a position that was on par with that of Xerox.[82]

Over the years, UNICOR has sought to rebrand itself and diversify its products and services. Federal prison administrators view expanding UNICOR's production and contracts as a key means to offset the costs of the growing federal prison system and to enhance prison security and safety by keeping inmates busy. For the federal government, it is cheaper to keep inmates occupied by investing in prison factories rather than by investing in counseling, drug treatment, and educational programs to keep them busy.[83]

The 13,000 inmates employed full and part time in federal prisons as of 2013 labor largely outside the workplace protections that shield civilian workers in the United States and elsewhere.[84] While prisoners in Germany are entitled to many of the same workplace protections as civilian workers, including vacation and unemployment benefits, U.S. inmates working for UNICOR do not even accrue Social Security benefits. Furthermore, U.S. courts have decreed that the federal Fair Labor Standards Act generally does not apply to prisoners because they do not work voluntarily and thus are not really "employees."[85] In 2010, a federal appeals court ruled that the government could fix prison wages at any price—even zero. The court noted that the Thirteenth Amendment to the Constitution, which outlawed slavery and involuntary servitude, made an exception for people convicted of crimes.[86] Being forced to work without pay was the leading complaint of inmates in seven Georgia prisons who went on strike in December 2010 in one of the biggest prison protests in recent memory.[87]

Since its early days, FPI has had to contend with charges that it undercuts private businesses and the civilian labor force. In recent years, attacks on UNICOR have escalated. The main focus of these attacks has not been the unbridled exploitation of penal labor but rather the unfair monopoly that the federal government allegedly enjoys thanks to its use of penal labor. At the center of the controversy is a provision dating back to the 1930s that requires the federal government to purchase items from UNICOR, sometimes even when those goods can be bought more cheaply elsewhere.[88]

In recent years, UNICOR has been a target of leading conservatives, and some business executives and business organizations.[89] A bipartisan coalition of lawmakers has been seeking to overhaul UNICOR's operations. They want to eliminate its preferential status, subject it to greater congressional oversight, impose federal work-safety standards, and raise the hourly wage.[90] Budget cuts stemming from congressional hostility and the poor economy have forced UNICOR to shutter factories and cut staff in recent years.[91]

Slaves of the Private Sector

At the same time that legislators have been pushing back against UNICOR, they have been pushing hard to liberate the private sector to enter the inmate labor market in a big way. With the decline of organized labor and the onset of the neoliberal era in the closing decades of the twentieth century, the hard-fought restrictions on the sale of prison-made goods and the use of prison labor have been eroding. The Prison Industries Enhancement Act, which was part of the Justice System Improvement Act of 1979, essentially repealed the Depression-era restrictions on interstate commerce in prisoner-made products.[92] It authorized the establishment of several pilot joint public-private penal enterprises under the Prison Industries Enhancement Certification Program (PIECP or PIE). Over the years, Congress has enacted legislation to expand this program. By 2011, programs in thirty-eight states and six counties had received PIECP certification.[93]

Certification is contingent on satisfying nine mandatory requirements. However, in a neoliberal era in which regulation is viewed with disdain, organized labor is on life support, and the private sector has the will, resources, and organizational capacity to dominate politics, these regulations have been easy to maneuver around. "Virtually all of the mandatory requirements for PIECP program are being ignored or openly violated," according to one expert on prison industries.[94] For example, prison industries routinely fail to consult with unions and local businesses to see if a new PIE program will undercut local workers and employers. PIE workers rarely receive wages comparable to those of civilian workers. Prison industries levy improper deductions on inmates' wages and ignore applicable state labor laws for their captive workers.[95] Like many penal programs, PIECP is subject to little independent oversight and essentially oversees itself.[96]

The number of people employed by PIE programs is relatively tiny—only about 5,000 inmates scattered in 190 operations in thirty-nine states and six counties as of 2011.[97] Although PIE and UNICOR operations are too small to alter the general market in any economic sector, they have had an enormous impact in certain localities. There are numerous examples of how prison industries are undercutting local wages and displacing civilian workers performing a huge range of jobs—everything from assembling circuit boards to repairing copiers to laundering hospital linens.[98]

Initially most PIE partnerships were with small businesses that had difficulty hiring or retaining employees due to low wages and fluctuating schedules. That changed radically beginning in the 1990s as state bans or restrictions on prison-made goods began to topple and gaping holes in PIE restrictions appeared. A who's who of corporate America—including Wal-Mart, Victoria's Secret, Boeing, and Starbucks—discovered the potential windfall of a captive labor force as their subcontractors began to harness penal labor.[99] Even Whole Foods got into the captive labor market by purchasing hormone-free, prison-raised tilapia.[100]

ALEC and Penal Labor

As with many penal innovations in the age of mass incarceration, the American Legislative Exchange Council (ALEC), the conservative lobbying organization, has been a key player in liberating the private sector to employ penal labor and expand the privatization of corrections. Since it was established in the early 1970s, ALEC has been an important pipeline for coordinating the introduction and enactment of conservative and corporate-friendly laws in state legislatures nationwide.[101] This nonprofit organization, which now sits at the epicenter of the privatization and anti-union movements, claims more than 2,000 state legislators as members (or about one-third of the nation's total state lawmakers), as well as more than two hundred corporations and special-interest groups.[102] Its ten task forces are each responsible for developing "model legislation," which ALEC members then sponsor back home. ALEC runs a "sophisticated operation for shaping public policy at a state-by-state level," according to the *New York Times.* "[S]pecial interests effectively turn ALEC's lawmaker members into stealth lobbyists, providing them with talking points, signaling how they should vote and collaborating on bills affecting hundreds of issues."[103]

Over the years, private prison companies and the National Rifle Association (NRA) have played leading roles in ALEC. Both the Corrections Corporation of America (CCA) and The GEO Group, the country's two largest private prison companies, have been longtime members and supporting contributors to ALEC. CCA paid an additional annual membership fee to secure a seat on ALEC's Public Safety Task Force, a key incubator of the signature law-and-order legislation that fueled the prison boom in the 1980s and 1990s, including mandatory minimums, truth in sentencing, and three-strikes laws.[104] CCA and The GEO Group reportedly are no longer members of ALEC.[105]

ALEC's generally low political profile was blown in spring 2012 with the controversy surrounding the shooting death of Trayvon Martin in Florida. His death put the Stand Your Ground laws that ALEC had been promoting in dozens of states under intense public scrutiny. More than a dozen corporations withdrew funding from ALEC, including big-name firms like McDonald's, Pizza Hut, and Coca-Cola. In the wake of the controversy surrounding Martin's death, ALEC announced in April 2012 that it was disbanding its Public Safety Task Force.

For at least two decades now, ALEC has been pushing to expand PIECP and to make prison industries more attractive to the private sector, especially the organization's large corporate benefactors.[106] In 1995, ALEC began promoting its Prison Industries Act. This measure was modeled on a controversial bill that the Texas legislature had enacted with the help of state representative Ray Allen, who was active with ALEC and also was a lobbyist for the National Correctional Industries Association (NCIA).[107]

Other state bans or restrictions on penal labor began tumbling in the 1990s. California voters repealed the state's constitutional ban on hiring out inmates to the private sector in 1990. Four years later, Oregon voters overwhelmingly approved a ballot initiative that requires all state inmates to work full time. This measure propelled the state's prison industries and joint correctional ventures with the private sector. Oregon's "Prison Blues" line of jeans and other denim products has garnered a national and international following and is perhaps the best known of any inmate-made goods produced in the United States. Oregon and other states have sought to expand their overseas exports of prison-made products. Meanwhile, U.S. importation of inmate-made goods from other countries has been at the center of charged disputes over human rights, especially between the United States and China.[108]

With the budget crunch brought on with the Great Recession, the number of PIE programs has been shrinking as states struggle to fund their prison industries.[109] At the same time, interest has grown in figuring out how to get a better return on penal labor. This typically translates into figuring out how to give the private sector a freer hand to exploit inmate labor. Across the country, legislators from both parties have been introducing measures to facilitate the private sector's use of penal labor.[110]

Lax Regulation

As in the days of convict leasing, inmates have once again been enlisted to do some of the dirtiest and most dangerous jobs with little regard for their health, safety, or dignity. Workplace conditions at UNICOR's operations are not closely monitored by outside inspectors. A 2010 government report revealed that inmates and staff at ten UNICOR recycling programs had been exposed for many years to extremely hazardous working conditions as they smashed computer monitors and cathode rays and dismantled devices marked with radiation symbols and skulls and crossbones. The federal Bureau of Prisons had only one certified industrial hygienist to serve 115 institutions and 103 UNICOR factories, according to the report.[111]

The government investigation found that UNICOR officials had a pervasive disregard for inmate and staff safety.[112] The searing report concluded that the program to recycle electronic waste, which was established in the mid-1990s, violated more than thirty safety requirements. This program repeatedly exposed prison staff and inmates (whose protective gear was often just gloves and steel-toed boots) to high levels of cadmium and lead. It was not until mid-2003 that UNICOR began making safety improvements to its recycling programs. By 2009—a decade and a half after the recycling operation was established—it was finally deemed to be in compliance with occupational standards.

Some of the worst abuses of PIE programs have occurred in the agricultural sector, especially in states like Arizona where the immigration crackdown has resulted in a shortage of farm workers in some locales. A state law in Arizona requires all able-bodied inmates to work. In Arizona and elsewhere, inmates who refuse to work jeopardize the "good time" credits they have been accumulating for early release.[113] Arizona contracts out inmates to agricultural producers and has the distinction of having the country's only female chain gangs. At one point, it contracted out female chain gangs to Martori Farms, one of Wal-Mart's leading suppliers. The women worked for fifty cents an hour, far below the prevailing wage, in blistering heat without proper water, breaks, or protection from the sun. Asked how Martori Farms and other private contractors could get away with what is arguably forced labor in violation of PIE's own regulations, a spokesman for NCIA "explained that the PIE program classifies certain work functions as a 'service' rather than an actual 'job.'" Thus "services" like picking crops in the blazing desert sun are exempt from its mandatory requirements.[114]

After the massive Deepwater Horizon oil spill in 2010, BP's use of inmate labor to clean up Gulf Coast beaches was an open secret. Local residents were outraged that the oil company first turned to inmates to clean up the mess rather than to people who had lost their livelihoods because of the disaster. Like other private employers, BP had a huge financial incentive to hire inmate labor thanks to the

Work Opportunity Tax Credit, which was instituted in the mid-1990s as part of the welfare-to-work movement. This provision rewards employers with a tax credit—typically around $2400—for hiring risky "target groups"—in this case, inmates from Louisiana's extensive work-release program.

The labor contractors for BP did make one concession to local outrage. In the first few days of the cleanup, workers wearing scarlet pants and white t-shirts with the words "Inmate Labor" emblazoned across them worked on the beaches shoveling contaminated sand into trash bags for hours on end in the searing sun. These uniforms soon disappeared, replaced by BP shirts and jeans.

Some of the inmates enlisted for the cleanup were ferried back and forth to jail in unmarked white vans. Others were housed in converted shipping containers with "Jails to Go" marked on the side. The containers, with their barred windows and deadbolt locks on the doors, appeared to be modern-day reincarnations of the dreaded "rolling cages" that carried leased convicts from one work site to another a century ago.[115]

Cells for Sale

For more than four decades now, the ardent push to privatize more government services—everything from education to national security—has been a defining feature of the neoliberal turn in American politics. Champions of privatization contend that the government should step aside—or be pushed aside—because the private sector can deliver better services at lower cost. The economic crisis fostered an extremely favorable climate for the prison industry and its supporters to promote not just penal labor but also privatization as a solution to escalating penal costs. Prison companies have viewed the crisis as a great opportunity to buy up more penal facilities as hard-pressed states and municipalities seek infusions of quick cash and as a virulently anti-government movement vilifies public workers and public services. "Desperate government is our best customer," explained the head of a finance company that specializes in infrastructure privatization.[116]

Since the 1980s, privatization has been transforming the character of punishment, "reducing the punitive enterprise to a question of price point and logistics."[117] The quality of life in private penal facilities generally has been incidental to discussions of privatization among lawmakers and other government officials.[118] But it has become a major issue for coalitions of human rights, labor, and immigrant groups mobilizing against privatization of the carceral state.[119] Private prisons have an extremely checkered record in terms of cost savings and performance, which should raise serious questions about their value to the public. These questions have not received much of a hearing in the stampede to privatize more penal services and facilities in the wake of the Great Recession, however. Recent debates over prison privatization have focused primarily on potential cost savings with little regard for whether private prisons deliver better services and whether contracting out everything from prisons to probation may be fundamentally changing the character of punishment and the character of U.S. democracy.

Over the years, states have taken various approaches to prison privatization. Some have allowed and encouraged the spread of private facilities while others have banned them outright. The recent economic crisis has turned the tide toward more privatization, not less. Private prisons once again are serving "as a kind of escape valve that relieves the pressures we might otherwise feel" to undertake a penetrating critical evaluation of our penal policies and practices.[120]

Recently governors and other state officials have presented breathtaking plans to privatize their penal operations in the face of scant evidence that privatized facilities and operations offer major cost savings and alarming evidence that they are more likely to jeopardize the health and safety of inmates and staff. Many of these state officials have close ties to the prison industry, thanks to the revolving door between the private and public sectors and the huge investments that the corrections industry has made in lobbying and campaign contributions.[121] In 2009, Arizona legislators approved a plan to turn over the operation of nearly every state prison to private companies as part of a wild sell-off of numerous state properties, including the state capitol building, to raise quick cash. After no credible bidder came forward, the plan was repealed.[122] Republican governor Rick Scott's proposal to privatize at least twenty-seven of Florida's state prisons came within a hair's breadth of passing in early 2010. Governors John Kasich (R-OH) and Bobby Jindal (R-LA) have doggedly sought a massive sell-off of their state prisons to the private sector.[123] In 2011, Ohio became the first state to sell a state-owned prison to a private firm. That same year, the administration of Governor Rick Perry (R-TX) created an uproar with its behind-the-scenes discussions of a private-sector takeover of the state's correctional health-care system.[124]

Contrary to what many critics of the prison industrial complex claim, the private prison industry was not a leading cause of the prison boom. Rather, mass incarceration helped transform the private prison sector into a powerful and nimble political player that today poses a major obstacle to dismantling the carceral state. Leading for-profit prison firms like CCA and The GEO Group have been pivotal in helping the carceral state adapt to shifting political and economic circumstances. Moreover, the private prison industry has become an integral part of a broader conservative political movement to hollow out the state and turn many public functions and services over to the private sector.

With the onset of the Great Recession, privatization in corrections entered a new phase. Previously, the prison industry's market largely consisted of supplying additional beds for county, state, and federal prisoners and immigrant detainees.[125] That began to change rapidly as an increasingly consolidated and powerful prison industry sought to take over existing state prisons and lease them back to the states. Private prison companies also sought to diversify into probation, parole, reentry, and other community-based services for profit (including assisting local law enforcement agencies in carrying out lockdowns and drug raids at public schools).[126]

As discussed earlier, profiting from penal labor was a common practice in the nineteenth and early twentieth centuries. After decades of hard-fought political battles, the public eventually recoiled against the rapacious and often brutal exploitation of inmates by private contractors working hand-in-hand with corrupt government officials. By the early decades of the twentieth century, imprisonment and the administration of other criminal justice functions were viewed in the United States and elsewhere as primarily government responsibilities. By the middle of the twentieth century, the idea that these were "core" government functions appeared to be a settled question.[127]

Contracting out for penal services did not completely disappear. States and local governments relied on the private sector for a range of services to run their penal systems, including medical care, food services, counseling, community treatment, juvenile detention, and halfway houses. In the 1960s, contracting out for penal services accelerated, but direct state administration and ownership of adult prisons and jails remained the norm. That began to change in the late 1970s and early 1980s, thanks largely to the federal government, not the private prison industry, which was still in its infancy. Faced with a need to house more undocumented immigrants quickly, the federal Immigration and Naturalization Service (INS) began contracting with private prison firms in the early 1980s to design, build, and operate detention facilities. These federal contracts "provided the seedbed for the contemporary private imprisonment industry in the United States."[128]

Some activists fighting the carceral state have directed much of their wrath at the companies that build and administer private prisons. Although the private corrections industry is certainly a major player in penal policy today, for-profit prisons are a relatively new phenomenon. CCA, the world's largest private prison company, was founded in 1983, the year the first privately run prison for adults opened and a full decade into the prison boom. The emerging market in immigrant detention and a federal court decision declaring that Tennessee's overcrowded prison system was unconstitutional were catalysts for the creation of CCA (which unsuccessfully sought to privatize Tennessee's entire prison system in the early 1980s).[129]

CCA and other for-profit prison firms began to press on state governments to contract out prison beds just at the moment when many states and localities were under court orders to improve the conditions in their severely overcrowded jails and prisons. It was not until the mid-1980s—more than a decade and a half after the incarceration rate had begun its steep upward climb—that for-profit prison firms secured their first contracts to manage major adult facilities. As late as 1987, only 3,000 inmates were housed in private adult jails and prisons in the United States. About a decade later, this number had soared to 85,000 but still constituted a relatively small portion of all adult inmates—just 3 percent.[130]

In the wake of glowing reports on Wall Street in the mid- to late 1990s about the potential financial windfall of private prisons, stock prices for the publicly traded prison firms skyrocketed, only to plummet shortly thereafter. CCA and other private prison companies overbuilt speculative prisons in the 1990s on the assumption that demand for prisons would continue to grow indefinitely in the tough-on-crime era. By the late 1990s, the private prison industry was at the brink of bankruptcy due to this overspeculation, as well as a series of highly publicized riots, escapes, and scandals at privately run prisons, and growing doubts about the potential cost savings from private facilities. Failed efforts to reorganize as Real Estate Investment Trusts (REITs) also were to blame for the downturn in the prison industry.[131]

Around this time, the federal government emerged as a financial godsend for the private prison industry. The growing market for immigrant detention, as elaborated in chapter 10, was a leading factor in turning the fortunes of CCA and other private prison firms around. So was the Clinton administration's aggressive push to contract with the private sector for more beds to hold federal prisoners.

With passage of the draconian crime bill in 1994, federal budget officials predicted that the number of employees in the federal Bureau of Prisons would need to grow by the thousands to handle all the projected new inmates.[132] Committed to reducing the size of the government, the Clinton administration sought to keep these new employees "off the books" through privatization. The White House's proposal to increase the number of federal inmates housed in private facilities initially received a frosty reception from senior officials at the Department of Justice, the Bureau of Prisons, and elsewhere. They bluntly questioned the findings of a White House analysis that suggested privatization might save money. A DOJ-commissioned report at the time concluded that private prisons saved little, if any, money; did not necessarily improve the performance of prisons; and posed thorny legal and constitutional issues.[133]

The Clinton administration plowed ahead anyway with its plans to contract out more beds to the prison industry to house federal prisoners. The revolving door between the private prison industry and top officials in the Clinton administration helped transform the DOJ and BOP from critics to champions of privatization.[134] The tens of millions of dollars that the private prison industry invested in the government over the years through lobbying and campaign contributions at the local, state, and national levels also helped turn the tide in favor of privatization despite growing evidence that private prisons did not do it better for less.

As of 2010, 8 percent of all state and federal prisoners were held in private facilities. This figure understates the large and growing influence of the private prison industry on penal policy and American politics more broadly. The industry has targeted its lobbying efforts in certain key state capitals and in Washington, DC, in order to create powerful beachheads to push the privatization cause nationally.[135] At the same time, it has forged tight linkages with pivotal conservative groups, most notably ALEC, whose neoliberal agenda is highly compatible with privatizing corrections.

There is enormous regional and state-by-state variation in the use of private prisons. About half of all states have no prisoners or just a handful serving time in private facilities. In one-third of the states, however, 10 percent or more of the inmates are imprisoned in private prisons. The private prison industry has been highly concentrated in certain regions and locales. In the South and Southwest, 7–9 percent of all prisoners are incarcerated in private facilities, compared to just 2–3 percent in the Northeast and Midwest. At the very high end are New Mexico (43 percent), Montana (40 percent), Alaska (34 percent), and Hawaii (33 percent).[136] People of color are overrepresented in private prisons, which tend to provide fewer educational and rehabilitative programs and services than public facilities.[137]

The federal system has been the most dynamic sector of the prison industry, with about 16 percent of all federal prisoners serving time in private prisons compared to about 7 percent of all state prisoners.[138] In 2011, nearly half of all immigrant detention beds were in private facilities, up from 10 percent a decade earlier.[139] The federal government is the largest client of publicly traded prison companies, accounting for about 40 percent of CCA's business in recent years.[140] Private operators have been capturing a huge share of the growth in new prison construction. Of the 153 new prisons and jails that opened between 2000 and 2005, only two were public facilities.[141] In 2005, private facilities accounted for about a quarter of all adult corrections facilities, up from 16 percent in 2000.[142]

Too Big to Fail

The prison industry has been shrewdly repositioning itself to take advantage of the shifting political and economic environment. For more than a decade now, CCA and other firms have sought to move from a focus on managing prisons to outright owning them. At the start of the twenty-first century, CCA owned three-quarters of all beds under its control. A decade later, that had increased to about 90 percent.[143] Owning prisons outright gives private prison companies enormous bargaining power. When states retain the prison as an asset, they have more leverage to cancel or rebid contracts. But if the state has ceded ownership to a private firm, its only leverage is to build a new prison or find another company to house its inmates, a very tough proposition when CCA and GEO so decisively dominate the market. Like the consolidated banking sector with its megabanks that the government keeps propping up because they are "too big to fail," federal, state, and local authorities are becoming dependent on a couple of private prison companies that are "too big to fail."

A few players dominated the prison industry from its inception in the 1980s. Since then, the industry has become even more concentrated. Thanks to a series of mergers, GEO and CCA now control about 80 percent of the private prison and jail beds in the United States.[144] Put another way, the for-profit prison industry constitutes the country's fourth largest prison system. CCA is the fifth largest prison operator, just behind the federal Bureau of Prisons, California, Texas, and Florida.[145]

Despite some unease about state budget cutbacks and pressure to cancel or reopen contracts, the private prison industry generally viewed the Great Recession as a great opportunity. One industry executive predicted in his company's 2008 annual report that the demand for inmate beds would increase because released offenders would have a harder time finding employment and would be more likely to recidivate.[146] In 2011, Damon Hininger, CCA's chief executive, cheered that for two years in a row, no state had appropriated any money for new public prisons. He predicted that this would soon result in a crunch for prison space, forcing more states to turn to the private sector for relief.[147]

It has not been completely smooth sailing for the private prison industry. In recent filings with the Securities and Exchange Commission, CCA acknowledged that the company could be disadvantaged by new developments in criminal justice. It noted "the relaxation of enforcement efforts, leniency in conviction or parole standards and sentencing practices . . . [and] the decriminalization of certain activities."[148] CCA reportedly quit ALEC in 2010 because the conservative lobbying organization had backed some initiatives to reduce the incarceration rate.[149] And in 2012, students and faculty forced Florida Atlantic University to rescind its agreement to award GEO naming rights to its football stadium in exchange for a $6 million donation to its athletic program. This brouhaha even caught the eye of *The Colbert Report*, the political satire program on the Comedy Central network.[150]

To offset some of the volatility in the corrections industry as the Great Recession battered state and local government budgets, prison companies looked to the federal government as a safe haven. They aimed to secure long-term contracts to house federal prisoners and to profit from the booming market in immigrant detention.[151] At the same time, they intensified their lobbying of state officials.[152] In 2012, Harley G. Lappin, CCA's chief corrections officer, sent a letter to prison officials in forty-eight states, announcing that the prison giant had set aside $250 million to buy state prisons and lease them back to the states. The company pushed states to sign twenty-year management contracts with guaranteed occupancy rates of 90 percent.[153] Lappin had joined CCA in June 2011, months after he had retired as director of the federal Bureau of Prisons shortly after being arrested for drunk driving.[154]

Diversification has been another key survival strategy for the prison industry. Riding the reentry and recidivism wave in public policy debates, private prison companies have sought to become leaders in providing what GEO describes as the "corrections lifecycle." This includes substance abuse and mental health treatment, probation and parole services, and electronic monitoring.[155] In 2010, GEO acquired BI Incorporated, the largest provider of electronic monitoring services to track offenders and former offenders, including GPS equipment, electronic ankle bracelets, and remote alcohol monitoring.

Hard economic times have not hit CCA or GEO hard. In 2010, political contributions for the three largest prison companies were at their highest point in a decade.[156] Between 2004 and 2014, stock values for CCA and GEO increased by 250 percent and 500 percent respectively.[157] CCA and GEO have been corporate pioneers in exploiting the 1960 REIT Act to avoid paying federal taxes. Following previous failed attempts, CCA and GEO convinced the Internal Revenue Service in 2013 that they should qualify for REIT status because the money they collect from the government for housing prisoners is essentially rent. CCA expected to save $70 million on its 2013 tax bill thanks to its new REIT designation.[158] (REIT stands for real estate investment trust.)

Elusive Savings and Hidden Costs

The big selling point for privately operated or owned penal facilities is that they cost less. But comparing costs between private and public facilities can be a bit like comparing apples and oranges. Studies that claim private prisons save considerable amounts of money—usually in the range of 10–20 percent—generally do not take into account fundamental differences between public and private facilities.[159] Independent studies that factor in differences between their inmate populations, accounting practices, and operations show that privatization saves little, if any, money.[160] A 2001 report commissioned by the DOJ's Bureau of Justice Assistance found that savings from private prisons averaged only about 1 percent, largely due to lower labor costs, or much lower than earlier estimates.[161] A 2007 GAO report, which the BOP disputed, concluded that the bureau had not collected enough data to assess accurately the cost savings and quality of private facilities compared to public ones.[162]

Much like the health insurance industry, the prison industry engages in a lot of cherry-picking and cost-shifting to maintain the illusion that the private sector does it better for less. The private prison industry has concentrated on running low- and medium-security facilities, leaving the comparatively more expensive maximum-security inmates on the government's tab. CCA reportedly prefers to fill its penal facilities in Arizona with Native Hawaiians because of a belief that they are more docile than prisoners from other states and therefore less costly.[163] Private contractors try to avoid taking in inmates with serious medical or mental health issues that are expensive to treat. Many private prisons provide only basic medical care. Their contracts typically require the government to pick up expenses for hospitalizations and advanced treatments.

Studies indicate that, all things being equal, private facilities tend to be more dangerous places for inmates and correctional officers.[164] One key reason for this is staffing. Private prisons typically pay their correctional officers considerably less than public facilities do, spend less on training, and have higher inmate-to-staff ratios.[165] As a consequence, staff turnover is generally higher in private facilities. Some evidence suggests that guards at privately run facilities also are more likely to issue disciplinary infractions, thus jeopardizing inmates' "good time" credits and lengthening the time they must serve before release.[166] This should not be so surprising since the private prison industry is in the business of making money by keeping its beds filled. A recent analysis of dozens of private prison contracts found that the majority of them guarantee that states will maintain 80–100 percent occupancy rates or else pay a fine to the company running the prison.[167]

Some of the most notorious, headline-grabbing incidents of prisoner abuse in recent memory have involved private prisons. These include the "gladiator school" at the Idaho Correctional Center run by CCA; rampant physical and sexual abuse at the privately run Walnut Grove Correctional Facility in Mississippi; the $40 million-plus settlement against GEO in the case of Gregorio de la Rosa, Jr., who was beaten to death by two fellow inmates in a Texas prison as corrections officials looked on; years of pervasive sexual abuse and gross lapses in medical care at a CCA-run facility in Kentucky for female inmates; and two huge insurrections sparked by abysmal conditions at GEO's immigrant detention center in Pecos, Texas, which is the world's largest privately run prison.

The privatization question highlights how vexing an issue the carceral state poses for organized labor. Unionized guards are generally better paid and better trained. They are a more stable workforce than their nonunionized counterparts and have been at the front lines in the battle against prison privatization. Scapegoating them in public debates over privatization of the penal system is part of a wider political assault that casts public employees as overindulged parasites whose wages, benefits, and pensions are strangling government budgets and services. These claims fly in the face of numerous studies going back decades showing that government employees actually earn less than their private-sector counterparts once age, educational level, and other key variables are factored in.[168]

Correctional officers' unions periodically have drawn public attention to prison overcrowding and other unsafe and unhealthy conditions that jeopardize staff members and inmates.[169] At the same time, some unions have ardently supported punitive legislation and fiercely opposed sentencing and other reforms to reduce the inmate population and shutter prisons. The California Correctional Peace Officers Association (CCPOA), which the prison buildup in the Golden State helped transform from a scrappy prison officers' association into a powerful, militant, and fiercely independent union, has championed some of the state's signature punitive measures, including the country's toughest three-strikes law. The union has moderated its position slightly in recent years.[170] The American Federation of State, County, and Municipal Employees (AFSCME), one of the country's most progressive unions, was a major opponent of closing the supermax facility in Tamms, Illinois. Other unions also have been strong supporters of solitary confinement.[171]

Back to the Future

A major theme of U.S. penal history throughout the nineteenth and twentieth centuries is how the quest to profit from inmates produced such abominable and exploitative conditions and such corrupt practices that individual states were eventually forced to assume primary control of their penal systems. Today's champions of privatization claim that the situation is vastly different from years ago because the courts now serve as active watchdogs of private prison operations. They contend that the carrot of ACA accreditation and the stick of possible inmate lawsuits and court-mandated consent decrees serve as major deterrents to abusive behavior.[172] However, over the last two decades, the courts have become more indifferent to lawsuits brought on behalf of prisoners, partly thanks to the Prison Litigation Reform Act. Enacted in 1995 just as the private prison industry was poised for takeoff, the PLRA has severely limited judicial oversight of penal affairs and greatly constricted inmates' access to the courts to challenge the conditions of their confinement, as discussed in chapter 2.[173] Defenders of privatization note that most contracts require private facilities to obtain ACA accreditation. But, as discussed in the previous chapter, ACA accreditation is a very low bar to jump over and is not much of an independent check on prison administrators in the public or private sectors.[174]

Private prisons and corrections services are subject to even less accountability and scrutiny than public ones. Like other privatized industries and social services, private jails and prisons generally are not subject to the federal Administrative Procedure Act (APA) and federal and state freedom of information acts (FOIAs).[175] Administrators of private facilities regularly rebuff FOIA and other requests for information regarding key issues, such as inmate deaths, health-care conditions, the use of deadly force, and the mistreatment of inmates. In at least one case, CCA said it was turning down a request because the information sought was deemed to be a trade secret.[176] In 2013, *Prison Legal News* filed a lawsuit against CCA because the company refused to comply with an open records request regarding inmate deaths and health care at Dawson State Jail in Dallas. This CCA-run facility has been at the center of controversy over allegations of mistreatment of offenders, including the 2012 death of a four-day-old baby girl, whose mother gave birth to her in a toilet.[177]

CCA and the rest of the private prison industry have strongly opposed the Private Prison Information Act. This measure would require private facilities holding federal prisoners and detainees to release the same information that public facilities are required to make available. This bill has made little headway in Congress, despite the support of dozens of leading criminal justice, civil rights, and public interest organizations.[178]

One way to make private prisons more accountable is to require greater state and public oversight and input. But most privatization decisions are made in a climate of haste, driven foremost by cost concerns. Legislators and other state officials are largely inattentive to accountability and transparency issues, let alone human rights issues, raised by privatizing penal operations. Moreover, calls for privatization are often loudest during periods of heightened hostility toward the government and regulation.[179] Few states require that government privatization schemes be subject to public hearings or that states provide the public with adequate information to make an informed decision.[180]

Florida and Arizona are two good cases in point. Florida has had extensive experience with prison privatization since the first enabling legislation was enacted in 1993. Almost 10 percent of the state's 100,000 prisoners are held in private facilities today. The 1993 statute required, among other things, that private correctional facilities provide at least 7 percent in savings relative to comparable state facilities. Over the years, the evidence has been underwhelming that the state's seven private prisons achieved that goal. A 2010 report by the Florida Center for Fiscal and Economic Policy (FCFEP), an independent research organization, found no evidence to support the claim that privatization had saved the state money, as required by law.[181] Moreover, privatization in Florida "has been marred by mismanagement by

state monitors, lax contracts, overbilling by prison contractors, a corruption investigation, and a legal loophole that allowed sexual misconduct in private facilities
to go unpunished."[182]

Despite this questionable record, Florida legislators attempted in 2011 to privatize twenty-seven prisons and detention facilities holding 16,000 prisoners
through a backdoor proviso slipped last minute into the budget.[183] They had the
strong support of Rick Scott, the newly elected Republican governor. On the campaign trail, Scott had vowed to cut $1 billion from the state's $2.2 billion corrections budget. The private prison industry, led by CCA and the Boca Raton-based
GEO Group, contributed nearly $1 million to Florida politicians and lawmakers
during the 2010 election cycle.[184] The Police Benevolent Association (PBA), which
at the time represented state prison employees, fiercely opposed Scott's plan.

The PBA challenged the privatization plan in the courts.[185] Ruling in favor of
the PBA, a judge found that the rush to privatize dozens of penal facilities by a
January 1, 2012, deadline skirted the state's statutory requirements built into prior
privatization legislation. The judge also ruled that the proviso has been enacted in
the absence of any cost-benefit analysis by the Florida Department of Corrections
(FDOC), again in violation of state statutes. Remarkably, Edwin Buss, the state's
secretary of corrections, testified that he had not been consulted about the massive privatization plan until after the budget bill with the controversial proviso had
become law. Buss ended up resigning just six months after taking office, reportedly forced out by the administration because he was not an ardent champion of
the administration's hasty privatization plan. The judge also took issue with the
request for proposals issued by the FDOC, which sought only one contract for
all twenty-seven facilities and considered no other options. As one criminologist
testified at the time, "awarding such a massive privatization contract to just one
company renders the state captive to a single corporation that will then have enormous power over a major part of the state budget."[186] After Governor Scott's plans
to privatize dozens of state prisons was thwarted, at least for the time being, he did
succeed in engineering a private-sector takeover of Florida's correctional health-
care system in 2013.

The Arizona Sell-Off

In 2009, lawmakers in Arizona, with the strong support of Republican governor
Jan Brewer, sought a quick infusion of cash by selling off the state's entire prison
system. They planned to lease back the prison beds at a cost that would greatly
exceed the original purchase price. They doggedly pursued privatization despite
government and independent reports that Arizona's existing private facilities were
relatively more costly and were vexed with serious security, health, and safety
lapses.

Prying information on prison privatization out of Arizona officials has not been
easy. A 1987 law requires the Arizona DOC to produce cost and quality reviews for

its private prisons and to assess how they measure up against state-run facilities. The DOC continued to collect the required information but stopped releasing it. A lawsuit filed by the American Friends Service Committee (AFSC) finally forced the department to release the data in late 2011. The AFSC discovered that the corrections department and auditor general had concluded that private beds were on average more expensive than public ones for nearly every year since 2005.[187] A 2010 report by Arizona's auditor general concluded that the state paid private prisons a higher per capita inmate rate than it spent for comparable state-run facilities in 2009.[188] The auditor general report also suggested that repealing the state's harsh mandatory minimum statutes and expanding community corrections were more "fiscally sound" solutions compared to building new prisons.[189]

In the end, Arizona did not privatize its entire prison system, partly because it could not find a buyer. However, the compromise budget in 2012 paved the way for five hundred new maximum-security beds in state prisons and one thousand more private beds. While Arizona legislators continued to slash spending for education, health care, and nearly every other public service, funding for corrections continued to hold steady or increased. The state planned to pay for the new prison beds by diverting $50 million of the $98 million settlement with financial institutions that had been intended to help homeowners hurt by foreclosure abuses.[190]

Arizona lawmakers slipped a provision into the budget that would eliminate the requirement for an annual quality and cost review of prison contracts. Legislators voted to eliminate the annual review less than two years after a notorious incident in which three inmates, two of whom had been convicted of murder, escaped from Kingman prison, a medium-security private facility, and murdered an Oklahoma couple before being captured. That incident, which made national headlines, prompted outcries to clean up lax security at Kingman and other private prisons in Arizona. Among its numerous problems, Kingman had a broken alarm system that routinely gave hundreds of false alarms each day.[191]

The company to which Arizona contracted out prisoner health care in April 2012 had such a terrible record that the state was forced to terminate its three-year contract in January 2013. State corrections officials then contracted with a different for-profit company that has a history of abuses and neglect.[192] In 2012, the ACLU, joined by a coalition of other human rights organizations, filed a major class-action suit charging the Arizona DOC with providing inadequate health care and with routinely keeping mentally ill prisoners in solitary confinement under abhorrent conditions.[193]

The Growing For-Profit Prison beyond the Prison

The budget crisis brought on by the Great Recession has opened up new frontiers in the privatization of corrections that extend way beyond the prison gate. The private sector has sought to cast the spell of the free market over a growing range of correctional services and operations, including probation, parole, and bail. The financial sector and government officials have been experimenting with new mechanisms to fund the carceral state "off the books." And states also have been devising new ways to directly turn a profit from criminal justice activities, including the brokering of excess prison beds, the greater use of civil forfeitures, and levying more fees and other legal financial obligations on prisoners, probationers, and parolees, as discussed in chapter 2.

On the finance side, New York City and Goldman Sachs signed a path-breaking and controversial contract in 2012 for the country's first major "social impact bond."[194] Goldman agreed to invest nearly $10 million in a prison program for adolescents at Rikers Island. Under the terms of the agreement, Goldman's return on investment depends on how much the program reduces the recidivism rate for program participants. In theory, if recidivism rates do not fall, Goldman would lose its investment. In practice, Mayor Michael Bloomberg's foundation sweetened the agreement by guaranteeing Goldman repayment for much of the loan even if recidivism rates remain unchanged. Interest in social impact bonds to fund corrections and other public services skyrocketed after New York City signed the Goldman contract.[195]

Some nonprofit organizations, social service providers, and advocates for disadvantaged groups have been alarmed by these "pay-for-success" bonds. Linking repayment to recidivism is a slippery and narrow way to gauge "what works," as elaborated in chapter 5, and provides an incentive to cherry-pick participants. Furthermore, carrying out multiple randomized or quasi-experimental trials for each program that meet minimum scientific standards is expensive. It may not even be feasible for programs that have a small number of participants. Fears are growing that these bonds will siphon off government and philanthropic resources that would otherwise go to nonprofit organizations and government agencies to provide vital services to needy groups and communities. As in the case of LRBs, a new industry of expensive intermediaries, including consultants, lawyers, and accountants, is emerging to put together social impact bond deals. In January 2014, Bank of America Merrill Lynch announced it had raised $13.5 million for the largest social impact bond to date. With a potential annual return of 12.5 percent, it will fund reentry programs for former prisoners in New York State.[196]

Convict Leasing in the Twenty-First Century

Along with major figures in the Right on Crime coalition, including Newt Gingrich and Pat Nolan, ALEC and the for-profit bail industry have become leading advocates of solving the prison overcrowding and budget crises by creating a private market for probation and parole modeled after the commercial bail system.[197] They also have stridently opposed pretrial bail reforms that would permit more defendants to be released prior to trial (or settlement of their cases) without requiring them to post bail. The United States is one of just two countries that permit for-profit bail bonding.[198] Only a handful of states prohibit commercial bondsmen.

Most others have statutes that permit and at times promote the use of private bail companies.

The American Bail Coalition (ABC) has been a major player in ALEC since joining the organization in 1993 and considers ALEC its "life preserver."[199] Together with ALEC, it has promoted model legislation that calls for releasing people from prison before they have served their full sentence if they have the means to post conditional bail.[200] This would essentially establish bonding companies as private probation and parole agents in ways reminiscent of how the ignominious convict-leasing system operated.[201] Under ALEC's conditional release plan, offenders who sought release from prison prior to completing their full sentence would be required to post a bond. If a bonding company determined that the released offender had violated the terms of parole, it would return the parolee to prison.

In making their case for how the private sector could do a better job than the public sector in managing probation and parole, proponents have highlighted sensational instances of released "killers" and rapists who went on to kill and rape again.[202] Left unsaid is the fact that few released offenders go on to commit a serious crime, and that former prisoners are not the main drivers of crime rates, as elaborated in chapters 5 and 8. Also left unsaid is that numerous problems and scandals have plagued the commercial bail market and have been the subject of scathing exposés and reports.[203]

The commercial bond system has contributed to disturbing distortions in the criminal justice system. Until the late 1950s, the for-profit bail bond industry was comprised primarily of bondsmen who used their own money and property as collateral for bonds. After bail agents began seeking out insurers to underwrite bail bonds, national and regional insurers became important players in the bond market. Bondsmen had an incentive and growing capacity to push for a large bail bond market with bail set at ever higher amounts.[204]

Two decades ago, bail bondsmen typically were only necessary in cases of high bond set by the court for defendants charged with serious crimes or repeat offenses. Most defendants were released on their own personal recognizance through publicly funded pretrial services. But today many people in the United States who pose no significant threat to society languish needlessly behind bars as they await their day in court because they cannot afford to post bail.[205] An estimated 500,000 people accused of crimes remain in jail each year because they cannot afford to make bail.[206] Many of them are so destitute that a bail set at just a couple of hundred dollars might as well be a million dollars. Defendants often are not guaranteed legal representation at bail hearings.[207] Those who remain in jail while awaiting trial are at a distinct disadvantage. They are more likely to be convicted and are more likely to receive a tougher sentence if convicted or if they plead guilty.

An award-winning NPR series on bail in the United States concluded that "pretrial release programs across the country are increasingly locked in a losing battle with bonding companies trying to either limit their programs or shut them down entirely."[208] Bondsmen have put enormous lobbying and financial resources into their fight to slash local pretrial programs and resources and into persuading law-makers that bondsmen should not have to pay the bond if a defendant out on bail commits a new crime.[209] In Broward County, Florida, they triumphed in gutting a successful pretrial release program that had been instituted to reduce overcrowd-ing and to avoid spending $70 million to build a new jail.

The private sector is penetrating the prison beyond the prison in other ways. A decade or two ago, many jurisdictions gave up trying to pursue fees owed by misdemeanants because it was too costly and time-consuming. Private firms iden-tified a potential windfall and stepped into the breach. They would charge public authorities little or nothing for running parole and probation services. Instead, they would make their money by loading additional fees and fines on defendants unable to pay their fines. Those who could not or would not pay risked being sent to jail.

In 2001, when Georgia discontinued providing probation services for state courts, many counties turned to private firms to operate these programs.[210] About three dozen for-profit firms now operate in hundreds of courts. People languish in Georgia jails and are deeply in debt for failing to pay a modest initial fine of $100 or $200 for a trivial infraction like speeding or failing to yield to a pedes-trian in a crosswalk. Over time, that legal financial obligation has mushroomed into a sizable debt as loosely regulated for-profit firms pile on more fees and fines. Since these people are misdemeanants, they are not guaranteed legal representa-tion even if they are indigent and run the risk of jail. As a consequence, they "often end up lost in a legal Twilight Zone."[211] To shroud this practice from public eyes, the Georgia legislature enacted a statute in 2006 that rendered all the reports, files, and records of private probation companies a confidential state secret.[212]

Conclusion

The carceral state is highly resilient and adaptable. It has zigged and zagged with the twists and turns of the new political economy that emerged with the ascen-dance of neoliberalism in the United States. This helps explain a paradoxical out-come: how a costly prison boom that entailed a major extension of the public sector and state power occurred amidst a sharply anti-government, anti-tax turn in American politics. The emergence of the carceral state was first and foremost a political project, not an economic project. However, it has since created pow-erful private-sector interests with close political allies. These interests are deeply invested in the carceral state and quite capable of recalibrating their strategies in light of the Great Recession and other political and economic developments. This helps explain why budgetary pressures alone will not spur a major rollback of the carceral state, nor will political strategies focused primarily on the racial dispari-ties and inequities of the carceral state, as discussed in chapters 6 and 7.

An enormous gap exists between the stated ideals and tenets of neoliberalism and how neoliberalism operates on the ground. Neoliberalism in practice has had to finesse some fundamental contradictions, as Bernard Harcourt demonstrates in his dissection of the deep historical and philosophical origins of the late-twentieth-century embrace of neoliberalism.[213] It took political chutzpah to engineer such a massive, expensive, and intrusive expansion of the penal system while ardently championing deregulation, lower taxes, and shrinking the public sector. Political actors and private interests finessed these contradictions in varied ways, and specific institutional and political factors, especially at the state level, shaped their choices. As such, they built a carceral state that has been hiding in plain sight. They also emboldened certain interests that have become major impediments to dismantling the carceral state.

The Great Recession created momentum to rethink U.S. penal policies. But in the wake of the 2008 financial collapse, the tenets of neoliberalism remain remarkably intact. Most of the political energy at the elite level has been focused on the three R's—recidivism, reentry, and justice reinvestment. As shown in the next two chapters, the three-R approach will at best stabilize the carceral state. It is a DIY social policy focused on remaking individuals, not remaking social, political, and economic structures.

CHAPTER FOUR

What Second Chance?

Reentry and Penal Reform

Because really, prison isn't designed for you to leave, it's designed to keep you.
And I don't care what anybody says—you don't go in there to get better.
Only the strong survive, and you have to fight to get better,
and you have to fight and win.[1]

—SHERI DWIGHT

The Great Recession created momentum to reconsider U.S. penal policies. But as in other areas of public policy, the extensive neoliberal consensus at the elite level has radically diminished the sense of what's possible. Most of the political energy among legislators, other government officials, leading foundations, and think tanks has been fixated on the three R's—reentry, recidivism, and justice reinvestment. Left unaddressed and unacknowledged is the R question—that is, the gross racial and other disparities and injustices on which the carceral state rests.

The three-R solution, as shown in this and the next chapter, is infused with the core tenets of neoliberalism. It rests on creating DIY social policies that stress individual solutions and personal responsibility while slighting the responsibilities that the state and the society have to the country's most disadvantaged citizens. The three-R solution promises to give people a second chance, never acknowledging that many of the people cycling in and out of prison and jail were never really given a first chance, let alone an equal chance. It shuns state-led solutions aimed at addressing deep-seated structural problems.

The three R's have fostered public policies that promise short-term budget payoffs, but that are more costly in terms of dollars and lives over the long run. They reinforce a bias in the public mind that the only penal reforms worth pursuing are ones that save money and reduce recidivism. This reinforces in the public mind a tight connection between incarceration rates and crime rates, even though the link between the two is tenuous at best.

Over the past decade, reentry has caught the imagination of penal reformers across the board. Many of them have promoted reentry programs as a key vehicle to reduce incarceration and crime rates and to repair the individuals and communities most directly affected by the carceral state. In his 2004 State of the Union address, President George W. Bush declared, "America is the land of second chance, and when the gates of the prison open, the path ahead should lead to a better life."[2] Four years later, he signed the Second Chance Act, which awarded nearly $300 million in block grants over the next four years to help states and localities develop reentry programs.[3] These included a wide range of programs for substance abuse treatment, mentoring, risk assessment, housing, education, employment, and other needs.[4]

Jeremy Travis defined reentry a decade ago in a very open-ended way. It was simply the "process of leaving prison and returning to society."[5] Many academics and practitioners initially equated the embrace of reentry as a return to a more rehabilitative, less punitive approach to offenders. Over the years, reentry has morphed into something else, however. The surge in enthusiasm for reentry has not fundamentally changed the discourse over punishment and has further entrenched certain punitive tendencies.[6]

The reentry solution as currently conceived has several serious shortcomings. Reentry charts a very narrow path to a better life that many ex-offenders have trouble navigating due to factors that are not under their control or even the control of corrections departments. Many champions of reentry portray successful reentry largely as a matter of helping ex-offenders acquire the right individual skills to become employable. They ignore or downplay the enormous structural obstacles that stand between ex-offenders and full economic, political, and social membership in the United States. As elaborated in this chapter, many of these obstacles are historically deep-seated and predate the run-up in incarceration rates than began in the 1970s.

Framing reentry in narrow human capital terms focuses public attention on correcting the reported inadequacies of offenders and ex-offenders. It deflects public policy away from correcting the deeper structural problems in the U.S. economy. In a pattern that has become distressingly familiar in the making of U.S. economic and social policy in recent decades, supply-side solutions are promoted to address demand-side problems.[7] Furthermore, even if reentry programs could substantially reduce the recidivism rates of ex-offenders—a big if, for reasons discussed in this chapter—major reductions in the overall crime rate would not necessarily result. Criminal offenses committed by repeat offenders are not the major drivers of crime rates, as elaborated in the next chapter.

The enthusiastic embrace of a narrow conception of reentry defined primarily by reducing recidivism rates and increasing employment rates for ex-offenders has a compelling political logic. It resonates with earlier trends in penal policy: the "rehabilitative ideal" of the 1960s and 1970s, with its emphasis on treatment and intervention; the incapacitative turn in the 1980s and 1990s, which was defined by crime control and retribution, with little regard for fiscal and other costs; and the "new managerialism" that coalesced in the early 1990s and borrowed heavily from the ostensibly neutral language and tools of economics and statistics (including their fixation on efficiency, cost-benefit analyses, risk assessment, and evidence-based research).[8]

Drawing from these three prior turns in penal policy, the reentry model has a veneer of nonpartisanship or bipartisanship that obscures the highly charged political and economic assumptions that undergird it. The narrow conception of reentry that prevails is fully compatible with a neoliberal vision of public policy that is persistently inattentive to or dismissive of the larger structural forces that have been remaking the life chances of historically disadvantaged groups in the United States and broader swaths of the population. The deeper socioeconomic and other factors that prevent offenders and ex-offenders from securing gainful employment that lifts them out of poverty and keeps them out of prison often are rendered invisible or inconsequential. As Magnus Hörnquist explains, "The response to social exclusion and unemployment is not seen to lie in structural change. More or less everything except the excluded individuals themselves is excluded from policy considerations."[9] Employability is misleadingly considered "an intrinsic property of individuals" rather than a reflection of the existing structure of the labor market.[10] The current enthusiasm for reentry with its emphasis on human capital as a gateway out of recidivism fails to reckon with the wide-ranging consequences of two key structural factors discussed in this chapter: the profound restructuring of the U.S. labor market and vast shifts in the historic pattern of black inequality over the last half century.

After a brief discussion of the state of reentry today, this chapter situates the embrace of reentry in a deeper historical, economic, and political context. It examines important structural transformations in the U.S. economy in the decades since World War II that have a bearing on the development of the carceral state and that continue to impede the economic, political, and social integration of ex-offenders. It also identifies important similarities between the welfare reform movement of two decades ago and the reentry movement today. Such comparisons underscore the shortsightedness of the human capital approach to penal reform on which the reentry project rests. The chapter concludes by examining broader conceptions of reentry that view former offenders as returning citizens who need to be fully integrated not only into the workforce but also the wider society and polity.

From Rehabilitation to Reentry

The terms reentry, rehabilitation, and "second chance" are gross misnomers. They suggest that ex-offenders "are being returned to a level of habilitation, integration and civic participation that they formerly enjoyed."[11] Yet many former offenders never got a first chance, let alone a second one. As one prison educator quipped, "How can an individual reenter a society of which he has never truly been a member?"[12] Moreover, for all the talk about investing more in reentry and alternatives to incarceration, many correctional programs today are being "asked to deliver the impossible—greater public safety and more rehabilitation with stagnant or declining funding," as detailed in chapter 2.[13]

The chronically marginalized and the chronically disadvantaged are the people most likely to end up in jail or prison. One-third of inmates in state prisons were unemployed at the time of their arrest, and barely half were working full time. Nearly one in five state prison inmates have less than an eighth-grade education; only 22 percent are high school graduates.[14] About one-quarter of state prisoners have a recent history of mental health problems, and 13 percent reported having attempted suicide in the previous year or since admission to prison.[15] As of 2012, ten times as many people with severe mental illnesses were housed in U.S. prisons and jails compared to the number of people with such illnesses who were residing in state psychiatric hospitals.[16]

The prevalence of psychiatric symptoms is about twice as high among formerly incarcerated men compared to the general population.[17] Some of these former inmates are afflicted with disorders that typically emerge in childhood or adolescence and thus pre-date their incarceration. However, a stint in jail or prison apparently increases the prevalence of mood disorders for former inmates, especially bipolar disorder and major depression.[18] For example, incarceration is associated with a 45 percent increase in the risk of lifetime major depression.[19] Research suggests that these mood disorders may be more disabling for returning citizens than substance abuse or impulse control problems.[20]

During the heyday of the rehabilitation era in the 1960s and 1970s, intensive general education and professional counseling programs were thought to be the best way to provide offenders and ex-offenders with "the tools they need to overcome histories of social disadvantage."[21] Since then, the focus has narrowed considerably, due partly to the ascendance of reentry in public policy discussions and to the tightening of government budgets. Expanding formal education and job training programs is not a main thrust of reentry. The emphasis instead is on improving personal traits that presumably determine employability and reduce recidivism, including social skills, personal appearance, and attitude. Reentry-related counseling programs aim to provide techniques for inmates to manage themselves, such as lessons in conflict resolution, anger management, and applying for a job. Reentry programs are popular with public officials and prison administrators partly because they are shorter in duration than more traditional education and rehabilitation programs. Reentry programs also tend to require fewer staff members overall, as well as fewer staff members with advanced or professional training. This makes them relatively less expensive.[22]

Participation in prison-based academic programs, including GED programs, college classes, and adult basic education, has been falling since the early 1990s. Recently, some states have been disbanding or shrinking the handful of prison-based post-secondary and liberal arts education programs that were able to soldier on in the wake of the 1994 congressional decision to begin denying Pell grants to inmates to fund higher education.[23] A 2011 survey of forty-three states by the

Institute for Higher Education Policy found that only 6 percent of prisoners were enrolled in vocational or academic post-secondary programs in the 2009–10 academic year. Of the inmates who were enrolled, 86 percent were serving time in thirteen states, which suggests that most states provide little access to higher education or vocational training for inmates.[24]

Participation in non-educational programs appears to have held steady, and participation in reentry programs has jumped.[25] Still, for all prison-based programs, participation rates by both state and federal inmates "are distressingly low" and waiting lists are long.[26] In California, a six-month wait for parolees to be admitted to a residential substance abuse treatment program is not uncommon.[27] A decade ago, Joan Petersilia concluded, "U.S. prisons today offer fewer services than they did when inmate problems were less severe."[28] That is probably even truer now in the aftermath of the Great Recession.

The surge in enthusiasm for reentry has not been matched by a surge in dollars for reentry programs. Federal spending to foster reentry has been infinitesimal at a time when departments of corrections have been slashing budgets for prison education, vocational training, substance abuse, and other programs, as discussed in chapter 2. In fiscal 2012, Congress agreed to appropriate just $63 million for the Second Chance Act after the Senate Appropriations Committee initially zeroed out all funding (but approved $300 million in new money for federal prisons).[29] This appropriation was truly a drop in the bucket compared to the nearly $60 billion spent annually by the federal Bureau of Prisons and by state departments of corrections. It amounts to less than $100 for each of the more than 700,000 people released annually from state and federal prisons.

Employment and Recidivism

A guiding assumption of many reentry programs is that improving the human capital of former offenders will help keep them employed and out of the criminal justice system. Cutting recidivism rates by half over the course of five years was a major condition for receiving federal reentry funds under the Second Chance Act.[30] But the very best reentry programs have had at best only a modest impact on lowering the unemployment and recidivism rates of former offenders, who constitute a sizable 6–7 percent of the total working-age population or about one in fifteen working-age adults.[31] Moreover, for all their successes, the best programs are not replicable on a large scale.

The research findings on the relationship between human capital and recidivism are compelling. Apparently human capital is a major factor in determining the recidivism and unemployment rates of ex-offenders—but it is the human capital they already have at the time they are swept up into the penal system, not whatever skills or education they acquire while incarcerated. Pre-prison employment, pre-prison education, and prior criminal history are the best predictors of post-prison employment and recidivism.[32] Prison-based GED, basic education, life skills, cognitive skills, and secondary and post-secondary education programs appear to be associated with an initial bump in earnings and employment for released offenders that is often not sustained.[33] A "growing literature on 'what works' in correctional programming has found that many programs have no impact on recidivism rates."[34] The more rigorous the program evaluation, the less likely it is to show a significant impact on recidivism. Not surprisingly, evaluations conducted by program developers demonstrate larger reductions in recidivism rates than those carried out by independent evaluators.[35]

A 2006 meta-analysis of the program evaluations conducted since the mid-1960s of nearly 300 in-prison and community-based treatment programs for adult offenders in the United States and abroad concluded that 40 percent of the programs had no impact on recidivism.[36] Only about one-quarter of the treatment programs that were deemed effective were prison- or jail-based. The reduction in recidivism rates for these prison-based and jail-based programs was extremely modest, ranging from a mere 5 percent for basic adult education programs to 13 percent for vocational education programs.[37] This is consistent with the findings of "other major evaluations of 'what works' (or doesn't work). Notably, many other programs do not reduce recidivism and may actually increase rates of failure."[38]

Among the handful of well-designed studies that demonstrate positive gains in earnings or employment or reductions in recidivism, the program effects are extremely modest.[39] Recidivism reductions tend to be in the 10–15 percent range and often are evident in only certain groups, such as older or low-risk offenders. "Program effects of this magnitude might thus reduce a re-arrest rate of 60 percent to 50 percent in the best-case scenario," explains Bruce Western.[40] In short, the best research to date indicates that desistance "does not come in the shape of a 'prison program.'"[41]

Local social and economic conditions largely out of their hands often determine who ends up on a path out of the criminal justice system and who does not. Gainful employment is often a condition of parole in the United States despite compelling evidence that most of the challenges that former offenders face are well beyond their own control and well beyond the control of criminal justice agencies. For example, about two-thirds of the inmates released each year in the state of Illinois return to neighborhoods on the West and South sides of Chicago where the unemployment rate for black males exceeds 40 percent.[42] Ex-offenders who return to economically disadvantaged neighborhoods have a harder time finding employment and are more likely to recidivate.[43] African American men released to areas with higher unemployment rates for blacks are more prone to violent recidivism.[44] Higher levels of residential stability and denser networks of nonprofit groups offering economic and other resources tend to dampen the effect of returning parolees on neighborhood crime rates.[45] In short, the "deterioration of low-skill urban labor markets, racial discrimination, punitive sentiment among voters and lawmakers, and anxiety among employers about hiring ex-offenders all create substantial obstacles to successful prisoner reintegration."[46] As Christopher

Uggen, Sara Wakefield, and Bruce Western suggest, measures of policy success need to be "calibrated by the standards of poor communities that supply prisoners."[47] After all, local labor-market and other conditions considerably affect the prospects of finding a job and going straight.[48]

Deindustrialization and the Changing Nature of Black Inequality

Deeper structural factors fundamentally impede the successful integration of citizens returning from prison. Analysts of the carceral state have not ignored the importance of structural factors entirely. A handful identify the deindustrialization and related hollowing out of wide swaths of urban America beginning in the 1950s and 1960s as key factors in the origins, development, and entrenchment of the carceral state. The deindustrialization thesis rests on several related claims: a vast expansion of the penal system emerged as the dominant means to control young black men and other disadvantaged groups who were rendered economically superfluous by widespread urban deindustrialization; these groups appeared to pose a particular threat to the social, political, and economic order because deindustrialization coincided with the social and political upheavals of the 1960s and 1970s; and politicians ushered in a new era of penal populism as they stoked or exploited rising anxieties among whites about the civil rights movement, urban unrest, and the wider consequences of the vast economic restructuring (as discussed further in chapter 7).

A closer look at the changing nature of inequality after World War II reveals that the standard deindustrialization thesis understates the enormity of the structural problems that blacks—especially young black men—faced in the immediate postwar decades and subsequently. In doing so, it underscores the gross inadequacies and misguided direction of the reentry mission as currently conceived.

The deindustrialization thesis implies that there was a "golden age" when black men, the demographic group that predominates in U.S. prisons, had access to steady jobs in the manufacturing sector. But as Michael Katz, Mark Stern, and Jamie Fader persuasively show, midcentury discrimination denied most African American men access to the industrial sector just at the moment when employment in the agricultural sector was collapsing and record numbers of blacks were migrating to urban areas. A "stunning disparity" in labor force participation opened up between black and white men in the 1940s, prior to wide-scale deindustrialization and the escalation of incarceration rates. This disparity grew considerably over the second half of the twentieth century.[49] Displaced from agriculture, black men were often pushed to the margins of the urban economy due to "discrimination and bad luck with timing."[50] They were moving out of agriculture just as the number of semiskilled manufacturing jobs was contracting. When black employment in manufacturing hit its peak in 1970, only about 12 percent of employed black men actually held blue-collar jobs in the manufacturing sector.[51]

For black women, the transition out of agriculture came sooner and was comparatively more successful. Black women found employment in private households and then increasingly in the non-household service sector and in government-related jobs, notably in education, health services, and public administration. Thanks largely to gains in education and government-related employment, "black women made stunning economic progress."[52]

Education was a key factor in lifting many African American men and women out of poverty. But the impact of education cannot be understood in isolation from other important shifts in the wider economic and political context. Advances in education for African Americans had such a big payback partly because they coincided with a vast expansion of the public sector. Government-related employment "provided more high and middle-status occupations for black men than did the private sector employment," according to Michael Hout. It thereby played "an important role in both occupational upgrading among black men and the emergence of class cleavages within the black population."[53] Reflecting on his classic *The Declining Significance of Race* in 2011, two decades after it was first published, William Julius Wilson acknowledged that if he were to write the book today, he would put more emphasis on the importance of public-sector employment for the economic and social advancement of African Americans.[54]

Spending on social programs and services more than doubled between 1965 and 1972.[55] This increase in public spending brought on by the war on poverty and Great Society in the 1960s spurred a large increase in public-sector jobs, which African Americans—especially African American women—disproportionately filled.[56] The vast expansion of public-sector employment is credited with helping narrow the income gap between blacks and whites and with lifting large numbers of African Americans out of poverty.[57] Rising public employment for African Americans had a two-pronged impact on poverty: it provided steady, well-paying jobs and was associated with generous and effective public assistance programs.[58]

Despite major gains in employment and income, the middle class remained out of reach for the majority of blacks, as it has throughout the history of the United States.[59] The subsequent contraction of public-sector spending and employment that began in earnest in the 1980s struck African Americans "with special ferocity and undermined their often fragile achievements" in employment and income.[60] For decades now, the unemployment rates for minority members of the workforce have been between two and four times higher than the aggregate unemployment rate.

Conventional unemployment statistics grossly underestimate the structural problems in the U.S. job market. They do not include millions of discouraged workers who have given up looking for a job, part-timers who have been unable to find full-time positions, and other workers who are marginally attached to the labor force. About one-quarter of black men and nearly that many black women are unemployed or underemployed, or about 50 percent more than enumerated in standard unemployment statistics.[61] The underemployment and unemployment rates for young, uneducated minority workers today rival the national rate of unemployment during the Great Depression.[62]

In short, over the course of the twentieth century, the nature of black inequality changed fundamentally. Inequality "based on social, economic, and political exclusion largely shattered" and was replaced "by a new configuration of inequality with rearranged features."[63] Access to education and to public-sector employment helped narrow the income and earnings gaps between whites and blacks but also became major sources of economic differentiation among blacks. Despite important income gains, a sharp earnings gap persisted between black and white men in the same occupational category, as did huge and growing differences in labor force participation. African American men coming of age from the mid-1970s onward fared much more poorly than the generation that came of age in the decades immediately after World War II.

The public sector is the leading employer of black men and the second-largest employer of black women. In 2011, about 19 percent of employed African Americans held government jobs compared to about 14 percent for whites and 10 percent for Hispanics.[64] Since the public sector has been the primary avenue for black advancement, "reductions in government employment are likely to be especially detrimental to blacks."[65] The recent contraction of the public sector threatens to unhinge the black middle class. Cuts in public-sector employment disproportionately hurt middle-class blacks. This is also true of cuts in spending on public goods because blacks are more likely to rely on public services, such as public schools and public hospitals, two main targets of the current "war on government."[66]

The focus on improving the human capital of returning citizens through a work-first approach to reentry ignores these larger structural forces that have been remaking the labor market and altering the contours of inequality, especially for African Americans but also for poor whites and members of other disadvantaged groups. In many cities, reentry has become one of the preeminent issues on the urban agenda. As more criminal justice agencies jump on the reentry bandwagon, the carceral state has become the social safety net of last resort. But improving the life skills of individual offenders and ex-offenders through reentry programs will not have a transformative effect on crime rates or on the communities to which released offenders return.

As champions of reentry rally so doggedly on behalf of this cause, the proven roads out of poverty and crime have come under vicious attack in recent years. These include a good public education, labor market reform, public job creation, a robust safety net, a strong labor movement, and aggressive anti-discrimination activity at the federal level. Notably, some of the key figures in the Right on Crime coalition have been leading the assault on public education, labor unions, the public sector, and the social safety net, as discussed in chapters 1 and 5.

Welfare, Workfare, and Reentry

The structural obstacles that returning citizens face are considerable and have grown with the onset of the Great Recession. Yet these obstacles are largely incidental in discussions of reentry. Instead, the reentry mission has been cast in terms remarkably reminiscent of the quest for workfare, a central pillar of the landmark

1996 welfare reform legislation that marked the culmination of four decades of conservative welfare state-building. In fact, some of the chief architects of welfare reform see the reentry movement as a promising new frontier for the new paternalism that guided welfare reform.[67]

Much like the push for welfare reform in the 1990s, reentry efforts have tended to focus on the supply side of the employment problem. As one leading proposal for a major national reentry program explained, "[t]he very low level of work experience among released prisoners" is "perhaps the key barrier to steady post-prison employment." The proposal goes on to say, "Sobriety and the habits of regular work offer the best chances of improving employment among released prisoners."[68]

A guiding assumption of the Second Chance Act and other reentry efforts is that returning citizens are disadvantaged in the job market because they lack key skills, training, education, or personal traits, such as punctuality, a service-oriented personality, and a will to work. Likewise, the central focus in debates over workfare and welfare "was on the likely behavior of current and potential *workers*—not on the conditions and constraints of *work* in the existing labor market."[69] As such, workfare failed to confront the abysmal and deteriorating state of the labor market since the 1970s.

A closer look at the evolution of the debate over workfare illuminates some of the shortcomings of the mainstream conception of reentry today. The Personal Responsibility and Work Opportunity Act enacted during the Clinton administration dismantled Aid to Families with Dependent Children (AFDC), a signature New Deal program that guaranteed a minimal level of public assistance to poor mothers and their children. It replaced AFDC with the Temporary Assistance for Need Families (TANF), which conditions most public assistance "on individual success in the labor market, with no government-guaranteed safety net if that market fails."[70] An overriding principle of workfare is that most people on public assistance lack the will or the necessary human capital to get and keep a job. Welfare reform singled out individual deficiencies, not structural economic factors—like the shortage of jobs that pay a living wage and that provide adequate health and other benefits—as largely to blame for why people seek public assistance rather than paychecks.

The welfare reform debate of the 1980s and 1990s revolved around two competing visions of workfare, as Eva Bertram shows.[71] The human capital vision was based on the assumption that a lack of skills or suitable education largely explained why more poor people could not move up the ladder to better-paying jobs. This fueled calls to impose a kinder, gentler version of workfare programs that included sufficient investment in education, job training, childcare, and other support services. Over the course of the 1990s, however, the human capital model of workfare lost out to the "work first" conception of workfare that conservatives had been pushing in earnest for more than a quarter of a century.

"Work first" programs sought to "facilitate immediate entry into the first available job for which the participant was currently qualified."[72] These programs largely abandoned the core principle of traditional job training and employment programs, which was to raise the wages and employment prospects of participants "*beyond* what they could otherwise be expected to achieve in the labor market."[73] The overriding assumption was that what mattered most to employers at the lower rungs of the employment ladder was not formal training but rather finding workers with the right attitude and other key personal attributes. As a 1994 policy brief of the Democratic Leadership Council explained, the "surest and most direct route" to financial independence for people on public assistance was a job, not more education and training.[74] The DLC was at the epicenter of the movement by Bill Clinton and other "New Democrats" to reposition the Democratic Party to the right in order to woo back the disaffected Reagan Democrats.

Champions of the human capital approach to workfare charge that the "work first" alternative largely abandons job training and education as strategies for upward mobility. But the problems with workfare run even deeper than that. As Eva Bertram and Gordon Lafer suggest, an emphasis on workfare—be it the more conservative work-first approach or the more expansive human capital version—was a fundamentally flawed strategy in the face of a rapidly changing labor market that since the 1970s has been hemorrhaging good middle-class jobs.[75]

Among the advanced industrialized countries, the United States has the highest proportion of low-wage workers—about one-quarter of the workforce.[76] Between 1968 and 2012, the real value of the federal minimum wage fell from $10.38 to $7.25 per hour, which is about 35 percent below the federal poverty level for a family of four.[77] Creation of the Earned Income Tax Credit (EITC) has offset a portion of these lost wages, but only for certain eligible employees. Low-wage workers in the United States are much less likely than their counterparts in other countries to have access to core benefits (such as health insurance, sick leave, vacation time, and the contractual protections of collective bargaining agreements).

In his exhaustive study of the employment impact of job training, Lafer concludes that no skills-based, education-based, or attitude-based employment programs have succeeded in lifting a large proportion of poor people out of poverty. Four decades of experimentation with job training programs demonstrate that "poverty and unemployment cannot be solved on the supply side, that is, by changing something about workers; instead, we must focus on the demand side of the labor market by working to improve the quality of jobs available to working-class Americans."[78] Otherwise, we are doing little more than "building a better underclass."[79] This is a sober evidence-based finding that is largely absent from most discussions of reentry.

The new paternalism that guided welfare reform bolsters some of the most debilitating experiences associated with poverty: "feeling that your fate rests in other people's hands, experiencing yourself as an object rather than an agent of authority, realizing that others do not trust you with the reins of control and the available responses have been defined as compliance or failure."[80] As such, welfare recipients have been unable to develop feelings of efficacy, control, and participation that are critical for meaningful civic and economic incorporation.[81] The reentry model as currently conceived shares many of these same shortcomings. Like the push for welfare reform, it does not address a fundamental structural issue: the absence of good jobs that pay living wages so that ex-offenders, like welfare recipients, "are not pushed into low-wage, dead-end jobs that fail to accommodate family needs and force them to cobble together precarious survival strategies well below the poverty line."[82]

Thanks to welfare reform and the reentry movement, people are being forced to accept "the meanest work at the meanest wages," with few opportunities to secure a living wage and dignified work conditions or to advance up the job ladder.[83] The benchmarks for "success" are very narrow. In the case of welfare reform, it is how many people have been moved off the welfare rolls—not how many people have been lifted out of poverty. In the case of reentry, recidivism is the main performance measure, even though this is a very slippery metric, as discussed in the next chapter. In both cases, little serious attention has been paid to the deep structural problems that have exacerbated the "disabilities, life problems, family needs, and resource deficits" found among the poor and truly disadvantaged.[84]

The Hamilton Project and National Reentry Proposals

Given the changing nature of black inequality and the wrenching structural shifts in the U.S. economy, even the most ambitious reentry proposals fall far short. Take, for example, a 2008 proposal for a national prisoner reentry program that was published under the auspices of the Hamilton Project, a neoliberal think tank associated with The Brookings Institution that was established in 2006 by financier Robert Rubin with the help of funding from Goldman Sachs. The Hamilton Project plan called for an $8.5 billion-per-year reentry program centered on providing up to a year of transitional employment in minimum-wage community service jobs for the estimated 245,000 men and women who are discharged annually from prison under supervised release and do not have a job when they get out.[85]

Compared to other reentry efforts, this one looks wildly generous and ambitious. It calls for spending each year more than thirty times the total amount spent during the first four years of the Second Chance Act. But providing a year of transitional employment and other services to parolees is unlikely to have a major impact on recidivism rates, the overall crime rate, or parolees' employment and earnings over the long term.

Claims that minimum-wage transitional jobs in the community service sector will reduce recidivism significantly and render people released from prison more employable at higher wages over the long run are highly debatable. The fact is that there have been few well-designed evaluations of such programs, and much of the existing evidence is based on programs from two or even three decades ago.[86] The Hamilton proposal acknowledges that even the very best transitional employment programs will likely have only a modest impact on re-arrest rates, reducing them by about 20 percent at most.[87] Moreover, the employment impacts of the programs may be short-lived. Claims that these transitional jobs will render people released from prison relatively more employable after the one-year transitional placement ends may be true. But if no good jobs are available, their enhanced employability is largely irrelevant.

The Hamilton proposal conservatively estimates that transitional employment would raise the future earnings of ex-prisoners by 15 percent over the short term, though it could be as high as almost 40 percent.[88] Even under the most optimistic estimates, transitional employment would barely raise the earnings capacity of former offenders back to what it would have been if they had never been sent to prison in the first place. Under more conservative and perhaps realistic assumptions, reentry programs centered on transitional employment in the marginal labor market would fall far short of restoring the earnings and employment prospects of former prisoners. In *Punishment and Inequality*, Bruce Western estimates that the effects of imprisonment on personal income are quite large, reducing the annual earnings of released offenders by 30–40 percent.[89]

Western demonstrates that low wages and joblessness among former prisoners are not simply the predictable results of skill deficiencies and anti-social behavior. The effects of incarceration itself help explain why ex-prisoners earn less, are employed less, and toil at "bad jobs characterized by high turnover and little chance of moving up the income ladder" than people from the same demographic and socioeconomic background who have never been sent to prison.[90] Western contends that incarceration has become a fast track to the low-wage, unstable marginal labor market for several reasons. A stint in prison erodes referral networks and social contacts that provide critical information about good job opportunities. A prison record and the stigma of conviction impede the development of long-term relationships founded on trust that are so crucial for entering white-collar, skilled trade, and public-sector jobs. The civil disabilities that deny ex-felons entry into licensed occupations impede their access to stable, well-paying jobs in the primary labor market.[91]

The Hamilton proposal calls for expanding prison-based educational programs. It recommends that state prisons adopt the standard for schooling that is in effect in federal penitentiaries. But this is unlikely to significantly increase the educational levels or employability of released offenders. Federal prisoners who are functionally illiterate or who lack a high school diploma or GED are required to enroll in 240 hours of education programs. This is equivalent to a mere nine weeks of high school on the outside. Moreover, an hour of in-prison instruction is not necessarily comparable to an hour of schooling on the outside. Prison-based education programs face challenges that arguably surpass those faced by some of the most challenging urban high schools. These include everything from the absence of any quiet space for studying to deep tensions between prison educators and prison guards over the utility of educational programming for inmates.[92]

The Hamilton plan makes a number of worthwhile recommendations that do not directly deal with increasing labor force participation. These include greatly restricting the use of imprisonment for technical parole violations, eliminating bans on federal benefits for returning citizens (such as restrictions on receiving public housing, food stamps, and student loans for people with criminal records), restoring Pell grants to prisoners, and guaranteeing public housing for people re-leased from prison who do not have a home. But in advocating for these laudable measures, penal reformers need to be wary of falling into the reentry-recidivism trap. If we are truly committed to integrating former offenders back into society, recommendations like these need to be evaluated through the lens of a more inclu-sive logic of restoring citizenship rather than by the narrow evidence-based stan-dard of whether they reduce the recidivism rate or not. If judged primarily by the recidivism yardstick, reentry—like rehabilitation before it—will come up short and will increasingly look like yet another failed experiment in penal reform.

At the public launch of the Hamilton Project proposal, Glenn Martin of the Fortune Society expressed considerable doubt about staking so much of the penal reform mission on reentry and transitional employment. "Even though we should be focusing on reentry, we shouldn't lose sight of the fact that we put way too many people in prison to begin with," he implored.[93] Martin suggested that a transitional employment program was not appropriate for some ex-offenders; furthermore, it would do little to offset the enormous structural barriers that prevent released offenders from securing employment in the secondary labor market of unstable, low-wage employment, let alone the primary labor market of good middle-class jobs that lift people out of poverty. As Bruce Western succinctly puts it, "reentry policy cannot successfully substitute for real social policy."[94] Even the best reentry programs are too weak and too limited in scope to address the deep-seated eco-nomic and social problems discussed earlier.

Got HOPE?

The modest impact that reentry efforts centered on services and employment have had on reducing recidivism rates has spurred some policy makers to search for alternative ways to engineer reentry. In 2004, Circuit Judge Steven Alm of Ha-waii established Hawaii's Opportunity Probation with Enforcement program, which has become one of the most widely acclaimed alternatives.[95] HOPE was initially directed at felony probationers, most of whom were substance abusers. Under HOPE, probationers receive clear warnings that failure to comply with the conditions of probation will be met with immediate graduated sanctions. HOPE also provides enhanced substance abuse treatment for offenders who repeatedly fail drug tests. It subjects substance abusers on probation to frequent drug tests and quickly dispatches them to short stints in jail for repeat violations. Most of these infractions tend to be quite trivial—such as a "dirty urine" test or a missed appointment with a probation officer. (Not surprisingly, the multi-billion-dollar a year drug-testing industry has been a fierce champion of HOPE.)[96] The HOPE ex-periment eliminated the hours of paperwork that had been required for a motion to revoke someone's probation. Under HOPE, the revocation form now takes pro-bation officers just twenty minutes to complete.[97]

The rationale behind HOPE is that "[j]ust as the threat of severe sanctions is largely impotent at controlling behavior if the sanctions are uncertain and deferred, the threat of even a mild sanction can be potent if the consequence follows the act swiftly and certainly."[98] Studies show that HOPE participants spend on average about the same number of days in jail for probation violations as a comparison group. But they spend only about a third as many days in prison due to revocations or new convictions, and had only half as many arrests for new crimes.[99]

Pilot HOPE programs have been sprouting up on the mainland in the wake of the reputed success in Hawaii. It remains an open question how transferable the HOPE model is to major urban centers on the mainland and to high incarceration states, which tend to differ markedly from Hawaii in terms of political culture, demographics, crime rates, poverty rates, and the extent of the social safety net. For all its celebrated merits, HOPE's approach appears to be out of sync with calls to end the war on drugs and scale back the role of law enforcement in drug policy.

A key mantra of the war on the war on drugs is that substance abuse should be treated primarily as a public health issue rather than as a criminal justice matter. HOPE portends a possible future of widespread "outpatient incarceration" that appears to be at odds with this public health model. It is questionable whether HOPE-style programs will be endowed with the resources and safeguards necessary to ensure that outpatient incarceration is truly restricted to those "who would otherwise face, with high probability, repeated spells of actual incarceration."[100]

HOPE was partly born out of a frustration that overburdened probation and parole officers faced with huge caseloads, outdated technology, and burdensome court procedures were unable to detect instances in which parolees and probationers exploit a system of loose supervision. But thanks to technological and other innovations and a reallocation of resources to parole and probation, the capacity of the authorities to detect infractions and swiftly punish them is growing exponentially. As a consequence, the growth possibilities for HOPE-style "virtual" or "outpatient" incarceration are enormous.[101] Beefing up the "pee 'em and see 'em" approach to supervised release and community corrections that has prevailed in the United States is likely to foster net widening.[102] Regular drug tests cost as little as five dollars each.[103] As of fifteen years ago, more than one-third of all U.S. probationers and parolees were under court orders for drug testing.[104] The number is certainly higher today, but there are no recent figures on how much higher.[105] Round-the-clock GPS monitoring can be had for perhaps as little as $15 per month.[106]

In a number of urban neighborhoods, police officers and parole officers work the streets in tandem. After the police officer runs a check on a license plate, the parole officer looks up the licensee's parole status, often with a handheld computer. If they find a "hit," the parolee is then subject to search without the usual Fourth Amendment protections that shield full citizens, as discussed in chapter 11.

Supervision and surveillance remain the dominant approaches to reentry even though it is not clear that the extensive post-release apparatus reduces crime significantly.[107] A large body of evidence suggests that investing more in probation and parole without fundamentally changing the mission of parole and probation officers will not reduce recidivism rates and the number of people returned to prison. Offenders monitored by parole and probation officers with smaller caseloads are not less likely to be re-arrested for a new crime. But they are more likely to have their parole or probation revoked for technical violations due to closer surveillance.[108]

Behind much of the talk about reentry and reintegration is often "a deep cynicism about the prospects for positive offender change."[109] In his recent ethnographic study of California parole officers, Robert Werth concluded that the punitive orientation that Mona Lynch documented a decade earlier had changed surprisingly little for all the talk about reentry. Parole officers did not disregard the new turn toward reentry and the renewed embrace of rehabilitation. They just incorporated it into their "'tough love' approach that emphasizes surveillance, sanctioning perceived misconduct, and utilizing (or threatening to utilize) reimprisonment."[110] Parole officers viewed parolees as primarily responsible for their own transformations and put little faith in educational, substance abuse, and other programs. As California's online handbook for parolees proclaims in its opening lines: "It's Your Choice—Successful Parole."[111]

As long as recidivism remains the main yardstick by which to measure penal success, and as long as recidivism is defined so capaciously (including anything from re-arrest for a missed appointment with a parole officer to conviction for a major new crime), detecting infractions will remain the central preoccupations of parole and probation officers. Their primary allegiance, attachments, and identity will remain in law enforcement, not in social welfare, education, economic development, or the needs of the community more broadly. The central focus will continue to be on how to do a better job at detecting parole and probation violations and quickly sanctioning them. It will not be on why the United States places so many conditions on its parolees and probationers and provides them and their communities with so few resources to meet these conditions. All of this greatly enhances the likelihood of net widening with the expansion of "outpatient" or "virtual" incarceration.

Stay to Play

As authorities impose or lengthen prison terms reportedly to foster a defendant's rehabilitation, reentry runs other risks of net widening. In the 2011 *Tapia v. United States* decision, the Supreme Court unanimously ruled that the language of the federal Sentencing Reform Act of 1984 recognized that "imprisonment is not an appropriate means of promoting correction and rehabilitation," and that the main purpose of prison was retribution, public safety, and deterrence.[112] It reversed a lower-court ruling that had permitted imposition of a longer sentence on a thirty-two-year-old woman than she would have received otherwise under the federal sentencing guidelines so that she could be eligible for a drug treatment program in a federal prison. Because this opinion was based on an interpretation of the federal sentencing act, it does not preclude state courts from requiring longer-than-usual prison stints to facilitate rehabilitation or from conditioning sentences and release dates on completion of treatment. In Texas and elsewhere, parole boards frequently extend prisoners' time to release because they have not completed a specific treatment program. This is often due not to any fault on the part of the inmate but because of lengthy waitlists for substance abuse treatment and other programs.

The *Tapia* decision and the reentry era's renewed emphasis on treatment also raise the question, when is a prison not a prison? The *Tapia* decision equates drug treatment in a secure facility as "pure 'imprisonment' with no rehabilitative goals." But Texas law specifically allows imprisonment in a secure facility in the name of rehabilitative goals. As part of its Right on Crime initiative, Texas has expanded the number of dedicated substance abuse treatment beds in such facilities. In political debates in Texas, treatment in a secure facility that looks like a prison, smells like a prison, and controls like a prison is nonetheless considered "community corrections" and an alternative to incarceration.[113]

Returning Citizens

A massive investment in reentry and rehabilitation, even on the scale of the Hamilton Project plan, would likely have only a modest impact at best on the recidivism and employment rates of former offenders. However, the foregoing analysis of the Hamilton proposal and reentry more generally should not be interpreted as a call to give up on reentry or rehabilitation. The evidence is overwhelming that providing incarcerated men and women with the opportunity to participate in meaningful employment, education, and self-improvement programs helps create safer, more humane, and less degrading prisons.[114] Prison programming also may provide employers with important signals about who is ready to desist from crime upon release, thus making them more willing to hire former felons.[115] Good reentry and rehabilitation programs also can improve considerably the quality of life for offenders and their families even if they make only a small dent in recidivism rates. Furthermore, even though the evidence is mixed that literacy and other prison education programs significantly reduce recidivism, they still have intrinsic value. Improving the reading and writing skills of people at the bottom rungs of society and helping them to become better parents, for example, enhances the quality of life for them and their families. Such programs also are symbolically important, for they represent a public commitment to replace some of the "degrading character of punishment" with a "more inclusive logic of renewal and social citizenship."[116]

The need is pressing to reclaim the rehabilitative ideal and embrace the reentry mission as worthy goals in their own right and not as means to an end defined largely by reducing recidivism. Doing so is recognition that the wider community has some connection to and responsibility for those it banishes behind bars.[117] It also helps further what is so lacking in the care and treatment of many prisoners and ex-offenders in the United States—a concern with upholding their dignity and avoiding their degradation.[118]

The U.S. approach to its returning citizens stands in striking contrast to how prisoners and ex-offenders are treated in other Western countries. The U.S. parole system "seems to be designed to catch a person doing something wrong, rather than provide the services to prevent an offense."[119] Western European countries "primarily use parole and probation services as a way of ensuring that the person leaving prison is receiving appropriate services and treatment to help ensure reintegration into the community."[120] In Finland, for example, only about one in five people on parole has a supervision or surveillance component to their release. All released prisoners in Finland have access to services regardless of whether or not a parole officer is supervising them closely. In the United States, about 200,000 people are released from prison each year without supervision (either because it is the conclusion of their sentence or because they are under some other kind of mandatory release). They are generally left largely on their own to integrate back into society without housing, employment, or other assistance.[121] In Germany and France, punishment law and penal practices are expressly designed to avoid creating "any sense of status differentiation between prisoners and the general population. On the contrary, practices in both countries are supposed to dramatize the fact that inmates are *just like everybody else*."[122]

European countries have largely abolished "civil death," the expulsion from political and public life that is so commonplace for convicted felons in the United States. European offenders do not lose membership in the political community, but perhaps more importantly, they do not lose membership in what James Q. Whitman calls the "social community." By contrast, the collateral consequences of a criminal conviction in the United States take a huge toll on ex-offenders and their families and communities, as elaborated in chapter 11.[123] In many states, a criminal conviction renders a former offender ineligible to vote, reside in public housing, receive public benefits (like welfare and student loans), obtain a driver's license, and work in certain occupations. No wonder a former prisoner titled his article on collateral consequences, "My Sentence Is Over But Will My Punishment Ever End?"[124]

European efforts to keep offenders "symbolically integrated into society" involve some striking measures, especially when compared to U.S. penal practices.[125] Prisoners in Germany are expected to be employed in jobs that resemble "real jobs" in the free world. German prisoners who are employed are eligible for key benefits and protections that German workers on the outside are entitled to, including a generous paid vacation each year and protection against arbitrary dismissal.[126] Germans who were employed while imprisoned but who cannot find work upon release are eligible for unemployment benefits.[127] The German government even covers the outside housing costs for prisoners for up to one year so they do not lose their homes while serving time. By contrast, prisoners in the

United States generally receive no housing relief while they are incarcerated, and many former felons in the United States are banned from public housing after they are released.

Conclusion

When he convened the inaugural meeting of the Reentry Council in January 2011, Attorney General Eric Holder said, "Reentry provides a major opportunity to reduce recidivism, save taxpayer dollars and make our communities safer."[128] But defending reentry, treatment, and rehabilitation programs in terms of their potential to reduce recidivism rates, trim penal budgets, and cut the prison population is an extremely risky and ultimately self-defeating strategy. The very best treatment and reentry programs are capable of making only modest contributions to reducing recidivism rates, and prison-based ones are the most ineffective on this score. Furthermore, as discussed in the next chapter, recidivism is an extremely slippery concept, and crimes committed by ex-offenders are not the main drivers of crime rates.

If crime rates escalate or if the recidivism rate remains stubbornly unchanged despite all the reported investment in reentry, the moment is ripe for another public outcry that "nothing works." Once again, "imprisonment will be regarded as the only viable answer to the crime problem."[129] Reentry and rehabilitation programs will be discredited, much as the Great Society social programs and the "root causes" approach to crime were discredited because they coincided with the mid-1960s spurt in national crime rates. Support for programs for offenders and ex-offenders—always tenuous—will likely erode even further, contributing to a further decline in the conditions of confinement and life prospects for the millions of people caught up in the penal system.

The enthusiasm for reentry as a path out of the carceral state is blithely detached from a deeper understanding of important shifts in the U.S. political economy since World War II on which the carceral state rests. These include widening income disparities among African Americans, which have fragmented black politics and contributed to growing political disparities (as discussed further in chapters 6 and 7). They also include the incomplete economic incorporation of African Americans, especially black men, after the Great Migration, the deindustrialization of wide swaths of urban America, the push to build up human capital rather than address the disappearance of good jobs, and the retreat of the public sector, which had been an important avenue of upward mobility for African Americans, as discussed in this chapter. The justice reinvestment movement, which has emerged on the heels of the reentry movement, is woefully inadequate to address these deeper structural issues, as discussed in the next chapter.

CHAPTER FIVE

Caught Again

Justice Reinvestment and Recidivism

I lay down, thinking thoughts that
Were one time real,
But are now like houses that have been torn down,
and families that have moved away.[1]

—CAROLYN BAXTER

The justice reinvestment movement was born more than a decade ago during the 2001–2003 recession. Its original premise was that a sizable portion of the billions of dollars spent on prisons and jails each year could be better spent on rebuilding the communities devastated by mass incarceration. Susan B. Tucker and Eric Cadora, who coined the term justice reinvestment, called for redirecting much of that money toward improving health care, education, employment programs, and public infrastructure in these communities.[2] They did not pitch justice reinvestment primarily as a way to save money and slash government budgets. Instead, they emphasized how spending so much on criminal justice rather than community development was inefficient, misguided, and undermined public safety.

Their original notion of justice reinvestment rested on a vague notion of community empowerment in which local communities would take the lead in developing solutions for their problems. Tucker and Cadora expressed some concerns about the reportedly high recidivism rates of released offenders. But their main focus was on rebuilding communities to enhance public safety and not on devising better prison-based and reentry programs to remake the individuals who cycle in and out of prison. In the years since Tucker and Cadora introduced the idea of justice reinvestment, it has morphed into something quite different. It now "runs the danger of institutionalizing mass incarceration at current levels."[3]

As originally sketched out, justice reinvestment took a holistic approach to public safety and the quality of life in low-income communities. Thanks to the quest to forge a broad elite-level political alliance on penal reform, a much narrower conception of justice reinvestment prevails today. Justice reinvestment now often amounts to reallocating resources within the criminal justice system and avoiding future prison costs rather than redirecting large sums of money and other resources from law enforcement and the penal system to schools, health care, social services, and economic development. Furthermore, the focus is on how to reorder spending priorities as budgets contract rather than on challenging the anti-tax, anti-government crusade and the related economic and regulatory policies that triggered the Great Recession and exacerbated preexisting economic and political inequalities.

For all the talk about the dawning of a new age in penal reform with the emergence of the justice reinvestment and Right on Crime movements, the actual impact of these initiatives on the reach of the carceral state has been remarkably modest. In most of the states that were forerunners in justice reinvestment, including Connecticut, Kansas, Texas, Rhode Island, and Arizona, we have not seen major reductions in prison populations or major shifts in spending from corrections to education, employment, housing, health care, and other programs to revitalize local communities hit hardest by the carceral state.[4] Much of the money that has been saved has been channeled into community corrections and law enforcement agencies.[5] Furthermore, funding for community-based substance abuse and mental health programs have been prime targets for budget cuts.

Justice reinvestment has at best acted as a brake on some future prison growth.[6] Claims about just how much new prison construction has been averted thanks to justice reinvestment are likely overstated. This is due to miscalculations or misrepresentations of future trends in prison growth, prison admissions, and crime rates. Another factor is the failure to consider the impact of policy shifts unrelated to justice reinvestment, including changes in the release rates of parole boards.[7]

The current push for justice reinvestment has been coming primarily from the top down, not the bottom up. The Pew Charitable Trusts, one of the biggest movers and shakers in penal reform today, and the U.S. Department of Justice have been major funders and champions of numerous state-level justice reinvestment initiatives and groups.[8] The primary vehicle for many of these state-level efforts is the Council of State Governments Justice Center (CSG). As of 2013, at least twenty-seven states had participated in justice reinvestment initiatives, and about two-thirds of them had enacted justice reinvestment legislation.[9]

As a condition of its involvement in a state, the CSG requires a bipartisan letter of invitation signed by top officials in all three branches of the state government. This assures, according to Todd Clear, that "the work is nonpartisan."[10] But elite-level bipartisan approaches to penal reform are not necessarily nonpartisan and have proven problematic in the past. The construction of the carceral state was a deeply bipartisan project, as elaborated in chapter 7. Leading politicians of both parties exploited fears of crime and racial anxieties. They excommunicated from public policy discussions members of the very communities most hurt by high crime rates and the exponential growth in incarceration rates. State and national lawmakers were able to "press forward with ever more punitive programs, independent of whether they worked or how much they cost," because they often had "little accountability to neighborhoods and communities that face the most serious crime."[11] Since crime and violence are highly stratified by race and class in the United States, those most victimized by crime and mass incarceration have had the least capacity to hold government officials accountable for the penal and other public policies they pursue.[12]

It remains an open question whether the CSG approach fundamentally changes this dynamic. CSG's justice reinvestment strategy calls for consulting at the start with a broad range of stakeholders, including law enforcement, service providers, and victims' advocates, but that consultation has consisted largely of periodic town meetings.[13] The key decision-making task forces and committees charged with furthering penal reform under the justice reinvestment model are composed almost exclusively of current and former public officials drawn from law enforcement and the three branches of government.[14]

In 2013, a group of some of the nation's leading criminal justice advocates and researchers, including Tucker and Cadora, released a sharply critical report of the justice reinvestment movement. Among other things, they castigated it for marginalizing knowledgeable and "well-established local advocates and justice reformers."[15] In response to the report, Adam Gelb, director of The Pew Charitable Trusts' Public Safety Performance Project, defended his foundation's "focus on nonpartisan, fact-based policymaking" that "has found strong resonance among decision makers once paralyzed by public safety rhetoric."[16]

Justice reinvestment, as practiced today, raises a fundamental political question: is it truly possible to make serious reductions in the size and gross inequities of the carceral state through a largely top-down process that is ostensibly nonpartisan and politically bloodless? The top-down justice reinvestment approach is not designed to tap into and nurture the growing movement in many states and communities to challenge the enormous size and wide-scale injustices of the carceral state. Indeed, it may be thwarting the emergence of a broad-based political movement with the power, resources, wherewithal, and vision to mount a sustained attack on the carceral state that will result in sizable reductions in the prison population and its retrenchment in other areas.

Dismantling the carceral state will necessitate constructing a political movement from a network of state-level political coalitions that have ties to citizen-based groups spanning many localities, as Heather Schoenfeld explains.[17] It is not clear that the CSG and Pew justice reinvestment strategy could ever be a catalyst for that kind of movement. Even though their approach is stridently bipartisan, it is not necessarily nonpartisan or apolitical. It is premised on three key political decisions that have enormous and potentially far-reaching consequences for the course of penal reform: keep budgetary concerns—not concerns about racial justice, morality, or justice writ large—at the center of the debate over penal reform; eschew calls for fundamental sentencing reform; and embrace reductions in the recidivism rate as a central yardstick of success.

As in many other areas of American politics, the call for a nonpartisan path to penal reform through justice reinvestment cloaks "a particular ideological politics under an anti-ideology banner."[18] The narrow focus on recidivism and on other quantifiable goals like efficiency and effectiveness is part of what Sarah Armstrong and Lesley McAra decry as the "economization of social life and governance." Beneath the apolitical, nonpartisan veneer, "problems of control still matter and are taking on new forms."[19]

The Slippery Concept of "Recidivism"

Reducing the recidivism rate now dominates all discussions of justice reinvestment and of penal policy more broadly. It has displaced broader public safety goals and more encompassing visions of how to improve the quality of life in the neighborhoods and communities that have borne the brunt of the carceral state. The mass incarceration crisis appears at times to be morphing into a recidivism crisis, or what Pat Carlen characterizes as a bout of "risk-crazed governance."[20]

The recidivism rate of released offenders has become a leading penal policy goal and indeed the preeminent yardstick by which to judge the success or failure of justice reinvestment and other penal reforms. As Jeanne Woodward, formerly a top corrections official in California, succinctly put it: "People will measure our success by our ability to lower the recidivism rate."[21] The penchant among criminologists, policy makers, and many penal reform advocates for data-driven, evidence-based solutions has reinforced this focus on recidivism. Stung by the hyper-politicization of penal policy since the 1970s, they have sought refuge in the illusionary promise that a focus on a narrow, quantifiable goal like recidivism provides an escape from politics.[22] But as Ian Loader and Richard Sparks remind us, "[T]here is always more at stake in crime reduction than reducing crime, and hence more to evaluation than finding out 'what works.'"[23]

The country's purportedly high recidivism rates have raised public alarms, even as crime rates fall to historic lows. Heather MacDonald of the Manhattan Institute warns about the "walking crime wave" released every day from U.S. prisons.[24] At the first-ever national summit on justice reinvestment held in 2010, Representative Frank Wolf (R-VA) expressed deep concerns about the "recidivism crisis that is straining our corrections system at all levels."[25] In a 2011 NAACP report on education and mass incarceration, James Bell, an attorney and youth justice activist, blamed the "unaccountable justice system" for the country's "70 percent recidivism rate."[26]

Bell and others have drawn much public attention to the key findings of a 2002 Bureau of Justice Statistics study that about two-thirds of released prisoners are re-arrested within three years, and four in ten are returned to prison in that time.[27] In doing so, they have fostered the mistaken public belief that many released prisoners go on to become serious repeat offenders and are the main drivers of crime rates. This foments the view that prisons are more like "graduate schools of crime" than places of correction and rehabilitation.[28] These misperceptions have impaired the political climate for pursuing the far-reaching sentencing and other penal reforms that are necessary if we are to make any serious dent in the incarceration rate and in the number of people under state surveillance.

Recidivism rates have been valorized as the key indicator of the return that states, municipalities, and taxpayers are receiving for their investments in the corrections system. But recidivism is a "notoriously slippery concept that is difficult to operationalize and reliably measure."[29] It has been "variably defined as rearrest, reconviction, or reincarceration, and does not always refer to the original offence(s)."[30] One analysis counted nine different definitions of recidivism in a survey of ninety studies of recidivism in the United States.[31]

Critics of the carceral state frequently claim that two-thirds of released offenders recidivate within three years, without noting that this is the re-arrest rate, not the rate at which released offenders are returned to prison for committing new crimes. Often left unsaid is that the number of people who are sent back to prison for committing a new serious crime is trivial compared to the overwhelming majority who are reimprisoned for committing a minor crime or a technical parole violation, such as a "dirty urine" test, a curfew infraction, or a missed appointment with a parole officer. For example, a recent study found that only 2–3 percent of released prisoners in New York State who had been incarcerated for a violent offense were returned to prison for committing a new felony offense. A drug-related offense or a technical parole violation, not a new violent crime, was the main reason these released offenders were sent back to prison.[32]

In 2011, Pew released the results of the first comprehensive state-by-state survey of recidivism.[33] When the report was released, Adam Gelb of Pew proclaimed, "Policies aimed at reducing recidivism offer perhaps the ripest opportunities for achieving the twin goals of less crime and lower costs."[34] Pew chose to use an expansive definition of recidivism—the proportion of released offenders who were returned to prison within three years. According to this definition, Pew found that about 43 percent of prisoners released in 2004 and nearly 45 percent of those released in 1999 were reincarcerated within three years. Pew's findings were comparable to those of the 2002 Bureau of Justice Statistics recidivism report and of studies of recidivism rates in other developed countries.[35]

The Pew study generated a spate of headlines about how four in ten ex-convicts ended up back in prison. In presenting its findings, Pew stressed how the national recidivism rate remained stubbornly high despite massive increases in state spending on prisons. Pew neglected to underscore that corrections costs had skyrocketed because the total number of prisoners and prisons had skyrocketed. It was not because states were spending so much more per prisoner on programming and other services to improve their lives and reduce recidivism rates.

The Pew report acknowledged that many of the people who return to prison had not necessarily committed new crimes. It also acknowledged that recidivism measures are complex and subject to misinterpretation. Nonetheless, the report still contributed to the common misperception that most released prisoners are habitual offenders who cycle in and out of prison and pose major threats to public safety.[36] Pew chose an expansive definition of recidivism (ex-convicts returned to prison, for whatever reason) and a subtitle closely associated with conservative attacks on the correctional system ("The Revolving Door of America's Prisons"). A follow-up BJS recidivism study released in 2014 reported three-year recidivism rates that were comparable to those of the Pew report and the pioneering 2002 BJS study.[37] The more recent BJS report, like its predecessor, largely defined recidivism based on rearrest rates. However, it did include some data on alternative conceptions of recidivism, including conviction rates for new crimes and also returns to prison for technical violations.

The portrait of crime and recidivism looks quite different depending on how recidivism is defined and framed in public discussions. For example, the state of Wyoming employs a much narrower definition of recidivism in assessing the performance of its penal system. In its 2009 annual report, the Wyoming Department of Corrections emphasized its "success rate," which it based on the percentage of released inmates who are not returned to prison for a *new felony conviction* within three years. In 2009, Wyoming boasted that its "success rate" was 99 percent, up from 85 percent in 2005. The Pew portrait of Wyoming is starkly different. Pew reports that Wyoming has a recidivism rate of 26 percent, with 15 percent returned to prison for technical violations and the remaining 11 percent for new, unspecified crimes. Unlike Wyoming's annual report, the Pew report does not distinguish between re-admissions for new felonies and re-admissions for more minor crimes or infractions.[38]

The Pew report concedes that recidivism rates can be potentially misleading indicators of correctional success. Nonetheless, it strongly recommends that correctional systems be judged and rewarded according to how good a job they do at lowering their recidivism rates. But a lower recidivism rate is not necessarily evidence of sound penal policy. States that cast a wide net that sweeps up many low-level offenders in their jails and prisons rather than sentencing them to probation or some other alternative to incarceration tend to have lower recidivism rates. But they pay a high social and economic cost for their over-incarceration of low-level and low-risk offenders. Likewise, states that make extensive use of parole for large numbers of released prisoners will generally have higher recidivism rates. Since they put more former offenders under the watchful eye of parole officers, they will detect more technical violations of parole.

California is a good case in point. Prior to the transformation of parole and other penal policies beginning in 2011 as part of "realignment," nearly every prisoner released was subject to at least three years of supervised parole.[39] As a result, the state had a huge parolee population, and many prison admissions were the result of technical parole violations. Prior to realignment, more than two out of every three offenders released from California's prisons were re-arrested within three years. Over half of them were returned to prison for a parole violation, which was a much higher rate of re-admission for technical violations than in most other states. Barely a quarter of released offenders in California were returned to state prison for a new crime.[40] Since realignment, California has been reporting recidivism rates in a more nuanced fashion based on arrests, returns to prison, and new convictions.[41]

States vary enormously in the proportion of former prisoners subject to supervised release. In Texas, about one-quarter of released inmates are not subject to parole supervision; in North Carolina, the number is more than 40 percent; and in

Florida it is over 60 percent.[42] Nationally, about four out of five released prisoners are placed under some form of supervision, which can range from a period of a few months to a lifetime.[43]

The Pew study reported that the recidivism rates in Texas (32 percent) and Oklahoma (26 percent) were among the lowest in the country.[44] This sparked wide praise for both states. But the kudos that Texas and Oklahoma received may have been undeserved because these are high-incarceration states that lock up large numbers of low-level offenders who do not pose much of a threat to society.[45] By comparison, Minnesota has a relatively high recidivism rate of 61 percent, which puts it at the top of Pew's list, but a relatively low incarceration rate.

The Pew recidivism study likely overstates the money to be saved by reducing state recidivism rates. It suggests that if the forty-one states that participated in its survey could reduce their recidivism rates by a mere 10 percent, they could save more than $635 million in annual incarceration costs. These calculations are based on multiplying each state's operating cost per inmate by one-tenth of the number of offenders returned to prison. But most of the costs of running a prison are fixed costs, as discussed in chapter 2. "The savings to a prison system with 10 or a 100 fewer prisoners is the marginal cost of food, toilet paper, laundry, and paperwork," explains Michael Tonry.[46] Not much money will be saved unless penal facilities are closed, corrections staffs are reduced, and large numbers of offenders are diverted out of the penal system.

The Recidivism-Crime Connection

This fixation on recidivism rates in discussions of penal reform fosters the misperception with the general public and with government officials who should know better that released offenders are the primary drivers of crime rates. For example, Attorney General Eric Holder told the American Bar Association several years ago, "Most crimes in America are committed by people who have committed crimes before." He went on to say, "About 67 percent of former state prisoners and 40 percent of former federal prisoners are re-arrested within three years of release. If we can reduce the rate of recidivism, we will directly reduce the crime rate."[47] But using the re-arrest rates of released offenders in this way to gauge recidivism and wider crime trends is problematic for many reasons.

The arrest rate of released offenders does not tell us much about what is driving the crime rate. It is well established that arrest rates are as much a function of police activities as they are of criminal activities. People subject to greater police attention, notably young minority men, residents of high crime areas, and people with prior criminal records, tend to be arrested more often.[48]

Although people released from prison are arrested at a far higher rate than the general population even after adjusting for age, race, and other factors, they are responsible for only a small fraction of all the crime reported each year. The 2002 BJS recidivism study concluded that offenders released in 1994 accounted for only about 5 percent of all arrests for serious crimes from 1994 to 1997.[49]

Richard Rosenfeld, Joel Wallman, and Robert Fornango calculate that the contribution of released offenders to the overall crime rate has been rising since the 2002 BJS study.[50] They estimate that the 1994 cohort of released offenders accounted for 10–16 percent of all arrests for violent, property, and drug offenses in the three-year period following their release. The 2001 cohort accounted for 30 percent of the arrests for violent crime, and about one-fifth of property and drug crime arrests.[51]

However, Rosenfeld, Wallman, and Fornango emphasize that these figures do not necessarily mean that released prisoners are becoming more criminogenic and are the main engines of the crime rate. During periods when the overall crime rate is falling and the number of released prisoners is rising, as has been the case since the mid-1990s, the overall contribution of released prisoners to the arrest rate—and presumably the crime rate—is likely to grow. This is so even though former prisoners are not necessarily committing more crimes than they once did.[52] "All else equal, the lower the general population's crime rate, the greater will be the proportion of all crime attributable to ex-prisoners," they explain.[53] Rosenfeld, Wallman, and Fornango conclude that the overall impact of released prisoners on the crime rate is "nontrivial but small."[54]

Recidivism Rates, Public Opinion, and Politics

Experts on crime and punishment often use the metaphor of a broken thermostat to explain the stubbornly persistent view among members of the general public that crime rates are out of control and rising despite ample evidence that they have been falling for years. All the attention on the reportedly high recidivism rates of released offenders does nothing to fix this broken thermometer. Reports of spectacular crimes committed by released offenders that lead the nightly news further distort public understandings of the degree to which released offenders drive the crime rate. Instead of clarifying this relationship, public officials often fuel these misunderstandings.

Democratic governor Ed Rendell of Pennsylvania, who left office in 2011 after serving two terms, is a good case in point. In fall 2008, Rendell suspended parole for all violent offenders in Pennsylvania's prisons after a man released on parole reportedly killed a Philadelphia police officer. Six months earlier, three men on parole had also been accused of killing a police officer in Philadelphia. In the wake of these incidents, Rendell stoked public hysteria that Pennsylvania's parole system was deeply flawed and that it was releasing many violent criminals who would go on to commit violent crimes once again.[55]

Rendell did not draw public attention to findings by the state's Board of Probation and Parole that strongly suggested otherwise. According to Catherine C. McVey, chair of the board at the time, 95 percent of offenders released on parole in Pennsylvania between 2005 and 2007 had not been convicted of a new crime while under supervision. Of the 5 percent who were convicted of a new offense, less than one-half of 1 percent (or 149 people out of nearly 39,000 released offenders) had been convicted of a new violent offense.[56] As Renee Cardwell Hughes, a Philadelphia judge specializing in homicides cases, lamented at the time, "If you live in the moment, if you live in the media," there is a widespread belief that "everyone who is out on parole is ready to shoot a cop."[57] In the case of Philadelphia, that would be about 57,000 people, which is the number of city residents who are serving parole or probation on any given day.[58]

Rendell's three-month parole suspension set off a severe and costly prison-overcrowding crisis in Pennsylvania that lasted well after the moratorium ended. In December 2008, Rendell lifted the moratorium once a report he commissioned had concluded that the state's parole process was generally sound but could be tweaked a little. Despite these findings, in his first official act in 2009, Rendell called on the Pennsylvania legislature to eliminate parole for certain violent and gun-related offenses and to enact stiffer and fixed sentences for such violations.[59] Mired in a budget standoff to close a $3 billion deficit at the time, Pennsylvania nonetheless continued full steam ahead on breaking ground for four new penal facilities, estimated to cost more than $800 million, to accommodate the projected 4 percent annual growth in the state's penal population through 2012.[60]

Structural Factors, Crime Rates, and the Quality of Life

The fixation on recidivism rates to gauge the performance of correctional systems is problematic for other reasons. It ignores the fact that larger political, social, and economic forces—not penal policies alone—drive recidivism and crime rates. Just as students' scores on standardized achievement tests are not just a factor of school and teacher performance, recidivism rates are not just a consequence of penal policies and penal programs.

Large numbers of returning parolees tend to be associated with increases in a neighborhood's crime rate. But few studies have focused on how neighborhood and community characteristics affect recidivism rates. We do know that releasing someone to an economically disadvantaged neighborhood increases the likelihood that he or she will recidivate.[61] Communities with greater residential stability and more voluntary organizations tend to dampen the effect of returning parolees on the crime rate.[62] High levels of single-parent families in a neighborhood apparently also dampen this effect. As more offenders are released in such neighborhoods, more families are reunited, which may increase the community's capacity to provide informal social control, John Hipp and Daniel Yates speculate.[63]

The single-minded focus on recidivism has diverted public attention from other important yardsticks by which to gauge the performance of correctional systems. For example, virtually no public attention has been paid to disquieting research findings that the mortality rates for released prisoners are considerably higher than for the general population, even after adjusting for factors like age, gender, and socioeconomic background.[64] In the first two years following release, the adjusted rate of death for former prisoners was 3.5 times higher than the rate for the general population, according to one study.[65]

The risk of death immediately after release is astronomical. In the first two weeks after release, it is nearly thirteen times higher than the adjusted mortality rate for the general population. During this period, a released prisoner is 129 times more likely to die of an overdose compared with the general population.[66] Studies also show that people are at enormous risk of suicide shortly after they leave prison.[67] Moderately higher rates of mortality persist for many years for people who have served time.[68] A study of parolees in New York State found that each year served in prison translated into a two-year decline in life expectancy. The risk was highest upon release and declined over time.[69]

As a consequence of the public and political obsession with recidivism rates as the primary gauge of what works, programs that improve the quality of life for offenders while they are in prison and once they are released have less political standing. Such programs are extremely vulnerable to budget cuts if they cannot demonstrate a measurable direct impact on recidivism rates of released offenders in the short term. For example, the report on the first national justice reinvestment summit acknowledged that some prison-based substance abuse treatment programs greatly improve the health outcomes and quality of life for low-risk offenders but have little impact on recidivism rates. Instead of using findings like these to defend prison-based treatment programs, the report recommended prioritizing access to programming based on risk level. To its credit, the report did criticize the practice of keeping low-level offenders in prison until they complete a mandated treatment program, for which there are often long waiting lists, and singled out community-based treatment programs supported by health insurance as essential elements of reentry planning.[70] However, it went on to declare: "If a program doesn't reduce recidivism, agencies are wasting their investments in these efforts."[71]

This is largely the sentiment expressed in Kentucky's Public Safety and Offender Act of 2011, which sailed through the state legislature as a main plank of its justice reinvestment initiative. This widely hailed statute includes a number of commendable reforms, including reduced penalties for minor drug sales and simple possession, greater restrictions on the use of sentencing enhancements, and some modest bail reforms.[72] It also requires that all supervision and treatment programs for offenders be subject to evidence-based evaluations. But the act bluntly states that reducing recidivism is the primary, if not exclusive, criterion by which to judge such programs.[73]

Justice Reinvestment and Pennsylvania

For all the attention justice reinvestment initiatives have garnered, their actual and projected impacts on the size of state prison populations have been extremely modest. In summer 2012, the Pennsylvania legislature unanimously enacted a justice reinvestment initiative that expanded alternative sentencing programs, diverted lower-level offenders to local jails, and reduced returns to state prison for technical violators of parole. Months later, the lawmakers enacted a companion

bill that earmarked most of the anticipated savings for law enforcement and victims programs, not reinvestment in the communities most hurt by the carceral
state. To the dismay of prisoners and many critics of the carceral state, the measure
also curtailed pre-release, a program that for decades had allowed well-behaved
state prisoners nearing the end of their sentences to serve their time in community
corrections facilities, which tend to be closer to home.

Republican governor Tom Corbett signed these bills with great fanfare. As
lawmakers extolled that the legislation would allow Pennsylvania to shut down
one state prison in the near future, the Corbett administration continued moving ahead on three new prison construction projects initiated under Rendell that
would add more than 5,000 prison beds at a cost of about $700 million.[74] The
justice reinvestment initiative in Pennsylvania is projected to result in a slight reduction in the prison population over five years—perhaps 3,000 fewer inmates
out of a total prison population of more than 51,000. The incarceration rate is
not likely to budge considerably because many of these would-be state prisoners
will be diverted to local jails and secure community corrections facilities.[75] At the
same time that the state was pursuing its justice reinvestment initiatives, lawmakers were seeking to impose tougher new mandatory minimum sanctions for gun-
related offenses.[76]

Don't Mess with Texas?

Policy makers, politicians, journalists criminologists, and penal reformers have
widely hailed Texas as a model in criminal justice reform for its pioneering role in
putting the principles of justice reinvestment into action.[77] As Tony Fabelo of the
Council of State Governments Justice Center said, " 'Be more like Texas' may not
be a bad thing."[78] Champions of justice reinvestment have been deeply invested
in portraying Texas, a Southern state with an indisputable get-tough reputation,
as a success story even though the roots of the Texas miracle in corrections are
shallow.

Praise began raining down on Texas largely thanks to its decision in 2007 not
to spend an estimated $2 billion on new prison construction to accommodate
projections that it would need an additional 17,000 prison beds by 2012. Legislators decided instead to allocate $241 million to invest in cheaper alternatives to
incarceration. These included expanding community corrections programs and
substance abuse and mental health treatment programs and beds, which had been
slashed and shuttered due to draconian budget cuts a decade earlier.[79]

The precise impact of Texas's justice reinvestment and other reforms is hard to
gauge, partly because of differences between the federal government and the state
of Texas in who counts as a state prisoner.[80] According to the Texas Department of
Criminal Justice (TDCJ), the state's prison population has largely stabilized since
the start of the justice reinvestment initiative. The total was 152,000 in 2012, a drop
of just 0.3 percent since 2008.[81] The federal Bureau of Justice Statistics reports that
the state prison population in Texas remained largely unchanged at about 172,000

between 2008 and 2011, before dropping to 166,000 in 2012, which was a decline of about 3.5 percent.[82]

The federal and state figures likely differ because the TDCJ does not include the thousands of state prisoners and parolees held by county jails. It also does not count the hundreds of state inmates that the TDCJ confines to fully secured substance abuse treatment facilities and the thousands more it confines in intermediate sanction facilities (ISFs). Many of these state prisoners are enumerated in Texas's jail population counts, which reportedly fell by 9.5 percent from 2008 to 2012, but many are not.[83]

ISFs are fully secured facilities used to incarcerate people who have violated the conditions of parole or probation.[84] First introduced in the early 1990s, the ISFs look and operate very much like prisons and have been a big growth area for the private prison industry in Texas and elsewhere. As of 2012, the state had about 1,800 people held in ISF facilities.[85] The ISF term of confinement is typically two to six months. Offenders detained in ISFs technically have not had their parole or probation revoked, and thus are not included in the state's prison population totals or when calculating recidivism rates.

The justice reinvestment initiative in Texas has created some momentum for modest measures that should improve the quality of life for some released offenders.[86] But it has not spurred major reductions in the state's prison population or major savings that have been reinvested in community development. The decline in numbers of Texas state prisoners from 2011 and 2012 recorded by the Bureau of Justice Statistics was probably due primarily to a surge in parole release rates between 2011 and 2012, not to the much heralded justice reinvestment initiatives.[87]

The Texas District & County Attorneys Association aptly summed up the legislature's ever so modest record on prison-related matters in 2011: "Most of the let-'em-out-early bills failed to pass, thanks to the opposition of prosecutors."[88] Meanwhile legislators continued to propose and enact new felonies and felony enhancement statutes.[89] The state's Legislative Budget Board is required to assess the budgetary impact of such measures. But the LBB has a habit of claiming that the costs of such enhancement bills are "insignificant," thus perpetuating the "convenient fiction that enables the tuff-on-crime [sic] crowd each session to write checks that the budget writers can pretend they'll never have to cash."[90]

All the credit that Texas has garnered due to the prisons it did not build (and the substance abuse and mental health programs it restored) has overshadowed the fact that the Lone Star State's incarceration rate remains stubbornly among the highest in the nation (see figure 1.2, p. 12). It was about 50 percent higher than that of California just as "realignment" was about to take off in the Golden State (about 900 per 100,000 for Texas compared to about 600 per 100,000 for California).[91] By numerous measures, Texas continues to be one of the most punitive states.[92] It incarcerates about one-quarter of a million people in its jails and prisons—or more than the total number of prisoners in Germany, France, Belgium, and the Netherlands combined. If parolees and probationers are added in, about 750,000 people are under the control of the correctional system in Texas, a population nearly equivalent to the size of Austin, the booming state capital.[93] Remarkably, one in twenty-seven people in Texas are either in jail or prison or on probation, parole, or under some other form of state supervision.[94]

All the acclaim for the Texas model of criminal justice reform has created some what's-wrong-with-this-picture moments. For example, in 2013, Texas lawmakers, policy makers, and Grover Norquist flocked to Oregon, with the blessing of the Pew Foundation, to proselytize about the Texas model for criminal justice reform. At the time, lawmakers in Oregon were considering several measures aimed at reducing its incarceration rate, which is already about 40 percent lower than that of Texas.[95] "It is deceptive to suggest that because other states started out with outrageously high incarceration rates and reduced those rates slightly, Oregon should follow suit," said one exasperated district attorney. "Other states should follow our lead and reduce their incarceration rates to the rates we have always had."[96]

So far, Texas has closed few penal facilities. In 2011, it finally shuttered the century-old Sugar Land prison, immortalized in the song "Midnight Special," which sat on prime Houston real estate coveted by developers. This was the first closure of an entire maximum-security facility in the state's history. Two years later, Texas announced plans to close a state jail in downtown Dallas and a pre-parole center elsewhere in the state, which would still leave the state with 109 lockups and the largest prison system of any state.[97]

The high praise for Texas as a model of penal reform is remarkable in other respects. Texas is exceptional not just for the sheer number of people under state control but also for the persistently brutal and inhumane conditions of their confinement, as discussed in chapters 3 and 6. The Lone Star State ranks fifth from the bottom in what it spends on average to house and care for each inmate under its control, or 43 percent less than the national average.[98] It is dead last in per capita spending on indigent criminal defense services.[99] Several years ago, Texas was forced to shut down the state's juvenile detention agency and transform its juvenile justice system after a media exposé documented widespread physical and sexual abuse of youths in detention that state officials were aware of but had not acted upon. Incidents of major force used against Texas prisoners have been rising over the last decade, likely because of high staff turnover, more inexperienced correctional officers, and brutally overheated penal facilities in the record-breaking summer heat.[100]

In the 1990s, Texas and Arizona were forerunners of the extensive use of supermax cells, where inmates are locked down nearly round-the-clock and denied any meaningful human contact for months, years, or sometimes even decades. The number of inmates in administrative segregation has been falling slowly in Texas since 2006. But it still stands at about 5.5 percent or about twice the proportion of inmates nationwide.[101] In 2013, legislators in Texas ordered a study of the state's use of administrative segregation, largely in response to concerns raised by mental health advocates (including the high rate of suicide among segregated inmates in Texas prisons).[102]

Along with Arizona, Texas has been a ruthless pioneer in thwarting federal judicial and other oversight of the conditions of confinement in state prisons, as discussed in chapter 3. This helps explain why, since the mid-1990s, Texas has faced fewer major court challenges compared to California about deteriorating medical and other conditions in its penal system. The fact that the TDCJ has had more success beating back major litigation is not necessarily a sign that it does a better job managing its penal system than California does, as some champions of the Texan model of penal reform claim.[103]

With an allocation of barely $10 per day per inmate, Texas spends far less on health care than other states with large prison systems. California, whose prison health-care system was deemed unconstitutional by the U.S. Supreme Court in 2011 because of the life-threatening and inadequate level of care in its state prisons, spends about three times as much per inmate on health care.[104] Texas universities responsible for providing most of the health care in its prisons through state contracts warned that, even prior to the 2012–13 cutbacks, the level of care was barely constitutional. As one commentator declared, "The system is clearly going California."[105]

The quality of life in Texas prisons has been declining in big and small ways with the onslaught of budget cuts. Along with several other states, Texas stopped serving lunch to inmates on weekends in some prisons to save money. This move did not provoke any outcry from leading advocates of the justice reinvestment movement in Texas. Democratic state senator John Whitmire, a national proselytizer for Right on Crime and Texas-style penal reforms, quipped, "If they don't like the menu, don't come there in the first place."[106]

The Deeper Political Context of Penal Reform in Texas

Texas only looks like a model of nonpartisan penal reform if it is viewed in isolation from the deeper political currents shaping American politics today. The ostensibly nonpartisan model of justice reinvestment in Texas needs to be understood within the context of broader economic and political developments that are deeply ideological and bitterly partisan. Texas has been at the epicenter of the roaring Tea Party movement, whose *raison d'état* is deep cuts in taxes and savage cuts in certain government-funded programs. The Lone Star State has been leading the nation in cutting taxes and shredding its safety net, which was already one of the most threadbare.

The focus on the prisons that Texas did not build has deflected attention away from the fact that Texas has been energetically disinvesting from the very items proven to reduce crime and improve the quality of life in the disadvantaged communities hurt most by crime and by get-tough policies. These include high-quality schools, good health care, living-wage jobs, and adequate resources for family planning, mental health, and social services. It also has deflected attention from the fact that the budget crisis in Texas was not an act of nature but rather a crisis that was politically engineered by some of the very people who are being hailed as leaders in penal reform today.

In Texas and many other states, the political debate has centered on what is to be cut and on how to maneuver within a tight budget climate. The conversation has not been about who should pay how much to maintain an equitable and just level of public spending on education, health care, infrastructure, and social services. When Texas faced a $10 billion budget shortfall in 2003, Republican governor Rick Perry enlisted the help of Grover Norquist, the country's most prominent anti-tax, anti-government crusader. Norquist came to Texas to help persuade Republicans on the fence to close the budget gap with spending cuts alone and to hold the line on no new taxes. This entailed cutting 200,000 children from the Children's Health Insurance Program and another 500,000 children from Medicaid and making steep cuts in mental health and substance abuse programs. In January 2011, Texas faced a $27 billion budget deficit for fiscal 2012 and 2013 combined.[107] This budget shortfall was the direct result of a huge property tax cut Perry had pushed through in 2006 in keeping with the Norquist formula to cut taxes in order to force drastic cuts in spending, especially for social programs. As Norquist toured the state with Perry in early 2011, he urged legislators to hang tough on no new taxes. He told them, "Now is not the time to get wobbly."[108]

The state's biennial budget for 2012 and 2013 did not include any tax increases to address the budget shortfall but did massively cut spending for education and social services. Texas, already near the bottom in state spending on education and dead last in percentage of adults with a high school diploma, slashed the budget for public schools by more than $4 billion, forcing districts to lay off thousands of teachers. This was the first reduction in per-student spending on education in Texas since World War II. Legislators also drastically cut funding for health and human services by 17 percent, even though Texas has the highest proportion of uninsured residents, ranks last in children's access to health care, and is forty-ninth in state spending per capita on mental health.[109] Texas also has one of the lowest drug treatment admission rates in the country and long waiting lists for substance abuse treatment.[110] Mental health services are so underfunded in Texas that the state faces a "court order declaring long wait times for forensic hospital beds unconstitutional."[111]

Texas has been a national leader in defunding health-care services for women and teenagers, even though it has one of the highest teen pregnancy and teen birthrates in the country. A leading cause of school dropouts, teen pregnancies increased under the Perry administration. Rates of sexually transmitted diseases have skyrocketed in a number of Texas counties since 2006, the first year that the budget for family-planning programs was cut.[112] In fall 2011, more than a dozen women's health clinics were forced to close in Texas after the legislature slashed financing for women's health care by two-thirds as part of a wider national assault on Planned Parenthood and abortion providers. None of these clinics, even the ones affiliated with Planned Parenthood, performed abortions. In 2012, the state decided to forfeit about $35 million in federal money that finances the Medicaid

Women's Health Program in order to prevent Planned Parenthood from receiving any of the federal money that funds many clinics for low-income women in Texas.[113]

Texas legislators left the overall size of the budget for the state's adult prisons largely untouched in the 2012–13 budget crunch, trimming a mere $5 million out of the nearly $5 billion allocation. But they cut $124 million from the state's juvenile justice agencies and nearly $72 million from prison health care in order to accommodate, among other things, increases in spending on correctional security, private prisons, and contracting out state inmates to county jails. Although the 2012–13 budget modestly increased funding for substance abuse programs, the lion's share of the cuts to the TDCJ budget came from community supervision and diversionary programs, which were supposed to be two of the state's main weapons to keep the incarceration rate in check. Texas also eliminated Project RIO, the primary state program for helping former felons find employment.[114]

Obamacare and Correctional Health Care

The unfolding political drama over implementation of President Obama's Patient Protection and Affordable Care Act (PPACA) starkly calls into question claims that fiscal pressures in Texas and elsewhere will force states to forge bipartisan coalitions centered on curtailing the carceral state because they cannot afford not to. Texas and many other states have decided to forfeit gargantuan sums of federal dollars for their health-care and correctional systems because of their ideological opposition to Obamacare.

In June 2012, the U.S. Supreme Court upheld the major provisions of the Affordable Care Act, except for the federal mandate that required states to expand Medicaid or else forfeit federal funding. Following that decision, most Republican governors announced that they would not expand Medicaid coverage for the uninsured, even though the federal government would pick up 100 percent of the tab for the first three years and 90 percent of the costs after 2019. As of December 2013, about twenty-three states had declared that they would not participate in the Medicaid expansion or were leaning against participating, including eight of the ten states with the nation's highest incarceration rates.[115]

Governor Perry decided to opt out because "Obamacare is bad for the economy, bad for health care, bad for freedom." His decision will cost Texas, which has the highest proportion of the uninsured of any state, an estimated $100 billion in federal funds over the next decade. Texas also forfeits the boost in jobs and consumer spending that comes with major injections of federal funds thanks to the "multiplier effect."[116] Perry's decision riled the state's health insurers and health-care providers, who expected a windfall from Medicaid expansion.

Although it may make ideological sense for Perry and other Republican governors and legislators to opt out of Medicaid expansion, from a fiscal point of view this decision is highly irrational. It also casts doubt on the expressed commitment in Texas and elsewhere to charting a new nonpartisan path in penal policy through justice reinvestment and greater investments in reentry. By opting out of Medic-aid expansion, Texas and other states forgo funds desperately needed to support health care, substance abuse, and mental health programs that are key for treating low-income people in the community and keeping them out of jail and prison.

The opt-out states also forfeit the opportunity to shift a huge chunk of correc-tional health-care costs onto the federal tab. Under the 1965 law that established Medicaid, inmates generally did not qualify for this means-tested federal-state health insurance program for low-income people. In 1997, however, the Depart-ment of Health and Human Services modified the "inmate exception" rule. It de-clared that the costs of treating inmates who were transferred to independent hospitals or other health-care facilities could be reimbursed by Medicaid if they were otherwise eligible and enrolled in the program.[117] Despite the rule change, the portion of inmate hospitalizations covered by Medicaid remained relatively small because many states were unaware of the change or lacked the bureaucratic capacity or expertise to implement it.[118] Furthermore, federal law only required states to provide Medicaid to low-income children, mothers with young children, pregnant women, and the disabled. Low-income men—the main population of correctional systems—were generally not eligible for Medicaid unless they had been certified as disabled.

All this has changed with enactment of the PPACA in 2010. States now have the option to expand Medicaid coverage to all adults under the age of sixty-five whose incomes are at or below 133 percent of the federal poverty level, with Washing-ton picking up most of the tab. Furthermore, adults of modest means who earn too much to qualify for Medicaid are now eligible to receive subsidized health insurance through the new exchanges that states and the federal government have established in accordance with the PPACA. The majority of inmates are likely to qualify for Medicaid under the new regulations. Nearly all hospitalizations and nursing home admissions of inmates at independent facilities will be eligible for federal funding under Medicaid, but only if states opt in to the Medicaid expan-sion.[119] In order to receive the full benefit, states also need to establish mechanisms to enroll inmates in Medicaid and maintain their coverage while they are incarcer-ated and after they are released. Some states and counties have been working ag-gressively to do that so that more correctional health-care expenses can be shifted onto the federal tab.

For states that opt in, the expansion of Medicaid will provide a major new stream of revenue for departments of corrections to cover offsite health-care costs. But the potential impact of the PPACA on the carceral state goes far beyond that. Since millions of low-income people cycle through U.S. jails each year, local jails could become major sites to enroll people in Medicaid and to obtain health in-surance for them through the exchanges.[120] The PPACA does not permit people who are serving time after their cases have been adjudicated to participate in the new health-care exchanges. However, it does permit people who are in custody or in the community pending disposition of the charges against them to obtain or maintain coverage through the exchanges. This could decrease the health-care tab of county jails considerably, since about six in ten inmates in jail are awaiting adjudication of their cases.[121]

Thanks to the Medicaid expansion and subsidized health insurance, states that opt in will be better able to ensure a continuity of care for people released from prison or jail, who tend to have higher rates of addiction, mental illness, infections, and chronic illnesses.[122] Many parolees, probationers, and other people serving time in community corrections will be eligible for full Medicaid coverage or for subsidized insurance through the health-care exchanges.[123] This will make it easier for them to access the substance abuse and mental health treatment and other care they need, which is a key factor in successful reintegration. Furthermore, the surge of new Medicaid money will provide states and counties with new resources and capacity to provide such care.[124]

The PPACA has great potential to expand critical services for low-income men and women in ways that could keep them out of the criminal justice system. However, as the opportunities to provide primary health-care services on the outside grow, prisons and jails will likely have even more trouble attracting qualified medical and mental health professionals, many of whom do not consider penal facilities desirable places to work.[125] Furthermore, by providing a way for state and county correctional systems to offload some of their correctional health-care costs onto the federal government, the PPACA could reduce the modest pressure that budgetary concerns have been putting on legislators and public officials to rethink the carceral state.

Texas and other states have gone chasing after federal Second Chance and justice reinvestment dollars, which are a relative pittance. Meanwhile they have been eschewing the billions of dollars in Medicaid funding that could provide real second chances to offenders and ex-offenders, many of whom, truth be told, never had a first chance. Top Republicans in the House have added to their pile of complaints against the Affordable Care Act that it will help incarcerated people.[126] Opting out of Medicaid expansion flies in the face of all the bipartisan talk about needing to provide greater support for reentry, second chances, alternatives to incarceration, and justice reinvestment.

Conclusion

Robert Perkinson's sweeping and searing account of the Lone Star State's penal system from the days of slavery to now is a sober reminder that budgetary pressures in Texas and elsewhere will not necessarily reverse the prison boom.[127] If Perkinson's analysis is correct, Texas will not begin shuttering its prisons without enormous political pressure. The "Texas tough" style of justice is not only deeply embedded in the state's budget but also in its political, cultural, and social fabric. In Texas and elsewhere, penal policies also are caught up in the broader national political currents that have captured American politics and created an enormous disjuncture between the problems facing the country and the will and capacity of the political system to address them.

Arguments centered primarily on the purported economic burden of the carceral state and on stemming recidivism rates are not up to the political task of challenging the fundamental legitimacy of the carceral state and the hyper-incarceration of the most disadvantaged groups in the United States. Elite-level bipartisan coalitions centered on the three R's also are not up to the political task, which helps explain why penal reforms thus far have been so modest. As discussed further in chapter 8, these reforms have been directed primarily at drug offenders and other nonserious, nonviolent, and nonsexual offenders—the so-called non, non, nons—which is unlikely to bring about a major retrenchment of the carceral state. Furthermore, all the recent attention on the non, non, nons has diverted public attention away from the ways in which the carceral state continues to grow, as discussed in chapters 8, 9, and 10, and how it distorts democratic institutions and conceptions of citizenship, as discussed in chapter 11. Moreover, the three R's are a color-blind strategy to criminal justice reform that ignores the stark racial and other injustices on which the carceral state rests, as discussed in the next two chapters. It blithely keeps them at arm's length. It does not tap into the growing political ferment and anger at the local level and among some advocacy groups to address these injustices.

PART II

The Politics of Race and Penal Reform

CHAPTER SIX

Is Mass Incarceration the "New Jim Crow"?

Racial Disparities and the Carceral State

I am invisible, understand, simply because people refuse to see me.
—RALPH ELLISON, *Invisible Man*

Some leading critics of the carceral state contend that racial animus, cloaked by institutional racism and ostensibly color-blind policies and laws, is the main engine of mass incarceration in the United States. In their view, any penal reform movement seeking to dismantle the carceral state must first and foremost target the country's deep, widespread, and persistent racism in its many manifestations.[1] In the words of Michelle Alexander, the carceral state is best understood as a new type of "racial caste system" akin to Jim Crow.[2]

Many criminologists, practitioners, and other experts on crime and punishment recoil from likening the causes and consequences of mass incarceration to those of Jim Crow.[3] Nonetheless, many of them have been preoccupied with assessing the racial disparities of the criminal justice system. Their efforts to measure these disparities have made some important contributions to our understanding of the carceral state. But the preoccupation in criminology and other disciplines with measuring racial disparities has come at a cost. It has impeded our understanding of some key developments in American politics and public policy not only with respect to the carceral state, but also other leading social, political, and economic problems.

Much of the research on racial disparities and the carceral state has fallen into what Adolph Reed and Merlin Chowkwanyun characterize as the trap of "interpretive pathologies."[4] Researchers have devised ever more sophisticated statistical models to measure the extent of black-white disparities in criminal justice and other realms like education, employment, health care, and income. But the deep and complex sources of those disparities and how to alleviate them often go largely unexamined beyond broad-brushed assertions of "institutional racism," deep-seated white racial animus toward blacks, or the "long and unbroken arc of American racism."[5] Also left largely unexamined is "the extent to which particular inequalities that appear statistically as 'racial' disparities" may in fact be embedded in other political, social, and economic social relations.[6] Furthermore, much of this work focuses nearly exclusively on disparities between whites and blacks. It largely ignores other racial and ethnic groups, including Latinos. Now the largest minority group in the United States, Latinos are the largest ethnic or racial group in federal prisons.[7]

This is not just an analytical problem. It is also a political problem. Key inequalities—such as the economic and political ones associated with the seepage of neoliberalism into all aspects of public policy—end up marginalized in debates over public policies if they do not fit neatly into a racial disparities framework.[8] This thwarts the development of a broader political and social movement to challenge the underlying forces that sustain the carceral state and other gross injustices in the United States today.

Too tight a focus on the racial disparities of the carceral state is problematic for other reasons. The focus on numbers—that is, how many African Americans or other minorities are serving time relative to whites—has overshadowed the qualitative dimension of the penal crisis. The racial disparities lens obscures the brutal and degrading conditions in which many prisoners, regardless of their race or ethnicity, serve their time. It also obscures how conditions in many prisons and jails deteriorated as corrections budgets contracted in the wake of the financial crisis and the Great Recession, as discussed in chapter 2. Some predominantly white states operate some of the most dehumanizing and dangerous prisons in the country. Idaho's largest prison was widely known as a "gladiator school" due to inmate-on-inmate violence allegedly fostered by guards at this CCA-run facility near Boise.[9] For many years, Maine, the whitest state in the country, operated one of the worst supermax facilities.[10] By contrast, Mississippi, a deep South state where more than two-thirds of the state prisoners are black and which has a long history of operating some of the country's most notorious penal facilities, has been a national pioneer in shrinking and regulating the use of supermax cells.[11]

This chapter identifies some of the key analytical and political pitfalls of viewing the carceral state primarily through a narrow lens of racial disparities that is not more attentive to the underlying mechanisms that reproduce these disparities. Such a narrow lens has obscured key aspects of the development of the carceral state, including important demographic changes in who is being incarcerated for what crimes, and the proliferation of degrading and inhumane conditions for people who are serving time.

This chapter begins with a brief overview of the changing racial, ethnic, and gender demographics of the carceral state with the waning of the war on drugs. It then surveys some of the major contributions of research on racial disparities in the criminal justice system. Next it examines the qualitative dimension of the carceral state, which does not fit neatly into a black-white racial disparities framework. A central contention is that the U.S. carceral state is exceptional not just because it locks so many people up but also because of the inhumane and degrading conditions that are unexceptional in jails and prisons throughout the United

States. The chapter concludes by identifying some of the shortcomings of uncritically staking a penal reform agenda too narrowly on the goal of ameliorating racial disparities in punishment.

The Changing Demographics of the Carceral State

The sheer magnitude of the U.S. incarceration rate and the vast racial and ethnic disparities between those who serve time and those who do not are two of the most distinctive features of the U.S. carceral state. These two features are frequently mentioned together, which has fostered the common assumption that they occurred simultaneously and have similar underlying causes. But new research suggests that "the greatest and most durable increases in racial disparity took place before the national incarceration rate began its rapid ascent."[12] Between 1880 and 1950, the nonwhite to white ratio of imprisonment rates roughly doubled, going from about 2.4:1 to 5:1.[13] Since then, the increase has been far less steep. The black-white ratio peaked at about 7:1 in the 1990s and then fell back to about 5:1 today.[14] Christopher Muller argues that the Great Migration of the early twentieth century is a key factor in explaining why racial disparities in imprisonment steeply escalated prior to the onset of the era of mass incarceration in the 1970s. During the Great Migration, he explains, millions of blacks left the South, an area of comparatively low nonwhite incarceration rates, and headed to the North, a region of relatively high nonwhite incarceration rates.[15]

Although racial disparities in incarceration have narrowed slightly since peaking in the mid-1990s, they remain breathtaking. As of 2009, the incarceration rate was about 2,300 per 100,000 for non-Hispanic blacks, 1,000 per 100,000 for Hispanics, and 400 per 100,000 for non-Hispanic whites (see figure 1.1 in chapter 1).[16] The black-white ratio in incarceration greatly exceeds all other major social indicators of black-white inequality, including unemployment (2:1), infant mortality (2:1), and wealth (1:5).[17] If current trends continue, one in three black males and one in six Hispanic males born in 2001 are expected to spend time in prison during their lives. The figure for white males is about one in seventeen.[18] The incarceration rate for black males is about 4,700 per 100,000, or several times the rate that South Africa was locking up black men on the eve of the end of apartheid in the early 1990s (see figure 1.1, p. 5).[19]

The U.S. incarceration rate for whites is low in comparison to the rates for African Americans and Hispanics. But it is high when compared to the overall incarceration rates of other industrialized democracies. The U.S. incarceration rate of 400 per 100,000 for whites is about two-and-a-half to seven times the incarceration rates of other Western countries and Japan.[20] One out of ten whites surveyed report they have a friend or relative currently incarcerated. This finding only looks unremarkable when compared to the survey results for African Americans, half of whom answered yes to this question.[21]

The incarceration rate for non-Hispanic whites varies enormously across the United States. In a handful of states in the Midwest or Northeast, it hovers around

200 per 100,000 people. This is about 25 percent higher than the national incarceration rates for England and Spain, two of the most punitive countries in Western Europe. But several states are locking up non-Hispanic whites at a pace that places them at the top of charts of incarceration rates worldwide (see figure 1.1, p. 5). These include Oklahoma (740 per 100,000), Texas (667 per 100,000), and Idaho (675 per 100,000).[22] The incarceration rates of these three states surpass the rate for Russia (568 per 100,000), which is second in the world after the United States.[23]

The cumulative risks of imprisonment for Latino and white men have followed strikingly similar patterns. For white and Latino males born in the late 1970s, the risk of being sent to prison by the time they turn thirty-four was about four times what it was for their cohorts born three decades earlier. For blacks, it was two and a half times higher.[24] Young African American men who have dropped out of high school now have an incarceration rate nearly fifty times the national average. For young white male dropouts, it is ten times the national average.[25] Nearly one-third of white high school dropouts have served time by the age of thirty-four. That figure only looks unremarkable when compared to the plight of the 68 percent of African American high school dropouts who have served time by that age.[26] These figures understate the likelihood of serving time because they do not include stints in jails, which house about a third of all U.S. inmates.

Incarceration rates have increased much faster for women than for men, thanks largely to the war on drugs. In 2001, a woman's chance of being sent to prison was six times greater than in 1974; for men, the increase was threefold.[27] In 2012, about 7 percent of inmates in state and federal prisons were female, up from just 3 percent in 1970. Women constituted 13 percent of inmates held in local jails, nearly double the proportion held in the mid-1980s.[28]

After passage of the federal Anti-Drug Abuse Acts of 1986 and 1988, with their stiff punishments for drug crimes, the number of women—especially black women—serving time for drug offenses in federal prisons soared, as did their length of sentence. Tough new drug laws at the state level likewise had a disparate impact on women, especially African American women.[29] Although the incarceration rate for black women has begun to decline with the recent waning of the war on drugs, it still stands at 333 per 100,000, far exceeding the overall incarceration rates for many other countries (see figure 1.1, p. 5).[30]

In recent years, the number of women imprisoned for violent offenses and property offenses has increased substantially, mostly driven by growth in imprisonment among white and Hispanic women.[31] For example, 80 percent of the women sentenced to prison in Ohio in fiscal 2013 were white, and many of them came from rural counties.[32] Between 2000 and 2009, the incarceration rate increased by nearly half for white women and one-fifth for Latinas, while falling by about 12 percent for black women.[33] The rising rates of contact with the criminal justice system for low-income white women are likely a consequence of the recent sharp deterioration in their health and social conditions.[34]

Research on Racial Disparities and the
Criminal Justice System

Between the 1930s and the 1980s, the U.S. penal system experienced a major transformation as it went from being majority white to majority black and Latino. This transformation coincided with the political awakening of the civil rights movement, which spurred political and analytical interest in whether racial bias and discrimination could explain the enormous racial disparities in punishment.

Before delving into what is wrong with too narrow an analytical and political focus today on the question of racial disparities in punishment, it is important to highlight some of the important prior contributions of research in this area. Partly due to the lack of credible research in the 1970s and early 1980s on racial disparities in the criminal justice system, anecdotal evidence and hunches of extensive racial bias in sentencing propelled policy-making. Prominent liberals and their sympathizers, most notably Senator Edward M. Kennedy (D-MA), Judge Marvin Frankel, and the American Friends Service Committee, pushed for an overhaul of the penal system to make it more fair and more consistent.[35] They sought determinate sentences and mandatory guidelines to end what they charged were extensive sentencing disparities between blacks and whites.[36] This call for one-size-fits-all sentences based primarily on the offense and not on the circumstances of the offender was also appealing because it resonated with the deeper egalitarian ethos on which the distinctive U.S. common-law system was built.[37]

Conservatives, up in arms at the time over what they charged were excessively lenient judges and parole boards, seized this political opening to enlist liberals in the cause of sentencing reform built around a set of mandatory guidelines. The result was the imposition of a complex sentencing grid that the new federal U.S. Sentencing Commission developed and monitored. The commission ratcheted up sentences across the board in the federal system. Meanwhile, many states followed the federal lead and imposed tough determinate sentences, mandatory minimums, and sentencing guidelines.[38]

At the time, the evidence to support allegations of extensive racial bias in sentencing was slim or nonexistent. Indeed, a National Research Council (NRC) panel concluded in 1983 that much of the research on sentencing disparities was vexed with measurement errors and sample selection problems that called into question many claims of defendant race effects on punishment outcomes.[39] In his assessment three decades later of the state of research on racial disparities in sentencing, Eric Baumer reaches a similar conclusion.[40]

Despite the persistent statistical and measurement obstacles noted by the NRC, Baumer, and other experts, we still know more than we think we know today about racial disparities in punishment. We now know that the significance of racial bias and race of the defendant in fostering sentencing disparities was grossly overstated, especially for serious and violent crimes. Comprehensive reviews of the research on racial disparities in sentencing have found that race of the defendant has only a relatively weak influence on sentence length.[41] As for the decision on whether to sentence someone to prison or impose an alternative sanction, the defendant's race has a significant but relatively modest effect overall and is highly variable across studies. We also know that race effects are highly contingent on many other factors, including age, gender, socioeconomic and employment status, quality of legal representation, offense type, criminal record, and jurisdictional location.[42]

We now have a more subtle understanding of how racial discrimination and bias operate in the criminal justice system. Recent research strongly suggests that the flagrant Scottsboro-type discrimination is not a primary driver of racial disparities in criminal justice outcomes. Rather, it appears that a little bias can still go a long way in a system that has many decision-makers—police who must decide whether to make an arrest or not; prosecutors who determine whether to dismiss the case, what to charge, and what plea bargains to seek; and judges who determine bail and sanctions. A recent review of dozens of studies of racial disparities in punishment concluded that small differences in treatment can accumulate such that they add up to substantial disparities in criminal justice outcomes between whites and people of color.[43]

Work on racial disparities also brought into sharp focus the relationship between race of the defendant and race of the victim in punishment. This research undermined the conventional wisdom that the defendant's race is the leading factor in determining who is sentenced to death. As David Baldus demonstrated in the landmark research at the center of the Supreme Court's 1987 *McCleskey v. Kemp* decision, the race of the victim is a far more significant factor than the race of the defendant in determining who is spared the death penalty and who is not.[44] Another notable study found that whites convicted of first-degree murder in Illinois were sentenced to death at a rate two-and-a-half times that of blacks convicted of the same crime. It appears that people convicted of murder in the largely white rural parts of Illinois were more likely to receive a death sentence than those living in urban areas that have more diverse populations.[45] In noncapital cases as well, the harshest penalties tend to be imposed on blacks who victimize whites, while blacks who victimize other blacks generally are treated more leniently.[46]

To sum up, Senator Edward M. Kennedy and Judge Frankel were not entirely wrong. Racial discrimination and unwarranted racial disparities in punishment did vex the criminal justice system. But they were not as extensive as many had thought they were in the sentencing phase, which is one act in a punishment play with many important actors taking center stage before the sentencing judge appears in the final act. Moreover, we now know that the imposition of sentencing guidelines, mandatory sentences, and determinate sentencing over the past four decades has not eliminated these unwarranted racial disparities.[47]

Racial Disparities and Public Opinion

Thanks to work on racial disparities and public opinion, we now have a better understanding of how shifts in public opinion on race manifest themselves in the criminal justice system and public policy. Public opinion survey research indicates a major shift in white attitudes toward blacks since the 1940s. Overt racial hostility appears to be less pervasive. Overwhelming majorities of whites report that they subscribe to norms of desegregation and racial equality and do not consider African Americans to be an inferior race.[48] "Still, other viewpoints about race have been remarkably resistant to change and, in some cases, moved toward greater intolerance and assent to inequalities," explains Berkeley political scientist Taeku Lee.[49]

Many Americans still appear to harbor anti-black and anti-Hispanic attitudes, and there are large and in some cases widening gaps in white, black, and Hispanic public opinion on key issues.[50] For example, nearly half of white Americans surveyed in 2008 said they believed blacks had achieved racial equality compared to only 11 percent of African Americans. Nearly three-quarters of blacks surveyed agreed that racism is still a major problem compared to more than half of Latinos surveyed and about one-third of whites.[51]

More sophisticated survey- and experiment-based research on public opinion reveals that latent and often unconscious stereotypes and prejudices persist and likely influence political and policy choices in subtle but still powerful ways. The existence of widely held conscious and unconscious stereotypes about black criminals and black criminality is now well documented, as is the impact that these stereotypes have on punishment outcomes. Defendants with darker skin are more likely to be punished more severely, as are defendants with more stereotypically African American facial features.[52] The expansive research on race, crime, and public opinion persuasively shows that people who harbor anti-black attitudes and resentments tend to support more punitive policies. Whites are more punitive than blacks and are more likely than blacks to perceive the criminal justice system as fair and legitimate.[53] Racial resentment is also a strong predictor of whites' support for capital punishment.[54] When whites are informed of racial disproportionality and bias in the imposition of the death penalty, their support does not waver much.[55]

Race and Crime Patterns

Although the persistence of racial biases and discrimination in the criminal justice system is deeply troubling, we now know that these are not the only reasons why African Americans are disproportionately incarcerated. Two other key factors are that blacks disproportionately commit the types of crimes that usually draw a long prison sentence, and that the sentences and time served for those offenses have escalated since the 1970s. Cassia Spohn concludes that the evidence is "irrefutable" that seriousness of the offense and the offender's prior record are the primary determinants of who goes to prison and for how long.[56]

In his classic 1982 study, Alfred Blumstein attributed about 80 percent of the racial disparity in imprisonment to differences in arrests and offending.[57] He suggested that the remaining 20 percent could be based on a variety of other factors that include discrimination but also "arguably legitimate" factors. These other factors were differences in prior criminal record between whites and blacks, disproportional representation of blacks "among the more serious versions *within* each of the offense types (e.g., in the *stranger-to-stranger* homicides, in the *armed* robberies, etc.)," and differences in socioeconomic status.[58] Blumstein suggested that some of these factors may be legitimate, but they "may also reflect some unknown degree of discrimination based on race."[59]

Although bias and stereotyping exist, they were not the main cause of racial disparities in imprisonment, Blumstein concluded. The most significant factor was that African Americans committed homicides, rapes, robberies, aggravated assaults, and other serious crimes at higher rates than whites did. For less serious offenses, however, variations in offending patterns were less likely to explain wide racial disparities in imprisonment, he suggested. In the case of crimes like burglary and drug abuse, police, prosecutors, and judges exercise much more discretion over whom to round up, charge, convict, and imprison. As a consequence, racial factors likely hold more sway with respect to these crimes.

Michael Tonry and Matthew Melewski replicated Blumstein's study using 2004 data and likewise concluded that "the more serious the crime, the more fully offending patterns appeared to explain racial disparities in imprisonment."[60] But they found that differential offending accounted for only about 60 percent of the racial disparities in imprisonment—not the 80 percent Blumstein originally found.[61] Tonry and Melewski attributed the lower figure to major changes in penal policy since Blumstein's pioneering work in the early 1980s. These included the fierce mobilization of the war on drugs and the imposition of tougher sentencing laws and policies, specifically three-strikes and other habitual offender laws, truth in sentencing, stiffer mandatory minimums, and the proliferation of life sentences, including life sentences without the possibility of parole (LWOP).[62]

African Americans have been disproportionately affected by the toughening of sentences for violent crimes. "Partly this is because black people more often commit violent crimes and are arrested for them, even though their relative overinvolvement in violent crime has been declining," explains Tonry.[63] For that reason, even if we could somehow end the ubiquitous and pernicious impact of implicit bias and conscious and unconscious stereotyping in punishment, Tonry argues, this would only marginally reduce the racial disparities in the prison population and "the damage American criminal justice does to its black citizens as a class."[64]

Racial Disparities and the War on Drugs

Drug cases present the most compelling evidence of the disparate treatment of blacks in the criminal justice system.[65] The evidence is overwhelming that the war on drugs has been far from color-blind. Police and prosecution tactics, including racial profiling, intense surveillance of poor inner-city neighborhoods, and the widespread use of buy-and-bust and stop-and-frisk tactics in these neighborhoods, help explain the vast racial disparities in who is arrested and who serves time for a drug offense. The social scientific evidence largely supports the *Wire*-esque world portrayed on the award-winning HBO television series in which young African American men in distressed Baltimore neighborhoods are the main targets of a war on drugs that has few heroes.

The war on drugs disproportionately targeted African Americans despite surveys showing that they are no more likely to use or sell illegal drugs than whites.[66] African Americans represented 12 percent of the total population of drug users as of 2005, but more than one-third of those arrested for drug crimes, and nearly half of those serving time in state prisons for drug offenses.[67] Drug arrests set in motion a racial chain reaction, as blacks are disproportionately arrested for drug crimes, and then disproportionately charged, convicted, and imprisoned for them.[68] A 2013 ACLU report found that a black person is about four times more likely to be arrested for marijuana possession than a white person, even though blacks and whites use marijuana at similar rates.[69]

Towering over all discussions of racial disparities and the war on drugs is the 100:1 disparity in penalties for powder cocaine and crack offenses that was a central feature of the federal Anti-Drug Abuse Act of 1986. Thirteen states also imposed sentencing distinctions for crack-powder cocaine offenses, although they were generally not as severe as the federal 100:1 disparity. Until the federal law was changed in 2010, a federal conviction for distributing five grams of crack cocaine— the equivalent of about one packet of sugar—triggered a mandatory five-year sentence, while it took 500 grams of powder cocaine to trigger the same penalty.[70]

No sophisticated statistical analyses were necessary to establish that this law, which was ostensibly color-blind, fueled troubling and unwarranted racial disparities in punishment. African Americans are more likely than whites to use crack, which pharmacologically is nearly identical to powder cocaine but much cheaper, while whites are proportionally more likely to use powder cocaine.[71] A special report to Congress by the U.S. Sentencing Commission in 1997 found that African Americans accounted for nearly 90 percent of all the people convicted of federal crack offenses, even though the majority of crack users are white.[72] From 1988 to 1995, federal prosecutors did not bring a single white person to trial under the crack provisions in seventeen states, which included major cities such as Boston, Denver, Miami, Los Angeles, Dallas, and Chicago.[73]

As Alexander shows in her masterful overview of the seminal cases regarding enforcement of the 100:1 crack-powder cocaine statute, racial profiling, the administration of the death penalty, and the rules governing jury selection, the courts also have largely shuttered the courthouse door to claims of racial discrimination or racial bias in the administration of the criminal justice system.[74] Law enforcement officials have been granted wide discretion regarding whom to stop, search, arrest, and charge with drug offenses.[75] Thanks to a series of landmark cases, the courts have essentially created a "virtual drug exception" to the Fourth Amendment's protections against illegal search and seizure.[76] In 2012, the U.S. Supreme Court went so far as to declare that police and corrections officers have the right to strip search anyone who is arrested, even for a minor offense like a traffic violation.[77]

As the war on drugs took off in the mid-1980s, the number of African Americans in prison spiked sharply. The high political profile of the war on drugs, the gross racial disparities in how drug cases were pursued, which were epitomized by the 100:1 disparity in cocaine penalties, and the courts' persistent indifference or hostility to claims of racial bias in the criminal justice system, solidified the view among many critics of U.S. penal policy that the war on drugs has been the main driver of mass incarceration. This bolstered the claim that race and racism are the defining features of the carceral state. According to Alexander, "The uncomfortable reality is that convictions for drug offenses—not violent crime—are the single most important cause of the prison boom in the United States, and people of color are convicted of drug offenses at rates out of proportion to their drug crimes."[78]

However, the impact of the war on drugs on the size of the prison population is often overstated.[79] As Franklin Zimring notes, the era of mass incarceration that began in the 1970s is not a unitary phenomenon. It is composed of at least three distinct periods driven by different engines of growth.[80] From the early 1970s to the mid-1980s, the main engine was a general rise in committing more marginal felons to prison, with few discernible patterns by type of crime or type of offender.[81] The 1985–1992 period was the heyday of the war on drugs as "the growth of drug commitments and drug sentences far outpaced the rate of growth of other offense commitments."[82] From the early 1990s onward, longer sentences and time served for a range of offenses due to a more punitive political climate that fostered penal innovations like three-strikes and truth-in-sentencing laws propelled the prison population upward. It is a sobering fact that if all drug cases were eliminated, the U.S. imprisonment rate would still have quadrupled over the past thirty-five years.[83]

Since the mid-1990s, we have seen important shifts in drug enforcement policy as enthusiasm for the war on drugs has waned, and the push to provide alternatives to incarceration for drug offenders has gained momentum. In 1996 and 2004 respectively, voters in Arizona and California endorsed important ballot initiatives to divert some substance abusers from prison. In 2009, Minneapolis became the first major U.S. city without a narcotics squad when it disbanded its special drug unit to save money. The following year, President Barack Obama signed the Fair Sentencing Act, which reduces the penalty disparity between crack and powder cocaine from 100:1 to 18:1. This was the first rollback in federal mandatory minimums in thirty-five years.[84] A growing number of jurisdictions have designated enforcement of marijuana laws a low priority. In 2012, voters in Colorado and Washington State approved ballot initiatives to legalize personal possession of marijuana. As of early 2014, more than half of the states were considering decriminalizing marijuana or legalizing it for medical or recreational use.[85]

These policy shifts have coincided with some important demographic shifts in the carceral state and drug offenses. The war on drugs is no longer a primary driver of new prison admissions. From 2000 to 2008, violent offenders accounted for 60 percent of the growth in the size of the state prison population. During this period, the number of sentenced drug offenders in state prisons actually declined by 8 percent.[86]

African Americans continue to be much more likely than whites (relative to their proportion of the population) to be arrested, charged, convicted, and imprisoned for drug crimes. But the racial gap in the war on drugs is narrowing.[87] The percentage of blacks among all drug arrests rose from 27 percent in 1980 to a peak of 42 percent in 1993 and then declined fairly steadily to the current 35 percent.[88] The disparities in drug arrests between whites and blacks has been shrinking and is now only slightly higher than it was in 1980, just as the war on drugs was taking off.[89] After peaking in 2000, the number of black drug offenders in state prisons fell steadily and was about 20 percent lower by 2008. The number of Hispanic drug offenders fell by approximately 5 percent during this period. Meanwhile, the number of white drug offenders in state prisons rose substantially—by about 35 percent.[90] Moreover, drug offenders—including black drug offenders—constitute a relatively small and shrinking proportion of the total state prison population. Drug offenders composed about 18 percent of all inmates in state prisons in 2008—or about 118,000 people. Non-Hispanic blacks imprisoned for drug offenses made up just 8 percent of the total state prison population; non-Hispanic white drug offenders constituted about 5 percent, as did Hispanic drug offenders.[91]

Although the war on drugs began slowing in many states in the 1990s, it continued to barrel along at the federal level. As the total number of drug offenders in state prisons fell at the dawn of the twenty-first century, it continued to grow at the federal level by an average of 3 percent annually from 2000 to 2008 before stabilizing somewhat.[92] Federal prisons are the only penal facilities in which people convicted of drug offenses constitute a near-majority of the inmate population. In 2011, drug charges were the primary offense of nearly half of all federal inmates.[93] Furthermore, the racial and ethnic patterns of drug offenses at the federal level are starkly different from those at the state level. Since the late 1990s at least, the ethnic and racial mix of drug offenders in federal prisons has remained remarkably stable (leaving aside gender). The total number of drug offenders in federal penitentiaries grew by about 33 percent between 1999 and 2005, and this growth was equally distributed among whites, blacks, and Hispanics. As of 2005, the proportion of drug offenders serving time in federal penitentiaries who were white, black, or Hispanic was nearly identical to what it had been in the late 1990s—or about 23 percent for whites, 43 percent for blacks, and 32 percent for Hispanics.[94]

National figures obscure great variations in how the war on drugs has been fought in states and cities around the country. Black-white disparities in drug arrests range from a low of 2:1 in Hawaii to a high of 11:1 in Minnesota and Iowa.[95] The rate at which individual states arrest whites for drug offenses also appears to vary greatly.[96] Figures on the black-white racial disparities in drug arrests likely underestimate the extent of such disparities because official national arrest data do not identify Latinos as a distinct racial group, thus conflating white and Latino arrests. This may explain why many of the states with the lowest disparities in black-white marijuana arrests are among the states with the highest Latino populations. It may also explain California's seemingly high drug arrest rate for whites.[97]

The argument that racial animus is the primary engine of the war on drugs and thus of the carceral state is further complicated by the fact that some overwhelmingly white states have been some of the most enthusiastic recruits in the war on drugs.[98] A decade ago, the Drug Enforcement Administration (DEA) and public officials began warning that "crystal meth could become the new crack." This has fostered a white drug scare in rural areas, even though the limited data available do not appear to support claims that meth use is dramatically on the rise.[99] The war against meth has been racialized but in different ways than the earlier war on drugs. Meth has been cast as a "drug of White status decay: poor White users are 'White trash,' middle-class White users are falling from privilege, and rotten teeth become the physical marker of decline," explains Naomi Murakawa.[100] States with apparently higher rates of meth use—notably Iowa and Minnesota—have experienced considerable increases in the number of incarcerated meth offenders.[101] Relatively few states have sizable numbers of meth users, so additional factors likely explain the shifting racial and ethnic complexion of the war on drugs. These include the substantial decline in crack use among blacks and changes in law enforcement and prosecution, to be discussed in greater detail in later chapters.[102]

Enthusiasm for waging the war on drugs varies enormously not only between the states but between cities. The number of drug arrests increased in forty of the forty-three largest cities between 1980 and 2003, but the differences in the growth rates of drug arrests were vast. The average rate of increase in drug arrests for the top ten cities was nearly 600 percent, or almost twice the average growth rate for the ten cities at the bottom of the list. Patterns of drug arrests can vary greatly even between nearby cities in the same state. The most striking example is Tucson, Arizona, where drug arrests soared nearly 900 percent during this period compared to an increase of 52 percent in Phoenix, Arizona.[103]

In short, the war on drugs is no longer a primary driver of new prison admissions, and the ratio of black to white drug arrests has been falling since it peaked in the early 1990s.[104] Nonetheless, the political and public policy reverberations of the war on drugs continue to be seismic. The war on drugs has bequeathed a starkly racialized framework through which to view the carceral state. It has helped obscure the more complex ways that race and other factors shape penal policy and the politics of penal reform, as elaborated in later chapters. As shown in this chapter, it has obscured important demographic shifts in the development of the carceral state over the past fifteen years or so.

Methodological Rabbit Hole

In 2010, shortly before his death, David Baldus summed up the findings of decades of research on racial disparities and punishment. He affirmed that Gary Kleck's earlier conclusions on racial bias in criminal sentencing and in imposition of the death penalty by race from the 1930s to the 1970s still largely held up for the post-1980 period as well. Quoting Kleck, Baldus concluded that, leaving aside the early capital rape cases in the South, there was no convincing evidence of "general or widespread overt discrimination against black defendants, although there is evidence of [such] discrimination for a minority of specific jurisdictions, judges, crime types, etc."[105] Baldus then posed an often overlooked puzzle: why, despite substantial evidence of persistent anti-black prejudice in the white population generally and among those involved in the criminal justice system, is there little evidence of statewide sentencing disparities for black defendants?

Baldus suggested that statewide studies of racial disparities in sentencing can be misleading if they fail to account for differences in the policies and practices of local jurisdictions, most notably at the county level. "[A]nti-black discrimination or other race effects in some counties may be neutralized by pro-black or no discrimination in other counties," thus cancelling out the statewide effects, according to Baldus.[106] This likely explains, for example, why statewide studies find no race of defendant effects in capital punishment cases in Texas and Pennsylvania, but closely controlled studies of Harris County, Texas, and Philadelphia, Pennsylvania—ground zero for the death penalty in these two states—find substantial black defendant disparities.[107] Similarly, in their analysis of state-level racial disparities in offending, Robert Crutchfield, George Bridges, and Susan Pitchford found support for Blumstein's finding that 80 percent of racial differences in U.S. prisons could be accounted for by higher rates of black offending, but that this finding masked large differences in the individual states.[108]

Findings like these should spur greater interest in examining the specific institutional, political, social, and economic factors at the local, state, and national levels—of which racial bias is but one—to better understand what fuels variations in punitiveness. Doing so would help identify which key political and public policy pressure points to push in the quest to dismantle the carceral state. But much of the research on racial disparities has gone in a different direction, down a methodological rabbit hole. The focus remains on devising ever more complex models to capture the omitted and confounding variables so as to measure ever more precisely what accounts for racial disparities in punishment.[109] This parallels the seemingly unending search for ever more sophisticated statistical models to quantitatively identify and measure what caused the exponential growth in the U.S. incarceration rate.[110] As a consequence, "the emphasis on disparity has taken away from direct research on the policies themselves" and from how to reverse the prison boom.[111] This "excessive focus" in detecting unwarranted disparities has come at the cost of examining fundamental questions about how and why certain laws, policies, and sentencing regimes brought about harsher penalties across the board—regardless of race or ethnicity.[112]

For example, analyzing racial disparities has become something of a cottage industry for the U.S. Sentencing Commission. This is not so surprising, since allegations of widespread racial discrimination in punishment helped bring the commission into being, as discussed earlier. In the 2005 *Booker* decision, the U.S. Supreme Court declared that the federal sentencing guidelines are "effectively advisory," not mandatory, thus granting federal judges more leeway to depart from the guidelines in sentencing.[113] Subsequently, the commission produced a couple of technically sophisticated reports showing that racial disparities in federal sentencing have increased in the wake of *Booker*.[114] The commission's 2010 report on *Booker* and racial disparities concluded that sentencing disparities for black males increased by 10 or 23 percent (depending on what methodology is used) in the post-*Booker* era compared to similarly situated white males.[115] With its extensive discussion of what multivariate regression analysis is and of its utility in measuring racial disparities, much of the report reads like a college-level textbook on statistics.

The main body of the commission's 2010 report does not provide a systematic accounting or discussion of what have been the actual changes in average sentence lengths for blacks and whites in the pre- and post-*Booker* eras. In other words, did average sentence lengths grow or shrink, regardless of race? The commission's report kept the focus on the narrower question of whether the guidelines in the pre-*Booker* era reduced racial disparities in sentencing and, if so, by what proportion. The fact that the average federal sentence actually *increased* in the immediate aftermath of *Booker* was not a central issue for discussion and analysis.[116]

Lacking the expertise and legitimacy to develop an alternative sentencing framework, the commission has functioned until recently as little more than the sentencing police to monitor judicial compliance with the guidelines.[117] "The Commission elevated two sentencing goals—retribution and the minimization of disparity—above all other goals, such as deterrence or rehabilitation," explains former federal judge Nancy Gertner.[118] Its fealty to eliminating disparities, especially racial disparities in punishment, deflected attention away from the fact that until recently the commission has "rarely passed up an opportunity to increase the severity of punishments."[119] The most rigorous studies of the guidelines suggest that they have not had much success in reducing sentencing disparities between judges, but they have been wildly successful in raising the severity of sentences in most crime categories.[120] "The cruelest irony of the modern American sentencing reform movement is that the diminution of racial discrimination in sentencing was a primary aim and exacerbation of racial disparities is a major result," laments Tonry.[121]

The past few years, the commission has demonstrated greater interest in tackling the larger question of the overall punitiveness of the U.S. penal system. In a massive report issued in October 2011, the commission concluded that federal mandatory minimum sentences are often "excessively severe" and not "applied consistently."[122] In April 2014, the commission voted unanimously to lower the guideline ranges for some drug trafficking sentences. In a major shift, the commission agreed in July 2014 to make recent changes in the guidelines for drug offenses retroactive. Nearly 50,000 federal drug offenders now serving time will be eligible for reduced sentences thanks to this change (as long as Congress does not void the commission's decision, which is not expected).[123]

The Complexities of Racial Disparities

Michelle Alexander and other penal reformers have identified ending or greatly reducing racial disparities in punishment as a top priority. The Annie E. Casey Foundation requires that jurisdictions participating in its Juvenile Detention and Alternatives Initiative "strive to not only reduce their detained population but to do it in a way that reduces racial disparity as well."[124] Support is growing for requiring racial impact statements for any proposed changes in criminal law or penal policy. Connecticut, Iowa, and Oregon are pioneers in enacting such legislation, which is modeled after the mandated fiscal and environmental impact statements that have become commonplace in many states. These racial impact statements are intended to prod policy makers to consider alternatives that would meet their public safety goals "without exacerbating racial disparities in imprisonment."[125]

Tethering a penal reform agenda too tightly to the goal of reducing racial disparities in incarceration could have a perverse result—smaller disparities but not necessarily more racial or social justice. Many of the most commonly talked about measures to reduce the detained population—such as diverting more low-level offenders from prison, ending the war on drugs, and reserving prison sentences for the most serious crimes—might actually result in greater, not smaller, racial disparities in imprisonment.

The black-white disparity in imprisonment is a complicated and potentially misleading yardstick by which to gauge how fairly a state's criminal justice system treats African Americans. States that have some of the largest racial disparities in their prison populations may nonetheless have—comparatively speaking—some of the nation's more progressive criminal justice systems. Minnesota is a good example. In the 1980s and early 1990s, Minnesota's black-white imprisonment ratio was about 20:1, the highest in the nation. Since then, it has fallen to about 11:1, which is still well above the national average. But Minnesota's overall imprisonment rate is still far below the national average (see figure 1.2, p. 12).[126] "This reflects Minnesota sentencing policies that discourage incarceration and benefit offenders of all races," explains Richard S. Frase.[127] "Minnesota blacks benefit from those policies when compared to blacks in other states, but they do not benefit nearly as much as Minnesota whites do."[128]

More lenient sentencing policies tell only part of the story for Minnesota. By other measures, Minnesota is comparatively less progressive compared to other states, which also helps explain its gaping black-white disparities in imprisonment. Here race matters, but it is not a simple case of persistent racial bias on the part of police, prosecutors, judges, and the public driving law enforcement and penal policy. Minnesota's whites tend to be better off economically than the national average for whites, while blacks in Minnesota are substantially more likely to be living in poverty.[129] Minnesota's blacks are much less likely to reside in low-crime rural areas not only when compared to whites in Minnesota but also when compared to blacks in other states.[130] Socioeconomic and residential variations like these probably account for some of the variations in black-white imprisonment ratios in Minnesota and elsewhere.[131] "With high degrees of black poverty and inner-city residential concentration and a small, politically weak black population, the risks are much greater that blacks will be drawn into crime and apprehended by highly targeted law enforcement measures," explains Frase.[132]

The uncomfortable fact is that states that reserve their prisons primarily for people who have committed the most serious crimes are more likely to have greater racial disparities in their inmate populations. Other states that take a more equal opportunity approach and throw the book at both serious and relatively minor offenders will likely have lower racial disparities in imprisonment.[133] The states with the highest rates of racial disproportionality in incarceration "tend to be the politically liberal states of the Northeast and upper Midwest, whereas most of the states with the lowest ratios are in the South."[134]

Since the 1990s, the black-white imprisonment gap in Minnesota has been narrowing. But the reasons for this development complicate any claim that associates the rise and fall of racial disparities in imprisonment with the rise and fall of racial bias (implicit or explicit) in law enforcement or the wider society. The narrowing of the gap is partly due to an increase in the number of whites sentenced for drunk driving and methamphetamine and other drug offenses, according to Frase. He also attributes it to important demographic shifts, notably substantial growth in the state's black population due to the large influx of recent immigrants from Africa that was not matched by a corresponding rise in the number of black criminal defendants and inmates.[135]

The states with the lowest black-white ratios in incarceration tend to be concentrated in the South and generally have lower-than-average socioeconomic disparities. This is partly because whites in these states are "more disadvantaged than U.S. whites generally," and because "blacks in these states have a disadvantage equal to or less than that of U.S. blacks generally."[136] The thirteen states that have the country's lowest black-white ratios in incarceration, most of which are in the South, "had higher than average white incarceration rates in 2005, and eight had lower than average black rates."[137] In short, having a white population that is comparatively poorer than the national average tends to be associated with lower black-white disparities in imprisonment but above-average imprisonment rates for whites.

Leveling Down

Political strategies to unhinge the carceral state by calling for an end to the stark racial and ethnic disparities that permeate U.S. prisons, jails, and death row are problematic in other respects. If not skillfully anchored in a larger penal and political reform agenda, they could perversely result in more punishment, not less. There is a risk that penal conservatives, confronted with evidence of the growing racial and ethnic disparities of the U.S. carceral state, will respond with another wave of "leveling down" in penal policy.[138] Instead of lessening the punishments for blacks and other minorities, they may attempt to raise the ante for whites by subjecting them to tougher prison sentences and invoking the death penalty more often for them in another expression of brute liberal egalitarianism.

In the United States, such "leveling down" remains a real risk. For example, confronted with substantial evidence of race-of-victim discrimination in capital punishment cases, some supporters of capital punishment argued for seeking the death penalty in more cases in which blacks were convicted of murdering blacks.[139] After Minnesota's Supreme Court invalidated the state's crack-powder cocaine penalty distinction, state legislators responded by raising the penalty for powder cocaine rather than reducing the penalty for crack. President Bill Clinton and members of Congress suggested a similar solution when confronted with evidence of stark racial disparities in federal sentencing for crack and powder cocaine offenses in the mid-1990s.[140] Over the strenuous objections of black legislators, Florida enacted the 10–20–LIFE bill in 1998, which mandates one of the country's toughest sentencing enhancements for the use of a gun in the commission of a crime. The state's black caucus did succeed in amending the bill to require prosecutors to report 10–20–LIFE cases by age, gender, and race. But this may have been a mixed victory. The reporting requirement likely helped to decrease racial disparities in the enforcement of 10–20–LIFE but at the cost of encouraging prosecutors to seek the same harsh sentences for both blacks and whites.[141]

The reinstitution of chain gangs in the South in the mid-1990s provides the most striking example of how an emphasis on racial egalitarianism in penal policy does not necessarily result in a fairer, less punitive carceral state. When Alabama lawmakers reinstituted chain gangs in the 1990s, they did so on the condition that they reflect the racial composition of the state's prison population. Florida considered a similar provision. But Charlie Crist, who embraced the nickname "Chain Gang Charlie" as he led the charge to reinstate chain gangs in the Sunshine State, ultimately rejected it.[142]

Color-blind Degrading and Abusive Conditions

Leveling down is consequential in other respects. African Americans and Latinos may be disproportionately subjected to certain abusive and degrading conditions, like solitary confinement. But skin color is scant protection from the brutal and dehumanizing conditions that are endemic to many penal facilities in the United States.[143] In 2004, the public and the media expressed shock and outrage upon discovering that guards imported from U.S. prisons were abusing inmates at Iraq's Abu Ghraib prison.[144] For many prisoners, human rights advocates, and some corrections officials, the shock was that the public and the media were so shocked. Back at home, "in hundreds of state and federal prisons, widespread rape and assault, prolonged sensory deprivation, and other abuses approach and even surpass the scale of violence and degradation meted out to suspected enemy combatants elsewhere."[145] Such abuses rarely make the news and rarely are identified as human rights abuses.

U.S. prisons and jails are exceptional for the extensive use of demeaning and degrading practices that would be considered flagrant human rights violations in most other industrialized countries. The Abu Ghraib scandal provided a brief moment to turn the spotlight on such practices. These include brutal cell extractions carried out with the help of trained attack dogs, routine and often unnecessary strip searches and body cavity searches, and everyday humiliations like forcing male inmates to wear women's pink underwear.[146] They also include double and triple celling inmates, confining suicidal prisoners to 3' by 3' "squirrel cages," and feeding inmates inedible "food bricks" (a mash-up of all of that day's food).[147] Female prisoners are routinely shackled during labor and childbirth. Dozens of states have no law banning this unsafe medical practice and assault on human dignity.[148] Since 2007, at least fourteen inmates have died of heat-related causes in Texas prisons.[149] With less than one-fifth of the state's prisons fully air-conditioned, "there is literally no escape from triple-digit temperatures" for many Texas inmates.[150] In 2013, the state's leading prison guards' union announced it would support an inmate lawsuit about the excessive heat in Texas prisons. The union acted after learning that the Texas Department of Criminal Justice (TDCJ) was constructing climate-controlled barns to cool pigs raised for inmate consumption.[151] Asked about whether Texas inmates should be allowed to reside in air-conditioned facilities, Democratic state senator John Whitmire, the long-term chairman of the Senate Criminal Justice Committee and a national leader in the Right on Crime coalition, remarked, "[T]he people of Texas don't want air-conditioned prisons, and there's a lot of other things on my list above the heat."[152]

On any given day, at least 80,000 U.S. inmates, including 25,000 housed in supermax prisons, are confined nearly round the clock to sparse cells where they are denied meaningful human contact for days, weeks, months, years, or even decades.[153] Most prisoners on death row serve out their years in solitary confinement, where they are denied not only access to employment, educational, and vocational programs, but also the companionship of fellow prisoners and even the touch of family members and loved ones during rare visits.[154] The total number of people held in administrative segregation in the United States has been extremely difficult to determine because most states do not release the relevant data or in many cases do not even collect it.[155] Human Rights Watch calls the proliferation of solitary confinement "the most troubling development in US corrections in recent decades."[156] Other industrialized countries do not routinely rely on such extreme isolation to control and punish prisoners. In 2011, the U.N. Special Rapporteur on Torture proposed an international standard of a fifteen-day limit on use of solitary confinement for prisoners.[157]

U.S. corrections officials claim that administrative segregation is reserved for the "worst of the worst." But minor infractions, such as tattooing, possessing too many postage stamps, or exiting the shower too slowly, can be cause enough to land someone in solitary confinement.[158] So can mere allegations of gang membership. Many prisons and jails in the United States use solitary confinement to punish, protect, house or treat children under the age of 18.[159] The mentally ill are more likely to end up in solitary confinement units, which are "virtual incubators of psychoses—seeding illness in otherwise healthy inmates and exacerbating illness in those suffering from mental infirmities," according to the findings of one district court.[160] A 2014 DOJ report concluded that Pennsylvania uses solitary confinement in ways that violated the constitutional rights of mentally ill prisoners and with "devastating consequences."[161]

Political and religious beliefs deemed to be out of the mainstream or dangerous—like Rastafarianism and what Burl Cain, warden of Louisiana's infamous Angola prison, dismissively calls "Black Pantherism"—also are cause to be banished to administrative segregation.[162] In the wake of 9/11, the Bureau of Prisons established Communications Management Units in a couple of federal penitentiaries. In these special units, inmates—predominantly Muslim prisoners—are subjected to extreme isolation "for their constitutionally protected religious beliefs, unpopular political views, or in retaliation for challenging poor treatment or other rights violations in the federal prison system," according to a lawsuit filed in 2010.[163]

In the United States there is a general acceptance of "violence—and particularly brutal sexual violence—as an inevitable consequence of incarcerating criminals," according to two leading experts on prison conditions.[164] The public, state officials, and the judicial system have readily "come to accept the brutality of our prisons and absorbed it into mainstream culture"—so much so that jokes about prison rape are standard fodder for comedy shows, television commercials, and even some public officials.[165]

Sexual assault is endemic to many prisons and jails in the United States. A 2012 study by the Bureau of Justice Statistics found that about one in ten former state prisoners were sexually abused while serving their most recent sentences and that about half of this abuse was committed by staff members, not fellow inmates.[166] The Justice Department reported that an estimated 209,000 out of the 2.2 million inmates in U.S. jails and prisons were victims of rape or sexual abuse in 2008.[167] To put that number in some perspective, the DOJ's National Crime Victimization Survey estimated that 164,000 females age twelve and older (excluding prisoners) were victims of rape or sexual assault in the *entire* United States in 2008.[168] Although sexual violence is part of the prison experience for many people, LGBT people are disproportionately targeted by staff and inmates.[169]

The general public and government officials often treat prisoner rape as a rite of passage, even though it is an "eminently preventable problem" and not an inevitable consequence of incarceration.[170] Enactment of the Prison Rape Elimination Act (PREA) in 2003 was supposed to change that. But, faced with intense opposition from the corrections sector, it took nearly a decade for the DOJ to promulgate the standards and regulations for PREA.[171] PREA's standards are legally binding for federal facilities operated by the Bureau of Prisons, but not for state prisons and local jails, which run the risk of a moderate cut in federal funding if they do not comply. While some experts on sexual abuse in prison have characterized the PREA standards as "conscientious and enlightened," others lament that they are "a hollow shell of what was originally envisioned by prisoners' rights advocates."[172] Many agree that the enforcement mechanisms are extremely weak, as are the provisions for independent monitoring of sexual abuse in penal facilities.[173] In March 2014, Governor Rick Perry (R-TX) sent a defiant letter to Attorney General Eric Holder declaring that his state would not be complying with PREA.[174]

Conclusion

Michelle Alexander notes that mass incarceration "directly harms far more whites than Jim Crow ever did." Nonetheless, she characterizes the harm done to whites as largely "collateral damage" in her portrayal of mass incarceration as primarily a racial caste system.[175] Her analysis in *The New Jim Crow* suggests that the carceral state can only be undone by forging a social movement in which the country's color-blind racist ideologies and entrenched racial hierarchies are the central targets. The foregoing analysis in this chapter, however, raises thorny political and public policy questions about how to forge such a movement. For example, should it concentrate its energies on closing the racial disparities gap and ending the war on drugs? Or should it aim to devise strategies to roll back excessive sentences and other highly punitive policies across the board?

In light of the persistent and deeply troubling racial and ethnic disparities of the U.S. criminal justice system, identifying and addressing the sources of these disparities in punishment should continue to be a high priority. In particular, we need greater attention to how "indirect race effects may be embedded" in "seemingly legitimate race-neutral" factors in processing (such as pretrial detention and the quality of defense counsel) and sentencing (such as a defendant's prior criminal record and employment status).[176] We also need a better understanding of how race interacts with other factors like geography (especially rural versus urban) and socioeconomic status in determining who receives what punishments. But too much of the research attention and resources has been shoehorned for too long into a relatively narrow set of questions, many of them premised on some aspect of more precisely measuring racial disparities in punishment.

The focus on developing ever more sophisticated models and experiments to measure racial disparities and racial bias and discrimination in the operation of the criminal justice system diverts intellectual energy and resources from critical issues that need to be addressed if we are to dismantle the carceral state. As a consequence, many key questions and issues remain largely off the table for research and wider public discussion. This has helped perpetuate the mistaken view that the problem of the carceral state is a problem confined primarily to African Americans and members of other minority groups, and that the emergence of color-blind racism is the main source of the problem. According to this view, the carceral state is only a problem for whites and the larger society to the extent that they must bear the heavy economic burden of sustaining such an expansive and expensive penal system without getting their money's worth in terms of enhancing public safety. Furthermore, an excessive focus on the extent of racial disparities slights an important and troubling qualitative dimension of the carceral state—the degrading and abusive conditions that many inmates, regardless of race or ethnicity, are subjected to.

In addressing the problem of the carceral state, the persistence of deep racial disparities in punishment cannot be ignored. We also cannot ignore the persistence of hostile white attitudes around questions of race and punishment. But, as shown in the previous and coming chapters, the specific actions and calculations of politicians, government officials, policy makers, interest groups, political movements, and leaders of historically disadvantaged groups need to be more central to the discussion. So do the changing political, social, and economic conditions in which they operate, to which we now turn.

CHAPTER SEVEN

What's Race Got to Do with It?

Bolstering and Challenging the Carceral State

There is also the danger in our culture that, because a person is called upon to give public statements and is acclaimed by the establishment, such a person gets to the point of believing he *is* the movement.

—ELLA BAKER

Punitive sentiments and punitive policies emerge from many sources, including but certainly not limited to racial factors. Race becomes more politically salient in penal policy under certain conditions, especially when public figures give their permission "to dislike 'others.' "[1] But this "permission to dislike" takes many forms, as politicians and other public figures recalibrate their strategies and rhetoric in light of changing political, economic, social, and demographic circumstances.

Broad explanations like the new Jim Crow, color-blind racism, and racial animus can obscure the varied, shifting, and subtle forms that this "permission to dislike" has taken in the development of the carceral state. Racial explanations that are too narrowly constructed tend to keep the focus on the role of whites—especially elite politicians and other public figures—in the construction and defense of the carceral state. This has come at the cost of slighting the varied roles that African Americans and members of other racial and ethnic groups have played in challenging and bolstering the carceral state. It also gives short shrift to other important political, economic, and institutional factors that built the carceral state and now stand in the way of devising successful political strategies to dismantle it. These other factors help explain substantial differences among the fifty states in the mechanisms, political actors, and timing of the prison boom.

There is a grand narrative of neoliberalism and race that helps explain the resiliency of the carceral state, but the specific chapters and main actors have shifted considerably depending on place, time, and context. Analytical attention to the role of political elites in mass incarceration has generally centered on how leading white politicians from Barry Goldwater to Bill Clinton sought to refashion their political bases in the wake of the seismic political shifts set in motion by the civil rights movement. According to this account, politicians began invoking the law-and-order card, which was really a thinly veiled race card, to woo disaffected white voters. This explanation largely omits the role of African Americans in bolstering and challenging the carceral state.

As Michelle Alexander pointedly notes, until recently, leading black politicians, public figures, and advocacy groups have been largely unwilling to address the issue of mass incarceration. She attributes their silence to the challenges of shoehorning the problem of mass incarceration into the traditional civil rights framework, especially in this era of color-blind racism.[2] But deeper historical and institutional factors also are critical in explaining why they have not been more strident critics of the carceral state.

The full story of black politics and the rise of the carceral state has yet to be written. What follows in this chapter is a suggestive rather than a comprehensive analysis that seeks to identify some of the deeper historical and institutional factors that have stood in the way of forging a broad penal reform movement with the wherewithal to mount a serious challenge to the carceral state. This chapter begins by examining the varied ways black elites have responded to the growing public and political association between blackness and criminality since the late nineteenth century. It then traces the strange career of the term "law and order" from the 1940s to the 1960s and major shifts within leading identity-based civil rights organizations with the demise of more radical civil rights groups and the Black Power movement. Next it examines the political impact of widening political and economic inequalities among African Americans that coincide with escalating rates of violence and substance abuse in poor urban communities. It identifies key electoral and party developments at the local and state levels that were influenced by the Republican Party's Southern strategy but not wholly determined by it. Taken together, these factors help explain why identity-based civil rights organizations have been slow to challenge the growing tentacles of the carceral state. They also explain why some leading African American politicians and public figures have supported the punitive turn rhetorically and substantively at key moments in the debate over U.S. penal policies.

Race and the Deeper Historical Origins of the Carceral State

Politicians so readily identified today as penal hard-liners, such as Richard Nixon, Ronald Reagan, and even segregationist Lester Maddox of Georgia, did not immediately march in lockstep toward the prison and the execution chamber after Goldwater denounced the "growing menace" to personal safety in his electrifying speech before the Republican convention in 1964.[3] Nor did these public officials single-handedly impose the carceral state. It is now clear that the construction of the carceral state was deeply bipartisan from early on and not merely a case of "New Democrats" like Bill Clinton belatedly following in the punitive footsteps firmly taken years earlier by Goldwater, Nixon, George H. W. Bush, and other leading Republicans.

Furthermore, political developments that pre-date the 1960s are critical to understanding two important issues: how and why the carceral state became so entrenched after incarceration rates began their decades-long ascent in 1973; and why the carceral state has not faced more organized political opposition, especially from the groups that have been most directly harmed by its growth. A new wave of historians and historically oriented political scientists and sociologists has identified key developments from earlier periods that are cause to rethink the 1960s as the founding moment of the carceral state and to reconsider the precise role of race in building the carceral state.

In his magisterial study of what he calls the "biography of the idea of black criminality in the making of modern urban America," Khalil Gibran Muhammad excavates the varied and changing set of claims about black criminality that were constructed from the late nineteenth century to the World War II era. In doing so, he shows how even during the heyday of Jim Crow, justifications for the "permission to dislike" were not embalmed in a primordial time capsule of racial animus.

Muhammad identifies how the Progressive era was a formative one for the carceral state.[4] He challenges the conventional wisdom that the racist Jim Crow South was the primary cauldron of racial criminalization that laid the foundations for the punitive turn that gave birth to the carceral state. Muhammad artfully shows how Progressive-era academics, journalists, politicians, and public figures located primarily in the North refashioned blackness through crime statistics. "[W]hite criminality gradually lost its fearsomeness," as Irish, Italian, Polish, and other white immigrant groups were "able to shed their criminal identities" but African Americans were not. A key and enduring legacy of Progressive-era social reformers, he argues, was to sever any sense that the fate of black people was linked to the fate of poor whites and urban immigrants.[5]

An optimistic vision of white criminality took root, according to Muhammad. It was premised on the view that white criminality in urban areas with high concentrations of immigrants was largely a symptom of industrial capitalism and urban life and thus could be ameliorated though greater public and private investments in education, social services, social programs, and public infrastructure. By contrast, the release of the 1890 census riveted public attention for the first time on the disproportionate number of blacks in U.S. prisons (especially Northern prisons). The absolute and relative growth of the black prison population was "interpreted as definitive proof of blacks' true criminal nature."[6] The 1890 census findings were used to justify many discriminatory laws that targeted blacks and treated them more harshly than whites. Blacks were portrayed as heralding from an inferior culture, one so scarred by centuries of slavery that government intervention would be of little help until blacks uplifted their own race on their own. In short, white criminality was considered society's problem, but black criminality was considered blacks' problem.

Some social scientists, journalists, social reformers, and anti-racist activists hotly contested these claims. But their activities had relatively little impact on the wider public understanding of the relationship between race, culture, and crime until about 1928, when Thorsten Sellin called into question the dominant thrust of nearly four decades of research on black criminality. Sellin argued that African Americans were being unfairly stigmatized by misinterpretations of the prison census data, as well as by the glaring limitations of existing research on crime, punishment, and law enforcement.

Sellin's claims fell on more receptive ears, according to Muhammad, because he was one of the nation's most respected white sociologists. Moreover, the widespread racial violence that erupted in the North in the 1920s in the wake of the first phase of the Great Migration had focused public attention on white police officers' complicity in that violence and on police corruption and brutality more generally. Furthermore, a second generation of black scholars and social workers was documenting how police, prosecutors, the courts, and prison officials treated blacks disparately in the criminal justice system, which helped to explain why blacks were disproportionately arrested and imprisoned.

Muhammad pointedly focuses on the critical role of black elites in the racialization of crime in the late nineteenth and early twentieth centuries. Many black elites, including W.E.B. DuBois, often embraced Victorian ideals of morality and respectability. They sought to distinguish themselves from the "uncouth" and "criminally inclined" poor blacks, especially recent migrants from the South, and emphasized the need for self-improvement.[7] But many black reformers also simultaneously or alternately singled out structural factors, including but not limited to white racism, to explain black criminality. Furthermore, they challenged claims that disproportionate arrest and imprisonment rates for blacks accurately reflected the degree of differential offending between blacks and whites. Then, as now, this was treacherous political ground. "By debating the meaning of high versus low criminality or increasing versus decreasing crime rates," explains Muhammad, "black writers unwittingly reinforced the importance of crime in defining black life."[8]

Muhammad's detailed and nuanced analysis of shifts in the racialization of crime over the course of the first half of the twentieth century illustrates how broad claims about racism or racial animus driving penal policy do not tell us much on their own. Such claims do not illuminate how and why specific penal policies, law enforcement tactics, and conceptions of criminality prevail at a given moment and who or what brought about their demise. Furthermore, such broad claims tend to direct much of the analytical attention to the role of whites in the construction of penal policy and away from that of blacks and other racial and ethnic groups.

Muhammad elucidates the difficult and often impossible terrain that black public figures have had to navigate on the issue of race and criminality. At times, they have been self-serving and moralizing as they have sought to preserve their privileged status as gatekeepers of the race by castigating poor blacks for their alleged cultural pathologies. When they have raised specific structural issues to explain differential criminality, it has not been an easy hill to climb. Any call to address the structural roots of differential offending between blacks and whites draws attention to those very differences, thus giving ammunition to conservative whites and others who blame blacks for the pathologies of black criminality.

The Strange Career of Law and Order

Naomi Murakawa picks up the story where Muhammad leaves off—the 1940s and 1950s, which she identifies as a key moment in the development of the carceral state.[9] In tracing the strange career of the term "law and order," she challenges the conventional wisdom about how, when, and why law and order became such a defining feature of U.S. politics. Law and order first took center stage in national politics as early as the 1940s, not the mid-1960s, as is commonly understood, according to Murakawa. Moreover, it was race liberals associated with Harry Truman in the 1940s and 1950s—not race conservatives associated with Goldwater, Wallace, and Nixon in the 1960s—who first made it a national issue.

Furthermore, the meaning of the phrase "law and order" was for a time politically indeterminate and thus hotly contested. In the 1940s, race liberals invoked law and order as a rallying point to push for measures to protect African Americans from interpersonal and state violence directed at them by white citizens and law enforcement officials. By the late 1960s, law and order had come to mean something very different. By then, calls for more law and order were widely understood to be calls for tougher laws, tougher sanctions, and tougher police and prosecutors to protect whites from street crime and from disorderly protests by blacks and their allies.

Long before the national crime rate began its sharp decade-long climb upward in the mid-1960s, law and order had already catapulted to the forefront of national politics. The dramatic, often violent, confrontations of the 1940s, including the lynchings of black veterans returning home to the South after World War II and the hundreds of urban disturbances (most notably the 1942 Zoot Suit riots in Los Angeles and the 1943 race riot in Detroit) sparked a national debate over race and law and order even as national crime rates were relatively low and stable. The varied political responses from white liberals, leading African Americans, identity-based civil rights organizations, and opponents of desegregation and civil rights set an important context for the subsequent construction of the carceral state and help explain its tenacity.

The numerous disputes and protests over instances of police brutality and police inaction in the face of organized and widespread white violence in the 1940s directed at blacks, Mexican Americans, and other people of color forced white liberals to take action. In signing the executive order creating the Presidential Committee on Civil Rights (PCCR) in December 1946, Truman pointedly referred to the many lynchings and other violent attacks on blacks that were being carried out with the tacit or explicit support of local authorities. He lamented how in some places "the local enforcement of law and order has broken down, and individuals—sometimes ex-servicemen, even women—have been killed, maimed, or intimidated."[10]

For a fleeting moment, Truman and other race liberals embraced an encompassing vision of the law-and-order problem, according to Murakawa. As articulated by the PCCR, defending law and order meant defending the "first civil right," which it defined as freedom from violence in all its manifestations. Foremost among them was violence perpetrated by the state and organized groups of whites against blacks and others who were challenging the country's entrenched color line. But Truman and other race liberals also adopted an individualized, psychological framework for understanding both white prejudice and black criminal behavior, as Murakawa explains. They rejected a more structural understanding derived from the anticolonial movement that viewed racism as a deeper systemic problem that pervaded the country's social, economic, and political structures.

Race liberals singled out prejudice itself as the main source of lawlessness and called for greater federal leadership and enhanced law enforcement resources to purge the criminal justice system of bias and discrimination. They told a causal story in which decades of state-sanctioned segregation and discrimination under Jim Crow had acutely damaged the psyche and culture of many blacks and had rendered the legal system illegitimate in their eyes. As a consequence, blacks were more prone to criminality. For race liberals, ending Jim Crow and building a more procedurally fair, neutral, and uniform criminal justice system that constrained the discretion of whites to act on their racial prejudices would resolve both the law-and-order problem and the civil rights problem.

This turned out to be a costly and risky strategy. Murakawa notes that, as early as 1943, Phileo Nash, a special adviser to Truman, was warning that tethering the cause of civil rights to promises that more civil rights would yield less crime would leave the civil rights agenda and the Democrats who promoted it politically vulnerable. In what turned out to be a chillingly prescient observation, Nash noted, "If any public relations program in race relations is developed around a pronouncement from a high official on the importance of law-and-order, then every breach of law-and-order is a slap in the face at the program and the speaker."[11]

With Truman at the helm, race liberals sought a greatly expanded role for the federal government in the administration of criminal justice and law enforcement at the local and state levels and in the prosecution and punishment of civil rights crimes. They introduced a flurry of bills in the 1940s and 1950s to provide federal assistance to equip, train, and professionalize local and state police forces so that they would be better able to protect African Americans and their allies from violence directed at them by whites defending the color line. They also introduced dozens of bills to federalize many crimes, including anti-lynching legislation and numerous proposals to create federal criminal penalties for the use of explosives.

Most of these bills were not enacted. Nonetheless, all this legislative activity in the 1940s and 1950s profoundly influenced how future discussions of law and order, crime, and the federal role in law enforcement would unfold, according to Murakawa. In pushing these bills, race liberals helped legitimize the idea that greater federal intervention in law enforcement was needed to contain lynchings and other organized violence directed at African Americans. But in doing so, they further bolstered the association between blackness and criminality that Muhammad demonstrated was so critical in the development of a more punitive state directed at blacks.

In the 1950s and 1960s, the American Bar Foundation spearheaded a flurry of research that centered on the problem of discretion and arbitrary power. This work reinforced the push for more uniformity and proceduralism in law enforcement and sentencing to resolve the law-and-order problem.[12] So did the American Law Institute's pursuit of a Model Penal Code and the string of Supreme Court decisions under Chief Justice Earl Warren in the 1960s. These decisions imposed new procedural limits on state and local law enforcement and thereby expanded the procedural rights of suspects, defendants, and prisoners.[13]

Race liberals mistakenly believed that more procedures and guidelines would produce less punishment. Furthermore, the intense national spotlight at this time on instances of sensational violence in the South—most notably the murder of Emmett Louis Till, the fourteen-year-old youth from Chicago who was killed and thrown into Mississippi's Tallahatchie River in 1955, and the lethal bombings of black churches—drained political attention away from what Murakawa characterizes as the "routine violence of standard policing and legal incarceration" throughout the country.[14]

Meanwhile, conservative Southern Democrats opposed to desegregation and civil rights were challenging race liberals by formulating their own association between civil rights, criminality, and blackness. These race conservatives began strategically wielding the street crime issue well before national crime rates began to escalate and well before leading Republicans took up the law-and-order charge. As Murakawa explains, "Even as battles against civil rights *generated* violence against black people and their allies—with beatings, arson, and explosives directed at civil rights advocates—race conservatives *displaced* the root of violence onto civil rights liberalization itself."[15]

Southern Democrats initially cast their opposition to major civil rights legislation in criminological terms, arguing that "segregation maintains law-and-order, while integration breeds crime."[16] This was a doctrine not just of words but also of deeds. They shrewdly used civil rights bills as vehicles to stiffen and broaden criminal penalties.[17] They also began pushing for enhanced police forces and law enforcement but for different reasons than those of the race liberals associated with Truman. They sought an expanded criminal justice apparatus as a way to stem what they charged was the increased lawlessness on the part of African Americans and their supporters who sought to bring down the Jim Crow regime.

The Johnson Administration and Law and Order

As riots broke out in major cities across the country in the mid- to late 1960s, opponents of civil rights reformulated the connection between civil rights and crime. They worked "vociferously to conflate crime and disobedience, with its obvious extensions to civil rights."[18] Many urban white voters in the North initially maintained a delicate balancing act on the civil rights issue. While they opposed racial integration at the local level, they supported national candidates who were pro–civil rights. This split political personality became less tenable as crime and disorder "became the fulcrum points at which the local and national intersected," thus weakening the New Deal coalition.[19]

The enormous social and political unrest of the 1960s took shape amidst a crime shock. The national homicide rate doubled between the mid-1960s and early 1970s, and violence became far more geographically concentrated in poor urban areas with high concentrations of African Americans. New York City's homicide rate increased more than sixfold between 1960 and 1990.[20] The homicide rates in Chicago, Philadelphia, and many other cities also considerably outpaced the national average.

These developments were not entirely unprecedented. As discussed earlier, the waves of immigrants that flowed into urban areas in the nineteenth and early twentieth centuries prompted "widespread fears and predictions of social deterioration." Many feared that crime would increase as the number of immigrants increased in U.S. cities.[21] Yet during the Progressive era, an optimistic view took hold that white criminality in U.S. cities was rooted primarily in the strains of industrial capitalism and urban life, and that it could be alleviated through greater public and private investments in education, social welfare, and public infrastructure in cities with high concentrations of European immigrants.

By contrast, in the last quarter of the twentieth century, the faith in the power of the government to ameliorate social problems by addressing their root causes was rapidly evaporating. Escalating attacks from penal conservatives were to blame. So was indifference from race liberals who had become fixated on a procedural solution to the law-and-order issue. Furthermore, violent crime was becoming highly concentrated geographically in certain urban neighborhoods at a time of growing class inequalities among African Americans. This greatly enhanced the public policing power of black elites, which has been a persistent theme of racial politics in the United States, as discussed further below.

The lack of a consensus on what caused the alarming increase in violent crime opened up enormous political space to redefine the law-and-order problem and its solutions. Foes of civil rights sought to associate concerns about crime with anxieties about racial disorder, the transformation of the racial status quo, and wider political turmoil, including the wave of urban riots and the huge demonstrations against the Vietnam War that gripped the country in the 1960s and 1970s.[22]

Aiming to neutralize conservative critics, Johnson Democrats reformulated the law-and-order problem, as Murakawa shows. In 1968, President Lyndon B. Johnson signed the Omnibus Crime Control and Safe Streets Act of 1968, which accorded the federal government a new and much larger role in criminal justice and law enforcement with creation of the Law Enforcement Assistance Administration (LEAA).[23] Liberal Democrats still viewed modernizing, professionalizing, and federalizing the criminal justice system as a solution to the problem of state and interpersonal violence directed at minorities. But the emphasis was shifting toward how an expanded, professionalized law enforcement apparatus would render the criminal justice system fairer and more legitimate in the eyes of blacks and thereby would reduce black criminality.[24]

As the Safe Streets Act moved through the legislative process, Southern Democrats and their Republican allies outmaneuvered race liberals time and again. They enshrined funding formulas that gave state governments—not cities or the federal government—enormous leeway to distribute the money as they saw fit. In the face of massive urban unrest that was increasingly criminalized and racialized in public debates, many states opted to accord riot control and militarization of the police priority over crime prevention and rehabilitation, two of the stated goals of the Safe Streets Act.

The ups and downs of LEAA's budget over the years and its eventual demise in 1982 belie the agency's significance. LEAA helped to legitimize a major role for the federal government in crime policy. It also legitimized and institutionalized the idea that greater law enforcement capacity was needed to combat crime and political unrest, two problems that were often conflated in public debates. Furthermore, LEAA created incentives for state and local governments to inflate their crime statistics in order to tap into more of the federal largesse.

In launching his war on crime, Johnson linked it to the war on poverty. He stressed the need to address the "root causes" of crime. So did several presidential commissions appointed in the 1960s to examine the causes of the crime wave and the numerous disturbances that gripped U.S. cities at the time, most notably the Watts riots of 1965. But the root causes approach—which called for addressing these problems by investing more in education, health, welfare, and social and economic programs, not just law enforcement—lost out in public debates for a number of reasons.

The mid-1960s escalation of the national crime rate coincided with the launch of Lyndon Johnson's Great Society. This created a chasm of political space for claims that greater investment in social and other programs did not reduce crime and indeed may be contributing to personal pathologies that were reportedly the real roots of crime—such as poor parenting and the emergence of a culture of dependency blamed on welfare programs and other public assistance. Pointing to how rising crime rates coincided with the welfare state expansion of the Great Society, leading conservatives sought to cast doubt on claims from some liberals about the structural causes of crime and poverty.[25] This helped foster what Lawrence D. Bobo calls "laissez faire racism" in which blacks themselves are blamed for the black-white disparities in socioeconomic status and other measures of inequality, like the incarceration rate. This contributed to the persistence of negative stereotypes of African Americans and fostered public resistance to changes in public policy to ameliorate racism and other structural factors responsible for these disparities.[26]

The escalation in the crime rate took place amidst the beginning stages of a vast economic restructuring as the manufacturing base of major urban areas was hollowed out, as discussed in chapter 4. The high rates of unemployment and poverty in pockets of urban America that coincided with this economic restructuring and the extraordinarily high rates of violent crime in these areas prompted some politicians to stoke public fears of a marauding "underclass."[27] As popular faith in the government's ability to ensure public safety and manage the economy dwindled, so did confidence in elite expertise to guide government policies. This gave wide berth to politicians to define the crime problem and its solutions.[28] All this provided a fertile environment for public fears of crime to escalate and for politicians to exploit those fears even after crime rates began to ebb.

The Emergence of the Southern Strategy

Leading strategists of the Republican Party developed what became widely known as the Southern strategy to exploit this new political context. It was centered on employing coded race-based appeals to law and order and launching attacks on welfare to woo Southern and working-class white voters.[29] They sought to appeal to whites' anxieties about the rising crime rate, which were entangled with other anxieties about their "loss of stature and privileges as economic opportunities narrowed and traditionally marginalized groups gained new rights" during a time of vast social, political, and cultural changes.[30]

The Republican Party was well situated to exploit these fears for political and electoral gain if it chose to do so. As the Democratic Party sundered over civil rights issues, the South became politically competitive for the first time since the end of Reconstruction a century earlier. This ushered in a major political realignment. Furthermore, exceptional features of the institutional structure of the United States—most notably the widespread use of elections to select judges and prosecutors—made it especially vulnerable to politicians seeking to stoke the public's fears of crime and to politicize law-and-order issues.[31]

Moreover, some liberals did not take the escalation in the crime rate as real and serious, treating it instead as a product of political *Sturm und Drang* or an artifact of inaccurate and misleading crime statistics. They did not do enough to separate the real from the imagined fears of urbanites and suburbanites.[32] Those liberals who did take the crime jump seriously often failed to challenge conservatives when they attributed the crime increase to the launch of the Great Society and to the mixing of the races with the demise of segregation. They also did not do more to challenge conservatives who conflated riots, street crime, and civil rights protests. Indeed, liberal senator Robert Kennedy of New York was gearing up to make get-tough measures against urban disorder a centerpiece of his campaign for the Democratic nomination for president when he was assassinated in June 1968.[33]

Another key factor was that, since the 1940s, race liberals had been consistently promoting greater investments in law enforcement and neutral procedures as the best way to resolve the law-and-order problem, as discussed earlier. The legislative struggle to reform the federal criminal code that began in the mid-1960s and that culminated in passage of the Sentencing Reform Act of 1984, which was discussed in chapter 6, reveals how deep and steadfast this faith in proceduralism was among some leading race liberals. With each iteration of this proposed legislation, race liberals lopped off another anti-carceral plank, as Murakawa explains. They remained confident that establishment of a modernized, rationalized, and uniform sentencing structure was the best insurance against fostering a criminal justice system that was excessively punitive and excessively biased against minorities.

Senator Edward M. Kennedy (D-MA), a leader in the cause of sentencing reform, viewed enhanced proceduralism as a way to strike a compromise between those who sought to stem crime through more punishment and those who sought to stem crime through addressing its root causes. In seeking the support of archly conservative Southerners like Senator John McClellan (D-AR) and Senator Strom Thurmond (R-SC), Kennedy ran roughshod over deep concerns expressed by other liberal legislators (including leading Democrats in the House of Representatives), interest groups, and some experts on crime and punishment. These liberals worried that the quest for sentencing guidelines untethered to substantive goals in criminal justice would yield a more punitive criminal justice system at a time when the United States already had the highest incarceration rate among Western democracies.[34] "It is futile," Kennedy retorted in 1975, "to counter the law-and-order fallacy with the opposite fallacy that crime cannot be controlled unless we demolish city slums and eliminate poverty and discrimination."[35]

By the late 1960s, Southern Democrats, Republicans, and some Northern liberals had converged on some important common ground with respect to aspects of the law-and-order question. For Republicans and Southern Democrats, the expansion of civil rights fostered crime "by disrupting the harmonious segregation of the races and by validating black civil disobedience."[36] For race liberals like Hubert Humphrey and Robert F. Kennedy, the incomplete civil rights agenda was the main cauldron of crime. Both explanations identified "blacks as default subjects in the crime problem" and thus generated support for a vast expansion of the law enforcement apparatus, but for different reasons, as Murakawa elaborates.[37] By the 1970s, combating the root causes of crime and discrimination was a distant secondary concern for some—but certainly not all—race liberals, including Senator Edward M. Kennedy.

African Americans and the Postwar Consolidation of the Carceral State

The two major political parties came to align themselves in some remarkably similar ways on the law-and-order question. What still has not been adequately explained is why they did not face more political resistance as they embarked on this enormous expansion of the law enforcement apparatus. We now know that some key social movements and liberal interest groups, including the victims' rights movement, the women's movement, the prisoners' rights movement, and the anti–death penalty movement, developed in ways that reinforced the punitive turn in penal policy.[38] Although black leaders, politicians, and advocacy groups were clearly not the main instigators of the punitive turn, their actions also contributed to the consolidation of the carceral state, in many cases unwittingly.

As crime rates began to increase in the 1960s, residents of inner-city neighborhoods had growing concerns and fears about the escalation of violence and substance abuse in their communities. However, these concerns and fears alone do not explain why some African American politicians and other leading black public figures supported get-tough measures, even as crime rates began to plummet in the 1990s. They also do not satisfactorily explain what Michelle Alexander calls the "awkward silence" of civil rights organizations and their political allies as incarceration rates skyrocketed.[39] Three other factors are key: widening class divisions among African Americans; the altered political calculus for civil rights organizations and other advocacy groups in the face of these demographic and other changes; and the altered political calculus of a new generation of black politicians who came of age in the wake of the seismic electoral and institutional shifts of the post–Jim Crow era.

Politicians often do not stray far from the status quo—especially on questions of race—unless forced to do so by wider social and political movements.[40] For the most part, mainstream civil rights organizations have not exerted much pressure on politicians to dismantle the carceral state. The disincentives and challenges to represent the poor and disadvantaged have always been enormous.[41] Advocacy on their behalf "is expensive, politically unpopular, and often involves trade-offs with other issues" that are more central to the mission of these organizations.[42] The disincentives and challenges to represent poor people who have run afoul of the law are even higher.[43]

In the decades immediately following World War II, competition from more radical organizations was key in prodding mainstream identity-based civil rights organizations to make the cause of the truly disadvantaged part of their mission and not just a rhetorical flourish. As Catherine Paden shows, even during the war on poverty in the 1960s, older mainstream civil rights organizations like the NAACP and National Urban League gave only intermittent support to the cause of poverty alleviation. When they did act, it was often because younger organizations that aggressively challenged the status quo posed a competitive threat to their funding and membership bases. With the demise of the Black Power movement and the atrophy of groups such as the Southern Christian Leadership Conference (SCLC), the Student Nonviolent Coordinating Committee (SNCC), and the Congress of Racial Equality (CORE), mainstream civil rights organizations faced less political pressure to embrace issues such as poverty alleviation and prisoners' rights. Furthermore, their priorities and strategies shifted substantially as they, like many interest groups, became professionally managed organizations that emphasized mass membership rather than mass mobilization.[44]

These developments coincided with the emergence of new patterns of racial inequality that would have important consequences for the politics of crime and punishment and the development of the carceral state. Up until the civil rights era, the predominant pattern was based largely on the exclusion of African Americans.

The pattern that emerged subsequently was rooted in selective incorporation in the context of widening education and income gaps among blacks and greater residential mobility for more affluent blacks.[45]

As social, political, and economic inequalities have grown within historically disadvantaged groups in recent decades, many leading advocacy organizations have been increasingly unable or unwilling to give meaningful attention to the needs and interests of the most marginalized people within their more complex constituencies. These advocacy groups are not necessarily uninterested in advancing the interests of the most disadvantaged within their broad constituencies. But they generally do not consider the plight of the truly disadvantaged to be a central part of their mission, as Dara Strolovitch explains.[46] They tend to privilege the interests of their most privileged members.

This general silence with respect to the carceral state stands in sharp contrast to the central place that criminal justice matters previously had occupied for leading identity-based civil rights organizations, most notably the NAACP. Together with the NAACP Legal Defense Fund, the country's oldest civil rights organization had been one of the primary litigants in a string of landmark court cases dating back to the 1920s involving African Americans that greatly expanded the rights of criminal defendants.[47] In the late 1940s and 1950s, a broad range of civil rights organizations, including the NAACP, the National Negro Congress, and the Civil Rights Congress, promulgated a conception of the law-and-order problem that stretched far beyond what race liberals had staked out.[48] They contended that the law-and-order problem was not primarily a problem of individual prejudice on the part of whites, and individual social and psychological dysfunction on the part of blacks confronted with white prejudice. Aligning themselves with the anti-colonial movement, these organizations adhered to group-based rather than individual-based explanations of violence that centered on the enormous range of state violence perpetrated against blacks and other minorities by leading political and governmental institutions infected by white supremacy.

They contended that this violence encompassed far more than just police brutality and the failure of local law enforcement to halt lynchings and stem white attacks on civil rights protesters. In their view, state violence ranged widely, including everything from discrimination in arrests, convictions, and sentencing to job discrimination, poverty, poor schools, violence in prisons, and limited access to higher education. From the mid-1940s to the early 1950s, a wide range of civil rights groups periodically petitioned the United Nations to indict the U.S. government for promoting genocidal criminal violence against African Americans.[49]

Over the next few decades, many civil rights organizations and leading black public figures retreated from this more expansive understanding of the law-and-order problem. The growing convergence between race liberals and race conservatives discussed earlier left civil rights organizations politically isolated as the law-and-order problem was redefined. It increasingly was understood to mean the street crime problem associated with blacks and not the wide-scale violence perpetrated against blacks by the state and organized groups of whites.

By the 1960s, prisoners' rights had become an integral plank of the civil rights movement. By the 1970s, this issue had become strongly associated with celebrated and reviled figures of the Black Power movement who themselves had been imprisoned, including George Jackson, Angela Davis, and Huey Newton.[50] In 1982, the NAACP featured the U.S. prison crisis on the cover of *The Crisis*, its monthly flagship publication. That issue included several articles denouncing the crowded and inhumane conditions in U.S. prisons, the growing number of incarcerated African Americans, and the belief that prisons can be sites for rehabilitation.[51]

As the inmate population continued to rise over the next two decades, the NAACP's attention to prisoners' rights issues and the prison crisis would wane.[52] Nearly fifteen years would elapse before *The Crisis* featured the prison crisis on its cover again in 1996.[53] By then, the number of inmates in state and federal prisons topped one million, compared to about 400,000 in 1982.[54] Between 1980 and early 2010, *The Crisis* ran nearly two dozen covers that celebrated the achievements of the NAACP and of heroes of the civil rights movement. But the prison crisis made the cover only three times. All told, *The Crisis* featured criminal justice–related issues on its cover about half a dozen times during those three decades, far less than the number of times that black entertainers and black athletes appeared.[55]

A host of internal problems plagued the NAACP during this period, which diminished its effectiveness on a broad range of issues, not just criminal justice, well into the 1990s.[56] The same was true for the Urban League, which has been comparably quiet on the issue of mass incarceration and is the only other of the "big five" identity-based civil rights organizations of the 1960s that is still relatively prominent in national politics.[57] However, these internal difficulties alone do not account for why these organizations turned their gaze away from prisoners' rights issues and the problem of the prison.

African Americans and the War on Drugs

With the onset of the war on drugs in the 1970s, substantial fissures began to open up among African Americans on the crime and punishment issue. Some leading black officials and public figures began to distance themselves from the cause of prisoners' rights and to abandon their earlier focus on prisons as key sites of state violence. They also started backing, at times quite enthusiastically, some of the signature punitive measures that helped build the carceral state, including the war on drugs. The conventional wisdom is that the Republicans launched the war on drugs in the 1970s, and that the Democrats, including leading black politicians, became belated conscripts in the 1980s to avoid what they perceived to be electoral Armageddon if they did not wrest the crime issue back from them. But new historical research suggests that some leading African Americans supported aspects of the war on drugs and other get-tough measures from much earlier on.

President Nixon declared his own war on drugs in 1971. This was an about-face for his administration, which had initially embraced greater investment in treatment, rehabilitation, and public health to combat substance abuse. Two years later, Republican governor Nelson Rockefeller of New York, who was aiming to reposition himself politically in the face of the Southern strategy and a possible run for the White House, pushed through the nation's toughest drug laws. States across the country adopted new drug laws modeled after what became widely known as the "Rockefeller laws." At the time, Nixon, Rockefeller, and other drug warriors constructed addicts and pushers as noncitizens who were "responsible not only for their own condition, but also for many of the problems plaguing society, such as crime, deteriorating urban infrastructure, and mass social and economic insecurity."[58] We now know that some black newspapers and public officials also initially championed the draconian and pioneering Rockefeller drug laws in New York State. They did so for a complex set of reasons, including rising fears of crime and rampant substance abuse but also growing fears of a black "underclass."[59]

The war on drugs continued to escalate in the 1980s, even though reported drug use reached its peak in the late 1970s and continued to fall until the early 1990s.[60] As a moral panic over the introduction of crack cocaine into urban drug markets erupted, Congress and the White House rushed to enact tough new federal drug laws in the wake of the 1986 overdose death of All-American basketball player Len Bias. These new drug laws, which resulted in historically unprecedented rates of imprisonment for drug use and possession, initially garnered key support from some leading African Americans. Before turning against it in the 1990s, Congressman Charles Rangel (D-NY) of Harlem ardently backed the Anti-Drug Abuse Act of 1986 with its controversial 100:1 sentencing disparity for crack and powder cocaine. Thirteen of the twenty voting members of the Congressional Black Caucus (CBC) supported this measure. Two years later, nearly one-third of the CBC backed the Anti-Drug Abuse Act of 1988.[61] Even though the White House was instrumental in passing these two pieces of landmark drug legislation, civil rights leader Jesse Jackson castigated President Ronald Reagan in the 1988 presidential campaign for being a faint-hearted general in the war on drugs.[62]

Divisions over criminal justice issues among African American politicians and other public figures deepened and were on full display during the debate over the Violent Crime Control and Law Enforcement Act of 1994. The CBC vowed to oppose President Clinton's massive and draconian crime bill if it did not include the Racial Justice Act, which would have allowed statistical evidence of racial discrimination to be introduced in capital punishment cases. But Clinton, who maintained a strategic silence on the Racial Justice Act, shrewdly outflanked the CBC by mobilizing black mayors to speak out on behalf of the crime bill, which, among other things, rendered sixty additional crimes punishable by death. Thanks in part to the billions of dollars that the crime bill allocated for crime prevention programs in urban areas and to its ban on assault weapons, many members of the CBC ended up supporting this legislation. They did so even though the bill included many highly punitive measures, and even though the Racial Justice Act had been removed in the conference committee.[63]

Black Public Opinion on Crime and Punishment

Historical, ethnographic, and public opinion scholarship suggests that rising crime rates, the heroin epidemic of the 1960s and 1970s, and the crack epidemic of the 1980s were great sources of concern for residents of inner-city neighborhoods. To underscore this point, James Forman notes how Supreme Court Justice Clarence Thomas in his 1999 dissent in *City of Chicago v. Morales* emphasized that blacks themselves had endorsed severe sanctions on the grounds that tougher laws benefit law-abiding blacks.[64] Such concerns help explain why Clinton was able to mobilize black mayors in support of his crime bill. But black sentiment on crime and punishment is extremely complex.

As Nixon, Wallace, and George H. W. Bush were using racially coded language to fan fears of crime to bolster their political bases among people least likely to be victims of serious crime, African Americans in poor and isolated urban neighborhoods were contending with high levels of violence. While leading white politicians were emphasizing the need for tougher sanctions to deal with the crime and punishment problem, black officials and other public figures took a more complex and nuanced stance that James Forman characterizes as "all of the above."[65] They supported tougher penalties and aggressive law enforcement in some instances. However, they also called for addressing the deteriorating economic and social conditions in urban areas that were facilitating these high rates of violence. This helps explain why Washington, DC has pursued get-tough penal policies and law enforcement tactics similar to those that have prevailed in much of the rest of the country, even though African Americans have dominated its political leadership.[66] The capital's incarceration rate for African Americans is one of the highest in the country, while its rate for whites is one of the lowest in the country (and rivals the rates of Norway and Sweden, two of the least punitive countries in the world).[67]

Public opinion research on criminal justice is a booming area of scholarship. This work has focused primarily on identifying variations in support for punitive measures between racial groups, especially blacks and whites, and variations in perceptions of bias or discrimination in law enforcement between these groups. Relatively little work has been done on differences of opinion within whites, blacks, and other groups on criminal justice issues, especially how people understand the causes of criminal behavior and the solutions to the crime problem.[68]

Some public opinion research appears to support Forman's claim of an "all-of-the-above" approach to crime and punishment among African Americans. What is less clear is whether support for "all of the above" is widespread among blacks. It might be the consequence of the fragmenting of black public opinion. Some African Americans may lean toward structural explanations and solutions for the crime problem, while others may lean toward individualistic explanations that suggest more punitive solutions.

Even after controlling for factors like education and income, large portions of blacks share a common sensibility about crime and punishment, according to James Unnever. They attribute high rates of incarceration of young African American men to structural factors, such as high unemployment, poor schools, and discrimination, as well as individual factors, such as poor parenting and bad values.[69] However, Thompson and Bobo found that nearly one-third of blacks surveyed attribute crime primarily to individual-level factors, while one-third attribute it primarily to structural factors, and one-third to both.[70] Individualists are much more likely than structuralists to support spending more on police and prisons rather than on education and job training, according to Victor Thompson and Lawrence Bobo.[71] But people who have greater fears of crime tend to support a mixed strategy predicated on spending more on law enforcement and prisons but also spending more to address the social and economic conditions that lead to crime. Thompson and Bobo speculate that the people who fear crime the most tend to live in areas of higher exposure to crime and therefore are likelier "to take a more holistic approach to solving the crime problem."[72]

As Ian Haney López emphasizes, these preferences cannot be understood separately from the constrained choices of people residing in poor neighborhoods of concentrated crime and violence. If given a choice between decent schools, effective job programs, affordable day care, and good housing on the one hand or more policing to combat crime and violence on the other, most would choose the former. But if they are "[f]orced into a 'choice' between governmental neglect versus neglect combined with aggressive policing, it seems cruel to defend such policing on the ground that it is 'preferred' by those trapped in impoverished nonwhite neighborhoods."[73]

Public opinion research suggests that differences are growing among blacks over a variety of issues—not just crime and punishment—and that some of those differences are stratified by income and education levels.[74] Inequality within the black population has probably never been greater than it is today.[75] The family income gap between poor and better-off African Americans has continued to grow since William Julius Wilson drew wide public attention to this gap in *The Declining Significance of Race* more than three decades ago. The situation of the bottom one-fifth of black families has been eroding.[76] A 2007 Pew poll found that nearly four in ten blacks say that blacks can no longer be considered a single race because the black community is so diverse.[77] Notably, a majority of blacks polled say that the values of poor and middle-income blacks are diverging more than they are converging. This perception of a values gap has widened over the past two decades, and the greatest shift has been among the most and the least educated blacks.[78] Polls also suggest that blacks are much more likely than whites or Hispanics to report that the communities they live in lack moral values.[79] Summing up the complexities of interpreting this research on black public opinion, Fredrick Harris says, "Either a significant number of blacks have internalized stereotypes about blacks lacking moral values or moral failings have become a self-fulfilling prophecy in the lives of many black people."[80]

Harris, Cathy Cohen, Michael Dawson, and other experts on black politics and public opinion suggest that these public opinion survey results need to be understood within a wider political context that takes into account, among other things, how black leaders shape black public opinion. In her detailed study of the views of black youths, Cohen shows how young blacks invoke individual and structural factors in complex and nuanced ways to explain why some blacks misbehave and run afoul of the law. She and others suggest that such worldviews cannot be understood separately from the emergence of a new generation of post-racial black politicians and public figures who have been emphasizing individual and cultural explanations over structural ones.[81]

The Emergence of the Post-Racial Generation of Black Leaders

Just as the political and organizational incentives and constituency base changed for civil rights organizations, they also have changed for African American politicians. Analyses of House roll call votes, for example, indicate that black elected leaders in Washington are not as liberal as they were in the mid-1970s.[82] Scholars of black politics have identified the emergence of a new generation of "post-racial" black politicians who have sought to catapult into higher office in majority-white jurisdictions by pursuing "deracialization" strategies. These post-racial politicians have sought to defuse racial issues by refusing to talk directly about race unless pushed to the wall by events.[83] However, they have not remained silent about the problem of law and order.

As the urban crisis worsened, some leading black politicians and public figures endorsed a causal story that focused on individual flaws, not structural problems, and that singled out the addict, the drug pusher, and the street criminal as part of the "undeserving poor" that posed the primary threat to working- and middle-class African Americans.[84] They emphasized individual explanations and solutions rather than structural ones that highlighted racial and economic factors. They burnished their post-racial credentials by lecturing those who had run afoul of the law, many of whom happened to be African American.

The new generation of post-racial black leaders has contributed to a broader moral panic in which young black Americans have been "increasingly vilified," as Cathy Cohen explains.[85] For example, in 2011, Mayor Michael Nutter of Philadelphia responded to several assaults by black youths in Center City (the affluent cultural and economic hub of Philadelphia) that made national headlines by channeling his inner Bill Cosby. Nutter took to the pulpit of a black church in West Philadelphia for a thirty-minute rant in which he castigated black fathers "for being nothing more than 'sperm donors'" and "called out 'doggone hoodie-wearing teens' who'd never get jobs with their underwear or 'the crack of your butt' showing." He accused these black youths of not only damaging themselves and their peers but also "your own race."[86]

Outbursts like these from leading African Americans help to legitimize an exaggerated public fear of black youths and to justify the heightened policing and criminalization of young blacks.[87] But such public vilifications do more than that. They also stoke sympathy among some African Americans for cultural explanations of black criminality and poverty. They also contribute to the political silencing of black youths who are pursuing what Cohen characterizes as a "politics of invisibility." These young people have largely disengaged from politics. They have sought "to remain invisible to officials who possibly could provide assistance but were more likely to impose greater surveillance and regulations on their lives."[88]

Black communities have long engaged in a "politics of respectability, attempting to win acceptance into the mainstream white society by demonstrating their worth and adherence to dominant norms."[89] The anti-elitist rhetoric of the Black Power movement helped to mute the "politics of respectability" somewhat, as Harris explains.[90] But the politics of respectability has come roaring back thanks to several factors. These include the decline of the Black Power movement, expanding class differences between blacks, growing violence and decay in inner-city neighborhoods, and the new political and institutional landscape that emerged in the aftermath of Jim Crow. As violent crime became highly concentrated in certain urban communities and as class divisions widened among African Americans, we have witnessed the deepening of what Cohen characterizes as the "secondary marginalization" of those who are "most vulnerable in oppressed communities." Indigenous organizations, institutions, and leaders have increasingly denied "community recognition and resources to those labeled deviant in black communities."[91]

In addition to Mayor Nutter, other notable post-racial black politicians and public figures include President Obama, Senator Corey Booker (D-NJ), Governor Deval Patrick (D-MA), former congressman Harold Ford, Jr., of Tennessee, talk show host Oprah Winfrey, and Kweisi Mfume, the former head of the NAACP. In drawing public attention to the persistence of alarming levels of violence in pockets of urban America, their message has been decidedly mixed. They have made restrictions on gun manufacturers and gun sales and stiffer penalties for gun-related violations a leading issue. They have invoked kinder, gentler but no less troubling culture of moral poverty explanations for high rates of violence as they have called upon mothers and especially fathers in these communities to be better parents. They mention in passing the need to address some of the well-established structural causes of high rates of violence—including high levels of unemployment and poverty, not enough living-wage jobs, residential segregation, and inadequate funding for schools and heath care. Absent are any strident calls for a bold new urban agenda aimed at the country's most disadvantaged neighborhoods to reverse the public disinvestment in these communities and to address the structural causes of astronomical levels of crime that vex them, as discussed more in chapter 12.[92] Remarkably, Obama's State of the Union Address in 2011 was the first by any president since 1948 not to mention the poor or poverty.[93]

At the same time, these post-racial black leaders have generally maintained a public silence on race issues, "which conveys to the country that racism is no longer a problem."[94] For example, in his first two years in office, Obama talked less about race than any Democratic president had since 1961, according to political scientist Daniel Q. Gillion.[95] As a consequence of this silence, the color-blindness frame seeps into blacks' worldview, though not to the extent that it affects whites.[96]

This is politically enervating, for it hinders the development of the all-out oppositional ideology and utopian vision necessary to dismantle—not just chip away at—the carceral state.[97]

Wider Institutional and Political Context

The emergence of post-racial black politicians is part of the grand narrative of race and the future of the carceral state. But that narrative has played out in varied ways depending on the specific institutional and political context. Florida is a good case in point. Heather Schoenfeld persuasively shows how the political and institutional remedies to address disparities in electoral representation paradoxically were catalysts for a political realignment that ultimately ushered in a new era of punitiveness in Florida.[98] She singles out in particular the forced reapportionment of the state legislature after the 1962 *Baker v. Carr* Supreme Court decision and the opening up of the voting booth to more blacks thanks to the civil rights movement.

In the 1960s and 1970s, a broad coalition of black and white voters wrested political control from conservative rural Democrats in north Florida who had long dominated state politics, Schoenfeld explains. This brought about some moderation in Florida's racial politics and penal policies even as racially charged law-and-order politics flourished at the national level and in other states. Some of the most far-reaching and progressive reforms of the Florida prison system came about during this period under the leadership of Louie Wainwright, a former prison guard who presided over the Division of Corrections from 1962 to 1987. Wainwright undertook to modernize the division by centralizing, depoliticizing, and professionalizing the penal system and its staff. He sought to provide educational opportunities to all inmates, regardless of race, and to establish health, safety, and welfare standards for the state's jails and prisons. Wainwright also phased out the controversial road works program, which harkened back to the days of the chain gang.[99] He sought to lower Florida's above-average incarceration rate by expanding the use of parole and probation, standardizing sentences across counties, and shifting low-risk offenders to work release and community corrections programs.[100]

In keeping with these liberalizing tendencies, black legislators in Florida in the early 1990s succeeded in mitigating some of the state's harsher sentencing policies by, for example, abolishing mandatory minimums for many crimes. But this period of moderation in Florida's penal practices and policies did not last. This was partly due to the 1992 redistricting, in which black state Democrats worked with Republican legislators to create more majority-minority legislative and congressional districts. As a result, the number of black representatives in the state legislature increased, but so did the number of Republicans, paving the way for the Republican takeover of both chambers of the Florida legislature in 1996 for the first time since Reconstruction. "With Republicans essentially in control, legislator-driven crime control initiatives became more commonplace," explains Schoenfeld.[101] The conditions were ripe for one or two hard-liners in the legislature to drive penal policy in a more punitive direction.

In short, the downfall of the Jim Crow regime transformed electoral incentives and institutional arrangements in ways that have been consequential for the carceral state. These transformations help explain considerable local and state-level differences in the punitive turn and also the emergence of a new generation of post-racial black leaders. They also complicate explanations about the role of race in the construction, maintenance, and dismantling of the carceral state.

Rediscovering the Prison—Sort Of

In the 1990s, elite identity-based civil rights organizations became more outspoken about some criminal justice issues. But these tended to be issues that could be easily fit into a civil rights framework as conventionally understood, notably racial profiling, the crack-powder cocaine sentencing disparity, police brutality, felon disenfranchisement, and the plight of the Jena 6.[102] Criminal justice was not a top priority. Neither was mass incarceration.

The Leadership Conference on Civil Rights, which is composed of the leadership of nearly 200 civil rights organizations, failed to include criminal justice as part of a big 2008 initiative to document how members of Congress voted on the most important civil rights issues. A major conference organized by this broad coalition in 2007 did not include a single panel devoted to criminal justice reform.[103] In January 2009, the CBC sent a letter to hundreds of sympathetic community and organization leaders asking them to designate their top priorities. The CBC listed nearly three dozen possible areas of special interest to choose from, including the media, taxes, faith-based initiatives, and the census, but no mention of criminal justice reform except for reentry.[104]

Under the leadership of Benjamin Jealous, the NAACP broke its general silence on the issue of mass incarceration. Soon after he took over in 2008, Jealous designated mass incarceration the leading civil rights issue of the twenty-first century.[105] In 2009, the NAACP launched its "Smart and Safe" campaign built around the idea of public safety as a civil right. The first phase of that campaign focused on the critical need for national standards for police use of force and for civilian oversight boards with real teeth to ensure police accountability.[106]

At its annual convention in 2010, the NAACP approved a record sixteen resolutions concerning criminal justice matters, almost as many as it had approved during the previous decade. The civil rights organization staked out some bold positions that did not fit comfortably into its historic civil rights framework. Notably, it called for the repeal of all life-without-parole statutes, characterizing LWOP as a form of "modern barbarism" and a "de facto death penalty."[107] In early 2011, the NAACP released its "Misplaced Priorities" report documenting how corrections budgets have grown at the expense of funding for education. Shortly thereafter, the NAACP unveiled a national billboard campaign to draw attention to the problem of mass incarceration.[108] At its annual convention in 2011—the fortieth anniversary of the official launch of the war on drugs—the NAACP finally enacted an historic resolution calling for an end to the war on drugs.[109]

Although the NAACP recently broke its general silence on mass incarceration, it has fashioned its political challenge to the carceral state in a highly conservative cast in some respects. The NAACP's penal reform agenda appears to be based on short-term political expediency rather than on a long-term vision around which a durable and effective coalition to dismantle the carceral state can be built. The NAACP prominently allied itself with the Right on Crime coalition, the group of leading conservatives who have staked out a neoliberal, economistic stance to reducing the prison population. As elaborated in other chapters, this approach is unlikely to result in a major drop in the incarceration rate or in the number of African Americans in prison. But it will likely bolster the political and economic forces that sustain the carceral state and thwart the development of a viable political alternative to the deeply conservative hue of American politics.

The NAACP's press conference to launch its "Misplaced Priorities" report featured a number of prominent conservatives. It included Grover Norquist, the anti-tax and anti-government crusader discussed in other chapters, and Michael Jimenez, president of the California Correctional Peace Officers Association (CCPOA), the nation's largest and most powerful prison guards' union.[110] The CCPOA has repeatedly stymied sensible proposals to modestly reduce California's prison population. It also has aggressively challenged public officials and political candidates who have sought to reduce the incarceration rate and to prosecute guards who abuse prisoners.[111]

Challenges from Below

Although many national identity-based civil rights organizations and leading black politicians have been slow to challenge the carceral state, poor neighborhoods in urban areas have been "hotbeds of mobilization" around criminal justice issues.[112] So have some of the local affiliates of these national organizations. For example, the local chapters of the NAACP in Maine and Mississippi have been effective advocates of reforming the supermax facilities in their states. The Maine chapter also drew national attention in 2008 for its efforts to inform state prisoners of their voting rights and to register them to vote. (Maine is one of only two states that does not bar prisoners from voting.) The Georgia State Conference of the NAACP spurred the national headquarters to join in an investigation of possible human rights violations in the state prison system after inmates engineered a massive strike in December 2010 to protest prison conditions.[113]

The local and state chapters of national organizations cannot always be counted on to represent the interests of those hurt most by the carceral state, however. There are numerous examples of how local groups have lacked the capacity, will, or vision to challenge the carceral state. For instance, in the late 1980s and early 1990s, Florida NAACP officials "more often blamed a lack of 'self-control' and 'moral compass' than state or federal policy" for escalating crime and incarceration rates. They rejected government solutions and instead embraced church, community, and family as critical factors for ensuring that young African Americans did not turn to crime.[114]

Ex-offenders and their families have been reluctant to take a more public stance against the carceral state for many reasons, including reluctance to draw attention to the criminal pasts that they have been trying to live down.[115] But former offenders are starting to create their own organizations to challenge U.S. penal policies despite the severe constraints the carceral state places on their political activities. The stigma of a criminal conviction poses a substantial obstacle to political engagement and participation. So do commonplace parole and probation conditions, including bans on having a cell phone or driver's license, associating with known felons or ex-felons, and traveling outside of specified geographic areas without permission.[116] Under the right circumstances, former offenders can be enormously effective advocates. For example, they played a vital role in a successful 2006 ballot initiative to repeal felon disenfranchisement statutes in Rhode Island.[117] In Chicago, the newly formed Voice of the Ex-Offender (VOTE) has garnered public attention for employing a protest model of direct action aimed at the city's black political establishment, including Reverend Jesse Jackson's Rainbow/PUSH Coalition.[118]

Conclusion

This chapter upended the neat periodization of the rise of the carceral state that focuses on the 1960s, in particular the emergence of racially charged law-and-order politics fomented by Barry Goldwater, Richard Nixon, and other leading white politicians. Such neat periodizations and neat villains are problematic. They leave the transitions between periods "curiously under-explained" while underplaying the continuities between periods.[119] They reify the role of major political figures—especially presidents and presidential candidates—at the cost of ignoring how the national narrative can vary greatly depending on institutional and other differences at the local and state levels. Furthermore, they focus on white politicians and their followers while slighting how African Americans and members of other groups have been independent political actors in their own right in the debates over crime and punishment. As shown in this chapter, African Americans bolstered and challenged the carceral state at key moments and in complex ways.

Several factors complicate any account of mass incarceration that invokes race to explain the development of the carceral state and the possibilities for dismantling it. These include the shifting and varied ways in which a wide range of politicians, public figures, advocacy groups, and scholars—some of them white, some of them not—have fostered a deep association between blackness and criminality; the evolving ways in which law and order has been inserted into American politics; the changing politics and priorities of black elites and advocacy organizations in the aftermath of Jim Crow; and the political impact of escalating rates of violence and disorder in urban areas. Other important factors are the institutional, political, and electoral differences at the state and local levels that are responsible for considerable variations in the development of the carceral state. This combination of factors helps explain why the narrowly focused bipartisan quest to balance state budgets by pursuing the three R's—reentry, recidivism, and justice reinvestment—has succeeded in capturing the penal reform agenda at the elite level. And why the race question and other issues of social justice have not been more central to these elite-level discussions and to the framing of the problem of the carceral state.

PART III

The Metastasizing Carceral State

CHAPTER EIGHT

Split Verdict

The Non, Non, Nons and the "Worst of the Worst"

A people confident in its laws and institutions should not be
ashamed of mercy.

—JUSTICE ANTHONY KENNEDY

Legislators and policy makers at all levels of government have been exploring ways to reduce their prison and jail populations by revising their criminal codes, establishing new parole and probation policies, and pursuing alternatives to incarceration. They have concentrated their efforts on how to shorten the prison stays of nonviolent, nonserious, and nonsexual offenders (the so-called non, non, nons) and how to keep them out of prison altogether.[1]

This political strategy of drawing a firm distinction between the non, non, nons on the one hand, and violent offenders, sex offenders, and criminal aliens on the other has yielded some worthwhile penal reforms, especially in the area of drug policy. But if the ultimate aim is to slash the prison and jail population, render the criminal justice system more just, and dismantle the carceral state without jeopardizing public safety, this political strategy may be ultimately self-defeating.

Often the "good" and "bad" criminal offender—like the "good" and "bad" immigrant—hail from the same community, sometimes even from the same family. In some cases, the "good" and "bad" offender may be the same person, once all the complexities of his or her run-ins with the law or with the immigration authorities are fully considered. Furthermore, as time elapses, people age out of crime. Ramping up the penalties leveled against the "really bad guys" can end up exacting severe and lasting punishments on entire communities without greatly enhancing public safety. The same holds true in the case of deporting "criminal aliens" for minor infractions or for more serious offenses committed long ago for which they had already been punished (as discussed in chapter 10).

Drawing a firm line between the non, non, nons and other offenders has contributed to the further demonization of people convicted of sex offenses or violent crimes in the public imagination and in policy debates. It has impeded the enactment of more comprehensive changes in sentencing policies and parole practices. It reinforces the misleading view that offenders should be defined forever by the seriousness of the offense that initially sent them away. "Only a few decades ago, Americans saw the essential nature of the criminal as separable from the criminal act," explains Anne-Marie Cusac. "Now the crime is the essence of the criminal."[2]

The United States remains deeply attached to condemning huge numbers of offenders to extremely long sentences and to deporting large numbers of noncitizens. This remains so despite mounting evidence that such measures have at best a minimal impact on reducing the crime rate and are socially and economically very costly. The courts have been generally supportive of life sentences, de facto life sentences, and extremely disproportionate sanctions, as discussed in this chapter. Revitalizing the parole and commutation processes so that even people who committed very serious crimes and who are serving long—sometimes lifelong—sentences get a chance to prove they are rehabilitated has not been a priority. Neither has abolishing life in prison without the possibility of parole (LWOP) and making all life sentences eligible for parole consideration. The handful of successes in curtailing the use of life sentences for adult offenders has mostly involved drug-related offenses.[3] Although several states have enacted new measures intended to expand the use of geriatric or compassionate release for elderly or gravely ill inmates, few people are actually being released under these new provisions.[4]

The political and legal obstacles to seriously reconsidering the extensive use of life sentences and other excessively long sentences in the United States remain formidable. This chapter analyzes some of the major obstacles, as well as emerging strategies to challenge excessive sentences. It first examines how the war against the war on drugs is shaping penal policy more broadly. As will be shown, this new war may be constricting political opportunities to challenge excessively long sentences for people convicted of non-drug crimes and more serious offenses. This chapter then analyzes why an assault on life sentences waged primarily through the courts is not likely to reduce the lifer population significantly. Next it considers how the vast heterogeneity of the life-sentenced population, as measured by offense, is an impediment to developing effective political and legal strategies to challenge the frequent imposition of the "other death penalty," or what Jessica Henry terms "death-in-prison sentences."[5] The chapter concludes with a discussion of the long shadow that capital punishment continues to cast over penal policy in general and life sentences in particular. It assesses the degree to which the death penalty abolitionist movement has contributed to the proliferation of life sentences. It also identifies some important lessons that opponents of life sentences should draw from the setbacks and victories of the abolitionist movement.

The War against the War on Drugs

The most notable penal reforms of late have been in the area of drug policy as the war against the war on drugs has gained ground. All the recent attention on the missteps of the war on drugs has contributed to the misperception that the war on drugs has been the primary engine of mass incarceration in the United States.

The reality is that tougher sentences across the board for both serious crimes and petty offenses initially fueled the prison buildup. But the contribution of violent offenders to the prison population now significantly dwarfs the contribution of drug offenders, as elaborated in chapter 6. Ending the war on drugs—one of the top priorities for many penal reformers—will not necessarily end mass incarceration in the United States because drug offenders have not been the primary driver of recent growth in the prison population.

Some opponents of the war on drugs have supported easing up on drug offenders and other nonviolent offenders in order to get tough with the "really bad guys." This obscures the reality that the United States, relatively speaking, is already quite punitive toward violent offenders, sex offenders, and property offenders and has been for a long time now.[6] Legislators and other public officials have been pursuing penal reform packages that reduce the penalties for drug offenses and some other nonviolent crimes while ratcheting up or leaving largely untouched the punishments for other crimes. For example, Arizona's Proposition 200, which mandated treatment or other alternatives to incarceration for certain drug offenders, has long been hailed as a pioneering piece of penal reform legislation since voters approved it by wide margins nearly two decades ago. But in that same election, voters also endorsed Proposition 102, which required more juvenile offenders to be tried in adult court and sentenced to adult prison if convicted.[7]

There are numerous other examples of these split policy verdicts. In 2010, South Carolina legislators enacted several laudable sentencing reforms with broad bipartisan support. These included equalizing the penalties for possession of crack and powder cocaine, authorizing greater use of alternatives to incarceration for people convicted of nontrafficking drug offenses, and reducing the maximum penalty for burglary. However, South Carolina lawmakers also redefined twenty-two crimes as violent ones that qualify for enhanced penalties, expanded the list of crimes that are eligible for LWOP sentences, and further toughened up its habitual offender statutes.[8] Legislators in Florida have balked at endorsing proposals to deal more leniently with some drug offenders unless those measures are offset with new laws that impose tougher sanctions for crimes against the elderly and children.[9] The 2012 report of a blue-ribbon commission on public safety in Oregon recommended, among other things, rolling back some of the mandatory minimums for more serious crimes like robbery, assault, and sexual assault that voters had originally approved in 1994. But legislators removed most of those proposed mandatory minimum reforms for more serious crimes from the sentencing bill enacted in July 2013, partly because of intense opposition from the state's district attorneys.[10]

In August 2012, Governor Deval Patrick of Massachusetts signed what he described as "balanced" penal reform legislation. It included a harsh new three-strikes law together with some modest reductions in drug-related penalties at a time when prisons in his state were operating at nearly 150 percent of capacity.[11] Members of the state's Black and Latino Legislative Caucus opposed the bill. Months earlier, a state agency had released a master plan calling for $1.3 billion to $2.3 billion in new prison construction to meet a major projected shortfall in prison beds.[12]

Maverick district attorneys launched into office in major urban areas with the backing of broad penal reform coalitions have served as important beachheads to engineer wider statewide shifts in penal policy in recent years. These prosecutors have focused mostly on the shortcomings of the war on drugs. The plight of people serving lengthy sentences for serious or violent crimes has not been part of their reform agenda.

After many years of political agitation by the "Drop the Rock" campaign, the New York State legislature finally enacted a reform package in 2009 that eviscerated what remained of the draconian Rockefeller drug laws. At the same time, lawmakers rejected an extremely modest recommendation from the New York State Commission on Sentencing Reform to extend so-called merit time to a very limited pool of people convicted of violent offenses. If enacted, it would have made these incarcerated individuals eligible to have a few months shaved off their sentences. These were people who had served decades in the system, had stellar behavior records, and had other markers of rehabilitation, such as college degrees earned while serving time.[13]

Federal officials have also sought a split policy verdict in penal reform. In 2011, Attorney General Eric Holder testified that he supported applying the 2010 Fair Sentencing Act (which reduced but did not eliminate sentencing disparities between penalties for crack and powder cocaine) retroactively, but only for certain nonviolent offenders. He urged the U.S. Sentencing Commission to exclude violent offenders (even though criminal histories and any gun possession had already been factored into their original sentences under a separate part of the federal sentencing guidelines).[14] Holder's speech to the American Bar Association in August 2013 was widely heralded as a major shift in federal sentencing policy. But his main policy pronouncement at the time was that a restricted subset of "low-level, non-violent" drug offenders would no longer be subject to federal mandatory minimum sentences.[15]

Not Jean Valjean

Drawing a firm line between nonviolent drug offenders and serious, violent, or sex offenders in policy debates reinforces the misleading view that there are clear-cut, largely immutable, and readily identifiable categories of offenders who are best defined by the offense that sent them to prison. But such fixed categories of offenders are often an illusion. It is well established in the criminology literature that "the current offense that one commits is a very poor predictor of the next offense."[16] Many offenders are highly versatile, which should make penal reformers cautious about staking their proposals on "a typology of offenders presumed to reflect distinct behavior profiles," explains Robert J. Sampson. The charge or offense that results in a specific decision to send someone to jail or prison "is often arbitrary and depends on issues of evidence."[17]

Surveys suggest that four out of five state inmates serving time for a "nonviolent" offense meet at least one of the four criteria that define a "serious" offender.[18] Many people serving time for a nonviolent crime like drug possession have been convicted of a violent offense in the past. Only about a quarter of federal inmates and a fifth of state inmates are first-time offenders.[19] Furthermore, some scholars and law enforcement officials contend that drug charges are often levied as surrogates for more serious, often violent, crimes. This is due to the difficulties that the police and prosecutors face in trying to directly prosecute violent felonies in many poor inner-city neighborhoods thanks to "no snitchin'" norms, the vulnerability of eyewitnesses, and other factors.[20] In short, U.S. prisons are not filled with easily identifiable Jean Valjeans.[21]

Releasing low-level drug offenders or diverting more of them from prison will not dramatically reduce the state and federal prison population. Eric Sevigny and Jonathan Caulkins calculate that "unambiguously low-level drug offenders" comprise less than 6 percent of state inmates and less than 2 percent of federal inmates. The proportion of people in prison for drug-law violations because they were exclusively users amounts to 4 percent of drug offenders in state and federal prisons and just 1 percent of all prisoners. Although most drug offenders are not drug kingpins, most have had some involvement in drug distribution. "[T]here is a spectrum of drug offenders in prison, and the greatest numbers come from the ambiguous middle of that spectrum," according to Sevigny and Caulkins. Their analysis also suggests that drug decriminalization for possession of small amounts could actually increase the prison population. Public demand for drugs would likely rise, and the number of suppliers would likely expand to meet that growing public demand.[22]

Just as all drug convictions may not necessarily be what they first appear, on closer inspection, all "violent" offenders are not necessarily what they first seem. Many of the people sent to prison for violent offenses are not necessarily violent offenders years later. Nevertheless, the common perception is that they still are violent despite stellar prison conduct records, ample evidence of rehabilitation through education, volunteering, and other programs, and conclusive research findings that people tend to age out of crime.

Witness the uproar after the North Carolina Supreme Court declined to review a 2008 appellate court decision that a life sentence is to be considered eighty years under the state's statutes. After the ruling, North Carolina's Department of Corrections announced its intention to release dozens of lifers who were eligible for early release thanks to the "good time" and merit time credits they had accumulated. Democratic governor Beverly Perdue stepped in to stop the release amid numerous reports in the media that many "rapists and murderers" were about to go free. This brouhaha spurred a spate of news stories that featured outraged victims and their families and that recounted the gruesome details of crimes committed decades earlier. In August 2010, the North Carolina Supreme Court reversed course and ruled that these inmates sentenced to life in the 1970s were not eligible for parole.[23]

Run-On Sentences

Opposition to the war on drugs has dominated discussions of penal reform, over-shadowing the plight of the "really bad guys" left behind in North Carolina and elsewhere.[24] The U.S. commitment to life sentences and other excessively long sentences remains deep despite a consensus among many experts on sentencing and crime that such sanctions do not enhance public safety considerably. Life sentences have become so commonplace that approximately one out of every nine people imprisoned in the United States is serving what some critics call "the other death penalty." Nearly one-third of these life-sentenced offenders have been sentenced to LWOP. The total life-sentenced population in the United States is approximately 160,000, or roughly twice the size of the *entire* incarcerated population in Japan.[25] Indeed, the United States locks up people for life at a rate of approximately 50 per 100,000, which is comparable to the incarceration rate for *all* prisoners, including pretrial detainees, in Sweden and other Scandinavian countries.[26] About 10,000 of these lifers have been convicted of nonviolent offenses, mostly property and drug crimes.[27] These figures on life sentences do not fully capture the large number of people who will probably remain in prison until the end of their days. They do not include the so-called virtual or de facto lifers—people who received sentences that exceed a natural life span and who are likely to die in prison long before reaching their parole-eligibility or release dates.[28]

As reentry has skyrocketed to the top of the penal reform agenda, as discussed in chapter 4, lifers are facing the prospect of a further deterioration in their conditions of confinement. For all the recent talk about the need to invest more in reentry, the amount of money available for treatment, programs, and other services for all offenders is shockingly limited and continuing to shrink, as discussed in earlier chapters. In an age of tightening budgets and a fixation on reentry, more lifers are being denied access to programs and activities that might make their days without end more bearable. In a 2012 national survey of juvenile lifers, 62 percent of them reported that they were not enrolled currently in any prison programs.[29] Prison restrictions and the absence of programs, not disinterest on their part, appear to explain these low levels of participation. Denied educational and other programs, lifers are less able to demonstrate evidence of reform and rehabilitation to satisfy the conditions for parole consideration that the Supreme Court laid down in the *Graham v. Florida* and *Miller v. Alabama* decisions discussed below. As one lifer in California lamented, "The thinking goes that since we will never get out of prison there is no point in expending scarce resources on dead men walking."[30]

The explosion in the number of lifers in the United States since the 1970s represents a major shift in U.S. penal policy. For much of the past century, life in prison "never really meant life in prison" thanks to critical penal reforms enacted during the Progressive era a century ago.[31] These reforms were rooted in growing enthusiasm for early release as halfway houses, work-release programs, and use of parole proliferated. In 1913, a "life" sentence in the federal system was officially defined as fifteen years.[32] Many states had comparable limits on "life" sentences.[33]

Until the early 1970s, even in a hard-line state such as Louisiana, which today has the country's highest incarceration rate, a life sentence typically meant ten years and six months (the 10/6 law). Lifers were routinely released in Louisiana after serving a decade or so if they had good conduct records and the warden's support. The years that inmates spent in Louisiana's infamous Angola state prison were often brutal and dehumanizing, but they nearly always had an end date. Almost overnight that situation changed, as lawmakers first raised the minimum number of years before a prisoner could be considered for clemency and then mandated that all life sentences meant LWOP.[34] In 1970, only 143 people were serving LWOP sentences in Louisiana. By 2012, that number had mushroomed to about 4,600—or nearly 12 percent of the state's entire prison population.[35] Between 1992 and 2008, the number of prisoners serving LWOP sentences nationwide increased by 300 percent. Due to the elimination of the discretionary parole system in sixteen states and the federal system, all life-sentenced inmates in these jurisdictions are ineligible for release.[36]

Life sentences and other extraordinarily long sentences have important spillover effects. They set a "reference price for crime" that makes other extreme but less severe punishments seem appropriate.[37] For instance, a sentence of ten years, which would be considered a very severe and exceptional sanction in many European countries, is considered a relatively modest, run-of-the-mill sanction in the U.S. penal system, which is chock-full of lifers and de facto lifers who will likely die in prison.

The extensive use of LWOP and life sentences in the United States stands in sharp contrast with practices in other developed democracies. In much of Europe, all prisoners "are in principle regarded as worthy of consideration for release," according to Dirk van Zyl Smit and Alessandro Corda. Indeed "recognition of their dignity" requires this as a right.[38] Most European countries do not permit LWOP, and those that do use it sparingly.[39] In many European countries, if a "lifer" does not continue to pose a major threat to public safety, he or she is typically released after serving approximately twelve years. This is similar to the practice that used to prevail in many states.[40] Lately Germany and some other European countries have been imposing life sentences more frequently, but several recent judicial developments suggest that Europe may be at the brink of outlawing life sentences as a matter of international human rights law.[41] In a much watched case, the European Court of Human Rights ruled in a 16-to-1 decision in July 2013 that the life sentences handed down to three men convicted of murder in Britain constituted degrading and inhuman treatment because they had no hope of release. The Court ruled that this violated the European Convention on Human Rights.[42]

Thanks to the escalation in the number of people serving life and other lengthy sentences, prisons are becoming maximum-security nursing homes. Between 1999 and 2007, the number of people aged 55 or older in state and federal prisons increased by about three-quarters, and the number of those aged 45 to 54 increased by more than two-thirds.[43] A 2012 ACLU report estimates that by 2030, there will be more than 400,000 prisoners who are 55 or older, compared to about

9,000 in 1981.[44] Prisons spend two to three times as much to incarcerate an elderly inmate compared with a younger one—or on average approximately $60,000 to $70,000 a year—due to their greater medical needs.[45]

This practice is costly in many other respects. Elderly prisoners who need advanced medical care complain that they are being transferred to special skilled nursing units that are akin to solitary confinement. In these units, they are denied visits from fellow inmates, many of whom are like surrogate family members after the many years they have spent together in prison. They also are prohibited from leaving the unit to attend programs and religious services and to use the library. Some elderly and infirm inmates are refusing treatment or are not seeking medical attention so as to avoid facing the end of their days isolated and alone in one of these special units.[46]

No Judicial Promised Land

The U.S. public has been largely indifferent to the proliferation of life sentences and of disproportionate and arbitrary punishments in the United States. Likewise, the political process has failed to engage in a serious debate about these issues. As a consequence, the courts appear to some observers to be the most promising arena to check excessive punishments such as life sentences. In the *Graham v. Florida* (2010) decision, the U.S. Supreme Court outlawed LWOP sentences for juveniles convicted of crimes other than homicide. Two years later, in *Miller v. Alabama* (2012), a divided Court ruled that juveniles may never receive a mandatory LWOP sentence. These two decisions bolstered faith that the courts would reduce the lifer population. However, this faith in the judiciary's greater potential to lead the way in curtailing extreme sentences in the United States may be unwarranted. An excessive focus on judicial strategies may be coming at the cost of developing successful complementary political and legislative strategies to shrink the lifer population.

The Supreme Court has a "highly unsatisfactory and disappointing" record when it comes to defining and limiting disproportionate sentences.[47] Generally, the Supreme Court has been extremely supportive of life sentences. In *Schick v. Reed* (1974), it dismissed any notion that LWOP was unconstitutional.[48] In *Harmelin v. Michigan* (1991), it ruled that LWOP sentences do not require the same "super due process" procedures mandated in capital punishment cases.[49]

As a consequence of these decisions, LWOP has become a much cheaper and easier alternative penalty to seek compared with a death sentence.[50] For example, as the number of death sentences meted out in Texas has plummeted recently, the state's LWOP population has exploded to nearly 500 people since 2005, when Texas became the last of the death penalty states to enact LWOP statutes.[51] Few LWOP prisoners in Texas or elsewhere "have any reasonable chance of getting their sentences overturned or reduced."[52] Offenders sentenced to life have fewer legal resources to challenge their sentences because they are not entitled to the automatic appeals process available to prisoners on death row. Moreover, most post-conviction offices and organizations focus almost exclusively on capital cases.

The Supreme Court has consistently given legislators and judges wide berth to impose whatever punishments they see fit—short of death—without significant judicial oversight. A life sentence has become an acceptable punishment not only for murder but also for a wide variety of other crimes, some of them quite trivial, as evidenced by the popularity of draconian versions of three-strikes legislation. In *Lockyer v. Andrade* (2003), the U.S. Supreme Court affirmed two 25-years-to-life sentences for a California man whose third strike was the theft of $153 worth of videotapes intended as Christmas gifts for his nieces. In *Ewing v. California* (2003), it sanctioned a 25-years-to-life sentence under California's three-strikes law for the theft of three golf clubs. In rendering these decisions, the Supreme Court affirmed that proportionality is a valid constitutional principle but then rejected strong proportionality limits.[53]

The Supreme Court's persistent reluctance—or hostility—to meaningfully defining and imposing real proportionality limits in noncapital cases stands in sharp contrast to its behavior in other areas of law. With respect to fines, forfeitures, and punitive damages, it has proven itself willing and able to set limits and define excessiveness.[54] This observation suggests that the Supreme Court lacks the will—not the capability—to take up the task of reviewing noncapital sentences and to devise a meaningful definition of proportionality that limits excessive sentences.

Capital punishment is one area of criminal law in which the Supreme Court has sought to define a robust oversight process and curb excessive punishment.[55] The Court requires states to have clear guidelines for the imposition of a capital sentence so that the death penalty is not imposed capriciously and arbitrarily. It has banned mandatory death sentences and insisted that capital defendants have the opportunity to present all kinds of mitigating evidence in the sentencing phase of their trial. It has sought to make the punishment fit the crime in capital cases, thereby forbidding the execution of people convicted of rape and greatly restricting the use of the death penalty in felony murder cases.

By contrast, life sentences are currently imposed in a manner similar to how death sentences were meted out in the pre-*Furman* and pre-*Gregg* eras before the Supreme Court nationalized capital punishment and began to regulate it through its new death-is-different doctrine. This similarity has prompted some observers to argue that pushing the courts to extend the death-is-different doctrine to lifers may be the most fruitful way to curtail use of this extreme sentence.[56] The *Graham* decision, which was a rare instance when the Court stepped in to regulate a noncapital sentence and borrowed from the death-is-different canon to do so, has reinforced this view. However, it is doubtful that legal strategies derived from death penalty jurisprudence will significantly stem the flow of life sentences in the United States.

The Supreme Court has been scrupulous about keeping its death penalty jurisprudence from bleeding into other areas of criminal justice by repeating the truism that death is different.[57] Furthermore, both supporters and opponents of the death penalty agree that the Supreme Court's regulation of capital punishment has not been a success. As Supreme Court Justice Harry Blackmun declared in 1994, eighteen years after he voted in favor of reinstating the death penalty in the *Gregg* decision, "[T]he death penalty experiment has failed."[58] Today, the death penalty is "overlaid by a web of rules and procedures that is more complex than that of any other area of criminal law."[59] Yet opponents of the death penalty complain that capital defendants still are regularly denied due process. They also complain that the death penalty continues to be imposed in a capricious, arbitrary, and discriminatory fashion.[60] Meanwhile, supporters of capital punishment lament the lengthy, often unending, legal appeals process in death penalty cases that in their view denies victims' families the closure that a timely execution purportedly brings.

Compared with the "virtually nonexistent" oversight of noncapital cases, the death penalty review process may appear robust.[61] However, the rules, principles, and precedents that have developed over more than four decades to govern capital punishment are notoriously confusing and contradictory.[62] Moreover, since the early 1980s, the Supreme Court and Congress have been weakening or dismantling some of the legal protections erected for capital defendants in a push toward "deregulating death."[63]

It would be a mistake to view the *Graham* and *Miller* decisions as major departures from these general trends or to interpret them as signals that the judiciary is the Promised Land in which to roll back life sentences in the United States. In *Graham*, as in the *Atkins v. Virginia* (2002) and *Roper v. Simmons* (2005) decisions (which banned the execution of mentally retarded and juvenile offenders, respectively), the Court emphasized that it was dealing with an extremely rare sentencing practice.[64] The Court singled out the rare use of this sentence as evidence that these particular LWOP sentences were at odds with "evolving standards of decency," a key pillar of its death penalty jurisprudence, and therefore were cruel, unusual, and unconstitutional. To gauge these evolving standards of decency, the Court weighed not just how many states had this sentence on the books but also how few actually imposed it. The Court also noted that international opinion and practice were arrayed against LWOP sentences for juvenile offenders, as were some key professional associations.

Even though the Court borrowed from the capital punishment canon to invalidate LWOP for these particular juvenile offenders, the evolving standards of decency approach does not appear to be a promising way to mount a broader legal challenge to LWOP or other life sentences. It is hard to make the case that the American public has become disenchanted with LWOP or life sentences more generally for most adult offenders. Prior to the 1970s, LWOP was virtually nonexistent. Today forty-nine states have some form of LWOP on the books, up from sixteen in the mid-1990s.[65] During the past three decades, the U.S. incarceration rate has quadrupled, and the LWOP population has increased a hundredfold.[66] Public opinion polls indicate strong and growing support for LWOP as an alternative to the death penalty.[67] Although international practice and opinion are decidedly against LWOP and the widespread use of other kinds of life sentences, international sentiment has been at best a second-tier consideration for the Court in gauging evolving standards of decency.

In *Graham*, the Supreme Court identified the "denial of hope" as another reason to declare that these specific JLWOP sentences were unconstitutional. The Court indicated that LWOP sentences for certain juvenile offenders may be unacceptable because it "means denial of hope; it means that good behavior and character improvement are immaterial; it means that whatever the future might hold in store for the mind and spirit of [the convict], he will remain in prison for the rest of his days."[68] However, denial of hope does not appear to be a fruitful way to challenge life sentences more broadly. Lifers exhibit a wide range of behaviors and coping strategies, much as one would find among the terminally ill or chronically disabled at various stages of their diagnoses and illnesses.[69] Anyone who has spent some time with lifers—especially lifers who have been incarcerated for a decade or more—cannot fail to be impressed with how hopeful a number of them appear to be. Many lifers doggedly seek purpose in their lives despite what may appear to many outsiders to be bleak living conditions and bleak life prospects.

Research on the impact of prison on the people serving lengthy sentences is scant, partly due to the high barrier to access that prison administrators and Institutional Review Boards have constructed. These barriers have contributed to a dearth in ethnographic work on prisoners compared to years ago.[70] Until the 1980s, most studies appeared to support the claim that "long-term incarceration inevitably leads to a systematic physical, emotional and mental deterioration."[71] More recent research suggests that many lifers cope with the extraordinarily difficult circumstances of their confinement by cultivating optimism about their own personal efficacy, by compiling impeccable disciplinary records, and by strictly adhering to daily routines defined by a whirlwind of educational, volunteer, and other activities. These findings help explain why lifers tend to be leaders in creating a more stable and livable atmosphere in prisons.[72]

This discussion is not intended to deny or minimize the severe psychological distress that often comes with a life sentence. A "new and distinctive kind of 'prison pain'" is emerging with the proliferation of very long—often lifelong—sentences at the same time that penal conditions for long-timers have become much more austere and tightly restricted.[73] The conditions of confinement in the United States and other countries for lifers tend to be "far worse than those for the rest of the prison population and more likely to fall below international human rights standards."[74] Many lifers experience a wrenching "kind of existential and identity crisis."[75] Life sentences are like a death in slow motion for many prisoners, causing great mental and sometimes great physical distress.[76] As Lewis E. Lawes, warden of New York's Sing Sing prison in the 1920s and 1930s, once said, "Death fades into insignificance when compared with life imprisonment. To spend each night in jail, day after day, year after year, gazing at the bars and longing for freedom, is indeed expiation."[77]

Although *Graham* and *Miller* certainly provide important legal openings, they are likely to be limited openings, partly because the Court "seems to have left a notoriously opaque area of the law even less clear than it was before."[78] In the wake of the *Graham* and *Miller* decisions, juvenile lifers have not found much relief in the courts or from state legislators. Many of the juveniles who have returned to court for resentencing received staggering new sentences of fifty, sixty-five, and even ninety years, which amount to de facto life sentences.[79] Many juveniles have been denied resentencing hearings altogether as courts and legislators in some states have resisted applying the 2012 *Miller* decision to previously sentenced juveniles.[80] The governor of Iowa commuted all the mandatory life sentences of his state's juvenile offenders but declared that they would be eligible for parole only after serving sixty years. To the dismay of many penal reformers and juvenile advocates in Pennsylvania, the state responded to the *Miller* decision by hastily enacting a new law that preserves life without parole as a sentencing option for juveniles. Judges in Pennsylvania now have the option of sentencing a juvenile offender to LWOP or to a discretionary life sentence that requires the defendant to serve twenty to thirty-five years before being considered for parole.[81]

In the two years following the *Miller* case, three states abolished JLWOP, joining six others that had already eliminated this sanction.[82] In 2013, California enacted legislation to permit some offenders serving JLWOP to petition the courts for resentencing after they have served fifteen years. All of these sentencing changes fall short of the nonpartisan American Law Institute's recommendation that juvenile lifers should be eligible for parole consideration after they have served ten years.[83]

In short, opponents of LWOP and other extraordinarily long sentences should be wary of making some of the same missteps that death penalty abolitionists made in the 1960s and 1970s. At the time, death penalty abolitionists focused intently on judicial strategies and largely ignored the legislative and political arenas. A preoccupation with judicial solutions forces an issue to be framed within the constraints of prior legal texts, rules, and decisions. As a consequence, arguments and evidence that may be compelling in the political arena fall to the wayside because the courts have been unreceptive to them. For example, given the Supreme Court's persistent indifference or hostility to claims about racial discrimination in the administration of criminal justice, it is not surprising that legal strategies to challenge life sentences do not stress the racial aspects of this punishment.[84] However, the gross racial disparities in the administration of both capital punishment and LWOP sentences are potentially compelling political issues.[85] Nearly half of the lifers are African American, and one in six is Latino.[86] Lifers also are more likely to be poor and to lack access to adequate legal representation.

Lengthy Sentences and Public Safety

Recent state-of-the-art research in criminology has largely substantiated Italian philosopher Cesare Beccaria's claim from the eighteenth century that the certainty of punishment is a far greater deterrent to crime than the severity of punishment.

The most persuasive studies suggest that increases in the severity of punishment have at best only a modest deterrent effect.[87] Evidence is mounting that doing time likely increases the recidivism rates of certain offenders, and that for some people, the more time served, the greater the risk of reoffending.[88] Furthermore, all things being equal, placement in a severe high-security penal facility is associated with higher rates of reoffending compared with placement in a penal facility at a lower level of security.[89] The evidence is compelling that longer sentences are not associated with greater reductions in future offending. Furthermore, the evidence is highly suggestive that prisons, "especially gratuitously painful ones," may be criminogenic. Defendants sent to prison—especially low-level offenders—may be more likely to reoffend than those who receive noncustodial sanctions.[90]

The deterrent and incapacitative effects of lengthy sentences are modest for several reasons. Since offenders tend to be present oriented, lengthening the sentence for a certain offense from, say, fifteen years to a life sentence, is unlikely to have a major effect on whether someone commits that crime or not. Furthermore, the evidence that people age out of crime is compelling. Researchers have persistently found that age is one of the most important predictors of criminality. Criminal activity tends to peak in late adolescence or early adulthood and then declines as a person ages, a process that some have termed "criminal menopause."[91] Finally, many lifers are first-time offenders convicted of homicide. The phrase "one, then done" is commonly used to sum up their criminal proclivities.

Older offenders and lifers released from prison after serving lengthy sentences are much less likely to return to prison due to the commission of a new serious crime than are younger offenders who have served shorter sentences. Lifers released from prison were less than one-third as likely to be re-arrested compared with other released prisoners, according to an analysis by The Sentencing Project.[92] Of the 368 people convicted of murder who were granted parole in New York between 1999 and 2003, only six, or less than 2 percent, were returned to prison within three years for a new felony conviction, and none were reimprisoned for a violent offense, according to a 2011 study by the New York State Parole Board.[93] Another recent study found that the two-year return rate for men who had served eight years or more in New York State prisons was 20 percent. Nearly three-quarters of them were sent back because of a technical parole violation, not the commission of a new crime. The recidivism rates for women who had served lengthy sentences were even lower.[94] These findings are consistent with prior studies documenting the relatively low recidivism rates of people convicted of murder, people on death row, and people who have served lengthy sentences.[95]

The public perception is that the life-sentenced population is composed largely of people who are the "worst of the worst" and who would pose major threats to public safety if released. But the life-sentenced population in the United States is extremely heterogeneous. It includes not only drug offenders but also middle-aged serial killers, getaway drivers in convenience store robberies gone awry, aging political radicals from the 1960s and 1970s, women who killed their abusive partners, third-strikers serving twenty-five years to life for trivial infractions such as stealing two pieces of pizza, and men who, as teenagers decades ago, killed their girlfriends in a fit of jealous rage. Many of the people serving life sentences today were the main perpetrators of a violent crime such as homicide. However, a great many of them were sent away for life for far less serious infractions.

A central question facing any penal reform movement concerned about the lifer issue is whether to concentrate on challenging the fundamental legitimacy of all life sentences that are not subject to a meaningful parole review process or whether to concentrate on a subset of lifers who appear less culpable and more likely to garner public sympathy. In the 1980s and 1990s, the penal reform movement at Louisiana's Angola prison splintered and floundered over this very issue.[96] Long-timers sentenced during the more permissive 10/6 regime were at odds with more recent lifers sentenced under the tougher new statutes.[97] Angola's Lifers Association excluded "practical lifers," even though "there is little difference between a man with a life sentence and one doing 299 years without parole."[98] Lifers who were first-time offenders tired of the all-or-nothing push for parole eligibility for all lifers and attempted to form their own organization.[99]

The enormous heterogeneity of the life-sentenced population presents an enormous political challenge. It renders extremely attractive political and legal arguments based on going after "low-hanging fruit" by emphasizing degrees of culpability and relative fairness. Such strategies could be costly over the long term. They could sow divisions among lifers and among their advocates on the outside. Moreover, they threaten to undermine more universalistic arguments about redemption, rehabilitation, mercy, and aging out of crime that would encompass a broader swath of the life-sentenced population and of people serving other lengthy sentences. More narrowly tailored arguments may win the release of individual lifers or certain categories of lifers but may worsen the odds of the other lifers left behind. Four categories of lifers sharply illustrate this point: offenders convicted of felony murder, juveniles sentenced to LWOP, people sent away for life for trivial offenses under California's three-strikes law (which is among the toughest in the country), and finally, the "worst of the worst," who have been convicted of particularly brutal, offensive, or noteworthy crimes.

Felony Murder

The United States is exceptional not only for its extensive use of life sentences but also for the persistence of the felony murder rule, which other common-law countries have largely abolished. The felony murder doctrine generally permits charging someone with first-degree homicide, instead of the lesser charge of involuntary manslaughter, if he or she caused an unintended death during the commission of a felony. Accomplices also may be charged with first-degree murder even if they are not directly responsible for the homicide. Nearly all states have retained some kind of felony murder rule, even though the American Law Institute's Model Penal

Code recommended abolishing it.[100] Felony murder statutes vary enormously between states. They differ over key factors such as how broadly to define culpability, complicity, and qualifying felonies.[101] In the most expansively drawn felony murder statutes, an accomplice may be considered as culpable as the triggerman for any murder committed during the commission of any other felony. Moreover, the definition of accomplice can be quite capacious. In some states, lending a car to a friend who ends up using it to commit a murder could be cause to send a person away for life.[102]

Political and legal strategies highlighting the lesser culpability of people convicted of felony murder and the gross disproportionality of their sentences sometimes result in pitting one group of lifers and their advocates against another. One lifer appears more deserving of release by highlighting how less deserving other lifers are. This approach may win the eventual release of an offender who had only minimal involvement in a particular crime. But this victory may come at the cost of bolstering the view that the main perpetrators—or the "really bad guys"—got what they deserved and should be forever defined by the crime they committed.

Juvenile Lifers

The plight of juveniles sentenced to LWOP is another good case in point. At the time of the *Miller* ruling, approximately 2,500 people were serving LWOP sentences for offenses committed when they were juveniles. This sentencing practice violates the 1989 United Nations Convention on the Rights of the Child and other international human rights agreements and norms.[103] Many youths sentenced to LWOP are incarcerated in adult facilities while they are still juveniles. Despite efforts to segregate juveniles from the adult population, often in supermax-type conditions until they turn eighteen, many of them are still subject to physical and other abuses, including rape, by staff members and older inmates.[104]

As discussed previously, the *Roper*, *Graham*, and *Miller* decisions have been major catalysts for the reconsideration of JLWOP sentences. Even before the *Graham* and *Miller* decisions, some states were beginning to rethink their JLWOP statutes.[105] In 2006, Colorado banned JLWOP, and Texas followed suit three years later.[106]

Graham and *Miller* rested partly on new research in brain science and psychology about adolescent brain development. The evidence is compelling that the prefrontal cortex of the brain, which regulates impulse control, is not fully developed until people are in their twenties. As a consequence, teenagers have greater trouble controlling their impulses and resisting peer pressure, as nearly any parent of a teen knows. Opponents of executing juveniles and of condemning them to life in prison argue that children and teenagers should not be considered fully culpable for the crimes they commit, however heinous or violent, because their brains are not fully developed.

Political and legal strategies rooted in arguments about the underdevelopment of teenage brains have proven to be an extremely promising avenue to abolish or at least limit the use of JLWOP sentences. These strategies could be costly over the long term for those offenders who were sent away for life for crimes they committed as adults, and thus when they presumably had fully developed brains. Stressing that teenagers are not fully culpable reinforces in a backhanded way the idea that adults who commit serious crimes should have known better and therefore are fully culpable. The brain-scan approach to criminal justice also supports narrow, biologically deterministic arguments about why people commit crimes. Such arguments are enjoying a renaissance in criminology and in public debates about crime and punishment to a degree not seen since the heyday of the eugenics movement a century ago. Crass use of brain science research reinforces the popular view that people who commit serious crimes are biologically incapable of fundamentally changing.

The relative culpability of juveniles convicted of felony murder was a central issue in debates about JLWOP in Pennsylvania in the aftermath of the *Graham* and *Miller* decisions. Pennsylvania has approximately 500 juvenile lifers, or one-fifth of the country's total and more than any other jurisdiction in the world.[107] Until the state modified its homicide statutes in response to the *Miller* decision, mandatory life was the only sentence available to youths convicted of first- or second-degree murder. There is no minimum age for prosecuting a juvenile as an adult in Pennsylvania. For many years now, Pennsylvania's governors have been persistently unwilling to commute the sentences of juvenile lifers who have served decades behind bars. This has been so even in cases in which members of the homicide victim's family have called for mercy and release.[108]

JLWOP opponents in Pennsylvania have focused extensively on the adolescent brain development argument.[109] At one legislative hearing on JLWOP reform, Anita Colón (whose brother is serving a life sentence in Pennsylvania for a felony murder conviction when he was sixteen) underscored that almost 60 percent of Pennsylvania's juvenile lifers were first-time offenders who had never been convicted of a previous crime. She also noted that approximately one-third of them had been convicted of felony murder, which is slightly above the national average of approximately 25 percent.[110] In their testimony, Colón and other opponents of JLWOP stressed that rehabilitation and treatment have a greater impact on juveniles than they do on adults, and therefore that juveniles are not beyond redemption. Legislators at the hearing focused much of their attention on the relative fairness of felony murder for juvenile lifers rather than on additional arguments raised by Colón and others about redemption, aging out of crime, and the huge economic cost of incarcerating so many youths until the end of their days.

In defending JLWOP, the Pennsylvania District Attorneys Association (PDAA) commended the legislature's recent efforts to reduce the state's prison population by focusing on diversionary and other programs directed at people convicted of nonviolent offenses. "That is the cohort group our collective attention should be focused on—not on letting murderers out early," the association declared.[111] The

PDAA framed proposals to abolish this sanction as violations of the rights of victims and of Pennsylvania's commitment to truth in sentencing. Representatives of victims' organizations and other defenders of JLWOP echoed this view and devoted much of their testimony to recounting gruesome details of crimes committed by juvenile lifers.[112]

The debates over JLWOP in Pennsylvania and elsewhere illustrate one of the many ways that the death penalty continues to cast a long shadow over the broader politics of punishment and penal reform. As *Roper v. Simmons* wound its way through the courts, organizations representing the victims of juvenile offenders generally did not mobilize in support of executing juvenile offenders. Assurances that juveniles who were spared the death penalty would spend all their remaining days behind bars were an important reason for their quiescence. Representatives of victims' organizations have portrayed ending JLWOP retroactively and making juvenile lifers eligible for parole consideration as a betrayal. They contend that many victims' families had agreed not to push for the death penalty because of assurances from prosecutors that the perpetrator would be locked up for life, thus sparing families the seemingly endless appeals process of capital punishment cases.[113]

Striking Out in the Golden State

California operates the country's second largest state prison system and has the highest number of life-sentenced prisoners—approximately 40,000, or one-quarter of the nation's total. This number is almost four times as many as in 1992, shortly before the state enacted its infamous three-strikes law. Approximately one in three prisoners in California, or about three times the national average, is currently serving a life sentence.[114] California's life-sentenced population is exceptional not only for its sheer size but also for its extreme heterogeneity as measured by sentencing offense. The state's three-strikes law, which has become a towering symbol of California's commitment to crime victims and of its uncompromising stance toward offenders, has posed a huge hurdle to devising effective political and legislative strategies to dismantle the "other death penalty" in the Golden State.

In 1994, California enacted what became the nation's most severe three-strikes law. For defendants with two or more prior serious or violent strikes, a third conviction for *any* felony entailed a minimum sentence of twenty-five years to life if a prosecutor chose to invoke the three-strikes statute. Unlike three-strikes laws in many other states and the federal system, the third strike need not be for a serious or violent offense in California. Moreover, the Golden State has an extremely permissive definition of what constitutes a felony, and prosecutors have enormous leeway to upgrade misdemeanors to felonies. As a consequence, the state's prison population includes many people convicted under the three-strikes law who are serving lengthy sentences for trivial infractions such as petty theft, minor drug possession, or minor drug sales. In one of the most infamous cases, Jerry Dewayne Williams received a 25-years-to-life sentence for snatching a slice of pizza from a group of children.[115] In another infamous case, a defendant was sentenced to life for stealing a dollar in change from the coin box of a parked car.[116]

An important but less widely known part of California's three-strikes law is its second-strike provision. This measure doubles the minimum sentence for anyone convicted of a second felony who has one prior serious or violent felony. The overwhelming majority of people serving time under California's three-strikes law were actually charged under the second-strike provision. More than 32,000 inmates—or approximately 20 percent of the state's prison population—are second-strikers, and approximately 9,000 are third-strikers.[117]

The proportion of California prisoners who were sentenced under the state's three-strikes law has increased substantially. Between 1994 and 2001, it rose from approximately 2.5 percent to about 25 percent, where it has stabilized.[118] The readiness of California's district attorneys to invoke their three-strikes prerogative has varied enormously around the state and even between seemingly similar cases in a single county.[119] African American men, who constitute around 3 percent of the state's population, represent approximately 33 percent of second-strikers and 44 percent of third-strikers among California's prison inmates.[120] Offenders sentenced under the state's three-strikes law receive sentences that are, on average, nine years longer than they would have received otherwise.[121] A 2009 report by the state's auditor estimated that the 43,500 inmates then serving time under California's three-strikes law will cost the state approximately $19 billion in additional costs.[122] More than half of the people imprisoned under the three-strikes law were convicted of a felony that is not considered violent or serious, at an additional cost of $7.5 billion.[123] A significant number of them are not necessarily habitual offenders.[124] Rather, prosecutors chose to invoke the three-strikes law in instances of multiple offenses committed on a single day in a single incident. For example, an armed robbery committed by a first-time offender could, through creative prosecutorial accounting, be considered three strikes that warrant a sentence of twenty-five years to life.

In 2004, Proposition 66, a major attempt to reform the state's three-strikes law, was resoundingly defeated after the political establishment in California, including Governor Arnold Schwarzenegger and former governor Jerry Brown, rallied against the measure in the final days before the election. They joined a well-funded campaign against Proposition 66 spearheaded by conservative victims' groups allied with the California Correctional Peace Officers Association (CCPOA), arguably the most powerful union in the state and unquestionably the country's savviest correctional officers' union. The well-funded eleventh-hour blitz of television and radio commercials exploited negative racial stereotypes and fearsome images of reviled criminals to defeat the measure.[125]

The defeat of Proposition 66 raised broader questions about how best to challenge mass imprisonment in the United States. Should penal reformers concentrate on high-profile campaigns that may be defeated but may help to build a successful political movement to challenge the carceral state over the long run? Or should they concentrate on below-the-radar efforts that attract less public attention and controversy? Following the defeat of Proposition 66, several lawyers and law students centered at Stanford Law School turned to the courts to win the release of some third-strikers. Their primary weapon was a 1998 ruling by the California Supreme Court. It permits trial judges in three-strikes cases to weigh whether mitigating factors, such as a defendant's "background, character and prospects," place him or her outside the "spirit" of three strikes.[126] The Stanford Three Strikes Project has litigated other aspects of the three-strikes law in both state and federal courts.[127] It has concentrated its legal efforts on gaining the release of sympathetic third-strikers "who haven't done terrible things, who haven't actually hurt anyone," according to defense attorney Michael Romano, who helped found the Stanford clinic.[128]

In 2011–12, the Stanford Three Strikes Project emerged as the nucleus of another high-profile political effort to amend California's three-strikes law. Proposition 36, which California voters approved by a wide margin in November 2012, was much more narrowly drawn than Proposition 66. Its advocates sought to attract the support or buy the silence of key members of the political establishment who had opposed the earlier initiative to reform the three-strikes law.[129] The district attorneys of the state's three largest cities, including Republican Steve Cooley of Los Angeles, came out in favor of the ballot measure. The California State Sheriffs' Association publicly opposed Proposition 36, as did the California District Attorneys Association and almost all of the state's other district attorneys. Democratic governor Jerry Brown and the correctional officers' union, fierce opponents of Proposition 66 in 2004, remained largely silent on Proposition 36.

Like its predecessor, Proposition 36 called for restricting felonies that trigger a third strike to offenses that are violent or serious crimes. Unlike its predecessor, however, Proposition 36 also included some relatively minor offenses, notably burglaries of unoccupied homes, in that category. In addition, under Proposition 36, someone who had previously been convicted of a serious crime such as rape, murder, or child molestation and then subsequently was convicted of *any* listed felony, including a trivial infraction such as shoplifting, could receive a 25-years-to-life sentence. For third-strikers previously convicted of less serious offenses, Proposition 36 would restrict the use of the 25-years-to-life third-strike penalty to a third offense that was serious or violent and not simply a felony. These third-strikers would now face a doubling of penalties, rather than a life sentence. Notably, Proposition 36 did not alter the existing second-strike provision, which doubles the sentence length for many second-strike offenders, even if the second offense is not serious or violent.[130]

In promoting Proposition 36, supporters focused on the third-strikers who had not done "terrible" things. They also employed some of the negative, demonizing language that opponents of Proposition 66 had used in 2004. "We're making absolutely sure that these (hard-core) criminals get no benefit whatsoever from the reform, no matter what third strike they commit," implored Dan Newman, a spokesman for the Proposition 36 campaign.[131] Feeding into popular beliefs that people who have committed the most serious crimes are irredeemable, they stressed how "[n]o rapists, murders [sic], or child molesters will benefit from Prop. 36."[132] Advocates of Proposition 36 also made the strategic decision to distance themselves from a more controversial criminal justice measure that also was on the ballot in November 2012—Proposition 34, which would have abolished the death penalty in California and which was ultimately rejected by voters.[133]

The Proposition 36 victory was symbolically important. It was only the second time in a century that California voters had backed a ballot initiative that ratcheted sentences down, compared with the nearly forty times they had endorsed tougher measures at the polls.[134] For all the talk about Proposition 36 heralding a new direction in penal policy, the measure is unlikely to result in the release of many lifers and other long-timers because it was so narrowly drawn. California's Legislative Analyst's Office projected that approximately 2,000 people would probably be released thanks to Proposition 36. Other experts estimated that the number might be as few as several hundred—not even 1 percent of the state prison population. This would leave the vast majority of third-strikers and second-strikers serving long—and in many cases lifelong—sentences.[135] As Los Angeles District Attorney Cooley commented, Proposition 36 is "a very modest reform of a very good tool" that will protect the three-strikes law from future court challenges and more comprehensive reforms such as Proposition 66.[136]

The "Worst of the Worst"

What to do about "the worst of the worst" lurks in the background of any discussion of life sentences. For many years, arguments about the "worst of the worst" dominated all discussions of capital punishment. Likewise, simply reciting the names Charles Manson, Jeffrey Dahmer, Ted Bundy, and Hannibal Lecter is enough to abort any serious discussion about developing political and legislative strategies to challenge the fundamental legitimacy of *all* LWOP sentences and of *all* life sentences that are not subject to meaningful parole reviews.

Arguments about the worst of the worst arise in many discussions of penal reform, even though the Ted Bundys, Charles Mansons, and Jeffrey Dahmers are exceptional cases. Most people sentenced to life or the death penalty are not "monstrous others" who pose infinite threats to public safety that only can be contained by executing them or warehousing them until the end of their days.[137] Homicide is a very serious crime "typically performed by relatively ordinary people" who are caught up in "deviant and criminal group dynamics" or in "hostile and stressful, even threatening," relationships.[138] As Catherine A. Appleton concludes in her study of lifers in Britain, "even those who have committed some of the gravest crimes are capable of, and do, change."[139] A significant minority of lifers have not even been convicted of murder, as elaborated earlier.

In discussions of the worst of the worst, the three key issues are retribution, risk, and political reality. Some people mistakenly interpret calls to abolish all LWOP sentences and to entitle all prisoners to a parole eligibility hearing after a certain number of years as an assault on the whole idea of retribution. For decades retribution has been a guiding principle, if not the preeminent philosophy, of the criminal justice system in the United States.

The retribution issue is familiar from debates over capital punishment. As demonstrated most starkly with the death penalty, what constitutes an acceptable punishment is culturally, politically, and socially constructed and thus varies enormously over time. Centuries ago, mere execution was not enough to express society's reprobation. The condemned often were publicly tortured and mutilated. Then their bodies were dissected for good measure and left on public display. By contrast, the maximum sentence available today to the International Criminal Court, which tries the gravest of crimes, including war crimes, genocide, and crimes against humanity, is a life sentence reviewable every twenty-five years.[140] Under California law, Charles Manson has been receiving a parole eligibility hearing every two years for decades, as has Sirhan Sirhan, who assassinated Senator Robert F. Kennedy of New York when he was running for president in 1968. Their parole hearings are hardly a sign that California, whose prison population has increased by more than 800 percent since Manson and Sirhan were sent away, has somehow forsaken retribution. As Dan Markel argues, retributive justice, properly understood, "hinges on modesty and dignity in modes of punishment" and is at odds with "the apparently ineluctable slide towards ever-harsher punishments in the name of justice."[141]

Unlike in the United States, several European countries make explicit the relative weights of retribution and risk in meting out life sentences. England and Wales, for example, have adopted a two-part process in which the court sets a minimum term for the purposes of deterrence and retribution. "However, once that period has been served, the release of the offender must be considered by a judicial body that meets the requirements of due process similar to those of a full trial but considers only the danger that the offender may still present to the public," as Catherine Appleton and Bent Grøver explain.[142]

In Germany, all life-sentenced prisoners are constitutionally entitled to be considered for release after fifteen years. If someone does not still pose a major threat to public safety and was not convicted of crimes involving "exceptional gravity of guilt," he or she is usually set free after serving fifteen years. Crimes involving "exceptional gravity of guilt" include multiple homicides and instances of particularly cruel, brutal, reckless, or antisocial acts. "In practice, most prisoners whose guilt is so exceptionally grave will serve 18 or 20 years," according to Frieder Dünkel and Ineke Pruin.[143] As of 2007, approximately 2,000 people in Germany were serving life sentences—around the same number as in the state of Mississippi, whose total population is barely 4 percent of Germany's population.[144]

A movement to abolish life imprisonment has been active for some time in Germany. It has focused on the need for limits on the legitimate power of the state to punish. One of its central contentions is that life sentences violate a key provision of the German Constitution, which declares, "Human dignity is inviolable. To respect and protect it is the duty of all state authority."[145]

Survey and public opinion research indicate that when people are asked about what they think are appropriate sentences, they tend to think of the worst cases of murder, which then generate the most punitive responses.[146] But public opinion may not be as daunting an obstacle to curtailing or abolishing the use of life sentences as it initially appears. There is a vast difference between informed and uninformed public opinion. Recent experiment-based research on public opinion found that the more knowledgeable respondents were about the particulars of a crime and punishment, the less punitive they tended to be. Even a brief communication that took just a few seconds to read had a "demonstrable effect" in dampening public enthusiasm for a life sentence.[147] This observation suggests that it may be possible to shift public opinion on lifers with messages that are brief enough to be adapted to a mass media environment.[148]

Executive Clemency, Risk, and the Waning of Mercy

Governors and other public officials remain deeply opposed to releasing serious and long-time offenders, no matter how many decades they have served behind bars, no matter the pile of evidence showing that they have turned their lives around, and no matter the compelling research findings about deterrence and aging out of crime. In 2008, Governor Schwarzenegger and prosecutors in California vehemently opposed the compassionate release of Susan Atkins, a former follower of Charles Manson who was convicted of the infamous 1969 Tate-LaBianca murders. Atkins, who was paralyzed and dying of brain cancer, had become a model prisoner during her forty years behind bars. After he refused to commute Atkins's sentence when she was gravely ill, Schwarzenegger said, "[T]hose kinds of crimes are just so unbelievable that I'm not for compassionate release."[149] For Schwarzenegger and many other politicians, the retributive endpoint for certain crimes is infinity.

Over the past forty years or so, a narrow conception of retribution has become a central feature of U.S. penal policy, supplanting rehabilitation and even public safety as the chief aims of the criminal justice system. Mercy, forgiveness, and redemption, which have been central considerations in religious, philosophical, and political debates about punishment for centuries—indeed millennia—have been sidelined. This shift is starkly evident not only in the sharp drop in the use of executive clemency but also in the marked change in how public officials justify the few pardons and commutations that they do grant.

Pardons and commutations were vital features of the U.S. criminal justice system throughout the nineteenth century and much of the twentieth century. Executive clemency was a key mechanism to manage the prison population, correct miscarriages of justice, restore the rights of former offenders, and make far-reaching public statements about the criminal justice system.[150] Presidents and governors continued to wield their powers of executive clemency even in the face of public uproars over particular pardons or commutations. On Christmas Day in 1912, Governor George Donaghey of Arkansas, a fierce opponent of convict leasing, "pardoned 360 state prisoners in one fell swoop" in a gesture that made national headlines.[151] In the 1930s, at the height of the Jim Crow era, Governor Mike Con-

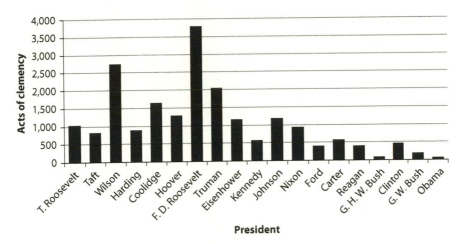

Figure 8.1. Individual Acts of Clemency by Presidents, 1901–January 2014

Source: Preliminary figures from George Lardner, Jr., and P. S. Ruckman, Jr., *Guilty No More* (New York: Public Affairs, forthcoming). Includes individual pardons, commutations, respites, remissions, and reprieves but not amnesties or general pardons.

ner traveled to Parchman Farm to investigate the "forgotten men" of Mississippi's infamous penal farm. At his "mercy courts," Conner freed dozens of black prisoners in the face of charges that he was granting "amnesty for ancient coons."[152]

In the first half of the twentieth century, Presidents Woodrow Wilson, Franklin D. Roosevelt, and Harry Truman issued hundreds and in some cases thousands of pardons and commutations. The number began to ebb during the Eisenhower administration and severely dropped off with President George H. W. Bush and his successors (see figure 8.1).[153] At the dawn of his sixth year in office in late 2013, President Barack Obama had by far the worst record on executive clemency since the modern era of pardons and commutations began more than a century ago (see figure 8.2).[154] A 2011 ProPublica investigation of federal pardons granted during the previous decade documented how "the pardon process has devolved into a mockery of itself; riven by arbitrariness, racial disparity, and charges of abuse."[155] ProPublica calculated that whites seeking presidential pardons have been nearly four times as likely to succeed as minorities. African Americans had by far the poorest chance of receiving executive clemency.[156] In what may portend a shift for the Obama administration in early 2014, it requested that defense attorneys suggest inmates in low-level drug cases who should be considered for executive clemency.[157]

Executive clemency is largely a thing of the past at the state level as well. Pennsylvania is one of six states in which life means life because all life sentences meted out to adults are automatically LWOP sentences. Since the early 1970s, the state's

President	Rate
Richard Nixon	1 in 3
Gerald Ford	1 in 4
Jimmy Carter	1 in 5
Ronald Reagan	1 in 8
George H. W. Bush	1 in 19
Bill Clinton	1 in 16
George W. Bush	1 in 55
Barack Obama	1 in 175

Figure 8.2. Grants of Presidential Executive Clemency, per Application for Pardon or Commutation, since 1968

Source: "Updated Clemency Statistics," Pardon Power blog, http://www.pardonpower .com/2014/03/updated-clemency statistics.html (retrieved March 12, 2014). Data available through March 5, 2014.

lifer population has increased elevenfold.[158] Between 1967 and 1994, Pennsylvania's governors and pardon board commuted the life sentences of nearly 400 inmates.[159] Since then, only six commutations have been granted. Democrat Ed Rendell commuted only five life sentences during his two terms as governor.[160] Rendell and his predecessors vigorously battled a lawsuit filed on behalf of inmates sentenced prior to 1997, before the commutation rules changed considerably. That lawsuit dragged on for more than twelve years—or about as long as a typical Pennsylvania lifer spent in prison in the 1970s before being released.[161]

In 2004, the American Bar Association's Justice Kennedy Commission wisely recommended that states and the federal government revitalize the clemency process. It urged them "to establish standards and provide an accessible process by which prisoners may request a reduction of sentence in exceptional circumstances." These included but were not limited to "old age, disability, changes in the law, exigent family circumstances, heroic acts, or extraordinary suffering." The commission also called for instituting procedures to help prisoners seeking clemency.[162]

Standardizing clemency procedures and providing prisoners with more assistance to navigate the process are noble goals. On their own, however, they will not revitalize the use of clemency or considerably reduce the lifer and long-timer population. Public officials need to be willing to assume the political risks that come with granting executive clemency. Years ago, governors and presidents were willing to weather charges of being antidemocratic or corrupt when they invoked their clemency powers. Now that crime has become such a persistent political tripwire in the United States, government officials need to steel themselves—and prepare the public—for the rare but inevitable instance when a released prisoner goes on to commit a front-page crime.

Although the recidivism rate for older inmates who have served lengthy sentences is comparatively lower, it is not—and never will be—zero. Despite all the attention focused on developing better risk-assessment tools, we will never be able to predict with complete certainty who will commit a serious crime if released and who will not. Lifers are not likely to kill or assault in prison or after release. However, a few will.[163] If public officials are going to revitalize executive clemency and parole, they must improve their rehabilitation programs and risk-assessment tools. They also must do more to educate the public that inmates who are released after serving lengthy terms are unlikely to commit violent offenses, but they are not risk-free.

Governors who are willing to assume that risk remain the exception. Since returning to the governor's mansion in 2011, Jerry Brown (D-CA) has been paroling lifers at a much higher rate than his predecessors did.[164] Governor Janet Granholm (D-MI) and Governor Mike Huckabee (R-AR) granted many more clemencies than their predecessors.[165] More typical is Governor Deval Patrick (D-MA), who after seven years in office had yet to grant a single pardon or commutation for any offender, let alone a lifer.[166] At the end of his first three years in office, Governor Andrew Cuomo (D-NY) finally used his clemency powers to grant his first three pardons—all to people who were no longer serving time.[167] Governor Rick Perry (R-TX) has rejected about two-thirds of the clemency recommendations from the Texas Board of Pardons and Parole. That board is composed of his political appointees and is not known for being soft on crime and punishment.[168]

Some public officials have expressed interest in early release of infirm or elderly inmates who do not pose a threat to society. By late 2009, fifteen states and the District of Columbia had established provisions for geriatric release. However, these jurisdictions have rarely released elderly inmates due to many factors. These include political considerations, public opinion, the narrow criteria for eligibility, Byzantine procedures, and the complicated and lengthy referral and review process that often drags on right up until an inmate dies in prison.[169] A major obstacle is that older prisoners are more likely to have been incarcerated for a serious violent offense. A 2006 report on North Carolina prisoners found that almost 60 percent of inmates aged fifty and older were serving time for violent or sex crimes. More than half of them were serving a sentence of life or ten years to life.[170]

Released long-time prisoners do not pose a major public threat, but they do pose a potential risk to political careers. Huckabee's commutation and pardon record came under national scrutiny and spurred a spate of political obituaries after a man he had granted clemency to in 2000 killed four police officers in Tacoma, Washington, in 2009. After a released parolee shot and killed a Massachusetts police officer in December 2010, Governor Patrick replaced much of the parole board with law enforcement appointees and introduced legislation that would further restrict parole eligibility for lifers in the Bay State. Patrick appointed a former prosecutor to head the parole board, which quickly adopted tougher new guidelines for release. The governor also successfully pushed for passage of one of the toughest three-strikes laws in the country, as discussed earlier.[171]

Changes in the institutional structure of parole and pardon boards could provide public officials with some important political insulation from potentially controversial release decisions. States almost always staff these boards with political appointees, who are extremely vulnerable to the wrath of public opinion. In 1968, the President's Commission on Law Enforcement and the Administration of Justice recommended that the boards be composed of psychologists, social workers, corrections officials, and other professionals with specialized training and expertise to evaluate offenders' suitability for release. That recommendation remains largely unrealized. In nearly every state, governors appoint all members of the parole board.[172] Two-thirds of the states have no professional qualifications for parole board membership.[173] Another major issue is that many states now require the governor to sign off personally on any decision by a parole or commutation board to release a lifer. This puts the governor directly in the line of political fire if a paroled or commuted offender goes on to commit a major crime. Grants of discretionary parole have plummeted—from a high mark of 72 percent of all prisoners released in 1977 to a bottoming out of just 23 percent in 2008.[174] This is thanks to wide-ranging statutory changes that eliminated parole for certain offenders and to a "palpable and growing reluctance on the part of parole boards" to release inmates before they complete serving their maximum sentence.

As Senator James Webb (D-VA) once said at a conference on prisoner reentry, "The real question is about fear. And I think it invades the political process."[175] Politicians and public officials can help neutralize that fear by educating the public about the nuances of deterrence, the limited utility of lengthy sentences for fighting crime, the phenomenon of aging out of crime, and the strengths and limits of risk-assessment tools. However, they cannot guarantee that releasing offenders will be risk-free. As Glenn Martin of the Fortune Society once said, "[W]e need to increase our appetite for risk. . . . [W]e have to at least accept the fact that some people are going to fail and some people are going to fail pretty significantly."[176]

The public's and politicians' low appetite for risk is not the only obstacle to expanding the use of executive clemency and rethinking the practice of condemning so many people to the "other death penalty." As several observers have noted, the retributive theory of clemency has been ascendant for some time now.[177] There is a widespread belief that clemency should be used only to remedy "miscarriages of justice," as Supreme Court Justice William Rehnquist said.[178] Governors are largely unwilling to treat mercy as a permissible reason for granting clemency. The few commutations and pardons that are granted today are frequently justified as a means to rectify some shortcoming of the judicial process: The offender is innocent or has a credible claim of innocence; he or she did not receive a fair trial; or the sentence is disproportionately severe compared with what other participants in the crime received.[179] These "anti-mercy conceptions of clemency" wholly reject redemption, forgiveness, reconciliation, and mercy as legitimate claims for clemency, greatly narrowing the pool of prisoners who might petition for a pardon or commutation.[180] But they do more than that.

The impact of executive clemency extends far beyond all the individuals lucky enough—or not—to receive a pardon or commutation. Executive clemency is an important vehicle with which to make a statement about the criminal justice system and, more broadly, about what kind of society we want. As such, it shapes the wider political environment in which issues of crime and punishment are debated, and criminal justice policy is forged. Governor Donaghey's wholesale pardon a century ago was intended as a searing denunciation of Alabama's brutal system of convict leasing. Woodrow Wilson was an ardent supporter of temperance but opposed the Volstead Act, which imposed Prohibition. As president, he pardoned hundreds of alcohol-related offenders.[181] His pardons were widely understood at the time as an indictment of Prohibition. In one of the most notable acts of mercy and forgiveness, President Jimmy Carter enraged veterans' groups the day after his inauguration in 1977 by fulfilling a campaign pledge to grant a broad amnesty to the tens of thousands of people who had dodged the draft to avoid military service during the Vietnam War. Governors Lee Cruce of Oklahoma (1911–1915), Winthrop Rockefeller of Arkansas (1967–1971), and Toney Anaya of New Mexico (1983–1987) issued mass commutations to empty their death rows. They justified their actions with calls for mercy for the condemned.[182] By contrast, of the four dozen executive commutations granted to people sentenced to death between 1976 and 2003, "only four were based on what could arguably be characterized as merciful reasons."[183]

When Illinois Governor George Ryan pardoned four inmates on death row and commuted the sentences of 167 others in 2003, he rejected "mercy and compassion as legitimate responses to criminals."[184] He said his actions were warranted because of problems in the way capital punishment was administered, not because the death penalty was fundamentally immoral. At the time, Ryan went out of his way to reaffirm his law-and-order credentials and to herald life in prison without the possibility of parole as a fate perhaps worse than death.[185]

In a 2003 speech to the American Bar Association, Supreme Court Justice Anthony Kennedy lamented, "The pardon process, of late, seems to have been drained of its moral force."[186] As a consequence, many crimes remain eternally unforgivable and unforgettable. Their perpetrators are forever defined by the crime, despite all the evidence accumulating over the decades that they are not the same people who committed those crimes, and that they do not pose major threats to public safety.

Capital Punishment and the "Other Death Penalty"

The tenacity of capital punishment in the United States poses an additional challenge to reducing the lifer population. Over the years, many leading abolitionists have ardently supported LWOP. They have uncritically accepted LWOP as a viable alternative to the death penalty. In doing so, they have helped to legitimize the wider use of a sentence that has many features in common with capital punishment.

These abolitionists have helped normalize a sanction that, like the death penalty, does not accord with human rights and sentencing norms in other advanced industrialized countries. In Western Europe, the number of life sentences did increase in the wake of the abolition of capital punishment, most notably in the United Kingdom, but remained considerably lower than in the United States.[187]

One has to be careful about how much blame to apportion to death penalty abolitionists for the proliferation of life sentences in the United States, however. Seven states already had LWOP statutes on the books or in practice prior to the 1972 *Furman* decision, which declared that capital punishment as then practiced in the United States was unconstitutional. Some of these statutes dated back to the nineteenth century.[188] The increasingly punitive climate in the aftermath of *Furman* helps explain why more states enacted LWOP or tougher life statutes. But the timing and triggering events appear to have varied enormously among the states.[189]

Neither opponents nor supporters of capital punishment could have predicted the fierce conservative backlash after the *Furman* decision or how it would spur the push for more punitive penal policies.[190] At that time, the abolitionist movement was not really a movement at all but rather a consortium of elite public-interest lawyers. They could not have done much to stem the punitive stampede in the immediate wake of *Furman* as states rewrote their death penalty statutes and began to rethink life sentences. Moreover, executive clemency still appeared to be a viable mechanism to secure the release of many lifers. Abolitionists could endorse LWOP or a life sentence as an alternative to capital punishment, figuring that most lifers—even those serving LWOP sentences—would be released after a decade or two at the most.[191] Indeed, there was an expectation that as states returned to determinate sentencing systems, the importance of executive clemency as a release mechanism was likely to grow.[192]

Abolitionists helped establish the legitimacy of LWOP in the 1970s, 1980s, and 1990s but in most cases were probably incidental to the final legislative outcome. Some abolitionists ardently opposed promoting LWOP as an alternative to the death penalty. As long-time abolitionist Hugo Adam Bedau once declared, "The death penalty is not the only outrageous form of punishment active in our society, even if it is the worst."[193] A number of prominent abolitionists, including Governor Mario Cuomo (D-NY), Sister Helen Prejean of *Dead Man Walking* fame, and Steven Brill, the founder of *The American Lawyer*, enthusiastically promoted LWOP as an equally tough—or even tougher—sanction.[194] Leading abolitionist organizations generally took an ambiguous or agnostic position on LWOP in the 1980s and 1990s.[195]

Capital defense attorneys have been vested in retaining LWOP. Evidence suggests that the possibility of parole in capital cases, however remote, is often a key factor for jurors when deciding whether to impose the death penalty or a life sentence. In those death penalty states where LWOP is an alternative option, capital defense attorneys, in making their pitch for life over death, often emphasize how the defendant will never be released from prison. Some of them also stress that a life sentence that stretches out for decades is actually more punitive than condemning someone to death. Prosecutors in capital punishment states have been some of the fiercest opponents of LWOP statutes. In states where parole is a possibility—however remote—for life-sentenced offenders, prosecutors often focus their closing arguments on warnings about the future threat the defendant poses if released on parole.[196] This commonplace prosecutorial strategy spurs jurors to choose death over life.[197]

LWOP statutes appear to have played only a minor role in the recent drop in the number of executions in the United States. But they probably have contributed to a doubling or even tripling of the sentence lengths for offenders who never would have been sentenced to death in the first place or even been eligible for the death penalty.[198] Lifers currently serve an average of twenty-nine years in prison, up from approximately twenty-one years in 1991.[199] In revising its Model Penal Code, the American Law Institute, an organization composed of leading judges, lawyers, and legal scholars, reluctantly gave its support to LWOP. But it was careful to say that LWOP was only warranted in those few cases in which the defendant would otherwise receive the death penalty.[200]

The exploding lifer population and the growing understanding of the similarities between how life sentences and death sentences are imposed and on whom have not prompted a fundamental rethinking of the connections between death penalty abolitionism and penal reform more broadly. Attorney Barry Scheck, a leading figure in the innocence movement, and other foes of capital punishment did not raise any critical questions about New Jersey's growing lifer population when they appeared before the state's Death Penalty Study Commission in 2006.[201] In 2012, abolitionists celebrated Connecticut's repeal of the death penalty. Less widely known is an alarming provision in the repeal legislation that requires the LWOP sentences that replaced capital punishment to be served under supermax-type conditions.[202]

The abolitionist movement still operates quite independently of the wider penal reform movement to roll back the carceral state. Typical of many mainstream abolitionist organizations, Amnesty International remains notably agnostic on the question of alternatives to the death penalty, except in the case of JLWOP, which it has stridently opposed. In 2002, Amnesty International rejected a recommendation by its own internal review committee to "initiate a thorough discussion of alternatives to the death penalty." It did so even though its unwillingness to recommend or oppose substitute punishments might be undermining "the credibility of its overall argument for abolition."[203] Number ten on the National Coalition Against the Death Penalty's list of "Ten Reasons Why Capital Punishment Is Flawed Public Policy" is: "Life without parole is a sensible alternative to the death penalty."[204] The Campaign to End the Death Penalty is one of the few anti-death penalty organizations that clearly opposes replacing the death penalty with LWOP.[205]

Noted abolitionist and capital defense attorney David R. Dow stridently denounced the campaign on behalf of California's Proposition 34, the 2012 ballot initiative to repeal the death penalty and replace it with LWOP. "The justifications given by death penalty opponents who have embraced life without parole reveal the extent to which abolitionists have surrendered the moral basis of their position," he argued.[206] Dow noted that many inmates on California's death row opposed the measure. If enacted, California's 725 death row inmates would have automatically lost their right to state-appointed lawyers to pursue their habeas corpus appeals.[207]

The Other Death Penalty Project, founded in 2008 and composed exclusively of prisoners, has called on death penalty abolitionist groups to stop promoting LWOP as a "supposedly humane alternative to lethal injection." The group rejects the proposition that LWOP "is a necessary first step toward ultimate abolition of the death penalty."[208] Kenneth E. Hartman, the group's founder, describes a life sentence as an "execution in the form of a long, deliberate stoning that goes on for as long as I draw breath."[209]

In deciding how best to challenge the proliferation of LWOP sentences and whether to declare all such sentences unacceptable, penal reformers certainly need to consider the realities of the broader political environment. But as Hugo Adam Bedau reminds us, "[I]t is not the task of penal reform—or of the movement against the death penalty—to present to the public whatever it will accept. The task, rather, is to argue for a punitive policy that is humane, feasible, and effective, whatever the crime and whoever the offender, and regardless of the current climate of public opinion."[210]

In keeping with that spirit, one of the premier penal reform groups in the United States recently made an important shift in its stance on the abolition of LWOP. The Sentencing Project has published three path-breaking reports on life sentences that have been invaluable in drawing public, journalistic, and scholarly attention to this invisible issue. In the first report, The Sentencing Project called for abolishing LWOP sentences "in all but exceptional cases."[211] In the follow-up reports, it recommended eliminating *all* LWOP sentences.[212]

The prospects are bleak that the plight of lifers and the large number of other people serving extraordinarily long sentences will become a leading issue on the penal reform agenda any time soon. This political quiescence in the face of exponential growth in the lifer population is particularly striking given the intense legal and political mobilization against capital punishment over the years. Thanks in part to the innocence movement, with its intense focus on people wrongly condemned to death, the use of the death penalty in this country is declining. The number of people executed each year has fallen by more than half since the high point in the late 1990s, and public opinion polls show that support for capital punishment is waning.[213] There are currently approximately 3,100 inmates on death row in the United States. Nearly all of them will die in prison of natural causes or suicide—not lethal injection. Compare that number with the nearly 160,000 people now serving life sentences in the United States. The reinstatement and transformation of capital punishment have been central legal and political issues for nearly forty years. Meanwhile, the United States has been nonchalantly condemning tens of thousands of people to the "other death penalty" with barely a legal or political whimper.

Conclusion

Maintaining and reinforcing the distinction between the non, non, nons and other offenders perpetuates the idea that there is a "dangerous class" of people who must be contained at all costs. The term "dangerous classes" was coined nearly a century and a half ago but has much deeper roots in U.S. history.[214] Being black and being cast as dangerous has a long and nearly uninterrupted history dating back to the days of slavery. Periodically certain other groups have been singled out as particularly dangerous, including Chinese immigrants, Mexican Americans, and people from southern and eastern Europe during the various campaigns against opium, marijuana, Zoot suits, and organized crime in the late nineteenth and early twentieth centuries.

Meaningful penal reform ultimately has to rest on "abandoning the discourse of the dangerous classes and avoiding even the temptation to claim it for progressive purposes."[215] Unfortunately, the main thrust of penal reform seems to be moving in the opposite direction toward drawing clear and often unwarranted distinctions between the non, non, nons and other offenders, as discussed in this chapter. With the emergence of new wars against sex offenders and immigrants, additional categories of offenders are being defined as dangerous and in need of being confined, contained, internally exiled, or deported, as discussed in the next two chapters.

CHAPTER NINE

The New Untouchables

The War on Sex Offenders

Now if you are to punish a man retributively, you must injure him. If you are
to reform him, you must improve him. And men are not improved by injuries.

—GEORGE BERNARD SHAW

Over the past two decades, sex offenders have become a major target of political energy and public fears in the United States. It is hard to
imagine a group of offenders that has fewer advocates than they do. De-
spised, vilified, and misrepresented in the media, sex offenders are widely viewed
as noncitizens entitled to little more than a "bare life" that has been "stripped of
the political and legal rights" that shield much of the rest of the society.[1] The incapacitation, containment, and banishment of convicted sex offenders dominate
discussions of how to stem sexual abuse in the United States.

The broader public has been a willing conscript in this new war on sex offenders, which has uncanny parallels with the war on drugs. These include the unbridled demonization of a group of offenders, skyrocketing incarceration rates for
sex offenses, eroding civil liberties, and the federalization of what had once been
largely a matter for local or state law enforcement.[2] Evidence-based research and
budgetary considerations have been no match for politicians, other public figures,
and members of the media willing to exploit public fears of sex offenders for political and other payoffs.[3]

One important difference is that the war on sex offenders does not fit readily into the new Jim Crow framework for understanding the origins and tenacity
of the carceral state. In the war on sex offenders, legislators and policy makers
have been less likely to invoke reflexively the racially coded language that they employed so often in the war on drugs to justify locking up so many young black men
and women.[4] Major sex offender laws tend to valorize white victims—especially
young white women and girls, who are memorialized in the names of many of
these laws.[5] But these measures have disproportionately swept up older white men,
not young men and women of color.[6]

Another difference is that registered sex offenders are subject to an Alice-in-
Wonderland maze of civil commitment laws, and community notification, registration, and residency restrictions that amount to a kind of ritual exile.[7] The
punitive maze of laws and restrictions that ensnare sex offenders in the United

States is exceptional. No other industrialized democracy imposes such lengthy criminal sanctions on sex offenders or keeps them so ensnared long after they have completed their criminal sentences. Thanks to the undifferentiated view of sex offenders that now prevails, the war on sex offenders imposes tough sanctions and restrictions on a wide array of infractions classified as "sex offenses"—everything from making obscene phone calls to urinating in public to consensual sex between teenagers to the rape and murder of a child.[8]

Intense campaigns against sex offenders are not something new in U.S. history. In the 1930s and 1940s, "sexual psychopaths" were a central target.[9] This earlier moral crusade against sexual psychopaths was incredibly vociferous at the rhetorical level. But its punitive consequences on the ground were relatively mild compared to today's war on sex offenders.

Chrysanthi Leon and others have identified important institutional and political differences between then and now that help explain why. In the 1950s, the view of sex offenders as psychopaths who needed to be incapacitated was dominant but not hegemonic. Alternative views that stressed sex offenders' potential for rehabilitation and reintegration, sanctions other than incarceration, and public education campaigns to stem sexual abuse were not entirely silenced in public discussions.[10] Thanks to the absence of single-issue victims' rights groups, policy makers and law enforcement officials at the time "were sufficiently insulated from the public and sufficiently confident in the legal system's ability to deliver justice that they could acquiesce in public but resist in practice more calls for harsh sanctions against sex offenders."[11] That changed in the 1980s with the emergence of a well-endowed and well-connected victims' rights movement with strong connections to law enforcement, especially prosecutors, that was centered on imposing severe sanctions on sex offenders.[12]

As discussed in this chapter, the latest war on sex offenders has employed three main weapons: tougher sentences across the board, registration and community notification laws, and indefinite civil commitment of sex offenders who have completed their criminal sentences. It also has legitimized the wider use of degrading punishments, including castration, a practice that had fallen into disuse in the United States because of its ignominious history associated with the Black Codes, the Jim Crow South, the Nazis, and the eugenics movement of a century ago.[13] Taken together, these measures amount to what some have characterized as an "apartheid regime" for convicted sexual offenders.[14] The spate of laws targeting sex offenders raises troubling questions about the misallocation of resources and about the creation of yet another group of permanent "internal exiles" or second-class citizens in the United States.

Rising Incarceration Rates for Sex Offenses

Over the years, the war on drugs bled into the rest of the criminal justice system. It paved the way for the wide-scale militarization of police forces and the evisceration of key constitutional protections in both drug and non-drug cases. It also set important precedents for radically expanding the prison beyond the prison that consigns released offenders to permanent second-class citizenship. Likewise, the war on sex offenders is setting important punitive precedents for expanding the prison beyond the prison not just for released sex offenders but also for a whole range of other groups and individuals deemed undesirable by law enforcement officers, government officials, and the broader public.

As discussed in earlier chapters, the war on drugs reached its zenith in the mid-1990s, after which arrest and incarceration rates for drug offenses began to fall. As the war on drugs started losing its momentum, states and the federal government were erecting an enormous legal and institutional architecture directed at sex offenders. Several high-profile sexual assaults and murders of children by strangers were important catalysts that helped propel the moral panic against sex offenders.

Rape-murder, especially of children, is an exceedingly rare crime. It is but "a thin sliver" of all sexual offenses committed in the United States.[15] But lawmakers, determined to do battle against an alleged epidemic of sexual violence against children by incorrigible pedophiles, enacted a stampede of tough measures beginning in the mid-1990s that swept up a wide range of sexual offenders. Leading public figures championed this cause, including talk-show host Oprah Winfrey, herself a survivor of child sexual abuse, and Fox television's Bill O'Reilly.[16]

Waging intense, large-scale moral panics against people and behavior singled out as sexually deviant is hardly something new in U.S. history. Government officials, politicians, other public figures, and the media have long portrayed sex offenders as people with "permanently depraved soul[s]" who are beyond redemption.[17] However, up until the 1970s or so, these moral panics ran their course without spurring major increases in imprisonment or other sanctions levied at sex offenders.

Between the 1930s and the early 1960s, "dirty old men" and "middle-aged sex fiends" were the primary targets of intense campaigns against "sexual psychopaths" that demonized them as monsters. These earlier sexual psychopath campaigns prompted passage of tough new laws aimed at sex-related crimes. But police generally did not respond by arresting more people for sex offenses. Furthermore, prosecutors and judges did not wield their new charging and sentencing prerogatives to get tougher on sex offenders, despite new laws that permitted them to do so. As a result, prison sentences and other punishments levied against people convicted of sex crimes did not jump markedly during these earlier campaigns against sexual psychopaths.[18] That began to change in the 1980s, as rapists and then pedophiles became the leading targets of moral panics. Pedophiles came to be viewed as interchangeable and synonymous with all sex offenders, despite the enormous range of offenses considered sex crimes.

This latest war against sex offenders has unfolded in two phases, as Leon explains. In the period running roughly between 1980 and the mid-1990s, sex crimes were not uniquely singled out for harsher sanctions. Much of the increase in punishments levied against sex offenders during this period was a consequence of a "tailwind effect" as tougher punishments were meted out across the board for all sorts of crimes, everything from drug abuse to homicide to child molestation.[19] Since the early 1990s, however, more sex offenders have been singled out as exceptional criminals deserving of exceptionally punitive penal and civil sanctions. As with the war on drugs and war on immigrants, the federal government has fostered joint operations with state and local law enforcement officers to pursue sex crimes. One of the most notable is Project Safe Childhood. Launched in 2006 by the U.S. Department of Justice, this program created partnerships with state and local authorities and nongovernmental organizations to investigate and prosecute Internet-based crimes against children.

Politicians and other public figures began mobilizing against an alleged epidemic of sexual abuse in the early 1990s despite official statistics showing that actual rates of rape and sexual assault were plummeting. After peaking in the 1980s, these rates fell considerably in a pattern that paralleled wider trends in violent crime.[20] Even though the rate of sex crimes was dropping, convictions for sex offenses increased by 400 percent between 1993 and 2000.[21] Nonrape sex offenses drove most of the increase in convictions and prison sentences for sex offenses.[22]

In the 1980s and 1990s, state-level incarceration rates for murder, sexual offenses, robbery, assault, burglary, and drugs generally continued to climb upward, but at varying rates. Between 2000 and 2010, however, incarceration rates for sex offenses continued to climb steadily while falling or stabilizing for these other offenses.[23] Thanks to tougher sanctions, sex offenders have become the fastest growing segment of state and federal prison populations. Between 10 and 20 percent of state prisoners are now serving time for sex offenses; in some states, however, the rate is nearly 30 percent.[24] The number of people serving time for possession of sexually explicit materials, typically child pornography, in the federal prison system increased more than sixtyfold between 1996 and 2010, compared to an 80 percent rise in drug offenses over this same period.[25]

Sentence lengths for sexual offenses have escalated at the state and federal levels thanks to tough new laws and sentencing guidelines. A number of states enacted two-strike laws specifically aimed at sex offenses and made more sex crimes eligible for a life sentence or the death penalty. The 2003 federal PROTECT Act included a two-strike provision that calls for a mandatory life sentence for most offenders convicted a second time of sexually abusing a child. It also made computer-generated child pornography that looks like the real thing a federal crime.[26] In 2010, the Ninth Circuit Court of Appeals ruled that a life sentence handed down to a Washington State man with a previous sex conviction who had briefly touched a five-year-old girl between her legs as she was going down a slide at a McDonald's play area was not grossly disproportionate under the state's two-strikes law.[27] In 2010, legislators in Oklahoma overwhelmingly approved a bill to permit the execution of repeat offenders who sexually abuse children. They were undeterred by the Supreme Court's decision two years earlier in *Kennedy v. Louisiana* that imposition of the death penalty in cases of child rape was unconstitutional.[28] In the wake of that decision, at least six other states considered legislation to impose the death penalty on people who sexually assault children.[29]

Nearly three dozen states have enacted some version of Jessica's Law. These statutes are modeled after Florida's 2005 Jessica Lunsford Act, which imposes a mandatory minimum of twenty-five years to life for certain sex offenses against children. That pioneering Florida law also required additional registration and monitoring requirements for released sex offenders and placed new restrictions on where they may live.[30] In 2006, California voters overwhelmingly approved their own version of Jessica's Law, despite fiscal projections included on the ballot initiative that the measure would cost the state hundreds of millions of dollars in coming years.[31] Four years later, California legislators voted unanimously for Chelsea's Law, which imposes further sanctions on sex offenders.[32]

States and the federal government have sharply increased their penalties for child pornography offenses, in some instances creating de facto life sentences for violations.[33] Several states and the federal government have set tough mandatory minimums for each illegal image. In Arizona, that minimum is ten years. Several years ago, an Arizona teacher with no prior criminal record received a 200-year sentence for possessing twenty such images.[34]

Hard to believe, but prior to the 1990s, simple possession of child pornography was not a federal crime. In 1990, Congress criminalized possession of child pornography for the first time. Over the next decade and a half, it successfully pushed to ramp up the statutory penalties and toughen the federal sentencing guidelines for child pornography offenses, against in some cases the recommendations and advice of the U.S. Sentencing Commission.[35] Federal case filings involving sexually explicit materials quickly soared, rising about seventeenfold between 1993 and 2013. Most of this increase was for receipt and possession of child pornography, not production and trafficking.[36]

As the number of federal child pornography cases skyrocketed, so did the severity of the sentences. In the early 1990s, a person without a criminal history who was convicted of possessing violent child pornography images and sharing them with others would face a maximum federal prison sentence of two years. Today, that same person could be looking at a sentence of twenty years or more.[37] The federal mandatory minimum sentence for receipt of child pornography is currently five years. The sanction for possession is zero to twenty years. But since the line between receipt and possession is thin or nonexistent, prosecutors have great leeway to charge these cases under the stiffer receipt category. In the overwhelming majority of child pornography cases, the actual sentence is much greater than five years due to aggravating factors stipulated in the federal sentencing guidelines. In 1996, the average federal sentence length for child pornography was about two-and-a-half years. In 2010, it was nearly three times that—surpassing sentence lengths for all other federal crimes except murder and kidnapping.[38] As one federal judge remarked, people who possess child pornography are being treated as "modern-day untouchables."[39]

Possession of child pornography has been conflated with actual child sex abuse, despite weak or inconsistent evidence about the likelihood that people who possess child pornography also sexually abuse children.[40] The vast majority of people convicted of receipt or possession of child pornography have little or no criminal history.[41] Conflating child pornography and sexual abuse of children has perpetuated the popular myth that stranger-danger is the main threat to children. It also has contributed to public misperceptions about what law enforcement is doing to successfully detect and prosecute sex offense cases that involve actual contact abuse of children.[42] The recommended sentences for viewing child pornography on a computer can actually be higher than the sentences received by people who troll online chat groups in search of minors to engage in sex with. In 2010, the average sentence for a federal child pornography conviction was actually a year longer than a federal conviction for actual sexual abuse.[43]

Civil Commitment Statutes

Lengthier prison sentences have been but one weapon in the war on sex offenders. Long after they have completed their criminal sentences, many sex offenders remain enmeshed in the carceral state and pariahs in their communities thanks to the wave of civil commitment, registration, residency, and community notification laws. For the most part, the courts have upheld these laws and have dismissed claims that they violate fundamental rights to due process, equal protection, and privacy.[44] At least twenty states and the federal government have enacted civil commitment laws directed at sex offenders, up from eight in 1998.[45] The number of people confined under civil commitment programs has mushroomed, as has the cost of these programs. Many civilly committed offenders are now serving de facto life sentences even though technically they have been released from prison.

In 1990, Washington State enacted a pioneering law that permits the authorities to send sex offenders to detention facilities for "treatment" after they have completed their prison sentences. A number of states considered and then rejected establishing their own civil commitment programs, largely because of opposition from professional groups, notably mental health professionals, and concerns about cost.[46] But in many states, budgetary concerns and evidence-based research that cast doubt on the efficacy of civil commitment to combat sexual abuse were incidental to the passage of so-called sexually violent predator statutes.

These laws are distinct in several ways from the civil commitment statutes that were a core feature of the "sexual psychopath" legislation enacted in the first half of the twentieth century and that had been largely rescinded by the 1980s. Today civil commitment is typically an add-on to the original prison sentence rather than an alternative to a criminal sanction, as it was years ago. Alleged sexual predators may be civilly committed even though they do not suffer from "a serious mental disorder," which was often a requirement of the earlier civil commitment laws. Furthermore, states are permitted to seek civil commitment based on offenses committed in the distant past—not just the recent past.[47] In some instances, offenders who have had no prior record of having been convicted of a sex offense have nonetheless been certified as "sexually dangerous" and thus candidates for civil commitment. Offenders serving time for no-contact sex offenses like possession of child pornography or making obscene calls also have been civilly committed.[48]

In some states, people who are checked into civil commitment programs are never checked out.[49] A New York State judge blasted the state's Office of Mental Health in 2010 for setting such high hurdles that people in civil commitment have little chance of qualifying for release and thus have little incentive to cooperate with treatment.[50] As of 2013, only one of the nearly 700 offenders committed under Minnesota's civil commitment program had been discharged in the eighteen years since this pioneering program was first established. In 2003, primary responsibility for making civil commitment decisions was shifted from Minnesota's Department of Corrections to the state's attorney general and its eighty-seven county attorneys, all of whom are elected public officials. After that change, the number of civilly committed sex offenders in Minnesota soared to the highest in the country on a per capita basis.[51] In June 2012, a British court refused to extradite a man accused of sexually assaulting three girls to face criminal charges in Minnesota because he might eventually end up in the state's controversial civil commitment program. In the court's view, this would amount to a life sentence and a "flagrant denial" of his human rights.[52] In late 2013, a state-appointed task force issued a report that was sharply critical of Minnesota's civil commitment program. It recommended a major overhaul or else risk a federal takeover because of potential constitutional violations.[53]

Critics contend that civil commitment statutes are actually "criminal laws masquerading as civil laws."[54] In their view, these statutes subject sex offenders who otherwise would be released from prison to further punishment, thus violating the double jeopardy and ex post facto protections of the Constitution. The U.S. Supreme Court largely rejected these arguments in its 1997 *Hendricks* decision. The Court upheld state civil commitment statutes as long as they were "non-punitive," and it accorded states wide berth to implement these statutes.[55]

The *Hendricks* decision rests on the claim that civil commitment laws are primarily civil, not criminal, in nature. As such, they do not run afoul of the constitutional protections accorded criminal defendants. Ironically, state civil commitment statutes that apply more broadly and that offer less protection for individual rights will "be *more* likely to be held constitutional."[56] In the Court's view, civil commitment laws that offered the "full panoply of constitutional safeguards of a criminal trial" would be deemed primarily criminal and punitive—not civil and non-punitive—and therefore unconstitutional.[57]

Since the courts have determined that civil commitment is a civil rather than a criminal proceeding, people who are candidates for possible civil commitment have fewer guaranteed rights. They are permitted to have defense counsel and to subpoena and cross-examine witnesses. They are not guaranteed other rights that are foundational in criminal proceedings, including the right to discovery, to remain silent, and to have a jury trial. In many states, civil commitment is a closed process, carried out without a jury or a public hearing. Many convicted sex offenders do not have legal representation at civil commitment proceedings because they are not entitled to an attorney if they are indigent. People facing civil commitment often languish in prison long after they have completed their criminal sentences because they are not entitled to bail or a speedy trial.[58] The U.S. Supreme Court raised no objections to keeping Graydon Earl Comstock, Jr. in federal prison for an additional three-and-a-half years after he had completed his child pornography sentence as he awaited the outcome of his civil commitment case.

The courts generally have not found fault with the vague criteria for determining when someone warrants release. They have tended to uphold the limited independent oversight of civil commitment decisions, even though many of the people who have been civilly committed are essentially serving de facto life sentences.[59] The constitutionality of civil commitment programs rests partly on the claim that successful completion of treatment programs is good cause for release. But in many states, offenders are confined to civil commitment units within prisons or prison-like complexes that do not offer any legitimate sexual offender treatment programs.[60] Even when treatment is available, many sex offenders are eschewing it because the courts have determined that any evidence obtained from in-prison treatment programs may be used against them in civil commitment hearings.[61]

In the 2010 *Comstock* decision, the Supreme Court determined that the federal civil commitment statute included as part of the 2006 Adam Walsh Act was constitutional. In its ruling, the Supreme Court strongly indicated that federal and state authorities have "virtually unfettered power to preventatively detain sex offenders."[62] The lower courts and the Bureau of Prisons have taken up these new powers with gusto. Federal regulations implementing the Adam Walsh Act grant the BOP the authority to designate anyone in federal custody as "sexually dangerous" and thus a candidate for possible civil commitment. The BOP reviewed the files of *all* inmates in federal custody—not just people convicted of sex crimes—to determine who might be a candidate for civil commitment. Although the Adam Walsh Act was ostensibly aimed at violent sex offenders, "nothing in the statute requires a person to have been convicted of such a crime."[63] The federal government has defined "sexually dangerous" quite capaciously to include offenses that do not involve violence or force, such as statutory rape and possession of child pornography. In making a case for civil commitment, the government is permitted to invoke offenses for which someone in federal custody was never charged or convicted.[64]

States and the federal government also are permitted to set the burden of proof in civil commitment cases much lower than in criminal proceedings. The federal government, for example, has adopted a standard of "clear and convincing evidence" in civil commitment proceedings rather than the more rigorous "beyond a reasonable doubt" that prevails in criminal proceedings. Due to the lower burden of proof and the fewer rights accorded to defendants in civil proceedings, the government has a tempting incentive to transfer certain cases onto the civil commitment track where it has a better chance of success. Corey Yung provides several examples of how federal authorities have been doing just that.[65]

Sexual predator commitment programs and facilities tend to be expensive compared to the costs of a typical state prison. In many states, they have been consuming a large and growing portion of the total resources available to combat sexual abuse and domestic violence while addressing only a small portion of the problem. In 2010, the twenty states that have civil commitment programs for sex offenders spent nearly $500 million to confine and treat the 5,200 people in these programs.[66] To put that figure in some perspective, all the major federal funding for domestic and sexual violence programs, which is funneled largely through the Violence Against Women Act (VAWA), totaled about $413 million in fiscal 2012.[67]

The average cost of confining a sexual offender in a civil commitment program is four times that of keeping someone in jail or prison.[68] In some states, the costs are astronomical—about $175,000 per person each year in New York State and California.[69] In 2004, California spent nearly $80 million to confine 535 people at $400 per day under its civil commitment program. The following year, California constructed a 1,500-bed facility for civilly committed sex offenders at an estimated cost of nearly $400 million. Soon after California enacted its version of Jessica's Law in 2006, which expanded the list of sex offenses that qualified for civil commitment, the number of people referred for civil commitment evaluations in the state skyrocketed from 50 to 750 per month.[70] Meanwhile, California was providing no meaningful sex offender treatment for the 17,000 people serving time for a sex offense in its state prisons, many of whom will return to the community.[71]

The annual costs of Virginia's civil commitment program ballooned from $2.4 million in 2004 to an expected $27 million in 2011. In early 2011, Republican governor Bob McDonnell proposed spending nearly $70 million over the next two years to meet the rising demand for civil commitment, including adding an additional facility because the new 300-bed center that opened in 2008 would soon be full. Alarmed at the $100,000 per year cost for each civilly committed sex offender, a Virginia state senator sought to revive a controversial measure, vetoed by Democratic governor Tim Kaine four years earlier, that would allow Virginia to join the handful of states that now permit the castration of sex offenders.[72]

Registries and Community Notification Laws

Even if they are not subject to civil commitment after serving their time, many former sex offenders remain deeply enmeshed in the carceral state. This is thanks to the proliferation of registration, community notification, and residency restrictions. These measures are creating important barriers to reentry for sex offenders. They impose many hardships on registered sex offenders, including well-documented cases of harassment, threatening phone calls, property damage, loss of employment and residence, physical assaults, and, in a few cases, death by vigilantes.[73]

The huge number of post-release restrictions imposed on sex offenders in the United States is exceptional. At least half a dozen other countries have sex offender registries, and others are contemplating establishing them. The United States is exceptional in the broad scope of the registries. In other countries that require certain sex offenders to register, the registration period is typically brief, and the information is only available to law enforcement officials, not to anyone with Internet access. Countries that considered wide-scale community notification laws have largely rejected them. Based on the experience of the United States, they have determined that these laws do not greatly enhance public safety but do spark vigilante violence and other negative consequences that impede the successful reintegration of former sex offenders back into society.[74]

One month after the 1994 rape and murder of seven-year-old Megan Kanka by a neighbor who was a released sex offender, New Jersey enacted Megan's Law. This measure required sex offender registration, community notification of registered sex offenders, and life in prison without the possibility of parole for certain sex offenders. New Jersey's Megan's Law rapidly became a template for other states and the federal government as lawmakers and other public officials sought to target sex offenders with tough new sanctions. In 1994, as part of the omnibus crime bill, Congress enacted the Jacob Wetterling Act, which required states to establish sex offender registries or forfeit some federal funding.

California enacted the nation's first sex offender registration law in 1947.[75] Today the federal government and all fifty states require certain adults and juveniles convicted of sex offenses to register with law enforcement authorities. Some states make their entire registries accessible to the public, while others are more selective. As of 2012, there were about 725,000 registered sex offenders in the United States—or about one in five hundred people. Since nearly all of them are men, this means that about one in 160 adult males is a registered sex offender—or about double the number from a decade ago.[76] Just as incarceration rates vary markedly between the states, so do sex offender registration rates. At the high end are Oregon and Arkansas, with rates of 400 to 500 registered sex offenders per 100,000 people, or about twice the national average of 230. At the low end is Pennsylvania, with about 100 registered sex offenders per 100,000 people.[77]

Over the years, Congress has extended the reach of these registries, as well as the federal government's role in sex offender policy. In 1996, it enacted a law to foster the development of enhanced state registries that are more accessible to the public. A decade later, the federal government became the preeminent government voice in sex offender policy when both houses of Congress unanimously passed the Adam Walsh Child Protection and Safety Act. This legislation included several major departures from earlier federal policy. It established a new federal crime of failure to register, laid the groundwork for a national registry for sex offenders, imposed tougher sentences for a wide variety of sex-related crimes, authorized a federal civil commitment system for sex offenders, set strict limits on bail for certain sexual offenses, and instituted new discovery rules in child pornography cases.[78]

Title I of the Adam Walsh Act, better known as the Sex Offender Registration and Notification Act (SORNA), created a new office within the Department of Justice to enforce and administer the statute. The Office of Sex Offender Sentencing, Monitoring, Apprehending, Registering, and Tracking (SMART) brings to mind creation of the Drug Enforcement Administration (DEA) decades ago when Richard Nixon launched the war on drugs. SORNA broadly defines sex offenders as any "individual who was convicted of a sex offense."[79] It requires convicted sex offenders to register in any jurisdiction where they live, work, or go to school. Registered sex offenders have only three days to report in person to the authorities any changes in name, address, employment, or student status. Failure to keep registration information accurate and up to date is punishable by a sentence of up to ten years in prison.[80]

SORNA also requires states to link their online registries to the national registries. One of its most controversial provisions requires states to list certain juvenile sex offenders on the national registry, sometimes for life. In early 2007, Attorney General Alberto Gonzales issued a rule that permits the Adam Walsh Act to be applied retroactively to people who had been convicted of sex offenses prior to passage of the measure.

With the creation of a national registry for sex offenders, federal criminal cases involving registry violations have skyrocketed as more states have joined the federal program. Between 2009 and 2013, federal registry cases more than doubled.[81] State-level studies of the implementation of SORNA in Ohio and Oklahoma suggest that the federal law's classification scheme for sex offenders could end up subjecting the majority of the country's sex offenders to lifetime registration and strict, expensive, and burdensome reporting requirements. The Ohio case suggests that nearly half of all registered juvenile sex offenders would end up classified at the highest risk level, making them likely candidates for lifetime registration.[82]

President Obama has been an outspoken supporter of the Adam Walsh Act, as have some leading Democrats, including Senator Barbara Mikulski (D-MD). His 2009 economic stimulus package originally included a proposal for $50 million to enforce SORNA.[83] The reauthorization of the Adam Walsh Act, which was approved by the House in August 2012 and then died in the Senate, called for about $66 million in annual support to maintain federal and state sex offender registries and pursue violations over the next five years. This is more than three times what Congress appropriated in fiscal 2012.[84]

Some states have hurried to amend their sex offender statutes and policies to comply with SORNA. Others have decided to opt out, thus risking some federal funding, because they view the federal registry requirements as onerous, expensive, and unlikely to enhance public safety significantly.[85] The federal financial penalty for failing to comply is relatively minor compared to the cost of fully implementing the federal SORNA requirements. Texas estimated it would have to spend nearly $39 million to comply with SORNA but would lose only $1.4 million in federal funds if it did not comply.[86] As of early 2014, only seventeen states were deemed to have substantially implemented SORNA.[87]

Washington State, which established the country's first public registry in 1990, is one of the states that has not implemented SORNA. Over the years, it has invested heavily in narrowing its registry and community notification efforts to focus on the truly high-risk offenders and to educate the public about the best research findings about sex offending and recidivism. SORNA would put these efforts in jeopardy by forcing the state to subject more of its sex offenders to stringent registration and community notification requirements. SORNA also would force the state to end the practice of not making public the names and addresses of low-level offenders.[88]

SORNA does not prevent states from setting up even more expansive registries than the federal government requires. The common assumption is that a registered sex offender is someone who has sexually assaulted a child or adult. But many states require people to register as sex offenders for actions that do not necessarily involve coercion or violence (for instance, flashing, consensual sex between teenagers, or prostitution-related offenses) or that may have had little or no connection to sex (such as public urination).[89] Many of the people currently required to register as sex offenders today were convicted of consensual sodomy years ago before the U.S. Supreme Court ruled in the 2003 *Lawrence v. Texas* decision that criminalizing such behavior was unconstitutional.[90]

In a number of states, all registered sex offenders, regardless of the seriousness of their crime, are listed in the publicly accessible online registries. These registries typically include not only information about a person's criminal conviction, which is part of the public record (except in the case of certain juveniles), but also such items as residential and email addresses, photo, place of employment, and license plate number.[91] At least seventeen states require all registrants to register for life—whether they were convicted of a relatively minor infraction like visiting an adult prostitute or a major offense like raping a child.[92]

Many registries and community notification schemes include inaccurate, misleading, or opaque information about the circumstances and the nature of the crime. For example, few states provide information about the registrant's age at the time of the offense, although all state registries include the registrant's current age.[93] This leads to many mistaken assumptions. As the years go by, the man convicted of a Romeo-and-Juliet offense when he was a teenager grows older on the registry, but the teenager he had sex with does not. As time goes by, what was originally a case of underage consensual teenage sex looks more like a case of child rape on the Internet registry.

Georgia has more than 17,000 registered sex offenders. Some of them are potentially quite dangerous, while many others are not. It is "fiendishly hard for anyone browsing the registry to tell one from the other" because of inaccurate, misleading, or incomplete information.[94] In 2008, the state's Sex Offender Registration Review Board concluded that about two-thirds of them posed little threat.

Failing to register on time and to inform authorities of any changes in address or other required information are felonies in many jurisdictions and can draw stiff penalties. In 2005, a jury sentenced a Texas man to fifty-five years in prison for missing by a few days the one-week deadline to inform authorities he had moved. Two prior convictions for failure to register had enhanced his sentence. In 2008, a Texas appeals court upheld this verdict and sentence. It ruled that when the man moved out of a motel room and into a vehicle parked in the motel's lot he was required to notify the authorities of an address change.[95]

Many states do not have the funding, personnel, and technical capacity to maintain updated registries, leaving registrants who do comply at risk of sanctions through no fault of their own. States that have conducted audits of their registries have found high rates of misinformation.[96] New York State discovered that one-quarter of the registry entries had errors.[97] After Michigan enacted a new sex offender registry law in 2011, local police were unprepared for the flood of registered sex offenders seeking to provide the new required information to update the registry. Offenders who supplied this information on time were nonetheless marked as "non-compliant" on the registry due to law enforcement delays in updating the registries.[98]

Listing juveniles on publicly accessible sex-offender registries, which is a fairly common practice in about thirty-five states, has been highly controversial. Under SORNA, states are required to include certain juveniles as young as fourteen years of age on their registries. Texas, which only has a public registry, not a separate nonpublic registry for law enforcement, permits children as young as ten years of age to be listed on its registry. Human Rights Watch has called for exempting youths and teenagers from registration, community notification, and residency requirements. The National District Attorneys Association strongly opposes such blanket exemptions and wants prosecutors to be the final arbiters of which sex offenders are required to register.[99]

Registration laws work hand-in-hand with community notification laws. Notification laws often provide few specific guidelines to law enforcement officials regarding who is to be informed and by what means. Some courts and legislators have sanctioned degrading measures, such as requiring special yard signs posted on the front lawns of registered sex offenders. Law enforcement officials have been known to expand the scope of community notification beyond what is necessary to protect public safety. In one case, an older man who had had consensual sex with his sixteen-year-old underage girlfriend when he was twenty years old was dismayed to learn that the police had been informing neighbors that he had raped a young girl.[100] Actions like these "mislead the public about the actual risk a sex offender poses, and inflame community hostility and fear."[101]

Residency Restrictions and Internal Exile

In addition to community notification and registration statutes, restrictions on where registered sex offenders are permitted to live, work, and visit have ballooned in the United States over the past decade. Residency restrictions have largely withstood numerous court challenges, although some courts have started to question their legislative intent and to find certain regulations unconstitutional.[102] When someone is sent to prison, "due process is afforded, a trial occurs, and appeals are made," explains Yung. "However, when a sex offender is internally exiled through residency and other restrictions, it is performed extra-judicially, often with no warning and no recourse for the offender."[103] Yung contends that the emerging regime to manage and contain registered sex offenders in the United States has disturbing similarities with the Soviet Union's *propiska* system of residency and migration controls that Stalin revived in the 1930s to create an extensive system of internal exile and banishment.[104]

Many states and municipalities in the United States have enacted laws that designate wide swaths of localities off-limits to registered sex offenders. Before 2000, only five states had such restrictions. Today, at least thirty do. So do hundreds of municipalities.[105] These statutes and ordinances have essentially banished sex offenders from entire cities or towns as a result of requirements that they live a certain distance from places where children tend to congregate, such as schools, childcare facilities, movie theaters, parks, and even pet stores. In most cases, these places are designated off-limits to *all* registered sex offenders, regardless of whether their crimes involved children or not.[106] Communities and neighborhoods across the country have even been erecting tiny pocket-sized parks as a way to force sex offenders, who are not permitted to reside near a park, out of their neighborhoods.[107]

Thanks to residency restrictions enacted as part of Jessica's Law and Chelsea's Law, many registered sex offenders have virtually no legal place to reside in the city of San Francisco.[108] In Miami, an encampment under a bridge became the shelter of last resort for released sex offenders because residency restrictions had rendered much of the rest of the city out of bounds to them.[109] Some jurisdictions in Florida have even barred sex offenders from seeking safety at public shelters during natural disasters like hurricanes.[110] Many registered sex offenders across the country are on virtual lockdown each year on Halloween, banned from even going trick-or-treating with their own children.

Residency and registration requirements have created Catch-22 situations for many former sex offenders. Rendered essentially homeless or forced to shift residences frequently due to residency restrictions, sex offenders have had greater difficulty complying with requirements that they register with the authorities. For example, in 2007, a Georgia man was sentenced to life in prison for failing to register. The fact that he was homeless because some of the toughest residency restrictions in the country had left him with virtually nowhere to live was not considered an acceptable excuse.[111] In 2010, Georgia modified some of the most egregious provisions of its sex-offender registration statutes.[112] Penalties for failing to register properly in Georgia are still severe: one to thirty years in prison for a first offense, and five to thirty years for a second offense.[113]

The Fiscal Burden and the Limits of Evidence-Based Research

Policy makers and government officials have promoted sex offender registries, community notification, residency restrictions, and electronic monitoring as low-cost measures that would greatly reduce incidents of sexual abuse. But these measures are not cheap. Moreover, research suggests that they do not significantly reduce sexual abuse.

Violations for failing to register properly with the authorities have become a growing source of new prison commitments and a new burden on state and federal corrections budgets. Failure to register is a common recidivism offense for sex offenders. In Minnesota, it has surpassed sexual conduct as the most common recidivism offense for sex offenders.[114] As of 2012, about 2,000 people were serving time in Texas jails and prisons for failing to register as a sex offender.[115]

GPS monitoring of sexual and other offenders is proving to be more expensive than originally suggested.[116] California now runs the country's largest electronic monitoring program, thanks in part to Jessica's Law and Chelsea's Law, which mandate lifetime GPS supervision for many sex offenders. GPS programs in California cost an estimated $36 per sex offender per day—or about $13,000 a year, which is nearly one-third more than the cost of traditional parole supervision. In 2011, the state spent about $88 million to electronically monitor nearly 7,000 sex offenders. Projecting that the financial burden will continue to grow as the number of released sex offenders rises, a government-funded report on California's GPS program recommended that the state consider imposing supervision fees on paroled sex offenders.[117] Recent research suggests that such fees raise little money but can be extremely burdensome to parolees and may possibly increase the risk of recidivism.[118] A modest proposal to end the lifetime registration of all sex offenders and create a tiered registry based on severity of offense stalled in the California legislature in 2013. Many lawmakers characterized this proposal as "radioactive."[119]

As punishments and restrictions for sex offenders have proliferated, research on the specific impact of key policies like registration, community notification, residency restrictions, and GPS monitoring has been relatively scarce.[120] The existing research strongly suggests that these measures have at best only an extremely modest or no general deterrent effect on would-be adult sex offenders and no or only a slight effect on lowering the recidivism rates of convicted sex offenders. Those effects probably vary considerably depending on the specifics of the locale or state.[121] One of the most extensive state-level studies found that New Jersey's Megan's Law had no significant effect on reducing sexual offending or sexual re-offending, and that the growing financial burden of implementing the law might not be justifiable.[122] Research also suggests that the sharp line drawn between sex offenders and non–sex offenders in public policy debates over criminal justice reform may not be warranted. The released offenders most likely to be re-arrested for a serious sex crime tend to be the ones with the most extensive histories of prior arrests for crimes of all kinds—not just sex offenses.[123]

The extant research refutes many of the common notions that fueled the stampede for get-tough policies targeted at sex offenders. In the media and public policy discussions, sex offenders often are portrayed as members of a homogeneous group with high probabilities of reoffending and who are best dealt with through a highly punitive one-size-fits-all approach. The research clearly demonstrates that sex offenders are a strikingly diverse group with vast differences in their risk levels and in the dangers they pose to public safety. The common belief that all or most sex offenders reoffend is incorrect. The recidivism rates of sex offenders vary greatly depending on many factors, such as the specific sexual offense they were originally convicted of, their age at the time of conviction and release, the victim's age, whether their victim was a stranger, family member, or acquaintance, and the treatment that offenders received.

Calculating accurate recidivism rates for sex offenders poses even more methodological challenges than calculating them for non–sex offenders.[124] Experts in this area generally agree that the widespread public perception that sex offenders will inevitably commit more sex crimes after discharge is incorrect. In a number of cases, the evidence suggests that their recidivism rates may be considerably lower.[125]

People who have served time for the most serious sex offenses like rape or sexual assault are more likely than released non-sex offenders to be re-arrested for another serious sex crime, according to one of the most extensive surveys of sex offenders and recidivism.[126] Their re-arrest rates within the first three years of discharge are still relatively low—about 5.3 percent.[127] Released sex offenders are considerably less likely to be re-arrested for any offense compared to non-sex offenders.[128] Certain subgroups of sex offenders do pose comparatively higher risk of reoffending, including same-sex child serial abusers and men who sexually assault women.[129]

Sex offender registries appear to have little impact on sex offender recidivism (except perhaps for a slight reduction in reoffending by registered sex offenders who were acquainted with their victims).[130] Offenders who fail to register are no more likely to recidivate than those who do—but they are more likely to be less educated, a member of a minority group, and an urban dweller.[131] States and the federal government have pushed to expand their sexual registries to include more juvenile sex offenders despite evidence suggesting that a juvenile convicted of a sex offense is not necessarily more prone to commit additional sex offenses as an adult.[132]

Community notification appears to have a slight deterrent effect. As for whether it reduces recidivism, the evidence is mixed or inconclusive.[133] Residency restrictions do not appear to be effective in lowering recidivism. In fact, the evidence suggests that they may pose a threat to public safety. These restrictions make it harder for registered sex offenders to reintegrate into society by forcing them to live in marginal areas with few opportunities for steady work, housing, social services, and public transportation.[134] Registration, community notification, and residency restrictions may actually increase recidivism rates by contributing to social isolation, unemployment, residential instability, depression, harassment, and feelings of shame, fear, and hopelessness, all of which are factors associated with a greater risk for reoffending.[135]

The claim that repeat sex offenders are responsible for committing the lion's share of all sex offenses has been a major justification for creating such far-reaching and publicly accessible registries. But a study of all males arrested for sex offenses in New York State between 1987 and 2006 that compared arrest patterns before and after creation of the state registry found that 95 percent of the arrests were of people who had not previously been convicted of a sex crime.[136] Another study found that barely 4 percent of the identified perpetrators in attacks on clients at a sexual assault agency were listed on a registry at the time that the attack occurred.[137] One extensive government survey of released offenders found that they were responsible for only about 4 percent of all arrests for rape in a three-year post-release period.[138]

The rush to enact tougher sex offender legislation highlights the fundamental disconnect between criminal justice policy making and empirical research.

Legislators admit that media reports and constituents' views—not empirical research—were their most important sources of information as states developed these policies. Research findings about who sex offenders are, their relative risks and recidivism rates, and their chances for reintegration have been largely irrelevant.[139]

Sex Offenders, Public Opinion, and Penal Reform

As with the war on drugs and other tough-on-crime crusades, the war on sex offenders has been fueled by public fears, ignorance, and misperceptions. A 2005 Gallup poll suggests that Americans fear child molesters more than they fear terrorists in their communities.[140] Survey data indicate strong public support for sex offender registries, despite their shortcomings, as well as for creating additional registries for all sorts of other offenses.[141] In one poll, three out of four people surveyed said they would support such policies "even if there is no scientific evidence showing that they reduce sexual abuse."[142] The public also tends to grossly overestimate the likelihood that sex offenders will reoffend and also the proportion of sexual assaults that are committed by strangers. Furthermore, the public tends to dismiss treatment of sex offenders as largely ineffective.[143]

Public opinion polls indicate that the public is implacably punitive when it comes to punishing and ostracizing sex offenders. But, as in the case of other surveys of public attitudes toward crime and punishment, public opinion toward sex offenders may be more fluid and less punitive than is commonly believed. For example, as legislators began piling on penalties for sex offenses from the mid-1990s onward in Washington State, the proportion of respondents who said sex offenders should be given every opportunity for a fresh start as lawful citizens actually began to rise.[144]

Although the main thrust has been toward more, not less, punitive policies for sex offenders, some political resistance is emerging. As discussed earlier, many states have balked at complying with SORNA. Several states moderated their penalties for "Romeo and Juliet" offenses in the wake of the national uproar over a Georgia case in which a seventeen-year-old boy received a mandatory ten-year sentence in 2005 for having consensual oral sex with a fifteen-year-old girl.[145]

Some victims' rights advocates and women's groups have begun to raise important objections to aspects of the new war on sex offenders, as have mental health professionals, including the American Psychiatric Association.[146] Patty Wetterling, whose son Jacob's abduction and disappearance spurred creation of the first federal sex offender registry in 1994, has become one of the leading critics of residency and many other restrictions imposed on released sex offenders.[147] Statewide coalitions of rape crisis centers and sexual assault programs in California and elsewhere have mobilized to oppose highly punitive measures directed at sex offenders, such as Jessica's Law. They charge that these measures waste valuable resources that could be better spent battling sexual abuse. They also have raised concerns that these laws might discourage victims of sexual abuse from reporting their abuse to the authorities, especially in cases that involve abuse by family members.[148] The once moribund California Reform Sex Offender Laws (CARSOL) has transformed itself into a genuine civil rights organization and has been battling the avalanche of laws and restrictions aimed at sex offenders in the courts and in the legislature.[149] In the debate over reauthorization of the Second Chance Act of 2007, exclusion of sex offenders from the benefits and programs of the original act has been an important issue. The reauthorization legislation introduced in late 2013 repeals controversial Section 212, which had excluded sex offenders.[150]

Within the federal judiciary, the tectonic plates of punishment appear to be shifting slowly with respect to child pornography offenses. They seem to be shifting in ways reminiscent of the growing disenchantment with the crack-powder cocaine sentencing disparity that began in the 1990s and reached a crescendo two decades later. A 2010 U.S. Sentencing Commission survey found that most federal district judges agreed that the sentencing guidelines generally rendered appropriate sentences, except in the case of three offenses—crack cocaine infractions and possession and receipt of child pornography. The judges' rate of dissatisfaction with the harshness of the sentences was nearly identical and remarkably high for each of these three crimes—about 70 percent.[151] This likely explains the relatively high rate of downward departures from the sentencing guidelines in cases involving receipt or possession of child pornography. Some prosecutors have tried to circumvent these downward departures through more creative and coercive charging and plea bargaining.[152]

In 2012, the U.S. Sentencing Commission issued a report to Congress calling for a major overhaul of the guidelines and statutes for child pornography. It recommended, among other things, a serious reconsideration of the harsh mandatory minimums and stiff guidelines for possession and receipt of child pornography.[153] As one judge said, "The resulting punishment under the Guidelines may be more a reflection of our visceral reaction to these images than a considered judgment of the appropriate sentence for the individual."[154] In its response to the Sentencing Commission report, the U.S. Department of Justice affirmed its opposition to eliminating or considerably reducing any of the mandatory minimums for child pornography but appeared receptive to some of the commission's other recommendations.[155]

Conclusion

A major theme of American political development has been the struggle to end the practice of limiting the rights of certain people based on categories like race, gender, national origin, sexual orientation, or disability. Many recent laws targeted at sex offenders have resurrected a concept of the "degraded other" that had been falling out of favor in U.S. law.[156] In one of the most notable recent examples, the Agricultural Act of 2014 prohibits certain convicted sex offenders (and people convicted of homicide) from receiving food stamps.[157]

Sex offender laws have not greatly enhanced public safety and have been very costly in many other respects. They have infringed on a wide range of protected rights, including the right to privacy, freedom of movement, and physical safety.[158] The push over the past two decades to create reduced-rights zones for sexual offenders has established disturbing precedents to expand those zones to other groups or individuals deemed undesirable. Civil commitment statutes that permit the lifetime confinement of sex offenders in "treatment" centers after they have completed their criminal sentences are the most striking example of this. Thanks to media and public indifference and a series of unfavorable court decisions, the United States is well on its way to establishing largely unchecked powers to preventively detain not only the "worst of the worst" sex offenders but also a whole range of people convicted of lesser sex crimes. This includes people convicted of offenses such as statutory rape and possession of child pornography, and even people who have never been convicted of a sex-related crime. "While sex offenders are easy targets because of their political vulnerability, there is no legal reason to distinguish the internal exile of sex offenders from other potentially undesirable populations," explains one expert.[159]

States and municipalities have created or are considering creating registries for all sorts of other offenders, including people convicted of gun crimes, arson, abusing animals, and abusing methamphetamine. Some have even considered establishing a registry for dogs deemed dangerous.[160] After the 2012 school massacre in Newtown, Connecticut, the National Rifle Association aggressively lobbied for establishment of a national registry of people who are mentally ill as an alternative to stricter gun control laws.[161]

Today's "sexual predator" laws, reportedly designed to capture and contain the "worst of the worst," cast an extremely wide net. They have provided politicians and other public figures with a highly visible symbol to express their commitment to fighting sexual violence without addressing the primary sources of such violence. Ritual exile, one of their main weapons in the war against sex offenders, misleads society into thinking that the primary threat to public safety comes from strangers who must be banished. However, friends, acquaintances, and family members are responsible for more than 90 percent of all sexual abuse of children and nearly 90 percent of all sexual abuse.[162] This misguided ritual exile undercuts feminist claims, now substantiated by a considerable body of social scientific research, that sexual violence is not primarily the result of depraved social misfits unable to control their sexual urges. Rather, it is the consequence of wider "social values, attitudes, and beliefs that tolerate, and even facilitate, sexual violence."[163]

The war on sex offenders poses perhaps the greatest political challenge for those seeking to dismantle the carceral state. It does not fit easily into the new Jim Crow critique of the carceral state. All the expensive punishments and restrictions heaped on sex offenders over the past two decades show that states, municipalities, and the federal government are willing to bear enormous social and fiscal costs to wage this war. Talk of embracing the plight of sex offenders makes even some of the most progressive penal reformers squeamish.

CHAPTER TEN

Catch and Keep

The Criminalization of Immigrants

Comprehensive immigration reform is a crime bill in disguise.[1]
—VICTOR NARRO, 2014

Major changes in immigration policy and in the government's capacity to implement these changes have become important new drivers of the carceral state. Federal and local authorities have been detaining a rising number of immigrants—both documented and undocumented—in jails, prisons, and detention centers. The Obama administration has deported a record number of immigrants, many of whom pose no risk to public safety and have extensive family and other ties to the United States. The amount that the federal government now spends on immigration enforcement exceeds funding for all principal federal law enforcement agencies combined.[2] These developments have fostered what some are calling a "crimmigration" or "immcarceration" crisis.[3] To the dismay of many immigrant advocates, most discussions of the carceral state ignore how the line between immigration enforcement and law enforcement is rapidly disappearing in the United States.

The brittle legal status of immigrants today is not unique to the United States.[4] Neither is the growing merger between law enforcement and immigration enforcement as immigration control takes "on the language and, in many respects, the spirit of crime control."[5] What makes the U.S. case exceptional is that the law enforcement and penal systems in this country are so much more extensive compared to those of other advanced industrialized countries. Therefore, the potential for the criminalization of immigration policy is much greater. At the same time, because these systems are comparatively decentralized in the United States, local communities here have potentially more avenues to resist the new get-tough immigration policies if they so choose.[6] This explains why the growing entanglement of immigration enforcement and law enforcement has become a flashpoint in local politics across the United States.

For the first time, Hispanics now compose the largest ethnic or racial group in federal prisons and courts. About 35 percent of all federal prisoners are Hispanic, and nearly half of all the defendants sentenced in federal courts in 2012 were Hispanic.[7] This shift is a consequence of the escalation in criminal prosecutions for immigration-related offenses and the relative decline in prosecutions for other offenses, including drug crimes and white-collar crimes (see figure 10.2).[8] The U.S. Department of Homeland Security (DHS), which absorbed the Immigration and Naturalization Service (INS) when it was established in 2003, now refers more cases to the Justice Department for prosecution than do all other major law enforcement agencies combined.

Despite a sharp downward trend in net migration from Mexico and in apprehensions at the border, prosecutions for immigration violations (mostly illegal entry and reentry) have exploded over the last decade.[9] Between 1998 and 2010, growth in the number of immigrant offenders accounted for 56 percent of the rise in federal prison admissions and 17 percent of the growth in federal prisoners.[10] As of 2013, nearly 11 percent of the inmates in federal prisons were serving time for immigration-related offenses.[11] In fiscal 2011, incarceration costs alone for those sentenced for illegal entry and reentry reached an estimated $1 billion.[12] This "browning" of federal penitentiaries and other penal facilities has fed the common misperception that immigrants commit a disproportionate amount of serious or violent crimes, which has fueled pressure for even more aggressive immigration enforcement.[13]

Deportations of immigrants, both documented and undocumented, have soared under the Obama administration, totaling nearly 2 million by the end of 2013 (see figure 10.1). A huge political schism has opened up between the White House and immigrant advocacy groups, who have derisively nicknamed President Obama the nation's "deporter in chief." Upon entering office, the Obama administration escalated prosecutions and deportations of immigrants who entered or re-entered the country without proper authorization. The Obama administration also stepped up deportations of immigrants with criminal records. Furthermore, it expanded the use of expedited deportation proceedings, thus closing off opportunities for immigrants to seek legal advice, pursue political asylum, or explain their extenuating circumstances to immigration judges.

President Obama repeatedly affirmed that his deportation policies were aimed at the "criminals" and "gang bangers" who pose serious threats to public safety. But nearly two-thirds of the deportations during the first five years of his administration involved noncitizens who had committed only minor infractions, including traffic violations, or had no criminal record at all. Only about one in five involved people convicted of serious crimes.[14]

Arrests for minor violations have become a major pretext to funnel noncitizens into deportation proceedings, where they are not entitled to defense counsel and other legal protections accorded people who have been charged with crimes. U.S. law defines deportation as an "administrative measure," not a type of punishment. But in fact deportation is one of the most extreme forms of punishment, for it precipitates the loss of home, family, and property for people who are members of U.S. society. The administration's aggressive deportation campaign depends heavily on the active participation of local law enforcement agencies and departments of corrections.

The United States has been steadily accruing its capacity to pursue a more punitive stance toward immigrants. Important legislative and institutional changes dating back to the 1990s have made possible the localization and criminalization of immigration policy. Over the last two decades, a whole new apparatus to apprehend, detain, and punish immigrants, including undocumented migrants as well as permanent residents with green cards and other authorized noncitizens, has been quietly under construction.

This huge and costly system operates today under the auspices of Immigration and Customs Enforcement (or ICE, which was formerly the INS) and the U.S. Marshals Service (USMS) but has been largely shielded from wider public and legal scrutiny. It has been built by importing many of the theories, objectives, and methods of law enforcement into immigration enforcement, as well as some of the inflammatory law-and-order and racial rhetoric that fostered the punitive turn in criminal justice policy.[15] It also rests on deploying state and local law enforcement agencies to the front lines of immigration enforcement. The new system grants sentencing courts wide berth to facilitate deportations, largely bypassing immigration judges, even in cases of lawful permanent residents and other authorized noncitizens.[16]

Most criminal justice policy makers and scholars of crime and punishment have not considered the punitive revolution in immigration policy that has unfolded over the last two decades to be part of the mass incarceration crisis.[17] Yet the parallels between the injustices, interests, and incendiary rhetoric that fueled the prison boom of the 1980s and 1990s and that have propelled the more recent punitive turn in immigration enforcement are striking, as discussed in this chapter. As the United States journeyed down the road to mass incarceration, it blithely ignored markers along the way about the human and economic costs of this radical shift in public policy. Politicians and policy makers continued to promote prisons as the best way to deter and contain crime despite mounting evidence that locking up a huge proportion of the population did not make the country a much safer place and might actually be jeopardizing public safety. In mobilizing for the war on immigrants, politicians and other public figures have been retooling the law enforcement tactics and inflammatory rhetoric deployed in the war on crime and the war on drugs.

Mass incarceration created powerful new political players—notably the private-sector interests that build, manage, service, supply, and finance prisons and jails, as discussed in chapter 3. In the course of the prison boom, these new players amassed considerable lobbying resources, political influence, and political expertise. They now are enlisting these in the pursuit of the criminalization of immigration enforcement and the expansion of private facilities to detain immigrants, as discussed in this chapter.

A "thick nativist mood is palpable" in the United States today and is finding expression in record numbers of anti-immigrant measures, many of which call for raising the criminal penalties for immigration-related violations.[18] Public officials defend the criminalization of immigration enforcement as a way to reduce serious and violent crime and to deter unauthorized immigrants from entering the country. A century of convincing research findings that influxes of immigrants tend to reduce—not increase—crime rates has been no match against politicians exploiting false stereotypes that equate more immigrants with more crime.[19]

The federal government—in particular the executive branch—has been the indisputable leader in the criminalization of immigration policy. It has had great leeway to determine how tough to be. Just as the war on drugs served as a bridge to bring local, state, and federal law enforcement authorities closer together, the criminalization of immigration policy rests on mobilizing state and local law enforcement agencies to help implement the new tough stance on immigration. These controversial joint ventures have been subjected to little federal oversight, much like the local anti-drug task forces established under the Byrne Justice Assistance Grants, which were discussed in chapter 2. Thanks to these new programs, local and state law enforcement partnerships with federal immigration authorities now account for well over half of the immigrants who are apprehended and detained. This chapter discusses several programs and institutional developments that have been instrumental in the localization and criminalization of immigration enforcement.[20]

Like the turn toward mass incarceration, the turn toward the criminalization of immigration enforcement has been remarkably bipartisan. Comprehensive immigration reform proposals in 2005–07 and 2012–14 to provide a path to citizenship for the estimated 11–13 million undocumented migrants in the United States were predicated on vastly increasing the power, authority, and capacity of the government to capture, detain, punish, and deport noncitizens, both documented and undocumented. The immigration bill that the U.S. Senate passed in June 2013 allocated an additional $46 billion to "secure the border" by 2021 through stepped-up law enforcement and military-style operations. The massive increase in resources that legislators of both parties are ready to devote to the further criminalization of immigration policy calls into question claims that budgetary pressures will inevitably force a retrenchment of the carceral state.

A Revolution in Immigration Enforcement

Since the mid-1990s, the immigration enforcement system has morphed into a vast and ever-growing web of Border Patrol agents, police, prosecutors, courts, jails, prisons, and detention centers with a well-documented history of human rights violations and procedural shortcuts that have "imperil[ed] the due process rights of immigration defendants."[21] With these shifts in policy and institutional capacity, the USMS and ICE have morphed into a mini Bureau of Prisons. In 2011, the average daily number of people in custody of the USMS was about 60,000, an increase of about 80 percent since 2000.[22] This is because of the growing role the USMS now plays in immigration enforcement, especially Operation Streamline, which is discussed later.[23]

The number of people that ICE holds in special detention centers and other fa-cilities on any given day has increased more than elevenfold since the early 1970s.[24] A little known congressional directive, referred to on Capitol Hill as the "bed man-date," requires ICE to keep an average of 34,000 detainees per day.[25] These figures understate the reach of the immigration apparatus of the carceral state. The total number of immigrants who passed through ICE detention facilities each year has more than doubled, rising from about 200,000 people in 2001 to more than 400,000 people in 2010.[26] ICE detainees include political asylum seekers, people who have violated administrative law by being in the United States without proper authorization, and noncitizens, including green card holders, charged or con-victed of a crime that subjects them to deportation. ICE holds adult immigrants as well as families. Residing in the United States without proper authorization is technically a civil code violation—the kind of infraction for which detention can-not be used as punishment. But most ICE detention facilities are modeled after jails and prisons.[27]

ICE not only detains but also deports. Under President Obama, the number of annual deportations soared to record levels, peaking at about 410,000 in fiscal 2012 (see figure 10.1).[28] This is more than double the annual average during Presi-dent George W. Bush's first term and more than 30 percent higher than when he left office.[29] It is about ten times the yearly average in the early 1990s. The number

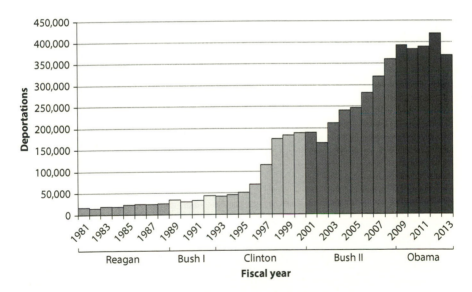

Figure 10.1. Annual Deportations, Fiscal 1981–Fiscal 2013

Sources: U.S. Department of Homeland Security, *2012 Yearbook of Immigration Statistics*, table 39, http://www.dhs.gov/yearbook-immigration-statistics (retrieved March 13, 2014); ICE, "FY 2013 ICE Immigration Removals," n.d., https://www.ice.gov/removal-statistics/ (retrieved March 13, 2014).

of annual deportations under Obama dwarfs the number of removals during the country's last major deportation campaign, which was back in the early 1930s.[30] Mexicans are the leading targets once again, accounting for nearly three-quarters of all deportations in 2010.[31]

Some of the deportees have committed serious crimes. But most are being exiled for having committed minor offenses like petty larceny, simple assault, drunk driving, drug violations, traffic offenses, or entering the country without proper authorization. Many of these deportees face discriminatory, inhumane, and, in some cases, life-threatening conditions upon return to "home" countries that they have not lived in for years, decades, or lifetimes.[32] In the case of immigrants who came to the United States as young children, they may not even speak the language of the homeland they have been deported to.

Imprisoning and deporting vast numbers of immigrants, both documented and undocumented, is a major shift in U.S. policy that is a throwback to immigration practices of the early to mid-twentieth century.[33] When the U.S. government closed the active immigration center at Ellis Island in 1954, it largely closed the door on routinely imprisoning immigrants who enter the country without proper documentation. This practice was largely abandoned until the early 1980s, when the purpose of immigration detention was recast as a deterrent to illegal immigration. The immediate catalyst was the influx of tens of thousands of immigrants from Cuba in 1980 in what became known as the Mariel boatlift and of large numbers of asylum seekers from Haiti. Prior to that, the government employed immigration detention for much narrower purposes and circumstances.[34]

In the decades since, the immigration authorities have been amassing the legal means and institutional capacity to implement this shift. Over the years, Congress has greatly stiffened the penalties for illegal reentry. In 1952, the maximum sanction for anyone convicted of illegal reentry was two years in prison. The Immigration Reform Act of 1986 raised the maximum penalty to 20 years in prison for people who reenter the country after prior convictions for aggravated felonies. Since then, by statute and practice, the definition of what constitutes an "aggravated felony" has expanded to include many nonviolent or trivial felonies and even certain misdemeanors.[35] Congress also has broadened the categories of documented and undocumented immigrants eligible for mandatory detention and deportation and restricted their rights to an administrative deportation hearing before an immigration judge.[36]

The strikingly punitive turn in immigration policy has been fiercely bipartisan. The Reagan administration ended the prevailing practice of routinely releasing most undocumented immigrants pending administrative proceedings.[37] President Bill Clinton implemented "Prevention through Deterrence," which militarized border control at key urban crossing areas in the Southwest and doubled the number of Border Patrol agents in that region.[38] Clinton's signature crime bill contained several little-noted provisions that hastened the criminalization of immigration enforcement, including enhanced penalties for immigration-related violations and new federal money to help states pay for the deportation of "criminal aliens."[39]

Clinton also championed the Antiterrorism and Effective Death Penalty Act (AEDPA) and the Illegal Immigration Reform and Immigrant Responsibility Act (IIRIRA), dubbed the "Mexican Exclusion Act" by many of its critics. These two measures laid the foundation for the vast criminalization of immigration infractions and for the sharp increase in the annual number of detentions and deportations beginning in the mid-1990s. They provided the legal means to expand the use of mandatory detention of noncitizens without bond. They also enlarged the categories of crimes for which lawful permanent residents could be deported by greatly expanding what constitutes an "aggravated felony" and applying it retroactively. Congress expanded the definition of "aggravated felony" so that it now includes a broad range of offenses, "many of which are neither 'aggravated' nor felonies."[40] For example, a conviction in the recent past or even the very distant past for a minor crime that received a minor sanction (such as simple battery or shoplifting with a one-year suspended sentence) could be cause to trigger mandatory detention and deportation for a green card holder.[41] The AEDPA and IIRIRA also removed many of the legal hurdles that protected immigrants from expedited deportations. They curtailed judicial review and due process in immigration cases and restricted granting relief for immigrants with family ties in the United States.[42]

Expanding Federal Capacity

Although hard to believe, until the 1990s, there was little coordination between the criminal justice and immigration enforcement bureaucracies. Since then, Congress has been generously funding a number of programs to knit them together.[43] As a result, the federal government's capacity to implement more punitive immigration policies has increased considerably. Much of this expansion has rested on creating new institutions that deploy law enforcement tactics and strategies in the cause of immigration enforcement.

In 2003, ICE launched its Fugitive Operations Program (FOP), which created seven-member Fugitive Operations Teams (FOTs). Over the last decade, the number of FOTs skyrocketed, as did the federal funding for these operations.[44] These teams are supposed to focus on apprehending and deporting fugitive aliens who have committed serious crimes or who are threats to national security. But in practice, the program has served as "a facade for persecuting undocumented immigrants in general."[45] From 2003 through early 2008, almost three-quarters of the individuals apprehended by FOTs did not have criminal convictions.[46]

Home raids are a primary enforcement tactic of FOTs. These raids are conducted under the auspices of administrative warrants issued by ICE. These warrants do not require immigration officials to present evidence under oath before an independent judge to show probable cause that a law has been violated. Many of the raids are carried out based on information in a database that the DHS's Inspector General has characterized as grossly inaccurate.[47]

In a typical raid, "armed FOT agents arrive at the homes in the early morning hours, bang hard on the doors and windows, and falsely identify themselves as the 'police,' whereupon they force the door open to enter the homes with guns drawn."[48] Although FOTs are legally obligated to obtain prior consent before entering a home, in many instances they do not seek such consent. Once inside, FOT agents often expand their focus far beyond apprehending the person identified in the administrative warrant as the target of the raid. They question everyone in the residence about his or her immigration status, even before a probable cause to do so has been established. Those deemed to be in the United States illegally may end up being arrested without a warrant.

In 2006, ICE's Worksite Enforcement Unit (WEU) began conducting more high-profile workplace raids in which hundreds of workers were rounded up on the job. These military-style raids typically involved dozens of armed agents who surrounded the workplace to prevent employees from leaving. Threatened with more serious charges and interrogated for hours without access to an attorney, many of these workers end up signing deportation papers or pleading guilty to lesser criminal charges. They typically appeared en masse in court, handcuffed or shackled to one another. Denied access to immigration attorneys, many of these accused workers were unaware of the immigration consequences of a guilty plea. The plea agreements that they signed typically required them to waive their rights to further immigration proceedings and rendered presiding judges largely powerless to alter the terms of the plea agreement.[49] In many instances, ICE did not coordinate its raids with local schools and social services to ensure that the children of the workers who were rounded up were properly looked after.[50]

These worksite raids, which are highly controversial, intensified at the very start of the Obama administration. In April 2009, ICE issued new guidelines to change the principal focus of the WEUs from undocumented employees to the criminal prosecution of employers who knowingly hire immigrants without proper paperwork. However, ICE also reaffirmed its commitment "to arrest and process for removal any illegal workers" encountered during these worksite enforcement operations.[51] In 2010, ICE director John Morton said his agency had audited the employment records of nearly 3,000 companies since Obama took office. These audits, which employers dubbed "silent raids," have resulted in mass firings. Despite its vow to shift the focus from punishing workers to punishing employers who exploit low-wage immigrants, ICE often grants immunity to audited companies that agree to fire unauthorized workers.[52] Of the nearly 92,000 immigration-related prosecutions in 2009, only thirteen employers in eight cases were prosecuted for the felony offense of hiring undocumented workers.[53]

Operation Streamline

Illegal entry and reentry have long been defined statutorily as federal misdemeanors. But this fact was largely ignored until about a decade ago. Border Patrol officers typically would permit immigrants apprehended at the border to be voluntarily repatriated or would refer their cases to the civil immigration system for processing. That changed dramatically with the establishment of Operation Streamline in 2005 as "catch and release" yielded to "catch and keep." Begun in Del

Rio, Texas, Operation Streamline quickly expanded to eight of the eleven federal district courts that span the Southwest border of the United States. Some border districts chose more evocative names for this expedited removal program, including Operation Lock Down in New Mexico, Operation No Pass in Texas, and Operation Arizona Denial. These zero-tolerance programs are known collectively as Operation Streamline.

Under these fast-track, zero-tolerance programs, first-time border crossers with no criminal record are usually charged with a misdemeanor that is punishable with a sentence of up to six months in prison. Typically they are sentenced to time served and then deported. Nearly everyone who is penalized for illegal reentry in federal court receives a prison sentence. Sentences have averaged about two years but sometimes are as high as 20 years.[54] These fast-track programs have prompted a jump in immigration violators sent to federal prison—from about 6,500 in 2000 to nearly 20,000 in 2010.[55] Sentencing for felony immigration crimes—which overwhelmingly involve instances of illegal border crossing, not more serious crimes like human smuggling—accounted for nearly 90 percent of the rise in the number of Hispanics sentenced to federal prison in the first decade of the twenty-first century.[56]

Thanks to these fast-track programs, the number of criminal case filings in the judicial districts along the 2,000-mile border with Mexico has skyrocketed, paralyzing the courts.[57] Processing so many petty border crossers without any criminal records has severely taxed the USMS and the federal courts, which must provide transportation, housing, food, defense attorneys, courtrooms, clerks, and judges. The $600 million border security plan that President Obama signed into law in summer 2010 failed to include any additional money for overworked courts or overworked defense attorneys handling immigration cases.[58] At the time of his death in the 2011 Tucson shooting spree that severely injured Representative Gabrielle Giffords (D-AZ), Arizona's chief federal judge John Roll was waiting to speak with the congresswoman to thank her for her efforts to secure more funding for federal courts overburdened with Operation Streamline cases.[59]

Operation Streamline and related programs have severely compromised the rights and dignity of immigrant defendants. In some jurisdictions, Border Patrol attorneys have been deputized as special assistant U.S. attorneys to prosecute Operation Streamline cases. These deputies generally operate out of the Border Patrol offices with little oversight from the United States Attorney's Office. Their dual appointments raise some troubling conflicts of interest, especially as concerns escalate about excessive use of deadly and other force by Border Patrol agents and local residents along the Southwest border.[60]

To handle the massive increase in immigration prosecutions, overtaxed courts have been conducting expedited hearings in which they arraign, convict, and sentence dozens of border crossers—sometimes upwards of eighty or a hundred—en masse in a single court appearance. Human rights groups have denounced these as "rapid-fire group trials." Immigrant defendants often arrive in court shackled to one another after a brief meeting with a defense attorney that sometimes lasts barely five minutes. Since the number of public defenders has not increased to meet the tidal wave of new criminal immigration cases, an appointed defense attorney often represents dozens of clients in a single hearing.[61]

The rapid speed and the manner in which these defendants are prosecuted "is a clear violation of due process," according to many public defenders and some legal and human rights critics.[62] In December 2009, the Ninth Circuit agreed that these en masse hearings violate federal criminal procedure rules that require judges to address defendants "personally in open court and determine that [a guilty] plea is voluntary."[63] This ruling, which does not apply to districts outside of the Ninth Circuit, has not spurred fundamental changes in how these group hearings are conducted.[64] More importantly, by grounding its decision in a procedural rule subject to congressional amendment, the appeals court signaled that "the issue of criminal defendants' procedural rights be subject to the will of Congress," rather than the Constitution.[65]

Public Safety at Risk

As in the case of the prison buildup that began in earnest in the 1980s, Operation Streamline and other efforts to criminalize immigration infractions have proceeded under the assumption that capturing more people and branding them as criminals enhances public safety. But the intense focus on petty immigration violators has come at the cost of diverting resources from more serious threats to public safety, like sophisticated drug, human trafficking, and firearms smuggling enterprises responsible for much of the border violence. Since 2004, immigration prosecutions have topped the list of federal criminal prosecutions nationwide (see figure 10.2). No other category of crime has so dominated the work of federal prosecutors.[66]

Requiring assistant U.S. attorneys along the border to focus most of their time and energy on low-level immigration prosecutions has come at the expense of developing the skills necessary to successfully investigate and prosecute more serious crimes, especially complex criminal enterprises. The repetitive and high-volume nature of Operation Streamline and other fast-track programs has also contributed to low morale and burnout among federal prosecutors, especially in border districts.[67]

Slow to join the stampede for fast-track prosecution of all unauthorized immigrants, California was an exception to these trends in prosecution. It focused its resources on border crossers deemed most likely to cause violence in U.S. cities rather than on petty immigration violators. This likely helps explain why the Southern District of California has ranked first in the nation in per capita prosecutions for drug trafficking and human smuggling.[68] In 2007, Carol C. Lam was ousted as United States Attorney for Southern California after Justice Department officials castigated her for not prosecuting enough unauthorized immigrants.[69]

It is now widely recognized that stiff mandatory minimums, three strikes, and other draconian measures that fueled the prison boom were not major deterrents to crime. Likewise, Operation Streamline and its progenitors have not served as major deterrents to unauthorized immigration, even though they have been

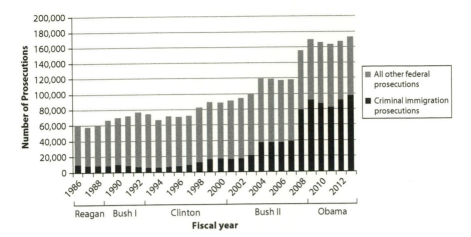

Figure 10.2. Criminal Immigration Prosecutions as a Share of All Federal Criminal Prosecutions, Fiscal 1981–Fiscal 2013

Source: Transactional Records Clearinghouse (TRAC), "Federal Judicial District: U.S. Immigration, # prosecuted," and "Federal Criminal Enforcement: prosecutions filed," from "Going Deeper" tool, http://tracfed.syr.edu/trachelp/tools/help/godeep.shtml (retrieved March 21, 2014).

promoted as such.[70] Like the criminal defendants who were confronted with the tougher new sentencing regime imposed in the 1980s and 1990s, many border crossers are unfamiliar with the legal and other consequences of the new immigration enforcement regime. This impairs the deterrence value of these programs. Many unauthorized immigrants do not grasp that a guilty plea essentially guarantees that they will be prohibited from legal entry and that any future attempt at reentry will likely draw a stiffer prison sentence.[71]

Immigration authorities and other government officials continue to fiercely defend these programs, crediting them for the decrease in streams of unauthorized immigrants entering the United States. But border apprehensions began declining as early as 2000—five years before the start of Operation Streamline. They have continued to fall almost steadily since then until a recent uptick, fueled partly by an influx of unaccompanied children from Central America, which became a heated political issue in summer 2014.[72]

Immigration experts attribute much of the recent drop in unauthorized immigrants entering the country to the faltering U.S. economy. (In 2013, the number of unauthorized immigrants in the United States appeared to be rising again after falling during the Great Recession.)[73] Another key factor is the intense militarization of the border, which has raised the cost and risk of crossing into the country. More immigrants now must rely on expensive "coyotes" to help smuggle them into the United States. They face a much higher risk of dying as they are forced to attempt crossings in more desolate and physically dangerous desert and mountain areas.[74] In a perverse outcome for those who want to slash the number of unauthorized immigrants residing permanently in the country, more immigrants are now settling down in the United States. This is because crossing back and forth—a common pattern in the past—has become so expensive and risky.[75] In another perverse outcome, the growing reliance on professional smugglers has heightened border violence.[76]

Localization of Immigration Enforcement

The criminalization of immigration policy hinges on more than just increasing the federal government's capacity to capture, detain, and punish immigrants. It also rests on radically changing the role of local and state law enforcement agencies in immigration enforcement. In the century after the federal government secured the exclusive responsibility to determine immigration policy in the 1880s, it largely abstained from mobilizing local and state jurisdictions in immigration enforcement.[77] That changed radically in the 1990s. Provision 287(g) of IRRIRA permits the federal government to deputize local and state police as enforcers of federal civil immigration laws and policies. Two other important institutional developments were the establishment of the Criminal Alien Program (CAP) in 2007 and the Secure Communities program in 2008.

These three programs have not necessarily enhanced public safety, according to many immigrant advocacy groups and even many law enforcement officials. Rather, they have contributed to the corrosion of trust "between immigrant communities and local law enforcement, allowing spheres of criminality to exist in immigrant neighborhoods where crime goes unreported because of individuals' fears of deportation."[78] This problem is especially acute with victims of domestic violence.[79] The criminalization of immigration violations also has contributed to jail overcrowding and has stressed some county budgets.

Provision 287(g) grants state and local authorities certain tools in immigration cases that would be violations of constitutional rights if they were used in criminal investigations. The 287(g) agreements with the federal government allow state and local authorities to incarcerate people for violations of civil immigration laws, often without any possibility of bond. These agreements also permit state and local police officers to make administrative arrests and issue administrative removal warrants without having to first secure authorization from an independent judge.[80]

The federal government entered into its first 287(g) agreement in 2002 in the immediate aftermath of 9/11. That year, Attorney General John Ashcroft issued a classified memo contending that state and local police have inherent authority to make arrests for violations of immigration laws.[81] By 2011, sixty-eight state and local law enforcement agencies spanning more than two dozen states had signed 287(g) agreements, and ICE had trained and certified more than 1,500 state and local law enforcement officers in immigration enforcement.[82] In late 2012, ICE announced a partial scale-back of the 287(g) program, saying it would no longer be training and deputizing local law enforcement officers to carry out immigration enforcement. At the same time, ICE reaffirmed its intentions to aggressively expand the Secure Communities program, which is discussed later.[83]

Another pivotal institution for criminalizing and localizing immigration enforcement is CAP. Beginning around 2005, the federal government consolidated the several programs that immigration authorities had relied on since the mid-1980s to screen for "criminal aliens" in prisons and jails into a single program that became known as CAP.[84] As of 2013, CAP was active in all federal and state prisons and in more than 300 local jails. Under CAP, participating law enforcement authorities, notably prisons and jails, notify ICE officials when they have arrested or convicted someone whom they suspect may be deportable.[85] ICE agents then are allowed to interview the detainee "regardless of the seriousness of the offense and without regard to innocence or guilt."[86]

ICE agents place immigration holds, known as "detainers," on people held by the authorities whom they deem potentially deportable. People with detainers enter a whole different legal universe. The courts are more likely to levy high bails on them or to deny bail altogether. They end up spending more time in jail and are put at a major disadvantage in mounting a defense against the criminal charges they face. After their criminal cases have been resolved, some of them continue to languish in jail, sometimes for weeks or months, long past the forty-eight-hour deadline for ICE to take them into custody.[87]

ICE purports to focus its efforts on immigrants with serious criminal backgrounds. But CAP, like Secure Communities, is mostly sweeping up noncitizens charged with trivial infractions. For example, in Travis County, Texas, anyone who is arrested is booked into the jail, where his or her personal information is collected and shared with ICE agents, who have unrestricted, round-the-clock access to the jail. This process occurs regardless of whether the charge "is a misdemeanor, a traffic offense, or even if the person is a victim of or witness to a crime."[88]

CAP provides police with an incentive to arrest someone, rather than merely issue a citation, in order to check his or her immigration status. CAP has spurred concerns about racial profiling and about the large number of people, most of them Latinos, who have been arrested and detained for low-level misdemeanors that are not punishable by jail time. Police in some counties in the United States regularly set up roadblocks in areas with a high number of immigrants to check whether drivers have proper licenses, registration, insurance, working tail lights, and the like. Immigrants—or suspected immigrants—who do not are at risk of being sent to the local jail, where an ICE detainer may await them. Wake County, North Carolina, which has been a staging ground to test new immigration enforcement tactics, erected nearly 200 such roadblocks over a three-year period between 2007 and 2009.[89] Immigrants often are mistreated during arrest and detention, according to several studies that document the excessive force and demeaning racial slurs that immigrants experience. Studies suggest that local police are more likely than trained Border Patrol agents to use excessive force against immigrants.[90]

Insecure Communities

The Secure Communities program is one of the most controversial weapons in the criminalization and localization of immigration enforcement. Established in 2008, this program provides police, jails, and other booking facilities with ready access to the DHS's immigration database to crosscheck fingerprints when an arrest is made. All local, state, and federal law enforcement officers also have access to ICE's Law Enforcement Support Center (LESC), which provides them with immediate immigration status and identity information round-the-clock for anyone they stop, not just people who are arrested or charged.[91] Secure Communities enables the police to determine quickly the immigration status of all arrestees and to enter their fingerprints into both criminal and immigration databases. If the person is found to be undocumented, ICE is alerted immediately. Immigrants detained due to Secure Communities and related programs are not necessarily entitled to a hearing before an immigration judge before being deported. In cases of so-called administrative and expedited removals, ICE officers determine on their own whether to deport someone or not.[92]

Just months after taking office, President Obama sought to expand the Secure Communities program to include all of the country's correctional institutions within a few years. If fully implemented, approximately one-and-a-half million deportable immigrants would be identified annually, an ICE official estimated.[93] Since its inception in 2008 with just 14 jurisdictions, Secure Communities has expanded to over 3,000 counties within all 50 states and the District of Columbia.[94] Faced with growing opposition from law enforcement officials and immigrant groups, many cities and states have attempted to opt out of the program or to terminate their agreements with the federal government, which initially portrayed the program as a voluntary partnership. Federal officials have been at odds with themselves and with local and state jurisdictions about whether or not states and municipalities are permitted to opt out of the program.

ICE claims that the main aim of Secure Communities and related programs is to apprehend and deport immigrants who pose major threats to public safety. But nearly 80 percent of the people deported through the Secure Communities program had no criminal conviction or had been found guilty of only traffic violations or other minor offenses.[95] Branded as hard-core criminals, U.S. deportees sometimes become public targets in the countries they are sent back to, even though most of them were removed from the United States for relatively minor infractions.[96] The "most serious" convictions for nearly 20 percent of criminal aliens removed in 2010 were traffic-related offenses.[97] Driving without a license is a common infraction among unauthorized immigrants because most states require proof of legal residence in the United States in order to be issued a permit or license to drive.[98]

Opposition to the localization of immigration enforcement and to the massive increase in deportations under Obama has been escalating. Many state and local officials and immigrant advocacy groups have spoken out against the growing role of the police in immigration enforcement.[99] In 2011, the Congressional Hispanic Caucus and more than two hundred immigrant groups asked the Obama administration to suspend the Secure Communities program.[100]

Some police chiefs have championed Secure Communities and related programs. Others have warned that drawing police officers into immigration enforcement jeopardizes the ties that they have cultivated with immigrant communities. They contend that these programs have a "chilling effect" on the willingness of immigrants to report crime and to aid police investigations. Furthermore, they expose police departments to charges of racial profiling.[101] In some communities, police involvement with ICE has been one of the most divisive issues in recent memory.[102] Many police chiefs have opposed legislation modeled after Arizona's controversial SB 1070. Signed into law in 2010, SB 1070 requires, among other things, that state and local law enforcement officers determine someone's immigration status if they suspect he or she is an unauthorized immigrant. A 2011 report by the leading policy research group for police chiefs recommended that police officers be explicitly prohibited from arresting or detaining people solely on the basis of their immigration status.[103]

In 2011, immigrant advocacy groups mounted major demonstrations at the public hearings of the DHS-appointed task force to study Secure Communities.[104] The task force's final report charged that the program had severely eroded public trust and was to blame for the detention of massive numbers of immigrants who had not committed serious crimes.[105] Five of the nineteen members of the task force resigned rather than endorse the final report, and major divisions persisted among the remaining members of the committee.

In responding to the task force report, ICE forcefully reaffirmed its support for the Secure Communities program. It also asserted that the program is not voluntary, and that it essentially can be implemented over the objections of states and local communities.[106] ICE also announced that it would no longer immediately place detainers on unauthorized immigrants stopped for minor traffic violations who do not have criminal records. However, ICE affirmed that federal agents retained the prerogative to place a detainer on them if and when they are convicted. Benjamin E. Johnson, a member of the task force and executive director of the American Immigration Council, a pro-immigration group in Washington, sharply criticized ICE's new stance. "In a traffic setting, we were very clear that ICE should just get out of the business of issuing detainers," Johnson explained.[107] In late 2012, ICE issued stricter detainer guidelines, but they had little discernible impact. Only about 11 percent of ICE's detainers met the agency's new stated aim to target noncitizens who pose a serious threat to public safety or national security. Most detainers continued to be placed on people without criminal records or histories of serious criminal conduct.[108]

Worst of Both Worlds

Apprehended noncitizens face the worst of both worlds. Key legal decisions dating back to the late nineteenth century established that detention and deportation are not akin to punishments meted out in criminal cases.[109] Thus, detainees facing possible deportation are governed primarily under administrative law, not criminal law, and are denied many of the legal protections that citizens charged with a criminal offense receive. Immigrant detainees find themselves situated beyond the protections of criminal law at a time when the immigration authorities are increasingly reliant on law enforcement tactics and on the local and state police to execute their tougher stance on immigration.[110] As one attorney representing a detainee put it: "You'd rather be charged with a serious murder where you have some rights than a visa overstay. Because it's civil in nature, the safeguards don't apply."[111]

Some legal scholars convincingly argue that the "enemy combatants" held at Guantánamo Bay have more legal protections than immigrant detainees, including lawful permanent residents who are held under mandatory detention.[112] Secret detentions, physical abuse, closed court proceedings, and notoriously arbitrary administrative reviews have long been the standard operating procedures of the parallel universe of immigrant detention.[113] So have institutionalized racial and ethnic biases, indefinite detentions, state resistance to habeas corpus reviews, and denial of contact with family members, attorneys, and the media.

Since detention of immigrants is not considered punishment, detained immigrants generally are not entitled to access to lawyers.[114] In 2010, more than half of the people appearing in civil proceedings before an immigration judge did not have counsel.[115] For detainees who do have legal representation, the quality of their defense is compromised by language barriers, inability to make private phone calls and, perhaps most significantly, abrupt transfers to other facilities.

Noncitizens residing in the United States typically are first detained at a facility near where they live. But ICE then routinely transfers many of them hundreds or even thousands of miles away, often to remote detention centers. The proportion of detainees who are transferred has skyrocketed with the imposition of the tougher immigration enforcement regime. These transfers "often erect insurmountable obstacles" to marshaling an effective defense, according to Human Rights Watch.[116] The Sixth Amendment protects the right of criminal defendants to stand trial in the jurisdiction where the crime was allegedly committed. But immigrant detainees facing possible deportation have no comparable right. They routinely find themselves transferred far away from the witnesses, evidence, and lawyers they need to defend themselves in deportation proceedings. In the remote locations where they are often sent, the opportunities to secure legal representation are far fewer.

At any point in the immigration proceedings, immigrant detainees can be transferred. Until ICE finally launched an online publicly accessible system to locate detainees in 2010, some detainees were "literally 'lost' from their attorneys and family members for days or even weeks after being transferred."[117] Transfers of detainees take place between and within almost every state. Three states—Texas, California, and Louisiana—are most likely to receive transferred detainees. The federal Court of Appeals for the Fifth Circuit, which covers Louisiana, Mississippi, and Texas, is the jurisdiction that receives the most transfers. This court "is widely known for decisions that are hostile to the rights of non-citizens."[118] Furthermore, the states within its jurisdiction have the lowest ratio of immigration attorneys to immigrant detainees in the country.

Detained immigrants have fewer legal options to challenge not only deportation and other immigration proceedings but also the conditions of confinement in the jails and detention centers that hold them. The nation's immigration detention system operates behind a veil of official secrecy and is subject to little independent public accountability. Virtually no independent research is available on USMS detention, and ICE "is at times unable or unwilling to provide complete and reliable information on its detainees and facilities."[119] Detainees are scattered across literally hundreds of federal, state, local, and private facilities, which compounds the oversight problem. Getting a complete list of all the USMS and ICE facilities is next to impossible, as is confirming which ones are privately run.[120] The federal government contracts with numerous state and local jurisdictions to house detainees. These jurisdictions often then subcontract with private providers, clouding the lines of responsibility and accountability. The Sentencing Project calculated that 43 percent of all ICE detainees were privately held, up from about one quarter of them in 2002. About 30 percent of USMS detainees were privately held as of 2011, more than a fourfold increase since 2000.[121]

Private prison companies are even more secretive and publicly unaccountable than public departments of corrections, as discussed in chapter 3. Even Jorge Bustamante, the U.N. Special Rapporteur on Human Rights of Migrants, was not permitted to visit the notorious T. Don Hutto Residential Center, a CCA-run immigrant detention facility in Texas. At this retrofitted former state prison, children were kept behind barbed wire, and parents were separated from their children as punishment for not obeying the detention facility's rules. Hutto was reportedly harder to visit than the death row wing in most publicly run prisons.[122]

Over the years, ICE and its predecessor, the INS, have established dozens of standards to govern the conditions in immigrant detention facilities. But these standards "are not legally enforceable by detainees in court or any other administrative judicial process," so violations are "substantial and pervasive."[123] Short of termination of the contract, ICE has no legal mechanisms to ensure compliance with its detention standards.[124] A 2009 report by the National Immigration Law Center concluded that immigrant detainees are held in conditions that are often "as bad as or worse than those faced by imprisoned criminals."[125] People detained by ICE are not even entitled to have their injuries, illnesses, or deaths in custody reported to family members in a timely fashion.[126] Privately operated detention centers have been sites for major uprisings over poor conditions. Two disturbances over a lack of adequate medical care wracked GEO's detention center in Pecos, Texas, in December 2008 and January 2009. The May 2012 riot at CCA's facility in Natchez, Mississippi, left one guard dead.

Noncitizens held in local jails and prisons due to ICE detainers often do not receive the basic services and opportunities provided to fellow inmates who are citizens. They have been denied opportunities to participate in educational, vocational, work release, and substance abuse programs because such rehabilitative programs "are reserved for inmates who will be released into 'society.'"[127] They also have been denied assignment to minimum-security correctional facilities despite the minor nature of their offense. They do not qualify for "good time" credits for sentence reductions, even in cases where a detainer has yet to be issued.[128] Immigrants confined in privately run detention centers have been put to work in "voluntary" work programs where they are paid on average $1 a day to clean and maintain the facilities and work in the kitchen.[129]

ICE also runs an extensive network of secret detention jails. "If you don't have enough evidence to charge someone criminally but you think he's illegal, we can make him disappear," John Pendergraph, a top ICE official, boasted to a conference of police officers and sheriffs in 2008. In addition to ICE's publicly listed field offices and detention sites, it also confines people in nearly 200 "unlisted and unmarked subfield offices, many in suburban office parks or commercial spaces revealing no information about their ICE tenants." Reportedly designed to confine individuals who are in transit, these subfield offices often lack basic facilities like beds, showers, and sanitary toilets and are not subject to ICE's Detention Standards.[130]

Top immigration officials in the Obama administration, many of whom were held over from the Bush years, have intentionally tried to conceal the brutal mistreatment of immigrant detainees. According to documents obtained by the ACLU and exposés by the *New York Times*, this mistreatment has contributed to more than one hundred in-custody deaths since 2003.[131] In August 2009, the Obama administration announced it would overhaul the immigration detention system. But widespread abuses persist.[132] The administration vowed to consolidate more detainees in centers under direct control of ICE but run by private prison companies, including CCA and GEO. In an ICE-commissioned report, the agency acknowledged that the facilities that detain immigrants were built and operated primarily as jails or prisons, and that they impose more restrictions and costs than are necessary for most people detained for immigrant violations.[133] But soon after the report was released in fall 2009, John T. Morton, the head of ICE, affirmed that his agency would continue to detain noncitizens "on a grand scale."[134]

The Obama administration has left intact the key features that make the detention system so excessively punitive, despite DHS Secretary Janet Napolitano's concession in 2009 that the "paradigm was wrong" and Morton's vow to build a "truly civil detention system."[135] It has declined to promulgate legally enforceable detention standards. It has not adopted meaningful standards to restrict transfers and make them more transparent and publicly accountable. The administration generally has not supported giving detainees enhanced due process protections. It also has continued the practice of detaining immigrant families in prison-like conditions, just no longer at the notorious Hutto Residential Center.

The Private Sector and Immigration Detention

The prison buildup of the 1980s and 1990s depended on fiscal sleights of hand that concealed the real costs of mass incarceration and rendered them less subject to democratic accountability, as elaborated in chapter 3. Likewise, the real financial burden of the criminalization of immigration violations has been obscured. For example, no one knows how much Operation Streamline actually costs because it is not an explicit item in the federal budget and has been subjected to little systematic federal oversight. ICE has been promoting the tougher immigration enforcement regime as a way for local communities to raise extra revenue by contracting with the federal government to house detainees in city and county jails.[136] Many communities, especially in the Southwest, have explicitly turned to immigration detention to help ease the budget pinch in the wake of the 2008 financial meltdown.[137] But the economic benefits of immigrant detention are likely to be as illusionary as those of the earlier prison buildup, for many of the same reasons discussed in chapters 2 and 3.

Although detention facilities have not been economically profitable for many local communities, they have been a booming business for private, for-profit prison companies. As discussed in chapter 3, immigration detention was a financial godsend for leading private prison firms in the 1980s and 1990s and was a leading factor in turning their fortunes around. CCA and other private-prison companies have been pushing for punitive measures that target immigrants (like Arizona's SB 1070 discussed earlier) and that expand the use of immigrant detention. They have invested heavily in lobbying government officials at all levels and in promulgating punitive legislation. Aggressive marketing and lobbying by the prison industry have induced local communities to invest in public-private partnerships, this time to finance and construct new immigration detention facilities. Private prison consultants have emerged as major players in brokering private-public partnerships that technically place the financial risk of building these speculative facilities on the backs of bondholders but in reality put it on the backs of local communities.

Financial arrangements modeled after the lease revenue bonds discussed in chapter 3 ensure that the bonds to build immigrant detention facilities do not need to go before voters for approval. Local governments contract with the federal government to house detainees and then typically subcontract with a private company for a set fee to run the detention facility. If the number of detainees and the revenue streams from them fall short of expectations, the local government is still saddled with the bond payments. If it defaults, the municipality imperils its credit rating, as has happened in a number of communities.[138] ALEC's Public Safety and Elections Task Force, which was chaired by the National Rifle Association and whose membership included CCA and the American Bail Coalition, was the incubator for Arizona's controversial SB 1070 and copycat legislation in other states.[139]

Immigrants and Crime

Mass incarceration was fueled in part by stoking public anxieties that crime was out of control. Likewise, support for tougher immigration policies has been whipped up by charges that immigrants are a major source of crime, and that "border violence is out of control," in the words of Representative John Culberson (R-TX).[140] When 2,200 immigrants were released from detention in early 2012 due to the "sequester" budget cuts, Republicans berated the Obama administration for allegedly releasing dangerous foreign criminals to the streets.[141]

The belief that immigrants are responsible for a disproportionate amount of serious crime is widespread in the United States and elsewhere.[142] Throughout U.S. history, politicians and other public leaders have periodically exploited such anti-immigrant sentiments to ignite crackdowns on immigration, especially on migrants from Mexico.[143] What makes the current crackdown so exceptional is its tenacity in the face of a wide consensus among experts on crime and immigration that immigrants do not pose an exceptional threat to public safety. The reality is that rates of violent crime along the U.S.-Mexico border have been falling for years. This decline began prior to the massive increase in Border Patrol and other law enforcement officials and the construction of a giant fence along the border. U.S. border cities are actually statistically safer on average than other cities in their states.[144]

Counter to public perceptions, immigrant communities have helped to stabilize economically disadvantaged and socially disorganized neighborhoods. Communities with concentrated populations of immigrants tend to have lower rates of violence.[145] These findings appear to hold up across time and place.[146] Research suggests that the much celebrated drop in crime since the early 1990s is partly the result of rising levels of immigration.[147]

Bipartisanship and the Criminalization of Immigration Policy

The criminalization of immigration enforcement has enjoyed strong bipartisan support, much as the prison buildup of the 1980s and 1990s was stridently bipartisan. It is not just the product of conservative Republicans like Mitt Romney, who championed "self-deportation" in his race for the Republican presidential nomination in 2012. When he chaired the Homeland Security Subcommittee, Representative David Price (D-NC) pushed to extend Operation Streamline.[148] In 2005, Representative Sheila Jackson Lee (D-TX), an African American legislator generally known as sympathetic to immigrants, introduced a bill in the U.S. House to add 100,000 more immigration beds, which would have more than tripled the size of the federal government's immigrant detention capacity. Jackson's proposal only looks moderate when compared to the bill introduced in the Senate with bipartisan support that called for a 200,000-bed increase.[149]

It is not just Republican Tea Partiers who have exploited the unsubstantiated claim that crime waves follow immigration waves. When Representative Gabrielle Giffords (D-AZ) announced in 2010 that the Obama administration would be sending 1,200 more National Guard troops to police the border with Mexico, she held up a photo of Robert Krentz, the soft-spoken rancher shot to death weeks earlier on his Arizona ranch. After his death, Krentz quickly became the poster child for the war on immigrants and a cause célèbre among conservatives.[150]

For more than a decade now, leading Democrats and Republicans have been guilty of using hyperbolic language to sound the alarm about the growing threat posed by gangs that have reportedly migrated from overseas and become entrenched in hundreds of cities and communities in the United States. The two major immigration bills introduced in Congress in 2005–06 and 2013 included provisions to expedite the apprehension and deportation of alleged gang members. ICE regularly trumpets the activities of Operation Community Shield and its other anti-gang initiatives. In doing so, it reinforces the public perception that immigrants are responsible for a large, growing, and disproportionate amount of serious and violent crime in the United States, despite much evidence to the contrary. These anti-gang efforts are controversial in immigrant communities, for ICE has no legal or uniform standards to define who constitutes a gang member. The agency usually relies on local law enforcement officers to identify gang members, which has encouraged discriminatory law enforcement practices that are troubling.[151]

Even Jim Webb, widely hailed as a crusader against mass incarceration when he served in the U.S. Senate, was not been immune to the anti-immigrant, anti-gang political hysteria. In introducing his laudable 2009 proposal to create a national criminal justice commission to study the problem of mass incarceration, the Democratic senator from Virginia invoked the specter of powerful violent gangs from Mexico and elsewhere that reportedly were infiltrating and threatening hundreds of U.S. cities. He argued for easing up on the war on drugs so that resources could be shifted to the real threat to public safety posed by the country's reported one million gang members, many of whom allegedly belong to transnational gangs.[152]

The Obama administration made a big show of its opposition to Arizona's SB 1070 and copycat legislation in other states. But White House opposition to this measure has obscured the administration's strong, growing, and consistent support for the criminalization of immigration infractions and for expanding the government's institutional capacity to apprehend, detain, and deport both unauthorized immigrants and permanent residents holding green cards. As Paul Begala, a former top aide to Bill Clinton, observed, "President Obama has put more boots on the ground on the Mexican border than any president since Woodrow Wilson was chasing Pancho Villa."[153]

For all of the Obama administration's talk about fostering alternatives to detention for immigrants and treating them more humanely, it has pushed deportations and detentions to record levels. It dramatically and aggressively expanded programs like Secure Communities and Operation Streamline and has been a reliable supporter of further militarization of the border. President Obama has boasted how under his watch the number of Border Patrol agents along the Southwest border has increased to 20,000, or double what it was a decade ago and a sixfold increase since the early 1990s.[154] In fiscal 2012, the Obama administration spent nearly $18 billion on immigration enforcement, or about $4 billion more than spending for all other federal law enforcement agencies combined.[155]

The Obama administration has justified its tough-on-immigration stance in the name of creating fertile political space for comprehensive immigration reform legislation. It periodically has vowed to end the most grievous excesses of that war on immigrants but has done little to challenge fundamentally the core premises of that war or the politics that sustain it. With Latino electoral support ebbing, largely because of its punitive stance on immigration enforcement, the White House made some conciliatory gestures toward the end of Obama's first term. In 2011, ICE announced it would restrict the use of deportations to dangerous offenders, but no significant drop in the actual number of deportees resulted.[156] In June 2012, Obama announced that many of the hundreds of thousands of undocumented immigrants who came to the United States as children would no longer be subject to deportation. Thanks to an executive action, they also would be legally permitted to work and obtain driver's licenses. This shift in policy was unquestionably an important step forward in allowing large numbers of noncitizens to come out of the shadows and out of legal limbo. But it was not likely to have much of an impact on the number of deportations because undocumented immigrant children had not been a main target of the deportation apparatus.

In fiscal 2012, which ended months after the new policy was announced, the United States deported a record 410,000 people, one-quarter of whom were the parents of children who were U.S. citizens.[157] The following year, the United States deported about 370,000 people, a 10 percent drop. Nonetheless, that brought the total number of people deported under Obama to 1.9 million, by far the most for any American president (see figure 10.1).[158] In fiscal 2013, immigration prosecutions reached an all-time high of nearly 100,000 (see figure 10.2, p. 225).[159]

The White House fought SB 1070 all the way to the U.S. Supreme Court. The main arguments it raised against the Arizona legislation were not rooted in civil rights claims but rather in claims about the rights of the federal government. The Justice Department argued that SB 1070 was unconstitutional not based on equal protection principles enshrined in the Constitution, but rather because it usurped federal prerogatives to enforce immigration laws. The Supreme Court largely sided with the administration in striking down most of the measure's provisions on federalism grounds. The Court unanimously left standing the law's most controversial provision, which requires state law enforcement officers to determine the immigration status of anyone they stop or arrest if they have "reasonable suspicion" that the person is in the United States illegally.[160]

As with many issues, the Obama White House is trying to have it both ways. On June 25, 2013, the same day that the Supreme Court handed down its decision in SB 1070, Janet Napolitano announced that the DHS was suspending the 287(g) program throughout Arizona.[161] Weeks earlier, the Justice Department had filed a lawsuit against Joe Arpaio of Maricopa County, who bills himself as "America's toughest sheriff." The federal government charged that Arpaio and law enforcement officials were waging a campaign against illegal immigration based on a "pattern of unlawful discrimination" directed at Latinos, regardless of their status or citizenship.[162]

The political battles in Congress over comprehensive immigration reform in 2005–07 and 2012–14 exposed growing cleavages within both parties over the criminalization of immigration policy. They also revealed a widening gulf between mainstream national immigration organizations and grassroots Latino groups and their allies. Many mainstream immigrant rights' organizations gave their qualified support to the Kennedy-McCain bill in 2006. They promoted it as a moderate alternative to the reviled House bill that had sparked massive nationwide protests in spring and summer of 2006. The main objections of mainstream immigration organizations focused on the creation of a guest worker program.[163] The fact that the so-called moderate Senate bill preserved many provisions from the House legislation that would intensify the war on immigrants through the further criminalization and localization of immigration enforcement was not a central concern of theirs.

Grassroots Latino groups and their coalition partners raised alarms about provisions in the Kennedy-McCain bill that would expand the Border Patrol and detention facilities and foster even closer cooperation between local police and federal authorities to track down undocumented immigrants. They also opposed stretching the already bloated definition of an "aggravated felony" to target more immigrants for deportation. They objected to a measure to make alleged gang membership a deportable offense even for people who had never even been convicted of a criminal act. About one hundred immigrant, human rights, social justice, and civil rights groups signed a statement that called for rejecting the Senate bill.[164]

When Congress again took up the cause of comprehensive immigration reform in 2013, divisions over the criminalization of immigration policy persisted.[165] To the dismay of many immigrant rights groups and their allies, the Senate agreed to make "securing the border" a precondition for opening up the path to citizenship for millions of undocumented immigrants. The Senate measure, passed by a 68 to 32 vote in June 2013, allocates $46 billion to secure the border, including $30 billion to double the number of Border Patrol agents.[166] This is a staggering figure— roughly equal to what all fifty states together spend on corrections each year, or approximately seven times the annual budget of the federal Bureau of Prisons. The Senate bill also increases the criminal penalties for illegal entry and reentry, expands the list of offenses that warrant automatic detention, further restricts the granting of detention waivers, expands the purview of Border Patrol agents to conduct warrantless searches, and deploys the National Guard to the Southwest border for immigration enforcement operations.

Grassroots immigrant rights groups and their supporters in Congress de-nounced what they nicknamed the "border surge" amendment, which was added in the final days of the Senate negotiations over the bill.[167] They also denounced other provisions in the bill that would enhance the capacity and authority of fed-eral, state, and local officials to further criminalize immigration enforcement and that would expand rather than abolish the loathsome Operation Streamline pro-gram. Congressman Filemon Vela (D-TX) created a stir when he resigned from the Congressional Hispanic Caucus to protest the group's tacit support of the Sen-ate bill with its "border surge" provisions.[168]

As the debate over immigration reform shifted to the U.S. House, the Repub-lican leadership focused its efforts on the further criminalization of immigration enforcement, including the border surge, and creation of a new temporary worker program, not a path to permanent citizenship, for unauthorized immigrants. In June 2013, the House Judiciary Committee passed the Strengthen and Fortify En-forcement Act (SAFE), which was modeled after the controversial 2005 House bill. The SAFE Act would grant state and local law enforcement officers enormous new powers to enforce immigration law and policies with little federal oversight and would deny federal funding to any states that prohibit their police from using these powers. It also would further stiffen criminal penalties for immigration vio-lations and expand the federal government's capacity to detain and deport.[169]

The focus on Republican obstructionism on immigration reform obfuscates how the executive branch has been the most critical player in the criminalization of immigration enforcement and the expansion of immigrant detention. Obama's immigration policies, especially the record number of deportations, have become one of the most contentious domestic issues of his administration. Under enor-mous political pressure from immigrant groups, Obama vowed once again in early 2014 to review his administration's deportation policies to make them "more hu-mane" and selective.[170] There is much more the Obama administration could do on its own to rein in what has become the most dynamic sector of the carceral state, but it has consistently lacked the political will to do so. Operation Streamline was largely a creation of the executive branch, not Congress. The DHS could use its administrative powers to essentially repeal this program. The attorney general also could direct U.S. States Attorneys to stop prosecuting petty immigration violators and to revert to the long-standing practice of turning these cases over to the civil immigration system.

Ending the detention and criminal prosecution of petty border crossers would greatly reduce the government's dependence on the for-profit detention industry and would save millions of dollars each year. It also would reduce the crushing burden now shouldered by magistrate and district courts, the U.S. Attorney's Of-fice, the Federal Public Defender, and the U.S. Marshals Service. This would allow law enforcement agencies to refocus their efforts on dangerous criminal enter-prises rather than using their scarce resources to prosecute migrants who pose no significant threat to public safety. ICE also could suspend all 287(g) agreements and the Secure Communities program, which is being imposed by the federal gov-ernment on many jurisdictions against their will. Furthermore, the administration could challenge more forcefully the hyperbolic claims about the criminality of immigrants rather than feeding into them with calls to step up border security based on unsubstantiated reports of increased border crime. In a meeting with local law enforcement officials in May 2014, Homeland Security Secretary Jeh Johnson reportedly indicated that the administration was planning to revamp the Secure Communities program to address some of the objections raised to it.[171]

Immigration became a combustible partisan issue in summer 2014 with the surge in border crossings of unaccompanied children from Central America. In June 2014, Obama vowed to issue broad directives by the end of the summer to overhaul the immigration system if Congress remained at an impasse. The administration reportedly was considering expansion of a program that would provide many undocumented immigrants with work permits that would allow them to live and work in the United States without fear of deportation. In early September, the president announced that he would delay taking executive action until after the midterm elections in November. He said he was yielding to pressure from fellow Democrats in tight races. His decision infuriated many immigration advocates, who had been pushing the president for months to sidestep Congress.

Conclusion

The political battles over comprehensive immigration reform in 2005–07 and 2012–14 shined a very public spotlight on the growing criminalization of immigration enforcement. They also exposed the diversity of the growing pool of the dispossessed in the United States—be they undocumented workers laboring alongside other low-wage workers in the peripheral economy or detained immigrants sharing jail cells alongside citizens charged with a crime. Furthermore, they exposed important political opportunities and cleavages that have major implications for the future of the carceral state and American politics more broadly.

Grassroots Latino groups have been at the center of some of the most dynamic political activity in the United States today. Young Latinos advocating on behalf of the DREAM Act have kept immigration reform on the national agenda. Young immigrants have been at the forefront of the movement pressing Obama to expand the deportation deferral program he created by executive action in 2013.[172]

Latino and other immigrant-based workers' centers have injected new energy into the moribund labor movement.[173] In 2006, immigrant rights' advocates and their labor supporters chose May Day, recognized around the world as International Workers Day, to launch major street demonstrations on behalf of immigration reform. A coalition of social justice, labor, and immigrant groups joined together in 2012 to oust Joe Arpaio, the notorious sheriff of Maricopa County, Arizona. That year "Sheriff Joe" faced his toughest reelection battle ever.[174] Labor and immigrant activists fought side-by-side in California on behalf of the Trust Act, which Governor Jerry Brown signed in October 2013. Under this measure, law enforcement agencies may not detain for possible deportation immigrants charged or convicted of minor crimes.[175] Immigrant rights groups, criminal justice groups, religious organizations, and remnants of Occupy Wall Street launched the National Prison Industry Divestment Campaign in 2011 to pressure investors in the private-prison industry (including Wells Fargo, General Electric, Fidelity, and Wellington Management Group), to divest from CCA and GEO.[176] These coalitions are not unproblematic. For example, the rallying cry of many immigrant rights' demonstrators—"We are workers. We are not criminals."—could further stigmatize prisoners and former prisoners by creating an image of good, law-abiding noncitizens pitted against a native-born criminal underclass.

In discussions of the politics of mass incarceration, much media and political attention has tended to focus on the emergence of the Right on Crime coalition and the growing bipartisan commitment to the three R's. The percolating political ferment at the grassroots level has been largely ignored. But this ferment has the potential to ignite a wider political movement that sets the United States on course to dismantle the carceral state and address other injustices and inequities in U.S. society today. The criminalization of immigration policy could become an important cauldron that helps galvanize a broader political movement among immigrant rights' groups, social justice groups, labor groups, and human rights groups to challenge not only the carceral state but also the neoliberal turn in American politics. For this broad array of activists, chasing after Grover Norquist or Newt Gingrich to get their blessing for modest shifts in penal policy such as the three R's creates a serious case of political cognitive dissonance that is politically enervating. It also denies the numerous other ways the carceral state is metastasizing in the United States and impairing the health of vital democratic and other institutions.

CHAPTER ELEVEN

The Prison beyond the Prison

The Carceral State and Growing Political and Economic Inequalities in the United States

No man can put a chain about the ankle of his fellow man without
at last finding the other end fastened about his own neck.

—FREDERICK DOUGLASS

Alexis de Tocqueville's paeans to democracy in *Democracy in America*
are widely cited. Less well known is that Tocqueville originally came to the
United States in the early nineteenth century to study its penitentiaries,
which had become world-famous by the 1830s. Tocqueville collected notes for his
classic study of the social and political conditions of the new republic as he traveled from prison to prison, interviewing wardens and prisoners and collecting
information about everything from living conditions to disciplinary practices.

Tocqueville's dark observations about the connection between the penal system and American democracy are seldom noted. But nearly two centuries ago
he warned: "While society in the United States gives the example of the most extended liberty, the prisons of the same country offer the spectacle of the most
complete despotism."[1] This bleak assessment is even truer today.

The United States has developed an awesome power and an extensive apparatus to monitor, incarcerate, and execute its citizens and residents that is unprecedented in modern U.S. history and among other Western countries. This development raises deeply troubling questions about the health of democratic institutions
in the United States and the character of the liberal state. It also challenges the
common understanding of the U.S. state as comparatively weak.

After nearly four decades of steadily climbing incarceration rates, mass incarceration is emerging finally as a major public issue in the United States. But the
enormous prison beyond the prison that consigns millions of people who are not
fully in prison or fully a part of society to legal and civil purgatory remains largely
invisible. People with criminal records are enmeshed in a series of rules, regulations, and controls about working, voting, residency, and personal behavior that
severely limit their political and civil rights and that tightly control their daily
lives, as discussed in this chapter.

Elaborate gradations of citizenship are on their way to becoming the new normal in the United States. The carceral state has helped to legitimize the idea of creating a highly distinct political and legal universe for numerous categories of people. These "partial citizens" or "internal exiles"—be they felons, ex-felons, parolees, probationers, convicted sex offenders, legal resident aliens, undocumented immigrants, or people burdened with banishment orders—are now routinely denied a range of political and civil rights and also access to many public benefits, as discussed in this chapter.[2]

Evidence is mounting that the carceral state fundamentally impedes not only the political advancement of the most disadvantaged people in the United States but also their economic advancement. As Bruce Western soberly concludes in his careful analysis of wage, employment, education, and other socioeconomic data, mass imprisonment has erased many of the "gains to African-American citizenship hard won by the civil rights movement."[3] The criminal justice system is serving increasingly as a gateway to a much larger system of stigmatization and permanent marginalization.[4] In short, the country's penal system is no longer just the creation of the larger political, social, and economic forces that shape U.S. society. It has become "one of those causal or shaping forces."[5]

The extent of the political, social, and economic disadvantages that the carceral state confers on the most disadvantaged members of American society has remained relatively invisible for many reasons, some analytical, some political, and some a combination of the two. On the analytical side, as discussed below, official statistical and other standard databases that track health and well-being exclude the incarcerated population. This skews findings about trends in important indicators, such as the unemployment rate, wages, education levels, and rates of disease transmission. As a consequence, the widening inequalities in the United States spurred by the carceral state and other developments remain invisible or understated.

Civil Death

The United States has constructed an enormous prison beyond the prison. Many of its bars are invisible to the wider public but are keenly felt by released prisoners, parolees, probationers, their families, and their communities. Many ex-felons (and even some former misdemeanants) are subjected to numerous acts of "civil death" that push them further to the political, social, and economic margins. Many of them face lifetime bans on key activities—like voting, working in certain occupations and professions, and serving on juries. These lifetime bans remain largely intact despite recent findings that the future offending risk of people who have gone several years without an arrest is nearly indistinguishable from people who have never been caught up in the criminal justice system.[6] A decade ago, the American Bar Association called upon sentencing judges to take into consideration the broad range of collateral consequences, including immigration consequences, when determining a sentence so that the "totality of the penalty is not unduly severe."[7] In 2011, the ABA identified 38,000 punitive provisions that apply to people convicted of crimes.[8] Soon after the ABA released its report, Attorney General Eric Holder urged states to eliminate some of those legal burdens on former offenders.[9]

For many former offenders, their time in purgatory never ends, even after they have served their prison sentence or successfully completed their parole or probation. Former felons often must forfeit their pensions, disability benefits, and veterans' benefits. State licensing regulations render many occupations and professions off limits to former felons. Many ex-offenders are ineligible for public housing, food stamps, or student loans.[10] (In an important shift, New York City and some other cities have initiated pilot programs that permit released prisoners to reside in public housing.)[11] A 2005 GAO report estimated that tens of thousands of students were ineligible each year for federal loans and grants for higher education due to a drug conviction. These students forfeited hundreds of millions of dollars in Pell grants and federal education loans aid between 2001 and 2004.[12] Dozens of states and the federal government ban ex-offenders from jury service for life. As a result, nearly one-third of African American men are permanently ineligible to serve as jurors.[13] The persistence of extensive racial discrimination in jury selection compounds the persistent problem of the underrepresentation of African Americans selected to serve on juries.[14]

Employment Discrimination

Employment holds a sacrosanct place in defining ideas of citizenship, especially in the United States.[15] By severing large numbers of people from the labor force and from certain occupations and professions, the carceral state also is severing their bonds of citizenship. Many jurisdictions forbid employers to discriminate against job applicants solely because of their arrest or criminal record unless their offense is directly relevant to performing the job. But applicants with criminal records are still disproportionately denied jobs and rejected job seekers have great difficulty getting redress in the courts.

The problem of employment discrimination against people with criminal records has grown as the number of individuals who have been arrested or convicted has escalated. An estimated sixty-five million people in the United States have a criminal record.[16] By age twenty-three, at least half of all black males in the United States have been arrested at least once, as have nearly 40 percent of all white males.[17] The problem is compounded in the United States because information about individual criminal history is widely available through public and private databases that are electronically accessible. As of 2003, states held approximately seventy-one million criminal records on individuals, and nine out of ten of these records were automated.[18] By contrast, European countries sharply restrict the dissemination of such information in recognition of an individual's right to privacy and of society's strong commitment to furthering the rehabilitation and reintegration of ex-offenders.[19]

In some major U.S. cities, 80 percent of young African American men now have criminal records and thus are subject to a "hidden underworld of legalized discrimination and permanent social exclusion."[20] A seminal audit study of employment, race, and criminal history found that the stigma of a criminal conviction presents a major barrier to employment for white job applicants in the United States and a nearly insurmountable barrier for black applicants.[21] White males without a criminal conviction received twice as many callbacks for job interviews as compared to white males with a criminal conviction (34 percent and 17 percent respectively). Only 5 percent of black job applicants with a criminal conviction received a callback. Black applicants appear to be paying a double penalty. Black job seekers *without* a criminal conviction were less likely to receive a callback than white job seekers *with* a criminal conviction (14 percent and 17 percent respectively).[22]

In 2012, the Equal Employment Opportunity Commission approved new guidelines that restrict employers' use of background checks to systematically rule out job applicants with a criminal record. The EEOC affirmed that employers are legally permitted to consider criminal records in the hiring process. However, it also acknowledged that across-the-board exclusions of all applicants with a conviction could violate employment discrimination law because of their potentially disparate effects on racial and ethnic minorities. In 2013, the federal agency sued Dollar General over its use of criminal background checks, the first lawsuit brought by the federal agency under its new guidelines.[23]

The pervasive inaccuracies of FBI records, widely considered the gold standard of criminal background checks, compound these problems.[24] Approximately one in four U.S. adults has an arrest or conviction record, and the FBI currently maintains records on an estimated seventy-five million people. Half of these FBI records are inaccurate or missing critical information, most notably the disposition of an arrest. This missing information is vital for people applying for jobs or professional licenses. After all, one-third of felony arrests do not result in a conviction, and many others are reduced to misdemeanors. The FBI routinely searches for this missing disposition information when someone seeks to purchase a gun but does not routinely do so in the case of employment or licensing background checks.[25]

The conditions of parole foster additional impediments to employment. Many states require that employers of people on parole permit parole officers to search their workplace premises at any time without advance warning. Many parolees are subject to house arrest and required to get permission from their parole agents any time they need to leave home. This makes it difficult to accept jobs with shifting work schedules and travel requirements.[26]

Felon Disenfranchisement

The widespread practice in the United States of denying voting rights to people with a criminal conviction raises additional troubling questions about how the carceral state is defining (and redefining) citizenship.[27] As Chief Justice Earl Warren declared in the landmark 1964 *Reynolds v. Sims* decision: "The right to vote freely for the candidate of one's choice is of the essence of a democratic society, and any restrictions on that right strike at the heart of representative government."[28]

A maze of state laws denies former offenders as well as probationers, parolees, and prisoners the right to vote. Other established democracies generally place far fewer restrictions on the right to vote for people with a criminal conviction, including those in prison.[29] The United States disenfranchises most of its prisoners. Numerous states also deny the right to vote to large numbers of people who have completed their sentences or who are serving probation or parole.[30]

The political impact of felon disenfranchisement in the United States is so huge because the number of people with criminal records is so huge. Furthermore, felon disenfranchisement laws have stark racial origins and racial consequences.[31] As of 2010, nearly six million people, or about 2.5 percent of the voting-age population, were ineligible to vote because of a current or prior criminal conviction. Only one-quarter of these disenfranchised individuals were serving prison sentences. About 2.6 million of them had completed their sentences. Most of the remainder were probationers or parolees.[32] In addition, hundreds of thousands of people are pretrial detainees held in jail who are legally entitled to vote but who in practice are often disenfranchised. Confined to jail at election time, they do not have ready access to a polling station or an absentee ballot.[33]

The distribution of disenfranchised felons varies enormously by state, race, and ethnicity because of great variations in state disenfranchisement statutes and state incarceration rates. At one end are Vermont and Maine, which permit everyone to vote, including state prisoners. At the other end is Florida, one of several states that impose a lifelong ban on voting for certain criminal convictions.[34] Florida disenfranchises 1.5 million people—or more than 10 percent of its voting-age population. In Florida, Kentucky, and Virginia, more than one in five voting-age African Americans is disenfranchised due to a criminal conviction.[35] The national disenfranchisement rate for African Americans is nearly 8 percent, or more than four times the rate for non–African Americans.[36] In Arizona and Florida, an estimated 9–10 percent of voting-age Latino citizens are disenfranchised as a consequence of their criminal records.[37] Tens of thousands of Latino votes have gone missing in each of the four states with the four largest Latino populations and the four largest prison populations—California, New York, Florida, and Texas.[38]

The disenfranchisement of offenders and ex-offenders may be a decisive factor in close elections. Jeff Manza and Christopher Uggen calculate that if Florida had not banned an estimated 800,000 former felons from voting in the 2000 election, Al Gore would have handily carried the state and won the White House.[39] They also conclude that the Democratic Party might have controlled the U.S. Senate for much of the 1990s, as well as several additional governorships since the 1970s, if former felons had been permitted to vote.[40] Their work implicitly challenges long-standing claims about the sources of the Republican Party's political dominance in the 1980s and 1990s. If felon disenfranchisement is factored in, the ascendancy of the Republican Party may have been as much a function of locking out wide swaths of the electorate as crafting a new, more conservative message that successfully resonated with disenchanted Reagan Democrats.

The first high tide for liberalizing felon disenfranchisement laws coincided with the high tide of the civil rights movement from the late 1950s to the early 1970s. The key catalysts for reform during this period were leading African American politicians. They fashioned their appeals on calls for redemption and inclusiveness and received critical support from advocacy organizations.[41] Latinos also have been at the center of some key legal challenges to felon disenfranchisement, most notably the 1974 *Richardson v. Ramirez* decision, in which the U.S. Supreme Court upheld California's felon disenfranchisement laws.[42]

In the mid-1990s, felon disenfranchisement statutes emerged once again as a central issue. The NAACP, ACLU, and some other civil rights organizations mobilized to focus public attention on the discriminatory nature of these laws, their stark racial consequences, and their roots in the Jim Crow era's efforts to push blacks out of the electorate. A broader array of groups subsequently joined the fight against these laws. The focus then began to shift from the racial aspects of these voting barriers to the importance of universal suffrage "for preserving the legitimacy of the democratic process."[43]

Increased attention to felon disenfranchisement policies beginning in the mid-1990s has yielded some important reforms. About two dozen states have amended their statutes and policies to expand the eligibility to vote for felons and ex-felons. By 2010, an estimated 800,000 people had regained the right to vote, thanks to repeals or amendments to lifetime disenfranchisement laws, expansion of voting rights to parolees and probationers, and relaxation of restrictions on the process to restore voting and other rights.[44] These gains have been precarious. For example, hours after taking office in January 2011, Republican governor Terry Branstad of Iowa made good on a campaign promise to rescind a 2005 executive order signed by his predecessor Tom Vilsack that allowed felons to vote after they had completed their sentences.[45] That order had been credited with reducing the number of disenfranchised people in Iowa by 80 percent, or by about 100,000 people.[46]

Pushback against easing felon disenfranchisement statutes and policies has become part of what some characterize as the Republican Party's "new Southern strategy" to shrink the voting population.[47] That strategy includes aggressive redistricting and gerrymandering, crowding more minorities into majority-minority districts, enacting voter identification laws in dozens of states, deliberate use of inaccurate voter registration lists, and efforts to deny the U.S. Department of Justice funds to enforce key provisions of the Voting Rights Act of 1965 (VRA).[48]

Florida, a perennial toss-up state in presidential elections, is infamous for having some of the country's most restrictive felon disenfranchisement policies. The state also has been a central arena for the new southern strategy.[49] Over the years, only a small number of ex-felons in Florida succeeded in getting their voting and other civil rights restored. They had to navigate an elaborate, capricious, intrusive, and daunting process that established a new standard of "worthiness" for political participation.[50] That changed somewhat in 2007, when Republican governor

Charlie Crist supported a rule change that allowed the automatic restoration of voting and other rights for many nonviolent ex-offenders. Crist attempted initially to have the new rules apply to all former felons, including people convicted of violent offenses, but was forced by his cabinet to compromise. More than 100,000 ex-offenders were able to have their voting rights restored in Florida thanks to the 2007 rule changes (despite inadequate implementation funding from the state legislature, which resulted in lengthy waits to process the required paperwork).[51]

In March 2011, Florida's clemency board reversed course and imposed much tighter restrictions on the restoration process for both violent and nonviolent offenders. Pam Bondi, Florida's newly elected attorney general and a former county prosecutor who served on the clemency board, proposed the rule change. Republican governor Rick Scott, also a member of the clemency board, portrayed the reinstatement of greater restrictions on voting as an important law-and-order initiative.[52]

The U.S. Congress and federal courts have been generally unreceptive to dismantling state barriers to voting by felons and ex-felons. Legal challenges to felon disenfranchisement statutes based on the equal protection clause of the Fourteenth Amendment and other constitutional provisions have been mostly unsuccessful, except in instances of glaring discriminatory intent.[53] After constitutional challenges based on the Fourteenth Amendment failed, opponents of felon disenfranchisement turned to Section 2 of the VRA, which bars any "voting qualification" that denies or abridges the right to vote on account of color or race. But this promising strategy appears to have hit a legal dead end as well.[54] The Democracy Restoration Act, which would reinstate the voting rights of an estimated four million former offenders in federal elections, has made little headway in Congress since it was first introduced in 2008. Nevertheless, opposition to felon disenfranchisement is growing. In February 2014, Attorney General Eric Holder made a very public call for states to restore the voting rights of ex-offenders. He pointedly focused on the racially discriminatory effects of such bans. Days later, U.S. Senator Rand Paul (R-KY) testified before a Kentucky Senate committee on behalf of restoring the voting rights of former felons.[55]

Other Barriers to Political Participation

The impact of the carceral state on political participation extends far beyond official barriers to voting like felon disenfranchisement statutes. Incarceration and other kinds of contact with the criminal justice system have had a ripple effect on political and civic participation. Having a criminal conviction may be a more significant factor in depressing voter turnout among offenders and ex-offenders than formal legal barriers to voting.[56] Contact with the criminal justice system, including everything from being stopped by the police to serving time in prison, appears to have a cumulatively negative effect not just on voter registration and turnout. It also depresses participation in civic groups, trust in the government, and belief in the legitimacy of the criminal justice system and other government institutions.[57]

Recent research suggests that people who have been incarcerated internalize the stigma of having been sentenced to prison. They view their prison time as a mark of disgrace rather than a rite of passage, even in high incarceration communities where many people have been sent to jail or prison.[58]

A basic social fact about penal and other law enforcement institutions is that "they confer and withhold dignity in ways that make them powerful mediators of status identity and belonging."[59] People who live in communities with high rates of incarceration, high rates of police surveillance, and high numbers of parolees and probationers are less likely to vote and to engage in other political and civic activities.[60] High concentrations of criminal convictions "destroy the social and human capital of individual offenders and, by extension, that of their families and neighborhoods."[61] New research suggests that incarceration reduces the political engagement of children who have experienced the incarceration of a parent and of the romantic partners of former offenders.[62] Since police stops, arrests, and convictions are concentrated in certain geographic areas and within certain racial groups, the carceral state appears to be creating a troubling phenomenon that Traci Burch calls "concentrated disenfranchisement."[63] It also has fostered the enormous gaps between white and black public opinion about the fairness and legitimacy of the police, courts, and the criminal justice system, which were discussed in chapter 7. These gaps likely help explain why blacks are less likely than whites to trust their local government and why the jury nullification movement is gaining ground.[64]

Widening Surveillance of Daily Life

Many of the five million people currently serving parole or probation in the United States are enmeshed in a matrix of controls. The rise of the carceral state has fostered a pernicious climate of fear and suspicion that penetrates all aspects of their daily life, including intimate and family relations, labor force participation, and access to medical care. Parole and probation officers are permitted to regulate many major and mundane aspects of their lives. This includes everything from where they reside and who they associate with to whether they are permitted to keep a beer in their refrigerator or carry a cell phone. Recently a West Virginia court upheld a parole condition that banned a woman from associating with her husband, who, like her, was a convicted felon.[65] Many people on parole or probation are subject to frequent unannounced drug tests. A failed drug test or two is often cause to bounce someone back to jail or prison.

Alice Goffman's ethnographic study of "life on the run" in Philadelphia is a chilling portrait of how the expansive systems of policing and surveillance have upended life in poor urban neighborhoods. Men on parole or probation and those with outstanding warrants, even for trivial offenses, avoid the police and the courts at all costs out of a justified fear they will be sent to prison or jail.[66] For these men, "the police and the courts become dangerous to interact with." They also avoid visits to the local hospital and steady employment at the same workplace because such activities make it easier for the authorities to track them down and apprehend them.[67] To cope, these young men avoid the police even when they are the visits to of serious crimes; they remain secretive; and they come and go in "irregular and unpredictable ways" to ensure that those close to them will not turn them over to the authorities.[68]

It is not clear whether the actual number of supervisory conditions levied on parolees and probationers has grown for most offenders.[69] It is clear that the number of supervisory conditions for sex offenders have soared, as discussed in chapter 9. Furthermore, parole and probation officers have increased their capacity to detect technical violations thanks to enhanced technology, favorable legal decisions, and other developments. Law enforcement officers are permitted to conduct warrantless searches of parolees and probationers that are not subject to the standard Fourth Amendment protections. Parole and probation officers and the police are increasingly going out on patrol as tag teams. In these joint patrols, police use their databases to look up names and vehicle registrations. Once someone is identified, the parole or probation officer runs the name through the department of corrections to check if the person is serving parole or probation and what are the conditions of his or her supervised release. If they get a hit, the agent and police officer do not need a warrant or probable cause to search the person and his or her vehicle and residence.[70] "The ability to arrest, confine, and, in some cases, reimprison the parolee for violating conditions of the parole agreement makes the parole agent a walking court system," explains Joan Petersilia.[71]

Return of Banishment

Banishment has become another important tool for law enforcement officers and other public officials to assert their authority and control in the prison beyond the prison. A widespread form of punishment and social control that fell into disfavor in the nineteenth century, banishment has been reinvented. It has become a popular mechanism to control people who are considered "undesirables" in urban areas. Banishment raises serious concerns about potential civil rights violations and also about political and social marginalization.[72] Modern-day banishment orders are reinvigorating the spirit of nineteenth-century vagrancy laws while eliding the constitutional obstacles that courts invoked in the 1960s and '70s to strike down vagrancy and loitering laws.

In the 1990s, many municipalities adopted "civility codes" that criminalized behavior often associated with homelessness, such as panhandling, sleeping on sidewalks, and camping out in city parks. In recent years, police have been enforcing these laws with renewed vigor. They also have been inventing new forms of social control aimed at eradicating social disorder. These new mechanisms often rest on an "innovative blend" of civil, criminal, and administrative laws and procedures that are ambiguous and vague.[73] This renders them especially difficult to challenge successfully in the courts. These "quality of life" regulations are disproportionately enforced against LGBT people.[74]

Specifically, municipalities have been refashioning their trespassing laws and procedures in creative ways. They have granted the police enormous leeway to issue trespassing admonishments, which forbid a person from being on a specified property or group of properties for a certain period of time, usually one year.[75] Police also have been granted enormous discretion to issue exclusion orders for minor civil violations, like being in a park after hours or having an unleashed pet. These admonishments and exclusions are technically civil penalties and generally do not require police officers to provide a reason for issuing them. These orders accord police sweeping powers to stop, search, and arrest people suspected of violating the order. Violations of these "civil" penalties are usually considered criminal offenses. They may result in a stint in prison or jail or in permanent banishment from certain places or areas.

Two other banishment mechanisms that are growing in popularity are SODA (Stay Out of Drug Areas) and SOAP (Stay Out of Areas of Prostitution) orders. Judges used to impose SODAs and SOAPs primarily as a condition of a sentence or deferred prosecution for people charged with a drug offense or prostitution. More judges now are leveling these exclusion orders against people convicted of other types of crimes. Violation of a SODA or SOAP order is considered a violation of the terms of parole or probation. This can be cause to send someone to prison to serve out the remaining sentence for the crime that he or she was originally convicted.

Police also are imposing these off-limits orders at the time of arrest or in lieu of arrest. Arrests and prosecutions for SOAP and SODA violations are much easier to carry out than arrests and prosecutions for drug or prostitution offenses. Often all that is needed is the police officer's assurance that the defendant had been in an area from which he or she had been banished.

Exclusion orders and trespassing admonishments have not considerably enhanced public safety. Prosecutors, local business groups, and some anti-crime neighborhood groups have championed them nonetheless. They remain popular with many politicians because they are important visible symbols that the government is responding to public concerns about crime and disorder.[76] SODAs and SOAPS are cordoning off wide swaths of public urban space from the "undesirables," who tend to include those who are poor, homeless, unemployed, and addicted. In Seattle, roughly half of the city, including the downtown core where many critical social and legal services are concentrated, is currently "defined as a 'drug area' from which someone may be banned."[77]

Modern-day banishment orders have had enormous and far-reaching negative consequences. They imperil the efforts of socially marginal people to reintegrate into society. In Seattle, where these orders have been closely studied, they have had a net-widening effect. They have created "crimes and criminal cases that would not otherwise exist."[78] People who have been banished report that the practice impairs their geographic mobility and sense of safety, and it affects their income, employment, and access to social services. They also report that the police are more likely to harass them, and that they tend to have more frequent contact with criminal justice institutions. For many of them, exclusion is a "powerful emotional experience" that confirms "their sense that they were no longer considered citizens, even fully human, by other residents."[79]

Invisible Economic and Social Inequalities

The carceral state is pushing more people not only to the political and social margins of U.S. society but also to the economic margins. It also is impairing the mental and physical health of a growing number of people. A prison sentence has a long-term impact, considerably reducing the lifetime wages, employment, and annual income of former inmates, who tend to be disproportionately poor, African American, and Latino.[80] Incarceration also decreases the likelihood that they will get married or stay married and increases the risk of domestic violence for their partners.[81] The hyper-incarceration of African Americans likely helps explain enduring racial disparities in morbidity and mortality.[82] These negative effects are concentrated among poor, uneducated, African American men, drawing a sharp demarcation between poor blacks and middle- and upper-class blacks. "By cleaving off poor black communities from the mainstream, the prison boom left America more divided," Western explains.[83]

The enormous growth in political, social, and economic inequalities in the United States due to the carceral state and other factors has remained invisible or understated. One reason why is because people who have been captured by the state in prison and jail are not captured in standard social surveys. Years ago, when the incarceration rate was much lower, excluding prisoners and ex-felons from major social surveys that track the health and welfare of American society did not have such major consequences. With the tremendous growth in the size of the carceral state, the failure to accurately and fully incorporate felons and ex-felons into leading surveys that measure key indicators like trends in unemployment, wage inequality, high school completion, voting participation, mortality, and morbidity has enormous implications. It calls into question the accuracy of the basic social facts used to assess the well-being of the U.S. population, especially that of historically disadvantaged groups. The failure to include felons and ex-felons in such surveys impairs the development of data-driven, evidence-based public policies. It also compromises evaluations of what works. Furthermore, it reinforces the liminal social and political status of prisoners, felons, and ex-felons in American society.[84]

Good public policy and good governance depend on having accurate assessments of pressing problems and their possible solutions. The founders recognized this more than two centuries ago when they included a provision for a decennial census in the U.S. Constitution. Politicians and policy makers at all levels of government—from Washington to state capitals to city halls—routinely use the decennial census and other federal surveys to identify problems and target resources. Since the 1930s, these federal surveys have been central to determining how government resources are allocated to state and local jurisdictions. By one calculation, 16 percent of the federal budget—or more than 3 percent of the gross domestic product (GDP)—is currently allocated to state and local governments through grants-in-aid based on formulas derived from the census and other federal surveys.[85]

The census and these other surveys are designed in ways that undercount or do not count at all some of the most marginalized groups in U.S. society. The undercount of historically disadvantaged groups has been a perennial problem for the census. Since the mid-twentieth century, the overall size of the census undercount has diminished. This is thanks to improvements in statistical techniques, greater investments in data collection, and growing political pressure, especially from urban areas and advocacy groups, to enumerate marginalized groups accurately. Nonetheless, the undercount of African Americans is still considerable, estimated to be as high as 3 percent in the 2000 census. The undercount of African Americans and other minorities is likely due to their higher rates of residential instability, homelessness, and urbanization. These are the very same factors that are highly correlated with people who have spent time in jail or prison.[86] From 1980 to 2000, census data on the size of the jail and prison population reasonably matched figures from the Bureau of Justice Statistics on the number of inmates. Since then, the census and BJS data have been diverging dramatically.[87]

Other major social surveys like the Current Population Survey do an even worse job than the census at incorporating marginalized populations, especially young black men, in their data collection. The CPS and many other leading federal surveys are based on periodic statistical sampling of people living in households. This practice leaves out the huge and growing population of people confined to jails and prisons. Furthermore, these household-based surveys tend to undercount young black men who are not in prison or jail because many of these men maintain a loose connection at best to a household. Becky Pettit estimates that 16 percent or more of black men are rendered invisible in standard household surveys because of these two factors.[88]

The leading surveys used to assess health outcomes are modeled on the CPS and therefore also undercount marginalized populations not attached to households.[89] Furthermore, they do not statistically sample inmates, even though it is well established that prisons and jails exacerbate many public health problems, including transmission of communicable disease like hepatitis C, tuberculosis, and HIV/AIDS, and that prisoners and former prisoners are much more likely to test positive for these diseases.[90]

The impact of excluding inmates and other marginalized groups in federal surveys of the U.S. population is seismic. This practice calls into question the validity of these major federal surveys, as well as the validity of social scientific research based on these surveys. By failing to account for the impact of the carceral state, these surveys are helping to foster illusions of progress by blacks and other historically disadvantaged groups.

Some researchers have begun to incorporate the impact of the carceral state in their assessments of trends in major measures of inequality. They paint a picture of widening inequalities that is strikingly at odds with conventional narratives that stress a narrowing of the black-white gap in critical areas like wages, employment, education, and political participation. For example, Bruce Western's work casts doubt on claims about the achievements of the 1992–2000 economic expansion, hailed as the largest peacetime expansion in U.S. history. If prison and jail inmates had been included in standard government databases, the U.S. unemployment rate for males would have been at least 2 percentage points higher by the mid-1990s (and the true jobless rate for young black males in 2000 would have been 32 percent, not the official 24 percent).[91]

Western's account also casts doubt on the popular claim that the United States, with its relatively unregulated labor market, weak unions, and stingy welfare benefits, has done a better job at reducing unemployment, especially for low-skilled workers, than "nanny states" like France, Italy, and Germany. "The invisible disadvantage produced by mass imprisonment challenges this account of how meager social protections benefit the least-skilled workers," he explains.[92] Moreover, state regulation of the poor did not recede in the United States in the 1990s. It merely shifted course. The government greatly increased its role in regulating the lives of poor, uneducated men and women by sweeping more of them up into the criminal justice system's growing dragnet.[93]

Decades of penal expansion have concealed persistent and in some cases growing black disadvantages from public view. Pettit calculates that the real high school dropout rate for young black men is 40 percent higher than conventional estimates and concludes that the black-white gap in high school graduation rates has not narrowed since the early 1990s.[94] Analyses of trends in educational attainment and wages that factor in the incarcerated population also cast doubt on longstanding claims that the U.S. population is relatively more educated compared to other advanced industrialized countries, and that the black-white gap in wages is shrinking.[95]

Invisible Political Inequalities

Failure to fully consider the impact of the carceral state is leading to misleading conclusions not only about trends in economic and social inequalities but also about trends in political inequality. For more than a half century now, the country's plummeting voter turnout rate has been a cause of national concern and vigorously debated. Overlooked in this debate is the fact that most analyses of voter turnout neglect to take into account the large and growing number of noncitizens, prisoners, people on parole or probation, and ex-felons who have been disenfranchised by electoral laws. As a result, estimates of the decline in voter turnout are likely overstated.[96]

Conventional accounts of growing black political participation based on national surveys like the Current Population Survey and National Election Survey also appear to be off the mark. The much celebrated narrowing of the black-white gap in voter turnout in recent years is likely not due to rising voter turnout among blacks but rather to the exclusionary effects of mass incarceration and to turnout declines among whites. The media have heralded reports from the U.S. Census

Bureau and others that African American voter turnout has been surging, and that it exceeded white voter participation in the 2012 presidential election.[97] These findings have prompted claims that lower socioeconomic status is far less of a barrier to voting for blacks than for whites. If the millions of people who are incarcerated and unable to vote are included when calculating turnout estimates, the portrait of voting trends for the most marginalized populations looks less rosy. "Among young black high school dropouts, only one in five voted in the historic 2008 election and the election of 2012—exactly the same fraction that voted in the 1980 election when Ronald Reagan defeated Jimmy Carter," Bryan Sykes and his collaborators conclude.[98]

Prison-Based Gerrymandering

The way the decennial census enumerates prisoners has distorted demographic and socioeconomic data, leading to misleading conclusions in vital areas like economic growth, migration, household income, and racial composition. How to tabulate prisoners was one of the most vexing issues for the U.S. Census Bureau as it prepared for the 2010 census. The bureau chose to enumerate prisoners as residents of the towns and counties where they are incarcerated. But most inmates have no personal or civic ties to these communities and almost always return to their home neighborhoods upon release. "Current census residency rules ignore the reality of prison life," according to Kenneth Prewitt, who opposed enumerating incarcerated people at their home addresses when he was director of the Census Bureau but has since changed his views. "Incarcerated people have virtually no contact with the community surrounding the prison. Upon release the vast majority return to the community in which they lived prior to incarceration."[99]

The way that prisoners are enumerated affects the accuracy and quality of demographic data. For example, in the 2000 census, 56 counties nationwide—or 1 in 50—with declining populations were misleadingly reported to be growing, thanks to the inclusion of their captive populations.[100] Pennsylvania's Union County, which has an archipelago of federal penitentiaries, is 90 percent white, according to the 2000 census. But without its 5,000 prisoners, Union would be 97 percent white.[101]

How prisoners are enumerated in the census also raises enormous and unsettling political questions. As mentioned earlier, in every state except Maine and Vermont, state prisoners are barred from voting. Yet disenfranchised prisoners are included in the population tallies used for congressional reapportionment and for redistricting state House and Senate seats, city councils, and other government bodies. Prison-based gerrymandering is a common practice even though nearly every state has a constitutional provision or statute affirming that someone does not gain or lose legal residence by virtue of being incarcerated.[102] This practice dilutes the votes of those urban and rural areas that do not have a prison within their jurisdictions. For example, nearly 40 percent of the inmates in

Pennsylvania's state prisons come from Philadelphia, which has no state prisons in its city limits.[103] For census and redistricting purposes, these Philadelphia citizens—nearly all of whom are black or Latino—are considered residents of the counties where they are imprisoned. These tend to be predominantly white, rural districts that are Republican strongholds.[104] Nearly 200 counties nationwide have at least 5 percent of their "residents" in prison, and about twenty counties have more than 20 percent of their "residents" incarcerated.[105] In one city council district in Anamosa, Iowa, 96 percent of the inhabitants were incarcerated.[106]

The evidence of political inequities resulting from how the Census Bureau enumerates prisoners is "compelling," according to a 2006 report by the National Research Council.[107] If Texas prisoners were enumerated in their home counties rather than where they are incarcerated, Houston would likely have one additional state representative in the latest round of redistricting.[108] A 2002 analysis by the Prison Policy Initiative suggested that several Republican Senate seats in New York State would be in jeopardy if prisoners in upstate correctional institutions were counted in their home neighborhoods in New York City.[109] Prison-based gerrymandering likely helps explain the Republican Party's ability to dominate the New York State Senate for decades.

The impact of prison-based gerrymandering on state legislative districting receives the most attention from policy makers and the media. But the redistricting issue is even more consequential in counties and towns with sparse populations. In these cases, the population of a single prison can easily constitute a majority of a local government district.[110]

Prison-based gerrymandering is reminiscent of the ignoble compromise of the Constitutional Convention when the founders agreed more than two centuries ago to count each disenfranchised slave as three-fifths of a white person. This decision allowed the slaveholding South to maintain its dominance in national politics for decades. Prison-based gerrymandering "makes a mockery of the one person, one vote principle and dilutes the voting strength of communities of color."[111]

The census is used to determine not only how states and local communities draw their political jurisdictions but also how the government distributes billions of dollars. Each of the ten largest federal assistance programs, including Medicaid, highway construction, public education, Temporary Aid for Needy Families (TANF), Section 8 public housing, and the Children's Health Insurance Program, rely to varying degrees on the census and related data to determine the allocation of public aid. In fiscal 2009, these ten programs totaled nearly $500 billion, or about 85 percent of all federal assistance.[112]

How prisoners are counted does have some fiscal consequences, but the political movement to challenge this practice has primarily emphasized political equity, not fiscal equity. This is partly because most federal assistance is distributed in the form of block grants to states. These allocations generally are not affected by where someone is enumerated since most prisoners are incarcerated within their home states. The programs that are most affected by prison-based gerrymandering tend to be small federal and state programs that provide funds for rural areas. This gives a slight financial boost to rural towns with prisons over rural communities without them.[113]

The non-profit Prison Policy Initiative has spearheaded the push to reform how prisoners are counted and has drawn leading civil rights groups into this cause, including the NAACP, the ACLU, and National Urban League. The Prison Policy Initiative has stressed the anti-democratic nature of the current practice. It emphasizes how this practice is at odds with the U.S. Supreme Court's admonition in *Reynolds v. Sims* four decades ago. The Court ruled then that comparable political jurisdictions should be comprised of roughly equal numbers of voters in accordance with the "one man, one vote" principle.

Under growing political pressure to revise the way it enumerates prisoners, in 2011, the Census Bureau began changing the way it publishes its data. The aim was to make it easier for states, counties, and municipalities to draw districts that exclude their prison populations if they so desire.[114] After the 2010 Census, more than 185 counties and municipalities chose to draw their districts without including the prison populations. Since 2010, legislators in several states, including New York, Delaware, California, and Maryland, have enacted measures to end prison-based gerrymandering. A few other states, including Michigan, Colorado, and New Jersey, already had laws mandating the exclusion of prisoners for redistricting purposes.[115]

Bursts of expansions in social programs have been accompanied by bursts in resources allocated to expand and improve the government's survey data collection. This was true during the New Deal in the 1930s and then again during the Great Society in the 1960s and 1970s.[116] Today the United States is caught in a period of rising calls for retrenchment of the welfare state and of intense political attacks on expertise of all kinds—from experts on climate change to experts on statistical sampling. The political will to improve the government's survey and data collection capabilities and to address well-identified shortcomings in major social surveys is wanting at the national level. Instead of trying to improve these databases, some legislators have been pushing in the opposite direction. In 2012, the Republican-led House of Representatives voted to eliminate funding for the American Community Survey, a key annual survey of U.S. households that has been around in some form since 1850.[117] Republicans renewed their efforts to eliminate the ACS in 2013 as part of a wider push to further slash the budget for the census.

Conclusion

The problem of the prison beyond the prison is enormous and growing. Millions of felons and ex-felons are ensnared in a web of controls that stretches far beyond the prison gate. These controls have a huge impact on their daily lives, their life prospects, their political participation, and their sense of political legitimacy. The prison beyond the prison excludes and stigmatizes. By branding people with criminal records as second-class citizens, it cuts them off from many of the things associated with forging healthy identities and desisting from crime over the long run—education, steady employment, supportive relationships, and meaningful community connections through civic and other activities. The prison beyond the prison helps to solidify the "condemnation scripts" in which former offenders cannot envision a different—and better—way of life.[118]

The carceral state is ensnaring more people who have never been arrested or spent a day in jail or prison. They include the children of the incarcerated. They also include the residents of high-incarceration neighborhoods that have been depopulated and destabilized as so many of their young men and women have been shipped off to jail or prison, and as law enforcement more intensely monitors those left behind.

As it continues to metastasize, the carceral state is not only upending individual lives and certain communities but is also upending key democratic and governing institutions in the United States. It is compromising election results, creating disturbing gradations of citizenship, and distorting major demographic and other databases. It also is exacerbating political, social, and economic inequalities and concealing the alarming extent of these inequalities. These developments raise acute questions about the vitality and legitimacy of many democratic and other institutions in the United States.

CHAPTER TWELVE

Bring It On

The Future of Penal Reform, the Carceral State, and American Politics

> Life is about transitions and transcending one's limitations,
> and sooner or later, for better or for worse, we all make or
> miss the transition that will define who we are and, most
> importantly, choose to be. No longer will the state define me.
> I will dare to define myself.[1]
>
> —ROBERT SALEEM HOLBROOK

The carceral state is deeply entangled in the political, economic, and social fabric of the United States. But in plotting a way out, we must guard against succumbing to "dystopian despair."[2] We need to resist the belief that the only way to raze the carceral state is to tackle the "root causes" of crime—massive unemployment, massive poverty, and unconscionable levels of social and economic inequality stratified by race, ethnicity, and gender. Ameliorating the deeper structural problems that foster such high levels of inequality in U.S. society is an admirable goal. But if the aim is to slash the country's incarceration rate and undo its harmful collateral consequences over the next few years, not the next few decades, the root causes approach to progressive penal reform, however well intentioned, is shortsighted.

Four decades ago, the United States had many of the same structural problems it has today—though not to the same degree—but it did not have such an expansive penal system. Since then, the United States has embarked on a war on drugs and a broader war on crime characterized by penal policies unprecedented in modern U.S. history and unheard of or disdained in other industrialized democracies. Experts on crime and punishment now generally agree that changes in public policies—not dramatic changes in criminal behavior—propelled the decades-long prison boom in the United States.[3] In short, it was about the time, not about the crime. The focus on structural problems overshadows the fact that numerous people are serving time today for nonviolent offenses, many of them property or petty drug offenses, that would not warrant a sentence in many other countries. Many others are serving savagely long sentences for violent offenses even though they no longer pose serious threats to public safety.

If we designate structural problems the centerpiece of any plan to dismantle the carceral state, we are essentially accepting that the extensive U.S. penal system is here to stay for a very long time to come. After all, structural problems call for comprehensive, often expensive, long-term solutions and commitments. Long-term fixes are problematic not just because they take a long time, but also because they are harder to sustain from one change of administration to the next (especially in the United States, which lacks a respected, expert, and politically insulated civil service). Furthermore, as elaborated in this chapter, a focus on structural problems conflates two problems that are actually quite distinct—the problem of mass incarceration and the problem of crime.

Major decarcerations that have occurred in other places and at other times came about primarily as a result of comprehensive changes in penal policy rather than by mounting a sustained attack on structural problems and the root causes of crime.[4] For the reasons discussed in chapters 4 and 5, the package of penal policies based on the three-R model that prevails in elite circles today—reentry, justice reinvestment, and reducing recidivism—is not up to the task. It has created a lot of motion but no major movement in razing the carceral state or considerably reducing the incarceration rate.

The changes needed in penal policy in order to slash the country's incarceration rate are no mystery. While reentry should be a priority, we cannot focus only on those who are being released. We need to reduce the number of people who are sent to jail or prison in the first place and to decrease sentence lengths and time served. In short, we need comprehensive sentencing reform guided by the principle that prison should be reserved primarily for people who pose grave threats to society.[5] Many leading policy makers are still acting as though "they can reduce the size of the prison population without directly taking on the rate and length of sentences."[6] They have deliberately pursued a strategy based on no fundamental changes in sentencing laws. That has begun to change.[7] But the limited sentencing reforms enacted so far have been directed almost exclusively at the non, non, nons—that is, the nonserious, nonviolent, non–sex-related offenders, as discussed in chapter 8.[8] And many state officials and policy makers have fiercely resisted applying these modest reforms retroactively to people already serving time.

Comprehensive sentencing reform directed at reducing the time served for a wider range of offenders is necessary. But it is not enough. The country's high incarceration rate is just one facet of the problem of the carceral state. Another is that too many people are serving time in U.S. jails, prisons, and detention centers that are abusive and degrading. These facilities need to be opened up to independent oversight to ensure that all prisoners and detainees are housed in safe, healthy environments that are respectful of human dignity. But we also need to begin laying the political groundwork for a constitutional amendment that enshrines respect for human dignity in the U.S. Constitution, as Jonathan Simon implores. The Eighth Amendment has proved to be scant protection against the degrading and abusive practices and conditions that prevail in too many U.S. jails and prisons.[9]

Comprehensive sentencing reform also will not rectify the enormous harm caused by the prison beyond the prison and the stark and pernicious gradations of citizenship that the carceral state has created. The widespread practice of condemning people with criminal records to "civil death" must be halted. Most of the barriers to receiving critical public services, such as public housing, student loans, and welfare, and to participating in civic life, including voting and jury duty, must be eliminated. Employment and licensing restrictions levied on ex-offenders should be narrowly tailored and reserved for very specific instances of compelling public safety concerns. The criminalization of immigration policy must end, and the creeping merger of the law enforcement and immigration enforcement systems needs to be reversed.

Major reforms in penal policy and law enforcement are necessary to slash the incarceration rate and begin dismantling the carceral state. In pursuing such reforms, we need to be clear that this will not resolve the crime crisis that persists in the United States despite the record crime drop of the past two decades. National crime rates are at nearly their lowest levels in half a century, but crime in poor communities—especially poor urban neighborhoods that are predominantly African American—remains a major social problem.

The crime crisis is directly related to deeper structural problems in ways that the crisis of the carceral state is not. The only legitimate long-term solution to this crime crisis is to alleviate the root causes of vast and growing inequalities in the United States. It goes without saying that this is going to take a long time and will require a major political struggle. But in the meantime, there is no compelling public safety justification for keeping so many people from poor communities locked up.

The necessary policy changes if we are serious about dismantling the carceral state are fairly straightforward. But the politics are not. As Glenn Loury and Bruce Western note, the "most challenging policy problems are not merely technical."[10] Issues of crime and punishment are so vexing because they are inextricably bound up with judgments about morality, how social benefits and burdens should be allocated, the proper reach of the government, and what kind of democratic society the United States is, was, and will be.[11] And all of these issues are to varying degrees tarnished by the patina of the country's troubled racial history.

What Doesn't Work

What is persistently missing in much of the current debate over mass incarceration and penal reform is any kind of inspiring, long-term vision against which the necessary short-term goals and strategic compromises can be measured.[12] In plotting an escape from the carceral state, we need to "distinguish between mere surface scratches on a policy that is otherwise intact and deep fissures in the core of the policy itself" that might mark the beginning of the end of the carceral state.[13]

The latest economic crisis provided an opportunity to redirect U.S. penal policy that opponents of the prison boom should continue to exploit. But framing the problem of the carceral state as primarily an economic one will not sustain the political momentum needed over the long haul to drastically reduce the prison population and will have other negative consequences, as discussed in chapter 2. It denies the reality that punishment in any society is never a purely rational act. Punishment is a means to regulate deviance, but it also is an expressive act "in which society talks to itself about its own moral identity," explains Philip Smith, channeling Durkheim.[14]

Successful decarceration will cost money. The people reentering society after prison need significant educational, vocational, housing, health, and economic support to ensure that the communities they are returning to are not further destabilized by waves of former prisoners. It is more expensive to process young people in the juvenile court system rather than to transfer them to adult court.[15] If we are serious about alternatives to incarceration, then community-based mental health and substance abuse programs will need major infusions of cash so that the penal system is no longer the primary line of defense to address these major public health problems.

A penal reform agenda delineated primarily by evidence-based research about "what works" will inevitably yield an agenda that is highly constrained and politically vulnerable. "What works" has a poor track record when it comes to engineering important shifts not just in penal policy, but all kinds of public policy.[16] In fact, a major preoccupation of scholars of public policy is seeking to explain why good scientific evidence often loses out in the contest against bad public policy. Just look at the tragedy of climate change. The fixation on emphasizing technocratic, expert-driven solutions to the problem of the carceral state denies the fundamental role that politics, emotion, and culture play in meting out punishment and in defining good and bad penal policy. Appeals to science are incapable of articulating a "public ideal around which reform can be mobilised."[17]

Furthermore, as Todd Clear emphasized in his 2009 presidential address to the American Society of Criminology, the "evidence-based policy paradigm is, at its core, extraordinarily conservative." The "what works" model is based on a narrowly constructed understanding of what counts as evidence—program evaluations based on the gold standard of multiple randomized trials. Such a narrow construction of evidence resting on what has already been shown to work fosters a "kind of slavery of the present." It also contributes to a denigration of other kinds of knowing and evidence that are not the result of controlled experiments, including policy studies and qualitative work.[18]

A penal reform agenda defined primarily by attacking racial bias and racial disparities in the criminal justice system, especially the war on drugs, racial profiling, and stop-and-frisk, will also not bring about the demise of the carceral state, for reasons elaborated in chapters 6 and 7. Even if every drug offender were released today, the United States would still have a sky-high incarceration rate. Furthermore, a movement to challenge the carceral state centered on black-white disparities in the criminal justice system ignores how the carceral state has been extending its reach to other marginalized groups, including immigrants, poor whites, and people charged with sex offenses. The racial disparities issue cannot be understood separately from key features of the wider political and economic context in which the carceral state was built, as discussed throughout this book. These include the ascendancy of neoliberalism, growing economic inequalities among blacks, and the emergence of a new generation of post-racial African American leaders.

The causes of extreme levels of racial disparity in the U.S. penal system (including the war on drugs, racial profiling, pernicious racial and ethnic stereotypes, and the savagely long sentences meted out for offenses that African Americans disproportionately commit) "are unjust and objectionable in themselves," as Michael Tonry argues. But it is the severity of sentences, not the disparities in sentences, "that does the most damage."[19] Tonry calculates that if imprisonment rates were reduced to their level in 1980, the black imprisonment rate would fall by two-thirds, and 700,000 fewer blacks would be in prison even though racial disparities in imprisonment would remain unchanged at about 5 to 1.[20]

For penal reformers troubled by the racial injustices of the criminal justice system, it is politically more challenging to put calls for across-the-board cuts in sentence lengths ahead of attacking policies that are so nakedly discriminatory, such as racial profiling, stop-and-frisk, and the war on drugs. It also is politically more challenging to formulate a nuanced argument in defense of people who committed serious or violent offenses and are serving such lengthy sentences even though they no longer pose serious threats to society.[21] Steven Raphael and Michael Stoll calculate that rolling back punishments for violent offenses to their 1984 levels would have reduced the state imprisonment rate in 2004 from about 500 per 100,000 to about 350 per 100,000, or a decrease of 30 percent.[22]

Sentencing Reform

Prisons and jails exacerbate many social ills that contribute to crime and poverty and are unlikely to significantly rehabilitate anyone. The findings of two centuries of research on mandatory sentences are compelling: they do not serve as major deterrents to crime but do contribute to wide unwarranted disparities in punishment, especially racial disparities.[23] We need to repeal high mandatory minimums, truth-in-sentencing, and habitual offender laws, including three-strikes statutes, and to rein in sex offender registration, notification, and civil commitment laws. We also need to reinvigorate the parole process and insulate it from politics to ensure that every offender is entitled to a meaningful parole review, including people serving life sentences. Furthermore, the bail bond system must be overhauled so that ability to pay is no longer the deciding factor in whether someone languishes in jail or not until his or her case is settled.[24]

Momentum has been growing for sentencing reform, though much of it has been focused on the non, non, nons. In May 2013, Congress created a bipartisan task force to pare down the criminal code with an eye toward reducing the number of people in federal prisons and reversing the encroachment of federal law enforcement into areas traditionally handled by the states. The following month,

Pew released a report highlighting how increases in time served have been a major contributor to the rise in incarceration rates.[25] The report called for some modest sentencing reforms directed primarily at nonviolent offenders. Months later, Senator Rand Paul (R-KY) created a sensation at a Senate hearing when he likened the war on drugs to Jim Crow and characterized low-level drug offenders as victims.[26] In January 2014, the U.S. Sentencing Commission proposed amendments to the sentencing guidelines to reduce the penalties for federal drug trafficking offenses.[27] Later that month, the Democrat-controlled Senate Judiciary Committee approved the Smarter Sentencing Act by a 13-to-5 vote with the support of Tea Partiers on the committee but not establishment Republicans. The act cuts some drug-related mandatory minimums in half, but the penalties still remain stiff—two, five, and ten years—and would not be applied retroactively. However, the act did modify the 2010 Fair Sentencing Act to make it somewhat retroactive.

Modest sentencing reforms have faced considerable political opposition. The Smarter Sentencing Act enacted by the Judiciary Committee was a greatly watered down version of the original legislation. In a fruitless eleventh-hour effort to win wider Republican support, legislators inserted some new mandatory minimums for sexual abuse, domestic terrorism, and domestic violence, to the dismay of some penal reformers, including the National Task Force to End Sexual and Domestic Violence.[28] In late 2013, federal prosecutors openly revolted against Attorney General Eric Holder's support of the Smarter Sentencing Act. The National Association of Assistant United States Attorneys, which represents the Department of Justice's 5,300 federal prosecutors, mounted an aggressive public campaign in defense of mandatory minimums and called on other leading law enforcement groups to join them. The association has also opposed important recent moves by the U.S. Sentencing Commission to reduce penalties for drug offenses, which were discussed in chapter 6.[29] In May 2014, dozens of former leaders in the DOJ, the DEA, and U.S. Attorney's Offices sent a letter to Senate leaders Harry Reid (D-NV) and Mitch McConnell (R-KY) urging them to defeat the Smarter Sentencing Act.[30]

Yes You Can

Comprehensive sentencing reform by definition requires statutory changes. The political logjam in Washington and many state capitals is a convenient foil to excuse why so little progress has been made in slashing the country's incarceration rate and ameliorating the collateral consequences of the carceral state. It justifies the pursuit of small-bore solutions like the three R's that are premised on splitting the difference without making any real difference in addressing the country's enormous and growing political, social, and economic inequalities, of which the carceral state is the starkest example.

Claims of legislative gridlock direct attention away from many nonlegislative means available to begin razing the carceral state. The carceral state was not built by punitive legislation alone. It also required a shift in the sensibilities of government officials and law enforcement officers on the front lines of the criminal justice system, particularly in its early years. Police officers, parole and probation agents, judges, corrections officials, attorneys general, local district attorneys, and federal prosecutors began to exercise their discretion in a more punitive direction as they read the new cues coming from law-and-order politicians. Rick Raemisch's blistering 2014 *New York Times* op-ed about the night he spent in solitary confinement as executive director of the Colorado Department of Corrections is a rare and noteworthy example of a bold individual challenge to the ingrained, taken-for-granted punitive sensibilities of the carceral state written by someone who is part of the system.[31]

Many observers attribute U.S. punitiveness to the exceptional politicization of prosecutors and judges, who are elected or otherwise chosen in a partisan manner. But this politicization can cut both ways. Prosecutors and judges have tended to use their discretion over the past three to four decades to lean in a more punitive direction. But that wide discretion also gives them great latitude to shift now and embrace alternatives to incarceration, as some district attorneys and judges have done.[32]

The widely misunderstood implementation of the draconian Rockefeller drug laws in 1973 is a good case in point.[33] At first, the Rockefeller laws had only a very modest impact on New York State's incarceration rate. This was due to the "selective pragmatic enforcement" by police, prosecutors, and judges, who initially viewed the new drug laws as wasteful and misguided. That changed in the late 1970s and early 1980s as Mayor Ed Koch of New York City and his new police commissioner embraced the "politics of fear and disorder" and sought to "retake the streets." Shortly thereafter, Democratic governor Hugh Carey promised major funding for new prison construction, and the state unveiled new joint state-local initiatives to target drug trafficking. Thanks to these political shifts, prison commitments for drug violations began to soar in the early 1980s as police, prosecutors, and judges in New York State belatedly embraced the Rockefeller laws and became willing recruits in the war on drugs. A decade later, some key law enforcement officials in New York State began to pull back from the war on drugs, and prison commitments for drug offenses began to fall. This was many years before the Rockefeller drug laws were largely repealed in 2009.

For all the talk about how mandatory minimums and mandatory guidelines built the carceral state, individuals serving on the front lines of the criminal justice system retain considerable discretion to choose a less punitive path. As discussed in chapter 8, the president and state governors have enormous discretion to grant executive clemency. So far, they have been largely unwilling to wield these powers to start righting the wrongs of the carceral state and to make a statement about how the time is long overdue to declare that the war on drugs and the war on crime are over. The Department of Justice could put an end to overcrowding in federal penitentiaries by calling a halt to the federal war on drugs. After all, the federal government "generally has no fundamental 'crime fighting' obligation to prosecute drug offenses in its jurisdiction" since "virtually every state has a body of criminal law devoted to drug offenses—from infractions to major felonies."[34]

Federal judges retain broad sentencing discretion. In more than 70 percent of federal cases, the statute does not impose a mandatory minimum.[35] The 2005 *Booker* and 2007 *Gall* decisions affirmed that federal judges have considerable leeway to depart from the mandatory sentencing guidelines. The 2011 *Pepper* decision affirmed that the courts are permitted to draw on a wide range of information at sentencing, and that "the punishment should fit the offender and not merely the crime."[36]

The Federal Bureau of Prisons

All the attention on the tough federal sentencing guidelines and the overzealousness of presidents and members of Congress to prosecute the war on drugs and the war on crime have created the impression that the federal Bureau of Prisons is largely a passive spectator in the carceral crisis. For all of its law-and-order zeal in the 1980s and 1990s, Congress nonetheless endowed the BOP with considerable discretionary powers to pursue early release of federal inmates. So far, the BOP has been generally unwilling to wield these powers. Without any changes in the federal sentencing guidelines or creation of new programs, the BOP could "eliminate thousands of years of unnecessary incarceration through full implementation of existing ameliorative statutes."[37] Instead, the BOP, which is under the authority of the Department of Justice, has continued to promulgate dire projections about the need for more prison beds as it has gone hat in hand to Congress year after year for more money to expand the federal prison system.

The BOP and many state departments of corrections have important compassionate release policies and laws on the books that would permit them to release infirm and elderly inmates. In 2013, the DOJ's inspector general issued a piercing report on the BOP's mismanagement of compassionate release cases. Months later, the Justice Department indicated it would revamp its policies so that more federal inmates would qualify for timely compassionate release.[38]

The BOP has mostly ignored the little known but potentially powerful "second look" provision of the Sentencing Reform Act of 1984. This measure permits a sentencing judge to reduce a sentence if the court finds "extraordinary and compelling" circumstances. Under the statute, the BOP plays a key gatekeeper function. It is responsible for filing a motion to the court for reconsideration of a sentence. The legislative history of this provision suggests that Congress sought to recognize a wide range of circumstances that would qualify for resentencing. Over the years, the BOP has interpreted this statute very narrowly to mean cases of imminent death and has filed only a handful of resentencing motions. In a quarter of the cases, the federal inmate died before the court had ruled on the motion.[39] In 2007, the U.S. Sentencing Commission adopted a new rule that set out no limit on what constitutes "extraordinary and compelling circumstances," but little changed at the BOP.[40] To the dismay of penal reform advocates and some members of Congress, the BOP has made scant use of several other important options at its disposal to reduce the time served for federal inmates.[41]

The "Real Lawmakers"

William Stuntz once characterized prosecutors as the "real lawmakers" of the criminal justice system because the penal code grants them such enormous leeway in charging decisions. As the violent crime rate started falling in the early 1990s, changes in prosecutorial behavior were one of the most important contributors to the ongoing rise in the state prison population. Much of the growth was not the result of judicial decisions to increase the use of prison sentences. Rather, it was due to an increase in the number of violent offenses (and, to a lesser extent, property cases) brought forward successfully for prosecution and to an increase in the time served by violent offenders.[42]

To reduce the imprisonment rate, prosecutors will have to be cajoled or pressured into embracing a commitment to send fewer people to prison and to reduce sentence lengths. In some cases, binding legislation may be necessary to force prosecutors to relinquish some of their discretionary powers and to make their activities and decisions more accountable and transparent to the public. But all paths to progressive penal reform do not have to run through state legislatures.

Attorneys general and district attorneys have enormous authority to set "the tone and culture of the office" and to determine the direction in which prosecutors working under them exercise their discretion in individual cases.[43] As a consequence, "the differences from one prosecutor's office to the next—even operating in the same jurisdiction—can be stunning."[44] National trends obscure "the profound variations in incarceration rates across states, cities, and especially local communities within cities."[45]

U.S. prosecutors are arguably the most powerful officials in the U.S. criminal justice system and the least understood and least transparent.[46] Historically, U.S. prosecutors have had enormous power relative to prosecutors in other industrialized democracies.[47] As states and the federal government revamped their sentencing structures in the 1980s and 1990s to curtail the discretion of judges (and, in some cases, the police), even more discretionary and other powers flowed to prosecutors. With the proliferation of mandatory minimum sentences and other get-tough policies, and the contraction of legal resources for public defenders, the already-enormous charging and plea-bargaining powers of U.S. prosecutors expanded even further.[48] Several landmark court cases challenging prosecutors' wide prerogatives that were decided in their favor further enhanced their powers.[49]

Prosecutors not only got tougher but also created powerful local, state, and national organizations to represent their interests and coordinate their political activities.[50] Furthermore, they forged close alliances with other law enforcement groups and helped create a conservative victims' rights movement premised on a zero-sum vision of justice that pitted victims against offenders.[51] Recently, statewide associations of district attorneys allied closely with other law enforcement organizations and with victims' rights groups have been leading opponents of sentencing and other penal reforms.[52]

So far, U.S. prosecutors "have escaped the kind of scrutiny and accountability that we demand of public officials in a democratic society."[53] While police forces have become substantially more transparent and publicly accountable over the past several decades, prosecutors' offices are actually far less transparent today than decades ago.[54] Most of their decisions are "totally discretionary and virtually unreviewable."[55]

By changing their behavior, prosecutors could have a profound impact on lowering incarceration rates and reducing racial disparities in sentences even without any statutory changes. For example, district attorneys could shift the standard for charging from "probable cause" to "likelihood of conviction." Or they could make a policy decision not to prosecute certain low-level offenders, as the Milwaukee district attorney did in the case of first-time offenders caught with drug paraphernalia.[56]

New research suggests that federal prosecutors, not federal judges, are the most persistent source of racial disparities in sentencing. Sonja Starr and Marit Rehavi found that, all things being equal, federal prosecutors were nearly twice as likely to charge African American men with an offense carrying a mandatory minimum sentence compared to white men.[57] With the help of a promising Vera Institute program, prosecutors in Milwaukee and in Mecklenburg, North Carolina, were able to reduce unwarranted racial disparities in their criminal justice systems by altering their seemingly race-neutral charging and plea-bargaining decisions.[58]

What incentives do prosecutors have to behave less punitively now? As prisons and jails eat up more state, municipal, and county budgets, prosecutors face the prospect of shrinking revenues to run their offices. But, more importantly, politics is all about forcing incentives to change. So far district attorneys and other prosecutors have faced little political pressure to change.

When he was president of the National Association for the Advancement of Colored People (NAACP), Benjamin Jealous designated mass incarceration as the leading civil rights challenge of this generation.[59] If that is so, then getting deeply involved in electoral contests for local district attorneys and otherwise putting political pressure on them should be a top priority for civil rights and other groups committed to dismantling the carceral state. If the aim is to shift penal policy in a less punitive direction, these local electoral contests are arguably as important—or even more important—than mobilizing for the quadrennial presidential elections.

Maverick district attorneys launched into office in major urban areas with the backing of broad penal reform coalitions have served as important beachheads to engineer wider statewide shifts in penal policy. The upset victory of David Soales in Albany's 2004 race for district attorney was a "watershed event" in the fight to reform the strict drug laws of the Rockefeller era in New York State.[60] His electoral victory, coming on the heels of the decade-old "Drop the Rock" campaign, paved the way for the beginning of the end of the Rockefeller drug laws.

The focus cannot be solely on electoral politics. Reform groups need to exert ongoing pressure on district attorneys to make their actions more transparent and publicly accountable. For example, a reform coalition launched Seth Williams, Philadelphia's first African American district attorney, into office to succeed long-time district attorney Lynne Abraham. A self-proclaimed "tough cookie," Abraham had garnered a national reputation as "the deadliest D.A." for her aggressive use of capital punishment.[61] But since taking office in 2010, Williams has faced remarkably little political pushback as he has tacked in a law-and-order direction.[62]

Five years into his tenure, Attorney General Eric Holder finally appeared ready to assert some of his vast discretion to challenge the carceral state. He created front-page news in August 2013 when he announced at the annual meeting of the American Bar Association that he had ordered federal prosecutors to omit specifying the quantities of illegal drugs in indictments for certain low-level drug offenders. By making this shift, prosecutors would avoid triggering the strict federal mandatory minimum penalties based on drug quantities. Although this announcement created a stir, its practical consequences might turn out to be quite minimal. The pool of federal defendants who would qualify for the new policies was drawn quite narrowly.[63] Furthermore, federal prosecutors retain enormous leeway on how to charge these cases.[64] The potentially more consequential change, which received less attention, was Holder's announcement at the time that the Justice Department was instituting new policies designed to leave more crimes for local and state courts and prosecutors to dispose of rather than have the federal government step in. Furthermore, Holder used his ABA speech as an opportunity to launch a broader rhetorical assault on mass incarceration and the racial disparities that run through the criminal justice system. He conceded that the system "is in too many respects broken."[65]

In short, comprehensive sentencing reform will not be enough on its own to reverse the prison boom because the criminal justice system is highly adaptive. To make major and lasting cuts, the penal sensibilities and penal culture of all components of the criminal justice system—police, prosecutors, judges, penal administrators, parole and probation officers—will have to change. They need to buy into the goal of major reductions in the prison population and to coordinate their behavior to achieve that end. Without that coordination, attempts to reduce the prison population will remain a complex and often futile game of Whack-a-Mole. Single-minded attention on "reforming" any one or two pieces of the criminal justice system to reduce the incarcerated population will not necessarily have the desired result because the system is highly adaptive.

Prosecutors remain the preeminent players in this game. By changing their actions and sensibilities, individual district attorneys, especially in large urban areas, have the potential to be important catalysts. They can help to facilitate the system-wide coordination and change in penal culture that are so critical to slashing the number of people in U.S. prisons and jails. But so far they have faced little political pressure to behave otherwise even though many of their constituents have been disproportionately harmed by the carceral state.

Realignment and Political Pushback in California

Recent developments in California are a bracing reminder of how the path toward decarceration remains steep and politically tortuous. In the acrimonious May 2011 *Brown v. Plata* decision, a sharply divided Supreme Court ruled 5 to 4 that the overcrowded conditions in California prisons were unconstitutional.[66] Specifically, the justices held that inadequate medical and mental health care was responsible for one inmate dying each week due to neglect. The Court ruled that the state needed to reduce the prison population to 137.5 percent of design capacity within two years. Anticipating the Court's decision, weeks earlier Governor Jerry Brown signed the Public Safety Realignment Act. Law enforcement officials, the correctional officers' union, and key legislators negotiated that measure behind the scenes with the Brown administration without any input from prisoners and their advocates or the wider public.[67]

"Realignment" in California seeks to divert many of the non, non, nons from state prisons and the state parole system to county jails and locally supervised community sanctions (such as probation and mandated substance abuse treatment). It bestows block grants on counties to implement realignment with virtually no strings attached, little state oversight, and no evaluations. Many counties have responded by investing heavily in jail expansion and by bolstering their law enforcement budgets. They have eschewed using the billions of new state dollars allocated for realignment to invest in mental health and substance abuse treatment and other social services for offenders diverted out of the state prison system.[68] This is not so surprising, since the legislation mandated the creation of Community Corrections Partnerships to be composed primarily of law enforcement officials.[69]

California appears on its way to substantiating Heather Schoenfeld's claim about the paradox of prison conditions litigation: if you litigate it, they very well may build it.[70] As of July 2012, the state had approved applications from twenty-one counties to build more than 10,000 new jail beds at a cost of $1.2 billion. The state had plans for an additional $500 million in jail construction. If all this construction is carried out, the total number of jail beds will increase by more than 17,000—a far cry from any decarceration. As one observer noted, "Prison building, essentially, has gone local."[71]

Although the state prison population fell substantially in the years immediately after realignment was first implemented, California's jail population rose somewhat. About one-third of the inmates realigned from California's prisons ended up in county jails.[72] Parolees with technical violations were returned to jail, not prison, and certain non, non, nons were diverted to local jails. The large decline in California's state prison population is responsible for much of the recent nationwide drop in the total state prison population.[73]

County jails have a well-deserved reputation as the "worst blight in American corrections."[74] Many jails in California were already seriously overcrowded before realignment came along. Designed and intended to house short-term, transient populations, jails do not have the medical facilities, programs, and security resources to meet the needs of inmates serving sentences counted in years, not months or weeks.[75] Security and other problems in California jails are mounting as long-term, high-security inmates are serving their time alongside the run-of-the-mill, low-level defendants who predominate in county jails. Civil rights lawyers and prisoners' rights advocates do not have the resources to monitor effectively the conditions in the more than 150 jails scattered throughout California's fifty-eight counties, let alone sue them all.

In late 2013, the California Department of Corrections and Rehabilitation projected that the state prison population would grow by more than 10,000 inmates over the next five years. State officials announced plans to house thousands of inmates in private out-of-state facilities, increase the capacity of the California prison system, and institute new parole programs to meet the expected demand for more prison beds. As of early 2014, about 9,000 California inmates were already serving their sentences in private CCA prisons in Arizona, Mississippi, Oklahoma, and California.[76] Even with the thousands of additional beds planned, California is expected to increasingly exceed the population cap affirmed by the Supreme Court. By 2017, the total jail and prison population might actually be 5,100 higher than it was before realignment took effect in 2011, according to some calculations.[77]

Governor Brown has resisted some modest sentencing reform measures to bring down the state's incarcerated population. In 2013, he vetoed a bill that would have permitted prosecutors or judges to charge simple drug possession as a misdemeanor instead of a felony, to the surprise and disappointment of the measure's sponsors.[78] However, in contrast to his predecessors and his counterparts in other states, Brown has been willing to parole more lifers—lots more of them. In his first three years in office, he signed off on paroling a total of 1,400 lifers.[79]

Realignment was drafted with the interests of law enforcement officials uppermost in mind. But many of them, especially prosecutors, remain disillusioned and opposed to key elements of the legislation.[80] Only a single Republican voted for the realignment bill. Opponents have sought to make realignment a major electoral issue and have blamed some recent blips in California's crime rates on realignment. It is hard to rebut these claims. Even though realignment is the "biggest penal experiment in modern history," the state provided no funding to evaluate its effects on public safety, the criminal justice system, and the size of the incarcerated population.[81] It also did not include any money for public information programs to educate people about the aims, rationale, and progress of realignment.[82]

For all the talk about a new bipartisan era that leans toward less punishment, not more, the ghosts of the law-and-order era have not been vanquished. Abel Maldonado, a gubernatorial hopeful, backed a brash campaign in May 2013 to repeal realignment. Republican legislative leaders launched a media campaign accusing Brown and other Democrats of undermining bipartisan legislation enacted in 2007 that called for building more prisons and local jails to alleviate overcrowding.[83]

The state's correctional officers' union has moderated its virulently anti-prisoner and pro–prison growth rhetoric and has staked out some progressive positions on penal reform. But many of its actions "indicate continued opposition to serious change."[84] In early 2014, three former governors, including Democrat Gray Davis, announced they would be spearheading a new ballot initiative to foreshorten the appeals process for people on death row so as to expedite executions. The measure also calls for returning death row inmates to the general inmate population, where it would be less expensive to house them as they get conveyed along a faster track to their lethal injection.[85]

The Politics of Dismantling the Carceral State

Developments in penal policy and practice are rarely the result of a single factor but rather of a wide variety of forces that interact with one another. These forces reflect and reproduce key features of a country's specific history, culture, polity, and institutions. This reality makes the political task of dismantling the carceral state all the more daunting.

Employing a wider historical and political lens to analyze the problem of the carceral state and the political possibilities for dismantling it is highly revealing. It is a striking reminder that some of the most successful penal reform movements in the United States over the last century and a half raised penetrating questions about economic and social justice. These movements did not act in isolation but were buoyed by contemporaneous political and social movements. The push to end the convict-leasing system that gripped the South for more than half a century drew some of its lifeblood from the Populist, Progressive, and feminist movements of the late nineteenth and early twentieth centuries.[86] A century ago, the exploitation of penal labor in Northern prison factories run by private entrepreneurs was central to wider political debates as the nation grappled with the wrenching economic and political upheavals brought on by industrialization and urbanization. How inmates were treated in these prison factories came to be seen as a crucial barometer of economic and social justice in the wider society.[87] In the 1960s and 1970s, the prisoners' rights and civil rights movements were deeply entangled with one another and drew important support from other political and social movements, including the labor movement.[88]

The most relevant historical example may be the movement to deinstitutionalize the mentally ill in the second half of the twentieth century. Deinstitutionalization was a rare instance in which states chose to shutter a vast archipelago of public institutions that they had invested in heavily for many years. That shutdown involved a protracted political drama that played out for decades and that did not have an entirely happy ending.[89]

Rising anxiety among state officials about the escalating costs of state mental institutions in the late 1940s did not on its own empty state asylums. Leadership at the federal level was critical to spurring deinstitutionalization. Another vital factor was the shift in the training, worldview, and identity of the psychiatric profession as the American Psychiatric Association split over the question of institutional care versus the community mental health model. The emergence of major new and interconnected social movements (including the civil rights movement and the senior citizens movement) also was pivotal in pushing policy makers to embrace deinstitutionalization of the mentally ill. So was growing journalistic and popular attention to the dire conditions in state mental hospitals. The final critical factor was the reconception of the mental health issue to include not just individuals and their individual diseases but also mental health as a barometer for the health of the whole community.[90]

Mental institutions were a huge and growing drain on state budgets for years, yet deinstitutionalization progressed very slowly. It wasn't until the 1990s—three decades after deinstitutionalization began—that whole institutions began to close in significant numbers. It took just as long for political leaders and the public to acknowledge that successful integration requires more than adequate medical treatment, and that the mentally ill needed access to good housing and jobs as well.[91] Deinstitutionalization was not an unqualified victory. With the closing of state mental hospitals and the contraction of federal money for treatment, services, and housing, jails and prisons unfortunately became the mental institutions of last resort for many seriously ill people. Cutbacks in mental health funds together with cuts in federal money for public housing and other services led to streams of apparently deranged people living on the streets. This outcome fueled a backlash against deinstitutionalization and community mental health. It overshadowed the fact that many mentally ill people made successful transitions to community life.[92]

The Invisibility of the Carceral State

Although important parallels exist, there are some key differences between the deinstitutionalization case and the problem of the carceral state. Engineering major cuts to the country's incarcerated population is likely to be an even greater political challenge than deinstitutionalizing the mentally ill. One key difference is that the problems of state asylums were far more visible to the wider public.

Prisons were not always the foreign, invisible worlds they are today for most Americans. Here I mean real prisons, not the prisons imagined by Hollywood and prime-time television. The prisons of popular culture have created a "troubling distance between the punisher and punished," as Michelle Brown explains. They foster spectacle but not a "critical self-awareness of the role of law and institutions in the production of pain and violence."[93]

Once upon a time, famous prisons like Sing Sing hosted thousands of visitors each year, including average citizens as well as celebrities like Babe Ruth and the Populist firebrand William Jennings Bryan. Inmates themselves also once played pivotal roles in making the prison a leading public issue. The escapes, strikes, mutinies, and riots of leased convicts, and their angry and mournful letters and memoirs, helped bring about the end of the brutal practice of convict leasing.[94] The strikes and protests of inmates in Northern prison factories in the late nineteenth and early twentieth centuries were catalysts for the enactment of state and federal legislation restricting the use of penal labor, as discussed in chapter 3.[95] The growing number of self-mutilations by convicts on state-run penal farms in the 1940s eventually made it impossible for state officials and enterprising journalists to ignore the abhorrent conditions that provoked these bloody and desperate acts of protest.[96]

Protests and riots no longer pose the political problems they once did for state officials and prison administrators. This is due partly to the development of tear gas and other anti-riot equipment beginning in the 1930s and of new management techniques (most notably the extensive use of supermax cells that so severely isolate and punish inmates).[97] Today the barriers to mobilizing and protesting from within are extraordinarily high. As such, the massive 2010 strike by Georgia inmates protesting prison conditions and the huge 2011–13 hunger strikes waged against supermax facilities in California are all the more remarkable.

Decades ago, the popular press and a vibrant prison press extensively covered penal issues and served as important prods to reform. Due to cutbacks and restructuring in the news business over the past three decades, investigative pieces documenting abuses in all kinds of institutions, including prisons, nursing homes, and hospitals, are rarer today. That may change somewhat with the recent founding of the Marshall Project. This is a new nonprofit news venture dedicated to covering the criminal justice system in the United States that Bill Keller, the former executive editor of the *New York Times*, has launched.[98]

Another challenge is that corrections administrators and other state officials have been erecting ever-higher barriers for journalists attempting to cover what happens behind prison walls, including complete bans on face-to-face interviews with inmates in some states.[99] The once vibrant in-house penal press is nearly extinct, thanks to a series of unfavorable court decisions since the mid-1970s. These decisions have whittled away First Amendment rights for prison journalists and have granted penal authorities enormous latitude to censor what publications inmates are allowed to read.[100] (An inmate in the federal supermax prison in Florence, Colorado, even had to go to court to fight for the right to read Barack Obama's two best-selling books. Prison authorities had deemed that the president's books were "potentially detrimental to national security.")[101]

Compared to prisoners today, the mentally ill and their legal advocates had considerable access to the courts in the 1960s and 1970s to press their civil rights claims and expose the dire conditions in state mental hospitals. Thanks to the Prison Litigation Reform Act, the Antiterrorism and Effective Death Penalty Act, and a string of unfavorable court decisions, prisoners and their legal advocates have had greater difficulty using the courts to pursue civil rights claims and to document and expose the conditions in U.S. jails and prisons, as discussed in chapters 2 and 3. The milestone 2011 *Brown v. Plata* decision is the exception that proves the rule. It took more than fifteen years for this case to reach the Supreme Court. After the Court rendered its decision, California officials continued to wage a legal war of attrition against it.

One cannot help but wonder whether the wider public turned its gaze away from prisons not just because corrections officials developed more sophisticated technologies and legal weapons to quell prison protests and render life behind the walls invisible. One of the big stories from the 1930s onward is how the country's prison population went from being predominantly white to being predominantly black and brown. This likely helps explain why the general public no longer identified with people on the inside, especially once law-and-order politicians decided to turn black into a synonym for violence and crime. Young minority men were a far less sympathetic population than the troubled young white women and elderly patients with dementia who filled state asylums years ago.[102]

The slave narratives of the antebellum period, which graphically rendered the physical pain that slaves suffered and made it widely visible, helped to propel the abolitionist cause.[103] Today, what happens in prison stays mostly in prison, making it harder to draw connections in the public mind between justice on the inside and justice on the outside. The ability to identify with an offender—or not—is a key predictor of why people differ in their levels of punitiveness.[104] The invisibility of the millions of people behind bars has made it extremely difficult to alter the negative portrait that members of the general public have in their heads of people who have been convicted of a crime. They are simply prisoners and criminals. As such, they often are denied their humanity and denied any right to democratic accountability, much as slaves were in the United States.

Public Opinion and Penal Reform

Although public opinion probably poses a greater hurdle to penal reform than it did to mental health reform, it is easy to overestimate how high this hurdle is. Politicians and policy makers seriously misperceive public opinion on penal matters, mistakenly seeing the public as inherently punitive. Legislators remain deeply reluctant to shift public policy toward greater leniency, even in the face of evidence that public opinion on crime and punishment can be quite malleable, and that support for hard-line policies has been falling. National surveys suggest considerable decreases since the early to mid-1990s in key indictors of public punitiveness, including public fear of crime, belief that the courts are too lenient, support for the death penalty, and designation of crime as a top priority.[105]

Public opinion looks more intractable and punitive than it is, partly due to the shortcomings of survey research in this area.[106] Qualitative gauges of public opinion, such as focus groups, and surveys that permit respondents to rank their policy preferences indicate that Americans have much more nuanced views of spending on criminal justice than the popular media or public policy debates suggest.[107]

As discussed in chapter 7, public opinion about crime and punishment is highly racialized, with considerable gaps between whites and blacks on key issues. Whites tend to associate crime and violence with being African American and are more likely than blacks to support harsh penal policies. This racialization of public opinion on crime and punishment should not be viewed as an implacable obstacle to dismantling the carceral state. Yes, public opinion on crime and punishment is highly racialized today. But when in U.S. history has it not been? Furthermore, as discussed in chapter 7, whites and blacks do not have monolithic views on criminal justice matters. Views vary considerably among whites and among blacks. Simplistic polls that ask whether one favors more or less punitive policies do not capture this complexity of views.

Political Quiescence and Resistance

Debates about crime, punishment, and law and order have been deeply entangled in wider political battles and electoral strategies in ways that the mental health issue never was. Republicans waged the rebirth of the modern Republican Party on the Southern strategy, which invoked law-and-order appeals to stoke racial anxieties and animosities. Democrat Bill Clinton staked his campaign for the White House on a kinder, gentler version of the Southern strategy to woo the so-called Reagan Democrats back to the party. Given that the crime and punishment issue has been a pillar for repositioning the major political parties, political openings to shift penal policy in a less punitive direction are fraught with risk and are hard to sustain. The opportunity for the emergence of the penal equivalent of a Robert Felix to put into motion a federal plan to spur a major decarceration of state prisons is less likely.[108]

The Southern strategy, the racialization of public opinion on crime and punishment, and the entrenched history of racial intransigence in the United States cannot on their own explain why the carceral state has not faced more opposition from the groups most harmed by it. As discussed throughout this book, the carceral state cannot be understood separately from the wider political, economic, and social context in which it was constructed. The rise of the carceral state coincided with what Michael Dawson has characterized as a "dangerous decline" in the black public sphere and black civil society since the 1970s.[109] A variety of factors discussed in earlier chapters are to blame—internal dissension, state repression, the ascendancy of neoliberalism, growing income and other inequalities between blacks, and the emergence of African American neighborhoods of extreme and concentrated poverty and crime. Residents of these poor neighborhoods are much more likely to view the problems in their communities as insolvable and to mistrust groups that have been key coalition partners in previous political movements, including unions, the working class, and the middle class.[110] These developments help explain their relative political quiescence in the face of the enormous injustices of the carceral state.

Moreover, as discussed in chapter 7, major national organizations committed to social and economic justice are vexed with subtle biases that keep them from mobilizing on behalf of the most marginalized groups in the United States, including offenders and ex-offenders. These organizations have failed to embrace "affirmative advocacy" to ensure that the plight of the most disadvantaged groups are more central to their mission.[111] This would include changing how decisions are made and ensuring greater representation for members of these groups on their staffs and boards. It also would entail developing stronger ties to local and state advocacy groups so that these groups serve as "democratic checks" on national organizations and as vehicles for more progressive ideas to "trickle up."[112]

These national organizations will not lead the way out of the carceral state without pressure from a more radical flank. Without that, they are unlikely to develop a penal reform vision that extends much beyond the three R's and the Right on Crime coalition. As Dawson notes, the three most successful periods of black political mobilization—Reconstruction, the Progressive era, and the combined civil rights and Black Power era—"were all marked by innovative initiatives in black civil society, a growing and robust black public sphere," and an active radical flank.[113] These movements did not single-mindedly focus on the problem of racial disparities and inequities but sought to forge a broader political agenda centered on racial, social, and economic justice.

All the focus on the three R's and the Right on Crime coalition has overshadowed the growing political ferment at the grassroots level against the carceral state. New groups have been forming at the state and local levels to battle various aspects of the carceral state, including felon disenfranchisement, supermax prisons, the abuse of transgender prisoners, exorbitant telephone rates for inmates, the shackling of pregnant women during labor, and employment discrimination against former offenders.[114] A new wave of prisoner and ex-prisoner-led groups—what some dub the "formerly incarcerated peoples' movement"—has been coalescing to fight the carceral state despite the special obstacles to political action that they face, which were discussed in chapter 7.[115] Since publishing The New Jim Crow, Michelle Alexander has become an outspoken advocate of forging a political movement to challenge the carceral state that is more encompassing than the race-centered approach she appeared to be endorsing in her book.[116] It remains an open question whether this ferment will coalesce into a broader movement to challenge not only the carceral state but also other growing inequities in the United States, including the unequal distribution of crime.

The Carceral State and Crime

The record drop in crime rates since the early 1990s in the United States is a major achievement that has received enormous attention. Less noted is that crime is distributed in highly unequal ways, and that unacceptably high rates of violent crime persist in certain urban neighborhoods.[117] Ignoring these disquieting facts is like heralding the record highs of the U.S. stock market or recent gains in U.S. per capita income without considering trends in income distribution or poverty rates. No other major city except Los Angeles has a homicide rate that comes close to New York City's relatively low rate of six per 100,000.[118] Most cities have homicide rates that are at least twice as large as New York's rate and, in many cases, several times or even dozens of times higher.[119]

Since the early 1990s, the homicide victimization rate for African Americans has fallen by more than half, but it remains extraordinarily high. Extremely high rates of violent crime persist in some urban neighborhoods.[120] The homicide rate in Chicago's affluent Hyde Park, home to Barack Obama, is 3 per 100,000. The rate in neighboring Washington Park, which is overwhelmingly poor and 98 percent African American, is 78 per 100,000.[121] The homicide victimization rate for young black men involved in criminally active groups in a high crime neighborhood on Chicago's west side is 3,000 per 100,000, or about 600 times the national rate. Put another way, this is three times the risk of stepping on a landmine in Afghanistan, a real war zone.[122]

The average rate of criminal violence for black neighborhoods is five times that for white neighborhoods; for minority areas, it is three and a half times that of white neighborhoods.[123] The homicide victimization rate for blacks is about six times the rate for whites.[124] Blacks constitute just 13 percent of the population but half of all homicide victims.[125] Despite the great crime drop, more than 78,000 black males were homicide victims between 2000 and 2010. This figure exceeds the total number of U.S. military casualties during the Vietnam War by about 25 percent.[126] And for every black male who died of gun violence, another twenty-four suffered nonfatal injuries.[127] Leaving aside homicide, the violent victimization rate for black girls and young black women is in many ways comparable to that of their male counterparts.[128]

Violent crime is highly stratified by race and class, but it is difficult—perhaps impossible—to determine which factor is more important. With the rise in the number of people living in residentially segregated neighborhoods of concentrated poverty, the deleterious effects of growing up and living in such neighborhoods are now well documented.[129] It is extremely hard—perhaps impossible—to disentangle the race effects from the class effects in violence because there are virtually no white neighborhoods as poor as the poorest black neighborhoods.[130] The "worst" urban neighborhoods in which whites reside are considerably better off than those of the average African American community, and the most advantaged black neighborhoods are no better off than the typical white neighborhood.[131]

Crime and Root Causes

The findings of decades of research on what explains variations in violent crime, especially homicide rates, are remarkably robust. Certain structural factors consistently predict higher rates of homicide: larger and denser populations, geographic location in the South, a higher proportion of divorced males, and higher rates of poverty and income inequality. Two other key structural factors that are related to income inequality—residential segregation and pervasive economic discrimination against certain groups—are likely consequential as well.[132] Over time, the relative weight of these factors has shifted, with structural economic factors related to poverty and income inequality now accounting for a greater proportion of the variance.[133] Differences in policing resources and policing strategies also likely explain variations in rates of violent crime, though experts do not agree on just how much to credit the police for sustained drops in rates of homicide and violent crime.[134]

If the United States is serious about addressing these high levels of concentrated violence, then it has to be serious about addressing the country's high levels of inequality and concentrated poverty. The only way out is to develop a new social and economic agenda that designates the alleviation of the unconscionably high rates of hunger, poverty, and joblessness that vex these communities a top priority, not a public policy afterthought. This would necessitate an infusion of resources and new policies and programs to address persistent residential segregation, inadequate investments in good housing, and disparate access to equitable residential loans and quality public education.[135] It also would also entail a renewed commitment to government intervention to bring down the unemployment rate and to foster the revitalization of organized labor and collective bargaining. All the handwringing and fatalism today about the government's purported impotency when it comes to creating jobs obscures the fact that expansion of the public sector beginning in the 1960s was a key factor in the sizable reductions in the poverty rate for blacks, as discussed in chapter 4.

Penal and social policies have long been two sides of the same coin in governing social marginality. Increasingly, penal policy has become the policy of first resort to address the massive economic and social dislocations of the last half-century and the related crime problem.[136] The main emphasis has been on the need for more police and new policing strategies to enhance public safety, most notably COMSTAT and "hot spots" policing. This has fomented a technicist approach that "depoliticizes crime prevention, by reducing it to the purely neutral scientific task of identifying 'best practice.'"[137] Such an approach is inattentive to the important political and symbolic dimensions of crime prevention and penal policy more generally.

Policing enthusiasts contend that policing strategies based on the proven deterrent effects of swift and certain apprehension and punishment are the key to lowering crime rates.[138] They have a point. It is "certainly better to prevent people from committing crime through a visible police presence than to wait for them to commit it and then put them behind bars," concedes Elliott Currie. But it is "one thing to prevent crime by improving social conditions or by making people more capable and productive," explains Currie. It is another thing altogether to prevent crime "by frightening unproductive, desperate, and alienated people with the threat of arrest and incarceration if they break the law."[139]

In recent decades, the resources available to many police departments and law enforcement agencies escalated.[140] This occurred largely without a commensurate increase in the accountability of the police to the communities they are supposed to serve. Police and their political benefactors have stridently resisted creating independent civilian review boards with real teeth to monitor and discipline their activities. Many prosecutors have been loath to aggressively pursue charges of police brutality and other criminal activities by police officers. Thanks to lucrative and highly permissive forfeiture laws and other measures discussed in chapter 2, police departments have expanded their paramilitary operations, their anti-drug task forces, and other controversial operations. The police also have been the main foot soldiers in the war on drugs and in carrying out massive stop-and-frisk campaigns in certain neighborhoods. And they have become important players in the local enforcement of federal immigration policies in some communities. As a consequence, the police are widely viewed in many inner-city neighborhoods and elsewhere in the country as an occupying army unaccountable to the local citizens. The uproar following the death of Michael Brown, an unarmed black teenager shot to death by a white police officer in Ferguson, Missouri, in August 2014 brought national and international attention to this issue.

Crime prevention policies have followed strikingly different trajectories in Europe compared to those in the United States. In Europe, they have been inextricably "bound up with concerns about social exclusion and urban renewal in disadvantaged communities."[141] The countries of the European Union have many more police per capita than the United States, but they also have more expansive social welfare and other programs that seek to reduce crime by ameliorating poverty and inequality.[142]

For decades conservatives have brazenly dismissed the claim that social welfare spending reduces crime. Indeed, many argued the exact reverse. Although the relationship between crime and spending on social welfare has been a hotly debated topic, research in this area is surprisingly sparse.[143] The limited research available suggests that certain types of social welfare spending and programs reduce crime.[144] What we do know conclusively is that states and countries that spend more on social welfare tend to have lower incarceration rates, and high rates of inequality are associated with higher rates of imprisonment and higher rates of crime.[145]

The unequal distribution of crime and the persistence of extraordinarily high levels of violent crime in certain urban neighborhoods is a major inequality that needs to be addressed. However, as discussed earlier, in addressing the crime problem, we must be careful not to conflate it with the problem of the carceral state. The United States needs a visionary agenda aimed at ameliorating the root causes of crime and other persistent and gaping inequalities in high-crime communities. But in the meantime, there is no excuse for keeping so many of the people from these communities locked up or otherwise ensnared in the carceral state.

"Bring It On" Politics

The distorted narrative of the urban crisis in the 1970s—especially New York City's fiscal crisis—was a vital "crucible for galvanizing new right intellectual activism" aimed at delegitimizing the remnants of the New Deal and Great Society, forging a "drop dead" urban policy, and facilitating the punitive turn.[146] In the aftermath of the Great Recession, cities may be poised to be the crucibles for the next big turn in politics and public policy in ways that have enormous implications not only for the carceral state but also for the future direction of U.S. social and economic policies. The optimists see the 2013 election of Bill de Blasio as the mayor of New York's "two cities" as a bellwether of a broader left-hand turn away from neoliberalism and heavy-handed law enforcement tactics.[147] The pessimists look to Detroit, Stockton, Central Falls, and other cities forced into bankruptcy where nothing is sacred—not the pensions of public workers or the priceless art collection of the Detroit Institute of Arts.

The incipient movements to challenge the carceral state and other inequalities in the United States certainly cannot ignore developments in electoral and party politics entirely. But they cannot bet their future on politicians and the two main political parties. Establishing vibrant and independent institutions and organizations—unions, women's groups, community and immigrant centers, an alternative press—were key to mounting successful challenges to gaping political and economic inequalities in the past and will be so in the future.[148]

The sobering reality is that "true criminal justice ultimately awaits true social justice," as Francis Cullen and Karen Gilbert once said.[149] Vast and growing economic inequalities rooted in vast and growing political inequalities are the preeminent problem facing the United States today. They are the touchstone of many of the major issues that vex the country—from mass incarceration to mass unemployment to climate change to the economic recovery of Wall Street but not Main Street and Martin Luther King Street. In the face of the enormous political chasm between the 99 percent and the 1 percent, a strategy of elite-led, bipartisan deal cutting premised on calls for "shared sacrifice" leaves this grossly inequitable economic and political fabric intact. As such, the 99 percent are caught in the vise of small-bore policies from their supposed friends and allies while their opponents encircle them with scorched-earth politics.

Faced with an economic meltdown widely understood to be the result of breathtaking malfeasance by the financial sector and its political patrons, President Obama and his key advisers first singled out health-care costs and then the deficit as the leading threats to the country's long-term economic health. Characterizing the country's economic problems this way was politically costly. It fostered an exaggerated faith in the possibilities to forge productive coalitions with elite political and economic interests. At the same time, it diminished interest in cultivating a wider political and social movement to press for far-reaching changes in issues ranging from mass unemployment to mass incarceration.

The Obama administration and much of the leadership of the Democratic Party have taken extreme care not to upset these basic interests. As a consequence, they squandered an exceptional political moment. There are not many times in American history when the previous administration and ruling party were so thoroughly discredited, as were President George W. Bush and the Republican Party on the eve of the 2008 election. Or when the business sector had been "stripped naked as leaders and strategists," in the words of Simon Johnson, former chief economist at the International Monetary Fund. The Great Recession was one of those moments. The Great Depression was another.

President Franklin D. Roosevelt came into office at an exceptional moment in 1933.[150] Four years into the Depression, the Hoover administration was thoroughly discredited, as was the business sector. FDR recognized that the country was ready for a clean break with the past as he symbolically and substantively cultivated that sentiment. The break did not come from FDR alone. Massive numbers of Americans mobilized in unions, women's organizations, veterans' groups, senior citizen associations, and civil rights organizations to ensure that the country switched course.

During the Depression, President Roosevelt was forced to broaden the public understanding of crime to include corporate crime. The Senate's riveting Pecora hearings during the waning days of the Hoover administration and the start of the Roosevelt presidency turned a scorching public spotlight on the malfeasance of the corporate sector and its complicity in sparking the Depression. As he put the House of Morgan and other bankers on trial, Ferdinand Pecora, chief counsel of the Senate Banking Committee, helped popularize during the age of Al Capone a term not heard today—the "bankster." These hearings compelled Roosevelt to support stricter regulation of the financial sector than he might have otherwise.[151]

One cannot talk about crime in the streets today without talking about crime in the suites. The growing public obsession over the past four decades with getting tougher on street crime coincided with the retreat of the state in regulating corporate malfeasance—everything from hedge funds to credit default swaps to workplace safety. Keeping the focus on street crime was a convenient strategy to shift public attention and resources from crime in the suites to crime in the streets.[152]

As billionaire financier Warren Buffet quipped in 2006, two years before the Great Recession descended, "There's class warfare, all right, but it's my class, the rich class, that's making war, and we're winning."[153] The signs of victory are everywhere. Income inequality rivals the Gilded Age. The labor movement is on life support. The economic recovery from the Great Recession was highly uneven.[154] Corporate profits have climbed to their highest share of the economy in seven decades while workers' wages have plummeted to their tiniest share over the same period.[155] Wealth has become even more concentrated than income.[156] The United States today has the largest proportion of low-wage workers of any advanced industrialized country.[157] In 2011, the official poverty rate was 15 percent, a steep increase from 12 percent a decade ago.[158]

Obama's persistent calls during his first term for a politics that rises above politics premised on "shared sacrifice" denied this reality and was politically demobilizing. It thwarted the emergence of a compelling alternative political vision on which new coalitions and movements could be forged to challenge fundamental inequities, including mass imprisonment and the growing tentacles of the carceral state. As political scientist E. E. Schattschneider once said, "The definition of the alternatives is the supreme instrument of power."[159] If the political and economic agenda needs to be fundamentally changed and not just tinkered with, we should expect more "bring it on" politics, not less.

Barack Obama is not suited to such politics by temperament or by experience. He rose up in the Democratic Party by cultivating powerful political and economic patrons in Chicago and then elsewhere. He made calls for a politics that transcends politics somehow sound transformative as he has pursued small-bore solutions.

But the problems run deeper than Obama's personality or the constrained political space he reportedly occupies as the country's first African American president.[160]

The political intransigence lavishly on display in the Republican Party that has repeatedly brought Congress to a caustic standstill obscures how a major segment of the Democratic Party is loath to mount any major challenge to the entrenched financial and political interests that have captured American politics today. For all the bluster about political polarization, the debate over what to do about the economy, the social safety net, and regulation of the financial sector—like the elite discussions over what to do about mass incarceration—oscillate within a very narrow range defined by neoliberalism and austerity policies.[161] President Obama has boasted repeatedly that the federal budget for discretionary spending on domestic programs has shrunk under his watch to the smallest share of the economy since Dwight Eisenhower was president.[162] Leading Democrats continue to reward Republican intransigence with more concessions. In 2011, Newt Gingrich succinctly summed up the Republican recipe for success: "I don't think you go to the middle. You bring the middle to you."[163]

The focus on the fratricide within the Republican Party as the establishment faces off against the Tea Party has obscured the deep tensions between the Wall Street wing and the Democratic wing of the Democratic Party. Buying into austerity politics means buying into the false idea that profligate spending by states and municipalities was at the root of the budget crises for state and local governments.[164] The primary cause was a perilous drop in the main sources of revenue for local and state governments—property, income, and sales taxes—as the housing bubble burst and the economy contracted thanks to Wall Street's malfeasance.[165] The budgetary shortfalls have been used as a pretext to dismantle key government functions and services or hive them off to the private sector—everything from schools to health care to prisons.

A number of progressives have sought to appear politically responsible by railing against the deficit and endorsing calls for fiscal constraint. Where they differ from other neoliberals is that they want to make the rich pay a fairer share to bring the deficit down. With some notable exceptions, progressives have generally been slow to mount an aggressive defense of expanding fiscal policy at a time when the private sector lacks the will or the capacity to invest in ways that reduce mass employment and that foster enlightened social and economic policies.[166] The Tea Party's histrionics have allowed the Democratic Party to postpone its own day of reckoning. "As long as a majority of the GOP is hell-bent on breaking bad," the Democratic Party can position itself as the "pragmatic, compromise-seeking adult technocrats."[167] This may be a winning political strategy for the short term. But it is wholly inadequate to address the enormous problems facing the country or to mobilize wide swaths of the public to bring on the convulsive politics from below that we need to dismantle the carceral state and ameliorate other gaping inequalities.

Acknowledgments

As C. Wright Mills once said, I have tried to be objective in this book but not detached. I feel sadness, rage, and despair as I write the final words of this book. This is not just because the United States is the world's warden. It is also because of the growing chasm between the enormous problems the country faces and the inability of the political system to resolve those problems, of which the carceral state is a leading example.

After completing *The Prison and the Gallows*, I did not expect to write another book about mass incarceration. Without realizing it, a number of kindred spirits coaxed *Caught* out of me. This book came to be thanks to the invitations I received to participate in various projects and conferences, to the dozens of letters sent to me from jails and prisons across the United States, and the passionate commitment of students of mine in classes held at Penn and behind the walls in Philadelphia's jails. Along the way, I discovered I was not writing another book about penal policy. Rather, *Caught* uses the problem of the carceral state as a lens to bring into acute focus the broader pathologies that vex American politics today.

A heartfelt thanks to the many people who directly and indirectly shaped this book in more ways than they know, including Freda Adler, Michelle Alexander, Katherine Beckett, Homi Bhabha, Thomas Blomberg, Traci Burch, Shawn Bushway, David Cameron, Patrick Carr, Bill DiMascio, Sharon Dolovich, Peter Enns, David Garland, Ruth Gilmore, Jacob Hacker, Craig Haney, Bernard Harcourt, Amy Lerman, Ian Loader, Glenn Loury, Mona Lynch, Hope Metcalf, Lisa Miller, Khalil Muhammad, Naomi Murakawa, Charles Ogletree, Jr., Joshua Page, Joan Petersilia, Lori Pompa, Ruth Peterson, Kevin Reitz, Judith Resnick, Paul Rock, David Rodovsky, Rick Rosenfeld, Austin Sarat, Margo Schlanger, Heather Schoenfeld, David Scott, Larry Sherman, Carol Steiker, Jordan Steiker, Heather Ann Thompson, Michael Tonry, Vesla Weaver, Tyrone Werts, Christopher Wildeman, Paul Wright, Takakazu Yamagishi, Malcolm Young, and the numerous participants in conferences, talks, seminars, and courses where I presented portions of this book. I apologize in advance to all the people I inadvertently left off this list.

A very special thanks to Mary Katzenstein, Ed Rhine, Marc Mauer, Nicola Lacey, and Jonathan Simon, who read the entire manuscript and made detailed and thoughtful suggestions that went far beyond the call of duty. I also benefited enormously from the sharp critiques of the anonymous reviewers of the manuscript for Princeton and other presses. Sarah Cate and Samantha Sye, my two main research assistants on this project, were indispensable, as were Thomas Dichter and Anthony Grasso in the final stages of the book.

I am deeply grateful to Jeremy Travis and Bruce Western for inviting me to join the National Academy of Sciences Committee on the Causes and Consequences of High Rates of Incarceration and for keeping the eyes of the committee on the big picture. Serving on that two-year project delayed the publication of *Caught*, but the sparring and Kumbaya moments on the NAS committee helped make this a better book.

Many people working with shoestring budgets and sometimes at great personal cost are chipping away at the carceral state by carefully documenting its tentacles. Their research, blogs, and reports were invaluable in writing *Caught*. I am particularly indebted to Lois Ahrens of the Real Cost of Prisons Project, Jean Casella and James Ridgeway of Solitary Watch, Scott Henson of the Grits for Breakfast blog, Marc Mauer and The Sentencing Project, P.S. Ruckman, Jr., who runs the Pardon Power blog, Douglas Berman of the Sentencing Law and Policy blog, Peter Wagner of the Prison Policy Initiative, and Paul Wright and his *Prison Legal News*.

Princeton University Press made the editorial process as smooth and enjoyable as is reasonably possible. Eric Crahan, my editor at Princeton, immediately got what *Caught* was about and did not flinch from its ambitious critique of American politics. He deftly guided the project along with patience, perseverance, and frank interventions. I am grateful to Debbie Tegarden, my production editor, and the rest of the Princeton University Press staff for keeping the trains running on time and for never appearing daunted by any bumps along the way.

Ralph Ellison once said, "We tell ourselves our individual stories so as to become aware of our general story." I cannot name all the men and women on the inside who have written from jail or prison to tell me their stories or to suggest a way out or to request legal aid. I have not been able to answer personally all of these letters. But I hope this book is a way of saying you have been heard, and we will find a way out. I also hope that you and your families and loved ones see your individual stories reflected in the general story I tell here.

This book is dedicated to Jai Dev Kohli, my beloved father-in-law who passed away just a week before this manuscript was due. In many ways, I knew him better than my own father, who died suddenly when I was a child. With his quiet reserve, my father-in-law bridged the enormous cultural, generational, and gender gaps that were between us and loved and accepted me for who I am.

Finally, I extend my deepest love and gratitude once again to Atul and Tara, who remain my toughest and most forgiving critics. With their levity, empathy, and distractions, they fortified me to confront the pathologies of the carceral state and American politics and yet not lose hope that forging a way out is possible and in our control.

Notes

Chapter One
Introduction

1. Lauren E. Glaze and Erinn J. Herberman, "Correctional Populations in the United States, 2012," *Bureau of Justice Statistics Bulletin*, December 2013, 3, table 2.

2. State supervision ranges widely between the 50 states, from a high of 1 in 13 adults in Georgia to a low of 1 in 88 in New Hampshire. Pew Center on the States, "One in 31: Behind Bars in America 2008" (Washington, DC: Pew Charitable Trusts, 2009), 1, 5, 10, and 42.

3. There are an estimated 16 million jail admissions each year. But surprisingly, no official national statistics are collected on the number of people jailed annually (which is quite different from the number of annual admissions, since many people cycle in and out of jail). One knowledgeable source unofficially reported that about 6.6 million people spent some time in jail in 2012. David Kaiser and Lovisa Stannow, "The Rape of American Prisoners," *New York Review of Books*, March 11, 2010, 19; Todd D. Minton, "Jail Inmates at Midyear 2012: Statistical Tables," Bureau of Justice Statistics, May 2013, http://www.bjs.gov/content/pub/pdf/jim12st.pdf (retrieved June 29, 2013); Christopher Uggen, Jeff Manza, and Melissa Thompson, "Citizenship, Democracy, and the Civic Reintegration of Criminal Offenders," *ANNALS of the American Academy of Political & Social Science* 605 (May 2006), 283.

4. Sesame Street's creation in 2013 of the first Muppet to have an incarcerated parent reflects the growing phenomenon of children with an incarcerated parent. A. Pawlowski, "'Sesame Street' Creates First Muppet to Have a Parent in Jail," June 17, 2013, http://www.today.com/moms/sesame-street-creates-first-muppet-have-parent-jail-6C10345061 (retrieved September 27, 2013). See also Jean M. Kjellstrand and J. Mark Eddy, "Parental Incarceration During Childhood, Family Context, and Youth Problem Behavior Across Adolescence," *Journal of Offender Rehabilitation* 50.1 (2011): 18–36; Lauren E. Glaze and Laura M. Maruschak, "Parents in Prison and Their Minor Children," Bureau of Justice Statistics Special Report, August 2008.

5. Lawrence D. Bobo and Victor Thompson, "Unfair by Design: The War on Drugs, Race, and the Legitimacy of the Criminal Justice System," *Social Research* 73.2 (2006): 445–72.

6. Jennifer L. Hochschild, *Facing Up to the American Dream: Race, Class, and the Soul of the Nation* (Princeton, NJ: Princeton University Press, 1995).

7. Christopher Uggen, Sarah Shannon, and Jeff Manza, "State-Level Estimates of Felon Disenfranchisement in the United States, 2010" (Washington, DC: The Sentencing Project, July 2012), 1.

8. The Adoption and Safe Families Act of 1997 puts strict time limits on reunification efforts for children separated from their parents and encourages states to terminate parental rights if reunification does not occur within a certain specified time frame. About half of the

states have enacted reunification statutes that apply to the children of imprisoned parents. Candace Krutttschnitt, "The Paradox of Women's Imprisonment," *Daedalus* 139. 3 (2010): 35; Vernetta D. Young and Rebecca Reviere, *Women Behind Bars: Gender and Race in U.S. Prisons* (Boulder, CO: Lynne Rienner, 2006), 111.

9. Marc Mauer, "Sentencing Reform Amid Mass Incarcerations—Guarded Optimism," *Criminal Justice* 26.1 (2011), n.p.

10. Frank R. Baumgartner, Suzanna L. De Boef, and Amber E. Boydstun, *The Decline of the Death Penalty and the Discovery of Innocence* (New York: Cambridge University Press, 2008), 224.

11. Michelle Alexander, *The New Jim Crow: Mass Incarceration in the Age of Colorblindness* (New York: New Press, 2010).

12. Lynn Davey, "Strategies for Framing Racial Disparities: A FrameWorks Institute Message Brief" (Washington, DC: Frameworks Institute, 2009), 11. Michelle Alexander originally made this point. See Michelle Alexander, "In Prison Reform, Money Trumps Civil Rights," *New York Times*, May 15, 2011, WK9.

13. Joe Soss, Richard C. Fording, and Sanford F. Schram, *Disciplining the Poor: Neoliberal Paternalism and the Persistent Power of Race* (Chicago: University of Chicago Press, 2011), 3.

14. Juan Cartagena, "Lost Votes, Body Counts and Joblessness: The Effects of Felon Disenfranchisement on Latino Civic Engagement," *Latino Studies* 6.1–2 (2008), 194.

15. Ray Walmsley, "World Female Imprisonment List," 2nd ed., International Centre for Prison Studies, 2010, http://www.prisonstudies.org/sites/prisonstudies.org/files/resources /downloads/wfil_2nd_edition.pdf (retrieved February 24, 2014), 1.

16. Federal Bureau of Prisons, "Inmate Ethnicity," December 28, 2013, http://www .bop.gov/about/statistics/statistics_inmate_ethnicity.js (retrieved February 2, 2014).

17. Kevin R. Reitz, "Don't Blame Determinacy: U.S. Incarceration Growth Has Been Driven by Other Forces," *Texas Law Review* 84.7 (2006), 1792. In the late 1990s, the Bureau of Justice Statistics decided to report separate figures for blacks, whites, and Hispanics in prisons and jails, thus complicating calculations of historical racial trends in incarceration. Previously, Hispanics were sometimes included in racial categories and sometimes broken out separately. Michael Tonry and Matthew Melewski, "The Malign Effects of Drug and Crime Control on Black Americans," in Michael Tonry, ed., *Crime and Justice: A Review of Research*, v. 37 (Chicago: University of Chicago Press, 2008), 8. For a more detailed analysis of trends in incarceration rates for Hispanics, see Jeremy Travis, Bruce Western, and Steve Redburn, eds., *The Growth of Incarceration in the United States: Exploring Causes and Consequences* (Washington, DC: National Academies Press, 2014), 61–64.

18. Silja J.A. Talvi, *Women Behind Bars: The Crisis of Women in the U.S. Prison System* (Emeryville, CA: Seal Press, 2007); Kruttschnitt, "The Paradox of Women's Imprisonment."

19. E. Ann Carson and William J. Sabol, "Prisoners in 2012," *Bureau of Justice Statistics Bulletin*, December 2012, 1.

20. Juliet Stumpf, "The Crimmigration Crisis: Immigrants, Crime, and Sovereign Power," *American University Law Review* 56.2 (2006): 367–419.

21. See, for example, Eduardo Bonilla-Silva, *Racism without Racists: Color-Blind Racism and the Persistence of Racial Inequality in the United States*, 3rd ed. (Lanham, MD: Rowman & Littlefield, 2010); Desmond S. King and Rogers M. Smith, *Still a House Divided: Race and Politics in Obama's America* (Princeton, NJ: Princeton University Press, 2011); David M. Oshinsky, '*Worse Than Slavery': Parchman Farm and the Ordeal of Jim Crow Justice* (New York: Free Press, 1996); Alex Lichtenstein, *Twice the Work of Free Labor: The Political Econ-*

omy of Convict Labor in the New South (London: Verso, 1996); Mary Ellen Curtin, *Black Prisoners and Their World, Alabama, 1865–1900* (Charlottesville: University of Virginia Press, 2000); Khalil Gibran Muhammad, *The Condemnation of Blackness: Race, Crime, and the Making of Modern Urban America* (Cambridge, MA: Harvard University Press, 2010); Robert Perkinson, *Texas Tough: The Rise of America's Prison Empire* (New York: Metropolitan Books, 2010); Douglas A. Blackmon, *Slavery by Another Name: The Re-Enslavement of Black Americans from the Civil War to World War II* (New York: Anchor Books, 2009).

22. James Q. Whitman, *Harsh Justice: Criminal Punishment and the Widening Divide Between America and Europe* (New York: Oxford University Press, 2003).

23. Mary Ellen Curtin, "'Please Hear Our Cries': The Hidden History of Black Prisoners in America," in Deborah E. McDowell, Claudrena N. Harold, and Juan Battle, eds., *The Punitive Turn: New Approaches to Race and Incarceration* (Charlottesville: University of Virginia Press, 2013), 38.

24. Craig Haney, "Counting Casualties in the War on Prisoners," *University of San Francisco Law Review* 43.1 (2008): 87.

25. Paul Wright, "From the Editor," *Prison Legal News*, September 2009, 14.

26. Commission on Safety and Abuse in America's Prisons, "Confronting Confinement" (New York: Vera Institute of Justice, June 2006), 10.

27. Francis Cullen, "Assessing the Penal Harm Movement," *Journal of Research in Crime and Delinquency* 32.3 (1995), 340.

28. Haney, "Counting Casualties," 88.

29. See, for example, Keith O. Lawrence, "Overview," in Keith O. Lawrence, ed., *Race, Crime, and Punishment: Breaking the Connection in America* (Washington, DC: Aspen Institute, 2011), vi.

30. For a critique of the prison-industrial complex framework for analyzing the carceral state, see Loïc Wacquant, "Prisoner Reentry as Myth and Ceremony," *Dialectical Anthropology* 34.4 (2010): 606–11.

31. See, for example, *Reason* magazine's special issue on criminal justice in July 2011; Jeffrey A. Miron and Katherine Waldock, "The Budgetary Impact of Ending Drug Prohibition," White Paper no. 30, The Cato Institute, Washington, DC, September 27, 2010; Sasha Abramsky, "The War Against the 'War on Drugs,'" *Nation*, June 17, 2009; Ethan Nadelmann, "Breaking the Taboo," *Nation*, December 27, 2010, 11–12; Kara Gotsch, "Bipartisan Justice: Fixing America's Punitive Penal System Has Politicians Crossing Party Lines," *American Prospect*, December 6, 2010, A22; David Dagan and Steven M. Teles, "The Conservative War on Prisons," *Washington Monthly*, November/December 2012, 25–31.

32. Newt Gingrich and Pat Nolan, "Prison Reform: A Smart Way for States to Save Money and Lives," *Washington Post*, January 7, 2011, http://www.washingtonpost .com/wp-dyn/content/article/2011/01/06/AR2011010604386.html (retrieved February 21, 2014).

33. Right on Crime, "Statement of Principles," n.d., http://www.rightoncrime.com /the-conservative-case-for-reform/statement-of-principles/ (retrieved October 31, 2011).

34. Jesse Washington, "NAACP Joins Gingrich in Urging Prison Reform," Associated Press, April 7, 2011, http://www.cnsnews.com/news/article/naacp-joins-gingrich-urging -prison-reform (retrieved May 28, 2013).

35. Ryan S. King, "The State of Sentencing 2008: Developments in Policy and Practice" (Washington, DC: The Sentencing Project, 2009); Lauren-Brooke Eisen and Juliene James, "Reallocating Justice Resources: A Review of 2011 State Sentencing Trends" (New York: Vera Institute of Justice, 2012).

36. David M. Reutter, "Economic Crisis Prompts Prison Closures Nationwide, but Savings (and Reforms) Are Elusive, *Prison Legal News*, September 2010, 1, 3–10; John Gramlich, "At Least 26 States Spend Less on Prisons," Stateline.org, August 11, 2009 (updated August 14, 2009), http://www.stateline.org/live/details/story?contentId=418338 (retrieved October 16, 2009); Judith Greene and Marc Mauer, "Downscaling Prisons: Lessons from Four States (Washington, DC: The Sentencing Project, 2010), 2; The Sentencing Project, "On the Chopping Block: State Prison Closings," n.d., http://sentencingproject.org/doc/publications/On_the_chopping_block_-_state_prison_closings_(2).pdf (retrieved September 27, 2013).

37. See, for example, the considerable differences that emerged between conservative groups and human rights, civil rights, and criminal defense organizations that were part of the Smart on Crime Coalition sponsored by The Constitution Project. The areas of difference included asset forfeitures, federal investigations, federal grand juries, forensic science, innocence issues, indigent defense, juvenile justice, federal sentencing, capital punishment, consular access for foreign defendants, reentry, pardon power, and executive clemency. The Smart on Crime Coalition, "Smart on Crime: Recommendations for the Administration and Congress" (Washington, DC: The Constitution Project, 2011).

38. The calculation for the Soviet Union only includes people incarcerated in gulag camps. It does not include people confined to labor colonies or prisons. Calculated from J. Arch Getty, Gábor T. Rittersporn, and Viktor N. Zemskov, "Victims of the Soviet Penal System in the Pre-War Years: A First Approach on the Basis of Archival Evidence," *American Historical Review* 98.4 (1993), 1048–49; and E. M. Andreev at al., *Naselenie Sovetskogo Soiuza, 1922–1991* (Moscow: Nauka, 1993), cited in Wikipedia, "Demographics of the Soviet Union," http://en.wikipedia.org/wiki/Demographics_of_the_Soviet_Union (retrieved April 28, 2014).

39. Calculated from Glaze and Herberman, "Correctional Populations in the United States, 2012," 3, table 2; and Lauren E. Glaze, "Correctional Populations in the United States, 2009," *Bureau of Justice Statistics Bulletin*, December 2010, 2, table 1.

40. In 2012, California had a total prison and jail population of nearly 212,000, a decrease of about 40,000 people since 2009. Calculated from Glaze and Herberman, "Correctional Populations in the United States, 2012," 5, table 5; Heather C. West and William J. Sabol, "Prisoners in 2009," *Bureau of Justice Statistics Bulletin*, December 2010, rev. October 27, 2011, http://www.bjs.gov/content/pub/pdf/p09.pdf (retrieved April 28, 2014), 16, appendix table 1; and Todd D. Minton, "Jail Inmates at Midyear 2012—Statistical Tables," Bureau of Justice Statistics, May 2013, http://www.bjs.gov/content/pub/pdf/jim12st.pdf (retrieved February 22, 2014), 2, fig. 2. For more on *Brown v. Plata* and California's "realignment," see pp. 269–71.

41. Pew Public Safety Performance Project, "More Than Half of States Cut Imprisonment Rates from 2006 to 2011," March 8, 2013, http://www.pewstates.org/news-room/press-releases/us-prison-count-continues-to-drop-85899457496 (retrieved February 22, 2014).

42. U.S. DOJ, "Federal Prison System: FY 2012 Performance Budget," n.d., http://www.justice.gov/jmd/2012justification/pdf/fy12-bop-se-justification.pdf (retrieved September 27, 2013), 2.

43. Tracey Kyckelhahn, "State Corrections Expenditures, FY 1982–2010," *Bureau of Justice Statistics Bulletin*, December 2012, rev. December 11, 2013, 1. The actual fiscal burden of the corrections system is probably considerably higher. Many corrections budgets do not include the full cost of key correction-related outlays, including capital expenses, health-

care and pension benefits for active and retired corrections employees, and hospital and other health-related expenses for the prison population. By one calculation, state corrections budgets would be on average 14 percent higher if these other expenses were fully incorporated in them. Christian Henrichson and Ruth Delaney, "The Price of Prisons: What Incarceration Costs Taxpayers" (New York: Vera Institute of Justice, January 2012), 2.

44. New York State had a higher than average proportion of incarcerated drug offenders due in part to the harsh 1973 Rockefeller drug laws. As these laws were rescinded by practice and then statute over the past 15 years, the state prison population has fallen by about one-quarter. Since 2011, the state has closed or announced plans to close at least 13 penal facilities, none of which are maximum-security ones. See various press releases from the New York State Department of Corrections and Community Supervision, including "Department of Corrections Details the State's Plan to Right-Size the New York's [sic] Prison System," February 5, 2014, http://www.doccs.ny.gov/PressRel/2014/Budget_Testimony_2014–15 .html (retrieved April 27, 2014).

45. Brandon Sample, "Violence on the Rise in BOP Facilities," *Prison Legal News*, August 2009, 10–12; David Reutter, "Report Cites Rising Violence, Other Problems at Illinois Maximum-Security Prison," *Prison Legal News*, October 2012, 30–31.

46. Center on Sentencing and Corrections, "The Continuing Fiscal Crisis in Corrections: Setting a New Course" (New York: Vera Institute of Justice, October 2010), 11.

47. Deborah Hastings, "Some States Are Charging Inmates for Prison Stay," Associated Press, August 16, 2009, http://www.boston.com/news/nation/articles/2009/08/16/some _states_charging_inmates_for_stay/ (retrieved May 19, 2014).

48. David Reutter, "Florida Jail to Discontinue Providing Underwear," *Prison Legal News*, March 2012, 40.

49. Barbara Ehrenreich, "Is It Now a Crime to Be Poor?," *New York Times*, August 9, 2009, WK9; Katherine Beckett and Steve Herbert, *Banished: The New Social Control in Urban America* (New York: Oxford University Press, 2010).

50. Stephen Bright, "The Independence of the American Lawyer," Florida Bar Association, Boca Raton, June 25, 2010, http://library.law.yale.edu/sites/default/files/counsel forpoor.pdf (retrieved September 23, 2013), 8; Andrew Cohen, "How the Sequester Threatens the U.S. Legal System," *Atlantic*, March 11, 2013, http://www.theatlantic.com/national /archive/2013/03/how-the-sequester-threatens-the-us-legal-system/273878/ (retrieved September 23, 2013).

51. U.S. DOJ, "Attorney General Eric Holder Speaks at the American Bar Association's National Summit on Indigent Defense," press release, February 4, 2012, http://www.justice .gov/iso/opa/ag/speeches/2012/ag-speech-120204.html (retrieved September 2, 2013).

52. Andrew Cohen, "The Lies We Tell Each Other About the Right to Counsel," Brennan Center for Justice, March 13, 2013, http://www.brennancenter.org/analysis/lies-we -tell-each-other-about-right-counsel (retrieved September 23, 2013). See also Brennan Center for Justice, "The Right to Counsel 50 Years After Gideon: A Resource Page," n.d., http:// www.brennancenter.org/analysis/right-counsel-50-years-after-gideon-resource-page (retrieved September 23, 2013); Karen Houppert, *Chasing Gideon: The Elusive Quest for Poor People's Justice* (New York: New Press, 2013).

53. In a major signal that it may be assuming a larger role in assuring that poor defendants have adequate legal counsel, in 2013, the DOJ filed a brief in an ACLU lawsuit against two towns in Washington State. Without taking a position on the merits of the ACLU's claims that the towns had failed to provide sufficient legal assistance, the brief recommended that a federal judge appoint a legal monitor of the towns' public defender systems

if the plaintiffs prevailed. In December 2013, the federal judge stopped short of ordering a federal takeover for the time being but did insist on several specific remedial measures. Matthew Mangino, "The DOJ Takes on Indigent Defense," *Crime Report*, September 17, 2013, http://www.thecrimereport.org/news/articles/2013-09—the-doj-takes-on-indigent-defense (retrieved February 9, 2014); Mike Carter, "Judge: Mt. Vernon, Burlington Failing Poor Defendants," *Seattle Times*, December 4, 2013, http://seattletimes.com/html/local news/2022396613_publicdefensexml.html (retrieved February 9, 2014).

54. Nicola Lacey, *The Prisoners' Dilemma: Political Economy and Punishment in Contemporary Democracies* (Cambridge, UK: Cambridge University Press, 2008); Nicola Lacey, "Political Systems and Criminal Justice: The Prisoners' Dilemma After the Coalition," *Current Legal Problems* 65.1 (2012): 203–39; Michael Cavadino and James Dignan, *Penal Systems: A Comparative Approach*, 4th ed. (London: Sage, 2006); Alessandro De Giorgi, *Re-Thinking the Political Economy of Punishment: Perspectives on Post-Fordism and Penal Politics* (Aldershot, UK: Ashgate, 2006).

55. Loïc Wacquant, *Punishing the Poor: The Neoliberal Government of Social Insecurity* (Durham, NC: Duke University Press, 2009), 306.

56. My conception of neoliberalism is based on Lisa Wedeen, *Peripheral Visions: Publics, Power, and Performance in Yemen* (Chicago: University of Chicago Press, 2008), 187.

57. Marie Gottschalk, "U.S. Health Reform and the Stockholm Syndrome," in Leo Panitch and Colin Leys, eds., *Socialist Register 2010: Morbid Symptoms: Health Under Capitalism* (Pontypool, Wales: Merlin Press, 2009): 103–24; Marie Gottschalk, "They're Back: The Public Plan, the Reincarnation of Harry and Louise, and the Limits of Obamacare," *Journal of Health Politics, Policy and Law* 36.3 (2011): 393–401; Marie Gottschalk, *The Shadow Welfare State: Labor, Business, and the Politics of Health Care in the United States* (Ithaca, NY: Cornell University Press, 2000); Joseph Stiglitz, "This Deficit Fetishism Is Killing Our Economy," Associated Press, August 9, 2012, http://www.huffingtonpost.com/2012/08/09/joseph-stiglitz-inequality_n_1760296.html (retrieved May 7, 2013).

58. Ari Berman, "The Austerity Class," *Nation*, November 7, 2011, 11–17.

59. Timothy Weaver, "Neoliberalism in the Trenches: Urban Policy and Politics in the United States and the United Kingdom," University of Pennsylvania, PhD dissertation, 2012.

60. Loïc Wacquant, "Crafting the Neoliberal State: Workfare, Prisonfare and Social Insecurity," in David Scott, ed., *Why Prison?* (Cambridge, UK: Cambridge University Press, 2013), 73.

61. Soss, Fording, and Schram, *Disciplining the Poor*, 16.

62. Bernard Harcourt, *The Illusion of Free Markets: Punishment and the Myth of Natural Order* (Cambridge, MA: Harvard University Press, 2011). See also Keally McBride, "California Penalty: The End/Price of the Neoliberal Exception," *Carceral Notebooks* 6 (2010), 133–34.

63. Soss, Fording, and Schram, *Disciplining the Poor*, 206, 301.

64. Wacquant, *Punishing the Poor*.

65. Lester Spence, "The Neoliberal Turn in Black Politics," paper presented at the University of Pennsylvania, American Politics Workshop, September 21, 2012.

66. Michael C. Dawson, "3 of 10 Theses on Neoliberalism in the U.S. During the Early 21st Century," *Carceral Notebooks* 6 (2010), 17.

67. This evocative phrase comes from Marc Mauer, *Race to Incarcerate* (New York: New Press, 1999).

68. Pat Carlen, "Carceral Clawback: The Case of Women's Imprisonment in Canada," *Punishment & Society* 4.1 (2002): 115–21.

69. Kelly Hannah-Moffat, *Punishment in Disguise: Penal Governance and Federal Imprisonment of Women in Canada* (Toronto: University of Toronto Press, 2001), 198.

70. Marie Gottschalk, *The Prison and the Gallows: The Politics of Mass Incarceration in America* (New York: Cambridge University Press, 2006).

71. Douglas A. Berman, "Reorienting Progressive Perspectives for Twenty-First Century Punishment Realities," *Harvard Law and Policy Review Online* 3 (December 8, 2008), http://www.hlpronline.com/Berman_HLPR_120808.pdf (retrieved October 28, 2011), 1.

72. Gottschalk, *The Prison and the Gallows*, 48–51.

73. Lichtenstein, *Twice the Work of Free Labor*, 16.

74. Perkinson, *Texas Tough*, 151.

75. For the left, rehabilitation had the "appearance of 'benevolence'" but really was "a mask for coercion" and unwarranted and unchecked discretion that disadvantaged blacks, other minorities, and low-income people. On the right, "treatment" was denigrated as "yet another social welfare program that undermined individual responsibility," encouraged bad behavior, and "coddled offenders." Francis T. Cullen and Cheryl Lero Jonson, "Rehabilitation and Treatment Programs," in James Q. Wilson and Joan Petersilia, eds., *Crime and Public Policy* (New York: Oxford University Press, 2011), 294.

76. Nancy Gertner, "Supporting Advisory Guidelines," *Harvard Law & Policy Review* 3.2 (2009), 267.

77. Mary Bosworth, *Explaining U.S. Imprisonment* (Thousand Oaks, CA: Sage, 2010), 178.

78. For a quick summary of research in this area, see James Austin et al., "Unlocking America: Why and How to Reduce America's Prison Population" (Washington, DC: JFA Institute, 2007), 13–14.

79. Travis, Western, and Redburn, eds., *The Growth of Incarceration in the United States*, 337. For a good overview of the complexities and limitations of research on the relationship between incarceration rates and crime rates, see chapter 5 of this report.

80. Ian Loader and Richard Sparks, *Public Criminology?* (Abingdon, UK and New York: Routledge, 2011).

81. David L. Bazelon, "The Hidden Politics of Criminology," *Federal Probation* 42.2 (1978): 3–9.

82. Loader and Sparks, *Public Criminology?*, 107. Emphasis in the original.

83. Loader and Sparks, *Public Criminology?*, 60, 108.

84. Stuart A. Scheingold, "Constructing the New Political Criminology: Power, Authority, and the Post-Liberal State," *Law and Social Inquiry* 23.4 (1998), 857.

85. Bosworth, *Explaining U.S. Imprisonment*, 196.

86. Nikolas Rose, "The Death of the Social? Re-figuring the Territory of Government," *Economy and Society* 25.3 (1996): 327–56; Kevin Stenson, "Beyond Histories of the Present," *Economy and Society* 27.4 (1998): 333–52.

87. Robert Reiner, Sonia Livingstone, and Jessica Allen, "Casino Culture: Media and Crime in a Winner-Loser Society," in Kevin Stenson and Robert R. Sullivan, eds., *Crime, Risk and Justice: The Politics of Crime in Liberal Democracies* (Devon, UK: Willan, 2001), 177.

88. Rose, "The Death of the Social?," 346.

89. Rose, "The Death of the Social?"

90. For an analysis of austerity politics from an historical and comparative perspective, see Mark Blyth, *Austerity: The History of a Dangerous Idea* (New York: Oxford University Press, 2013).

91. Half of the rise in the budget deficit since 2007 is a consequence of the recession. Another quarter can be explained by policies to ameliorate the recession, including the 2009 stimulus package and the extensions of unemployment insurance. War spending accounts for the remainder of the rise in the deficit. Josh Bivens, "Marching Backwards: The Consequences of Bipartisan Budget Cutting," *New Labor Forum* 20.3 (2011): 19–20.

92. The CBO forecast in 2011 that the budget deficit would shrink to 3.1 percent of gross domestic product by 2014 if the current tax and spending laws remained in place and the economy rebounded. CBO, "CBO Summary: Budget and Economic Outlook, Fiscal Years 2011–2021 (Washington, DC: CBO, January 2011), 1.

Under President Ronald Reagan, budget deficits averaged 4.2 percent of GDP. Calculated from CBO, "Budget and Economic Outlook: Historical Budget Data" (Washington, DC: CBO, January 2011), http://www.cbo.gov/ftpdocs/120xx/doc12039/HistoricalTables[1] .pdf (retrieved November 7, 2011), 2, table E-1. If Obama had not consented to extend all Bush tax cuts through 2012, the United States would have been well on its way to manageable budget deficits. David Cay Johnston, "Taxing Times," *American Prospect*, March 2012, 49.

93. William Greider, *The Education of David Stockman and Other Americans* (New York: Dutton, 1982).

94. "Rethinking Their Pledge," *New York Times*, editorial, April 22, 2011, A22.

95. Signatories of the pledge vowed to oppose efforts to increase taxes or reduce tax credits unless further tax cuts offset the resulting revenue increase. ATF highlights on its website how Norquist has been called the "dark wizard of the Right's anti-tax cult." In 2010, ATF received more than two-thirds of its budget from the Center to Protect Patient Rights, which is affiliated with the conservative Koch brothers, and from Karl Rove's Crossroads GPS. ATF, "Who Is Grover Norquist?," n.d., http://www.atr.org/about-grover (retrieved May 15, 2013); Lee Fang, "Grover Norquist, Lobbyist," *Nation*, January 21, 2013, 17–18.

96. Lee Fang, "Selling Schools Out: The Scam of Virtual Education Reform," *Nation*, December 5, 2011, 15.

97. About two dozen states have enacted Stand Your Ground legislation modeled on Florida's 2005 law. These laws are an extension of the so-called castle doctrine, which exonerates "from prosecution citizens who use deadly force when confronted by an assailant, even if they could have retreated safely." Jill Lepore, "Battleground America: One Nation, Under the Gun," *New Yorker*, April 23, 2012, 40. See also Eric Lichtblau, "Martin Death Spurs Group to Readjust Policy Focus," *New York Times*, April 18, 2012, A13.

98. The boycott cost ALEC hundreds of members and more than $1 million in funding. A who's who of corporate America—including Coca-Cola, Pepsi, McDonald's, Home Depot, General Electric, Amazon, Wal-Mart, Bank of America, and Visa—cancelled their memberships as ALEC's subterranean punitive policies came under harsh public glare following Trayvon Martin's death. "Task Force Linked to Harsh Sentencing Laws and Private Prison Firms Disbands Following Public Scrutiny, Boycott," *Prison Legal News*, January 2014, 22–23.

99. For example, in 2010 Obama established the National Commission on Fiscal Responsibility and Reform and appointed two conservative deficit hawks to head it—Erskine Bowles, White House chief of staff under Bill Clinton, and former senator Alan Simpson (R-WY). Although Obama did not endorse the commission's final report, in seeking a "grand bargain" with Congress on deficit reduction in 2012–13, he largely endorsed the

Simpson-Bowles target of reducing the deficit by $4 trillion by cutting roughly $2.50 in spending for every $1 in new taxes and other revenue. During the 2012 campaign, Obama largely abandoned his half-trillion-dollar American Jobs Act, which had been unveiled a year earlier. He vowed in his second inaugural address in January 2013 to defend Medicare and Social Security. But the budget he released weeks later proposed major cuts to these and other social welfare programs, which enraged members of his own party. Obama's stance was part of his ongoing illusive quest to secure a budget compromise with the Republicans. "Naturally, Republicans refused," the *New York Times* editorialized. "The President's Budget," editorial, *New York Times*, April 11, 2013, A22. See also Robert L. Borosage, "The Grand Betrayal?," *Nation*, December 3, 2012, 13–20.

100. Quoted in "Editorial: What's With All the Good News Lately?," *Drug War Chronicle* no. 583, May 1, 2009, http://stopthedrugwar.org/chronicle/583/fulltext (retrieved February 21, 2014).

Chapter Two
Show Me the Money

1. Kenneth E. Hartman, "The Trouble with Prison," in Doran Larson, ed., *Fourth City: Essays from the Prison in America* (East Lansing: Michigan State University Press, 2013), 184. Sentenced to LWOP, Hartman has served more than three decades in the California prison system. He is an award-winning author and founder of The Other Death Penalty Project.

2. Abdon Pallasch, "Prisons Not the Answer to Crime Problems: Attorney General," *Chicago Sun-Times*, August 3, 2009.

3. Marc Mauer, *Race to Incarcerate* (New York: New Press, 1999).

4. John Hagan, *Who Are the Criminals? The Politics of Crime Policy from the Age of Roosevelt to the Age of Reagan* (Princeton, NJ: Princeton University Press, 2011), 10–18.

5. The report allegedly was quashed at the last minute because it was out of step with prominent claims by the Reagan administration that violent victimization was on the rise, and that "welfare queens" and other peddlers of bad family values were to blame. Hagan, *Who Are the Criminals?*, 10–18.

6. Drake Bennett and Robert Kuttner, "Crime and Redemption," *American Prospect*, December 2003, 36.

7. Center on Sentencing and Corrections, "The Continuing Fiscal Crisis in Corrections: Setting a New Course" (New York: Vera Institute of Justice, October 2010), 7.

8. Tracey Kyckelhahn, "State Corrections Expenditures, FY 1982–2010," *Bureau of Justice Statistics Bulletin*, December 2012, 1.

9. For example, each additional inmate costs the state of Missouri about $6,200 in direct costs for food, health care, etc. George Lombardi, Director of the Missouri Department of Corrections, personal email communication, May 21, 2013. See also James Austin, "Myths and Realities in Correctional Cost-Benefit Analysis," *Corrections Today* 72.1 (2010): 54–74.

10. B. Jayne Anno et al., "Correctional Health Care: Addressing the Needs of Elderly, Chronically Ill, and Terminally Ill Inmates" (Washington, DC: National Institute of Corrections, 2004), 11. Between 1999 and 2007, the number of people who were 55 years of age or older in state and federal prisons grew by nearly 77 percent. Projections of the proportion of elderly people in prison by 2020 range from one-fifth to one-third of all prisoners. The

cutoff point for classifying inmates as elderly is usually set at 50 or 55 years of age because a combination of mental and physical declines renders inmates, on average, about a decade older physiologically than their counterparts on the outside. Tina Chiu, "It's About Time: Aging Prisoners, Increasing Costs and Geriatric Release" (New York: Vera Institute of Justice, 2010), 4; R.V. Rikard and Ed Rosenberg, "Aging Inmates: A Convergence of Trends in the American Criminal Justice System," *Journal of Correctional Health Care* 13.3 (2007): 150–51; Heather Habes, "Paying for the Graying: How California Can More Effectively Manage Its Growing Elderly Inmate Population," *Southern California Interdisciplinary Law Journal* 20.2 (2011): 395–423.

11. For example, in 2013, Connecticut opened its first forensic nursing home for ill and disabled prisoners, which allowed the state to transfer some of the costs of caring for them to Medicaid. David Drury, "First Patients Moved into Controversial Rocky Hill Nursing Home," *Hartford Courant*, May 3, 2013, http://articles.courant.com/2013-05-03/news/hc -rocky-hill-nursing-home-moving-in-20130503_1_nursing-home-patients-state-department (retrieved September 20, 2013).

12. David Garland, *The Culture of Control: Crime and Social Order in Contemporary Society* (Chicago: University of Chicago Press, 2001).

13. Garland, *The Culture of Control*, 132–33.

14. Amanda Matravers and Shadd Maruna, "Modern Penalty and Psychoanalysis," in Matt Matravers, ed., *Managing Modernity: Politics and the Culture of Control* (London: Routledge, 2005), 128.

15. Charles M. Blow, "The Morose Middle Class," *New York Times*, April 27, 2013, A19.

16. Michael T. Costelloe, Ted Chiricos, and Marc Gertz, "Public Attitudes Toward Criminals: Exploring the Relevance of Crime Salience and Economic Insecurity," *Punishment & Society* 11.1 (2009): 25–49.

17. The number of firearms available for sale or possessed by U.S. citizens has increased in recent years. It is extremely difficult to get a precise view of trends in the proportion of households owning guns because surveys of gun ownership are notoriously inaccurate due to respondent errors or misstatements. In 2012, Black Friday gun sales hit a high of nearly 155,000, an increase of about 20 percent over 2011 and almost 300 percent over 2008. Kevin Johnson, "Black Friday's Gun-Buyer Checks Set a Record," *USA Today*, November 26, 2012, http://www.usatoday.com/story/news/nation/2012/11/26/black-friday-gun-sales/1727409/ (retrieved September 20, 2013); Charles M. Blow, "Pitchforks and Pistols," *New York Times*, April 4, 2009, A17; Bob Johnson and Jeff Martin, "Researchers Report Sharp Rise in 'Patriot' Groups,'" Associated Press, March 5, 2013, http://news.yahoo.com/researchers-report-sharp -rise-patriot-groups-170121578.html (retrieved April 19, 2013).

18. Joe Keohane, "Imaginary Fiends: Crime in America Keeps Going Down. Why Does the Public Refuse to Believe It?," *Boston Globe*, February 14, 2010; Rasmussen Reports, "63% Favor Death Penalty, 47% Say It Deters Crime," June 29, 2011, http://www .rasmussenreports.com/public_content/politics/general_politics/june_2011/63_favor_death _penalty_47_say_it_deters_crime (retrieved July 1, 2011).

19. Pew Research Center, "Gun Homicide Rate Down 49% Since 1993 Peak; Public Unaware" (Washington, DC: Pew Research Center, May 7, 2013), 1, 4–5, 25–26.

20. Joanne Wood, "Local Macroeconomic Trends and Hospital Admissions for Child Abuse, 2000–2009," *Pediatrics* 130.2 (2012): 358–64; Seth Stephens-Davidowitz, "How Googling Unmasks Child Abuse," *New York Times*, July 14, 2013, SR5; Randall Roth, comments at workshop on "American Exceptionalism in Crime and Punishment," University of Minnesota Law School, Robina Institute, April 27, 2013.

21. Richard Rosenfeld, "Crime Is the Problem: Homicide, Acquisitive Crime, and Economic Conditions," *Journal of Quantitative Criminology* 25.3 (2009): 287–306; Richard Rosenfeld and Steven F. Messner, "The Crime Drop in Comparative Perspective: The Impact of the Economy and Imprisonment on American and European Burglary Rates," *British Journal of Sociology* 60.3 (2009): 445–71.

22. For a survey of earlier work on the relationship between unemployment and crime rates, see Theodore G. Chiricos and Miriam A. Delone, "Labor Surplus and Punishment: A Review and Assessment of Theory and Evidence," *Social Problems* 39.4 (1992): 421–46.

23. Michael J. Lynch, *Big Prisons, Big Dreams: Crime and the Failure of America's Penal System* (New Brunswick, NJ: Rutgers University Press, 2007), ch. 5; Robert Reiner, "Beyond Risk: A Lament for Social Democratic Criminology," in Tim Newburn and Paul Rock, eds., *The Politics of Crime Control: Essays in Honour of David Downes* (Oxford: Oxford University Press, 2006), 33–34.

24. Steven Raphael and Michael A. Stoll, "Why Are So Many Americans in Prison?," in Steven Raphael and Michael A. Stoll, eds., *Do Prisons Make Us Safer? The Benefits and Costs of the Prison Boom* (New York: Russell Sage Foundation, 2009), 55, 59; Eric D. Gould, Bruce A. Weinberg, and David B. Mustard, "Crime Rates and Local Labor Market Opportunities in the United States: 1979–1997," *Review of Economics and Statistics* 84.1 (2002): 45–61.

25. Rosenfeld and Messner, "The Crime Drop in Comparative Perspective"; Richard Rosenfeld and Robert Fornango, "The Impact of Economic Conditions on Robbery and Property Crime: The Role of Consumer Sentiment," *Criminology* 45.4 (2007): 735–69.

26. Alessandro De Giorgi, *Re-Thinking the Political Economy of Punishment: Perspectives on Post-Fordism and Penal Politics* (Aldershot, UK: Ashgate, 2006), 3–33.

27. Pershing Square Capital Management, "Prisons' Dilemma," October 20, 2009, http://thinkprogress.org/wp-content/uploads/2010/09/Bill-AckmanPresentation.pdf (retrieved August 4, 2012), 17.

28. For a succinct overview of the literature on the relationship between punishment and perceptions of social threat, see Bruce Western, Meredith Kleykamp, and Jake Rosenfeld, "Crime, Punishment, and American Inequality," in Katherine Neckerman, ed., *Social Inequality* (New York: Russell Sage Foundation, 2004), 782–85.

29. Western, Kleykamp, and Rosenfeld, "Crime, Punishment, and American Inequality," 785. Some state guidelines, notably those in North Carolina, explicitly instruct judges to consider employment as a mitigating factor. John F. Pfaff, "The Empirics of Prison Growth: A Critical Review and Path Forward," *Criminology* 98.2 (2008): 556.

30. Seung Min Kim, "Eric Cantor Calls Wall Street Protesters 'Mobs,'" *Politico*, October 7, 2012, http://www.politico.com/news/stories/1011/65419.html (retrieved July 13, 2012).

31. At the time, former Labor home secretary Jack Straw announced, "There is patently now an urgent need for more prison places." A panel established by Prime Minister Cameron attributed the riots to a broad range of factors, including high youth unemployment, volatile relations with the local police, and aggressive stop-and-frisk policies. Ed Vulliamy, "Broken Britain: Nothing Is Left of the Family Silver," *Harper's*, November 2011, 34, 41; Fiona Bawdon, "Verdict on UK Riots: People Need a 'Stake in Society,' Says Report," *Guardian*, March 27, 2012, http://www.guardian.co.uk/uk/2012/mar/28/verdict-uk-riots-stake-society (retrieved July 14, 2012).

32. Robert Fogelson, *America's Armories: Architecture, Society, and Public Order* (Cambridge, MA: Harvard University Press, 1989), 1, quoted in Samuel Bowles and Arjun Jayadev, "Garrison America," *Economist's Voice*, March 2007, http://www.bepress.com/ev/vol4/iss2/art3/ (retrieved March 11, 2009).

33. Michael Goldfield, "Worker Insurgency, Radical Organization, and New Deal Labor Legislation," *American Political Science Review* 83.4 (1989): 1257–82.

34. Tony Badger, "FDR: A Model for Obama?," *Nation*, January 7, 2009.

35. Marie Gottschalk, *The Prison and the Gallows: The Politics of Mass Incarceration in America* (New York: Cambridge University Press, 2006), 65–70.

36. Sudhir Venkatesh, "Feeling Too Down to Rise Up," *New York Times*, March 29, 2009, WK10.

37. Alexandra Bradbury, "Home Is Where the Fight Is: Unions Pitch in to Stop Evictions," *Labor Notes*, March 2013, 1–3.

38. The notable exceptions include the Liberty City, Miami, riots in 1980, the Los Angeles riots in 1992, the confrontations between police and protesters at the 1999 World Trade Organization meetings in Seattle, and the unrest in Ferguson, Missouri, after Michael Brown was shot to death in August 2014.

39. Michael B. Katz, "Why Don't American Cities Burn Very Often?," *Journal of Urban History* 34.2 (2008): 185–208.

40. Katz, "Why Don't American Cities Burn Very Often?," 193.

41. Katz, "Why Don't American Cities Burn Very Often?," 192.

42. Jarret S. Lovell, *Crimes of Dissent: Civil Disobedience, Criminal Justice, and the Politics of Conscience* (New York: NYU Press, 2009); Luiz A. Fernandez, *Policing Dissent: Social Control and the Anti-Globalization Movement* (New Brunswick, NJ: Rutgers University Press, 2008).

43. Michael Greenberg, "New York: The Police and the Protesters," *New York Review of Books*, October 11, 2012, 57–61; Michael Greenberg, "The Problem of the New York Police," *New York Review of Books*, October 25, 2012; Jeff Madrick, "The Fall and Rise of Occupy Wall Street," *Harper's*, March 2013.

44. David M. Reutter, "Economic Crisis Prompts Prison Closures Nationwide, but Savings (and Reforms) Are Elusive," *Prison Legal News*, April 2009, 1, 3–10.

45. Judith Greene and Marc Mauer, "Downscaling Prisons: Lessons from Four States" (Washington, DC: The Sentencing Project, 2010), 60. Since 2009, New York State's prison population has decreased by an additional 9 percent, and the state has closed seven prisons. But the corrections budget has not contracted significantly. New York State Commission of Correction, "Inmate Population Statistics," n.d., http://www.scoc.ny.gov/pop.htm (retrieved April 19, 2014); New York State Division of the Budget, "2012–13 New York State Executive Budget: Public Safety," n.d., http://www.budget.ny.gov/pubs/archive/fy1213archive /eBudget1213/fy1213littlebook/PublicSafety.pdf (retrieved April 19, 2014).

46. State officials in New Jersey blame contract settlements with unions for the lack of savings, as do corrections officials in Rhode Island, which also experienced a drop in its prison population without substantial savings in corrections spending. Ram Subramanian and Rebecca Tublitz, "Realigning Justice Resources: A Review of Population and Spending Shifts in Prison and Community Corrections" (New York: Vera Institute of Justice, September 2012), 12–13.

47. Michigan Department of Corrections, "Mound Correctional Facility (NRF) Closed January 8, 2012," n.d., http://www.michigan.gov/corrections/1,1607,7-119-1381_1388 -5352—,00.html (retrieved September 18, 2013); Jeff Gerritt, "In Ryan Prison Closing, State Makes Doubly Dumb Decision," May 24, 2012, http://www.freep.com/article /20120524/BLOG2505/120524068/In-Ryan-prison-closing-state-makes-doubly-dumb -decision (retrieved September 18, 2013).

48. David Downes, "The *Macho* Penal Economy: Mass Incarceration in the United States—A European Perspective," *Punishment & Society* 3.1 (2001), 74.

49. Katherine Beckett and Bruce Western, "How Unregulated Is the U.S. Labor Market? The Dynamics of Jobs and Jails, 1980–1995," *American Journal of Sociology* 104.4 (1999), 1040.

50. Michael Cavadino and James Dignan, *Penal Systems: A Comparative Approach* (London: Sage, 2006), 58.

51. In fiscal 2012, federal spending on corrections was $6.6 billion, and state spending on corrections totaled about $53.3 billion. Local government spending on corrections was about $25 billion in fiscal 2009, the latest figure available. A recent Vera Institute report suggests that state spending on corrections may be considerably higher. See p. 288, n. 43. DOJ, "FY 2013 Budget & Performance Summary: Federal Prison System, n.d., http://www.justice .gov/jmd/2013summary/pdf/fy13-bop-bud-summary.pdf (retrieved June 7, 2013); National Association of State Budget Officers, "State Expenditures Report: Examining Fiscal 2010–2012 State Spending," December 2012, http://www.nasbo.org/sites/default/files/State%20 Expenditure%20Report_1.pdf (retrieved June 7, 2013), 52; U.S. Census Bureau, "Annual Surveys of State and Local Government Finances," www.census.gov/govs/estimate/, cited in David R. Richenthal, "The Budget Case for Criminal Justice Reform," *Government Finance Review*, April 2012, 62; Christian Henrichson and Ruth Delaney, "The Price of Prisons: What Incarceration Costs Taxpayers" (New York: Vera Institute of Justice, January 2012).

52. Bureau of Justice Statistics, "Direct Expenditures by Criminal Justice Function, 1982–2007," 2008, rev. July 28, 2012, http://bjs.ojp.usdoj.gov/content/glance/tables/exptyptab .cfm (retrieved July 28, 2012).

53. This calculation includes the police, private security guards, military personnel, and others "who make up the disciplinary apparatus of society." Bowles and Jayadev, "Garrison America," 1.

54. Pew Center on the States, "The High Cost of Corrections in America: Info-graphic," June 12, 2012, http://www.pewstates.org/research/data-visualizations/the-high-cost -of-corrections-in-america-85899397897 (retrieved May 2, 2013).

55. Suzanne M. Kirchhoff, "Economic Impacts of Prison Growth," summary, Congressional Research Service, April 13, 2010, http://www.fas.org/sgp/crs/misc/R41177.pdf (retrieved October 23, 2013), n.p.

56. Grits for Breakfast, "Stimulus and the Police State," February 7, 2009, http://gritsfor breakfast.blogspot.com/2009/02/stimulus-and-police-state.html (retrieved May 20, 2014).

57. Calculated from Center for Sentencing and Corrections, "The Continuing Fiscal Crisis," 9, table 1.

58. Radley Balko, "Bad Cop: Why Obama Is Getting Criminal Justice Wrong," *Slate*, October 6, 2008 http://www.slate.com/id/2201632/ (retrieved March 11, 2009).

59. Neil A. Lewis, "Recovery Bill Has $1 Billion to Hire More Local Police," *New York Times*, February 6, 2009, A16.

60. See Inimai Chettiar et al., "Reforming Funding to Reduce Mass Incarceration" (New York: Brennan Center for Justice at NYU School of Law, 2013) for a critique of the Byrne grants and a proposal on how to restructure them to address the problem of mass incarceration.

61. Balko, "Bad Cop: Why Obama Is Getting Criminal Justice Wrong."

62. Balko, "Bad Cop: Why Obama Is Getting Criminal Justice Wrong."

63. The Tulia scandal forced the Texas legislature, Governor George W. Bush, and his

successor Rick Perry to rethink the Byrne drug task forces and largely phase them out. Grits for Breakfast, "Elimination of Drug Task Forces a Blessing in Disguise from Sequester Cuts," April 6, 2013, http://gritsforbreakfast.blogspot.com/2013/04/elimination-of-drug-task-forces.html (retrieved May 21, 2013).

64. David Hunt, "Obama Fields Questions on Jacksonville Crime," *Florida Times-Union*, September 22, 2008, quoted in Michelle Alexander, *The New Jim Crow: Mass Incarceration in the Age of Colorblindness* (New York: New Press, 2010), 82–83.

65. John Gramlich, "Stimulus Prompts Debate Over Police," *Stateline*, February 11, 2009, http://www.stateline.org/live/details/story?contentId=375802 (retrieved March 6, 2009).

66. Phillip Smith, "Federal Budget: Economic Stimulus Bill Stimulates Drug War, Too," *Drug War Chronicle*, no. 573, February 20, 2009.

67. Ted Guest, "Senate Likely to Save COPS; House Panel Wants U.S. Prison Study," *Crime Report*, July 17, 2013, http://www.thecrimereport.org/news/inside-criminal-justice/2013-07-senate-saves-cops-again (retrieved January 30, 2014); U.S. House, Committee on Appropriations—Democrats, "Summary of Omnibus Appropriations Act," n.d., http://democrats.appropriations.house.gov/top-news/summary-of-omnibus-appropriations-act/ (retrieved January 30, 2014).

68. Vernon Clark, "Biden Stands with Philadelphia Area Police in Push for Jobs Bill," October 19, 2011, *philly.com*, http://articles.philly.com/2011-10-19/news/30298040_1_vice-president-biden-jobs-bill-police-officers (retrieved July 15, 2012); Lucy Madison, "White House Stands by Biden on Murder, Rape Rates," CBS News, October 20, 2011, http://www.cbsnews.com/8301-503544_162-20123397-503544.html (retrieved July 15, 2012).

69. Grits for Breakfast, "Audits of Asset Forfeiture Funds Yield Questions, Felony Conviction of Brooks/Jim Wells DA," January 23, 2012, http://gritsforbreakfast.blogspot.com/2012/01/audits-of-asset-forfeiture-funds-yield.html (retrieved April 13, 2012).

70. Sarah Stillman, "Taken," *New Yorker*, August 12 and 19, 2013, 53.

71. Stillman, "Taken," 53.

72. Grits for Breakfast, "Making the Same Old Mistakes on Asset Forfeiture," February 26, 2011, http://gritsforbreakfast.blogspot.com/2011/02/making-same-old-mistakes-on-asset.html (retrieved April 13, 2013).

73. The Smart on Crime Coalition, "Recommendations for the Administration and Congress" (Washington, DC: Constitution Project, 2011), 19.

74. Alexander, *The New Jim Crow*, 77–83.

75. U.S. DOJ, "Annual Report of the Department of Justice Asset Forfeiture Program," "Total Net Deposits to the Fund by State of Deport," various years, http://www.justice.gov/jmd/afp/02fundreport/ (retrieved June 21, 2013).

76. Lise Olsen and Jason Buch, "Government Seizures Cloaked in Secrecy," *Houston Chronicle*, May 27, 2013, http://www.houstonchronicle.com/news/houston-texas/houston/article/Government-seizures-cloaked-in-secrecy-4548851.php#/0 (retrieved January 14, 2014).

77. Kevin Drum, "'Forfeiture Corridors' Are the New Speed Traps," *Mother Jones*, April 12, 2012, http://www.motherjones.com/kevin-drum/2012/04/forfeiture-corridors-are-new-speed-traps (retrieved June 21, 2013).

78. Stillman, "Taken," 50.

79. Stillman, "Taken," 53.

80. John W. Whitehead, "Governmental Highway Robbery: Asset Forfeiture and the Pillaging of the American People," *Prison Legal News*, May 2013, 16–17.

81. In the 2005 *Illinois v. Caballes* decision, the U.S. Supreme Court ruled that K-9 searches of the exterior of a vehicle during routine traffic stops are constitutional. But drug-sniffing dogs can be highly unreliable and are easily manipulated by law enforcement officers during traffic stops. Radley Balko, "Illinois Traffic Stop of Star Trek Fans Raises Concerns about Drug Searches, Police Dogs, Bad Cops," *Huffington Post*, March 31, 2012, http://www.huffingtonpost.com/2012/03/31/drug-search-trekies-stopped-searched-illinois_n_1364087.html (retrieved June 21, 2013).

82. Smart on Crime Coalition, "Recommendations," 19.

83. Smart on Crime Coalition, "Recommendations," 20.

84. Stillman, "Taken," 57.

85. Christopher Zoukis, "Missouri: Arrestees Billed for Cost of Police Tasers," *Prison Legal News*, September 2013, 25.

86. "In fact, incarcerating indigent defendants unable to pay their LFOs often ends up costing much more than states and counties can ever hope to recover." ACLU, "In for a Penny: The Rise of America's New Debtors' Prisons," October 2010, http://www.aclu.org/files/assets/InForAPenny_web.pdf#page=6 (retrieved May 21, 2013), 9.

87. "The New Debtors' Prisons," editorial, *New York Times*, April 6, 2009, A24.

88. David M. Reutter, "Florida DOC and Keefe Gouge Prisoners on Commissary Sales," *Prison Legal News*, October 2009, 21.

89. ACLU, "In for a Penny," 5.

90. Quoted in Ethan Bronner, "Poor Land in Jail as Companies Add Huge Fees for Probation," *New York Times*, July 3, 2012, A1.

91. Katherine Beckett and Alexes Harris, "On Cash and Conviction: Monetary Sanctions as Misguided Policy," *Criminology & Public Policy* 10.3 (2011): 505–37.

92. David M. Reutter, "Debtors' Prisons Returning to America," *Prison Legal News*, November 2013, 20.

93. Forrest Wilder, "Fast Cash: How Taking Out a Payday Loan Could Land You in Jail," *Texas Observer*, July 16, 2013, http://www.texasobserver.org/cash-fast-how-taking-out-a-payday-loan-could-land-you-in-jail/ (retrieved January 21, 2014).

94. Jessica Silver-Greenberg, "In Prosecutors, Debt Collectors Find a Partner," *New York Times*, September 15, 2012, A1.

95. ACLU, "In for a Penny," 6.

96. In 1983, the U.S. Supreme Court ruled in *Bearden v. Georgia* that imprisoning people unable to pay fines or restitution through no fault of their own violated the equal protection clause of the Fourteenth Amendment. The Court ruled that sentencing courts must determine a defendant's reasons for failing to pay a fine or restitution before sentencing him or her to prison. The Court held that imprisoning someone on account of his or her poverty would be fundamentally unfair. Yet over one six-month period, nearly one-quarter of the bookings in Ohio's Huron County Jail were related to failure to pay fines. ACLU of Ohio, "The Outskirts of Hope: How Ohio's Debtors' Prisons Are Ruining Lives and Costing Communities," April 2013, http://www.acluohio.org/wp-content/uploads/2013/04/TheOutskirtsOfHope2013_04.pdf (retrieved May 21, 2013), 6; ACLU, "In for a Penny," 5.

97. Gary Hunter, "Washington Jail a Modern-Day Debtor's Prison," April 2010, *Prison Legal News*, 8–9.

98. This account of Louisiana is based on Cindy Chang, "In World of Prisons, Some Rural Parishes' Economies Hinge on Keeping Their Jails Full," *Times-Picayune*, May 13, 2012, http://www.nola.com/crime/index.ssf/2012/05/in_world_of_prisons_some_rural.html (retrieved October 23, 2012); Cindy Chang, "North Louisiana Family Is a Major Force in the State's Vast Prison Industry," *Times-Picayune*, May 14, 2012, http://www.nola.com/crime/index.ssf/2012/05/jonesboro_family_is_a_major_fo.html (retrieved October 23, 2012).

99. Richard Harding, "Private Prisons," in Michael Tonry, ed., *Crime and Justice: A Review of Research*, v. 28 (Chicago: University of Chicago Press, 2001), 281.

100. Jail Bed Space.com, n.d., http://www.jailbedspace.com/jbs/ (retrieved October 27, 2012).

101. A 2011 federally funded report was sharply critical of Hawaii's practice of sending many of its prisoners to privately operated prisons on the mainland. Joe Watson, "Hawaii AG Study Confirms Ineffectiveness of Mainland Private Prisons," *Prison Legal News*, November 2012, 30.

102. Alfred Aman, Jr., "Privatisation, Democracy, and Human Rights: The Need to Extend the Province of Administrative Law," *Indiana Journal of Global Legal Studies* 12.2 (2005), 542.

103. Marilyn Brown quoted in Rena Morningstar Blumberg, "Too Many People Profit from Sending Prisoners Out of State," *Haleakala Times*, October 24, 2006, http://www.haleakalatimes.com/news/story2244.aspx (retrieved October 28, 2006).

104. Aman, Jr., "Privatisation, Prisons, Democracy and Human Rights," 543; "Schwarzenegger: Send Prisoners to Mexico," *Los Angeles Times*, January 25, 2012, http://latimesblogs.latimes.com/california-politics/2010/01/schwarzenegger-send-prisoners-to-mexico.html (retrieved October 26, 2012).

105. Harding, "Private Prisons," 280.

106. Aman, Jr., "Privatisation, Prisons, Democracy, and Human Rights," 543; Casey Newton, Ginger Rough, and J. J. Hensley, "Arizona Inmate Escape Puts Spotlight on State Private Prisons," *Arizona Republic*, August 22, 2010, http://www.azcentral.com/news/articles/2010/08/22/20100822arizona-private-prisons.html (retrieved October 26, 2012).

107. Silja J. A. Talvi, "No Room in Prison? Ship 'Em Off," *In These Times*, May 2006, 25.

108. See the three-part series "Unlocked" by Sam Dolnick that appeared in the *New York Times*, June 17–19, 2012.

109. David M. Reutter, "Montana, Michigan Towns Vie to Fill Prisons with Guantánamo Detainees," *Prison Legal News*, October 2009, 28.

110. Kirchhoff, "Economic Impacts of Prison Growth," 30.

111. Carol Cratty, "Obama Administration Proceeds with Controversial Prison Purchase," CNN, October 2, 2012, http://www.cnn.com/2012/10/02/politics/illinois-prison/index.html (retrieved October 22, 2012).

112. Craig Haney, "Riding the Punishment Wave: On the Origins of Our Devolving Standards of Decency," *Hastings Women's Law Journal* 9.1 (1998), 58.

113. Haney, "Riding the Punishment Wave," 58.

114. Public Safety Performance Project, "Public Safety, Public Spending: Forecasting America's Prison Population, 2007–2011" (Washington, DC: Pew Charitable Trusts, 2007), 27, table A1.

115. James Q. Whitman, *Harsh Justice: Criminal Punishment and the Widening Divide between America and Europe* (New York: Oxford University Press, 2003); Ann-Marie Cusac, *Cruel and Unusual: The Culture of Punishment in America* (New Haven, CT: Yale University Press, 2009); Jonathan Simon, "Dignity and Risk: The Long Road from *Graham v. Florida*

to Abolition of Life without Parole," in Charles Ogletree, Jr., and Austin Sarat, eds., *Life Without Parole: America's New Death Penalty?* (New York: NYU Press, 2012): 282–310.

116. Caitlin Dewey, "With Few Other Outlets, Inmates Review Prisons on Yelp," *Washington Post*, April 27, 2013, http://articles.washingtonpost.com/2013-04-27/business/3886 1994_1_yelp-juice-boxes-other-reviews (retrieved May 20, 2013).

117. This holds even after even after accounting for differences in economic development and family income. Besiki Kutateladze, *Is America Really So Punitive? Exploring a Continuum of U.S. State Criminal Policies* (El Paso, TX: LFB Scholarly Publishing, 2009), 183–96.

118. Henrichson and Delaney, "The Price of Prisons," 10, fig. 4; Marc Santora, "City's Annual Cost Per Inmate is $168,000, Study Finds," *New York Times*, August 23, 2013, A16.

119. Public Safety Performance Project, "Public Safety, Public Spending," 27, table A1 and 33, table A7.

120. Grits for Breakfast, "Tent Jail Idea Opens the Door for Expensive Litigation," April 5, 2011, http://gritsforbreakfast.blogspot.com/2011/04/tent-jail-idea-opens-door-for-expensive.html (retrieved April 8, 2011). See also William Finnegan, "Sheriff Joe," *New Yorker*, July 20, 2009, 42–53.

121. Mark Hornbeck, "Michigan Prisons Focus on Released Inmates," *Detroit News*, April 8, 2010, http://www.ri-familylifecenter.org/node/574 (retrieved July 19, 2012); "Oregon Rethinking Criminal Justice Policies to Avoid Fiscal Crisis," *Prison Legal News*, December 2012, 44–45.

122. Neil Nisperos, "Study Rips Prison Funding," InlandPolitics.com, August 7, 2011, http://inlandpolitics.com/blog/2011/08/08/the-sun-study-rips-prison-funding/ (retrieved July 19, 2012).

123. Bert Useem and Anne Morrison Piehl, *Prison State: The Challenge of Mass Incarceration* (New York: Cambridge University Press, 2008), 114; Jeremy Travis, Bruce Western, and Steve Redburn, eds., *The Growth of Incarceration in the United States: Exploring Causes and Consequences* (Washington, DC: National Academies Press, 2014), 161.

124. Kenneth E. Hartman, "The Recession Behind Bars," *New York Times*, September 5, 2009, WK9.

125. In October 2011, Texas started serving a meal it calls "brunch" between 5 am and 7 am on weekends, and serving dinner between 4 pm and 6:30 pm. Texas has a law requiring that inmates receive three meals a day, but the statute only applies to jails, not prisons. Texas also abolished the "last meal" ritual for prisoners about to be executed, though this apparently was done as much for political reasons as for economic ones. Matt Clarke, "Texas Abolishes Last Meals for Death Row Prisoners, Reduces Weekend Meals," *Prison Legal News*, October 2012, 28–29.

126. Some of them attributed the increase in cell robberies to the cutbacks in food. Correctional Institution Inspection Committee, "Inspection and Evaluation of Trumball Correctional Institution," June 16, 2010, http://ciic.state.oh.us/docs/trumbull_correctional_institution_may_3,_2010.pdf (retrieved May 20, 2014), 14.

127. *Rhodes v. Chapman* 452 U.S. 337 (1981), 349; *Wilson v. Seiter* 501 U.S. 294 (1991), 298.

128. Craig Haney, "The Wages of Prison Overcrowding: Harmful Psychological Consequences and Dysfunctional Correctional Reactions," *Washington University Journal of Law & Policy* 22 (2006), 266.

129. Stephanos Bibas, "Transparency and Participation in Criminal Procedure," *N.Y.U. Law Review* 81.3 (2006): 911–66.

130. Sarah Geraghty and Melanie Velez, "Bringing Transparency and Accountability to Criminal Justice Institutions in the South," *Stanford Law & Policy Review* 22.2 (2011), 458, 463–65.

131. Travis, Western, and Redburn, eds., *The Growth of Incarceration*, 164–66.

132. National Research Council, "Ensuring the Quality, Credibility, and Relevance of U.S. Justice Statistics" (Washington, DC: National Academy of Sciences, 2009), 253.

133. Kutateladze, *Is America Really So Punitive?*, 177.

134. Kurt Erickson, "Illinois Could Face California-style Prison Meltdown," *Quad-City Times*, August 24, 2011, http://qctimes.com/news/local/illinois-could-face-california-style -prison-meltdown-experts-say/article_c3390cb4-cebe-11e0-b9c3–001cc4c03286.html (retrieved April 19, 2013).

135. Julie Wernau, "CT: State's Prisons Are Overcrowded, But Officials Say Conditions Not Inhumane," *Day*, December 22, 2007, http://www.realcostofprisons.org/blog /archives/2007/12/ct_states_priso.html (retrieved August 4, 2011).

136. My calculation is based on the number of states that reported operating at above their design capacity (21 states) or above their operational capacity in cases where they did not specify their design capacity (5 states) as of year-end 2011. The Bureau of Justice Statistics defines design capacity as the number of inmates that planners or architects intended for a facility. Operational capacity is the number of inmates that can be accommodated based on existing facilities, staff, programs, and services. E. Ann Carson and William J. Sabol, "Prisoners in 2011," *Bureau of Justice Statistics Bulletin*, December 2012, 18 and 31, appendix table 14.

137. U.S. DOJ, "Federal Prison System: FY 2013 Congressional Budget, Building and Facilities," n.d., http://www.justice.gov/jmd/2013justification/pdf/fy13-bop-bf-justification .pdf (retrieved June 7, 2013), 1; Carson and Sabol, "Prisoners in 2011," 31, appendix table 14. Alabama's Donaldson Correctional Facility, which had a design capacity of 968, housed nearly 1,700 inmates by late December 2008. The former warden of DCF described the guard shortage at the facility as a "crisis." In one sector of the facility, only two guards watched over nearly 300 inmates, and in another unit there were only two or three guards for more than 500 prisoners, according to a class-action lawsuit settled in 2012. David Reutter, "Settlement in Alabama Overcrowding and Violence Suit," *Prison Legal News*, March 2012, 22–23. For a facility-by-facility calculation of overcrowding in the federal system, see Judith Resnick, Hope Metcalf, and Megan Quattlebaum, U.S. Senate Judiciary Committee, prepared statement, "Oversight of the Bureau of Prisons & Cost-Effective Strategies for Reducing Recidivism," November 12, 2013, http://www.law.yale.edu/documents/pdf/Liman /Senate_Judiciary_Committee_BOP_Oversight_Hearing_Liman_Statement_for_the _Record_Nov__12_2013.pdf_website.pdf (retrieved January 18, 2014).

138. Alison Liebling, "Moral Performance, Inhuman and Degrading Treatment and Prison Pain," *Punishment & Society* 13.5 (2011), 530.

139. Ann Chih Lin, *Reform in the Making: The Implementation of Social Policy in Prison* (Princeton, NJ: Princeton University Press, 2000).

140. Dr. Josiah D. Rich, Brown University Medical School, personal email communication, May 22, 2013.

141. Kutateladze, *Is America Really So Punitive?*, 194–95.

142. Margaret E. Noonan, "Mortality in Local Jails and State Prisons, 2000–2011," *Bureau of Justice Statistics, Statistical Tables*, August 2013, http://www.bjs.gov/content /pub/pdf/mljsp0011.pdf (retrieved September 17, 2013), 1, fig. 1; Erin Banco, "Suicides

Worry Experts at Big Jail in Capital," *New York Times*, August 20, 2013, A11; Jeff Gerritt, "After Closing Psychiatric Hospitals, Michigan Incarcerates Mentally Ill," *Detroit Free Press*, November 27, 2011, http://www.freep.com/article/20111127/OPINION02/111270434 /After-closing-psychiatric-hospitals-Michigan-incarcerates-mentally-ill (retrieved September 18, 2013).

143. Barbara Hoberock, "State Corrections Officer Staffing Historically Low," *Tulsa World*, April 16, 2010, in Grits for Breakfast, "Absolutely Irresponsible," April 16, 2010, http://gritsforbreakfast.blogspot.com/2010/04/absolutely-irresponsible-okies-boosting.html (retrieved October 23, 2013).

144. Naomi Spencer, "Georgia Prisoners Strike for Wages, Better Medical Care and Food," *Prison Legal News*, January 2011, 24–25.

145. David Reutter, Gary Hunter, and Brandon Sample, "Appalling Prison and Jail Food Leaves Prisoners Hungry for Justice," *Prison Legal News*, April 2010, 1–7; David Reutter, "Indian Country Gets Stimulus Money . . . to Build More Jails," *Prison Legal News*, April 2010, 28; Grits for Breakfast, "TDCJ Reduced Spending on Prisoner Food 13.5% Since 2009," January 30, 2011, http://gritsforbreakfast.blogspot.com/2011/01/tdcj-reduced -spending-on-prisoner-food.html (retrieved February 9, 2011); Michael Brodheim, "California Sheriffs Appropriate Rehabilitating Funds for Security Needs," *Prison Legal News*, October 2009, 21.

146. See, for example, Terri Langford, "Force Against Texas Inmates on The Rise," *Texas Tribune*, April 3, 2014, https://www.texastribune.org/2014/04/03/force-against-texas-inmates -rise/ (retrieved May 16, 2014).

147. Some prisons and jails are not collecting or reporting any information about assaults. Allen Beck, the chief statistician for the federal Bureau of Justice Statistics, told the Katzenbach commission, "I cannot measure well the level of assaults using administrative records as they exist today." Commission on Safety and Abuse in America's Prisons, "Confronting Confinement" (New York: Vera Institute of Justice, June 2006), 3.

148. Brandon Sample, "Violence on the Rise in BOP Facilities," *Prison Legal News*, August 2008, 10–12; Bryan Lowry and Phil Glover of the American Federation of Government Employees, Council of Prison Locals, prepared statement, U.S. House Committee on Appropriations, Subcommittee on Commerce, Justice and Science, March 10, 2009, 4.

149. U.S. DOJ, "Federal Prison System, FY 2011 Performance Budget," n.d., http://www .justice.gov/jmd/2011justification/pdf/fy11-bop-se-justification.pdf (retrieved July 28, 2012), 5–6.

150. Traci Billingsley quoted in Kevin Johnson, "2011 Budget Gives Federal Prisons $528M," *USA Today*, February 4, 2010. See also U.S. GAO, "Bureau of Prisons: Growing Inmate Crowding Negatively Affects Inmates, Staff, and Infrastructure," September 2012, http://www.gao.gov/assets/650/648123.pdf (retrieved May 7, 2014).

151. Commission on Safety and Abuse in America's Prisons, "Confronting Confinement," 12.

152. For example, about half of the inmates released from California prisons in 2006 had not participated in a single rehabilitation or job training program or had any work assignment while serving their sentences. Surveys show that nearly three-quarters of state prison inmates nationwide had work assignments in 1974 compared to only 60 percent a decade ago. Haney, "Counting Casualties," 114; and Useem and Piehl, *Prison State*, 113.

153. Useem and Piehl, *Prison State*, 113. Nationwide, the inmate-to-staff ratio for educational and vocational instructors has more than doubled since the 1970s. By 2005, it had

jumped to 112 inmates per instructor. Before the onset of the prison boom, only about one in five inmates in state prisons participated in educational programs. That proportion rose to a peak of 46 percent in 1991 before falling back to about 29 percent in 2004. Michelle S. Phelps, "Rehabilitation in the Punitive Era: The Gap Between Rhetoric and Reality," *Law & Society Review* 45.1 (2011), 48.

154. They reduced the budget for the school district that administers educational programs in Texas prisons by 25 percent. Matt Clarke, "Texas Slashes Prison Education Budget," *Prison Legal News*, December 2012, 24.

155. Matt Clarke, "Indiana Cuts Prison College Courses," *Prison Legal News*, March 2012, 40; John Howard Association of Illinois, "Cuts in Prison Education Put Illinois at Risk," 2010, http://thejha.org/sites/default/files/Prisoneducation.pdf (retrieved June 18, 2013).

156. Florida Department of Corrections, "Table 2A: Secure Drug Treatment Program Enrollment Data, by Fiscal Year," March 2011, http://www.dc.state.fl.us/pub/subabuse/probation /09-10/tab2a.html (retrieved September 22, 2013).

157. John Gramlich, "For State Prisons, Cuts Present New Problems," *Stateline*, May 19, 2010, http://www.pewstates.org/projects/stateline/headlines/for-state-prisons-cuts-present -new-problems-85899376814 (retrieved June 19, 2013).

158. Thanks to their shorter sentences, the transferred prisoners were given priority for educational and vocational training programs ahead of Angola's 5,000-plus lifers and long-termers. John Corley, "Squeezed," *Angolite*, November/December 2012, 22–25.

159. Michele Deitch, "The Need for Independent Prison Oversight in a Post-PLRA World," *Federal Sentencing Reporter* 24.4 (2012): 236–44.

160. Commission on Safety and Abuse in America's Prisons, "Confronting Confinement," 5.

161. Commission on Safety and Abuse in America's Prisons, "Confronting Confinement," 6.

162. Harding, "Private Prisons," 315–16; Little Rock Reed and Ivan Denisovich, "The American Correctional Association: A Conspiracy of Silence," in Bob Gaucher, ed., *Writing as Resistance: The Journal of Prisoners on Prisons Anthology, 1988-2002* (Toronto: Canadian Scholars' Press, 2002): 447–70; Lynn S. Branham, "Accrediting the Accreditors: A New Paradigm for Correctional Oversight," *Pace Law Review* 30.5 (2010): 1656–71; David M. Bogard, "Effective Corrections Oversight: What Can We Learn from ACA Standards and Accreditation?," *Pace Law Review* 30.5 (2010): 1646–55.

163. For an overview of how penal oversight in the United States compares with other countries, see the contributions to "Opening Up a Closed World: A Sourcebook on Prison Oversight," special issue, *Pace Law Review* 30.5 (2010). See also Dirk van Zyl Smit, "Regulation of Prison Conditions," in Michael Tonry, ed., *Crime and Justice: A Review of Research*, v. 39 (Chicago: University of Chicago Press, 2010): 501–63.

164. Silvia Casale, "The Importance of Dialogue and Cooperation in Prison Oversight," *Pace Law Review* 30.5 (2010): 1494–1500.

165. On the hurdles that the PLRA poses, see Human Rights Watch, "No Equal Justice: The Prison Litigation Reform Act in the United States" (New York: Human Rights Watch, June 15, 2009); Margo Schlanger, "Inmate Litigation," *Harvard Law Review* 116 (April 2003): 1557–1706; Margo Schlanger and Giovanna Shay, "Preserving the Rule of Law in America's Jails and Prisons: The Case for Amending the Prison Litigation Reform Act," *University of Pennsylvania Journal of Constitutional Law* 11.1 (2008): 139–54.

166. Benjamin Fluery-Stein with Carla Crowder, *Dying Inside: The HIV/AIDS Ward at Limestone Prison* (Ann Arbor: University of Michigan Press, 2008), 83.

167. State Health Care Spending Project, "Managing Prison Health Care Spending," October 2013, http://www.pewstates.org/uploadedFiles/PCS_Assets/2013/SHCS_Pew-Managing _Prison_Health_Care_Spending_Report.pdf (retrieved January 17, 2014), 5.

168. Elizabeth Alexander, "Prison Health Care, Political Choice, and the Accidental Death Penalty," *University of Pennsylvania Journal of Constitutional Law* 11.1 (2008), 1.

169. Elizabeth Alexander, "Michigan Breaks Political Logjam: A New Model for Reducing Prison Populations" (New York: ACLU, 2009), 14.

170. See Alexander's interpretation of *Wilson v. Seiter* in "Prison Health Care," 2, n.3.

171. Michele Deitch, "Independent Correctional Oversight Mechanisms Across the County: A 50-State Inventory," *Pace Law Review* 30.5 (2010), 1762. One notable exception is the Correctional Association of New York, "which has legislative authority, dating back to the 19th century, to enter any New York State prison, speak with whomever it chooses, and issue public reports and recommendations based on their findings." James Ridgeway and Jean Casella, "Oversight in British Prisons: Lessons for the U.S.?," *Crime Report*, August 12, 2013, http://www.thecrimereport.org/news/inside-criminal-justice/2013–08-over sight-in-british-prisons-lessons-for-the-us (retrieved January 14, 2014).

172. Deitch, "The Need for Independent Prison Oversight," 240–41.

173. Marvin Mentor, "California Corrections System Officially Declared 'Dysfunctional'—Redemption Doubtful," *Prison Legal News*, March 2005, 1–8; Geri Lynn Green, "The Quixotic Dilemma, California's Immutable Culture of Incarceration," *Pace Law Review* 30.5 (2010): 1453–75.

174. Maurice Chammah, "Report Supports Calls for Prison System Oversight Board," *Texas Tribune*, March 5, 2013, http://www.texastribune.org/2013/03/05/report-calls-prison -oversight/ (retrieved April 19, 2013); Bob Ray Sanders, "Prison Oversight Committee Not Likely to Happen This Session," *Star-Telegram*, April 9, 2013, http://www.star-telegram .com/2013/04/09/4762340/prison-oversight-committee-not.html (retrieved April 19, 2013).

175. Brandi Grissom, "Hundreds Die of Illnesses in County Jails," *Texas Tribune*, November 14, 2010, http://www.texastribune.org/texas-state-agencies/state-commission-on-jail -standards/hundreds-die-of-illnesses-in-county-jails/ (retrieved July 20, 2012).

176. Matt Clarke, "Inadequate Medical Care in Texas Jails Kills Hundreds of Prisoners," *Prison Legal News*, May 2011, 17; Texas Criminal Justice Coalition, "The Texas Commission on Jail Standards: The State's Solution for Implementing a Strong County Jail System, While Protecting Counties from Liability," 2012, http://www.texascjc.org/sites/default/files /uploads/TCJS%20State%20Solution%20(Dec%202012).pdf (retrieved September 13, 2013), 5.

177. Texas Criminal Justice Coalition, "The Texas Commission on Jail Standards," 4.

178. Gary Hunter, "Texas Prisoners Still Dying in Houston Jails, Among Other Problems," *Prison Legal News*, October 2009, 4.

179. "Dallas County Passes Jail Inspections . . . Finally," *Prison Legal News*, June 2012, 17.

180. Hunter, "Texas Prisoners Still Dying," 4.

181. Emily DePrang, "Harris County Jail Among Worst for Inmate Sexual Assault," *Texas Observer*, July 1, 2013, http://www.texasobserver.org/harris-county-jail-among-worst-for -inmate-sexual-assault/ (retrieved September 13, 2013).

182. Jennifer Medina, "Pressed, Sheriff Agrees to Jails Inquiry," *New York Times*, October 22, 2011, A15; Sarah Liebowitz et al., "Cruel and Unusual Punishment: How a Savage Gang of Deputies Controls L.A. County Jails," ACLU National Prison Project and ACLU

of Southern California, September 2011, https://www.aclu.org/files/assets/78162_aclu_jails_r2_lr.pdf (retrieved October 23, 2013); Mike Brodheim and Alex Friedmann, "Abuse in Los Angeles Jail System Leads to Investigations, Lawsuits and Eventual Reforms," *Prison Legal News*, March 2013, 1–12.

183. Thomas E. Perez and David J. Hickton, U.S. DOJ, Civil Right Division, letter to Governor Tom Corbett, "Re: Investigation of the State Correctional Institution at Cresson and Notice of Expanded Investigation," n.d., http://www.ada.gov/cresson-lof.htm (retrieved January 17, 2014); Andrew Cohen, "One of the Darkest Periods in the History of American Prisons," *Atlantic*, June 9, 2013, http://www.theatlantic.com/national/archive/2013/06/one-of-the-darkest-periods-in-the-history-of-american-prisons/276684/ (retrieved January 17, 2014); Laura Benshoff, "Federal Report Condemns Use of Solitary Confinement for Mentally Ill Prisoners in Pa.," February 27, 2014, http://www.newsworks.org/index.php/local/healthscience/65353-federal-report-condemns-use-of-solitary-confinement-for-mentally-ill-prisoners-in-pa (retrieved May 18, 2014).

184. U.S. GAO, "Improvements Needed in Bureau of Prisons' Monitoring and Evaluation of Impact of Segregated Housing," May 1, 2013, http://www.gao.gov/products/GAO-13-429 (retrieved January 17, 2014).

185. Barbara Ehrenreich, "Is It Now a Crime to Be Poor?," *New York Times*, August 9, 2009, WK9; Katherine Beckett and Steven Herbert, *Banished: The New Social Control in Urban America* (New York: Oxford University Press, 2009).

186. The National Law Center on Homelessness & Poverty and The National Coalition for the Homeless, "Homes Not Handcuffs: The Criminalization of Homelessness in U.S. Cities," July 2009, http://www.nationalhomeless.org/publications/crimreport/CrimzReport_2009.pdf (retrieved June 4, 2013), 9–11; Alfred Lubrano, "In Hard Times, Americans Blame the Poor," *Philadelphia Inquirer*, February 15, 2010, http://articles.philly.com/2010-02-15/news/25219526_1_poor-children-food-stamps-middle-class (retrieved September 20, 2013).

187. A. G. Sulzberger, "States Adding Drug Test as Hurdle for Welfare," *New York Times*, October 11, 2011, A1.

188. Up until then, Michigan had been the only state to ever force applicants to the Temporary Assistance for Needy Families (TANF) to submit to drug tests. In 2003, a federal appeals court voided the Michigan law after a challenge from the ACLU. Rania Khalek, "New Drug Tests Target the Poor," *In These Times*, September 2011, 10–11.

189. Frances Robles, "Florida Law on Drug Tests for Welfare Struck Down," *New York Times*, January 1, 2014, A10.

190. Sulzberger, "States Adding Drug Test." In 2012, Congress enacted a law that permits states to administer urine tests to recipients of unemployment benefits who are seeking positions in occupations that require such screenings. Isabel Macdonald, "The GOP's Drug Test Dragnet," *Nation*, April 22, 2013, 11.

191. Loïc Wacquant, *Punishing the Poor: The Neoliberal Government of Social Insecurity* (Durham, NC: Duke University Press, 2009); Katherine Beckett and Bruce Western, "Governing Social Marginality: Welfare, Incarceration, and the Transformation of State Policy," *Punishment & Society* 3.1 (2001): 43–59.

192. Emily DePrang, "Barred Care: Want Treatment for Mental Illness in Houston? Go to Jail," *Texas Observer*, January 13, 2014, http://www.google.com/search?client=safari&rls=en&q=Emily+DePrang,+"Barred+Care:+Want+Treatment+for+Mental+Illness+in+Houston%3F+Go+to+Jail,"&ie=UTF-8&oe=UTF-8 (retrieved January 18, 2014).

193. Robert E. Crew and Belinda Creel Davis, "Substance Abuse as a Barrier to Employment of Welfare Recipients," *Journal of Policy Practice* 5.4 (2006): 69–82; Harold A. Pollack

et al., "Substance Use among Welfare Recipients: Trends and Policy Responses," *Social Service Review* 76.2 (2002): 256–74.

194. Chris Brennan, "Gov. Corbett Blames Slow Job Growth on Failed Employee Drug Tests," philly.com, April 30, 2013, http://www.philly.com/philly/blogs/cityhall/Gov-Corbett-blames-slow-job-growth-on-failed-employee-drug-tests.html (retrieved June 4, 2013).

195. Tara Herivel, "Introduction," in Tara Herivel and Paul Wright, eds., *Prison Profiteers: Who Makes Money from Mass Incarceration* (New York: New Press, 2007), ix.

Chapter Three
Squaring the Political Circle

1. In the case of Florida, for example, welfare state retrenchment and increased spending on criminal justice were not initially part of a single, cohesive political and ideological agenda. Some leading penal conservatives favored a greater role for the state in crime prevention, education, and rehabilitating offenders. But once they decided to construct more prisons, cuts had to come from somewhere. As a consequence, education, public assistance, and health care ended up paying the price of the prison tab. Heather Schoenfeld, "The Politics of Prison Growth: From Chain Gangs to Work Release Centers and Supermax Prisons, Florida, 1955–2000," Northwestern University, PhD dissertation, 2009, 261–62, 256–61, 315–17.

2. This is twice as many as it constructed in the first century after statehood. California also added about two dozen smaller penal facilities. Ruth Wilson Gilmore, *Golden Gulag: Prisons, Surplus, Crisis, and Opposition in Globalizing California* (Berkeley: University of California Press, 2007), 7–8.

3. Joshua Page, *The Toughest Beat: Politics, Punishment, and the Prison Officers Union in California* (New York: Oxford University Press, 2011), ch. 7. In 2005, the department's name was changed to the California Department of Corrections and Rehabilitation.

4. Keith Edgerton, *Montana Justice: Power, Punishment, and the Penitentiary* (Seattle: University of Washington Press, 1976).

5. Gilmore, *Golden Gulag*; Mona Lynch, *Sunbelt Justice: Arizona and the Transformation of American Punishment* (Stanford, CA: Stanford University Press, 2010); Robert Perkinson, *Texas Tough: The Rise of America's Prison Empire* (New York: Metropolitan Books, 2010); Schoenfeld, "The Politics of Prison Growth."

6. In 2014, the American Bar Association adopted a resolution urging states to expand coverage of the notice-and-comment rule-making provisions of their administrative procedures acts to include correctional facilities. American Bar Association, Resolution 103B, adopted February 10, 2014, http://www.google.com/#q=americna+bar+assoicaiotn+resolution+103+B (retrieved March 1, 2014).

7. Gilmore, *Golden Gulag*, 96.

8. Alex Anderson, "Hiding Out in Prison Bonds," *Forbes*, October 22, 2008, http://www.forbes.com/2008/10/22/prison-correctional-bonds-pf-ii-in_aa_1022fixedincome_inl.html (retrieved October 25, 2012).

9. Anderson, "Hiding Out in Prison Bonds."

10. Brown and Wood LLP, "Alternatives for Financing Prison Facilities: Report for the Association of Correctional Administrators," 1999, http://www.asca.net/system/assets/attachments/2085/Alternatives_for_Financing_Prison_Facilities-3.pdf?1296161869 (retrieved August 6, 2012).

11. For example, the Florida Supreme Court ruled in 1990 that since lawmakers can decide to cancel the bond payments, LRBs are not "real debt." Katie Hayden, "A Billion Dollars and Growing: Why Prison Bonding Is Tougher on Florida's Taxpayers Than on Crime" (Miami and Tallahassee: Collins Center for Public Policy and Florida TaxWatch, April 2011).

12. Grits for Breakfast, "Are Counties on the Hook for Debt Issued by 'Nonprofits' They Create to Oversee Jail Bonds?," July 11, 2012, http://gritsforbreakfast.blogspot.com/2012/07/are-counties-on-hook-for-debt-issued-by.html (retrieved July 19, 2012).

13. Kevin Pranis, "Doing Borrowed Time: The High Cost of Backdoor Prison Finance," in Tara Herivel and Paul Wright, eds., *Prison Profiteers: Who Makes Money from Mass Incarceration* (New York: New Press, 2007), 37.

14. Pranis, "Doing Borrowed Time," 38.

15. In the aggregate, growth in correctional spending "primarily siphoned off funds from welfare expenditures" targeted at the poor and likely did not substantially crowd out state spending on health care and education. The story in any single state may be different. Joshua Guetzkow and Bruce Western, "The Political Consequences of Mass Imprisonment," in Joe Soss, Jacob S. Hacker, and Suzanne Mettler, eds., *Remaking America: Democracy and Public Policy in an Age of Inequality* (New York: Russell Sage Foundation, 2007), 238.

16. Hayden, "A Billion Dollars and Growing," 2, 9.

17. Hayden, "A Billion Dollars and Growing," 14.

18. Pranis, "Doing Borrowed Time."

19. Julie Turner, Texas Patriots PAC, "What Should Happen to Joe Corely Jail?," April 7, 2013, http://www.texaspatriotspac.com/articles/what-should-happen-joe-corley-jail (retrieved May 21, 2013).

20. Grits for Breakfast, "Just Don't Call It a 'Jail,'" October 21, 2013, http://gritsforbreakfast.blogspot.com/2013/10/just-dont-call-it-jail.html (retrieved January 21, 2014); Ronnie Crocker, "Texas Voters Have Their Say at the Polls," *Houston Chronicle*, November 5, 2013, http://www.chron.com/news/politics/article/Texas-voters-have-their-say-at-the-polls-4958304.php (retrieved January 22, 2014).

21. On the economic development pitch of Florida's Department of Corrections to rural areas, see Schoenfeld, "The Politics of Prison Growth," 224–25.

22. Gilmore, *Golden Gulag*, 104–5.

23. Gilmore, *Golden Gulag*; Ryan S. King, Marc Mauer, and Tracy Huling, "Big Prisons, Small Towns: Prison Economics in Rural America (Washington, DC: The Sentencing Project, February 2003); Gregory Hooks, Clayton Mosher, Shaun Genter et al., "Revisiting the Impact of Prison Building on Job Growth, Education, Incarceration, and County-Level Employment, 1976–2004," *Social Science Quarterly* 91.1 (2010): 228–44; Terry L. Besser and Margaret M. Hanson, "Development of Last Resort: The Impact of New State Prisons on Small Town Economies in the United States," *Journal of the Community Development Society* 35.2 (2004): 1–16; Amy K. Glasmeier and Tracey Farrigan, "The Economic Impacts of the Prison Development Boom on Persistently Poor Rural Places," *International Regional Science Review* 30.3 (2007): 274–99.

24. Gilmore, *Golden Gulag*, 149; Clayton Mosher, Gregory Hooks, and Peter B. Wood, "Don't Build It Here: The Hype Versus the Reality of Prisons and Local Employment," in Herivel and Wrights, eds., *Prison Profiteers*, 90–97.

25. For example, the feasibility study for a proposed jail in the small city of Hardin, Montana, based its financial assumptions largely on the money to be made by importing

prisoners from other states. The study failed to mention that this practice is potentially illegal under Montana law. The Hardin jail was built and remained empty, forcing the city to default on the bonds. Justin Elliott, "Behind Montana Jail Fiasco: How Private Prison Developers Prey on Desperate Towns," *Prison Legal News*, December 2009, 8–9.

26. Hayden, "A Billion Dollars and Growing."

27. Grits for Breakfast, "IRS Auditing Entrepreneurial Texas Jails That Improperly Used Tax-Exempt Bonds," October 17, 2013, http://gritsforbreakfast.blogspot.com/2013/10/irs-auditing-entrepreneurial-texas.html (retrieved January 21, 2014).

28. Mitch Mitchell, "Texas Prison Boom Going Bust," *Star-Telegram*, September 3, 2011, http://www.star-telegram.com/2011/09/03/3335901/texas-prison-boom-going-bust.html (retrieved July 29, 2012); John Burnett, "Private Prison Promises Leave Texas Towns in Trouble," NPR, March 28, 2011, http://www.npr.org/2011/03/28/134855801/private-prison-promises-leave-texas-towns-in-trouble (retrieved October 24, 2012).

29. In 2013, state senator John Whitmire (D-Houston) warned local officials that if the state took ownership of the local lockup, it might fill the new state prison with sex offenders. Mike Ward, "Legislative Fight Over Buying Empty West Texas Lockup Focuses on Bondholders," *Austin American-Statesman*, May 1, 2013, http://www.statesman.com/news/news/legislative-fight-over-buying-empty-west-texas-loc/nXdmZ/ (retrieved May 20, 2013).

30. Mary Williams Walsh and Michael Cooper, "Faltering City Testing Its Vow to Pensioners," *New York Times*, August 13, 2011, A1; "Public Pensions in Bankruptcy Court," editorial, *New York Times*, April 14, 2013, SR10.

31. Lynch, *Sunbelt Justice*, 25.

32. Lynch, *Sunbelt Justice*, 171.

33. Lynch, *Sunbelt Justice*, 172.

34. Lynch, *Sunbelt Justice*, 113, 149.

35. Leading state officials in Arizona were so committed to punitive segregation that the governor and director of corrections even supported turning down a private grant awarded to the state to develop alternatives to incarceration. Lynch, *Sunbelt Justice*, 165.

36. J. Ricketts, "Arizona Department of Corrections: Adult Institutional and Community Inmate Work Programs" (Phoenix: Arizona Department of Corrections, n.d.), 4, quoted in Lynch, *Sunbelt Justice*, 119.

37. Lynch, *Sunbelt Justice*, 213. Emphasis in the original.

38. Joe Arpaio, sheriff of Maricopa County since 1993, boasted how he spent only 20 cents a day feeding inmates in his jails, thanks in part to his infamous "green bologna." Lynch, *Sunbelt Justice*, 164.

39. Lynch, *Sunbelt Justice*, 142.

40. Lynch, *Sunbelt Justice*, 129.

41. Lynch, *Sunbelt Justice*, 172.

42. In defending the state's relatively measly expenditures on prison programming, one director of corrections in Arizona noted that Minnesota spent twice as much per inmate yet had a recidivism rate comparable to Arizona's rate. Lynch, *Sunbelt Justice*, 171–73.

43. Lynch, *Sunbelt Justice*, 128.

44. Lynch, *Sunbelt Justice*, 140.

45. Lynch, *Sunbelt Justice*, 169. A video produced by the Arizona DOC to teach its correctional officers how to use dogs to drag inmates out of their cells "evokes some of the infamous dog photos from Abu Ghraib." James Forman, Jr., "Exporting Harshness: How the War on Crime Helped Make the War on Terror Possible," *N.Y.U. Review of Law & Social*

Change 33 (2009), 350–51; Human Rights Watch, "Cruel and Degrading: The Use of Dogs for Cell Extractions in U.S. Prisons," 18.5 (2006), http://www.hrw.org/sites/default/files/reports/us1006webwcover.pdf (retrieved July 16, 2012).

46. Lynch *Sunbelt Justice*, 203; Perkinson, *Texas Tough*; Schoenfeld, "The Politics of Prison Growth."

47. Lynch, *Sunbelt Justice*, 186. *Lewis v. Casey* considerably narrowed the 1977 *Bounds v. Smith* decision, which had established prisoners' rights to adequate law libraries and other legal assistance.

48. Lynch, *Sunbelt Justice*, 197.

49. For more on the PLRA, see 43–44 and 273.

50. The account that follows of the politics that built the prisons in Texas is based largely on Michael Campbell, "Politics, Prisons, and Law Enforcement: An Examination of 'Law and Order' Politics in Texas," *Law & Society Review* 45.3 (2011): 177–99.

51. Campbell attributes the low level of civic involvement to several institutional factors, including Texas's frequent elections, its off-year gubernatorial contests, numerous constitutional amendments related to trivial aspects of government, and a deep-seated patriarchal political culture. See "Politics, Prisons, and Law Enforcement."

52. Perkinson, *Texas Tough*, 253.

53. Perkinson, *Texas Tough*.

54. See, for example, "Gramm Campaign Speech: National Rifle Association," May 20, 1995, C-Span Video Library, http://www.c-spanvideo.org/program/65284-1# 9 (retrieved July 21, 2012).

55. Ken Silverstein, "Tea Party in the Sonora: For the Future of GOP Governance, Look to Arizona," *Harper's*, July 2010, 36.

56. Gary Hunter, "Prison Labor Bails Out State and County Budgets," *Prison Legal News*, March 2010, 14–15; David M. Reutter, "Requests for Hawaiian Prisoner Workers Soar Due to Poor Economy," *Prison Legal News*, November 2011, 20; Rick Karlin, "CSEA Unhappy with Prison Call Center," Capitol Confidential, January 12, 2012, http://blog.timesunion.com/capitol/archives/105807/csea-unhappy-with-prison-call-center/ (retrieved July 27, 2012).

57. David M. Reutter, "Savings from North Carolina Prison Slave Labor Result in Additional Prison Beds," *Prison Legal News*, June 2011, 14.

58. A DOJ publication commemorating the 75th anniversary of the Federal Prison Industries program in 1996 presented "repatriating work currently performed outside the U.S." as a "potential growth opportunity" that would infuse the federal convict labor program "with new inmate jobs without undue impact on the American worker." J. W. Roberts, *Factories with Fences: The History of Federal Prison Industries* (Washington, DC: U.S. DOJ, Federal Prison Industries, 1996), 30. See also Nicholas Stein, "Former Reagan Attorney General Ed Meese Has a Way to Slow the Exodus of Jobs Overseas: Put Prisoners to Work," *Fortune*, September 15, 2003, http://money.cnn.com/magazines/fortune/fortune_archive/2003/09/15/349159/index.htm (retrieved August 3, 2011); Robert P. Weiss, "'Repatriating' Low-Wage Work: The Political Economy of Prison Labor Reprivatization in the Postindustrial United States," *Criminology* 39.2 (2001): 253–92.

59. National Institute of Justice study quoted in Heather Ann Thompson, "Why Mass Incarceration Matters: Rethinking Crisis, Decline, and Transformation in Postwar American History," *Journal of American History* 97.3 (2010), 723.

60. David M. Reutter, "Prison Slave Labor Replaces Freeworld Workers in Down Economy," *Prison Legal News*, May 2012, 1–7.

61. Ray Henry, "Ga. Gov.: Hire People on Probation for Farm Work," cncnews.com, June 14, 2011, http://cnsnews.com/news/article/ga-gov-hire-people-probation-farm-work (retrieved July 21, 2012); Laura Emiko Soltis, "Gov. Deal's Farm Labor Plan Recalls Convict Leasing," Creative Loafing Atlanta, June 29, 2011, http://clatl.com/atlanta/gov-deals-farm-labor-plan-recalls-convict-leasing/Content?oid=3402272 (retrieved July 27, 2012).

62. Calculated from James Stephan, "Census of State and Federal Correctional Facilities, 2005," Bureau of Justice Statistics, October 2008, 5; Pew Center on the States, "Prison Count 2010" (Washington, DC: Pew Charitable Trusts, March 2010); Todd D. Minton, "Jail Inmates at Midyear 2010—Statistical Tables," Bureau of Justice Statistics, April 2011, rev. June 28, 2011.

63. Stephan, "Census of State and Federal Correctional Facilities, 2005," 5–6.

64. Perkinson, *Texas Tough*, 235.

65. Rebecca M. McLennan, *The Crisis of Imprisonment: Protest, Politics, and the Making of the American Penal State, 1776–1941* (New York: Cambridge University Press, 2008), 45.

66. McLennan, *The Crisis of Imprisonment*, 85. Emphasis in the original.

67. Perkinson, *Texas Tough*, 73.

68. As one Alabama prison inspector said in a 1922 report, "Our jails are money-making machines." Quoted in Douglas A. Blackmon, *Slavery by Another Name: The Re-Enslavement of Black Americans from the Civil War to World War II* (New York: Anchor Books, 2009), 367.

69. Marie Gottschalk, *The Prison and the Gallows: The Politics of Mass Incarceration in America* (New York: Cambridge University Press, 2006), 47–52.

70. Blackmon, *Slavery by Another Name*, 289.

71. As late as the 1950s, Florida's penal system consisted of just one main state prison, one small prison farm, and dozens of self-sufficient road camps that were responsible for building and maintaining roads. These camps were direct descendants of county convict-leasing camps and had a reputation for extremely severe work and living conditions. Schoenfeld, "The Politics of Prison Growth," 82–83, 91.

72. McLennan, *The Crisis of Imprisonment*, 135.

73. McLennan, *The Crisis of Imprisonment*, 2.

74. McLennan, *The Crisis of Imprisonment*, 135.

75. McLennan, *The Crisis of Imprisonment*.

76. In 1905, President Theodore Roosevelt signed an executive order forbidding the use of convict labor on federal projects. James Austin and Garry Coventry, "Emerging Issues on Privatized Prisons" (Washington, DC: Bureau of Justice Assistance, National Council of Crime and Delinquency, February 2001), 11.

77. Thompson, "Why Mass Incarceration Matters," 718.

78. Thompson, "Why Mass Incarceration Matters," 718.

79. The 1929 Hawes-Cooper Act severely curbed interstate commerce of inmate-made products by granting the states authority to place almost any restriction on the trade of these goods. The 1935 Ashurst-Sumners Act required that all "prison-made" goods be labeled as such and made it a federal offense to ship inmate-produced goods to states that banned them. The 1936 Walsh-Healy Act prohibited most federal contractors from using goods produced by inmate labor. The Sumners-Ashurst Act of 1940 made it a federal crime to knowingly transport prison-made goods across state lines, regardless of prevailing laws about convict labor in those states. Asatar P. Bair, *Prison Labor in the United States: An Economic Analysis* (New York: Routledge, 2008), 115; Roberts, *Factories with Fences*, 13–14.

80. Roberts, *Factories with Fences*, 20; Harry Elmer Barnes, *Report on the Progress of*

the State Prison War Program Under the Government Division of the War Production Board (Washington, DC: War Production Board, 1944).

81. Ian Urbina, "The Prisoners of War," *AlterNet*, October 27, 2003, http://www .alternet.org/story/17042/the_prisoners_of_war (retrieved July 26, 2012).

82. UNICOR, "2011 Annual Financial Management Report," n.d., http://www.UNICOR .gov/information/publications/pdfs/corporate/CATAR2011_C.pdf (retrieved July 26, 2012); Washington Technology, "2011 Washington Technology Top 100," n.d., http://washington technology.com/toplists/top-100-lists/2011.aspx/ (retrieved July 26, 2012).

83. Urbina, "The Prisoners of War."

84. U.S. DOJ, Federal Prison Industries, Inc., "Management's Discussion and Analysis (Unaudited)," https://www.unicor.gov/information/publications/pdfs/corporate/FY2013.Q4 .FPI%20Annual%20Management%20Report%20Final%20121313_C.pdf (retrieved May 2, 2014).

85. Douglas MacDonald et al., "Private Prisons in the United States: An Assessment of Current Practice" (Cambridge, MA: Abt Associates, July 16, 1998), 62.

86. Bob Egelko, "Court Rejects Call for Fair Wages for Prisoners," *San Francisco Chronicle*, April 12, 2010, http://www.sfgate.com/bayarea/article/Court-rejects-call-for-fair -wages-for-prisoners-3192932.php (retrieved July 27, 2012). See also Raja Raghunath, "A Promise the Nation Cannot Keep: What Prevents the Application of the Thirteenth Amend-ment in Prison?," *William & Mary Bill of Rights Journal* 18.2 (2009): 1–43.

87. Naomi Spencer, "Georgia Prisoners Strike for Wages, Better Medical Care and Food," *Prison Legal News*, January 2011, 24–25.

88. A 1997 GAO investigation found that FPI-produced items tend to be more expen-sive, of lower quality, and slower to arrive than comparable goods produced in the private sector. Urbina, "The Prisoners of War."

89. Derek Gilna, "Business, Members of Congress Not Happy with UNICOR," *Prison Legal News*, March 2014, 52–53.

90. The current rate ranges from about 23 cents to $1.15 per hour. Diane Cardwell, "Private Businesses Fight Federal Prisons for Contracts," *New York Times*, March 15, 2012, B1.

91. As of 2011, UNICOR was operating 88 factories at 66 prison facilities, employing about 8 percent of all able-bodied federal inmates. This was down considerably from the peak of 23,000 inmates in 2007, or nearly 12 percent of the federal prison population. In 2000, one in four federal inmates was employed by FPI. Since at least 2013, FPI has sought to create more part-time rather than full-time positions so as to increase the total number of inmates employed. This complicates year-to-year comparisons of employment trends. U.S. DOJ, Federal Prison Industries, Inc., "Management's Discussion and Analysis"; UNICOR, "2011 Annual Financial Management Report," n.d., http://www.UNICOR.gov/about/reports /index.cfm (retrieved July 27, 2012); Federal Prison Industries, Inc., "Annual Report 2009," 13; Bryan Lowry and Phil Glover of the American Federation of Government Employees, Council of Prison Locals, prepared statement, U.S. House Committee on Appropriations, Subcommittee on Commerce, Justice and Science, March 10, 2009, 9.

92. For details about these restrictions, see 311, n. 79.

93. Barbara Auerbach, "The Prison Industry Enhancement Certification Program," National Correctional Industries Association, December 2011, http://www.nationalcia.org /piecp-2/pie-research (retrieved July 23, 2012), 23.

94. Bob Sloan, "The Prison Industries Enhancement Certification Program: Why Ev-eryone Should Be Concerned," *Prison Legal News*, March 2010, 1.

95. Sloan, "The Prison Industries Enhancement Certification Program."

96. Sloan, "The Prison Industries Enhancement Certification Program," 4–5.

97. Auerbach, "The Prison Industry Enhancement Certification Program," 23.

98. Sloan, "The Prison Industries Enhancement Certification Program"; Thompson, "Why Mass Incarceration Matters," 721–22.

99. Sloan, "The Prison Industries Enhancement Certification Program," 1.

100. Russell Nichols, "Working Prisoners Save Taxpayers' Money," *Governing*, May 2011, http://www.governing.com/topics/public-workforce/working-prisoners-saves-taxpayers-money.html (retrieved May 23, 2011).

101. Joel Rogers and Laura Dresser, "Business Domination Inc.," *Nation*, August 1–8, 2011, 19. In Bill Moyers's 2012 documentary "United States of ALEC," former Wisconsin governor Tommy Thompson confessed to ALEC members: "I always loved going to those meetings because I always found new ideas. Then I'd take them back to Wisconsin, disguise them a little bit and declare, 'That's mine.'" John Nichols, "Noted," *Nation*, October 22, 2012, 5.

102. Beau Hodai, "Corporate Con Game: How the Private Prison Industry Helped Shape Arizona's Anti-Immigrant Law," *In These Times*, July 2010, 17.

103. Mike McIntire, "Conservative Nonprofit Acts as a Stealth Business Lobbyist," *New York Times*, April 22, 2012, A1.

104. Paul Ashton and Amanda Petteruti, "Gaming the System: How the Political Strategies of Private Prison Companies Promote Ineffective Incarceration Policies" (Washington, DC: Justice Policy Institute, June 2011), 29.

105. "Task Force Linked to Harsh Sentencing Laws and Private Prison Firms Disbands Following Public Scrutiny, Boycott," *Prison Legal News*, January 2014, 22–23.

106. For example, its model Prison Industries Act included a provision that would allow money that was deducted from inmate wages to offset the costs of incarceration to be diverted to expanding prison industries. The model bill also sought to exploit a "critical PIE loophole that seemed to suggest that its rules did not apply to prisoner-made goods that were not shipped across state lines." Mike Elk and Bob Sloan, "The Hidden History of ALEC and Prison Labor," *Nation*, August 1, 2011, http://www.thenation.com/article/162478/hidden-history-alec-and-prison-labor (retrieved August 5, 2011).

107. Allen's lobbying activities on behalf of NICA forced his resignation from the Texas legislature in 2006. After resigning, he immediately became a lobbyist with The GEO Group, the country's second-largest prison conglomerate. Elk and Sloan, "The Hidden History of ALEC."

Bob Sloan, "Slave Labor, ALEC and the Federal Industry Program," Daily Kos, June 10, 2011, http://www.dailykos.com/story/2011/06/10/983992/-Slave-Labor-ALEC-and-the-federal-Prison-Industry-Program-Breaking-News (retrieved June 10, 2011); Lisa Sandberg, "Labor Leaders Fume Over Texas Prison Plan," *Houston Chronicle*, September 14, 2006, http://www.chron.com/news/houston-texas/article/Labor-leaders-fume-over-Texas-prison-labor-plan-1519077.php (retrieved July 29, 2012).

108. Curtis R. Blakely, *America's Prisons: The Movement Toward Profit and Privatization* (Boca Raton, FL: Brown Walker Press, 2005), 14.

109. Mike Ward, "Prison Industry Programs a Victim of Economic Recession," *Austin American-Statesman*, September 4, 2011, http://www.statesman.com/news/texas-politics/prison-industry-programs-a-victim-of-economic-recession-1820020.html?viewAsSingle Page=true (retrieved July 30, 2012).

110. "Pennsylvania Hopes to Allow Businesses to Employ Inmates," *Corrections Reporter*,

May 26, 2010, http://www.correctionsreporter.com/2010/05/26/pa-hopes-to-allow-businesses
-to-employ-inmates/?utm_source=feedburner&utm_medium=email&utm_campaign=Feed
%3A+correctionsreporter+%28The+Corrections+Reporter%29 (retrieved May 26, 2010);
Tom Beyerlein, "Proposed Bill Would Allow Inmates to Manufacture Goods for Market,"
Middletown Journal, August 22, 2011, http://www.middletownjournal.com/news/news/local
/proposed-bill-would-allow-inmates-to-manufacture-1/nMtYD/ (retrieved July 30, 2012).

111. The UNICOR recycling case was referred to the DOJ's environmental crimes
unit and to the U.S. Attorneys in Ohio and New Jersey for possible criminal prosecution.
After lengthy investigations, no action was taken due to "evidentiary, legal, and strategic
concerns," according to a report from the department's inspector general. Myron Levin,
"Bureau of Prisons Unit Guilty of Pervasive Safety Violations, U.S. Investigation Finds,"
FairWarning Reports, October 21, 2010, http://www.fairwarning.org/2010/10/bureau-of
-prisons-unit-guilty-of-pervasive-safety-violations-u-s-investigation-finds/ (retrieved July 27,
2012); "Report Finds Federal Prisoners Exposed to Toxic Metals in Recycling Jobs," *Prison
Legal News*, October 2011, 44; Anne-Marie Cusac, "Toxic Prison Labor," *Progressive*, March
2009, 26–31.

112. In an affidavit filed in a lawsuit against UNICOR by staff members and former prisoners, the factory manager of the first recycling program of the Bureau of Prisons charged
that the program was established in the mid-1990s "'on the fly' without any research into
potential hazards, health or safety matters, training or discussions of hazardous waste handling." Cusac, "Toxic Prison Labor," 29.

113. As one warden of a work-release center in Louisiana explained: "If they say no to a
job, they get that time that was taken off their sentence put right back on, and get sent right
back to the lockup they came out of." Abe Louise Young, "BP Hires Labor to Clean Up Spill
While Coastal Residents Struggle," *Nation*, July 21, 2010.

114. Sadhbh Walshe, "How US Prison Labour Pads Corporate Profits at Taxpayers'
Expense," *Guardian*, July 6, 2010, http://www.guardian.co.uk/commentisfree/2012/jul/06
/prison-labor-pads-corporate-profits-taxpayers-expense (retrieved July 30, 2012).

115. This account of inmate labor and the BP Deepwater Horizon cleanup is based on
Young, "BP Hires Labor to Clean Up Spill."

116. Joel Bleifuss, "GOP Land Grab," *In These Times*, September 2012, 5.

117. Mary Sigler, "Private Prisons, Public Functions, and the Meaning of Punishment,"
Florida State University Law Review 35.1 (2010), 27.

118. Sharon Dolovich, "State Punishment and Private Prisons," *Duke Law Journal* 55.3
(2005): 437–546.

119. For more on these coalitions and activities, see Grassroots Leadership at http://
grassrootsleadership.org/ (retrieved June 17, 2013); and the Private Corrections Working
Group at http://www.privateci.org/who.html (retrieved June 17, 2013).

120. Sigler, "Private Prisons, Public Functions," 29

121. Ashton and Petteruti, "Gaming the System."

122. Casey Newton, Ginger Rough, and J. J. Hensley, "Arizona Inmate Escape Puts Spotlight on State Private Prisons," *Arizona Republic*, August 22, 2010, http://www.azcentral
.com/news/articles/2010/08/22/20100822arizona-private-prisons.html (retrieved October 26,
2012).

123. Kasich had appointed Gary C. Mohr, a former managing director of CCA, as the
new head of the Ohio Department of Rehabilitation and Corrections. ACLU of Ohio, "Prisons for Profit: A Look at Prison Privatization" (Cleveland: ACLU of Ohio, April 2011), 4.

124. Sasha Abramsky, "No Escape From Debt by Selling Jails," *Guardian*, November 23, 2009, http://www.guardian.co.uk/commentisfree/cifamerica/2009/nov/21/arizona-prisons (retrieved August 2, 2010); David M. Reutter, "Florida Provides Lesson in How Not to Privatize," *Prison Legal News*, February 2012, 1, 3–8; Cell-Out Arizona, "Arizona's Budget Giveaway to the Private Prison Industry," TucsonCitizenAz.com, May 3, 2012, http://tucsoncitizen.com/cell-out-arizona/2012/05/03/arizonas-budget-giveaway-to-the-private-prison-industry/ (retrieved August 2, 2012); Charles Maldonado, "Privatizing Louisiana Prisons," Gambit, May 8, 2012, http://www.bestofneworleans.com/gambit/privatizing-louisiana-prisons/Content?oid=2001212 (retrieved August 2, 2012); Mike Ward, "Lawmakers Chafe as Push Continues to Privatize Prison Health Care," *Austin American-Statesman*, April 30, 2011, http://www.statesman.com/news/statesman-investigates/lawmakers-chafe-as-push-continues-to-privatize-prison-1445569.html (retrieved August 2, 2012); German Lopez, "Liberty for Sale: Should Ohio Prisoners Be Commodities in a For-Profit Venture?," *Prison Legal News*, November 2012, 16–19.

125. Douglas McDonald et al., "Private Prisons in the United States: An Assessment of Current Practice" (Cambridge, MA: Abt Associates, Inc., July 16, 1998), 5.

126. Beau Hodai, "America Eats Its Young: Arizona Communities Embrace Use of Private Prison Employees in Drug Raids at Public Schools," *Prison Legal News*, December 2012, 32–34.

127. McDonald et al., "Private Prisons in the United States," 4.

128. McDonald et al., "Private Prisons in the United States," 5.

129. Michael A. Hallett, *Private Prisons in America: A Critical Race Perspective* (Urbana and Chicago: University of Illinois Press, 2006), 56, 93.

130. If jails are excluded, the figure is 4.2 percent for all state and federal prisoners. McDonald et al., "Private Prisons in the United States," 7; Richard Harding, "Private Prisons," in Michael Tonry, ed., *Crime and Justice: A Review of Research*, v. 28 (Chicago: University of Chicago Press, 2001), 268.

131. Tom Barry, "A Death in Texas: Profits, Poverty, and Immigration Converge," *Boston Review*, November/December 2009, http://new.bostonreview.net/BR34.6/barry.php (retrieved May 20, 2014); Margaret Talbot, "The Lost Children: What Do Tougher Detention Policies Mean for Illegal Immigrant Families?," *New Yorker*, March 3, 2008, 66–67.

132. This paragraph is based largely on Jeff Gerth and Stephen Labaton, "Prisons for Profit: Jail Business Shows Its Weakness," *New York Times*, November 25, 2005, B18.

133. McDonald et al., "Private Prisons in the United States."

134. One of the most notable connections between the prison industry and the Clinton administration was Thurgood Marshall, Jr., the son of the Supreme Court Justice who was a leading crusader for the civil rights movement. He held a number of high-level positions in the Clinton administration. In 2002, he joined CCA's board of directors. "About CCA," http://www.cca.com/about/management-team/board-directors/ (retrieved August 4, 2012). From 1996 to 1999, Joseph Johnson, former executive director of Jesse Jackson's Rainbow Coalition, served on CCA's board. Texas Prison Bid'ness, "Superdelegate Has Ties to CCA," March 20, 2008, http://www.texasprisonbidness.org/lobbying-and-influence/super-delegate-has-ties-cca (retrieved September 27, 2013).

135. Two-thirds of CCA's $1 million total in state-level political giving between 2003 and 2010 went to just three states—California, Florida, and Georgia. The GEO Group exhibited a similar pattern, with two-thirds of its political donations flowing to California, New Mexico, and Florida. Lobbying efforts are similarly concentrated. Ashton and Petteruti,

"Gaming the System," 16, 25. See also Beau Hodai, "Legacy of Corruption: GEO Buys Off the Florida Political Establishment," *Prison Legal News*, March 2011, 1, 3–12.

136. Paul Guerino, Paige M. Harrison, and William J. Sabol, "Prisoners in 2010," *Bureau of Justice Statistics Bulletin*, December 2011, rev. February 9, 2012, 31, appendix table 20.

137. Christopher Petrella and Josh Begley, "The Color of Corporate Corrections: Overrepresentation of People of Color in the Private Prison Industry," *Prison Legal News*, March 2013, 16–17.

138. Guerino, Harrison, and Sabol, "Prisoners in 2010," 31, appendix table 20.

139. Laura Wides-Munoz and Garance Burke, "Immigrants Prove Big Business for Prison Companies," *Star Tribune*, August 2, 2012, http://www.startribune.com/printarticle /?id=164707756 (retrieved August 3, 2012).

140. Kirchhoff, "Economic Impacts of Prison Growth," 22.

141. Calculated from James Stephan, "Census of State and Federal Correctional Facilities, 2005," Bureau of Justice Statistics, October 2008, 9, appendix table 1.

142. Kirchhoff, "Economic Impacts of Prison Growth,"15.

143. Pershing Square Capital Management, "Prisons' Dilemma," October 20, 2009, http://thinkprogress.org/wp-content/uploads/2010/09/Bill-AckmanPresentation.pdf (retrieved August 4, 2012), 37.

144. Calculated from Pershing Square Capital Management, "Prisons' Dilemma," 6.

145. Pershing Square Capital Management, "Prisons' Dilemma," 2.

146. James E. Hyman, letter to shareholders, Cornell Companies, "2008 Annual Report," http://www.annualreports.com/HostedData/AnnualReports/PDFArchive/crn2008.pdf (retrieved August 6, 2012).

147. "Corrections Corporation of America's CEO Discusses Q2 2011 Results—Earnings Call Transcript," seekingalpha.com, August 4, 2011, http://seekingalpha.com/article/284806 -corrections-corporation-of-america-s-ceo-discusses-q2–2011-results-earnings-call-transcript (retrieved August 6, 2011).

148. Quoted in Terry Carter, "Prison Break: Budget Crises Drive Reform, But Private Jails Press On," *ABA Journal*, October 2012, http://www.abajournal.com/magazine/article /prison_break_budget_crises_drive_reform_but_private_jails_press_on/ (retrieved June 17, 2013).

149. Carter, "Prison Break."

150. Carl Takei, "Private Prison Company Doctors Its Own Wikipedia Page and Fabricates Facts to Fight Bad Publicity," *Huffington Post*, March 4, 2013, http://www.huffington post.com/carl-takei/private-prison-company-do_b_2807202.html (retrieved June 17, 2013).

151. James E. Hyman, letter to shareholders, Cornell Companies, "2009 Annual Report," http://idc.api.edgar-online.com/efx_dll/edgarpro.dll?FetchFilingConvPDF1?SessionID =4MgBHbWFlQkdwfS&ID=7216316 (retrieved August 6, 2012); George C. Zoley, letter to shareholders, The GEO Group, "2010 Annual Report," https://materials.proxyvote.com /Approved/36159R/20110303/AR_84939/HTML2/geo_group-ar2010_0004.htm (retrieved May 20, 2014), 2; George C. Zoley, letter to shareholders, The GEO Group, "2009 Annual Report," https://materials.proxyvote.com/Approved/36159R/20100303/AR_56789/HTML2 /default.htm (retrieved August 6, 2012), 1.

152. The GEO Group, "2010 Annual Report," 24.

153. Chris Kirkham, "Private Prison Corporation Offers Cash in Exchange for State Prisons," *Huffington Post*, February 14, 2012, http://www.huffingtonpost.com/2012/02/14 /private-prisons-buying-state-prisons_n_1272143.html?view=print&comm_ref=false (retrieved August 6, 2012).

154. Terry Frieden, "Retiring Head of Federal Bureau of Prisons Apologizes for DUI Arrest," CNN Politics, March 30, 2011, http://www.cnn.com/2011/POLITICS/03/30/prisons.director.dui.apology/ (retrieved February 28, 2014).

155. Zoley, letter to shareholders, The GEO Group, "2010 Annual Report," 2; The GEO Group, "Annual Report, Fiscal 2011," http://www.sec.gov/Archives/edgar/data/923796/0000 95012311020922/g25405e10vk.htm3 (retrieved October 10, 2013), 3.

156. Ashton and Petteruti, "Gaming the System," 16.

157. Corrections Corporation of America, wikinvest, n.d., http://www.wikinvest.com/stock/Corrections_Corporation_of_America_(CXW) (retrieved May 2, 2014); and The GEO Group, wikinvest, n.d., http://www.wikinvest.com/stock/Geo_Group_(GEO) (retrieved May 2, 2014).

158. Nathaniel Popper, "Restyled as Real Estate Trusts, Varied Businesses Avoid Taxes," New York Times, April 22, 2013, A1.

159. For more on the methodological problems involved in comparing private and public facilities, see McDonald et al., "Private Prisons in the United States," iv; Austin and Coventry, "Emerging Issues in Privatized Prisons," ch. 3; Dina Perrone and Travis C. Pratt, "Comparing the Quality of Confinement and Cost-Effectiveness of Public Versus Private Prisons," Prison Journal 83.3 (2003): 301–22.

160. For a good summary and analysis of these studies, see Kirchhoff, "Economic Impacts of Prison Growth," 23–24; and Ashton and Petteruti, "Gaming the System," 32–33. See also Brad W. Lundahl et al., "Prison Privatization: A Meta-analysis of Cost and Quality of Confinement Indicators," Research on Social Work Practice 19.4 (2009): 383–94.

161. Austin and Coventry, "Emerging Issues on Privatized Prisons," iii.

162. U.S. GAO, "Cost of Prisons: Bureau of Prisons Needs Better Data to Assess Alternatives for Acquiring Low and Minimum Security Facilities," Report GAO-08-6 (Washington, DC: GAO, October 2007); Kirchhoff, "Economic Impacts of Prison Growth," 23.

163. Ashton and Petteruti, "Gaming the System," 32–33.

164. Austin and Coventry, "Emerging Issues on Privatized Prisons," 52. See also Curtis R. Blakely and Vic W. Bumphus, "Private and Public Sector Prisons: A Comparison of Selected Characteristics," Federal Probation 68.1 (2004): 27–31.

165. In 2010, the median wage for federal correctional officers was $54,000; state correctional officers earned $39,000; and employees at private prisons earned $30,000. U.S. Department of Labor, Bureau of Labor Statistics, "Occupational Outlook Handbook: Correctional Officers," April 26, 2012, http://www.bls.gov/ooh/protective-service/correctional-officers.htm#tab-5 (retrieved August 5, 2012).

166. A 1992 study by the New Mexico DOC found that female inmates held at a CCA facility lost "good time" at a rate nearly eight times higher than male prisoners housed at a state facility. Eric Bates, "Private Prisons," Nation, January 5, 1998, 11.

167. In the Public Interest, "Criminal: How Lockup Quotas and 'Low-Crime Taxes' Guarantee Profits for Private Prison Corporations," September 2013, http://www.inthepublicinterest.org/sites/default/files/Criminal-Lockup%20Quota-Report.pdf (retrieved February 8, 2014), 2–3.

168. Robert Pollin and Jeff Thompson, "State and Municipal Alternatives to Austerity," New Labor Forum 20.3 (2011), 24; John Schmitt, "The Wage Penalty for State and Local Government Employees" (Washington, DC: Center for Economic and Policy Research, May 2010).

169. Heather Ann Thompson, "Downsizing the Carceral State: The Policy Implications of Prison Guard Unions," Criminology & Public Policy 10.3 (2011), 773.

170. Page, *The Toughest Beat*.

171. James Ridgeway and Jean Casella, "Solidarity and Solitary: When Unions Clash with Prison Reform," *Prison Legal News*, June 2013, 12–14.

172. Austin and Coventry, "Emerging Issues in Privatized Prisons," 17.

173. One notable exception is that the U.S. Supreme Court has recognized that private prisons and their employees are not as protected from lawsuits. Employees of private facilities generally are not protected by the qualified immunity that shields public employees. Alfred C. Aman, Jr., "Privatisation, Prisons, Democracy, and Human Rights: The Need to Extend the Province of Administrative Law," *Indiana Journal of Global Legal Studies* 12.2 (2005), 535.

174. McDonald et al., "Private Prisons in the United States," 49; and Dolovich, "State Punishment and Private Prisons."

175. Enacted in 1946, the APA established basic standards regarding transparency, judicial review, public participation, and rule making that govern federal agencies and other federal entities. Aman, Jr., "Privatisation, Prisons, Democracy, and Human Rights," 513–14.

176. Texas Prison Bid'ness, "Hill Briefing on Private Prison Information Act," February 1, 2010, http://www.texasprisonbidness.org/lobbying-and-influence/hill-briefing-private-prison-information-ac (retrieved August 10, 2012).

177. Maurice Chammah, "Lawsuit Targets Prison Company Over Records Request," *Texas Tribune*, May 1, 2013, http://www.texastribune.org/2013/05/01/private-prison-company-sued-rights-group/ (retrieved June 17, 2013).

178. Mel Motel, "Reintroducing the Private Prison Information Act: An Interview," *Prison Legal News*, February 2013, 14–15.

179. Aman, Jr., "Privatisation, Prisons, Democracy, and Human Rights," 540; Harding, "Private Prisons," 341.

180. Aman, Jr., "Privatisation, Prisons, Democracy, and Human Rights," 537–38.

181. Quoted in Reutter, "Florida Provides Lesson in How Not to Privatize," 5.

182. Scott Hiaasen, "Effort to Privatize Florida Prisons Raises Questions of Cost," *Miami Herald*, April 23, 2011, http://www.miamiherald.com/2011/04/23/v-print/2181158/effort-to-privatize-florida-prisons.html (retrieved April 23, 2011). For several years, a law banning correctional officers from engaging in "sexual misconduct" with prisoners—behavior that does not rise to the level of rape—applied only to Florida DOC personnel, not to correctional officers at private prisons. The DOC's inspector general uncovered multiple cases of sexual misconduct at private facilities, but the guards could not be prosecuted because of this loophole, which legislators finally closed in 2010.

183. This account of the recent push for privatization in Florida is based largely on Reutter, "Florida Provides Lesson in How Not to Privatize."

184. Report by the National Institute on Money in State Politics cited in Kathleen Haughney, "Florida Politics," *SunSentinel.com*, January 30, 2012, http://weblogs.sun-sentinel.com/news/politics/dcblog/2012/01/campaign_finance_group_highlig.html (retrieved August 10, 2012).

185. Dara Kam, "Florida Prison Privatization Stalls Despite Big Spending," *Palm Beach Post*, February 5, 2012, http://www.palmbeachpost.com/news/news/state-regional/florida-prison-privatization-push-stalls-despite-b/nL3rF/ (retrieved August 10, 2012).

186. Michael Hallett, quoted in Bill Cotterell, "Prison Privatization Under Fire: Plan Faces Challenge from All Sides," *Tallahassee Democrat*, October 2, 2011, http://www.privateci.org/private_pics/ArduinFla.htm (retrieved August 10, 2012).

187. The only exception was one recent report in which the Arizona DOC had changed the way it computed expenses. The AFSC faulted this report because its methodology was flawed. Bob Ortega, "Group: Facilities Hard to Oversee, Aren't Cost-effective," *Arizona Republic*, February 15, 2012, http://www.azcentral.com/news/articles/2012/02/15/20120215 arizona-private-prisons-slammed-by-report.html (retrieved August 10, 2012).

188. Arizona Auditor General, Performance Audit Division, "Department of Corrections—Prison Population Growth: A Report to the Arizona Legislature," September 2010, http://www.azauditor.gov/Reports/State_Agencies/Agencies/Corrections_Department_of /Performance/10–08/10–08.pdf (retrieved February 8, 2014), 19–20.

189. Performance Audit Division, "Department of Corrections—Prison Population Growth," 23–25, 37–46.

190. Carter, "Prison Break."

191. Bob Ortega, "Arizona Prison Oversight Lacking for Private Facilities," *Arizona Republic*, August 7, 2011, http://www.azcentral.com/news/articles/2011/08/07/20110807arizona -prison-private-oversight.html (retrieved August 10, 2012).

192. Joe Watson, "Arizona Prison System Plagued by Politics, Privatization and Prisoner Deaths," *Prison Legal News*, July 2013, 7.

193. Cecilia Chan, "Arizona Prison Health Lawsuit Gets Class-Action Status," *Arizona Republic*, March 6, 2013, http://www.azcentral.com/news/state/articles/20130306arizona -prisoner-lawsuit-class-action-status-abrk.html (retrieved May 18, 2014).

194. This discussion of social impact bonds is based on David W. Chen, "Goldman to Invest in City Prison Program, Reaping Profit if Recidivism Drops," *New York Times*, August 2, 2012, A14; NPR, "Goldman Sachs Hopes to Profit by Helping Troubled Teens," npr.com, March 24, 2013, http://www.npr.org/2013/03/24/175197680/goldman-sachs-hopes -to-profit-by-helping-troubled-teens (retrieved July 16, 2013); Sophie Quinton, "How Goldman Sachs Can Help Save the Safety Net," *National Journal*, May 30, 2013, http://www .nationaljournal.com/magazine/how-goldman-sachs-can-help-save-the-safety-net-2013 0509 (retrieved July 16, 2013).

195. President Obama requested $485 million for social impact bonds in his 2012 budget. Massachusetts authorized $50 million to finance two social impact bonds, and other states were exploring how to put together "pay-for-success" bond packages. Estimates of the potential size of the social impact bond market by 2020 range from $400 billion to $1 trillion. Quinton, "How Goldman Sachs Can Help Save the Safety Net."

196. "Bank of America Raises $13.5M for NY Ex-Inmate Social-Impact Bond Project," *Crime Report*, January 14, 2014, http://www.thecrimereport.org/news/crime-and-justice -news/2014–01-pay-for-success-new-project (retrieved January 22, 2014).

197. See the 2007 appearance before ALEC of Jerry Watson, ABC's general counsel and head of ALEC's Private Enterprise Board from 2006 to 2008. "Jerry Watson Speaks at the Annual Meeting of the American Legislative Exchange Council, Philadelphia, PA, July 25–27, 2007," YouTube, http://www.youtube.com/watch?v=O8nUeJmdf0g (retrieved October 24, 2012).

198. Spike Bradford, "For Better or for Profit: How the Bail Bonding Industry Stands in the Way of Fair and Effective Pre-trial Justice," executive summary (Washington, DC: Justice Policy Institute, September 2012).

199. American Bail Coalition, newsletter, October 2010, http://pretrial.org/Perspectives /ABC%20October%202010%20Newsletter.pdf (retrieved October 24, 2012), 3; "Jerry Watson Speaks at the Annual Meeting of the American Legislative Exchange Council."

200. ALEC, "Conditional Early Release Bond Act," January 2009, http://www.alec.org/wp-content/uploads/Conditional-Early-Release-Bond-Act.pdf (retrieved October 24, 2012).

201. Blackmon, *Slavery by Another Name*.

202. Morgan O. Reynolds, "Privatizing Probation and Parole," executive summary (Dallas: National Center for Policy Analysis, June 2000), 1–2.

203. See, for example, Melissa Neal, "Bail Fail: Why the U.S. Should End the Practice of Using Money for Bail" (Washington, DC: Justice Policy Institute, September 2012); and Jean Chung, "Bailing on Baltimore: Voices from the Front Lines of the Justice System" (Washington, DC: Justice Policy Institute, September 2012).

204. Tracy Velázquez, Melissa Neal, and Spike Bradford, "Bailing on Justice: The Dysfunctional System of Using Money to Buy Pretrial Freedom," *Prison Legal News*, November 2012, 1–13.

205. The use of financial release, primarily through commercial bonds, increased by about one-third between 1992 and 2006. In 1992, release on recognizance was the most common type of pretrial release. By 2006, about 70 percent of people charged with a felony were assigned bail money. During that time, average bail amounts increased by more than $30,000. Neal, "Bail Fail," 10.

206. David M. Reutter, "Bail Bond Companies Profit While Poorest Defendants Remain in Jail," *Prison Legal News*, September 2012, 36.

207. Instead, many jurisdictions "rely on their own sense as to when counsel should be appointed, if at all." Phyllis E. Mann, "Ethical Obligations of Indigent Defense Attorneys to Their Clients," *Missouri Law Review* 75 (October 2010), 732.

208. Laura Sullivan, "Bail Burden Keeps U.S. Jails Stuffed with Inmates," NPR, January 21, 2010, http://www.npr.org/2010/01/21/122725771/Bail-Burden-Keeps-U-S-Jails-Stuffed-With-Inmates (retrieved October 24, 2012).

209. Laura Sullivan, "Bondsman Lobby Targets Pretrial Release Program," NPR, January 22, 2010, http://www.npr.org/templates/story/story.php?storyId=122725849 (retrieved October 24, 2012).

210. David M. Reutter, "Georgia's Privatized Probation System Traps the Poor," *Prison Legal News*, June 2012, 22. See also Human Rights Watch, "Profiting from Probation: America's 'Offender-Funded' Probation Industry," February 2014, http://www.hrw.org/sites/default/files/reports/us0214_ForUpload_0.pdf (retrieved March 1, 2014).

211. Ethan Bronner, "Poor Land in Jail as Companies Add Huge Fees for Probation," *New York Times*, July 3, 2012, A1.

212. Sarah Geraghty and Melanie Velez, "Bringing Transparency and Accountability to Criminal Justice Institutions in the South," *Stanford Law & Policy Review* 22.2 (2011), 476.

213. Bernard E. Harcourt, *The Illusion of Free Markets: Punishment and the Myth of Natural Order* (Cambridge, MA: Harvard University Press, 2011).

Chapter Four
What Second Chance?

1. "Sheri Dwight," in Robin Levi and Ayelet Waldman, eds., *Inside This Place, Not of It: Narratives from Women's Prisons* (San Francisco: McSweeney's Books, 2011,) 54.

2. George W. Bush, "Text of President Bush's 2004 State of the Union Address," *Washington Post*, January 20, 2004, http://www.washingtonpost.com/wp-srv/politics/transcripts/bushtext_012004.html (retrieved March 6, 2012).

3. "The Second Chance Act," Council of State Governments Justice Center, n.d. http://reentrypolicy.org/documents/0000/1277/2.14.12_Second_Chance_Act_Fact_Sheet_.pdf (retrieved February 29, 2012).

4. For an excellent overview of the reentry movement, see Edward E. Rhine and Anthony C. Thompson, "The Reentry Movement in Corrections: Resiliency, Fragility and Prospects," *Criminal Law Bulletin* 47.2 (2011): 177–209.

5. Jeremy Travis, *But They All Come Back: Facing the Challenges of Prisoner Reentry* (Washington, DC: Urban Institute, 2005), xxi.

6. Sara Steen, Traci Lacock, and Shelby McKinzey, "Unsettling the Discourse of Punishment? Competing Narratives of Reentry and the Possibilities for Change," *Punishment & Society* 14.1 (2012), 29.

7. Michael B. Katz, Mark J. Stern, and Jamie J. Fader, "The New African-American Inequality," *Journal of American History* 92.1 (2005), 107.

8. Malcolm Feeley and Jonathan Simon, "The New Penology: Notes on the Emerging Strategy of Corrections and Its Implications," *Criminology* 30.4 (1992): 449–74. Of course, these periodizations simplify these trends and overstate how much of a break they were with the past. For example, the rehabilitative ideal left only a light touch on certain penal systems, even in its heyday, as shown in the discussions of Arizona and Texas in chapter 3. Likewise, rehabilitation was never fully abandoned, even in the incapacitative era. See Michelle S. Phelps, "Rehabilitation in the Punitive Era: The Gap Between Rhetoric and Reality," *Law & Society Review* 45.1 (2011): 33–68; Leonidas K. Cheliotis, "How Iron Is the Iron Cage of the New Penology? The Role of Human Agency in the Implementation of Criminal Justice Policy," *Punishment & Society* 8.3 (2006): 313–40.

9. Magnus Hörnquist, "The Imaginary Constitution of Wage Labourers," in Pat Carlen, ed., *Imaginary Penalties* (Devon, UK: Willan, 2008), 180.

10. Hörnquist, "The Imaginary Constitution," 181. Bosworth makes a similar point with respect to how much of the responsibility for self-improvement and for keeping good order in prisons has shifted from penal institutions and penal administrators to prisoners themselves. Mary Bosworth, "Creating the Responsible Prisoner: Federal Admission and Orientation Packets," *Punishment & Society* 9.1 (2007), 71.

11. Megan Comfort, "'The Best Seven Years I Could'a Done': The Reconstruction of Imprisonment and Rehabilitation," in Carlen, ed., *Imaginary Penalties*, 257.

12. Daniel Stageman, "Entry, Revisited," *Dialectical Anthropology* 34.4 (2010), 441.

13. Joan Petersilia, "Community Corrections: Probation, Parole, and Prisoner Reentry," in James Q. Wilson and Joan Petersilia, eds., *Crime and Public Policy* (New York: Oxford University Press, 2011), 503.

14. Allen Beck et al., "Survey of State Prison Inmates, 1991," Bureau of Justice Statistics, March 1993, http://www.bjs.gov/content/pub/pdf/SOSPI91.PDF (retrieved May 21, 2014), 3. A more recent Urban Institute survey of incarcerated men and women just prior to their release and in the year following their release found higher pre-prison rates of labor force participation, but not much higher. The surveyed men and women identified finding employment as their single largest concern. Christy A. Visher, "Returning Home: Emerging Findings and Policy Lessons about Prisoner Reentry," *Federal Sentencing Reporter* 20.2 (2007), 99.

15. Doris J. James and Lauren E. Glaze, "Mental Health Problems of Prison and Jail Inmates," Bureau of Justice Statistics Special Report, September 2006, rev. December 14, 2006, http://www.bjs.gov/content/pub/pdf/mhppji.pdf (retrieved May 21, 2014), 1–2.

16. Treatment Advocacy Center and National Sheriffs' Association, "The Treatment of

Persons with Mental Illness in Prisons and Jails: A State Survey," April 8, 2014, http://www
.tacreports.org/storage/documents/treatment-behind-bars/treatment-behind-bars.pdf (retrieved May 16, 2014).

17. Jason Schnittker, "The Psychological Costs of Incarceration," *ANNALS of the American Academy of Political and Social Science* 651 (January 2014): 122–38.

18. Jason Schnittker, Michael Massoglia, and Christopher Uggen, "Out and Down: Incarceration and Psychiatric Disorders," *Journal of Health and Social Behavior* 53.4 (2012):
448–64.

19. Schnittker et al., "Out and Down," 459.

20. Schnittker et al., "Out and Down."

21. Phelps, "Rehabilitation in the Punitive Era," 61.

22. Stefan LoBuglio, "Time to Reframe Politics and Practices in Correctional Education," *Annual Review of Adult Learning and Literacy*, v. 2 (Boston: National Center for the
Study of Adult Learning and Literacy, 2001).

23. For example, in 2011, the Department of Corrections in Indiana cancelled contracts with half a dozen colleges providing traditional liberal arts programs and shifted its
resources to vocational classes. Dan McFeely, "Prison Education Changes Course: Focus
on Job Training Will Save Money But Limit Classes, Degrees," The Real Cost of Prisons
Weblog, June 7, 2011, http://realcostofprisons.org/blog/archives/2011/06/in_prison_educa
.html (retrieved January 26, 2012). For more on prisoners and Pell grants, see Joshua Page,
"Eliminating the Enemy: The Import of Denying Prisoners Access to Higher Education in
Clinton's America," *Punishment & Society* 6.4 (2004): 357–78.

24. Kevin Helliker, "In Prison, College Courses Are Few," *Wall Street Journal*, May 4,
2011.

25. According to one survey, participation in reentry-related programs, including life
skills, community readjustment training, and other pre-release programs such as financial
planning, job application training, and anger management, increased significantly from
15 percent of inmates in 1991 to 25 percent of inmates in 2004. Phelps, "Rehabilitation in
the Punitive Era," 54–55.

26. Joan Petersilia, "From Cell to Society: Who Is Returning Home?," in Jeremy Travis
and Christy Visher, eds., *Prisoner Reentry and Crime in America* (New York: Cambridge
University Press, 2005), 38.

27. Robert Werth, "The Construction and Stewardship of Responsible Yet Precarious
Subjects: Punitive Ideology, Rehabilitation, and 'Tough Love' Among Parole Personnel,"
Punishment & Society 15.3 (2013), 234.

28. Petersilia, "From Cell to Society," 41.

29. Nathan James, Jennifer D. Williams, and John F. Sargent, Jr., "Commerce, Justice,
Science, and Related Agencies: FY 2013 Appropriations," Congressional Research Service,
March 26, 2012, 32; Sentencing Project, "The Sentencing Project Decries Senate Appropriations Committee Action on Second Chance Act," press release, October 19, 2011, http://
org2.democracyinaction.org/o/5269/t/0/blastContent.jsp?email_blast_KEY=1181757 (retrieved July 5, 2013).

30. Rhine and Thompson, "The Reentry Movement in Corrections," 192.

31. John Schmitt and Kris Warner, "Ex-offenders and the Labor Market" (Washington,
DC: Center for Economic and Policy Research, November 2010), 1.

32. Christy A. Visher and Vera Kachnowski, "Finding Work on the Outside: Results
from the 'Returning Home' Project in Chicago," in Shawn Bushway, Michael A. Stoll, and

David F. Weiman, eds., *Barriers to Reentry? The Labor Market for Released Prisoners in Post-Industrial America* (New York: Russell Sage Foundation, 2007), 102; William J. Sabol, "Local Labor-Market Conditions and Post-Prison Employment Experiences of Offenders Released from Ohio State Prisons," in *Barriers to Reentry?*: 257–303.

33. Stephen J. Steuer, Linda Smith, and Alice Tracy, "Three-State Recidivism Study," submitted to the Office of Correctional Education, U.S. Department of Education, Washington, DC, 2001; John H. Tyler and Jeffrey R. Kling, "Prison-Based Education and Reentry in the Mainstream Labor Market," in Bushway, Stoll, and Weiman, eds., *Barriers to Reentry?*, 249; Steven Raphael and David F. Weiman, "The Impact of Local Labor-Market Conditions on the Likelihood that Parolees Are Returned to Custody," in *Barriers to Reentry?*.

34. James Austin et al., "Unlocking America: Why and How to Reduce America's Prison Population," JFA Institute, November 2007, http://www.jfa-associates.com/publications/srs/UnlockingAmerica.pdf (retrieved February 10, 2014), 22.

35. Mark A. R. Kleiman, Jonathan P. Caulkins, and Angela Hawken, *Drugs and Drug Policy: What Everyone Needs to Know* (New York: Oxford University Press, 2011), 191.

36. Calculated from Steve Aos, Marna Miller, and Elizabeth Drake, *Evidence-Based Adult Corrections Programs: What Works and What Does Not* (Olympia, WA: Washington State Institute for Public Policy, January 2006), 3, exhibit 1.

37. Aos, Miller, and Drake, *Evidence-Based Adult Corrections Programs*, 3, exhibit 1.

38. Austin et al., "Unlocking America," 20.

39. Shawn D. Bushway, "Labor Markets and Crime," in Wilson and Petersilia, eds., *Crime and Public Policy*, 183–84.

40. Bruce Western, "The Penal System and the Labor Market," in Bushway, Stoll, and Weiman, eds., *Barriers to Reentry?* 353.

41. Shadd Maruna and Hans Toch, "The Impact of Imprisonment on the Desistance Process," in Travis and Visher, eds., *Prisoner Reentry and Crime in America*, 171. See also Michael Hallett, "Reentry to What? Theorizing Prisoner Reentry in the Jobless Future," *Critical Criminology* 20.3 (2012): 213–28.

42. Robert P. Fairbanks II, "The Illinois Reentry Imperative: Sheridan Correctional Center as National Model," *Carceral Notebooks* 6 (2011), 175.

43. Sabol, "Local Labor-Market Conditions"; Charles E. Kubrin and Eric A. Stewart, "Predicting Who Reoffends: The Neglected Role of Neighborhood Context in Recidivism Studies," *Criminology* 44.1 (2006): 165–97.

44. Xia Wang, Daniel P. Mears, and William D. Bales, "Race-Specific Employment Contexts and Recidivism," *Criminology* 48.4 (2010): 1171–1211.

45. John R. Hipp and Daniel K. Yates, "Do Returning Parolees Affect Neighborhood Crime? A Case Study of Sacramento," *Criminology* 47.3 (2009): 619–56.

46. Christopher Uggen, Sara Wakefield, and Bruce Western, "Work and Family Perspectives in Reentry," in Travis and Visher, eds., *Prisoner Reentry and Crime in America*, 237.

47. Uggen, Wakefield, and Western, "Work and Family Perspectives in Reentry," 237.

48. Raphael and Weiman, "The Impact of Local Labor-Market Conditions."

49. "Very few adult black men were outside the labor force before 1940, and their participation paralleled that of white men. . . . Among black men aged 21–25, the proportion not in the labor force rose from 9 percent in 1940 to 27 percent in 1990 and 34 percent in 2000. Between 1990 and 2000, nonparticipation increased for black men of other ages as well." Katz, Stern, and Fader, "The New African-American Inequality," 81.

50. Katz, Stern, and Fader, "The New African-American Inequality," 85.

51. Michael Hout, "Occupational Mobility of Black Men: 1962 to 1973," *American Sociological Review* 49.3 (1984), 308. See also Katz, Stern, and Fader, "The New African-American Inequality," 86.

52. Katz, Stern, and Fader, "The New African-American Inequality," 99.

53. Hout, "Occupational Mobility of Black Men," 308.

54. William Julius Wilson, "The Declining Significance of Race: Revisited and Revised," *Daedalus* 140.2 (2011), 61.

55. Katz, Stern, and Fader, "The New African-American Inequality," 87.

56. By the end of the century, almost half of employed black women (43 percent) were working in public or publicly funded agencies compared to about one in five black men. Katz, Stern, and Fader, "The New African-American Inequality," 87.

57. For example, a study of 15 representative cities found that government employment accounted for 60 percent of the variance in black poverty rates. Katz, Stern, and Fader, "The New African-American Inequality," 96.

58. This presumably was because "African-American access to public employment also signaled increasing black influence, which encouraged local welfare bureaucracies to respond more generously to black need." Katz, Stern, and Fader, "The New African-American Inequality, 96.

59. Reynolds Farley, *The New American Reality: Who We Are, How We Got Here, and Where We Are Going* (New York: Russell Sage Foundation, 1996), 248–55.

60. Katz, Stern, and Fader, "The New African-American Inequality," 91.

61. The more comprehensive unemployment figures were 13 percent and 12 percent respectively for white men and white women and 20 percent and 21 percent respectively for Latino men and women. John Schmitt and Janelle Jones, "America's 'New Class': A Profile of the Long-Term Unemployed," *New Labor Forum* 21.2 (2012): 57–65, 130–31.

62. Eva Bertram, *Building the Workfare State: The New Politics of Public Assistance* (Philadelphia: University of Pennsylvania Press, forthcoming), ms., ch. 5, p. 20.

63. Katz, Stern, and Fader, "The New African-American Inequality," 76.

64. U.S. Department of Labor, "The African-American Labor Force in the Recovery," February 29, 2012, http://www.dol.gov/_sec/media/reports/BlackLaborForce/BlackLabor Force.pdf (retrieved September 22, 2013).

65. Marshall I. Pomer, "Labor Market Structure, Intragenerational Mobility, and Discrimination: Black Male Advancement Out of Low-Paying Occupations, 1962–1973," *American Sociological Review* 51.5 (1986), 657.

66. Mary Pattillo, "Consumers as Well as Employees," nytimes.com, July 25, 2011, http://www.nytimes.com/roomfordebate/2011/07/25/how-budget-cuts-will-change-the -black-middle-class/the-black-middle-class-as-employees-and-consumers (retrieved July 3, 2013).

67. Lawrence M. Mead, *Expanding Work Programs for Poor Men* (Washington, DC: AEI Press, 2011). For two searing but somewhat distinct analyses of the connection between welfare reform and the rise of the carceral state, see Joe Soss, Richard C. Fording, and Sanford F. Schram, *Disciplining the Poor: Neoliberal Paternalism and the Persistent Power of Race* (Chicago: University of Chicago Press, 2011); and Loïc Wacquant, *Punishing the Poor: The Neoliberal Government of Social Insecurity* (Durham, NC: Duke University Press, 2009).

68. Bruce Western, "From Prison to Work: A Proposal for a National Prisoner Reentry Program," The Hamilton Project, Discussion Paper 2008–16 (Washington, DC: The Brookings Institution and The Hamilton Project, 2008), 14 and 16.

69. Bertram, *Building the Workfare State*, ms., ch. 5, p. 2. Emphasis in the original.

70. Bertram, *Building the Workfare State*, ms., ch. 1, p. 1.

71. My account of the deeper origins and development of workfare in the United States draws heavily on Bertram, *Building the Workfare State*.

72. Bertram, *Building the Workfare State*, ms., ch. 8, p. 40.

73. Bertram, *Building the Workfare State*, ms., ch. 8, pp. 39–40. Emphasis in the original.

74. Will Marshal, "Replacing Welfare With Work," in Bertram, *Building the Workfare State*, ms., ch. 8, p. 38.

75. Bertram, *Building the Workfare State*; Gordon Lafer, *The Job Training Charade* (Ithaca, NY: Cornell University Press, 2002).

76. The Organization of Economic Cooperation and Development defined low-wage jobs as ones that paid less than two-thirds of the national median hourly wage. John Schmitt, "Low-Wage Lessons," Center for Economic and Policy Research, January 2012, http://www.cepr.net/documents/publications/low-wage-2012-01.pdf (retrieved July 3, 2013), 1.

77. Chris Isidore, "Not Getting By on Minimum Wage," CNNMoney, September 27, 2011, http://money.cnn.com/2011/09/27/news/economy/minimum_wage_jobs/index.htm (retrieved July 3, 2013); U.S. Department of Health and Human Services, "2012 HHS Poverty Guidelines," n.d., http://aspe.hhs.gov/poverty/12poverty.shtml/#guidelines (retrieved July 3, 2013).

78. Lafer, *The Job Training Charade*, 197–98.

79. Douglas S. Massey, *Categorically Unequal: The American Stratification System* (New York: Russell Sage Foundation, 2007), ch. 4.

80. Soss, Fording, and Schram, *Disciplining the Poor*, 305.

81. Soss, Fording, and Schram, *Disciplining the Poor*, 305.

82. Soss, Fording, and Schram, *Disciplining the Poor*, 301.

83. Soss, Fording, and Schram, *Disciplining the Poor*, 5.

84. Soss, Fording, and Schram, *Disciplining the Poor*, 15.

85. About 70 percent of the more than 700,000 people who leave prison each year remain under some kind of supervised release and thus would be eligible for the proposed program. The proposal assumes that about half of these 490,000 new parolees would need work immediately after release from custody, or about 245,000 ex-offenders. Western, "From Prison to Work," 17.

86. For a summary of the results of these programs, see Western, "From Prison to Work," 11–12, table 2.

87. Western, "From Prison to Work," 10.

88. Western, "From Prison to Work, 24.

89. Western, *Punishment and Inequality*, 125.

90. Western, *Punishment and Inequality*, 125.

91. Western, *Punishment and Inequality*, 120–21.

92. Ann Chih Lin, *Reform in the Making: The Implementation of Social Policy in Prison* (Princeton, NJ: Princeton University Press, 2000). For example, my incarcerated students in the Philadelphia jail system complained that when guards "tossed" their cells looking for contraband they often confiscated teaching materials for our class.

93. "Hamilton Project From Prison to Work: Overcoming Barriers to Reentry," The National Press Club, Washington, DC, transcript, December 5, 2008, http://www.brookings.edu/~/media/Events/2008/12/05%20prison%20to%20work/20081205_prison_to_work.PDF (retrieved May 21, 2014), n.p.

94. Bruce Western, "The Penal System and the Labor Market," in Bushway, Stoll, and Weiman, eds., *Barriers to Reentry?*, 353.

95. For more on HOPE, see Mark A. R. Kleiman, "Toward Fewer Prisoners and Less Crime," *Daedalus* 139.3 (2010), 121–23; Mark A. R. Kleiman, "Justice Reinvestment in Community Supervision," *Criminology & Public Policy* 10.3 (2011): 651–59; Pew Center on the States, "One in 31: Behind Bars in America 2008" (Washington, DC: Pew Charitable Trusts, 2009), 27.

96. Robert DuPont, who served as drug policy director under Gerald Ford and Richard Nixon and has been in the drug-testing business since the 1980s, extolled HOPE at the 2012 annual meeting of the Drug & Alcohol Testing Industry Association. He told the gathering in a voice that rose to a high-pitched yell, "If they test positive, they go to jail that day! No discussion! . . . No discretion! To jail that day!" Isabel Macdonald, "Drug Test Dragnet," *Nation*, April 22, 2013.

97. Kleiman, "Toward Fewer Prisoners," 120.

98. According to Mark A. R. Kleiman, one of HOPE's leading advocates, "a judicial warning that the next positive drug test would draw an immediate jail term measured in days succeeded in virtually ending drug use for more than three-quarters of a group of chronically defiant felony probationers." Kleiman, "Toward Fewer Prisoners," 120.

99. Kleiman, "Toward Fewer Prisoners," 120.

100. Kleiman, "Toward Fewer Prisoners," 123.

101. The terms "outpatient" and "virtual" incarceration come from Kleiman, "Toward Fewer Prisoners," 122.

102. This is how one parole officer characterized the prevailing approach to supervision. Francis T. Cullen and Cheryl Lero Jonson, "Rehabilitation and Treatment Programs," in Wilson and Petersilia, eds., *Crime and Public Policy*, 294–95.

103. Kleiman, "Justice Reinvestment in Community Supervision," 654.

104. Camille Camp and George Camp, *The Corrections Yearbook 1998* (Middleton, CT: Criminal Justice Institute, 1999) in Petersilia, "Community Corrections," 513.

105. Petersilia, "Community Corrections," 513.

106. Kleiman, "Toward Fewer Prisoners," 121.

107. Edward E. Rhine, "The Present Status and Future Prospects of Parole Boards and Parole Supervision," in Joan Petersilia and Kevin Reitz, eds., *The Oxford Handbook of Sentencing and Corrections* (New York: Oxford University Press, 2012), 646.

108. Joan Petersilia and Susan Tucker, "Intensive Probation and Parole," in Michael Tonry, ed., *Crime and Justice: A Review of Research*, v. 17 (Chicago: University of Chicago Press, 1993), 281–335.

109. Rhine, "The Present Status and Future Prospects of Parole Boards," 640.

110. Werth, "The Construction and Stewardship," 219; Mona Lynch, "Rehabilitation as Rhetoric," *Punishment & Society* 2.1 (2000): 40–65. See also Rhine, "The Present Status and Future Prospects of Parole Boards," 638–40.

111. The handbook goes on to say, "Now that you are out of prison you will have a lot more freedom. How well you do while out on parole is up to you." Quoted in Werth, "The Construction and Stewardship," 229.

112. *Tapia v. United States* 564 S. Ct. 2387–88 (2011); Michael Doyle, "U.S. Supreme Court Rules Longer Prison Terms Not Allowed for Drug Rehab," *Sacramento Bee*, June 17, 2011, http://www.modbee.com/2011/06/17/1736074/us-supreme-court-rules-longer.html (retrieved March 9, 2012).

113. Grits for Breakfast, "Can Imprisonment Rehabilitate?," June 17, 2011, http://grits forbreakfast.blogspot.com/2011/06/can-imprisonment-rehabilitate.html (retrieved June 20, 2011).

114. Austin et al., "Unlocking America," 21. See also Cullen and Johnson, "Rehabilitation and Treatment Programs."

115. Shawn D. Bushway and Robert Apel, "A Signaling Perspective on Employment-Based Reentry Programming: Training Completion as a Desistance Signal," *Criminology & Public Policy* 11.1 (2012): 21–50.

116. Western, "The Penal System and the Labor Market," 356.

117. Stephen D. Sowle, "A Regime of Social Death: Criminal Punishment in the Age of Prisons." *N.Y.U. Review of Law and Social Change* 21.3 (1994–95): 497–565.

118. James Q. Whitman, *Harsh Justice: Criminal Punishment and the Widening Divide between America and Europe* (New York: Oxford University Press, 2003), 84–85.

119. Amanda Petteruti and Jason Fenster, "Finding Direction: Expanding Criminal Justice Options by Considering Policies of Other Nations" (Washington, DC: Justice Policy Institute, April 2011), 34.

120. Petteruti and Fenster, "Finding Direction," 34. See also Nicola Padfield, Dirk van Zyl Smit, and Frieder Dünkel, eds., *Release from Prison: European Policy and Practice* (Devon, UK: Willan, 2010).

121. Petteruti and Fenster, "Finding Direction," 41.

122. Whitman, *Harsh Justice*, 85. Emphasis in the original.

123. Rhine and Thompson, "The Reentry Movement," 189.

124. Brian E. Oliver, "My Sentence Is Over But Will My Punishment Ever End?," *Dialectical Anthropology* 34.4 (2010): 447–51.

125. Whitman, *Harsh Justice*, 86.

126. Whitman, *Harsh Justice*, 89.

127. Whitman, *Harsh Justice*, 88.

128. U.S. DOJ, Office of Public Affairs, "Attorney General Eric Holder Convenes Inaugural Cabinet-Level Reentry Council," press release, January 5, 2011, http://www.justice.gov/opa/pr/2011/January/11-ag-010.html (retrieved February 10, 2012).

129. Austin et al., "Unlocking America," 21.

Chapter Five

Caught Again

1. Carolyn Baxter, "On Being Counted," in H. Bruce Franklin, ed., *Prison Writing in 20th-Century America* (New York: Penguin Press, 1998), 250.

2. Susan B. Tucker and Eric Cadora, "Justice Reinvestment," *Ideas for an Open Society* 3.3 (2003): 2–5.

3. James Austin et al., "Ending Mass Incarceration: Charting a New Justice Reinvestment," 2013, http://www.justicestrategies.org/sites/default/files/publications/Charting%20a%20New%20Justice%20Reinvestment.pdf (retrieved June 22, 2013), 1; Christopher D. Berk, "Investment Talk: Comments on the Use of the Language of Investment in Prison Reform Advocacy," *Carceral Notebooks* 6 (2010): 115–29.

4. Todd R. Clear, "A Private-Sector, Incentives-Based Model for Justice Reinvestment," *Criminology & Public Policy* 10.3 (2011), 594–95.

5. Austin et al., "Ending Mass Incarceration," 2, 6.

6. For example, Kentucky's Public Safety and Offender Act of 2011 was projected to reduce the state's prison population by just 3,000 people—or about 15 percent—over the next decade. In the wake of the Public Safety Improvement Act that sailed through the Arkansas

legislature in 2011, the state's prison population is still projected to grow by more than 20 percent over the next decade (compared to a projected growth of 45 percent without the reforms). If the projections are on target, Arkansas will need to construct nearly 3,500 new prison beds. The Pew Center on the States, "Arkansas's 2011 Public Safety Reform," July 2011, http://www.pewcenteronthestates.org/uploadedFiles/Pew_Arkansas_brief.pdf (retrieved March 9, 2012), 3; The Pew Center on the States, "2011 Kentucky Reforms Cut Recidivism, Costs," July 1, 2011, http://www.pewstates.org/uploadedFiles/PCS_Assets/2011/2011_Kentucky_Reforms_Cut_Recidivism.pdf (retrieved May 9, 2012), 1.

7. Austin et al., "Ending Mass Incarceration."

8. James H. Burch II, "Encouraging Innovation on the Foundation of Evidence: On the Path to the 'Adjacent Possible'?," *Criminology & Public Policy* 10.3 (2011): 609–16.

9. Austin et al., "Ending Mass Incarceration," 1.

10. Clear, "A Private-Sector, Incentives-Based Model," 589.

11. Lisa Miller, "The Local and the Legal: American Federalism and the Carceral State," *Criminology & Public Policy* 10.3 (2011), 727.

12. Miller, "The Local and the Legal," 727; Ruth D. Peterson and Lauren J. Krivo, *Neighborhood Crime and the Racial-Spatial Divide* (New York: Russell Sage Foundation, 2010).

13. Council of State Governments Justice Center, "Justice Reinvestment: The Strategy," n.d., http://justicereinvestment.org/about (retrieved November 28, 2011).

14. See, for example, the membership list of the Task Force on the Penal Code and Controlled Substances, which was established in 2010 by the Kentucky General Assembly and was the incubator for the widely hailed penal reform bill enacted in 2011. See also the membership of Arkansas's Working Group on Sentencing and Corrections, which was the force behind the state's Public Safety Improvement Act enacted in 2011. The Pew Center on the States, "2011 Kentucky Reforms Cut Recidivism, Costs"; The Pew Center on the States, "Arkansas's 2011 Public Safety Reform," 3.

15. Austin et al., "Ending Mass Incarceration," 2.

16. Ted Gest, "Critics Say Justice Reinvestment Sidesteps Minority Communities," *Crime Report*, April 17, 2013, http://www.thecrimereport.org/news/inside-criminal-justice/2013-04-is-justice-reinvestment-as-good-as-it-looks (retrieved June 22, 2013).

17. Heather Schoenfeld, "Putting Politics in Penal Policy Reform," *Criminology & Public Policy* 10.3 (2011), 719.

18. Sarah Armstrong and Lesley McAra, "Audiences, Borders, Architecture: The Contours of Control," in Sarah Armstrong and Lesley McAra, eds., *Perspectives on Punishment: The Contours of Control* (Oxford: Oxford University Press, 2006), 21.

19. Armstrong and McAra, "Audiences, Borders, Architecture," 21.

20. Pat Carlen, "Imaginary Penalties: Risk-Crazed Governance," in Pat Carlen, ed., *Imaginary Penalties* (Devon, UK: Willan, 2008): 1–25. For another skeptical view of staking the penal reform agenda primarily on devising better carrots (such as greater levels of rehabilitative services) and sticks (such as swift and certain sanctions for probation and parole violations) to reduce recidivism, see James Austin, "Reducing America's Correctional Population: A Strategic Plan," *Justice Research and Policy* 12.1 (2010): 9–40.

21. Sasha Abramsky, "Prison Futures," *Sacramento News and Review*, March 9, 2006, http://www.newsreview.com/sacramento/prison-futures/content?oid=47640 (retrieved October 24, 2013).

22. Ian Loader and Richard Sparks, *Public Criminology?* (London: Routledge, 2011), 127–44.

23. Loader and Sparks, *Public Criminology?*, 127.

24. Heather MacDonald, "How to Straighten Out Ex-Cons," *City Journal*, Spring 2003, http://www.city-journal.org/html/13_2_how_to_straighten.html (retrieved February 9, 2014).

25. Marshall Clement, Matthew Schwarzfeld, and Michael Thompson, "The National Summit on Justice Reinvestment and Public Safety: Addressing Recidivism, Crime, and Corrections Spending" (New York: The Council of State Governments, Justice Center, January 2011), 1.

26. NAACP, "Misplaced Priorities: Overincarcerate, Under Educate" (Baltimore, MD: NAACP, April 2011), 12.

27. Patrick Langan and David J. Levin, "Recidivism of Prisoners Released in 1994," Bureau of Justice Statistics Special Report, June 2002, http://www.bjs.gov/content/pub/pdf/rprts05p0510.pdf (retrieved May 16, 2014).

28. Mark L. Earley and Kathryn Wiley, "The New Frontier of Public Safety," *Stanford Law & Policy Review* 22.2 (2011), 345.

29. Kelly Hannah-Moffat, "Actuarial Sentencing: An 'Unsettled' Proposition," paper presented at the Symposium on Crime and Justice: The Past and Future of Empirical Sentencing Research, SUNY at Albany, School of Criminal Justice, September 23–24, 2010, 12.

30. Hannah-Moffat, "Actuarial Sentencing," 12.

31. Michael Maltz, *Recidivism* (Orlando, FL: Academic Press, 1984), 61–62.

32. Carla Marquez et al., "How Much Punishment Is Enough? Designing Participatory Research on Parole Policies for Persons Convicted of Violent Crimes," paper presented at the Annual Meeting of the American Anthropological Association, Montreal, Canada, November 16–20, 2011, 10.

33. Pew Center on the States, "State of Recidivism: The Revolving Door of America's Prisons" (Washington, DC: The Pew Charitable Trusts, April 2011).

34. Pew Center on the States, "Pew Finds Four in 10 Offenders Return to Prison Within Three Years," press release, April 12, 2011, http://www.pewstates.org/news-room/press-releases/pew-finds-four-in-10-offenders-return-to-prison-within-three-years-85899371939 (retrieved November 18, 2011).

35. The Bureau of Justice Statistics actually found that just over half of released prisoners were returned to prison within three years. However, once California, whose large size skews the national data, is excluded, both the BJS and Pew studies concluded that recidivism rates have consistently remained around 40 percent between 1994 and 2007. Langan and Levin, "Recidivism of Prisoners Released in 1994"; Pew Center on the States, "Pew Finds Four in 10 Offenders Return to Prison." On recidivism rates in other countries, see Amanda Petteruti and Jason Fenster, "Finding Direction: Expanding Criminal Justice Options by Considering Policies of Other Nations" (Washington, DC: Justice Policy Institute, April 2011), 41–42.

36. For example, Governor Michael Dukakis (D-MA) was excoriated in the 1988 presidential campaign for his "revolving door" policy toward repeat and dangerous offenders that threatened public safety. See "George Bush Sr. 'Revolving Door' Attack Ad Campaign," YouTube, http://www.youtube.com/watch?v=PmwhdDv8VrM (retrieved November 18, 2011).

37. Matthew R. Durose, Alexia D. Cooper, and Howard N. Snyder, "Recidivism of Prisoners Released in 30 States in 2005: Patterns from 2005 to 2010," Bureau of Justice Statistics Special Report, April 2014, http://www.bjs.gov/content/pub/pdf/rprts05p0510.pdf (retrieved May 16, 2014), 15, table 16.

38. Wyoming Department of Corrections, "Annual Report FY2009," n.d., doc.state.wy .us/Media.aspx?mediaId=195 (retrieved November 28, 2011); Pew Center on the States, "State of Recidivism," 14.

39. "Realignment" is the package of measures California enacted in 2011 in response to its defeat in the decades-long *Brown v. Plata* prison overcrowding lawsuit. For more on California's realignment, see pp. 269–71.

40. Ryan G. Fischer, "Are California's Recidivism Rates *Really* the Highest in the Nation? It Depends on What Measure of Recidivism You Use," *Bulletin* 1.1 (Irvine: University of California–Irvine Center for Evidence-Based Corrections, September 2005).

41. CDCR, Office of Research, "2011 Adult Institutions Outcome Evaluation Report," November 23, 2011, http://www.cdcr.ca.gov/Adult_Research_Branch/Research _Documents/ARB_FY_0607_Recidivism_Report(11-23-11).pdf (retrieved June 29, 2013).

42. Fischer, "Are California's Recidivism Rates *Really* the Highest in the Nation?"

43. Jeremy Travis and Christy Visher, "Considering the Policy Implications," in Jeremy Travis and Christy Visher, eds., *Prisoner Reentry and Crime in America* (New York: Cambridge University Press, 2005), 252.

44. Pew Center on the States, "State of Recidivism," 14.

45. Grits for Breakfast, "Pew Recommendation on Recidivism Metric Wrong for Texas," April 17, 2011, http://gritsforbreakfast.blogspot.com/2011/04/pew-recommendation-on -recidivism-metric.html (retrieved May 9, 2011).

46. Michael Tonry, "Making Peace, Not a Desert: Penal Reform Should Be about Values not Justice Reinvestment," *Criminology & Public Policy* 10.3 (2011): 637–49.

47. Abdon M. Pallasch, "Prisons Not the Answer to Crime Problems: Attorney General," *Chicago Sun-Times*, August 3, 2009.

48. Robert Sampson and Janet Lauritsen, "Racial and Ethnic Disparities in Crime and Criminal Justice in the United States," in Michael Tonry, ed., *Ethnicity, Crime, and Immigration: Comparative and Cross-National Perspectives* (Chicago: University of Chicago Press, 1997): 311–74.

49. Langan and Levin, "Recidivism of Prisoners Released in 1994," 5–6.

50. Richard Rosenfeld, Joel Wallman, and Robert Fornango, "The Contribution of Ex-Prisoners to Crime Rates," in Travis and Visher, eds., *Prisoner Reentry and Crime in America*: 80–104.

51. Rosenfeld, Wallman, and Fornango, "The Contribution of Ex-Prisoners to Crime Rates," 91–92.

52. About 637,000 people were released from state and federal prisons in 2012, more than a threefold increase from three decades earlier. E. Ann Carson and Daniela Golinelli, "Prisoners in 2012: Trends in Admissions and Releases, 1991–2012," *Bureau of Justice Statistics Bulletin*, December 2013, 1.

53. Rosenfeld, Wallman, and Fornango, "The Contribution of Ex-Prisoners to Crime Rates," 88.

54. Rosenfeld, Wallman, and Fornango, "The Contribution of Ex-Prisoners to Crime Rates," 88.

55. Peter Jackson, "Rendell Orders Review of Pa. Parole System," Associated Press, September 29, 2008, http://abclocal.go.com/wpvi/story?section=news/local&id=6421419 (retrieved November 23, 2011).

56. Catherine C. McVey, testimony before the Pennsylvania Senate Judiciary Committee, January 27, 2009; Angela Couloumbis, "Officials Say Improvements Made to Parole System," philly.com, January 28, 2009, http://articles.philly.com/2009-01-28/news

/25279407_1_parole-system-high-risk-offenders-john-s-goldkamp (retrieved February 9, 2014).

57. Renee Cardwell Hughes, remarks made at "Parole: Why We Need It; Why It Works; Where It Needs Fixing," sponsored by the Pennsylvania Prison Society, Philadelphia, PA, February 24, 2009.

58. William M. DiMascio, "Parole Freeze Courts Danger," philly.com, October 9, 2008, http://articles.philly.com/2008–10–09/news/25265096_1_parole-state-prison-population -inmates-and-staff (retrieved October 22, 2013).

59. Reuters, "PA Gov. Rendell to Legislature: End Paroles for Repeat Violent Offenders to Keep Communities Safe," January 4, 2009, http://www.reuters.com/article/2009/01/04 /idUS79907+04-Jan-2009+PRN20090104 (retrieved February 9, 2014).

60. Keith Phucas, "New State Prison Planned," *Times Herald*, February 19, 2009.

61. Charis E. Kubrin and Eric A. Stewart, "Predicting Who Reoffends: The Neglected Role of Neighborhood Context in Recidivism Studies," *Criminology* 44.1 (2006): 165–97.

62. John R. Hipp and Daniel K. Yates, "Do Returning Parolees Affect Neighborhood Crime? A Case Study of Sacramento," *Criminology* 47.3 (2009), 619, 644.

63. Hipp and Yates, "Do Returning Parolees Affect Neighborhood Crime?," 620.

64. David L. Rosen, Victor J. Schoenbach, and David A. Wohl, "All-Cause and Cause-Specific Mortality Among Men Released from State Prison, 1980–2005," *American Journal of Public Health* 98.12 (2008): 2278–84; "Study: Risk of Murder, Overdose and Suicide Higher for Recently Released Jail Prisoners in New York City," *Prison Legal News*, January 2014, 31.

65. Ingrid A. Binswanger et al., "Release from Prison—A High Risk of Death for Former Inmates," *New England Journal of Medicine* 356.5 (January 11, 2007): 157–65.

66. The leading causes of death for released inmates were homicide, suicide, cardiovascular disease, and drug overdoses. Binswanger et al., "Release from Prison."

67. Daniel Pratt et al., "Suicide in Recently Released Prisoners: A Case-Control Study," *Psychological Medicine* 40.5 (2010): 827–35.

68. Anne C. Spaulding et al., "Prisoner Survival Inside and Outside the Institution: Implications for Health-Care Planning," *American Journal of Epidemiology* 173.5 (2011): 479–87.

69. Parolees able to "survive their parole without incident eventually return to the before-prison mortality curve." Evelyn J. Patterson, "The Dose-Response of Time Served in Prison on Mortality: New York State, 1989–2003," *American Journal of Public Health* 103.3 (2013), 526.

70. Clement, Schwarzfeld, and Thompson, "The National Summit on Justice Reinvestment," 21.

71. Clement, Schwarzfeld, and Thompson, "The National Summit on Justice Reinvestment," 24.

72. The Pew Center on the States, "2011 Kentucky Reforms."

73. Kentucky Legislature, 11 reg. sess., HB 463, unofficial copy as of March 3, 2012, http://www.lrc.ky.gov/record/11rs/hb463.ht (retrieved March 8, 2012), 1.

74. Upon entering office, Corbett did cancel one of these proposed prisons, saying he wanted to cultivate industries that "generate wealth, not sorrow." "The Text of Gov. Corbett's Budget Address," philly.com, March 8, 2011, http://articles.philly.com/2011–03–08/news /28668900_1_budget-address-first-budget-tree (retrieved June 22, 2013).

75. Mindy Bogue, "Justice Reinvestment Initiative to Decrease Prison Population," *Correctional Forum*, September 2012, 4–5; Hakim Ali and Layne Mullett, "True Prison Reform

Continues to Elude Pennsylvania," July 9, 2012, http://articles.philly.com/2012–07–09/news /32602281_1_prison-reform-elderly-prisoners-older-prisoners (retrieved June 22, 2013); Rep. Thomas Caltagirone, "Caltagirone Says Prison Reform Law Will Reduce Crime, Costs," press release, July 6, 2012, http://www.pahouse.com/pr/127070612.asp (retrieved June 22, 2013); Austin et al., "Ending Mass Incarceration," 10.

76. Allison Steele and Amy Worden, "Mandatory 2-year Prison Term Proposed for Illegal Firearm Users in Phila.," philly.com, April 6, 2013, http://articles.philly.com/2013–04 –06/news/38309721_1_gun-purchase-gun-violence-gun-control (retrieved June 22, 2013); Dana DiFilippo, "Gun Convictions Would Mean 5-Year Minimum If House Bill Passes," philly.com, August 17, 2013, http://articles.philly.com/2012–08–16/news/33233560_1 _illegal-gun-felons-time-for-gun-crime (retrieved February 9, 2014).

77. See, for example, John Buntin, "2010 Public Officials of the Year: The Correctionists," *Governing*, 2010 (retrieved February 15, 2011); "Conservatives and Criminal Justice: Right and Proper," *Economist*, May 26, 2011; Sasha Abramsky, "Is This the End of the War on Crime?," *Nation*, June 16, 2010; Tony Fabelo, "Texas Justice Reinvestment: Be More Like Texas?," *Justice Research and Policy* 12.1 (2010): 113–31; Laurie O. Robinson, "Exploring Certainty and Severity: Perspectives from a Federal Perch," *Criminology & Public Policy* 10.1 (2011), 89; Clement, Schwarzfeld, and Thompson, "The National Summit on Justice Reinvestment," 58.

78. Fabelo, "Texas Justice Reinvestment," 114.

79. Council of State Governments Justice Center, "Justice Reinvestment State Brief: Texas," n.d., http://www.pewcenteronthestates.org/uploadedFiles/TX%20State%20Brief.pdf (retrieved November 12, 2011); Council of State Governments Justice Center, "Justice Reinvestment in Texas: Assessing the Impact of the 2007 Justice Reinvestment Initiative," April 2009, http://www.ncsl.org/portals/1/Documents/cj/texas.pdf (retrieved February 9, 2014).

80. Grits for Breakfast, "On the Differences Between DOJ and TDCJ Prison Population Totals for Texas," September 10, 2013, http://gritsforbreakfast.blogspot.com/2013/09/on -differences-between-doj-and-tdcj.html (retrieved February 9, 2014).

81. Between 2008 and 2012, the number of people on parole rose by 8 percent while the number on probation fell by approximately 5 percent. These figures are calculated from TDCJ, "Fiscal Year 2012 Statistical Report," n.d., http://www.tdcj.state.tx.us/documents /Statistical_Report_FY2012.pdf (retrieved February 9, 2014), vi, 2, 6; and TDCJ, "Fiscal Year 2008 Statistical Report," n.d., https://www.tdcj.state.tx.us/documents/Statistical _Report_FY2008.pdf (retrieved February 9, 2014), 1, 4, and 6.

82. William J. Sabol, Heather C. West, and Matthew Cooper, "Prisoners in 2008," *Bureau of Justice Statistics Bulletin*, 17, appendix table 2E; Ann Carson, "Prisoners in 2012—Advance Counts," *Bureau of Justice Statistics Bulletin*, July 2013, 3, table 2.

83. Grits for Breakfast, "Texas Jail Population Down 9.5% since 2008," April 24, 2012, http://gritsforbreakfast.blogspot.com/2012/04/texas-jail-populations-down-95-since.html (retrieved February 9, 2014).

84. TDCJ, "Statistical Report Fiscal Year 2011," n.d., http://www.tdcj.state.tx.us/documents /Statistical_Report_2011.pdf (retrieved June 22, 2013), iv.

85. TDCJ, "Fiscal Year 2012 Statistical Report," 5.

86. For example, in 2009, the Texas legislature established a housing voucher program for parolees; relaxed restrictions on "good time" credits and on occupational licenses for certain offenders; and required the TDCJ to establish a comprehensive reentry and

reintegration plan for released prisoners and to make it easier for released prisoners to obtain some form of official state identification. Matt Clarke, "Justice Reinvestment Eliminates Texas Prison Overcrowding," *Prison Legal News*, November 2009, 18–19.

87. Between 2008 and 2011, parole approval rates in Texas averaged about 31 percent before jumping to nearly 37 percent in 2012. Texas Board of Pardons and Parole, "Annual Statistical Report: Fiscal Year 2012," June 2013, http://www.tdcj.state.tx.us/bpp/publications /FY%202012%20BPP%20StatisticalReport.pdf (retrieved February 9, 2014), 5.

88. Texas District & County Attorneys Association, "Legislative Summary of Regular Session," June 1, 2012, http://www.tdcaa.com/legislative/legislative-summary-regular -session-june-1-2011 (retrieved August 21, 2012).

89. For example, Texas legislators agreed to make cheating or lying about the size of a fish caught in a tournament a third-degree felony, punishable by as much as a 2- to 10-year prison sentence. They also enacted a measure to expand the use of life without the possibility of parole for certain sexual assaults. Texas District & County Attorneys Association, "Legislative Summary"; Grits for Breakfast, "Newest Felony: Misrepresenting Fish," May 10, 2011, http://gritsforbreakfast.blogspot.com/2011/05/newest-felony-misrepresenting-fish.html (retrieved August 21, 2012).

90. Grits for Breakfast, "Dozens of New Crimes Proposed at the Lege: Will LBB Man Up and Assign them Fiscal Notes?," February 3, 2012, http://gritsforbreakfast.blogspot .com/2011/02/dozens-of-new-crimes-proposed-at-lege.html (retrieved February 9, 2014).

91. The Sentencing Project, "Total Corrections Population," interactive maps for Texas and California, http://www.sentencingproject.org/map/map.cfm#map (retrieved February 9, 2014). For more on California's realignment, see pp. 269–71.

92. Texas is comparatively more punitive in both big and small ways. For example, the state also has 11 felonies on the books related to the handling and harvesting of oysters. In some communities in Texas, people with overdue library materials risk being arrested and sent to jail. Jessica Langdon, "Room Scarce at Jail," *Times Record News*, July 13, 2009, http:// www.timesrecordnews.com/news/2009/jul/13/room-scarce-at-jail/ (retrieved November 28, 2011); Marc Levin, "Overcriminalization: 2011–2012 Legislators' Guide to the Issues" (Austin: Texas Public Policy Foundation, September 13, 2010), http://www.texaspolicy.com/pdf /2011-Overcriminalization-CEJ-ml.pdf (retrieved November 28, 2011).

93. Robert Perkinson, *Texas Tough: The Rise of America's Prison Empire* (New York: Metropolitan Books, 2010), 16, 19.

94. Pew Center on the States, "One in 31: Behind Bars in America 2008" (Washington, DC: Pew Center on the States, 2009), 7.

95. The Sentencing Project, "Total Corrections Population," interactive maps for Oregon and Texas, http://www.sentencingproject.org/map/map.cfm#map (retrieved February 9, 2014).

96. Stephen M. Lilienthal, "Oregon: The 'Texas Model' Under Fire," corrections.com, September 16, 2013, http://www.corrections.com/news/article/34046-oregon-the-texas-model -under-fire (retrieved February 9, 2014).

97. Mike Ward, "Officials: Two Private Prisons to Close," *Austin American-Statesman*, June 11, 2013, http://www.statesman.com/news/news/officials-two-private-prisons-to-close /nYH3w/ (retrieved October 4, 2013).

98. National Institute of Corrections, "Texas: Overview of Correctional System; Annual Cost Per Inmate, 2008," n.d., http://nicic.gov/StateStats/ Annual Cost per Inmate (retrieved November 12, 2011).

99. Perkinson, *Texas Tough*, 4.

100. Terri Langford, "Force Against Texas Inmates on The Rise," *Texas Tribune*, April 3, 2014, https://www.texastribune.org/2014/04/03/force-against-texas-inmates-rise/ (retrieved May 16, 2014).

101. State-by-state comparisons of the use of administrative segregation are difficult because of the lack of complete and public information. Also, there is no standard definition of what counts as administrative segregation. Some states have been reducing their official supermax populations by double-celling and triple-celling people who were formerly held in solitary confinement—but still keeping these inmates locked down nearly round the clock. The main difference now is that they have a cellie or two. Eric Dexheimer, "Do Prisons Need So Many Inmates in Maximum Custody?," *Austin American-Statesman*, May 25, 2013, http://www.mystatesman.com/news/news/do-prisons-need-so-many-inmates -in-maximum-custody/nX3xN/ (retrieved October 4, 2013).

102. Dexheimer, "Do Prisons Need So Many Inmates in Maximum Custody?"; and Eric Dexheimer, "Texas Suicide Rate High Among Inmates in Isolation," *Austin American-Statesman*, May 25, 2013, http://www.mystatesman.com/news/news/crime-law/texas-prison -suicide-rate-high-among-inmates-in-is/nX3xK/ (retrieved October 4, 2013).

103. See, for example, Fabelo, "Texas Justice Reinvestment," 115.

104. Texans Care for Children, "A Session Recap on the Bottom Line: Children and the 82nd Texas Legislature" (Austin: Texans Care for Children, 2011), 7–10; Mike Ward, "Could Cuts to Prison Health Care Cost Texans More in the Long Run?," *Austin American-Statesman*, January 21, 2011, http://www.statesman.com/news/texas-politics/could-cuts-to-prison-health -care-cost-texans-1201681.html?viewAsSinglePage=true (retrieved February 9, 2011).

105. Grits for Breakfast, "TDCJ 'Going California'?: Prison Health Care Under-funded by Nine Figures," May 30, 2011, http://gritsforbreakfast.blogspot.com/2011/05/tdcj-going -california-prison-health.html (retrieved November 11, 2011).

106. Manny Fernandez, "In Bid to Cut Costs at Some Texas Prisons, Lunch Will Not Be Served on Weekends," *New York Times*, October 21, 2011, A22.

107. Bob Moser, "God Help Us: Will Rick Perry's Blend of Christian-Right, Small-Government, and Pro-Corporate Fervor Land Him in the White House?," *American Prospect*, December 2011, 18. In July 2012, Perry toured a new seminary program for offenders inside a Houston-area lockup. This was his first visit to a state prison during his nearly 12 years in office. Mike Ward, "Perry Visits Prison Seminary Program Near Houston," *Austin American-Statesman*, July 3, 2012, http://www.statesman.com/news/news/state-regional -govt-politics/perry-visits-prison-seminary-program-near-housto-1/nRpwN/ (retrieved June 21, 2013).

108. Moser, "God Help Us," 18.

109. Ross Ramsey, Emily Ramshaw, and Morgan Smith, "Texas Legislature Passes $15 Billion in Cuts," *Texas Tribune*, May 28, 2011, http://www.texastribune.org/texas-taxes/budget /liveblog-texas-legislature-passes-15-billion/ (retrieved November 11, 2011); Bob Moser, "Texas' Wild Tea Party," *Nation*, May 11, 2011; Texas Legislature, Legislative Budget Board, 82nd session, Summary of Conference Committee Report on House Bill 1 for the 2012–13 Biennium, May 2011, 4; Grits for Breakfast, "Texas Budget Ditches 'Smart on Crime' Approach, Reverting to Old Priorities," May 29, 2011, http://gritsforbreakfast .blogspot.com/2011/05/texas-budget-ditches-smart-on-crime.html (retrieved November 11, 2011); Paul J. Weber, "Texas School Budget Cuts, Teacher Layoffs Add to Unemployment," *Huffington Post*, September 29, 2011, http://www.huffingtonpost.com/2011/09/29

/shrinking-texas-school-pa_0_n_986909.html (retrieved November 11, 2011); Texas Early Childhood Education Coalition, "82nd Regular Legislative Session/June Special Session: Post Session Analysis," June 2011, http://www.tecec.org/files/82nd%20Texas%20Legislature%20Post%20Session%20Analysis%20June%202011.pdf (retrieved November 14, 2011); Kaiser Family Foundation, "State Mental Health Agency (SMHA), Per Capita Mental Health Services Expenditures, FY 2010," n.d., http://kff.org/other/state-indicator/smha-expenditures-per-capita/ (retrieved February 9, 2014).

110. Caitlin Dunklee, Travis Leete, and Jorge Antonio Renaud, "Effective Approaches to Drug Crimes in Texas: Strategies to Reduce Crime, Save Money, and Treat Addiction" (Austin: Texas Criminal Justice Coalition, January 2013), 9.

111. Grits for Breakfast, "Texas' Decision to Reject Medicaid Expansion Quickens Trend Toward Using Justice System as Mental Health Substitute," July 19, 2012, http://gritsforbreakfast.blogspot.com/2012/07/texas-decision-to-reject-medicaid.html (retrieved May 17, 2013).

112. Jordan Smith, "Rick Perry's War on Women," *Nation*, December 2011, 18–21.

113. Pam Bulluck and Emily Ramshaw, "Women in Texas Losing Options for Health Care in Abortion Fight," *New York Times*, March 8, 2012, A1.

114. See p. 334, n. 104 and n. 109.

115. These eight states are Alabama, Florida, Georgia, Louisiana, Mississippi, Oklahoma, South Carolina, and Texas. The two exceptions are Delaware and Arizona. Calculated from Kaiser Family Foundation, "Status of State Action on the Medicaid Expansion Decision, as of December 11, 2013," http://kff.org/health-reform/state-indicator/state-activity-around-expanding-medicaid-under-the-affordable-care-act/ (retrieved January 14, 2014); and Pew Center on the States, "One in 31: Behind Bars in America 2008," 34.

116. This estimate comes from the state's Health and Human Services Commission. Perry also likened expanding Medicaid to "adding a thousand people to the Titanic." See Jay Hancock, "Businesses Will Push Perry to Rethink Medicaid Expansion," Kaiser Health News, June 18, 2012, http://www.kaiserhealthnews.org/Stories/2012/July/18/Texas-Medicaid-expansion-business.aspx (retrieved May 16, 2013). See also William Bergstrom, "Rick Perry on Supreme Court Decision: 'Stomach Punch' to Economy," *Politico*, June 28, 2012, http://www.politico.com/news/stories/0612/77978.html (retrieved May 15, 2013).

117. The inmate would be eligible if he or she remained in that institution for longer than 24 hours and if that institution was open to the general public. National Association of Counties, Community Services Division, "County Jails and the Affordable Care Act," n.d., http://www.naco.org/research/pubs/Documents/Health,%20Human%20Services%20and%20Justice/Community%20Services%20Docs/WebVersion_PWFIssueBrief.pdf (retrieved May 16, 2013), 3; Ellen Rose Whelan-Wuest, "Medicaid Coverage for Inmates and Reentering Populations in North Carolina," mimeo, April 12, 2012, http://dukespace.lib.duke.edu/dspace/bitstream/handle/10161/5174/Whelan-Wuest_MastersProject_FinalDraft.pdf?sequence=1 (retrieved May 16, 2013), ii.

118. That has begun to change as more state and county correctional systems have developed programs and expertise to take greater advantage of the rule change. The State Health Care Spending Project, "Managing Prison Health Care Spending," October 2013, http://www.pewstates.org/uploadedFiles/PCS_Assets/2013/SHCS_Pew-Managing_Prison_Health_Care_Spending_Report.pdf (retrieved January 17, 2014), 17–18.

119. American Correctional Association, Coalition of Correctional Heath Authorities, "Key Elements of the Affordable Care Act: Interface with Correctional Settings and

Inmate Health Care," February 2012, http://www.nga.org/files/live/sites/NGA/files/pdf/ACA
CCHAAffordableCareActMonograph.pdf (retrieved May 17, 2013), 2.

120. In recent years, jail admissions have averaged about 12–13 million per year. Calculated from Todd D. Minton, "Jail Inmates at Midyear 2011—Statistical Tables," Bureau of Justice Statistics, April 2012, http://www.bjs.gov/content/pub/pdf/jim11st.pdf (retrieved May 21, 2014), 3.

121. Minton, "Jail Inmates at Midyear 2011," 1.

122. These include asthma, hypertension, tuberculosis, diabetes, hepatitis, and HIV/AIDS. The lack of access to adequate health care on the outside to treat these serious afflictions helps explain the extraordinarily high mortality rate among released prisoners. Binswanger et al., "Release from Prison."

123. By some estimates, one-third of prisoners released annually would be eligible for Medicaid and another quarter would qualify for subsidized health coverage through the exchanges. The numbers could be considerably higher. New York City, which expanded Medicaid eligibility to childless adults prior to the full implementation of the PPACA, reported that 80 percent of the people in its jails are either enrolled or eligible to be enrolled in Medicaid. Andrea A. Bainbridge, "The Affordable Care Act and Criminal Justice: Intersections and Implications," U.S. DOJ, Bureau of Justice Assistance, July 2012, https://www.bja.gov/Publications/ACA-CJ_WhitePaper.pdf (retrieved May 17, 2013), 6.

124. Binswanger et al., "Release from Prison."

125. Katti Gray, "The Prison Health Care Dilemma," *Crime Report*, August 2, 2012, http://www.thecrimereport.org/news/inside-criminal-justice/2012–08-the-prison-health-care-dilemma (retrieved May 18, 2013).

126. Tom Howell, Jr., "House GOP Wants to Know If Ex-Prisoners Benefit from Medicaid Expansion," *Washington Times*, October 9, 2013, http://www.washingtontimes.com/news/2013/oct/9/house-gop-wants-know-if-ex-prisoners-benefit-medic/ (retrieved February 10, 2014).

127. Perkinson, *Texas Tough*.

Chapter Six
Is Mass Incarceration the "New Jim Crow"?

1. See, for example, Keith Lawrence, "Overview," in Keith O. Lawrence, ed., *Race, Crime, and Punishment: Breaking the Connection in America* (Washington, DC: Aspen Institute, 2011), and some of the other essays in that volume.

2. Like Jim Crow and slavery, it functions "as a tightly networked system of laws, policies, customs, and institutions" that operate together to "ensure the subordinate status of a group defined largely by race," according to Michelle Alexander. See *The New Jim Crow: Mass Incarceration in the Age of Colorblindness* (New York: New Press, 2010), 13, 192, and 224. Likewise, Debra E. McDowell, Claudrena N. Harold, and Juan Battle note in the introduction to their edited volume that "the link between crime and punishment has become emphatically racialized." See *The Punitive Turn: New Approaches to Race and Incarceration* (Charlottesville: University of Virginia Press, 2013), 3.

3. See, for example, Judge Ricardo H. Hinojosa, supplemental statement, in Jeremy Travis, Bruce Western and Steve Redburn, eds., *The Growth of Incarceration in the United States: Exploring Causes and Consequences* (Washington, DC: National Academies Press, 2014), 419–20.

4. Adolph Reed, Jr., and Merlin Chowkwanyun, "Race, Class, Crisis: The Discourse of Racial Disparity and Its Analytical Discontents," in Leo Panitch, Gregory Albo, and Vivek Chibber, eds., *Socialist Register 2012: The Crisis and the Left* (New York: Monthly Review Press, 2011), 150.

5. Reed and Chowkwanyun, "Race, Class, Crisis," 150. See also Adolph Reed, Jr., "The 'Color Line' Then and Now: The Souls of Black Folk and the Changing Context of Black American Politics," in Adolph Reed, Jr., and Kenneth W. Warren, eds., *Renewing Black Intellectual History: The Ideological and Material Foundations of African American Thought* (Boulder, CO: Paradigm, 2010), 275.

6. Reed and Chowkwanyun, "Race, Class, Crisis," 151.

7. This is especially the case in research on racial disparities in the criminal justice system. Robert D. Crutchfield, April Fernandes, and Jorge Martinez, "Racial and Ethnic Disparity and Criminal Justice: How Much Is Too Much?," *Journal of Criminal Law & Criminology* 100.3 (2010), 910.

8. Reed, Jr., "The 'Color Line' Then and Now," 271.

9. Stephen Pevar of the ACLU said "he has sued at least 100 jails and prisons, but that none came close to the level of violence" at the privately run Idaho Correctional Center. CCA has settled several lawsuits filed on behalf of inmates of the facility. In September 2013, a federal judge ruled that CCA was in contempt for violating the terms of the class-action agreement. Associated Press, "ACLU Sues over Idaho Prison So Violent It's Called 'Gladiator School' by Inmates," March 11, 2010, OregonLive.com, http://www.oregonlive.com/news/index.ssf/2010/03/aclu_sues_over_idaho_prison_so.html (retrieved October 6, 2011); Rebecca Boone, "Idaho Inmates Settle Lawsuit over Prison Violence," Associated Press, September 20, 2011, http://www.utsandiego.com/news/2011/sep/20/idaho-inmates-settle-lawsuit-over-prison-violence/ (retrieved May 7, 2013); Rebecca Boone, "Judge: CCA in Contempt for Prison Understaffing," Associated Press, September 13, 2013, http://bigstory.ap.org/article/judge-cca-contempt-prison-understaffing (retrieved January 25, 2014).

10. In a major turnaround in early 2011, Maine's new director of corrections cut the state's supermax population by more than half, suspended the brutal "cell extractions," and relaxed some other conditions of confinement in supermax cells. Lance Tapley, "Reform Comes to the Supermax," *Phoenix*, May 25, 2011, http://portland.thephoenix.com/news/121171-reform-comes-to-the-supermax/ (retrieved June 3, 2011); Jean Casella and James Ridgeway, "In States That 'Reduce' Their Use of Solitary Confinement, Suffering Continues for Those Left Behind," Solitary Watch, November 13, 2013, http://solitarywatch.com/2013/11/13/states-reduced-use-solitary-confinement-suffering-continues-left-behind/ (retrieved January 25, 2014).

11. That said, Mississippi still has one of the highest incarceration rates in the country, and the conditions for inmates languishing in supermax cells in Mississippi and Maine remain grim. Terry A. Kupers et al., "Beyond Supermax Administrative Segregation: Mississippi's Experience Rethinking Prison Classification and Creating Alternative Mental Health Programs," *Criminal Justice and Behavior* 36.10 (2009): 1037–50; Mississippi Department of Corrections, "Fact Sheet," October 1, 2011, http://www.mdoc.state.ms.us/Research%20and%20Statistics/MonthlyFactSheets/2011MFS/October%202011%20Fact%20Sheet.pdf (retrieved October 5, 2011).

12. Christopher Muller, "Northward Migration and the Rise of Racial Disparity in American Incarceration, 1880–1950," *American Journal of Sociology* 118.2 (2012), 282.

13. Detailed data on Latino incarceration and migration rates for this period are not available. However, Latinos likely composed well below 1 percent of the total population

of the northern Great Migration states. Muller, "Northward Migration," 287, figs. 1 and 286, n. 2.

14. These figures are based on people held in state and federal prisons. They do not include the jail population. Travis, Western, and Redburn, eds., *The Growth of Incarceration in the United States*, 58, table 2.2.

15. Muller, "Northward Migration."

16. These figures are based on people held in both local jails and federal and state prisons. They do not include people held in special immigration detention facilities, who are overwhelmingly Latino. Data on the racial and ethnic disparities in the U.S. incarceration rate are more difficult to come by since 2006, when the Bureau of Justice Statistics stopped reporting the total combined jail and prison incarceration rates and the combined prison-jail incarceration rates broken down by ethnicity and race in its standard publications. My calculations are based on Heather C. West, "Prison Inmates at Midyear 2009—Statistical Tables," Bureau of Justice Statistics, June 2010, http://www.bjs.gov/content/pub/pdf/pim09st .pdf (retrieved February 11, 2014), 19, tables 16 and 21, table 18; U.S. Census Bureau, "Vintage 2009: National Tables, Annual Population Estimates," http://www.census.gov /popest/data/state/totals/2009/tables/NST-EST2009-01.csv (retrieved February 14, 2014).

17. Bruce Western, *Punishment and Inequality in America* (New York: Russell Sage Foundation, 2006), 16.

18. The comparable figures for black, Hispanic, and white females are 1 in 18, 1 in 45, and 1 in 110. These figures would be even more alarming if they included the likelihood of spending time in jail, not just prison. Thomas P. Bonczar, "Prevalence of Imprisonment in the U.S. Population, 1974–2001," Bureau of Justice Statistics Special Report, 2003, 1.

19. The rate in South Africa in the early 1990s was 681 per 100,000. Fox Butterfield, "U.S. Expands Its Lead in the Rate of Imprisonment," *New York Times*, February 11, 1992, A16.

20. Roy Walmsley, "World Prison Population List," 9th ed. (London: King's College, International Centre for Prison Studies, May 2011), http://www.kcl.ac.uk/depsta/law/research /icps/downloads/wppl-8th_41.pdf (retrieved February 11, 2014).

21. For black and white high school dropouts with incomes below $25,000 a year, the figures were about 60 percent and 20 percent respectively. Lawrence D. Bobo and Victor Thompson, "Racialized Mass Incarceration: Poverty, Prejudice, and Punishment," in Hazel R. Markus and Paula M. L. Moya, eds., *Doing Race: 21 Essays for the 21st Century* (New York: W.W. Norton, 2010), 350.

22. Marc Mauer and Ryan S. King, "Uneven Justice: State Rates of Incarceration by Race and Ethnicity" (Washington, DC: The Sentencing Project, July 2007), 6, table 2.

23. Walmsley, "World Prison Population List," 5. Rwanda is technically second, but its prison population includes thousands of people sentenced or awaiting trial in connection with the 1994 genocide.

24. Calculated from Bruce Western and Becky Pettit, "Incarceration and Social Inequality," *Daedalus* 139.3 (2010), 11, table 1.

25. Western, *Punishment and Inequality*, 17. But the risk of going to prison has been rising at a faster rate for poor whites than for poor blacks and Latinos. For black and Latino male high school dropouts born in the late 1970s, the risk was about five times higher than the risk for their counterparts born in the late 1940s; for white high school dropouts, it rose more than sevenfold. Calculated from Western and Pettit, "Incarceration and Social Inequality," 11, table 1.

26. Western and Pettit, "Incarceration and Social Inequality," 11, table 1.

27. Calculated from Bonczar, "Prevalence of Imprisonment in the U.S. Population," 1.

28. About 9 percent of all inmates in U.S. prisons and jails are women. E. Ann Carson and Daniela Golinelli, "Prisoners in 2012—Advance Counts," *Bureau of Justice Statistics Bulletin*, July 2013, 7, table 6; Todd D. Minton, "Jail Inmates at Midyear—Statistical Tables," Bureau of Justice Statistics, Statistical Tables, May 2013, 5, table 2; Meda Chesney-Lind, "Imprisoning Women: The Unintended Victims of Mass Imprisonment," in Marc Mauer and Meda Chesney-Lind., eds., *Invisible Punishment: The Collateral Consequences of Mass Imprisonment* (New York: New Press, 2004), 80–81.

29. Stephanie Bush-Baskette, *Misguided Justice: The War on Drugs and the Incarceration of Black Women* (New York: iUNiverse, Inc., 2010), 24; Marne L. Lenox, "Neutralizing the Gendered Collateral Consequences of the War on Drugs," *N.Y.U. Law Review* 86.1 (2011): 280–315.

30. This includes women incarcerated in prisons and jails. See figure 1.1, p. 5. Between 2000 and 2009, the imprisonment rate for black women in state and federal prisons fell by about one-third (from 205 per 100,000 to 142 per 100,000), and the black-white disparities in imprisonment for women fell from about 6:1 to 3:1. Marc Mauer, "The Changing Racial Dynamics of Women's Incarceration" (Washington, DC: The Sentencing Project, February 2013), 2, 8.

31. Between 2000 and 2009, the number of white women sentenced for drug, property, and violent crimes increased substantially. The number of black women sentenced for property and drug crimes, but not violent offenses, fell substantially. Mauer, "The Changing Racial Dynamics of Women's Incarceration," 13, table 4.

32. About three-quarters of Ohio's female prisoners are white. Ohio Department of Rehabilitation and Corrections, "2013 Annual Report," n.d., http://www.drc.ohio.gov/web /reports/Annual/Annual%20Report%202013.pdf (retrieved January 17, 2014), 22; John Caniglia, "White Women Sent to Ohio Prisons in Record Numbers, Reports Say," August 15, 2013, http://www.cleveland.com/metro/index.ssf/2013/08/white_women_sent_to_ohio _priso.html (retrieved January 17, 2014).

33. Calculated from West, "Prison Inmates at Midyear 2009," 21, table 18.

34. These include rising rates of uninsurance, chronic illness, poverty, and unemployment, and an exceptional five-year drop in life expectancy between 1990 and 2008 for white women who were high school dropouts. The life expectancy rate also fell for white male high school dropouts, but not for blacks and Hispanics of either sex. S. Jay Olshansky et al., "Differences in Life Expectancy Due to Race and Educational Differences Are Widening, and Many May Not Catch Up," *Health Affairs* 31.8 (2012), 1807, exhibit 2.

35. "Sentencing in America is a national scandal," Kennedy charged. "Every day our system of sentencing breeds massive injustice. Judges are free to roam at will, dispensing ad hoc justice in ways that defy both reason and fairness." Edward M. Kennedy, "Introduction to Symposium on Sentencing," *Hofstra Law Review*, 7.1–9 (1978): 1–3. See also Marvin E. Frankel, *Criminal Sentences: Law Without Order* (New York: Hill and Wang, 1973); American Friends Service Committee, *Struggle for Justice* (New York: Hill and Wang, 1971), 8.

36. For other examples of criticism of the vast discretionary powers of judges and other administrators of the penal system, much of it written by sympathetic liberals, see Erik Olin Wright, ed., *The Politics of Punishment* (New York: Harper and Row, 1973); Alvin J. Bronstein, "Reform Without Change: The Future of Prisoners' Rights," *Civil Liberties Review* 4.3 (September/October 1977), 30; Kenneth Culp Davis, *Discretionary Justice: A*

Preliminary Inquiry (Baton Rouge: Louisiana State University Press, 1969); Andrew von Hirsch, *Doing Justice: The Choice of Punishments: Report of the Committee for the Study of Incarceration* (New York: Hill and Wang, 1976); Twentieth Century Fund, *Fair and Certain Punishment: Report of the Twentieth Century Fund Task Force on Criminal Sentencing* (New York: McGraw-Hill, 1976).

37. James Q. Whitman, *Harsh Justice: Criminal Punishment and the Widening Divide between America and Europe* (New York: Oxford University Press, 2003).

38. Senator Edward M. Kennedy (D-MA) co-sponsored with Senator Strom Thurmond (R-SC) a series of federal sentencing reform bills that led to the establishment of the U.S. Sentencing Commission under the 1984 Sentencing Reform Act. The commission's guidelines, which went into effect in 1987, carried "a heavy presumption of imprisonment for most offenders" and gave "little regard for any mitigating circumstances involved in an offense." See Marc Mauer, *Race to Incarcerate* (New York: New Press), 58–59. See also Kate Stith and Steve Y. Koh, "The Politics of Sentencing Reform: The Legislative History of the Federal Sentencing Guidelines," *Wake Forest Law Review* 28 (1993): 223–90; Kate Stith and José A. Cabranes, *Fear of Judging: Sentencing Guidelines in the Federal Courts* (Chicago: University of Chicago Press, 1998).

39. Alfred Blumstein, Jacqueline Cohen, Susan E. Martin, and Michael H. Tonry, eds., *Research on Sentencing: The Search for Reform*, v. 1 (Washington, DC: National Academies Press, 1983), 109.

40. Eric P. Baumer, "Reassessing and Redirecting Research on Race and Sentencing," *Justice Quarterly* 30.2 (2013), 232. See also Richard S. Frase, "Research on Race and Sentencing: Goals, Methods, and Topics," *Justice Quarterly*, 30.2 (2013): 262–69.

41. For a brief overview of this research, see Baumer, "Reassessing and Redirecting Research." See also Cassia C. Spohn, "Thirty Years of Sentencing Reform: The Quest for a Racially Neutral Sentencing Process," in U.S. National Institute of Justice, ed., *Criminal Justice 2000*, v. 3 (Washington, DC: U.S. National Institute of Justice, 2000): 427–501.

42. Baumer, "Reassessing and Redirecting Research," 18; Spohn, "Thirty Years of Sentencing Reform," 460–62.

43. For example, if whites are differentially sorted out prior to sentencing, and then a sentencing study reports no racial difference, we cannot know if there really is no difference between comparable cases, or if minority defendants, of varying types, are being sentenced similarly compared to only the worst of white defendants. Crutchfield, Fernandes, and Martinez, "Racial and Ethnic Disparity and Criminal Justice," 929.

44. David C. Baldus, Charles Pulaski, and George Woodworth, "Comparative Review of Death Sentences: An Empirical Study of the Georgia Experience," *Journal of Criminal Law & Criminology* 74.3 (1983): 661–753.

45. Scott Turow, *Ultimate Punishment: A Lawyer's Reflections on Dealing with the Death Penalty* (New York: Farrar, Straus and Giroux, 2003), 72–73.

46. Spohn, "Thirty Years of Sentencing Reform," 469.

47. Spohn, "Thirty Years of Sentencing Reform," 475–76.

48. Howard Schuman, Charlotte Steeh, Lawrence Bobo, and Maria Krysan, *Racial Attitudes in America* (Cambridge, MA: Harvard University Press, 1997); Tali Mendelberg, *The Race Card: Campaign Strategy, Implicit Messages, and the Norm of Equality* (Princeton, NJ: Princeton University Press, 2001); Larry Bobo, "Racial Attitudes and Relations at the Close of the Twentieth Century," in Neil J. Smelser, William J. Wilson, and Faith Mitchell. eds.,

America Becoming: Racial Trends and Their Consequences, v. 1 (Washington, DC: National Academies Press, 2001).

49. Taeku Lee, "Polling Prejudice," *American Prospect*, March 9, 2011, http://prospect .org/article/polling-prejudice (retrieved July 16, 2013).

50. See, for example, Associated Press, "AP Poll: U.S. Majority Have Prejudice Against Blacks," *USA Today*, October 27, 2012, http://www.usatoday.com/story/news/politics/2012 /10/27/poll-black-prejudice-america/1662067/ (retrieved July 16, 2013). See also Donald R. Kinder and Lynn Sanders, *Divided by Color: Racial Politics and Democratic Ideals* (Chicago: University of Chicago Press, 1996).

51. Michael C. Dawson, *Not in Our Lifetimes: The Future of Black Politics* (Chicago: University of Chicago Press, 2011), 12–13, 148.

52. See, for example, Jennifer L. Hochschild and Vesla Weaver, "The Skin Color Paradox and the American Racial Order," *Social Forces* 86.2 (2007): 643–70. For a good overview of the research findings on the impact of skin color and facial features on criminal sanctions, see Michael Tonry, *Punishing Race: A Continuing American Dilemma* (New York: Oxford University Press, 2011), 77–97.

53. For good, succinct overviews of this research, see Bobo and Thompson, "Racialized Mass Incarceration," 336–46. For a more comprehensive overview, see James D. Unnever, "Race, Crime, and Public Opinion," in Sandra M. Bucerius and Michael Tonry, eds., *The Oxford Handbook of Ethnicity, Crime, and Immigration* (New York: Oxford University Press, 2014): 70–106; and Mark Peffley and Jon Hurwitz, *Justice in America: The Separate Realities of Blacks and Whites* (New York: Cambridge University Press, 2010).

54. James D. Unnever, Francis T. Cullen, and Cheryl Lero Jonson, "Race, Racism, and Support for Capital Punishment," in Michael Tonry, ed., *Crime and Justice: A Review of Research*, v. 37 (Chicago: University of Chicago Press, 2008): 45–96; Larry D. Bobo and Devon Johnson, "A Taste for Punishment: Black and White Americans' Views on the Death Penalty and the War on Drugs," *Du Bois Review* 1.1 (2004): 151–80.

55. Peffley and Hurwitz, *Justice in America*; Bobo and Johnson, "A Taste for Punishment."

56. Spohn, "Thirty Years of Sentencing Reform," 481.

57. Alfred Blumstein, "On the Racial Disproportionality of the United States' Prison Populations," *Journal of Criminal Law and Criminology* 73.3 (1982), 1267. A follow-up study by Patrick Langan addressed some of the shortcomings of Blumstein's original study and arrived at a comparable figure of 80 percent. "Racism on Trial: New Evidence to Explain the Racial Composition of Prisons in the United States," *Journal of Criminal Law and Criminology* 76.3 (1985), 679.

58. Blumstein, "On the Racial Disproportionality of the United States' Prison Populations," 1289, 1268. Emphasis in the original.

59. Blumstein, "On the Racial Disproportionality of the United States' Prison Populations," 1280.

60. Michael Tonry and Matthew Melewski, "The Malign Effects of Drug and Crime Control on Black Americans," in Michael Tonry, ed., *Crime and Justice: A Review of Research*, v. 37 (Chicago: University of Chicago, 2008), 5.

61. Tonry and Melewski, "The Malign Effects of Drug and Crime Control," 18 and 2, table 17.

62. Tonry and Melewski, "The Malign Effects of Drug and Crime Control," 23–30.

63. Tonry, *Punishing Race*, 29.

64. Tonry, *Punishing Race*, 171.

65. Alfred Blumstein, "Racial Disproportionality of U.S. Prison Populations Revisited," *University of Colorado Law Review* 64 (1993): 743–60.

66. For an excellent overview of the survey research data on illegal drug use and drug sales, see Tonry, *Punishing Race*, 59–70.

67. Marc Mauer, "The Changing Racial Dynamics of the War on Drugs" (Washington, DC: The Sentencing Project, April 2009), 4.

68. Tonry, *Punishing Race*, 71.

69. This probably understates the black-white disparity in marijuana arrests because official national arrest statistics do not identify Latinos as a distinct group, thus conflating white and Latino arrests. Indeed, many of the states with the lowest disparities in black-white marijuana arrests are among the states with the highest Latino populations. In 2013, the FBI announced it would begin collecting data on Latino arrests for its annual Uniform Crime Report. In 1987, it had abandoned efforts to collect crime data by ethnicity. Roque Planas, "FBI to Track Latino Arrests for Uniform Crime Report, *Huffington Post*, June 25, 2013, http://www.huffingtonpost.com/2013/06/25/fbi-latino-arrests_n_3492521.html (retrieved May 17, 2014); ACLU, "The War on Marijuana in Black and White: Billions of Dollars Wasted on Racially Biased Arrests" (New York: ACLU, June 2013), 4, 32.

70. Under the Fair Sentencing Act of 2010, Congress reduced the disparity from 100:1 to 18:1.

71. On patterns of alcohol and illicit drug use by race, see Tonry, *Punishing Race*, 59–60, table 3.1.

72. USSC, "Special Report to the Congress: Cocaine and Federal Sentencing Policy," April 1997, http://www.ussc.gov/Legislative_and_Public_Affairs/Congressional_Testimony _and_Reports/Drug_Topics/19970429_RtC_Cocaine_Sentencing_Policy.PDF (retrieved February 11, 2014).

73. Alec Karakatsanis, "Why *US v Blewett* Is the Obama Justice Department's Greatest Shame," *Guardian*, July 23, 2013, http://www.theguardian.com/commentisfree/2013 /jul/23/us-v-blewett-obama-justice-department-shame (retrieved December 31, 2013).

74. Alexander, *The New Jim Crow*, 106–20, 128–36. See also Doris Marie Provine, *Unequal Under the Law: Racism in the War on Drugs* (Chicago: University of Chicago Press, 2007), 140–61.

75. Alexander, *The New Jim Crow*, 60–71.

76. Alexander, *The New Jim Crow*, 60.

77. Roadside body cavity searches conducted in full view of passing motorists are standard policy among state troopers in Texas, according to lawyers and civil rights activists. Two women sued the state in 2013 because a Texas state trooper subjected them to such a search after allegedly smelling marijuana and searching their car but finding none. Deborah Hasting, "Texas State Troopers Caught on Camera Probing Women's Privates Aren't Isolated Incidents: Lawyers," *New York Daily News*, August 2, 2013, http://www.nydailynews .com/news/national/troopers-texas-probe-genitals-women-traffic-stops-article-1.1414668 (retrieved September 27, 2013); "Roadside Body Cavity Search: Angel and Ashley Dobbs Sue Texas State Troopers for Body Search," video, *Huffington Post*, December 19, 2012, http:// www.huffingtonpost.com/2012/12/19/roadside-body-cavity-search-texas-women-sue -state-troopers-for-humiliating-body-search_n_2333302.html (retrieved September 27, 2013).

78. Alexander, *The New Jim Crow*, 99.

79. John F. Pfaff, "The Empirics of Prison Growth: A Critical Review and Path Forward," *Criminology* 98.2 (2008), 559.

80. Franklin E. Zimring, "Imprisonment Rates and the New Politics of Criminal Punishment," *Punishment & Society* 3.1 (2001): 161–66.

81. Franklin E. Zimring and Gordon Hawkins, *Incapacitation: Penal Confinement and the Restraint of Crime* (New York: Oxford University Press, 1995), ch. 5.

82. Zimring, "Imprisonment Rates," 162.

83. William J. Stuntz, *The Collapse of American Criminal Justice* (Cambridge, MA: Belknap Press of Harvard University Press, 2011), 47.

84. Remarks by Rep. Robert C. "Bobby" Scott (D-VA), University of Pennsylvania Law Review Symposium, "Sentencing Law: Rhetoric and Reality," October 28, 2011.

85. Rick Lyman, "Pivotal Point Is Seen as More States Consider Legalizing Marijuana," *New York Times*, February 27, 2014, A1.

86. Heather C. West and William J. Sabol, "Prisoners in 2009," *Bureau of Justice Statistics Bulletin*, December 2010, 7, table 7.

87. Between 2000 and 2009, white arrests for drug offenses increased by 2 percent while black arrests for drugs fell by nearly 12 percent. FBI Uniform Crime Reports cited in Mauer, "The Changing Racial Dynamics," 11, table 2.

88. Human Rights Watch, "Decades of Disparity: Drug Arrests and Race in the United States" (New York: Human Rights Watch, March 2009), 5, table 1.

89. After peaking at 5.5:1 in 1989 and again in 1991, the ratio of black to white arrests for drug offenses began to decline steadily. By 2007, it was 3.6:1 or slightly above the 2.9:1 ratio in 1980. Human Rights Watch, "Decades of Disparity," 7, table 2.

90. Calculated from Mauer, "The Changing Racial Dynamics of the War on Drugs," 4, table 1; West and Sabol, "Prisoners in 2009," 29–30, appendix tables 16a, 16b, and 16c. The number of Hispanic drug offenders in state prison peaked in 2002. The number of white drug offenders in state prison peaked in 2005 at 72,300, which was 43 percent higher than in 1999.

91. Calculated from West and Sabol, "Prisoners in 2009," 30, appendix table 16c. In 1980, just before the war on drugs really took off, the figure was 6 percent. Todd R. Clear and James Austin, "Reducing Mass Incarceration: Implications of the Iron Law of Prison Populations," *Harvard Law & Policy Review* 3.2 (2009), 317.

92. West and Sabol, "Prisoners in 2009," 33, appendix table 18.

93. E. Ann Carson, "Prisoners in 2011," *Bureau of Justice Statistics Bulletin*, December 2012, 1.

94. Mauer, "The Changing Racial Dynamics of the War on Drugs," 6, table 2.

95. Human Rights Watch, "Decades of Disparity," 9.

96. Human Rights Watch, "Decades of Disparity," 11, table 4.

97. ACLU, "The War on Marijuana," 32; Human Rights Watch, "Decades of Disparity," 11, table 4.

98. Human Rights Watch, "Decades of Disparity," 11, table 4.

99. Naomi Murakawa, "Toothless: The Methamphetamine 'Epidemic,' 'Meth Mouth,' and the Racial Construction of Drug Scares," *Du Bois Review* 8.1 (2011), 220.

100. Murakawa, "Toothless," 220.

101. Mauer, "The Changing Racial Dynamics of the War on Drugs," 17.

102. Mauer, "The Changing Racial Dynamics of the War on Drugs," 12–15.

103. Ryan S. King, "Disparity by Geography: The War on Drugs in America's Cities" (Washington, DC: The Sentencing Project, May 2008), 2.

104. There are a few important caveats here. The war on drugs will continue to reverberate through the criminal justice system even if a ceasefire is declared. Although a drug conviction per se may not directly result in a prison sentence, it can count as a prior felony,

thus resulting in longer sentences for felons convicted of non-drug crimes. Furthermore, the war on drugs has had all kinds of spillover effects, from the militarization of policing to the widespread use of informants to the deterioration of Fourth Amendment constitutional protections. Finally, a failed drug test is a primary reason why people on parole are sent back to prison. Rodney Balko, *Rise of the Warrior Cop: The Militarization of America's Police Forces* (New York: Public Affairs, 2013); Peter B. Kraska, ed., *Militarizing the American Criminal Justice System: The Changing Roles of the Armed Forces and Police* (Boston: Northeastern University Press, 2001); Alexander, *The New Jim Crow*.

105. Gary Kleck, "Racial Discrimination in Sentencing: A Critical Evaluation of the Evidence with Additional Evidence on the Death Penalty," *American Sociological Review* 46.6 (1981), 799, quoted in David C. Baldus, "Racial Discrimination in Capital and Non-Capital Sentencing with Special Reference to the Evidence in Murder and Rape Prosecutions," paper presented at the Symposium on Crime and Justice: The Past and Future of Empirical Sentencing Research, SUNY at Albany, School of Criminal Justice, September 23–24, 2010, 3.

106. Baldus, "Racial Discrimination in Capital and Non-Capital Sentencing," 10.

107. David C. Baldus et al., "Racial Discrimination and the Death Penalty in the Post-*Furman* Era: An Empirical and Legal Overview, With Recent Findings from Philadelphia," *Cornell Law Review* 83.6 (1998): 1643–1770.

108. Robert D. Crutchfield, George S. Bridges, and Susan R. Pitchford, "Analytical and Aggregation Biases in Analyses of Imprisonment: Reconciling Discrepancies in Studies of Racial Disparity," *Journal of Research in Crime & Delinquency* 31.2 (1994), 166, 170.

109. See, for example, Ojmarrh Mitchell, "A Meta-analysis of Race and Sentencing Research: Explaining the Inconsistencies," *Journal of Quantitative Criminology* 21.4 (2005): 439–66.

110. For an overview of the statistical and other technical shortcomings of many quantitative accounts of prison growth, see Pfaff, "The Empirics of Prison Growth."

111. Brian Forst and Shawn Bushway, "Discretion, Rule of Law, and Rationality," paper presented at Symposium on Crime and Justice, 23.

112. Rodney L. Engen, "Assessing Determinate and Presumptive Sentencing—Making Research Relevant," *Criminology & Public Policy* 8.2 (2009), 332–33.

113. *United States v. Booker* 543 U.S. 220, 245 (2005).

114. USSC, "Final Report on the Impact of *United States v. Booker* on Federal Sentencing," March 2006, http://www.ussc.gov/Legislative_and_Public_Affairs/Congressional_Testimony_and_Reports/Submissions/200603_Booker/Booker_Report.pdf (retrieved February 11, 2014); USSC, "Demographic Differences in Federal Sentencing Practices: An Update of the *Booker* Report's Multivariate Regression Analysis," March 2010, http://www.albany.edu/scj/documents/USSC_Multivariate_Regression_Analysis_Report_001.pdf (retrieved February 11, 2014).

115. In this updated report on sentencing post-*Booker*, the period examined is from December 2007 to September 2009. USSC, "Demographic Differences in Federal Sentencing Practices," 3.

116. On the increase in federal sentences post-*Booker*, see Frank O. Bowman III, "The Sounds of Silence: American Criminal Justice Policy in Election Year 2008," *Federal Sentencing Reporter* 20.5 (2008), 292.

117. Nancy Gertner, "Supporting Advisory Guidelines," *Harvard Law & Policy Review* 3.2 (2009), 262.

118. Gertner, "Supporting Advisory Guidelines," 269.

119. Gertner, "Supporting Advisory Guidelines," 266.

120. Kate Stith, "The Arc of the Pendulum: Judges, Prosecutors, and the Exercise of Discretion," *Yale Law Journal*, 117.7 (2008), 1451, 1453. See also Stith and Cabranes, *Fear of Judging*, 59–63.

121. Michael Tonry, "Racial Disparities Getting Worse in U.S. Prisons and Jails," in Michael Tonry and Kathleen Hatlestad, eds., *Sentencing Reform in Overcrowded Times: A Comparative Perspective* (New York: Oxford University Press, 1997), 217.

122. USSC, "Report to Congress: Mandatory Minimum Penalties in the Federal Criminal Justice System" (Washington, DC: GAO, October 2011), xxx.

123. USSC, "U.S. Sentencing Commission Votes to Reduce Drug Trafficking Sentences," press release, April 10, 2014, http://www.ussc.gov/sites/default/files/pdf/news/press-releases-and-news-advisories/press-releases/20140410_Press_Release.pdf (retrieved May 6, 2014); and Jerry Markon and Rachel Weiner, "Thousands of Felons Could Have Drug Sentences Lessened," *Washington Post*, July 18, 2014.

124. Marc Mauer, "Addressing Racial Disparities in Incarceration," *Prison Journal* 91.3 (2011), 98S.

125. Mauer, "Addressing Racial Disparities in Incarceration," 97S.

126. Richard S. Frase, "What Explains Persistent Racial Disproportionality in Minnesota's Prison and Jail Populations?," in Michael Tonry, ed., *Crime and Justice: A Review of Research*, v. 38 (Chicago: University of Chicago, 2009), 219, table 3.

127. Frase, "What Explains Persistent Racial Disproportionality," 206.

128. Frase, "What Explains Persistent Racial Disproportionality," 224. A similar pattern can be found in Iowa, which has one of the highest black-white imprisonment ratios in the country but one of the lowest incarceration rates and one of the smallest proportions of its population under community supervision.

129. In 2000, the black-white poverty rate in Minnesota was more than 6:1, compared to the national black-white poverty rate of 3.4:1. Frase, "What Explains Persistent Racial Disproportionality," 231, table 5.

130. Frase, "What Explains Persistent Racial Disproportionality," 205–6.

131. Frase, "What Explains Persistent Racial Disproportionality," 206.

132. Frase, "What Explains Persistent Racial Disproportionality," 230.

133. There are a couple of important qualifications here. As Frase notes, this explanation works less well in explaining geographic patterns of racial disproportionality in jails, which tend to have fewer violent offenders than state prisons, yet exhibit similar but less pronounced geographic variations in racial disproportionality. Frase, "What Explains Persistent Racial Disproportionality," 224.

134. Frase, "What Explains Persistent Racial Disproportionality," 207.

135. Frase, "What Explains Persistent Racial Disproportionality," 220.

136. Frase, "What Explains Persistent Racial Disproportionality," 234.

137. Frase, "What Explains Persistent Racial Disproportionality," 223.

138. For an elaboration of the historic role of "leveling down" in U.S. penal policy, see the discussion of James Q. Whitman's work on p. 6.

139. In their dissent from a favorable report by the House Judiciary Committee on the proposed Racial Justice Act, Rep. Henry Hyde (R-IL) and others argued as much in 1994. Randall Kennedy, *Race, Crime, and the Law* (New York: Pantheon, 1997), 347.

140. Kennedy, *Race, Crime, and the Law*, 385.

141. Florida Department of Corrections, Office of Re-Entry, Bureau of Community Relations, "10–20-LIFE," n.d., http://www.dc.state.fl.us/oth/10–20-life/ (retrieved October 7, 2011); Heather Schoenfeld, "The Politics of Prison Growth: From Chain Gangs to Work Release Centers and Supermax Prisons, Florida, 1955–2000," Northwestern University, PhD dissertation, 2009, 302–4.

142. Crist even carried a ball and chain onto the floor of the Florida state senate to push this cause. Schoenfeld, "The Politics of Prison Growth," 283–84.

143. There is scant information on who is held in segregated confinement in U.S. prisons and jails. Preliminary data suggest that prisoners of color are disproportionately kept in solitary confinement. Margo Schlanger, "Prison Segregation: Symposium Introduction and Preliminary Data on Racial Disparities," *Michigan Journal of Race & Law* 18.2 (2013): 241–50.

144. For more on the "normalcy of exceptional brutality" on which penal facilities operated by the United States at home and abroad are premised, see Avery F. Gordon, "The United States Military Prison: The Normalcy of Exceptional Brutality," in Phil Scraton and Jude McCulloch, eds., *The Violence of Incarceration* (New York: Routledge, 2009): 164–86.

145. Rebecca McLennan, "When Felons Were Human," *On the Human*, August 16, 2011, http://onthehuman.org/2011/08/when-felons-were-human/ (retrieved November 14, 2012).

146. See, for example, Bob Herbert, "America's Abu Ghraibs," *New York Times*, May 31, 2004; Fox Butterfield, "Mistreatment of Prisoners Is Called Routine in U.S.," *New York Times*, May 8, 2004.

147. "Louisiana Sheriff Cages Suicidal Prisoners in Space Smaller than Required for Dogs," *Prison Legal News*, June 2011, 18–19.

148. ACLU Reproductive Freedom Project and ACLU National Prison Project, "ACLU Briefing Paper: The Shackling of Pregnant Women & Girls in U.S. Prisons, Jails & Youth Detention Centers," n.d., http://www.aclu.org/files/assets/anti-shackling_briefing_paper_stand _alone.pdf (retrieved April 16, 2013).

149. University of Texas School of Law Human Rights Clinic, "Deadly Heat in Texas Prisons," April 2014, http://www.utexas.edu/law/clinics/humanrights/workhighlights.php (retrieved May 6, 2014); Manny Fernandez, "Two Lawsuits Challenge the Lack of Air-Conditioning in Texas Prisons," *New York Times*, June 27, 2012, A15; Manny Fernandez, "In Texas, Arguing That Heat Can Be a Death Sentence for Prisoners," *New York Times*, July 29, 2013, A17; Fox News, "Texas Prison Guards to Join Inmate Lawsuit Over Sweltering Jails," September 2, 2013, http://www.foxnews.com/us/2013/09/02/texas-prison-guards-union -to-reportedly-join-inmate-litigation-over-hot-state/ (retrieved September 22, 2013).

150. A state law requires county jails to maintain temperatures in the 65–85 degree range, but that statute does not apply to state prisons. Fernandez, "In Texas, Arguing That Heat Can Be a Death Sentence."

151. Ann Zimmerman, "Extreme Heat Tests Prisons," *Wall Street Journal*, October 17, 2013, http://online.wsj.com/news/articles/SB100014240527023044414045791233812020 26834 (retrieved February 10, 2014).

152. "Failure to Communicate," editorial, *Houston Chronicle*, April 25, 2014, http:// www.chron.com/opinion/editorials/article/Failure-to-communicate-5430794.php (retrieved May 19, 2014).

153. Sharon Shalev, *Controlling Risk Through Solitary Confinement* (Devon, UK: Willan, 2009); Lorna A. Rhodes, *Total Confinement: Madness and Reason in the Maximum Security Prison* (Berkeley: University of California Press, 2004).

154. ACLU, "A Death Before Dying: Solitary Confinement on Death Row" (New York: ACLU, 2013).

155. Jean Casella and James Ridgeway, "How Many Prisoners Are in Solitary Confinement in the United States?," Solitary Watch, February 1, 2012, http://solitarywatch.com /2012/02/01/how-many-prisoners-are-in-solitary-confinement-in-the-united-states/ (retrieved November 16, 2012); Angela Browne, Alissa Cambier, and Suzanne Agha, "Prisons Within Prisons: The Use of Segregation in the United States," Federal Sentencing Reporter 24.1 (2011): 46–49.

156. Human Rights Watch, "US: Look Critically at Widespread Use of Solitary Confinement," written statement submitted to the U.S. Senate Judiciary Committee, Subcommittee on the Constitution, Civil Rights, and Human Rights, June 18, 2012, http://www.hrw.org /news/2012/06/18/us-look-critically-widespread-use-solitary-confinement (retrieved November 14, 2012).

157. U.N. General Assembly, Department of Public Information, "Special Rapporteur on Torture Tells Third Committee Use of Prolonged Confinement on Rise, Calls for Global Ban on Practice," October 18, 2011, http://www.un.org/News/Press/docs/2011/gashc4014 .doc.htm (retrieved May 22, 2014).

158. Five out of six transfers to solitary confinement in New York State are for nonviolent behavior, including infractions like having too many postage stamps, cutting class, and selling chewing tobacco. Scarlet Kim, Taylor Pendergrass, and Helen Zelon, "Boxed In: The True Cost of Extreme Isolation in New York's Prisons (New York: N.Y. Civil Liberties Union, 2012). For an excellent state-level case study of supermax, see Keramet A. Reiter, "Parole, Snitch, or Die: California's Supermax Prisons and Prisoners, 1997–2007," Punishment & Society 14.5 (2012): 530–63.

159. Human Rights Watch and ACLU, "Growing Up Locked Down: Youth in Solitary Confinement in Jails and Prisons Across the United States," October 2012, http://www .hrw.org/sites/default/files/reports/us1012ForUpload.pdf (retrieved May 20, 2013), 2.

160. Quoted in Alex Friedmann, "Solitary Confinement Subject of Unprecedented Congressional Hearing," Prison Legal News, October 2012, 6.

161. Jocelyn Samuels and David J. Hickton, U.S. DOJ, letter to Governor Tom Corbett, February 24, 2014, http://www.justice.gov/crt/about/spl/documents/pdoc_finding _2-24-14.pdf (retrieved March 1, 2014).

162. Friedmann, "Solitary Confinement," 5; James Ridgeway, "God's Own Warden," Prison Legal News, June 2012, 1, 3–11.

163. James Ridgeway and Jean Casella, "The Lonely Battle Against Solitary Confinement," Guardian, January 19, 2011, http://www.guardian.co.uk/commentisfree/cifamerica /2011/jan/19/bradley-manning-wikileaks (retrieved April 12, 2013). See also, Alia Malek, "Gitmo in the Heartland," Nation, March 28, 2011.

164. Robert Weisberg and David Mills, "Violence Silence: Why No One Really Cares About Prison Rape," Slate, October 1, 2003, http://www.slate.com/articles/news_and _politics/jurisprudence/2003/10/violence_silence.single.html (retrieved September 30, 2011)

165. When Bill Lockyer, California's attorney general, was asked about the prosecution of Kenneth Lay, the former Enron CEO who was convicted of securities fraud and related charges, he chuckled, "I would love to personally escort Lay to an 8-by-10 cell that he could share with a tattooed dude who says, 'Hi, my name is Spike, honey.'" Jennifer Warren, "Lockyer Fires Earthly Attack at Exec.," L.A. Times, May 23, 2001, quoted in Valerie Jenness and Michael Smyth, "The Passage and Implementation of the Prison Rape Elimination Act: Legal Endogeneity and the Uncertain Road from Symbolic Law to Instrumental Effects,"

Stanford Law & Policy Review 22.2 (2011), 491 n.11. In another egregious example, in 2002, 7UP "ran a TV advertisement in which a teasing threat of sexual assault in prison was part of a lighthearted pitch for selling soda. The advertisement ran for two months without objection and was only pulled after criticism from prisoners' rights groups." Weisberg and Mills, "Violence Silence." See also Kim Shayo Buchanan, "Impunity: Sexual Abuse in Women's Prisons," *Harvard Civil Rights-Civil Liberties Law Review* 42.1 (2007): 45–87.

166. Separate from that abuse, about one-third of the former prisoners reported that staff members had sexually harassed them. Allen J. Beck and Candace Johnson, "Sexual Victimization Reported by Former State Prisoners, 2008" (Washington, DC Bureau of Justice Statistics, May 2012), 5, 10; David Kaiser and Lovisa Stannow, "The Way to Stop Prison Rape," *New York Review of Books*, March 25, 2010, 37; David Kaiser and Lovisa Stannow, "Prison Rape and the Government," *New York Review of Books*, March 24, 2011, 26. If all sexual contact between staff members and inmates is considered nonconsensual—regardless of how inmates characterize it given their vulnerable position—then rates of sexual abuse of inmates by staff members considerably exceed rates of sexual abuse by fellow inmates, according to inmate surveys. Allen Beck et al., "Sexual Victimization in Prisons and Jails Reported by Inmates, 2008–09" (Washington, DC:, Bureau of Justice Statistics, August 2010), 5.

167. U.S. DOJ, "Prison Rape Elimination Act: Regulatory Impact Assessment," May 17, 2012, http://ojp.gov/programs/pdfs/prea_ria.pdf (retrieved March 1, 2014), 2. It has been more than a decade since Congress enacted PREA, but reliable data on the nature and extent of sexual violence in U.S. prisons and jails are still woefully lacking. PREA requires states to collect and report all allegations of sexual violence and to indicate whether these allegations had been "substantiated" through an investigation. The extreme variation between states in the numbers of "substantiated" claims of sexual abuse perpetrated by staff members against inmates prompted one researcher to conclude that some states are "suspiciously perfunctory in determining whether evidence was (in)sufficient to show the alleged incident occurred." For example, in 2006, Florida reported no substantiated claims out of 152 allegations, while West Virginia reported that six of the seven reported allegations were substantiated. Besiki Kutateladze, *Is America Really So Punitive? Exploring a Continuum of U.S. State Criminal Justice Policies* (El Paso, TX: LFB Scholarly Publishing, 2009), 201; Matt Clarke and Alex Friedmann, "State-by-State Prisoner Rape and Sexual Abuse Round-Up," *Prison Legal News*, April 2012, 1–17.

168. Michael R. Rand, "Criminal Victimization, 2008," *Bureau of Justice Statistics Bulletin*, September 2009, 5, table 6.

169. Joey L. Mogul, Andrea J. Ritchie, and Kay Whitlock, *Queer (In)Justice: The Criminalization of LGBT People in the United States* (Boston: Beacon Press, 2011), 99.

170. Studies suggest that institutional culture and facility leadership are key factors in determining the level of sexual victimization in prisons and jails. David Kaiser and Lovisa Stannow, "Prison Rape: Obama's Program to Stop It," *New York Review of Books*, October 11, 2012, 49. See also Sharon Dolovich, "Two Models of the Prison: Accidental Humanity and Hypermasculinity in the L.A. County Jail," *Journal of Criminal Law and Criminology* 102.4 (2012): 965–1118.

171. Joaquin Sapien, "In Effort to End Prison Rape, Questions about a Monitor's Independence," *ProPublica*, August 30, 2013, http://www.propublica.org/article/in-effort-to-end-prison-rape-questions-about-a-monitors-independence (retrieved September 21, 2013).

172. Kaiser and Stannow, "Prison Rape," 50. See also Alex Friedmann, "Prison Rape Elimination Act Standards Finally in Effect, But Will They Be Effective?," *Prison Legal News*, September 2013, 4. The standards specify, among other things, how inmates are to be super-

vised and monitored; the reporting procedures for sexual victimization; how inmates are to be classified and housed in a facility; and the responsibilities of the staff in investigating and responding to reports of sexual victimization. U.S. DOJ, "National Standards to Prevent, Detect, and Respond to Prison Rape," May 16, 2012, http://www.ojp.usdoj.gov/programs/pdfs/prea_final_rule.pdf (retrieved April 20, 2013).

173. Friedmann, "Prison Rape Elimination Act Standards"; Sapien, "In Effort to End Prison Rape."

174. Grits for Breakfast, "Perry: Texas Won't Comply with Federal Prison Rape Elimination Act," March 28, 2014, http://gritsforbreakfast.blogspot.com/2014/03/perry-texas-wont-comply-with-federal.html (retrieved May 7, 2014).

175. Alexander, *The New Jim Crow*, 199, 15.

176. Frase, "Research on Race and Sentencing."

Chapter Seven
What's Race Got to Do with It?

1. James D. Unnever and Francis T. Cullen, "The Social Sources of Americans' Punitiveness: A Test of Three Competing Models," *Criminology* 48.1 (2010): 99–129.

2. Michelle Alexander, *The New Jim Crow: Mass Incarceration in the Age of Colorblindness* (New York: New Press, 2010), 211. For an elaboration of the concept of "color-blind racism," see Eduardo Bonilla-Silva, *Racism without Racists: Color-Blind Racism and the Persistence of Racial Inequality in the United States*, 3rd ed. (Lanham, MD: Rowman & Littlefield, 2010).

3. Marie Gottschalk, *The Prison and the Gallows: The Politics of Mass Incarceration in America* (New York: Cambridge University Press, 2006), 10, 213–24, 234.

4. Khalil Gibran Muhammad, *The Condemnation of Blackness: Race, Crime, and the Making of Modern Urban America* (Cambridge, MA: Harvard University Press, 2010), 1.

5. Muhammad, *The Condemnation of Blackness*, 103.

6. Muhammad, *The Condemnation of Blackness*, 34.

7. Muhammad, *The Condemnation of Blackness*, 9–10. See also 67–70 on DuBois.

8. Muhammad, *The Condemnation of Blackness*, 93.

9. The discussion that follows on the role of white liberals and their supporters in the 1940s is largely based on Naomi Murakawa, *The First Civil Right: How Liberals Built Prison America* (New York: Oxford University Press, 2014), especially chs. 1–3.

10. President's Committee on Civil Rights, "To Secure These Rights: The Report of the President's Committee on Civil Rights" (Washington, DC: U.S. Government Printing Office, 1947), vii.

11. Quoted in Murakawa, *The First Civil Right*, 28.

12. William J. Stuntz, *The Collapse of American Criminal Justice* (Cambridge, MA: Belknap Press of Harvard University Press, 2011), 266–67.

13. Stuntz, *The Collapse of American Criminal Justice*, ch. 8.

14. Murakawa, *The First Civil Right*, 57, 67.

15. Murakawa, *The First Civil Right*, 57. Emphasis in the original.

16. Murakawa, *The First Civil Right*, 58.

17. These add-ons to civil rights legislation experimented with certain sanctions that later became central features of the major federal and state-level crime bills of the 1980s and 1990s, including stiff mandatory minimums, denial of federal benefits to people convicted

of certain felonies, and sentencing enhancements for vaguely and capaciously defined violations, such as rioting. Vesla M. Weaver, "Frontlash: Race and the Development of Punitive Crime Policy," *Studies in American Political Development* 21.2 (2007): 230–65.

18. Weaver, "Frontlash," 250.

19. Michael W. Flamm, *Law and Order: Street Crime, Civil Unrest, and the Crisis of Liberalism in the 1960s* (New York: Columbia University Press, 2007), 10.

20. Stuntz, *The Collapse of American Criminal Justice*, 133, fig. 2.

21. John MacDonald and Robert J. Sampson, "The World in a City: Immigration and America's Changing Social Fabric," *ANNALS of the American Academy of Political and Social Science* 641 (May 2012), 7.

22. Flamm, *Law and Order*; Heather Ann Thompson, "Why Mass Incarceration Matters: Rethinking Crisis, Decline, and Transformation in Postwar American History," *Journal of American History* 97.3 (2010), 729–31; Weaver, "Frontlash"; Katherine Beckett, *Making Crime Pay: Law and Order in Contemporary American Politics* (New York: Oxford University Press, 1997).

23. For more on the central role of the LEAA in the development of the carceral state, see Gottschalk, *The Prison and the Gallows*, 84–91 and 124–49.

24. Murakawa, *The First Civil Right*.

25. See, for example, the discussion of James Q. Wilson's work in Henry Ruth and Kevin R. Reitz, *The Challenge of Crime: Rethinking Our Response* (Cambridge, MA: Harvard University Press, 2003), 80–91; and William J. Bennett, John J. DiIulio, Jr., and John P. Walters, *Body Count: Moral Poverty . . . and How to Win America's War Against Crime and Drugs* (New York: Simon & Schuster, 1996), 191–208.

26. Lawrence D. Bobo, "Inequalities That Endure? Racial Ideology, American Politics, and the Peculiar Role of the Social Sciences," in Maria Krysan and Amanda E. Lewis, eds., *The Changing Terrain of Race and Ethnicity* (New York: Russell Sage Foundation, 2004), 16–22, 13–42.

27. Loïc Wacquant, *Punishing the Poor: The Neoliberal Government of Social Insecurity* (Durham, NC: Duke University Press, 2009).

28. David Garland, *The Culture of Control: Crime and Social Order in Contemporary Society* (Chicago: University of Chicago Press, 2001).

29. Kevin P. Phillips, *The Emerging Republican Majority* (New York: Arlington House, 1969).

30. Julilly Hohler-Hausmann, "'The Attila the Hun Law': New York's Rockefeller Drug Laws and the Making of a Punitive State," *Journal of Social History* 44.1 (2010), 73.

31. In most other advanced industrialized democracies, prosecutors and judges are career civil servants who are not selected through an electoral or highly political process. Michael Tonry, "Determinants of Penal Policy," in Michael Tonry, ed., *Crime, Punishment, and Politics in Comparative Perspective—Crime and Justice: A Review of Research*, v. 36 (Chicago: University of Chicago Press, 2007): 1–48.

32. Flamm, *Law and Order*, 49–50; Ruth and Reitz, *The Challenge of Crime*, 79–80.

33. Stuntz, *The Collapse of American Criminal Justice*, 239; Jonathan Simon, *Governing Through Crime: How the War on Crime Transformed American Democracy and Created a Culture of Fear* (New York: Oxford University Press, 2007), 49–53.

34. John Hagan, *Who Are the Criminals? The Politics of Crime Policy from the Age of Roosevelt to the Age of Reagan* (Princeton, NJ: Princeton University Press, 2011), 155.

35. Edward M. Kennedy, "Punishing the Offenders," *New York Times*, December 6, 1975, 29, quoted in Murakawa, *The First Civil Right*, 109.

36. Murakawa, *The First Civil Right*, 14.

37. Murakawa, *The First Civil Right*, 14.

38. Gottschalk, *The Prison and the Gallows*. See also Kristin Bumiller, *In an Abusive State: How Neoliberalism Appropriated the Feminist Movement Against Sexual Violence* (Durham, NC: Duke University Press, 2008); Beth Ritchie, *Arrested Justice: Black Women, Violence, and America's Prison Nation* (New York: NYU Press, 2012).

39. Alexander, *The New Jim Crow*, 211.

40. Russell Riley, *The Presidency and the Politics of Racial Inequality* (New York: Columbia University Press, 1999).

41. For the seminal statement on this, see John D. McCarthy and Mayer N. Zald, "Resource Mobilization and Social Movements: A Partial Theory," *American Journal of Sociology* 82.6 (1977): 1212–41.

42. Catherine M. Paden, *Civil Rights Advocacy on Behalf of the Poor* (Philadelphia: University of Pennsylvania Press, 2011), 2.

43. For an analysis of the challenges that activists on the outside have faced in forging links with women on the inside to pursue criminal justice reform, see Jodie Michelle Lawston, *Sisters Outside: Radical Activists Working for Women Prisoners* (Albany: SUNY Press, 2009).

44. Paden, *Civil Rights Advocacy*, 3; Theda Skocpol, *Diminished Democracy: From Membership to Management in American Civic Life* (Norman: University of Oklahoma Press, 2003).

45. Michael B. Katz, Mark J. Stern, and Jamie J. Fader, "The New African American Inequality," *Journal of American History* 92.1 (2005): 75–108.

46. Dara Strolovitch, *Affirmative Advocacy: Race, Class, and Gender in Interest Group Politics* (Chicago: University of Chicago Press, 2007).

47. Gottschalk, *The Prison and the Gallows*, chs. 7–9.

48. The Civil Rights Congress, for example, castigated the U.S. government in 1951 for "the willful creation of conditions making for premature death, poverty, and disease" of American blacks. Quoted in Murakawa, *The First Civil Right*, 56.

49. Murakawa, *The First Civil Right*, 55–56.

50. Gottschalk, *The Prison and the Gallows*, ch. 7; Donna Murch, *Living for the City: Migration, Education, and the Rise of the Black Panther Party in Oakland, California* (Chapel Hill: University of North Carolina Press, 2010).

51. "Inside U.S. Prisons with the NAACP," *Crisis* 89.4 (1982).

52. In 2004, the NAACP did launch a campaign to establish more prison-based branches to help prisoners develop leadership skills and learn about their voting and other civic rights. "NAACP Prison Program Returns," *New Crisis* 108.2 (2001): 55–56; and NAACP, "The Race Is On . . . NAACP 2004 Annual Report" (Baltimore, MD: NAACP, 2004), 17.

53. "Cops, Judges, Prisons and the Hall of Injustice," *Crisis*, January 1996.

54. U.S. Census Bureau, "Federal and State Prisoners by Jurisdiction and Sex: 1925 to 2001," 2012 Statistical Abstract: Historical Statistics, Table No. HS-24, http://www.census .gov/statab/his/HS-24pdf (retrieved April 19, 2014).

55. In addition to the three covers on the prison crisis in 1982, 1996, and 2002, *The Crisis* ran cover stories on racial discrimination in law enforcement (October 1995 and December 1991), rising violence in U.S. schools (April–May 1993), and careers in law enforcement (August–September 1991).

56. Linda Faye Williams, "Race and the Politics of Social Policy," in Margaret Weir, ed.,

The Social Divide: Political Parties and the Future of Activist Government (Washington, DC and New York: Brookings Institution and Russell Sage Foundation, 1998), 427.

57. For example, the Urban League's annual "State of Black America" report in 2009 issued at the dawn of the Obama presidency barely mentioned criminal justice. The 2010 report also did not list criminal justice as a leading issue. "State of Black America 2009: Message to the President" (New York: National Urban League, 2009); National Urban League, "The State of Black America 2010: Jobs, Responding to the Crisis" (New York: National Urban League, 2010). The remaining three members of the "big five" are the SCLC, CORE, and SNCC. Williams, "Race and the Politics of Social Policy," 427.

58. Hohler-Hausmann, "'The Attila the Hun Law,'" 74.

59. Vanessa Barker, *The Politics of Imprisonment: How the Democratic Process Shapes the Way America Punishes Offenders* (New York: Oxford University Press, 2009), 150–151; Michael Javen Fortner, "The Carceral State and the Crucible of Black Politics: An Urban History of the Rockefeller Drug Laws," *Studies in American Political Development* 27.1 (2013): 14–35.

60. In the early 1990s, drug use turned upward but remained considerably below the late 1970s peak. Lloyd D. Johnston et al., "Monitoring the Future: National Survey Results on Drug Use, 1975–2007," v. 2 (Bethesda, MD: National Institute of Drug Abuse, 2008), 155.

61. Murakawa, *The First Civil Right*, 124.

62. Murakawa, *The First Civil Right*, 118.

63. Williams, "Race and the Politics of Social Policy," 432–33.

64. James Forman, Jr., "Race, Crime, Punishment and Local Democracy in America," paper presented at the University of Minnesota Law School, Robina Conference, April 25, 2013, 29.

65. Forman, Jr., "Race, Crime, Punishment and Local Democracy," 29.

66. James Forman, Jr., "Racial Critiques of Mass Incarceration: Beyond the New Jim Crow," *N.Y.U. Law Review* 87.1 (2012), 38–42.

67. Marc Mauer and Ryan S. King, "Uneven Justice: State Rates of Incarceration by Race and Ethnicity (Washington, DC: The Sentencing Project, July 2007), 6, table 2; Roy Walmsley, "World Prison Population List," 9th ed. (London: King's College, International Centre for Prison Studies, May 2011), http://www.kcl.ac.uk/depsta/law/research/icps/downloads/wppl-8th_41.pdf (retrieved February 11, 2014).

68. Victor R. Thompson and Lawrence D. Bobo, "Thinking About Crime: Race and Lay Accounts of Lawbreaking Behavior," *ANNALS of the American Academy of Political and Social Science* 634.1 (2011), 19. For a comprehensive review of research in this area, see James D. Unnever, "Race, Crime, and Public Opinion," in Sandra M. Bucerius and Michael Tonry, eds., *The Oxford Handbook of Ethnicity, Crime, and Immigration* (New York: Oxford University Press, 2014): 70–106.

69. James D. Unnever, "Two Worlds Far Apart: Black-White Differences in Beliefs About Why African American Men Are Disproportionately Imprisoned, *Criminology* 46.2 (2008), 516.

70. Blacks are much more likely to be structuralists than whites. Only about 15 percent of whites surveyed attributed crime primarily to structural factors, while about half attributed it primarily to individual factors, and the remaining 30 percent to mixed factors. Thompson and Bobo, "Thinking About Crime," 29 and 24, fig. 1.

71. Thompson and Bobo, "Thinking About Crime," 29.

72. Thompson and Bobo, "Thinking About Crime," 31.

73. Ian F. Haney López, "Post-Racial Racism: Racial Stratification and Mass Incarceration in the Age of Obama," *California Law Review* 98.3 (2010): 1057–58.

74. Fredrick C. Harris, *The Price of the Ticket: Barack Obama and the Rise and Decline of Black Politics* (New York: Oxford University Press, 2012), 135.

75. Lawrence D. Bobo, "Somewhere between Jim Crow & Post-Racialism: Reflections on the Racial Divide in America Today," *Daedalus* 140.2 (2011), 14.

76. William Julius Wilson, "The Declining Significance of Race: Revisited & Revised," *Daedalus* 140.2 (2010), 63.

77. Pew Research Center, "Blacks See Growing Values Gap Between Poor and Middle Class," press release, November 13, 2007, http://www.pewsocialtrends.org/2007/11/13/blacks-see-growing-values-gap-between-poor-and-middle-class/ (retrieved September 20, 2013).

78. Harris, *The Price of the Ticket*, 117.

79. Harris, *The Price of the Ticket*, 134–35.

80. Harris, *The Price of the Ticket*, 135.

81. On the varied meanings attached to the term "post-racial," see Bobo, "Somewhere between Jim Crow & Post-Racialism," 13–14.

82. Katherine Tate, *What's Going On? Political Incorporation and the Transformation of Black Public Opinion* (Washington, DC: Georgetown University Press, 2010).

83. Harris, *The Price of the Ticket*, 147. In the case of Barack Obama, the most notable events include the revelations about Reverend Jeremiah Wright during the 2008 presidential campaign; the 2013 not guilty verdict rendered in the trial of George Zimmerman, accused of shooting Trayvon Martin to death; and the uproar over the death Michael Brown, an African American teenager shot to death in August 2014 by a police officer in Ferguson, Missouri.

84. Fortner, "The Carceral State and the Crucible of Black Politics."

85. Cathy J. Cohen, *Democracy Remixed: Black Youth and the Future of American Politics* (New York: Oxford University Press, 2010), 19.

86. Annette John-Hall, "Nutter Playing Shame Game," *Philadelphia Inquirer*, August 9, 2011, B1.

87. Cohen, *Democracy Remixed*, 23 and 39.

88. Cohen, *Democracy Remixed*, 196.

89. Cohen, *Democracy Remixed*, 4. For a succinct overview of the "politics of respectability," see Cheryl D. Hicks, "'Bright and Good Looking Colored Girl': Black Women's Sexuality and 'Harmful Intimacy' in Early Twentieth Century New York," in Deborah E. McDowell, Claudrena N. Harold, and Juan Battle, eds., *The Punitive Turn: New Approaches to Race and Incarceration* (Charlottesville: University of Virginia Press, 2013): 73–107; Harris, *The Price of the Ticket*, ch. 4.

90. Harris, *The Price of the Ticket*, 115.

91. Cohen, *Democracy Remixed*, 28.

92. See, for example, Obama's Father's Day speech at a black church in Chicago in 2008. "Obama's Father's Day Speech Urges Black Fathers to Be More Engaged in Raising Their Children," *Huffington Post*, June 23, 2008, http://www.huffingtonpost.com/2008/06/15/obamas-fathers-day-speech_n_107220.html (retrieved January 11, 2013).

93. Fredrick C. Harris, "The Price of a Black President," *New York Times*, October 28, 2013, WR9.

94. Cohen, *Democracy Remixed*, 21.

95. Daniel Gillion in Harris, "The Price of a Black President."

96. Bonilla-Silva, *Racism without Racists*, 172.

97. Here I am building on a point made by Bonilla-Silva in *Racism without Racists*, 172.

98. This account of the Florida case is based largely on Heather Schoenfeld, "The Politics of Prison Growth: From Chain Gangs to Work Release Centers and Supermax Prisons, Florida, 1955–2000," Northwestern University, PhD dissertation, 2009, especially 154, 171, 249–51, 271, 293, 308–12, 317.

99. In order to garner legislative support for education and training programs, Wainwright's Division of Corrections strategically portrayed the state's penal system as primarily a white institution, thus "disassociating the state prisons from black inmates," according to Schoenfeld. For example, under Wainwright, the division's biennial reports "began incorporating pictures of inmates engaged in various activities and drastically over-represented white inmates in the pictures." Schoenfeld, "The Politics of Prison Growth," 138–39.

100. Schoenfeld, "The Politics of Prison Growth," 146–47.

101. Schoenfeld, "The Politics of Prison Growth," 293.

102. For an excellent analysis of the case of the Jena 6, six African American teenagers charged with attempted murder in Louisiana for an altercation that was sparked by a series of racially charged conflicts, including the hanging of several nooses from a tree in the high school's main courtyard, see Alexander, *The New Jim Crow*, 209–11.

103. Alexander, *The New Jim Crow*, 9–10.

104. Alexander, *The New Jim Crow*, 10.

105. Adam Serwer, "The Other Black President: The NAACP Confronts a New Political—and Racial—Era," *American Prospect*, February 25, 2009. Jealous left the NAACP in 2013.

106. Hilary Hurd Anyaso, "NAACP Launches Public Safety Campaign," *Crisis* 116.3 (2009), 45.

107. "Resolutions," *Crisis* 117.4 (2010): 56–64. For other years, see NAACP, *NAACP Policy Handbook, 1976–2006: Resolutions Approved by the National Board of Directors*, draft (Maryland: NAACP, n.d.), http://naacp.3cdn.net/26f3b9bb801a1f73ae_lym6y7ax2.pdf (retrieved May 18, 2011); and the annual list of resolutions published in *The Crisis*.

108. NAACP, "Misplaced Priorities: Over Incarcerate, Under Educate" (Baltimore, MD: NAACP, April 2011).

109. Phillip Smith, "NAACP Calls for the End to the War on Drugs," StoptheDrugWar.org, July 26, 2011, http://stopthedrugwar.org/print/28244 (retrieved July 29, 2011).

110. NAACP, "NAACP Report Ties State Spending on Prison to Low Education Achievement," press release, April 6, 2011, http://www.naacp.org/press/entry/grover-norquist-rod-paige-join-naacp-to-call-for-reduced-incarceration (retrieved October 20, 2011).

111. Joshua Page, *The Toughest Beat: Politics, Punishment, and the Prison Officers Union in California* (New York: Oxford University Press, 2011).

112. Lisa L. Miller, "The Representational Bias of Federalism: Scope and Bias in the Political Process Revisited," *Perspectives on Politics* 5.2 (2007), 13.

113. Cynthia Yeldell, "Georgia Prisoners' Fight for Human Rights," *Crisis* 118.2 (2011).

114. Schoenfeld, "The Politics of Prison Growth," 234.

115. Forman, "Race, Crime, Punishment, and Local Democracy," 25.

116. Since so many people in certain urban neighborhoods have criminal records, the conventional wisdom was that serving time in jail or prison had been normalized and was even a "badge of honor" for some. More recent evidence suggests that ex-offenders and their families view involvement with the criminal justice system as deeply stigmatizing. Donald Braman, *Doing Time on the Outside: Incarceration and Family Life in America* (Ann Arbor: University of Michigan Press, 2007).

117. Michael Lee Owens, "Civic Lessons for People with Felony Convictions," *ANNALS of the American Academy of Political and Social Science* 651 (January 2014): 256–65.

118. VOTE is centered in Chicago's distressed North Lawndale neighborhood, where an estimated 70 percent of all men between ages 18 and 45 have a criminal record (three times the national average for this demographic group) and where the youth unemployment rate is 52 percent—the highest in the nation. Salim Muwakkil, "Black Chicago Divided," *In These Times*, August 2011, 20–23.

119. Ian Loader and Richard Sparks, "Beyond Lamentation: Democratic Egalitarian Politics of Crime and Justice," in Tim Newburn and Jill Peay, eds., *Policing: Politics, Culture and Control* (Oxford: Hart, 2012), 17; Garland, *The Culture of Control*, 167–68.

Chapter Eight
Split Verdict

Parts of chapter 8 originally appeared in Charles J. Ogletree, Jr., and Austin Sarat, eds., *Life without Parole: America's New Death Penalty?* (New York: NYU Press, 2012), and the *Annual Review of Law and Social Science*, v. 9, © Annual Reviews, http://www.annualreviews .org, and are used here with their permission.

1. Center on Sentencing and Corrections, "The Continuing Fiscal Crisis in Corrections: Setting a New Course" (New York: Vera Institute of Justice, 2010), 14.

2. Anne-Marie Cusac, *Cruel and Unusual: The Culture of Punishment in America* (New Haven, CT: Yale University Press, 2009), 14.

3. In 1998, Michigan reformed its notorious "650-lifer" law, reducing the mandatory LWOP sentence for drug offenders caught with more than 650g of heroin or cocaine to 20 years to life. In 2001, the Louisiana legislature reduced the punishment for distribution of heroin or cocaine from a life sentence to penalties ranging from 5–50 years. In 2010, West Virginia legislators extended parole review to lifers with nonviolent criminal records. Michigan Families Against Mandatory Minimums, "Michigan Enacts Reform of '650-Lifer' Law," *News Briefs*, July–August 1998, http://www.ndsn.org/julaug98/sent.html (retrieved January 26, 2011); Drug Policy Alliance, "Louisiana Passes Sweeping Drug Law Reform," June 18, 2001, http://www.drugpolicy.org/news/pressroom/pressrelease/pr_june18_01.cfm (retrieved January 26, 2011); Larry Sharp, "Coming Full Circle," *Angolite*, September/ October 2009, 25; West Virginia Legislature, 81st leg., 1st sess., Senate Bill 218, final version, March 13, 2010, http://www.legis.state.wv.us/bill_status/bills_text.cfm?billdoc=SB218 %20SUB1%20enr.htm&yr=2010&sesstype=RS&i=218 (retrieved September 9, 2013).

4. Tina Chiu, "It's About Time: Aging Prisoners, Increasing Costs, and Geriatric Release" (New York: Vera Institute of Justice, 2010).

5. Jessica S. Henry, "Death-in-Prison Sentences: Overutilized and Underscrutinized," in Charles J. Ogletree, Jr., and Austin Sarat, eds., *Life Without Parole: America's New Death Penalty?* (New York: NYU Press, 2012), 66–95.

6. Between 1980 and 2010, time served tripled for murder, doubled for sexual assault, and increased substantially for robbery, though not to this degree. These calculations are considered the lower bounds of the estimated increase. Jeremy Travis, Bruce Western, and Steven Redburn, eds., *The Growth of Incarceration in the United States: Exploring Causes and Consequences* (Washington, DC: National Academies Press, 2014), 54, fig. 2–29. On U.S. sentences and time served compared with those of other countries, see David P. Farrington, Patrick A. Langan, and Michael Tonry, eds., "Cross-National Studies in Crime and Justice" (Washington, DC: U.S. DOJ, Office of Justice Programs, September 2004).

7. Mona Lynch, *Sunbelt Justice: Arizona and the Transformation of American Punishment* (Stanford: Stanford University Press, 2010), 162–63.

8. Nicole D. Porter, "The State of Sentencing 2010: Developments in Policy and Practice (Washington, DC: The Sentencing Project, 2011), 5; South Carolina General Assembly, 118th Sess., 2009–10, "Omnibus Crime Reduction and Sentencing Reform Act," n.d., http://www.scstatehouse.gov/sess118_2009–2010/bills/1154.htm (retrieved September 11, 2013).

9. Mary Ellen Klas, "Push for Leniency in Drug Sentencing Has Been a Hard Sell in Florida," *Bradenton Herald*, August 19, 2013, http://www.bradenton.com/2013/08/19/4669761/push-for-leniency-in-drug-sentencing.html (retrieved September 21, 2013).

10. David Rogers, "Why Are the District Attorneys Opposing Public Safety Reform?," *Street Roots*, May 17, 2013, http://news.streetroots.org/2013/05/17/why-are-district-attorneys-opposing-public-safety-reform (retrieved January 27, 2014); House Bill 3194, *Oregonian*, Oregon Legislature Bill Tracker, n.d., http://gov.oregonlive.com/bill/2013/HB3194/ (retrieved January 27, 2014).

11. This measure had been languishing in the legislature for a dozen years. It will cost Massachusetts an estimated $125 million more per year. Glen Johnson and Brian R. Ballou, "Deval Patrick Signs Repeat Offender Crime Bill in Private State House Ceremony," *Boston Globe*, August 2, 2012, http://www.bostonglobe.com/metro/2012/08/02/deval-patrick-signs-repeat-offender-crime-bill-private-state-house-ceremony/nFg2i7ocGjNwc1kZUlVauI/story.html (retrieved January 27, 2014).

12. Executive Office of Public Safety and Security, Commonwealth of Massachusetts, "The Corrections Master Plan—The Final Report," December 2011, http://www.mass.gov/eopss/docs/eops/publications/masscorrectionsmasterplancombined.pdf (retrieved January 27, 2014).

13. New York State Commission on Sentencing Reform, "The Future of Sentencing in New York State: Recommendations for Reform," January 30, 2009, http://www.criminaljustice.ny.gov/pio/csr_report2-2009.pdf (retrieved February 5, 2014), 163–66.

14. Charlie Savage, "Retroactive Reductions Sought in Crack Penalties," *New York Times*, June 2, 2011, A15.

15. U.S. DOJ, "Attorney General Eric Holder Delivers Remarks at the Annual Meeting of the American Bar Association's House of Delegates," press release, August 12, 2013, http://www.justice.gov/iso/opa/ag/speeches/2013/ag-speech-130812.html (retrieved September 4, 2013).

16. Robert J. Sampson, "The Incarceration Ledger: Toward a New Era in Assessing Societal Consequences," *Criminology & Public Policy* 10.3 (2011), 823.

17. Sampson, "Incarceration Ledger," 823.

18. The figure for their federal counterparts is 55 percent. The four criteria are: "whether the offender carried or used a weapon in the current offense; had a prior violent conviction; committed the current offense while on probation, parole, or escape; or had two or more prior sentences." Bert Useem and Anne Morrison Piehl, *Prison State: The Challenge of Mass Incarceration* (New York: Cambridge University Press, 2008), 60–61.

19. Useem and Piehl, *Prison State*, 60–61.

20. William Stuntz, "Unequal Justice," *Harvard Law Review* 121.8 (2010), 2022. See also Tracey L. Meares, Neal Katyal, and Dan M. Kahan, "Updating the Study of Punishment," *Stanford Law Review* 56.5 (2004), 1178.

21. Jean Valjean is the protagonist of Victor Hugo's *Les Misérables* who was sentenced to prison for stealing a loaf of bread to feed his starving sister and was mercilessly pursued by Police Inspector Javert.

22. Eric L. Sevigny and Jonathan P. Caulkins, "Kingpins or Mules: An Analysis of Drug Offenders Incarcerated in Federal and State Prisons," *Criminology & Public Policy* 3.3 (2004), 401, 421–22.

23. Associated Press, "Rapists and Murderers Going Free Under Old Law," October 16, 2009, http://www.msnbc.msn.com/id/33340592/ (retrieved September 24, 2010); WSCOTV, "Victims, Families Outraged by N.C. Inmates' Release," October 20, 2009, http://www.wsoctv.com/news/21350656/detail.html (retrieved September 24, 2010); Mandy Locke, "Ruling Affirms 1970s Life Sentences," *Charlotte Observer*, August 27, 2010, http://www.charlotteobserver.com/2010/08/27/1647108/nc-supreme-court-life-sentences.html (retrieved September 24, 2010).

24. For example, sentencing and other relief for people convicted of violent crimes is not listed as part of the "abolitionist movement" agenda outlined by Dorothy Roberts. She calls for a moratorium on new prison construction; "amnesty for most prisoners convicted of nonviolent crimes, and repeal of excessive mandatory sentences for drug offenses; to abolish capital punishment; and to implement new procedures to identify and punish new patterns of police abuse." Dorothy Roberts, "Constructing a Criminal Justice System Free of Racial Bias: An Abolitionist Framework, *Columbia Human Rights Law Review* 39.1 (2007), 284.

25. Ashley Nellis, "Life Goes On: The Historic Rise in Life Sentences in America" (Washington, DC: The Sentencing Project, 2013), 1.

26. Michael Tonry, *Punishing Race: A Continuing American Dilemma* (New York: Oxford University Press, 2011), 36.

27. Nellis, "Life Goes On," 1.

28. A 2000 study estimated that approximately one in every four adult prisoners was serving a sentence of 20 years or more. C. G. Camp and G. M. Camp, *The 2000 Corrections Yearbook: Adult Corrections* (Middletown, CT: Criminal Justice Institute, 2000), 54.

29. Ashley Nellis, "The Lives of Juvenile Lifers: Findings from a National Survey" (Washington, DC: The Sentencing Project, 2012), 4, 35.

30. Kenneth E. Hartman, "The Other Death Penalty," in James Ridgeway and Jean Casella, "Voices from Solitary," May 19, 2010, http://solitarywatch.com/2010/05/19/voices-from-solitary-kenneth-e-hartman-on-the-other-death-penalty/ (retrieved November 22, 2010).

31. "A Matter of Life and Death: The Effect of Life-Without-Parole Statutes on Capital Punishment," *Harvard Law Review* 119.6 (2006), 1839.

32. Peter B. Hoffman, "History of the Federal Parole System, Part 1 (1910–1972)," *Federal Probation* 61 (1997), 24, in "A Matter of Life and Death," *Harvard Law Review*, 1840, n.16.

33. In the early 1950s, the average time served for a life sentence was 10 years in Kentucky, 11 years in Texas, and 14 years in North Carolina. Giovanni I. Giardini and Richard G. Farrow, "The Paroling of Capital Offenders," *ANNALS of the American Academy of Political and Social Science* 284 (1952), 93.

34. Lane Nelson, "A History of Penal Reform in Angola, Part I: The Immovable Object," *The Angolite*, September/October 2009, 17.

35. John Corley, "A Matter of Life," *Angolite*, September/October 2009, 29; Nellis, "Life Goes On," 6, table B.

36. Ashley Nellis, "Tinkering with Life: A Look at the Inappropriateness of Life Without Parole as an Alternative to the Death Penalty," *University of Miami Law Review* 67.2 (2013), 441.

37. Jonathan Simon, "The 'Hardback' of Mass Incarceration: Fear, Structural Racism, and the Overpunishment of Violent Crime," in Deborah E. McDowell, Claudrena N. Harold, and Juan Battle, eds., *The Punitive Turn: New Approaches to Race and Incarceration* (Charlottesville: University of Virginia Press, 2013), 200.

38. Dirk van Zyl Smit and Alessandro Corda, "American Exceptionalism in Parole Release and Supervision," paper presented at the University of Minnesota Law School, Robina Conference, April 26, 2013, 18.

39. Michael C. Campbell, "Homicide and Punishment in Europe: Examining National Variation," in Marieke C. A. Liem and William A. Pridemore, eds., *Handbook of European Homicide Research: Patterns, Explanations, and Country Studies* (New York: Springer, 2012): 273–84.

40. For a succinct overview of key European Court of Human Rights decisions regarding life-sentenced prisoners, see Dirk van Zyl Smit and John R. Spencer, "The European Dimension to the Release of Sentenced Prisoners," in Nicola Padfield, Dirk van Zyl Smit, and Frieder Dünkel, eds., *Release from Prison: European Policy and Practice* (Devon, UK: Willan, 2010), 18–21. On the evolution of the life sentence in England, see Catherine A. Appleton, *Life after Life Imprisonment* (Oxford: Oxford University Press, 2010), ch. 1; and Barry Mitchell and Julian V. Roberts, *Exploring the Mandatory Life Sentence for Murder* (Oxford and Portland, OR: Hart Publishing, 2012), chs. 1–3.

41. Dirk van Zyl Smith, "Outlawing Irreducible Life Sentences: Europe on the Brink?," *Federal Sentencing Reporter* 23.1 (2010): 39–48.

42. The decision was *Case of Vinter and Others v. The United Kingdom*. Owen Bowcott and Eric Allison, "Whole-Life Jail Terms without Review Breach Human Rights—European Court," *Guardian*, July 9, 2013, http://www.theguardian.com/law/2013/jul/09/whole-life-jail -sentences-without-review-breach-human-rights (retrieved September 21, 2013).

43. Chiu, "It's About Time," 4.

44. ACLU, "At America's Expense: The Mass Incarceration of the Elderly" (New York: ACLU, 2012), 1.

45. Jayne Anno et al., "Correctional Health Care: Addressing the Needs of the Elderly, Chronically Ill, and Terminally Ill Inmates" (Washington, DC: U.S. DOJ, National Institute of Corrections, 2004) in Chiu, "It's About Time," 5.

46. Shawn Fisher, "Voices from Solitary: Growing Old in Isolation," Solitary Watch, May 8, 2013, http://solitarywatch.com/2013/05/08/voices-from-solitary-growing-old-in -isolation/ (retrieved September 9, 2013).

47. Youngjae Lee, "The Constitutional Right against Excessive Punishment," *Virginia Law Review* 91.3 (2005), 681. See also Rachel E. Barkow, "The Court of Life and Death: The Two Tracks of Constitutional Sentencing Law and the Case for Uniformity," *Michigan Law Review* 107.7 (2009): 1145–1206.

48. Julian H. Wright, Jr., "Life-without-Parole: An Alternative to Death or Not Much of a Life At All?," *Vanderbilt Law Review* 43 (March 1990), 535–37.

49. J. Mark Lane, "'Is There Life Without Parole?' A Capital Defendant's Right to a Meaningful Alternative Sentence," *Loyola of Los Angeles Law Review* 26 (1992–93), 351–53.

50. Robert M. Bohm, "The Economic Costs of Capital Punishment: Past, Present, and Future," in James R. Acker, Robert M. Bohm, and Charles S. Lanier, eds., *America's Experiment with Capital Punishment: Reflections on the Past, Present, and Future of the Ultimate Penal Sanction*, 2nd ed. (Durham, NC: Carolina Academic Press, 2003), 591–92.

51. Texas Department of Criminal Justice, "Fiscal Year 2012 Statistical Report" (Austin: TDCJ, 2012), 17.

52. "A Matter of Life and Death," *Harvard Law Review*, 1853.

53. Its jurisprudence with respect to noncapital sentences has been a "meaningless muddle" in which "no clear definition of proportionality can be found." Richard S. Frase, "Excessive Prison Sentences, Punishment Goals, and the Eighth Amendment: 'Proportionality' Relative to What?," *Minnesota Law Review* 89 (February 2005), 574. See also Catherine Appleton and Bent Grøver, "The Pros and Cons of Life Without Parole," *British Journal of Criminology* 47.4 (2007), 599.

54. Frase, "Excessive Prison Sentences," 629. See also Barkow, "The Court of Life and Death," 1184.

55. Barkow, "The Court of Life and Death," 1145.

56. See, for example, Josh Bowers, "Mandatory Life and Death of Equitable Discretion," in Ogletree and Sarat, eds., *Life Without Parole*, 25–65.

57. Rachel E. Barkow, "Life Without Parole and the Hope for Real Sentencing Reform," in Ogletree and Sarat, eds., *Life Without Parole*, 190–226.

58. *Callins v. Collins* 510 U.S. (1994) 1141 at 1145 as quoted in David Garland, *Peculiar Institution: America's Death Penalty in an Age of Abolition* (Cambridge, MA: Belknap Press of Harvard University Press, 2010), 266.

59. Garland, *Peculiar Institution*, 43.

60. See, for example, Stephen B. Bright, "Discrimination, Death, and Denial: Race and the Death Penalty," in David R. Dow and Mark Dow, eds., *Machinery of Death: The Reality of America's Death Penalty Regime* (New York and London: Routledge, 2002), 45–78.

61. Barkow, "The Court of Life and Death," 1145.

62. Garland, *Peculiar Institution*, 258.

63. Robert Weisberg, "Deregulating Death," *Supreme Court Review* (1983): 305–95. See also John Paul Stevens, "On the Death Sentence," *New York Review of Books*, December 23, 2010, 14.

64. *Graham v. Florida* 569 U.S. 2010, 2.

65. Bohm, "The Economic Costs of Capital Punishment," 591; Nellis, "Life Goes On," 3.

66. Appleton and Grøver, "The Pros and Cons of Life Without Parole," 599–600.

67. Frank R. Baumgartner, Suzanna L. De Boef, and Amber E. Boydstun, *The Decline of the Death Penalty and the Discovery of Innocence* (New York: Cambridge University Press, 2008), 173–74; Death Penalty Information Center, "Public Opinion," n.d., http://www.deathpenalty info.org/category/categories/resources/public-opinion?page=2 (retrieved January 15, 2012).

68. *Naovarath v. State*, 105 Nev. 525, 526, 779 P. 2d 944 (1989) as quoted in *Graham v. Florida* 569 U.S. 2010, 19.

69. See Timothy J. Flanagan, ed., *Long-Term Imprisonment: Policy, Science, and Correctional Practice* (Thousand Oaks, CA: Sage, 1995).

70. Loïc Wacquant, "The Curious Eclipse of Prison Ethnography in the Age of Mass Incarceration," *Ethnography* 3.4 (2002): 371–97.

71. John Irwin, *Lifers: Seeking Redemption in Prison* (New York: Routledge, 2009); Robert Johnson and Ania Dobrzanska, "Mature Coping Among Life-Sentenced Inmates: An Exploratory Study of Adjustment Dynamics," *Corrections Compendium*, November/December 2005, 37, n.4.

72. Johnson and Dobrzanska, "Mature Coping Among Life-Sentenced Inmates," 8, 36–37; Margaret E. Leigey, "For the Longest Time: The Adjustment of Inmates to a Sentence of Life Without Parole," *Prison Journal* 90.3 (2010): 247–68.

73. Alison Liebling, "Moral Performance, Inhuman and Degrading Treatment and Prison Pain," *Punishment & Society* 13.5 (2011), 536.

74. Penal Reform International, "Alternatives to the Death Penalty: The Problems with Life Imprisonment," *Penal Briefing* no. 1 (2007), http://www.penalreform.org/publications /penal-reform-briefing-no1-alternatives-death-penalty-0 (retrieved May 25, 2011), 1 and 6.

75. Liebling, "Moral Performance," 536; Robert Johnson and Sandra McGunigall-Smith, "Life Without Parole, America's Other Death Penalty: Notes on Life Under Sentence of Death by Incarceration," *Prison Journal* 88.2 (2008): 328–46.

76. Sharon Dolovich, "Creating the Permanent Prisoner," in Ogletree and Sarat, eds., *Life Without Parole*: 96–137.

77. Lewis E. Lawes, "Why I Changed My Mind," in Philip E. Mackey, ed., *Voices Against Death: American Opposition to Capital Punishment, 1787–1975* (New York: Burt Franklin & Co., 1976), 194.

78. Michael M. O'Hear, "The Beginning of the End for Life Without Parole?," *Federal Sentencing Reporter* 23.1 (2010), 2; Richard S. Frase, "Graham's Good News—and Not," *Federal Sentencing Reporter* 23.1 (2010), 54–57.

79. A number of judges have interpreted *Graham* to mean that they are free to impose very long sentences as long as they are for a fixed term rather than for life. In his dissent, this is how Justice Samuel A. Alito, Jr., urged lower courts to interpret the *Graham* decision. Adam Liptak, "Is 100 Years a Life Sentence? Opinions Are Divided," *New York Times*, April 30, 2013, A11.

80. The U.S. Supreme Court was ambiguous about whether the *Miller* decision applied to juveniles sentenced prior to 2012, and state courts have been divided about this issue. Erik Eckholm, "Juveniles Facing Lifelong Terms Despite Rulings," *New York Times*, January 20, 2014, A1.

81. Beth Gallagher, "Pennsylvania Passes New Juvenile Sentencing Law," *Correctional Forum*, January 2013, 1.

82. "End Mandatory Life Sentences," *New York Times*, editorial, September 17, 2013, A22.

83. Ethan Bronner, "Juvenile Killers and Life Terms: A Case in Point," *New York Times*, October 13, 2012, A1; Larry Miller, "Corbett Signs Law to Spare Juvenile Lifers," PhillyTrib.com, November 2, 2012, http://www.phillytrib.com/cityandregionarticles/item/6483-corbett-signs -law-to-spare-juvenile-lifers.html (retrieved January 2, 2013).

84. For a good critical overview of the Supreme Court's record on race and criminal justice in noncapital cases, see Alexander, *The New Jim Crow*, ch. 3.

85. Ashley Nellis and Ryan S. King, "No Exit: The Expanding Use of Life Sentences in America (Washington, DC: The Sentencing Project, 2009), 11.

86. Nellis, "Life Goes On," 1.

87. Steven N. Durlauf and Daniel S. Nagin, "Imprisonment and Crime: Can Both Be Reduced?," *Criminology & Public Policy* 10.1 (2011): 13–54. See also Travis, Western, and Redburn, eds., *The Growth of Incarceration in the United States*, ch. 5.

88. See the meta-analysis by Paula Smith, Claire Goggin, and Paul Gendreau, "The Effects of Prison Sentences and Intermediate Sanctions on Recidivism: General Effects and Individual Differences" (Ottawa: Solicitor General of Canada, 2002), 9–11; and Travis, Western, and Redburn, eds., *The Growth of Incarceration*, 193–95.

89. Amy E. Lerman, *The Modern Prison Paradox: Politics, Punishment, and Social Community* (New York: Cambridge University Press, 2013).

90. Daniel S. Nagin, Francis T. Cullen, and Cheryl Lero Jonson, "Imprisonment and Reoffending," in Michael Tonry, ed., *Crime and Justice: A Review of Research*, v. 38 (Chicago: University of Chicago Press, 2009): 115–200; G. Matthew Snodgrass et al., "Does the Time

Cause the Crime? An Examination of the Relationship Between Time Served and Reoffending in the Netherlands," *Criminology* 49.4 (2011): 1149–86; Shelley Johnson Listwan et al., "The Pains of Imprisonment Revisited: The Impact of Strain on Inmate Recidivism," *Justice Quarterly* 30.1 (2013): 144–68.

91. John H. Laub and Robert J. Sampson, *Shared Beginnings, Divergent Lives: Delinquent Boys to Age 70* (Cambridge, MA: Harvard University Press, 2003); Cindy Chang, "Angola Lifers Are Taught Life Skills, Then Spend Their Lives Behind Bars," *Times-Picayune*, May 15, 2012, http://www.nola.com/crime/index.ssf/2012/05/angola_inmates_are_taught _life.html (retrieved January 14, 2013).

92. Marc Mauer, Ryan S. King, and Malcolm C. Young, "The Meaning of 'Life': Long Prison Sentences in Context (Washington, DC: The Sentencing Project, May 2004), 24.

93. "Low Recidivism Rate Reported for Paroled NY Murderers," *Crime Report*, January 7, 2011, http://www.thecrimereport.org/archive/low-recidivism-rate-reported-for-paroled -ny-murderers/ (retrieved March 28, 2011).

94. The two-year return to prison rate for women who had served at least eight years in New York State prisons was less than 5 percent. Only one of the 128 women who were followed over a two-year period after their release was returned to prison for the commission of a new crime. Carla Marquez et al., "How Much Punishment Is Enough? Designing Participatory Research on Parole Policies for Persons Convicted of Violent Crimes," paper presented at the Annual Meeting of the American Anthropological Association, Montreal, Canada, November 16–20, 2011, 10–11.

95. James W. Marquart and Jonathan R. Sorensen, "A National Study of the *Furman*-Commuted Inmates: Assessing the Threat to Society from Capital Offenders," *Loyola of Los Angeles Law Review* 23 (1989), 9–10; "Prison Statistics for England and Wales 1999" (London: Home Office, 2000), 100, n.43, cited in Andrew Coyle, "Replacing the Death Penalty: The Vexed Issue of Alternative Sanctions," in Peter Hodgkinson and William A. Schabas, eds., *Capital Punishment: Strategies for Abolition* (Cambridge, UK: Cambridge University Press, 2004), 107; Mark D. Cunningham, Thomas J. Reidy, and Jon R. Sorensen, "Is Death Row Obsolete? A Decade of Mainstreaming Death-Sentenced Inmates in Missouri, *Behavioral Sciences and the Law* 23.3 (2005): 307–20; Hugo Adam Bedau, "Recidivism, Parole, and Deterrence," in Hugo Adam Bedau, ed., *The Death Penalty in America*, 3rd ed. (New York: Oxford University Press, 1982): 173–80; Advisory Committee on Geriatric and Seriously Ill Inmates, "Report of the Advisory Committee on Geriatric and Seriously Ill Inmates" (Harrisburg: Joint State Government Commission, General Assembly of the Commonwealth of Pennsylvania, 2005), 77.

96. Nelson, "A History of Penal Reform in Angola, Part 1," 19.

97. Lifers also were divided over whether to keep their distance from the controversies surrounding the "Angola Three," the three former Black Panthers kept for decades in solitary confinement at Angola. Lane Nelson, "A History of Penal Reform in Angola, Part 2: The Immovable Object," *Angolite*, November/December 2009, 32.

98. Nelson, "A History of Penal Reform in Angola, Part 2," 28.

99. Nelson, "A History of Penal Reform in Angola, Part 2," 33.

100. Guyora Binder, *Felony Murder* (Stanford, CA: Stanford University Press, 2012), 7.

101. For details on these state-by-state differences, see Binder, *Felony Murder*, chs. 9–11.

102. Adam Liptak, "Serving Life for Providing Car to Killers," *New York Times*, December 4, 2007, A1.

103. Nellis and King, "No Exit," 42; Human Rights Watch and Amnesty International, "The Rest of Their Lives: Life without Parole for Child Offenders in the United States" (New

York: Human Rights Watch and Amnesty International, 2005), 5; Michelle Leighton and Connie de la Vega, "Sentencing Our Children to Die in Prison: Global Law and Practice," *University of San Francisco Law Review* 42.4 (2008), 990–92.

104. On any given day, as many as 7,500 youths are incarcerated in adult prisons and jails in the United States. Campaign for Youth Justice, "Jailing Juveniles: The Dangers of Incarcerating Youth in Adult Jails in America," 2007, http://www.campaignforyouthjustice .org/documents/CFYJNR_JailingJuveniles.pdf (retrieved July 22, 2013).

105. Porter, "The State of Sentencing 2010," 22.

106. Vince Beiser, "Kids Locked Up for Life," *Atlantic*, November 2009, http://www .google.com/#q=Vince+Beiser%2C+"Kids+Locked+Up+for+Life%2C"+The+Atlantic (retrieved February 5, 2014); Tresa Baldas, "More States Rethinking Life Sentences for Teens," *National Law Journal*, March 15, 2010, http://www.nationallawjournal.com /id=1202446216111/More-States-Rethinking-Life-Sentences-for-Teens (retrieved March 1, 2014).

107. Bradley Bridge, Defender Association of Philadelphia, Pennsylvania House Judiciary Committee, hearing on HB 1999, written testimony, August 4, 2010, 1.

108. Adam Liptak, "To More Inmates, Life Term Means Dying Behind Bars," *New York Times*, October 2, 2005, A1.

109. Robert G. Schwartz, Juvenile Law Center, hearing on HB 1999, written testimony, August 4, 2010, 10.

110. Anita Colón, Pennsylvania Coalition for the Fair Sentencing of Youth, hearing on HB 1999, written testimony, August 4, 2010; Marc Mauer, The Sentencing Project, executive director, letter to Reps. John Conyers, Jr., and Lamar Smith, May 7, 2009.

111. Pennsylvania District Attorneys Association, hearing on HB 1999, written testimony, August 2, 2010, 3–4.

112. See the written testimony of Dawn Romig, Larry Markel, Carol Schouwe, and Alyce C. Thompson, hearing on HB 1999, August 2 and 4, 2010.

113. Bobbi Jamriska, National Organization of Victims of "Juvenile Lifers," hearing on HB 1999, written testimony, August 2, 2010, n.p.

114. California figures come from Nellis, "Life Goes On," 6, table B; Solomon Moore, "Number of Life Terms Hits Record," *New York Times*, July 23, 2009, A24; Nellis and King, "No Exit," 6, table B.

115. Jack Leonard, "'Pizza Thief' Walks the Line," *L.A. Times*, February 10, 2010, http:// articles.latimes.com/2010/feb/10/local/la-me-pizzathief10-2010feb10 (retrieved November 22, 2010).

116. Emily Bazelon, "Arguing Three Strikes," *New York Times Magazine*, May 21, 2010.

117. Marisa Lagos, "Two Strikes Have Large Impact on Prison Population," *San Francisco Chronicle*, July 31, 2011, http://www.sfgate.com/politics/article/Two-strikes-have-large -impact-on-prison-population-2352565.php#page-2 (retrieved January 3, 2013).

118. Stanford Three Strikes Project, http://www.law.stanford.edu/program/clinics /threestrikesproject/ (retrieved March 30, 2011).

119. Samara Marion, "Justice by Geography? A Study of San Diego County's Three Strikes Sentencing Practices from July-Dec. 1996," *Stanford Law and Policy Review* 11.1 (1999–2000): 29–57; Franklin E. Zimring, Gordon Hawkins, and Sam Kamin, *Punishment and Democracy: Three Strikes and You're Out in California* (New York: Oxford University Press, 2001).

120. Elsa Y. Chen, "Impact of 'Three Strikes and You're Out' on Crime Trends in Cali-

fornia and Throughout the United States," *Journal of Contemporary Criminal Justice* 24.4 (2008), 365.

121. California State Auditor Report, "California Department of Corrections and Rehabilitation: Inmates Sentenced Under the Three Strikes Law and a Small Number of Inmates Receiving Specialty Health Care Represent Significant Costs," Report 2009.107.2 (Sacramento: California State Auditor, Bureau of State Audits, May 2010), 1.

122. California State Auditor, "California Department of Corrections and Rehabilitation: It Fails to Track and Use Data That Would Allow It to More Effectively Monitor and Manage Its Operations," Report 2009.107.1 (Sacramento: California State Auditor, Bureau of State Audits, September 2009), 2.

123. California State Auditor Report 2009.107.2, 2.

124. California State Auditor Report 2009 107.2, 23, table 2.

125. Joshua Page, *The Toughest Beat: Politics, Punishment, and the Prison Officers Union in California* (New York: Oxford University Press, 2011), 121–32; Joshua Page, "Fear of Change: Prisoner Officer Unions and the Perpetuation of the Penal Status Quo," *Criminology & Public Policy* 10.3 (2011), 747–48.

126. *People v. Williams*, 17 Cal. 4th 148 (1998), 161, as quoted in Rebecca Gross, "The 'Spirit' of Three Strikes Law: From the *Romero* Myth to the Hopeful Implications of *Andrade*," *Golden Gate University Law Review* 32.2 (2002), 179.

127. Among other claims, the Stanford Project has successfully argued that its clients were denied effective legal representation and that their sentences constitute cruel and unusual punishment. Stanford Three Strikes Project, "Three Strikes Basics," http://www.law .stanford.edu/program/clinics/threestrikesproject/, n.d. (retrieved March 30, 2011).

128. Bazelon, "Arguing Three Strikes." See also Matt Taibbi, "Cruel and Unusual," *Rolling Stone*, March 27, 2013.

129. KQED, "Prop. 36 Will Release Felons from Prison. Who Gets Out?," November 12, 2012, http://blogs.kqed.org/newsfix/2012/11/12/prop-36-may-release-felons-from-prison -but-how-many/ (retrieved January 13, 2013).

130. Unlike Proposition 36, Proposition 66 would have required that all strikes under the revised law be for serious or violent offenses. Moreover, most offenders serving 25 years-to-life sentences for nonviolent or trivial infractions would be eligible for resentencing. Proposition 66 also included provisions that would have made it more difficult to invoke the draconian three-strike penalties in instances of multiple infractions stemming from a single criminal incident such as an armed robbery.

131. Tracey Kaplan, "Stanford Law Professors Submit Proposed Initiative to Limit Three Strikes Law," *San Jose Mercury News*, November 2, 2011, http://www.mercurynews.com /ci_19242905 (retrieved February 5, 2014).

132. Yes on 36, Three Strikes Reform, "California Proposition 36: 3 Strikes Reform Act," n.d., http://www.fixthreestrikes.com/about (retrieved January 3, 2013).

133. KQED, "Prop. 36."

134. Tracey Kaplan and Howard Mintz, "California Has Chance to Change Three Strikes, Repeal Death Penalty," *San Jose Mercury News*, October 6, 2012, http://www .mercurynews.com/elections/ci_21711741/california-has-chance-change-three-strikes -repeal-death (retrieved January 3, 2013); Peter Henderson, "California May Lead Prison-Reform Trend, Ease '3 Strikes,'" NBC News.com, October 13, 2012, http://www.msnbc.msn .com/id/49400913/ns/politics/t/california-may-lead-prison-reform-trend-ease-strikes /#.UPWC5K6ttFo (retrieved January 15, 2013).

135. KQED, "Prop. 36."

136. KQED, "George Gascon, Steve Cooley Back Nov. Ballot Initiative Softening 3-Strikes Law," News Fix, August 23, 2012, http://blogs.kqed.org/newsfix/2012/08/23/video -george-gascon-steve-cooley-describe-their-positions-on-death-penalty-3-strikes-ballot -initiatives/ (retrieved January 3, 2013).

137. Appleton, *Life after Life Imprisonment*, 76.

138. Irwin, *Lifers*, 44.

139. Appleton, *Life after Life Imprisonment*, 218.

140. Appleton and Grøver, "The Pros and Cons of Life Without Parole," 608.

141. Dan Markel, "State, Be Not Proud: A Retributivist Defense of the Commutation of Death Row and the Abolition of the Death Penalty," *Harvard Civil Rights-Civil Liberties Law Review* 40.2 (2005), 407. But this more nuanced view of retribution also compels Markel to reject merciful interventions like pardons and commutations. Dan Markel, "Against Mercy," *Minnesota Law Review* 88.6 (2004): 1421–80.

142. Appleton and Grøver, "The Pros and Cons of Life Without Parole," 606.

143. Frieder Dünkel and Ineke Pruin, "Germany," in Padfield, van Zyl Smit, and Dünkel, eds., *Release from Prison*, 193–94.

144. Dünkel and Pruin, "Germany," 193.

145. Quoted in Dirk van Zyl Smit, "Abolishing Life Imprisonment?," 301.

146. Mitchell and Roberts, *Exploring the Mandatory Life Sentence*, 116.

147. Mitchell and Roberts, *Exploring the Mandatory Life Sentence*, 116.

148. Mitchell and Roberts, *Exploring the Mandatory Life Sentence*.

149. CNN.com, "Ailing Manson Follower Denied Release from Prison," July 15, 2008, http://www.cnn.com/2008/CRIME/07/15/release.denied/ (retrieved May 22, 2014).

150. James Q. Whitman, *Harsh Justice: Criminal Punishment and the Widening Divide between America and Europe* (New York: Oxford University Press, 2003); Christen Jensen, *The Pardoning Power in the American States* (Chicago: University of Chicago Press, 1922).

151. David M. Oshinsky, *"Worse Than Slavery": Parchman Farm and the Ordeal of Jim Crow Justice* (New York: Free Press, 1996), 67–69.

152. Oshinsky, *"Worse Than Slavery"*, 196–200.

153. P. S. Ruckman, "Executive Clemency in the United States: Origins, Development, and Analysis (1900–93)," *Presidential Studies Quarterly* 27.2 (1997), 261, table 1.

154. In the same news cycle that Obama announced eight commutations and thirteen pardons in late 2013, Russian President Vladimir Putin announced that he would free more than 20,000 prisoners from his country's prisons. Walter Olson, "Obama's Unpardonable Record on Pardons," bloomberg.com, December 22, 2013, http://www.bloomberg.com /news/2013-12-22/obama-s-unpardonable-record-on-pardons.html (retrieved January 26, 2014); Dafna Linzer, "Obama Has Granted Clemency More Rarely Then Any Modern President," *ProPublica*, November 12, 2012, http://www.propublica.org/article/obama-has -granted-clemency-more-rarely-than-any-modern-president (retrieved September 9, 2013).

155. "Pardon Rates Remain Low," editorial, *New York Times*, August 21, 2013, A26.

156. Dafna Linzer and Jennifer LaFleur, "Presidential Pardons Heavily Favor Whites," *ProPublica*, December 3, 2011, http://www.propublica.org/article/shades-of-mercy -presidential-forgiveness-heavily-favors-whites (retrieved September 9, 2013).

157. Matt Apuzzo, "Justice Dept. Starts Quest for Inmates to be Freed," *New York Times*, January 31, 2014, A13.

158. Calculated from Mark Rowan and Brian S. Kane, "Life Means Life, Maybe? An Analysis of Pennsylvania's Policy Toward Lifers," *Duquesne Law Review* 30.3 (1992): 661–80; also see Nellis and King, "No Exit," 9, table 2.

159. "Report of the Advisory Committee on Geriatric and Seriously Ill Inmates," 78.

160. Robert Moran, "Rendell to Commute Life Sentences for Three," December 30, 2010, http://articles.philly.com/2010–12–30/news/26356500_1_pardons-board-rendell-clemency (retrieved January 27, 2011).

161. Michael Rubinkam, "Pa. Lifers Seeking Clemency in Wake of U.S. Ruling," Associated Press, September 3, 2009, http://www.utsandiego.com/news/2009/sep/02/us-clemency -lifers-090209/all/?print (retrieved February 5, 2014).

162. American Bar Association Justice Kennedy Commission, "Reports with Recommendations to the ABA House of Delegates" (Chicago, IL: ABA, August 2004), 64, 67.

163. See, for example, studies of how many of the death row inmates whose sentences were commuted by the 1972 *Furman* decision went on to commit homicide or another violent act while in prison or after being paroled. Marquart and Sorensen, "A National Study of the *Furman*-Commuted Inmates," 21–28; Joan M. Cheever, *Back from the Dead: One Woman's Search for the Men Who Walked Off Death Row* (New York: Wiley, 2006), 4, 36, 206.

164. As of early 2014, Governor Brown had approved 82 percent of the recommendations from the Board of Parole to grant parole to inmates sentenced to life, compared to a rate of about 27 percent for his immediate predecessor, Governor Arnold Schwarzenegger, and just 1 percent for Governor Gray Davis. Fewer than 1 percent of these paroled lifers have been returned to prison for committing a new offense. Associated Press, "Prison 'Lifers' Being Released at Record Pace," February 25, 2014, http://losangeles.cbslocal.com /2014/02/25/prison-lifers-being-released-at-record-pace/ (retrieved March 1, 2014); John E. Dannenberg, "California Governor Approved Parole for 377 Life-Sentenced Murderers in 2012," *Prison Legal News*, March 2013, 52–53. For more on lifers in California and how the state's parole board operates, see Irwin, *Lifers*.

165. Bob Brenzing, "179 Commutations and Counting: Granholm Exits as Most Merciful Michigan Governor in Decades," *Detroit Free Press*, December 20, 2010, http://www .wzzm13.com/news/news_story.aspx?storyid=145281 (retrieved January 27, 2011); KFSM News, "By the Numbers: Huckabee's Clemency Record," July 28, 2004, in Austin Sarat, *Mercy on Trial: What It Means to Stop an Execution* (Princeton, NJ: Princeton University Press, 2005), 33.

166. Rick Karlin, "Ghosts Haunt Pardon Process," *Times Union*, December 24, 2014, http://www.timesunion.com/local/article/Ghost-haunts-pardon-process-5091811.php (retrieved January 26, 2014); Andy Metzger, "Governor to Look at Commuting Prison Sentences," *Taunton Daily Gazette*, December 24, 2013, http://www.tauntongazette.com /x919118809/Governor-to-look-at-commuting-prison-sentences (retrieved January 26, 2014).

167. Casey Seller, "Cuomo Announces First Pardons of His Tenure," December 31, 2013, http://blog.timesunion.com/capitol/archives/202322/cuomo-announces-first-pardons-of -his-tenure/ (retrieved February 6, 2014).

168. Grits for Breakfast, "Perry Ignores Most Recommendations for Clemency from Board of Pardons and Parole," September 26, 2013, http://gritsforbreakfast.blogspot.com /2013/09/perry-ignores-most-recommendations-for.html (retrieved January 27, 2014).

169. Chiu, "It's About Time," 2.

170. Charlotte A. Price, "Aging Inmate Population Study," North Carolina Department of Correction, Division of Prisons, May 2006, https://www.ncdps.gov/div/adultcorrection /AgingStudyReport.pdf (retrieved February 6, 2014).

171. Yvonne Abraham, "Without Mercy," *Boston Globe*, July 28, 2011, http://www .bostonglobe.com/1970/01/22/abraham/UCH4HkenS1BSWM2IgBqUPI/story.html (retrieved September 11, 2013); Michael Rezendes, "Paroled Lifers Pose High Risk of New Crimes;

Serious Offenders Often Back in Jail in 3 Years, Review Finds," *Boston Globe*, June 19, 2011, http://www.boston.com/news/local/massachusetts/articles/2011/06/19/paroled_lifers _pose_high_risk_of_new_crimes/ (retrieved September 11, 2013).

172. Mario A. Paparozzi and Joel M. Caplan, "A Profile of Paroling Authorities in America: The Strange Bedfellows of Politics and Professionalism," *Prison Journal* 89.4 (2009), 411–15.

173. Joan Petersilia, *When Prisoners Come Home: Parole and Prisoner Reentry* (New York: Oxford University Press, 2003), 191.

174. Edward E. Rhine, "The Present Status and Future Prospects of Parole Boards and Parole Supervision," in Joan Petersilia and Kevin Reitz, eds., *The Oxford Handbook of Sentencing and Corrections* (New York: Oxford University Press, 2012), 633.

175. Hamilton Project, "From Prison to Work: Overcoming Barriers to Reentry," The Brookings Institution, December 5, 2008, n.p., http://www.brookings.edu/~/media/Files /events/2008/1205_prison/20081205_prison_to_work.pdf (retrieved Oct. 8, 2010).

176. Hamilton Project, "From Prison to Work," n.p.

177. Sarat, *Mercy on Trial*; Daniel T. Kobil, "Should Mercy Have a Place in Clemency Decisions?," in Austin Sarat and Nasser Hussain, eds., *Forgiveness, Mercy, and Clemency* (Stanford, CA: Stanford University Press): 36–63; Elizabeth Rapaport, "Retribution and Redemption in the Operation of Executive Clemency," *Chicago-Kent Law Review* 74.4 (2000): 1501–35.

178. *Herrera v. Collins*, 506 U.S. (1993), 390, 412, in Sarat, *Mercy on Trial*, 107.

179. Kobil, "Should Mercy Have a Place in Clemency Decisions?," 37.

180. Sarat, *Mercy on Trial*, 139.

181. P. S. Ruckman, "The Pardoning Power: The *Other* Civics Lesson," paper presented at the Annual Meeting of the Southern Political Science Association, Atlanta, Georgia, November 7–10, 2001, 8.

182. Sarat, *Mercy on Trial*, 37–66.

183. Kobil, "Should Mercy Have a Place in Clemency Decisions?," 37

184. Sarat, *Mercy on Trial*, 28.

185. Sarat, *Mercy on Trial*, 10.

186. Anthony M. Kennedy, "Speech at the American Bar Association Annual Meeting," American Bar Association, press release, August 9, 2003, http://www.abanet.org /leadership/initiative/kennedyspeech.pdf (retrieved January 31, 2010), 5.

187. Penal Reform International, "Alternatives to the Death Penalty"; Appleton, *Life after Life Imprisonment*, 172–75.

188. See also Death Penalty Information Center, "Year That States Adopted Life Without Parole (LWOP) Sentencing," n.d., http://www.deathpenaltyinfo.org/year-states-adopted -life-without-parole-lwop-sentencing (retrieved January 14, 2011).

189. On the Louisiana case, see Nelson, "A History of Penal Reform in Angola, Part I," 17. For a discussion of Alabama and Georgia, see Jim Stewart and Paul Lieberman, "What Is This New Sentence That Takes Away Parole?," *Student Lawyer* 11 (1982–83): 14–17.

190. For a development of these points, see Marie Gottschalk, *The Prison and the Gallows: The Politics of Mass Incarceration in America* (New York: Cambridge University Press, 2006), chs. 8–9.

191. Derral Cheatwood, "The Life-without-Parole Sanction: Its Current Status and a Research Agenda," *Crime & Delinquency* 34.1 (1988), 49.

192. Susan E. Martin, "Commutation of Prison Sentences: Practice, Promise, and Limitation," *Crime & Delinquency* 29.4 (1983), 594.

193. Hugo Adam Bedau, "Imprisonment vs. Death: Does Avoiding Schwarzchild's Paradox Lead to Sheleff's Dilemma?," *Albany Law Review* 54 (1989–90), 495.

194. Herbert H. Haines, *Against Capital Punishment: The Anti-Death Penalty Movement in America, 1972–1994* (New York: Oxford University Press, 1996), 179; Steven Brill, "Trantino: Long Locked Up, Now Throw Away the Key," *New Jersey Law Journal* 126 (July 26, 1990): 9, 36–37.

195. Mary E. Medland and Craig Fischer, "Life Without Parole Offered as Alternative to Death Penalty," *Criminal Justice Newsletter*, January 16, 1990, 4; Stewart and Lieberman, "What Is This New Sentence?," 17.

196. "A Matter of Life and Death," *Harvard Law Review*, 1838.

197. *Simmons v. South Carolina* (1994) reinforced prosecutors' opposition to LWOP. The Supreme Court declared that prosecutors who raise the issue of the future dangerousness of a capital defendant in their closing arguments must inform the jury if the LWOP alternative exists in a state. However, jurors do not have to be informed about other parole conditions. William W. Hood III, "Note: The Meaning of 'Life' for Virginia Jurors and Its Effect on Reliability in Capital Sentencing," *Virginia Law Review* 75 (1989), 1605, 1624–25, cited in *Harvard Law Review*, "A Matter of Life and Death," 1838, 1844.

198. *Harvard Law Review*, "A Matter of Life and Death," 1829, 1847.

199. Mauer, King, and Young, "The Meaning of 'Life,'" 12.

200. American Law Institute, "Model Penal Code: Sentencing," Tentative Draft no. 2, March 25, 2011, 11–16.

201. New Jersey Death Penalty Study Commission, Trenton, New Jersey, July 19, 2010; CNN, "Newsnight with Aaron Brown: Interview with Innocence Project Cofounder Barry Scheck," December 10, 2004, in "A Matter of Life and Death," *Harvard Law Review*, 1838, n.2.

202. The repeal legislation authorized Connecticut's commissioner of corrections to determine if and when these lifers would be moved to a less severe environment. Shannon Young, "Conn. Senate Votes to Repeal Death Penalty Bill," *Christian Science Monitor*, April 5, 2012, http://www.csmonitor.com/USA/Latest-News-Wires/2012/0405/Conn.-Senate-votes-to-repeal-death-penalty-bill (retrieved January 14, 2013).

203. See Human Rights Watch and Amnesty International, "The Rest of Their Lives"; Amnesty International, "Review of AI Work Against the Death Penalty—Original Discussion Paper" (ACT 51/003/2002) and Full Draft Report (ACT 50.008/2002) in Peter Hodgkinson, "Replacing Capital Punishment: An Effective Penal Policy Approach," University of Westminster, Centre for Capital Punishment Studies, Occasional Paper Series—Special Edition, v. 3, "Managing Effective Alternatives to Capital Punishment: Conference Papers," June 24, 2005, n.p.

204. National Coalition Against the Death Penalty, "Death Penalty Overview: Ten Reasons Why Capital Punishment is Flawed Public Policy," n.d., http://www.ncadp.org/index.cfm?content=5 (retrieved March 31, 2011).

205. Rebecca Burns, "Is a Slow Death Any Better?," *In These Times*, May 2013, 8–10.

206. David R. Dow, "Life Without Parole: A Different Death Penalty," *Nation*, October 26, 2012.

207. Dow, "Life Without Parole."

208. "The Other Death Penalty Project Announces Letter-Writing Campaign to Anti-Death Penalty Groups," February 22, 2010, http://www.prnewswire.com/news-releases/the-other-death-penalty-project-announces-letter-writing-campaign-to-anti-death-penalty-groups-84945657.html (retrieved November 22, 2010); Gordon Haas and Lloyd

Fillion, "Life without Parole: A Reconsideration," Criminal Justice Policy Coalition, Jamaica Plain, Massachusetts, November 30, 2010.

209. Hartman's organization recently published an anthology of writings by people serving life sentences to raise public awareness of this issue. Kenneth E. Hartman, "The Other Death Penalty," February 22, 2010, http://www.theotherdeathpenalty.org/founding document.htm (retrieved October 20, 2010); Marlene Martin, "National Initiatives and Resolution," *Abolitionist*, January 2009, http://www.nodeathpenalty.org/new_abolitionist /Jan.-2009-issue-47/national-initiatives-and-resolution (retrieved January 27, 2011); Kenneth E. Hartman, ed., *Too Cruel, Not Unusual Enough* (California: The Steering Committee Press, 2013).

210. Bedau, "Imprisonment vs. Death," 495.

211. Mauer, King, and Young, "The Meaning of 'Life'," 32.

212. Nellis and King, "No Exit"; and Nellis, "Life Goes On," 19.

213. Baumgartner, De Boef, and Boydstun, *The Decline of the Death Penalty*, 173.

214. Charles Loring Brace, *The Dangerous Classes of New York, and Twenty Years' Work among Them* (New York: Wynkoop and Hallenbeck, 1872).

215. Alice O'Connor, "Changing the Conversation," in Keith O. Lawrence, ed., *Race, Crime, and Punishment: Breaking the Connection in America* (Washington, DC: Aspen Institute, 2011), 95.

Chapter Nine
The New Untouchables

1. Dale Spencer, "Sex Offender as Homo Sacer," *Punishment & Society* 11.2 (2009), 219–220; Heather Cucolo and Michael L. Perin, "Preventing Sex-Offender Recidivism Through Therapeutic Jurisprudence Approaches and Specialized Community Integration," *Temple Political & Civil Rights Law Review*, Fall 2012, http://papers.ssrn.com/sol3/papers .cfm?abstract_id=2116424 (retrieved January 31, 2014), 5.

2. Corey Rayburn Yung, "The Emerging Criminal War on Sex Offenders," *Harvard Civil Rights-Civil Liberties Law Review* 45.2 (2010), 436.

3. Jonathan Simon and Chrysanthi Leon, "The Third Wave: American Sex Offender Policies Since the 1990s," in Shlomo Giora Shoham, Ori Beck, and Martin Kett, eds., *The International Handbook of Penology and Criminal Justice* (Boca Raton, FL: CRC Press, 2008), 750.

4. When asked to conjure up the image of a sex offender in one survey, most legislators and policy makers reported that "sex offenders look like any average male they may encounter." Lisa L. Sample and Colleen Kadleck, "Sex Offender Laws: Legislators' Accounts of the Need for Policy," *Criminal Justice Policy Review* 19.1 (2008): 40–62.

5. For example, all of the 18 victims of sex crimes whom Congress chose to memorialize by name in its Adam Walsh Act "roll call" were white and, with one exception, children. Wayne A. Logan, *Knowledge as Power: Criminal Registration and Community Notification Laws in America* (Stanford, CA: Stanford University Press, 2009).

6. For example, non-Hispanic whites make up about 90 percent of all federal convictions for child pornography. Nearly all the defendants in these cases are men. Their average age ranges in the early 40s. USSC, "Report to the Congress: Federal Child Pornography Offenses," December 2012, http://www.ussc.gov/Legislative_and_Public_Affairs

/Congressional_Testimony_and_Reports/Sex_Offense_Topics/201212_Federal_Child _Pornography_Offenses/Full_Report_to_Congress.pdf (retrieved January 31, 2014), 142, table 6–8. A major government report on sex offenders released from state prisons who had been serving time for rape or other serious sexual crimes reported that more than two-thirds of the discharged offenders were white males. Studies of police practices suggest that people of color are not disproportionately targeted for police crackdowns on sex offenses, unlike in the case of the war on drugs. Patrick A. Langan, Erica L. Schmitt, and Matthew R. Durose, "Recidivism of Sex Offenders Released from Prison in 1994" (Washington, DC: Bureau of Justice Statistics, November 2003), 7; Chrysanthi S. Leon, *Sex Fiends, Perverts, and Pedophiles: Understanding Sex Crime Policy in America* (New York: NYU Press, 2011), 100.

7. The term ritual exile comes from Eric S. Janus, *Failure to Protect: America's Sexual Predator Laws and the Rise of the Preventive State* (Ithaca, NY: Cornell University Press, 2006), 89.

8. Spencer, "Sex Offender as Homo Sacer," 225.

9. Philip Jenkins, *Moral Panic: Changing Concepts of the Child Molester in Modern America* (New Haven, CT: Yale University Press, 1998).

10. See Leon, *Sex Fiends*, ch. 2.

11. See Leon, *Sex Fiends*, 52.

12. For more on the conservative turn in victims' rights, see Marie Gottschalk, *The Prison and the Gallows: The Politics of Mass Incarceration in America* (New York: Cambridge University Press, 2006).

13. Europe has been a pioneer in the use of castration to treat or punish sex offenders. Physical castration began to fall out of use in Europe due to advances in pharmacology and rising concerns about prisoners' rights, but chemical castration is a generally accepted practice there today. Walter J. Meyer III and Collier M. Cole, "Physical and Chemical Castration of Sex Offenders: A Review," *Journal of Offender Rehabilitation* 25.3/4 (1997): 1–18; "Germany Sex Offenders Castration Criticized," *Huffington Post*, February 22, 2012, http://www.huffingtonpost.com/2012/02/22/germany-sex-offenders -castration_n_1292943.html (retrieved September 22, 2012).

14. Keith Soothill and Brian Francis, "Sexual Reconvictions and the Sex Offenders Act 1997," *New Law Journal* 147 (September 5, 1997): 1285–86.

15. Janus, *Failure to Protect*, 2.

16. In 1991, Oprah Winfrey testified in Congress on behalf of creating a national registry of sex offenders. In 2005, she launched her "Child Predator Watch List," and three years later she encouraged her viewers to support the PROTECT Act and other legislation aimed at sex offenders. "Oprah Calls on Viewers to Demand Action Against Child Predators," Oprah.com, September 12, 2008, http://www.oprah.com/pressroom/Oprah-Calls-for -Action-Against-Child-Predators (retrieved September 5, 2012); Corey Rayburn Yung, "Sex Offender Exceptionalism and Preventive Detention," *Journal of Criminal Law & Criminology* 101.3 (2011), 990. On Bill O'Reilly, see Tom Patterson, Utah Sentencing Commission Weblog, March 24, 2006, http://utahsentencing.blogspot.com/ (retrieved October 3, 2012).

17. Spencer, "Sex Offender as Homo Sacer," 225.

18. Leon, *Sex Fiends*.

19. Leon, *Sex Fiends*, 169.

20. After peaking in the 1980s, rates of rape and sexual assault began falling. From 1995 to 2005, the total rate of sexual violence committed against females age 12 and above in the United States fell by almost two-thirds. Between 1992 and 2007, substantiated reports

of sexual abuse cases in the child welfare system fell by about half. The earlier increases do not appear to be the result of increased reporting due to rising public awareness. Eric Beauregard and Roxanne Lieb, "Sex Offenders and Sex Offender Policy" in James Q. Wilson and Joan Petersilia, eds., *Crime and Public Policy* (New York: Oxford University Press, 2011), 353; Michael Planty and Christopher Krebs, "Female Victims of Sexual Violence, 1994–2010," Bureau of Justice Statistics Special Report, March 2013, http://www.bjs.gov/content/pub/pdf/fvsv9410.pdf (retrieved February 28, 2014), 1, fig. 1.

21. "Sex Offenders: Will Tough New Laws Do More Harm Than Good?," *CQ Researcher* 16.31 (2006): 721–44 in Tracy Velázquez, "The Pursuit of Safety: Sex Offender Policy in the United States" (New York: Vera Institute of Justice, September 2008), 8.

22. The incarceration rate for rape remained largely stable from the early 1980s to the early 2000s, while the incarceration rate for all sex offenses skyrocketed from 5 per 100,000 to about 30 per 100,000. Leon, *Sex Fiends*, 165–66.

23. Alfred Blumstein and Allen J. Beck, "Trends in Incarceration Rates, 1980–2010," presented at The National Academies, Committee on the Causes and Consequences of High Rates of Incarceration, Washington, DC, July 9, 2012.

24. Velázquez, "The Pursuit of Safety," 1.

25. Blumstein and Beck, "Trends in Incarceration Rates, 1980–2010."

26. U.S. DOJ, "Fact Sheet: PROTECT Act," April 30, 2003, http://www.justice.gov/opa/pr/2003/April/03_ag_266.htm (retrieved August 12, 2012).

27. "Ninth Circuit Upholds Washington's 'Two Strikes Law' for Repeat Sex Offenders," *Prison Legal News*, June 2011, 16.

28. At the time of the *Kennedy v. Louisiana* decision, half a dozen states permitted executions in cases of child rape. Death Penalty Information Center, "Death Penalty Statutes for the Rape of a Child (before *Kennedy v. Louisiana*)," n.d., http://deathpenaltyinfo.org/death-penalty-offenses-other-murder (retrieved August 24, 2013).

29. Rachel Petersen, "Harsher Punishments Enacted Against Repeat Molestation Offenders," *McAlester News-Capital*, December 29, 2010, http://mcalesternews.com/local/x1758586206/Harsher-punishments-enacted-against-repeat-molestation-offenders (retrieved September 15, 2012).

30. At the time that Florida enacted the country's first Jessica's Law, the state was providing no sex offender treatment in its prisons. John Couey, the man convicted of murdering 9-year-old Jessica Lunsford, reportedly had been trying for nearly three decades to receive mental health assistance to help control his sexual attraction to young children. Janus, *Failure to Protect*, 157.

31. Velázquez, "The Pursuit of Safety," 4.

32. Chelsea's Law expands the list of sex offenses that qualify for life or LWOP sentences and broadens the use of civil commitment and GPS monitoring for sex offenders. Michael Gardner, "Chelsea's Law Could Launch National Movement," *Union Tribune*, August 19, 2010, http://www.theuniontribune.com/news/2010/aug/19/chelseas-law-could-launch-a-movement/ (retrieved September 15, 2012).

33. For a detailed account of these sentencing changes, see Carissa Byrne Hessick, "Disentangling Child Pornography from Child Sex Abuse," *Washington University Law Review* 88.4 (2010–11), 856–64.

34. Amir Efrati, "Making Punishments Fit the Most Offensive Crime," *Wall Street Journal*, October 23, 2008, http://online.wsj.com/article/SB122471925786760689.html (retrieved September 22, 2012).

35. For a scorching account of how Congress repeatedly ran roughshod over the USSC

as legislators toughened sanctions for child pornography, see Troy Stabenow, "Deconstructing the Myth of Careful Study: A Primer on the Flawed Progression of the Child Pornography Guidelines," January 1, 2009, http://www.fd.org/docs/Select-Topics—-sentencing /child-porn-july-revision.pdf (retrieved January 31, 2014).

36. Calculated from Administrative Office of the U.S. Courts, "Judicial Business of the United States Courts: 1997 Annual Report of the Director," http://www .uscourts.gov/uscourts/Statistics/JudicialBusiness/1997/appendices/d02sep97.pdf (retrieved May 23, 2014), 187, table D2 "Judicial Business of the United States Courts: 2013 Annual Report of the Director," http://www.uscourts.gov/uscourts/Statistics/JudicialBusiness/2013 /appendices/D02DSep13.pdf (retrieved May 23, 2014), 3, table D2. This escalation is likely even greater than seventeenfold because statistics collected from the early years were based on only two categories of sex offenses—sexual abuse and other. The latter category subsumed infractions related to sexually explicit materials as well as other offenses like adult prostitution.

37. Efrati, "Making Punishments Fit."

38. The 1996 figure also includes prostitution violations. USSC, *1996 Sourcebook of Federal Sentencing Statistics*, "Average Sentence Length by Primary Offense Category," table 13, http://www.ussc.gov/Data_and_Statistics/Annual_Reports_and_Sourcebooks/1996/tab -13.pdf (retrieved September 3, 2012); and USSC, *2010 Sourcebook of Federal Sentencing Statistics*, "Sentence Length in Each Primary Offense Category," table 13, http://www.ussc .gov/Data_and_Statistics/Annual_Reports_and_Sourcebooks/2010/Table13.pdf (retrieved September 3, 2012).

39. Quoted in Troy Stabenow, "A Method for Careful Study: A Proposal for Reforming the Child Pornography Guidelines," *Federal Sentencing Reporter* 24.2 (2011), 114.

40. For a good overview of this research, see Stabenow, "A Method for Careful Study," 117–21.

41. USSC, "Federal Child Pornography Offenses," 141.

42. Hessick, "Disentangling Child Pornography from Child Sex Abuse," 855–56.

43. USSC, *2010 Sourcebook of Federal Sentencing Statistics*, "Sentence Length in Each Primary Offense Category," table 13.

44. For a summary of some key court decisions, see Human Rights Watch, "No Easy Answers: Sex Offender Laws in the U.S." (New York: Human Rights Watch, September 2007), 125–29.

45. Velázquez, "The Pursuit of Safety," 26.

46. The American Psychiatric Association has repeatedly raised objections to civil commitment laws, likening them to a form of preventive detention. A 2005 APA task force report asserted that these laws represent "a serious assault on the integrity of psychiatry." Quoted in Rachel Aviv, "The Science of Sex Abuse," *New Yorker*, January 14, 2013, 41.

47. This comparison between today's civil commitment laws and statutes from the "sexual psychopath" era comes from Laura J. Zilney and Lisa Anne Zilney, *Perverts and Predators: The Making of Sexual Offending Laws* (Lanham, MD: Rowman & Littlefield, 2009), 85.

48. Derek Gilna, "Federal Sex Offender Civil Commitment Process Under Fire," *Prison Legal News*, August 2012, 1.

49. Some other states, notably Arizona, New Jersey, and California, have had better records on releasing civilly committed sex offenders back into the community. Hannah Rappleye, *Salon*, "America's Expensive Sex Offenders," April 17, 2012, http://www.salon .com/2012/04/17/americas_expensive_sex_offenders/ (retrieved September 5, 2012); Matt

Clarke, "Civilly Committing Sex Offenders Strains Some States' Budgets," *Prison Legal News*, January 2011, 35.

50. Gary Craig, "State's Sex Offender Program Questioned," *Democrat and Chronicle*, December 29, 2010, http://www.democratandchronicle.com/article/20101229/NEWS01/12290347/State-s-sex-offender-program-questioned (retrieved September 4, 2012).

51. The abduction and murder of a college student by a repeat sex offender in 2003 prompted the Minnesota DOC to shift this responsibility to these elected public officials. Janus, *Failure to Protect*, 137; State of Minnesota, Office of Legislative Auditor, "Evaluation Report: Civil Commitment of Sex Offenders," March 2011, http://www.auditor.leg.state.mn.us/ped/pedrep/ccso.pdf (retrieved February 8, 2014), x, 26.

52. Ian Evans, "Britain Denies Extradition of Minnesota Sex Suspect," *Star Tribune*, June 28, 2012, http://www.startribune.com/local/160704485.html?refer=y (retrieved October 2, 2012).

53. Chris Serres, "Lawmakers Weigh Changes to Minnesota's Sex-Offender Program," *Star Tribune*, January 16, 2014, http://www.startribune.com/local/240347761.html (retrieved January 31, 2014).

54. Janus, *Failure to Protect*, 37.

55. For a summary of civil commitment court cases involving sex offenders, see Janus, *Failure to Protect*, 36–41.

56. Yung, "Sex Offender Exceptionalism," 996. Emphasis in the original.

57. Yung, "Sex Offender Exceptionalism," 996.

58. Gilna, "Federal Sex Offender Civil Commitment Process Under Fire."

59. Yung, "Sex Offender Exceptionalism," 980.

60. For a riveting account of how the federal civil commitment program for sex offenders functions—or malfunctions, see Aviv, "The Science of Sex Abuse."

61. Yung, "Sex Offender Exceptionalism," 983–84.

62. Yung, "Sex Offender Exceptionalism," 972.

63. Yung, "Sex Offender Exceptionalism," 987.

64. Yung, "Sex Offender Exceptionalism," 987.

65. Yung, "Sex Offender Exceptionalism," 995–96.

66. Clarke, "Civilly Committing Sex Offenders Strains Some States' Budgets," 34.

67. U.S. DOJ, Office of Violence Against Women, "FY 2013 Budget Request at a Glance," n.d., http://www.justice.gov/jmd/2013summary/pdf/fy13-ovw-bud-summary.pdf (retrieved February 8, 2014).

68. Calculated from "A Profile of Civil Commitment Around the Country," *New York Times*, March 3, 2007, http://www.nytimes.com/imagepages/2007/03/03/us/20070304_CIVIL_GRAPHIC.html (retrieved February 1, 2014). There are some exceptions. The annual cost per offender of the civil commitment program in Texas is $27,000. In a controversial practice, Texas places sex offenders in designated halfway houses and boarding houses, where they are supposed to receive outpatient treatment as well as close supervision and monitoring. But not a single person has been released in 15 years from the civil commitment program in Texas. State of Minnesota, Office of the Legislative Auditor, "Evaluation Report: Civil Commitment of Sex Offenders," March 2011, http://www.auditor.leg.state.mn.us/ped/pedrep/ccso.pdf (retrieved February 8, 2014), xi; Mike Ward and Anita Hassan, "For Sex Offenders Who Completed Their Sentences, 'The Only Way Out Appears to Be to Die'," *Houston Chronicle*, April 26, 2014, http://www.houstonchronicle.com/news/houston-texas/houston/article/For-sex-offenders-who-completed-their-sentences-5432609.php (retrieved May 23, 2014).

69. Clarke, "Civilly Committing Sex Offenders Strains Some States' Budgets," 34.

70. Laura Mansnerus, "Locked Up in Limbo," *Nation*, December 31, 2012, 9.

71. Janus, *Failure to Protect*, 115.

72. In 1996, California became the first state to permit and mandate the use of chemical or surgical castration for certain sex offenders being released back into the community. Since then, at least eight other states have enacted some form of castration legislation. Charles L. Scott and Trent Holmberg, "Castration of Sex Offenders: Prisoners' Rights Versus Public Safety," *Journal of American Academy of Psychiatry Law* 31.4 (2003): 502–9; Brandon Benavides, "Virginia Lawmaker Wants to Castrate Sex Offenders," January 27, 2011, NBC Washington, http://www.nbcwashington.com/news/local/Va-Lawmaker-Pushing-for-Castrating-Sex-Offenders-114640604.html (retrieved September 22, 2012).

73. Richard Tewksbury, "Collateral Consequences of Sex Offender Registration," *Journal of Contemporary Criminal Justice Research* 21.1 (2005), 75, table 2; Richard Tewksbury, "Exile at Home: The Unintended Collateral Consequences of Sex Offender Residency Restrictions," *Harvard Civil Rights-Civil Liberties Law Review* 42.2 (2007), 532–34.

74. Human Rights Watch, "No Easy Answers," 10, 118; Human Rights Watch, "Raised on the Registry: The Irreparable Harm of Placing Children on Sex Offender Registries in the U.S." (New York: Human Rights Watch, 2013), 98–100.

75. Leon, *Sex Fiends*, 51.

76. Calculated from National Center for Missing and Exploited Children, "Registered Sex Offenders in the United States and Its Territories per 100,000 Population," July 11, 2012, http://www.missingkids.com/en_US/documents/sex-offender-map.pdf (retrieved September 21, 2012); U.S. Census Bureau, "State and County Quick Facts: USA," n.d., http://quickfacts.census.gov/qfd/states/00000.html (retrieved September 21, 2012); Devon B. Adams, "Summary of State Sex Offender Registries, 2001," Bureau of Justice Statistics, "Fact Sheet," March 2002, 1.

77. National Center for Missing and Exploited Children, "Registered Sex Offenders."

78. Yung, "The Emerging War," 451, 471.

79. U.S. Code Title 42, § 16911.

80. U.S. DOJ, Office of Sex Offender Sentencing, Monitoring, Apprehending, Registering, and Tracking (SMART), "Sex Offender Registration and Failure to Register FAQs," n.d., http://ojp.gov/smart/faqs/faq_registration.htm#10 (retrieved February 8, 2014).

81. Administrative Office of the United States Courts, "2013 Annual Report of the Director," 3, table D-2.

82. Andrew J. Harris, Christopher Lobanov-Rostovsky, and Jill S. Levenson, "Widening the Net: The Effects of Transitioning to the Adam Walsh Act's Federally Mandated Sex Offender Classification System," *Criminal Justice and Behavior* 37.5 (2010), 514.

83. This money was never appropriated, as Congress sought to trim "pork" from the stimulus package. Yung, "The Emerging War," 452.

84. U.S. Congress, 112th, 2nd sess., H.R. 3796: Adam Walsh Reauthorization Act of 2012, August 2, 2012, govtrack.us, http://www.govtrack.us/congress/bills/112/hr3796/text (retrieved September 22, 2012); Congressional Budget Office, "H.R. 3796: Adam Walsh Reauthorization Act of 2012," July 30, 2012, http://www.cbo.gov/sites/default/files/cbofiles/attachments/hr3796.pdf (retrieved August 24, 2013).

85. Brian Freskos, "Adam Walsh Act Reignites Debate Over Sex Offender Policies," *Star News*, February 3, 2012, http://www.starnewsonline.com/article/20120203/ARTICLES/120209899?p=5&tc=pg&tc=ar (retrieved September 29, 2012); Justice Policy Institute, "What Will It Cost States to Comply with the Sex Offender Registration and Notification Act," n.d.,

http://www.justicepolicy.org/images/upload/08–08_FAC_SORNACosts_JJ.pdf (retrieved September 29, 2012).

86. Ted Gest, "Feds Begin Penalizing States That Haven't Adopted U.S. Sex Offender Law," *Crime Report*, April 12, 2012, http://www.thecrimereport.org/viewpoints/2012–04 -sorna (retrieved October 5, 2012).

87. U.S. DOJ, Office of Justice Programs, SMART, "SORNA: Substantial Implementation Reports," n.d., http://www.ojp.usdoj.gov/smart/sorna.htm (retrieved February 1, 2014).

88. Steve Yoder, "Life on the List," *American Prospect*, May 2011, 31–32.

89. Human Rights Watch, "No Easy Answers," 39.

90. Yung, "The Emerging War," 455.

91. A 2012 survey of the 14 states deemed to be in substantial compliance with SORNA found that only three of those states exempt juvenile sex offenders from public websites. Sex offender registries established by private security companies "post the picture and information of all registrants regardless of what the state does." National Juvenile Justice Network, "Fighting Adam Walsh Act Legislation in Your State: Juvenile Specific Factsheet and Update," January 2012, http://www.njjn.org/uploads/digital-library/SORNA-Juvenile%20 Update-January-2012-2.pdf (retrieved October 9, 2013).

92. Human Rights Watch, "No Easy Answers," 42.

93. Human Rights Watch, "No Easy Answers," 55.

94. "Sex Laws: Unjust and Ineffective," *Economist*, August 6, 2009.

95. *James Burt Breeden v. The State of Texas*, no. 05–06–00862-CR, 2008 Court of Appeals Fifth District of Texas at Dallas.

96. Yung, "The Emerging Criminal War," 477.

97. Erik German, "State Shows Problems in Sex Offender Registry," *Newsday*, January 15, 2008, http://www.newsday.com/news/state-shows-problems-in-sex-offender-registry -1.583279 (retrieved October 1, 2012).

98. Matt Clarke, "Michigan Sex Offender's Suicide Results in Changes to Sex Offender Registry Law," *Prison Legal News*, June 2012, 18–19.

99. Associated Press, "Sex-Offender Registries: Should Kids Be Listed?," May 1, 2013, http://www.usatoday.com/story/news/nation/2013/05/01/sex-offender-registries/2125699/ (retrieved August 24, 2013).

100. Human Rights Watch, "No Easy Answers," 52.

101. Human Rights Watch, "No Easy Answers," 51.

102. For example, after losing a string of court battles over one of the toughest residency laws in the country, Georgia legislators were forced to scale back the measure in 2010 or else risk that a federal judge would void the entire law. Associated Press, "Georgia Forced to Soften Famously Strict Laws Against Sex Offenders," July 19, 2010, http://www.foxnews .com/us/2010/07/19/georgia-forced-soften-laws-targeting-sex-offenders/ (retrieved August 23, 2013).

103. Corey Rayburn Yung, "Banishment by a Thousand Laws: Residency Restrictions on Sex Offenders," *Washington University Law Review* 85.1 (2007), 146.

104. Yung, "Banishment by a Thousand Laws," 137–38.

105. Velázquez, "The Pursuit of Safety," 19.

106. Human Rights Watch, "No Easy Answers," 101. Sex offender exclusion zones generally apply to all registered sex offenders. Yung, "Banishment by a Thousand Laws," 128.

107. Ian Lovett, "Neighborhoods Seek to Banish Sex Offenders by Building Parks," *New York Times*, March 10, 2013, A22.

108. Lauren Smiley, "Chelsea's Law Threatens to Force San Francisco Sex Offenders into Homelessness for Life," *SF Weekly*, July 9, 2010, http://blogs.sfweekly.com/thesnitch /2010/07/chelseas_law_threatens_to_forc.php (retrieved September 21, 2012).

109. In 2010, Miami lawmakers partly relaxed the restrictions because the encampment had become an eyesore and public embarrassment. Valerie Jonas and Walter Bradley, "The End of 'Bookville' Homeless Camp Under the Tuttle?," *Miami Herald*, November 5, 2011, http://newsstand.x10hosting.com/archive2/2398.html (retrieved September 21, 2012).

110. Human Rights Watch, "No Easy Answers," 104.

111. Shaila Dewan, "Homelessness Could Mean Life in Prison for Offender," *New York Times*, August 3, 2007, http://www.nytimes.com/2007/08/03/us/03homeless.html (retrieved February 1, 2014).

112. Sarah Geraghty and Melanie Velez, "Bringing Transparency and Accountability to Criminal Justice Institutions in the South," *Stanford Law & Policy Review* 22.2 (2011), 476-77.

113. Georgia Bureau of Investigation, "42-1-12 State Sexual Offender Registry," n.d., http://gbi.georgia.gov/42-1-12-state-sexual-offender-registry (retrieved October 9, 2013).

114. Grant Duwe and William Donnay, "The Effects of Failure to Register on Sex Offender Recidivism," *Criminal Justice and Behavior* 37.5 (2010), 521.

115. Texas Department of Criminal Justice, "Statistical Report: Fiscal Year 2012," n.d., http://www.tdcj.state.tx.us/documents/Statistical_Report_FY2012.pdf (retrieved August 25, 2013), 9.

116. A 2012 report by the Iowa Sex Offender Research Council projected that the state's parole caseload would increase by three-quarters over the next decade at an additional cost of at least $35 million due to the special post-release sentences imposed on sex offenders. Joe Watson, "Iowa Reconsidering Costs, Benefits of Sex Offender Supervision Law," *Prison Legal News*, November 2012, 46.

117. Stephen V. Gies et al., "Monitoring High-Risk Offenders with GPS Technology: An Evaluation of the California Supervision Program, Final Report" (Bethesda, MD: Development Services Group, March 31, 2012), vii, 1-13, 3-21.

118. Some states use GPS systems that require individuals to remain at home for six hours a day for recharging the device, thus subjecting them to de facto house arrest. Defense attorneys contend that these devices amount to additional punishment, not mere supervision, for the devices are often heavy, conspicuous, and prone to technical difficulties (such as misfiring in public). In one incredible case, a man under electronic surveillance was arrested when he went to the police station to report a change of address after his house burned down, which cut off the signal. The rules of the monitoring program did not permit him to be out of the house at that time. "Interview with Monica Jahner, Northwest Initiative, Lansing, MI," Voice of the Monitored, May 6, 2014, http://voiceofthemonitored .com/2014/05/06/interview-with-monica-jahner-northwest-initiative-lansing-mi/ (retrieved May 16, 2014). See also Velázquez, "The Pursuit of Safety," 22.

119. Charlotte Silver, "No Justice: Sex Offenses, No Matter How Minor or Understandable, Can Ruin You for Life," *Prison Legal News*, August 2013, 36.

120. Lisa L. Sample, "Sexual Violence," in Michael Tonry, ed., *The Oxford Handbook of Crime and Public Policy* (New York: Oxford University Press, 2009), 53; Andrew J. Harris and Arthur J. Lurigio, "Introduction to Special Issue on Sex Offenses and Offenders: Toward Evidence-Based Public Policy," *Criminal Justice and Behavior* 37.5 (2010), 478.

121. Elizabeth J. Letourneau et al., "Effects of South Carolina's Sex Offender Registration and Notification Policy on Deterrence and Adult Sex Crimes," *Criminal Justice and*

Behavior 37.5 (2010), 549; J.J. Prescott and Jonah E. Rockoff, "Do Sex Offender Registration and Notification Laws Affect Criminal Behavior?," *Journal of Law & Economics* 54 (February 2011): 161–206; Paul A. Zandbergen, Jill S. Levenson, and Timothy C. Hart, "Residential Proximity to Schools and Daycares: An Empirical Analysis of Sex Offense Recidivism," *Criminal Justice and Behavior* 37.5 (2010), 478; Richard Tewksbury and Wesley G. Jennings, "Assessing the Impact of Sex Offender Registration and Community Notification on Sex-Offending Trajectories," *Criminal Justice and Behavior* 37.5 (2010): 570–82; Bob Edward Vásquez, Sean Maddan, and Jeffrey T. Walker, "The Influence of Sex Offender Registration and Notification Laws in the United States," *Crime & Delinquency*: 54.2 (2008): 175–92; Matt R. Nobles, Jill S. Levenson, and Tasha J. Youstin, "Effectiveness of Residence Restrictions in Preventing Sex Offense Recidivism," *Crime & Delinquency* 58.4 (2012): 491–513; Kelly M. Socia, "The Efficacy of County-Level Sex Offender Residence Restrictions in New York," *Crime & Delinquency* 58.4 (2012): 612–42.

122. Kristen Zgoba et al., "Megan's Law: Assessing the Practical and Monetary Effect," New Jersey DOC, Research & Evaluation Unit, December 2008, https://www.ncjrs.gov /pdffiles1/nij/grants/225370.pdf (retrieved February 1, 2014), 2.

123. Langan, Schmitt, and Durose, "Recidivism of Sex Offenders," 27, table 28 and 28, table 31; Franklin E. Zimring, Alex R. Piquero, and Wesley G. Jennings, "Sexual Delinquency in Racine," *Criminology & Public Policy* 6.3 (2007): 507–34.

124. For an overview of these challenges, see Keith Soothill, "Sex Offender Recidivism," in Michael Tonry, ed., *Crime and Justice: A Review of Research*, v. 39 (Chicago: University of Chicago Press, 2010): 145–211.

125. Sample, "Sexual Violence"; Soothill, "Sex Offender Recidivism"; Velázquez, "The Pursuit of Safety," 6, 12–13.

126. This widely cited government survey only examines the recidivism rate of people convicted of violent or serious sex crimes in which force was used or threatened or the victim did not give consent or was somehow coerced. It does include other crimes commonly categorized as sex crimes, such as prostitution, child pornography, and indecent exposure. Langan, Schmitt, and Durose, "Recidivism of Sex Offenders," 3.

127. The rearrest rate for sex crimes by released non–sex offenders was 1.3 percent. Langan, Schmitt, and Durose, "Recidivism of Sex Offenders," 1.

128. The rearrest rate for all crimes—not just sex offenses—was 43 percent for released sex offenders compared to 68 percent for released non–sex offenders, or about one-third lower. The reconviction rate for sex offenders for all crimes was 25 percent. Langan, Schmitt, and Durose, "Recidivism of Sex Offenders," 1–2.

129. Beauregard and Lieb, "Sex Offenders and Sex Offender Policy," 348.

130. For an overview of research on sex offender registration and recidivism rates, see Velázquez, "The Pursuit of Safety," 12–13.

131. Duwe and Donnay, "The Effects of Failure to Register."

132. Frequency of police contacts as a juvenile—rather than having committed a sexual offense during adolescence—appears to be a better predictor of which juveniles will go on to become adult sex offenders. Zimring, Piquero, and Jennings, "Sexual Delinquency in Racine," 529. See also Elizabeth J. Letourneau et al., "Do Sex Offender Registration and Notification Requirements Deter Juvenile Sex Crimes?," *Criminal Justice and Behavior* 37.5 (2010): 553–69.

133. Velázquez, "The Pursuit of Safety," 16–19.

134. Velázquez, "The Pursuit of Safety," 20–21.

135. Prescott and Rockoff, "Do Sex Offender Registration and Notification Laws Affect Criminal Behavior?"; Harris et al., "Widening the Net," 516; Michael P. Lasher and Robert J. McGrath, "The Impact of Community Notification on Sex Offender Reintegration: A Quantitative Review of the Research Literature," *International Journal of Offender Therapy and Comparative Criminology* 56.1 (2012): 6–28.

136. Jeffrey C. Sandler, Naomi Freeman, and Kelly M. Socia, "Does a Watched Pot Boil? A Time-Series Analysis of New York's Sex Offender Registration and Notification Law," *Psychology, Public Policy, and Law* 14.4 (2008): 284–302.

137. Sarah W. Craun, Catherine A. Simmons, and Kristen Reeves, "Percentage of Named Offenders on the Registry at Time of the Assault: Reports from Sexual Assault Survivors," *Violence Against Women* 17.11 (2011): 1374–82.

138. Patrick Langan and David J. Levin, "Recidivism of Prisoners Released in 1994," Bureau of Justice Statistics Special Report, June 2002, 5, table 6.

139. Lisa L. Sample and Colleen Kadleck, "Sex Offender Laws: Legislators' Accounts of the Need for Policy," *Criminal Justice Policy Review* 19.1 (2008): 40–62.

140. Joseph Carroll, "Crystal Meth, Child Molestation Top Crime Concerns," May 3, 2005, http://www.gallup.com/poll/16123/crystal-meth-child-molestation-top-crime-concerns .aspx (retrieved August 30, 2013).

141. Sarah W. Craun, Poco D. Kernsmith, and N. K. Butler, "'Anything That Can Be a Danger to the Public': Desire to Extend Registries Beyond Sex Offenses," *Criminal Justice Policy Review* 22.3 (2011), 375, 378.

142. Jill S. Levenson et al., "Public Perceptions About Sex Offenders and Community Protection Policies," *Analyses of Social Issues and Public Policy* 7.1 (2007), 150.

143. Stacey Katz-Schiavone, Jill S. Levenson, and Alissa R. Ackerman, "Myths and Facts About Sexual Violence: Public Perceptions and Implications for Prevention," *Journal of Criminal Justice and Popular Culture* 15.3 (2008), 293–94.

144. About 40 percent of the respondents also expressed concern that notifying the community about the highest risk offenders created a false sense of security. Washington State Institute for Public Policy, "Community Notification as Viewed by Washington's Citizens: A 10-Year Follow-Up" (Olympia: Washington State Institute for Public Policy, March 2008), 3.

145. He was released in 2007 after serving two years following a decision by the Georgia State Supreme Court that his sentence was disproportionate. Richard Fausset and Jenny Jarvie, "After Teen Sex Ruling, He's Free," *Los Angeles Times*, October 27, 2007, http://articles .latimes.com/2007/oct/27/nation/na-teensex27 (retrieved February 1, 2014).

146. Erica R. Meiners, "Never Innocent: Feminist Trouble with Sex Offender Registries and Protection in a Prison Nation," *Meridians* 9.2 (2009): 31–62.

147. Jennifer Bleyer, "Patty Wetterling Questions Sex Offender Laws," *City Pages*, March 20, 2013, http://www.citypages.com/2013-03-20/news/patty-wetterling-questions -sex-offender-laws/full/Citypages (retrieved August 24, 2013).

148. "Proposition 83 CALCASA Position Paper," n.d., http://www.calcasa.org/wp -content/uploads/2008/03/prop-83-position-paper.pdf (retrieved September 21, 2012), 2; Velázquez, "The Pursuit of Safety," 8.

149. Silver, "No Justice," 37.

150. S.1690: Second Chance Reauthorization Act of 2013, 113th Cong., 1st Sess., November 13, 2013, http://www.gpo.gov/fdsys/pkg/BILLS-113s1690is/pdf/BILLS-113s1690is .pdf (retrieved January 29, 2014), 28.

151. USSC, "Results of Survey of United States District Judges January 2010 through

March 2010," Question 8: Appropriateness of Guidelines Ranges, June 2010, http://www
.ussc.gov/Research_and_Statistics/Research_Projects/Surveys/20100608_Judge_Survey
.pdf (retrieved February 1, 2014), n.p.

152. Stabenow, "A Method for Careful Study," 111–14.

153. USSC, "Federal Child Pornography Offenses," xviii–xxi.

154. Quoted in Stabenow, "A Method for Careful Study," 114.

155. Anne Gannon, U.S. DOJ, Office of the Deputy Attorney General, letter to Patti B.
Saris, USSC, March 5, 2013, http://sentencing.typepad.com/files/doj-letter-to-ussc-on-cp
-report.pdf (retrieved February 1, 2014).

156. Janus, *Failure to Protect*, 5.

157. Christopher Doering, "Farm Bill Passes After Years of Partisan Bickering; Food
Stamps Cut," *Detroit Free Press*, February 4, 2014, http://www.freep.com/article/20140204
/NEWS07/302040113/farm-bill-subsidies-food-stamps (retrieved March 1, 2014).

158. Human Rights Watch, "No Easy Answers," 119–20.

159. Yung, "Banishment by a Thousand Laws," 147.

160. Craun, Kernsmith, and Butler, "'Anything That Can Be a Danger'," 376.

161. Erica Goode and Jack Healy, "Focus on Mental Health Laws to Curb Violence Is
Unfair, Some Say," *New York Times*, February 1, 2013, A13.

162. Howard N. Snyder, "Sexual Assault of Young Children as Reported to Law Enforcement: Victim, Incident, and Offender Characteristics" (Washington, DC: Bureau of Justice
Statistics, July 2000), 10, table 6.

163. Janus, *Failure to Protect*, 90. See also 87–88, 147.

Chapter Ten

Catch and Keep

1. Narro is an immigrant rights leader in California. Quoted in Alejandra Marchevsky
and Beth Baker, "Why Has President Obama Deported More Immigrants Than Any President in History?," *Nation*, March 31, 2014.

2. In 1986, funding for the INS, ICE's predecessor, amounted to only about one-
quarter of the total funding allocated to the FBI, DEA, Secret Service, USMS, and the Bureau of Alcohol, Tobacco, Firearms and Explosives. Doris Meissner et al., "Immigration
Enforcement in the United States: The Rise of a Formidable Machinery" (Washington, DC:
Migration Policy Institute, 2013), 20.

3. Juliet Stumpf, "The Crimmigration Crisis: Immigrants, Crime, and Sovereign
Power," *American University Law Review* 56.2 (2006): 367–419; Anil Kalhan, "Rethinking
Immigration Detention," *Columbia Law Review Sidebar* 110 (July 21, 2010), 43.

4. On the criminalization of immigration enforcement from a comparative perspective, see Katja Franko Aas and Mary Bosworth, eds., *The Borders of Punishment: Migration,
Citizenship, and Social Exclusion* (Oxford: Oxford University Press, 2013).

5. Hindpal Singh Bhui, "Introduction: Humanizing Migration Control and Detention," in Aas and Bosworth, eds., *The Borders of Punishment*, 7; Mathew Coleman, "The 'Local' Migration State: The Site-Specific Devolution of Immigration Enforcement in the U.S.
South," *Law & Policy* 34.2 (2012): 159–90.

6. Tom K. Wong, "287(g) and the Politics of Interior Immigration Control in the
United States: Explaining Local Cooperation with Federal Immigration Authorities," *Jour-

nal of Ethnic and Migration Studies 38.5 (2012): 737–56; Alexandra Filindra and Melinda Kovács, "Analysing U.S. State Legislative Resolutions on Immigrants and Immigration: The Role of Immigration Federalism," *International Migration* 50.4 (2012): 33–50.

7. U.S. BOP, "Inmate Ethnicity," n.d., http://www.bop.gov/about/statistics/statistics _inmate_ethnicity.jsp (retrieved May 10, 2014); Michael T. Light, Mark Hugo Lopez, and Ana Gonzalez-Barrera, "The Rise of Federal Immigration Crimes" (Washington, DC: The Pew Research Center's Hispanic Trends Project, March 2014), 11.

8. Light et al., "The Rise of Federal Immigration Crimes," 9.

9. Since about 2011, the number of migrants crossing illegally into the United States from the South Texas border area appears to be on the rise again. On migration trends, see Jeffrey Passel, D'Vera Cohn, and Ana Gonzalez-Barrera, "Net Migration from Mexico Falls to Zero—and Perhaps Less," The Pew Research Hispanic Trends Project," April 23, 2013, http://www.pewhispanic.org/2012/04/23/net-migration-from-mexico-falls-to-zero-and -perhaps-less/ (retrieved August 16, 2013); Julia Preston, "Hoping for Asylum, Migrants Strain Border," *New York Times*, April 11, 2014, A1.

10. Kamala Mallik-Kane, Barbara Parthasarathy, and William Adams, "Examining Growth in the Federal Prison Population, 1998–2010" (Washington, DC: Urban Institute Justice Policy Center, September 2010), 6.

11. U.S. BOP, "Offenses," December 28, 2013, http://www.bop.gov/about/statistics /statistics_inmate_offenses.jsp (retrieved February 2, 2014).

12. Alistair Graham Robertson et al., "Costs and Consequences," Grassroots Leadership, September 2012, http://grassrootsleadership.org/sites/default/files/uploads/GRL_Sept 2012_Report-final.pdf (retrieved August 16, 2013), 3.

13. Jennifer M. Chacón, "Managing Migration Through Crime," *Columbia Law Review Sidebar* 109 (December 12, 2009), 146. See also Doris Marie Provine and Roxanne Lynn Doty, "The Criminalization of Immigrants as a Racial Project," *Journal of Contemporary Criminal Justice* 27.3 (2011): 261–77.

14. Analysis by Ginger Thompson and Sarah Cohen, "More Deportations Follow Minor Crimes, Data Shows," *New York Times*, April 7, 2014, A1.

15. Teresa A. Miller, "Lessons Learned, Lessons Lost: Immigration Enforcement's Failed Experiment with Penal Severity," *Fordham Urban Law Journal* 38.1 (2010), 222.

16. Maureen A. Sweeney, "Fact or Fiction: The Legal Construction of Immigration Removal for Crimes," *Yale Journal on Regulation* 27.1 (2010), 87.

17. For example, a major National Research Council study on mass incarceration did not include a discussion of the impact of immigration policy on penal policy. See Jeremy Travis, Bruce Western, and Steve Redburn, eds., *The Growth of Incarceration in the United States: Exploring Causes and Consequences* (Washington, DC: National Academies Press, 2014). For some notable exceptions, see Jonathan Simon, "Refugees in a Carceral Age: The Rebirth of Immigration Prisons in the United States," *Public Culture* 10.3 (1998): 577–607; Mary Bosworth and Emma Kaufman, "Foreigners in a Carceral Age: Immigration and Imprisonment in the United States," *Stanford Law & Policy Review* 22.2 (2011): 429–54; Aas and Bosworth, eds., *The Borders of Punishment*; Katherine Beckett and Naomi Murakawa, "Mapping the Shadow Carceral State: Toward an Institutionally Capacious Approach to Punishment," *Theoretical Criminology* 16.2 (2012): 221–44.

18. Eduardo Bonilla-Silva, *Racism without Racists: Color-Blind Racism and the Persistence of Racial Inequality in the United States*, 3rd ed. (Landam, MD: Rowman & Littlefield, 2010), 211.

19. The crime-reducing effects tend to be greatest in gateway cities accustomed to large streams of immigrants. New research suggests that the influx of immigrants in non-gateway cities has no effect either positive or negative on crime rates. María B. Vélez and Christopher J. Lyons, "Situating the Immigration and Neighborhood Crime Relationship across Multiple Cities," in Charis E. Kubrin, Marjorie S. Zatz, and Ramiro Martínez, Jr., eds., *Punishing Immigrants: Policy, Politics, and Injustice.* (New York: NYU Press, 2012): 159–77.

20. Dora Schriro, "Immigration and Detention: Overview and Recommendations," ICE, October 6, 2009, http://www.ice.gov/doclib/about/offices/odpp/pdf/ice-detention-rpt .pdf (retrieved February 2, 2014), 12.

21. Human Rights Watch, "Turning Migrants into Criminals: The Harmful Impact of US Border Prosecutions" (New York: Human Rights Watch, 2013), 5. A *New York Times* editorial described the "cruelty and deficiencies" of this web as "appalling." "Border Injustice," May 28, 2013, A16.

22. Cody Mason, "Dollars and Detainees: The Growth of For-Profit Detention" (Washington, DC: The Sentencing Project, July 2012), 6–7.

23. About 40 percent of the people detained by the USMS were being held for immigration offenses. Mason, "Dollars and Detainees," 3.

24. Calculated from Mark Dow, *American Gulag: Inside U.S. Immigration Prisons* (Berkeley: University of California Press, 2004), 7–9; and Inter-American Commission on Human Rights, "Report on Immigration in the United States: Detention and Due Process," December 30, 2011, 8.

25. Nick Miroff, "Controversial Quota Drives Immigration Detention Boom," *Washington Post*, October 13, 2013, http://www.washingtonpost.com/world/controversial-quota -drives-immigration-detention-boom/2013/10/13/09bb689e-214c-11e3-ad1a-1a919f2ed890 _story.html (retrieved February 2, 2014).

26. The figure for the USMS was nearly 210,000 in 2011. Mason, "Dollars and Detainees," 3; ACLU and Georgia Detention Watch, "Securely Insecure: The Real Costs, Consequences and Human Face of Immigration Detention," January 14, 2011, http://www.detention watchnetwork.org/sites/detentionwatchnetwork.org/files/1.14.11_Fact%20Sheet%20 FINAL_0.pdf (retrieved August 15, 2013); John Simanski and Lesley M. Sapp, "Immigration Enforcement Actions: 2011," U.S. DHS, Office of Immigration Statistics, Annual Report, September 2012, http://www.dhs.gov/sites/default/files/publications/immigration -statistics/enforcement_ar_2011.pdf (retrieved August 15, 2013), 4.

27. Graham Kates, "Fast Track to Deportation," *Crime Report*, September 17, 2013, http://www.thecrimereport.org/news/inside-criminal-justice/2013–09-fast-track-to -deportation (retrieved May 10, 2014).

28. ICE, "Removal Statistics," n.d., http://www.ice.gov/removal-statistics/ (retrieved August 15, 2013); Detention Watch Network, "The History of Immigration Detention in the U.S.," n.d., http://www.detentionwatchnetwork.org/node/2381 (retrieved May 15, 2012).

29. U.S. DHS, Office of Immigration Statistics, Annual Report, "Immigration Enforcement Actions: 2010," June 2011, http://www.dhs.gov/xlibrary/assets/statistics/publications /enforcement-ar-2010.pdf (retrieved February 2, 2014), 4, table 2; Devin Dwyer, "Obama 'Softens' Immigration Policy with Mixed Results," ABC News, February 24, 2012, http:// abcnews.go.com/blogs/politics/2012/02/obama-softens-immigration-policy-with-mixed -results/ (retrieved June 16, 2012).

30. Douglas Massey quoted in Lourdes Medrano, "Obama as Border Cop: He's Deported Record Numbers of Illegal Immigrants," *Christian Science Monitor*, August 12, 2010, http://www.csmonitor.com/USA/Justice/2010/0812/Obama-as-border-cop-He-s-deported -record-numbers-of-illegal-immigrants (retrieved July 6, 2012).

31. Nationals from Guatemala, Honduras, El Salvador, and Mexico together accounted for more than 90 percent of all deportations that year. U.S. DHS, "Immigration Enforcement Actions: 2010," 4, table 3.

32. Daniel Kanstroom, *Aftermath: Deportation Law and the New American Diaspora* (New York: Oxford University Press, 2012).

33. Bosworth and Kaufman, "Foreigners in a Carceral Age," 431.

34. Faiza W. Sayed, "Challenging Detention: Why Immigrant Detainees Receive Less Process Than 'Enemy Combatants' and Why They Deserve More," *Columbia Law Review* 111.8 (2011), 1836.

35. Human Rights Watch, "Turning Migrants into Criminals," 11; Sweeney, "Fact or Fiction."

36. Sweeney, "Fact or Fiction," 63–67.

37. Rebecca Bohrman and Naomi Murakawa, "Remaking Big Government: Immigration and Crime Control in the United States," in Julia Sudbury, ed., *Global Lockdown: Race, Gender, and the Prison-Industrial Complex* (New York: Routledge, 2005): 109–26.

38. Jacqueline Hagan and Scott Phillips, "Border Blunders: The Unanticipated Human and Economic Costs of the U.S. Approach to Immigration Control, 1986–2007," *Criminology & Public Policy* 7.1 (2008), 84.

39. National Criminal Justice Reference Service, "U.S. Department of Justice, Fact Sheet: Violent Crime Control and Law Enforcement Act of 1994," n.d., https://www.ncjrs.gov/txtfiles/billfs.txt (retrieved April 19, 2014).

40. Sweeney, "Fact or Fiction," 65.

41. David Manuel Hernández, "Pursuant to Deportation: Latinos and Immigrant Detention," *Latino Studies* 6.1 (2008): 35–63; and Dow, *American Gulag*, 173–74.

42. Hagan and Phillips, "Border Blunders," 87. See also Shoba Sivaprasad Wadhia, "The Policy and Politics of Immigrant Rights," *Temple Political & Civil Rights Law Review* 16.2 (2006–07): 387–421; and Sweeney, "Fact or Fiction."

43. Sweeney, "Fact or Fiction," 61, 72.

44. Between 2003 and 2012, the number of FOTs multiplied from eight to 129, and their funding jumped from $9 million to $155 million. Margot Mendelson, Shayna Strom, and Michael Wishnie, "Collateral Damage: An Examination of ICE's Fugitive Operations Program," Migration Policy Institute, February 2009, http://www.migrationpolicy.org/pubs/NFOP_Feb09.pdf (retrieved February 4, 2014), 1; National Immigration Forum, "The President's FY 2013 Budget–Department of Homeland Security," 2012, http://www.immigrationforum.org/images/uploads/2012/dhs_fy_2013_budget_summary.pdf (retrieved October 9, 2013); ICE, "Fact Sheet: ICE Fugitive Operations Program," July 2, 2013 (retrieved August 30, 2013).

45. Inter-American Commission on Human Rights, "Report on Immigration," 55.

46. Mendelson, Strom, and Wishnie, "Collateral Damage," 1.

47. Inter-American Commission on Human Rights, "Report on Immigration," 55–57.

48. Inter-American Commission on Human Rights, "Report on Immigration," 56–57.

49. Inter-American Commission on Human Rights, "Report on Immigration," 48–50.

50. One infamous raid in New Bedford, Massachusetts, in 2007 left at least 100 young children on their own, in some cases for several days. National Council of La Raza and the Urban Institute, "Paying the Price: The Impact of Immigration Raids on America's Children" (Washington, DC: National Council of La Raza, 2007), http://www.urban.org/UploadedPDF/411566_immigration_raids.pdf (retrieved May 29, 2012), 19, 35–38.

51. ICE, "Worksite Enforcement," n.d., http://www.ice.gov/news/library/factsheets/worksite.htm (retrieved May 29, 2012). On the mixed results of this change in policy,

see Andorra Bruno, "Immigration-Related Worksite Enforcement: Performance Measures," Congressional Research Service, August 7, 2013, http://www.fas.org/sgp/crs/homesec/R40002.pdf (retrieved January 15, 2014).

52. For example, in late 2010, Chipotle, the fast-food restaurant chain, fired 450 workers across Minnesota, more than a third of its workforce in the state, after ICE told the company to dismiss the workers following an audit. David Bacon, "Fired for the Crime of Working: Not Much Has Changed for Undocumented Workers Since Obama Took Office," *In These Times*, April 2011, 30–31; Julia Preston, "In Crackdown on Immigrants, 800 Pink Slips," *New York Times*, September 30, 2009, A1.

53. TRAC, "FY 2009 Federal Prosecutions Sharply Higher," December 21, 2009, http://trac.syr.edu/tracreports/crim/223/ (retrieved June 8, 2012).

54. Light et al., "The Rise of Federal Immigration Crimes," 5.

55. Matt Clarke, "Dramatic Increase in Number of Hispanics Sentenced to Federal Prison," *Prison Legal News*, May 2012, 26.

56. Associated Press, "More Hispanics Go to Federal Prison," *USA Today*, June 4, 2011, http://www.usatoday.com/news/nation/2011-06-04-immigration-hispanic-offenders-federal-prison_n.htm (retrieved June 8, 2012).

57. Joanna Lydgate, "Operation Streamline: Border Enforcement That Doesn't Work," *L.A. Times*, May 14, 2010, http://articles.latimes.com/2010/may/14/opinion/la-oe-lydgate-immigration-20100514 (retrieved February 4, 2014); Tara Buentello et al., "Operation Streamline: Drowning Justice and Draining Dollars Along the Rio Grande," Green Paper, Grassroots Leadership, Charlotte, NC, July 2010, http://grassrootsleadership.org/sites/default/files/uploads/Operation-Streamline-Green-Paper.pdf (retrieved February 4, 2014), 1; Joanna Lydgate, "Assembly-Line Justice: A Review of Operation Streamline, *Policy Brief* (Earl Warren Institute, University of California, Berkeley Law School), January 2010, 2.

58. Amanda Lee Myers, "Overwhelmed Courts Need $40 Million for Border Plan," azcentral.com, June 29, 2010, http://www.azcentral.com/news/articles/2010/06/29/201006 29arizona-immigration-federal-court-costs.html (retrieved July 5, 2010).

59. Associated Press, "More Hispanics Go to Federal Prison."

60. When apprehended immigrants complain about misconduct by Border Patrol agents, it can be difficult to raise such complaints to the Border Patrol attorney, "who is a co-worker (and often also a friend) of the agent in question." Federal defender quoted in Lydgate, "Assembly-Line Justice," 15. For more on the improper use of deadly force along the border, see the special investigation by Bob Ortega and Rob O'Dell, "Deadly Border Incidents Cloaked in Silence," *Arizona Republic*, December 16, 2013, http://www.azcentral.com/news/politics/articles/20131212arizona-border-patrol-deadly-force-investigation.html (retrieved February 2, 2014). See also Daniel E. Martínez, Guillermo Cantor, and Walter A. Ewing, "No Action Taken: Lack of CBP Accountability in Responding to Complaints of Abuse" (Washington, DC: American Immigration Council, May 2014).

61. Lydgate, "Assembly-Line Justice," 13–14.

62. Buentello et al., "Operation Streamline," 9; and Human Rights Watch, "Turning Migrants into Criminals," 5.

63. Federal Rules of Criminal Procedure 11(b)(2) as quoted in Edith Nazarian, "Crossing Over: Assessing Operation Streamline and the Rights of Immigrant Criminal Defendants at the Border," *Loyola of Los Angeles Law Review* 44.4 (2011), 1407.

64. Lydgate, "Assembly-Line Justice," 14. In Tucson, for example, judges began taking pleas individually while still holding hearings en masse. Lauren Gambino, "Program

Prosecutes Illegal Immigrants Before Deporting Them," News21, August 2010, http://asu .news21.com/2010/08/prosecuting-illegal-immigrants/ (retrieved May 23, 2014).

65. It appears to be affirming that the plenary power doctrine, which has long served to restrict judicial review of congressional immigration acts, applies to criminal as well as civil immigration proceedings. Nazarian, "Crossing Over," 1411–12.

66. In 1992, drug offenses accounted for 45 percent of all convictions in federal courts, while immigration violations accounted for just 5 percent. By 2012, immigration convictions (30 percent) nearly equaled drug convictions (33 percent). Light, Lopez, and Gonzalez-Barrera, "The Rise of Federal Immigration Crimes," 9.

67. Lydgate, "Assembly-Line Justice," 8–10.

68. Lydgate, "Operation Streamline."

69. Solomon Moore, "Push on Immigration Crimes Is Said to Shift Focus," *New York Times*, January 12, 2009, A1.

70. In 2006, Michael Chertoff, head of the Department of Homeland Security, explained, "We are working to get [Operation Streamline] expanded across other parts of the border" because "it has a great deterrent effect." Tom Barry, "A Death in Texas: Profits, Poverty, and Immigration Converge," *Boston Review*, November/December 2009.

71. Lydgate, "Assembly-Line Justice," 7.

72. Light et al., "The Rise of Federal Immigration Crimes," 6.

73. Jeffrey S. Passel, D'Vera Cohn, and Ana Gonzalez-Barrera, "Population Decline of Unauthorized Immigrants Stalls, May Have Reversed," Pew Research Hispanic Trends Project, September 23, 2013, http://www.pewhispanic.org/2013/09/23/population-decline -of-unauthorized-immigrants-stalls-may-have-reversed/ (retrieved January 15, 2014).

74. The death rate has tripled for migrants attempting border crossings in more remote regions of the Southwest. Douglas S. Massey, "Backfire at the Border: Why Enforcement without Legalization Cannot Stop Illegal Immigration" (Washington, DC: Center for Trade Policies Studies, Cato Institute, 2005), 1.

75. Douglas S. Massey, U.S. Senate Committee on the Judiciary, testimony, May 20, 2009; and Wayne A. Cornelius et al., eds., *Mexican Migration and the U.S. Economic Crisis: A Transnational Perspective* (San Diego: Center for Comparative Immigration, 2010).

76. Lydgate, "Assembly-Line Justice," 10.

77. Doris Marie Provine et al., "Growing Tensions between Civic Membership and Enforcement in the Devolution of Immigration Control," in Kubrin, Zatz, and Martínez, eds., *Punishing Immigrants*, 47.

78. Andrea Guttin, "The Criminal Alien Program: Immigration Enforcement in Travis County, Texas," Immigration Policy Center, February 2010, http://www.immigrationpolicy .org/special-reports/criminal-alien-program-immigration-enforcement-travis-county -texas (retrieved February 2, 2014), 16.

79. As one police detective in Travis County notes, when a woman "is afraid of deportation, usually that is something that the batterer has used to keep her in line or to try to keep her from calling law enforcement." Quoted in Guttin, "The Criminal Alien Program," 15.

80. Inter-American Commission on Human Rights, "Report on Immigration in the United States," 67.

81. Provine and Doty, "The Criminalization of Immigrants," 268.

82. ICE, "Fact Sheet: Delegation of Immigration Authority Section 287(g) Immigration and Nationality Act," n.d., http://www.ice.gov/news/library/factsheets/287g.htm (retrieved May 29, 2012).

83. Ted Hesson, "As One Immigration Enforcement Program Fades Away, Another Rises," *ABC News*, December 27, 2012, http://abcnews.go.com/ABC_Univision/News /immigration-enforcement-program-287g-scaled-back/story?id=18077757 (retrieved August 15, 2013).

84. Guttin, "The Criminal Alien Program," 4.

85. Inter-American Commission on Human Rights, "Report on Immigration," 61.

86. Guttin, "The Criminal Alien Program," 8.

87. In Travis County, Texas, which includes the city of Austin, inmates on detainer have consistently spent three times longer in jail than general population inmates. Guttin, "The Criminal Alien Program," 12.

88. Guttin, "The Criminal Alien Program," 8.

89. Personal communication with Mat Coleman of Ohio State University, who has been researching these roadblocks in North Carolina and elsewhere.

90. Hagan and Phillips, "Border Blunders," 89.

91. ICE, "Law Enforcement Support Center," n.d., http://www.ice.gov/lesc/, (retrieved August 14, 2013).

92. Aarti Kohli, Peter L. Markowitz, and Lisa Chavez, "Secure Communities by the Numbers" (Berkeley: Warren Institute of Law and Social Policy, Berkeley Law School, October 2011).

93. Spencer S. Hsu, "U.S. to Check Immigration Status of People in Local Jails," *Washington Post*, May 19, 2009, http://www.washingtonpost.com/wp-dyn/content/article/2009/05 /18/AR2009051803172.html (retrieved May 30, 2011); Hagan and Phillips, "Border Blunders," 88.

94. ICE, "Secure Communities: The Basics," n.d., http://www.ice.gov/secure _communities/ (retrieved September 8, 2014).

95. Data from National Day Laborer Organization, Center for Constitutional Rights, and the Cardozo School of Law cited in Deepa Fernandes and Abdulai Bah, "Deported and Forgotten: Is the U.S. Government Responsible for the Fate of Deportees It Brands as Criminals?," *Nation*, February 20, 2012, 25.

96. Fernandes and Bah, "Deported and Forgotten," 23–26.

97. U.S. DHS, Office of Immigration Statistics, Annual Report, "Immigration Enforcement Actions: 2010," 4, table 4.

98. As of 2013, only eleven states permitted undocumented immigrants to obtain driver's licenses. Many of these states forbid use of these licenses as official identification. Sonia Nazario, "The Heartache of an Immigrant Family," *New York Times*, October 15, 2013, A27; Kristen Wyatt, "Driver's License Campaign for Immigrants in Peril," denverpost.com, May 22, 2012, http://www.denverpost.com/news/ci_20679637/co-immigrant-advocates -plan-drivers-license-push (retrieved June 21, 2012); Ivan Moreno, "Undocumented Immigrant Driver's Licenses Bill Signed Into Law In Colorado," *Huffington Post*, June 5, 2013, http://www.huffingtonpost.com/2013/06/05/immigrant-drivers-license_n_3391941.html (retrieved October 13, 2013).

99. Julia Preston, "Police Chiefs Wary of Immigration Role," *New York Times*, March 4, 2011, A18; Julia Preston, "Resistance Widens to Obama Initiative on Criminal Immigrants," *New York Times*, August 13, 2011, A11.

100. Preston, "Resistance Widens to Obama Initiative."

101. Police Executive Research Foundation, "Police Chiefs and Sheriffs Speak Out on Local Immigration Enforcement" (Washington, DC: Police Executive Research Foundation, April 2008), 15.

102. Police Executive Research Foundation, "Police Chiefs and Sheriffs Speak Out," 23.

103. Debra A. Hoffmaster et al., "Police and Immigration: How Chiefs Are Leading Their Communities through the Challenges" (Washington, DC: Police Executive Research Foundation, 2011), viii.

104. Julia Preston and Sarah Wheaton, "Meant to Ease Fears of Deportation Program, Federal Hearings Draw Anger," *New York Times*, August 26, 2011, A13.

105. Julia Preston, "Deportation Program Sows Mistrust, U.S. Is Told," *New York Times*, September 16, 2011, A12.

106. ICE contended that once a state or local law enforcement agency submits fingerprints to the FBI's national criminal database, which is standard operating procedure when someone is arrested, no further consent is necessary to forward that data on to ICE to check against its immigrant database. ICE, "ICE Response to the Task Force on Secure Communities Findings and Recommendations," April 27, 2012, http://www.dhs.gov/xlibrary/assets /hsac/ice-response-to-task-force-on-secure-communities.pdf (retrieved February 2, 2014).

107. Julia Preston, "Fewer Illegal Immigrants Stopped for Traffic Violations Will Face Deportation," *New York Times*, April 28, 2012, A14.

108. TRAC Immigration, "New ICE Detainer Guidelines Have Little Impact," October 1, 2013, http://trac.syr.edu/immigration/reports/333/ (retrieved February 4, 2014).

109. For a good summary of the implications for immigrant detainees today of two pivotal nineteenth-century U.S. Supreme decisions, *Fong Yue Ting v. United States* 149 U.S. 698 (1893) and *Wong Wing v. United States* 163 U.S. 228 (1896), see Hernández, "Pursuant to Deportation," 47–48.

110. Hernández, "Pursuant to Deportation."

111. Lisa Getter, "Freedom Elusive for Refugees Fleeing to the U.S.," *Los Angeles Times*, December 31, 2001, A4 in Hernández, "Pursuant to Deportation," 48.

112. Sayed, "Challenging Detention."

113. Dow, *American Gulag*.

114. In an important ruling in April 2013, a federal judge in California ordered immigration courts in three states to provide legal assistance for immigrants with mental disabilities who are being detained and facing deportation if they are unable to represent themselves. This decision was the first time that any court had ruled that the government is required to provide legal help for any group of people appearing before the nation's immigration courts. Julia Preston, "In a First, Judge Orders Legal Aid for Mentally Disabled Immigrants Facing Deportation," *New York Times*, April 25, 2013, A18.

115. Mark Motivans, "Immigration Offenders in the Federal Justice System," Bureau of Justice Statistics, July 2012, rev. October 22, 2013, http://www.bjs.gov/content/pub/pdf /iofjs10.pdf (retrieved February 2, 2014).

116. Human Rights Watch, "Locked Up Far Away: The Transfer of Immigrants to Remote Detention Centers in the United States" (New York: Human Rights Watch, December 2009), 2.

117. Heartland Alliance National Immigrant Justice Center, Detention Watch Network, and Midwest Coalition for Human Rights, "Year One Report Card: Human Rights and the Obama Administration's Immigration Detention Reforms," October 6, 2010, http:// www.immigrantjustice.org/sites/immigrantjustice.org/files/ICE%20report%20card%20 FULL%20FINAL%202010%2010%2006.pdf (retrieved August 17, 2013), 24.

118. Human Rights Watch, "Locked Up Far Away," 6.

119. Mason, "Dollars and Detainees," 16.

120. The Sentencing Project reported that lists provided by ICE omitted facilities

included on ICE's website and on the websites of private prison companies. Mason, "Dollars and Detainees," 9.

121. Mason, "Dollars and Detainees," 5, 7.

122. Hutto's deplorable conditions have been the subject of scathing media coverage and the target of an ACLU lawsuit. Margaret Talbot, "The Lost Children: What Do Tougher Detention Policies Mean for Illegal Immigrant Families?," *New Yorker*, March 3, 2008, 59–67; TRAC Immigration Reports, "Huge Increase in Transfers of ICE Detainees," December 2, 2009, http://trac.syr.edu/immigration/reports/220/ (retrieved June 21, 2012).

123. Inter-American Commission on Human Rights, "Report on Immigration in the United States," 88–89; Karen Tumlin, Linton Joaquin, and Ranjana Natarajan, "A Broken System: Confidential Reports Reveal Failures in U.S. Immigrant Detention Centers" (Los Angeles: National Immigration Law Center, 2009), vi.

124. ICE, "Detention Management," November 10, 2011, http://www.ice.gov/news /library/factsheets/detention-mgmt.htm (retrieved May 30, 2012).

125. Tumlin, Joaquin, and Natarajan, "A Broken System," vi. See also Detention Watch Network's report documenting conditions in what it classifies as the "ten worst" detention facilities in the United States. "Expose and Close," November 2012, http://detentionwatch -network.org/sites/detentionwatchnetwork.org/files/ExposeClose/Expose-Executive11–15 .pdf (retrieved August 15, 2013).

126. In 2011, the U.S. House passed a bill that would require federal detention facilities to report deaths in custody to the attorney general, but this measure stalled in the Senate. Rep. Bobby Scott, "Death in Custody Reporting Act of 2011," H.R. 2189, *Congressional Record*, June 15, 2011, http://beta.congress.gov/bill/112th/house-bill/2189/actions (retrieved October 13, 2013); Nina Bernstein, "Few Details on Immigrants Who Died in Custody," *New York Times*, May 5, 2008, A1; ACLU, "Deaths in Custody Reporting Act Must Demand Accountability in Federal Immigration Detention Facilities," press release, September 18, 2008, http://www.aclu.org/immigrants/detention/36849prs20080918.html (retrieved October 4, 2008).

127. Miller, "Lessons Learned," 239.

128. Miller, "Lessons Learned," 239–40.

129. This practice is legal because the detainees are technically receiving stipends—not wages—for voluntary work, according to an ICE spokesman. Yana Kunichoff, "'Voluntary' Work Program in Private Detention Centers Pays Detained Immigrants $1 a Day," *Prison Legal News*, August 2012, 46–48.

130. This paragraph is based on Jacqueline Stevens, "America's Secret ICE Castles," *Nation*, January 4, 2010, 13.

131. Will Matthews, "Immigration Detention: A Death Sentence for Far Too Many," Blog of Rights, ACLU, October 24, 2011, http://www.aclu.org/blog/immigrants-rights /immigration-detention-death-sentence-far-too-many (retrieved May 16, 2012).

132. Nina Bernstein, "U.S. to Reform Policy on Detention for Immigrants," *New York Times*, August 6, 2009, A1; Matthews, "Immigration Detention"; PBS Frontline, "How Much Sexual Abuse Gets 'Lost in Detention'?," October 19, 2011, http://www.pbs.org /wgbh/pages/frontline/race-multicultural/lost-in-detention/how-much-sexual-abuse -gets-lost-in-detention/ (retrieved May 16, 2012); Heartland Alliance et al., "Year One Report Card."

133. Schriro, "Immigration Detention Overview and Recommendations."

134. John T. Morton, speech before Migration Policy Institute, January 25, 2010, quoted in Kalhan, "Rethinking Immigration Detention," 44.

135. Nina Bernstein, "Ideas for Immigrant Detention Include Converting Hotels and Building Models," *New York Times*, October 6, 2009, A14.

136. "How to Make Money and Increase Safety by Working with ICE," corrections .com, June 8, 2010, http://www.correctionsone.com/facility-design-and-operation/articles /2080068-How-to-make-money-and-increase-safety-by-working-with-ICE/ (retrieved June 14, 2012).

137. Matt Clarke, "Southern California Jails Addicted to ICE Money," *Prison Legal News*, October 2009, 19.

138. Barry, "A Death in Texas."

139. Laura Sullivan, "Prison Economics Help Drive Arizona Law," NPR, October 28, 2010, http://www.npr.org/2010/10/28/130833741/prison-economics-help-drive-ariz-immigration -law (retrieved June 14, 2012); Beau Hodai, "Corporate Con Game: How the Private Prison Industry Helped Shaped Arizona's Anti-Immigrant Law," *In These Times*, June 21, 2010, 17.

140. John Culberson, "The Daily Caller: Secretary Napolitano Ignores Border Violence," March 16, 2011, http://culberson.house.gov/congressman-culberson-in-the-daily-caller/ (retrieved June 8, 2012).

141. Kirk Semple, "Mass Release of Immigrants Is Tied to Cuts," *New York Times*, February 27, 2013, A1; Julia Preston, "Administration Official Defends Release of Detainees," *New York Times*, March 20, 2013, A18.

142. For an overview of recent work on public opinion about immigrants and crime, see John Hagan, Ron Levi, and Ronit Dinovitzer, "The Symbolic Violence of the Crime-Immigration Nexus: Migrant Mythologies in the Americas," *Criminology & Public Policy* 7.1 (2008), 98. On the evolving debate in Europe about immigration and crime, see Alessandro De Giorgi, *Re-Thinking the Political Economy of Punishment: Perspectives on Post-Fordism and Penal Politics* (Aldershot, UK: Ashgate, 2006), ch. 5.

143. For a succinct overview of the central role that allegations of Mexican and Latino criminality have played in U.S. history, see José Luis Morín, "Latinas/os and U.S. Prisons: Trends and Challenges," *Latino Studies* 6.1–2 (2008), 15–17.

144. Alan Gomez, Jack Gillum, and Kevin Johnson, "U.S. Border Cities Prove Havens from Mexico's Drug War," *USA Today*, July 14, 2011, http://usatoday30.usatoday .com/news/washington/2011-07-15-border-violence-main_n.htm (retrieved June 12, 2012).

145. Robert J. Sampson, "Rethinking Crime and Immigration," *Contexts* 7.1 (2008): 28–33; John MacDonald and Robert J. Sampson, "The World in a City: Immigration and America's Changing Social Fabric," *ANNALS of the American Academy of Political and Social Science* 641 (May 2012), 9; Garth Davies and Jeffrey Fagan, "Crime and Enforcement in Immigrant Neighborhoods: Evidence from New York City," *ANNALS of the American Academy of Political and Social Science* 641 (May 2012): 99–124.

146. Ramiro Martinez, Jr., and Jacob I. Stowell, "Extending Immigration and Crime Studies: National Implications and Local Settings," *ANNALS of the American Academy of Political and Social Science* 641 (May 2012), 189; Hagan et al., "The Symbolic Violence," 99–104; John MacDonald and Jessica Saunders, "Are Immigrant Youth Less Violent? Specifying the Reasons and Mechanisms," *ANNALS of the American Academy of Political and Social Science* 641 (May 2012): 125–47.

147. Tim Wadsworth, "Is Immigration Responsible for the Crime Drop? An Assessment of Immigration on Changes in Violent Crime Between 1990 and 2000," *Social Science Quarterly* 91.2 (2010): 531–53; Robert J. Sampson, "Open Doors Don't Invite Criminals: Is Increased Immigration Behind the Drop in Crime?," *New York Times*, March 11, 2006, A27;

Marjorie S. Zatz and Hilary Smith, "Immigration, Crime, and Victimization: Rhetoric and Reality," *Annual Review of Law and Social Sciences*, v. 8 (2012): 141–59.

148. Barry, "A Death in Texas."

149. Edward Hegstrom, "Sheila Jackson Lee Proposes Stronger Border Security," *Houston Chronicle*, October 18, 2005, http://www.chron.com/news/houston-texas/article /Jackson-Lee-proposes-stronger-border-security-1943760.php (retrieved June 20, 2012); Christopher Nugent, "Towards Balancing a New Immigration and Nationality Act: Enhanced Immigration Enforcement and Fair, Humane and Cost-Effective Treatment of Aliens," *University of Maryland Law Journal of Race, Religion, Gender, & Class* 5.2 (2005), 252.

150. Krentz was the only American murdered by a suspected unauthorized immigrant in at least a decade within the Tucson sector of the Border Patrol, which is one of the busiest smuggling routes along the U.S.–Mexico border. Randal C. Archibold, "On Border Violence, Truth Pales Compared to Ideas," *New York Times*, June 20, 2010, A18; Dennis Wagner, "Violence Is Not Up on Arizona Border," *Arizona Republic*, May 2, 2010, http:// www.azcentral.com/arizonarepublic/news/articles/2010/05/02/20100502arizona-border -violence-mexico.html (retrieved July 5, 2012).

151. Jennifer M. Chacón, "Whose Community Shield?: Examining the Removal of the 'Criminal Street Gang Member,'" *University of Chicago Legal Forum* (2007): 1–41; Sarah Garland, "Suburban Ghetto: Segregation, Not Immigration, Is to Blame for the Growth of Hispanic Gangs," *American Prospect*, September 2009, 28–30.

152. James Webb, "Floor Speech to Introduce 'The National Criminal Justice Commission Act of 2009,'" March 26, 2009, b.senate.gov/newsroom/floorandcommitteestatements /2009–03–26–01.cfm (retrieved June 22, 2012).

153. Frank Clifford, "The Border Effect," *American Prospect*, September/October 2012, 63.

154. "Obama's Speech on Immigration from El Paso, Texas," *National Journal*, May 10, 2011, http://www.nationaljournal.com/whitehouse/text-obama-s-speech-on-immigration -from-el-paso-texas-20110510 (retrieved June 22, 2012); Peter Andreas, *Border Games: Policing the U.S.-Mexico Divide* (Ithaca, NY: Cornell University Press, 2000), cited in Hagan and Phillips, "Border Blunders," 84.

155. Meissner et al., "Immigration Enforcement in the United States," 22.

156. Julianne Hing, "DREAMers Welcome Obama's Immigration Shift, But Pledge Caution," *Colorlines*, June 18, 2012, http://colorlines.com/archives/2012/06/obamas_small _immigration_fix_for_dreamers_a_big_political_win.html (retrieved June 20, 2012); Devin Dwyer, "Obama 'Softens' Immigration Policy with Mixed Results," ABC News, February 24, 2012, http://abcnews.go.com/blogs/politics/2012/02/obama-softens-immigration-policy-with-mixed-results/ (retrieved June 16, 2012); Julia Preston, "Deportations Go On Despite U.S. Review of Backlog," *New York Times*, June 7, 2012, A12.

157. Julia Preston and John H. Cushman, Jr., "Obama to Permit Young Migrants to Remain in U.S.," *New York Times*, June 16, 2012, A1; Seth Freed Wessler, "Rep. Gutierrez: Stop Deporting Parents as Reform Debate Unfolds," *Colorlines*, December 18, 2012, http:// colorlines.com/archives/2012/12/advocates_and.html (retrieved August 15, 2013).

158. ICE, "FY 2013 ICE Immigration Removals," n.d., http://www.ice.gov/removal -statistics/ (retrieved February 2, 2014); Julia Preston, "U.S. Deportations Decline; Felons Made Up Big Share," *New York Times*, December 20, 2013, A20.

159. TRAC Immigration, "At Nearly 100,000, Immigration Prosecutions Reach All-Time High in FY 2013," November 25, 2013, http://trac.syr.edu/immigration/reports/336/ (retrieved February 2, 2014); TRAC Immigration, "Southern District of Texas Leading in

Record Year for Immigration Prosecutions," May 10, 2013, http://trac.syr.edu/immigration/reports/318/ (retrieved February 2, 2014).

160. The Supreme Court left open the door to future challenges to SB 1070 on other constitutional grounds. Julia Preston, "A Hearing and Rallies Over a Law in Arizona," *New York Times*, April 25, 2012, A14; Adam Liptak, "Court Splits Immigration Law Verdicts; Upholds Hotly Debate Centerpiece, 8–0," *New York Times*, June 26, 2012, A1.

161. Julia Preston, "Justices' Decision a Narrow Opening for Other States," *New York Times*, June 26, 2012, A12.

162. Fernanda Santos and Charlie Savage, "Lawsuit Says Sheriff Discriminated Against Latinos," *New York Times*, May 11, 2012, A18.

163. Hernández, "Pursuant to Deportation," 40; Wadhia, "The Policy and Politics of Immigrant Rights," 398.

164. Saurav Sarkar, "What They're Marching For," *Nation*, June 19, 2006, 18–20; Michelle Chen, "Activists See Broader Immigration Debate Beyond the Beltway," *NewStandard*, April 17, 2006, http://paceebene.org/nvns/nonviolence-news-service-archive/activists-seek-broader-immigration-debate-beyond-beltway (retrieved July 8, 2012).

165. Rebecca Burns, "The Devil's in the Details," *In These Times*, September 2013, 8–9.

166. It also included $8 billion to double the length of the controversial fence along the Southwest border and $4.5 billion to expand drone and other military operations directed at immigrants. Sen. Patrick Leahy (D-VT), chairman of the Senate Judiciary Committee, said the border security amendment "reads like a Christmas wish list for Halliburton," the military contractor. Alexander Bolton, "Leahy: Border Security Measure Reads 'Like a Christmas Wish List for Halliburton,'" *The Hill*, June 22, 2013, http://thehill.com/home news/senate/307205-leahy-border-security-measure-reads-like-a-christmas-wish-list-for -halliburton (retrieved August 16, 2013).

167. See, for example, National Network for Immigrant and Refugee Rights, "Open Letter to the Members of the Senate Judiciary Committee in Support of Fair and Just Immigration Reform," May 20, 2013, http://www.nnirr.org/%7Ennirrorg/drupal/sites/default /files/senate_judiciary_committee_letter_with_signatures.pdf (retrieved February 3, 2014); National Network for Immigrant and Refugee Rights, "'Border Surge' Approval Further Threatens Border Communities, Migrant Safety and Well-Being," press release, June 28, 2013, http://www.nnirr.org/~nnirrorg/drupal/senate-bill-dashes-hopes (retrieved February 3, 2014); and remarks by Reps. Beto O'Rourke (D-TX), Susan Davis (D-CA), Pete Gallego (D-TX), and Filemon Vela (D-TX), U.S. House, *Congressional Record*, "U.S.-Mexico Border," June 26, 2013, H4068-H4074.

168. Seung Min Kim, "Filemon Vela Quits Hispanic Caucus over Borer Surge," *Politico*, July 2, 2013, http://www.politico.com/story/2013/07/filemon-vela-quits-hispanic-caucus -border-surge-93676.html (retrieved August 15, 2013).

169. For a succinct comparison of the various immigration bills, see Migration Policy Institute, "Immigration Bills: Side-by-Side Comparison of 2013 Senate Immigration Bill with Individual 2013 House Bills," Issue Brief 7 (August 2013), http://www.migrationpolicy .org/pubs/CIRbrief-2013House-SenateBills-Side-by-Side.pdf (retrieved August 17, 2013). See also Human Rights Watch, "US: Reject Extreme Immigration Enforcement Bill," press release, June 19, 2013, http://www.hrw.org/news/2013/06/19/us-reject-extreme-immigration -enforcement-bill (retrieved August 16, 2013).

170. Thompson and Cohen, "More Deportations Follow Minor Crimes."

171. David Nakamura, "Obama Administration Likely to Refocus Deportation Policy, Police Chiefs Say," *Washington Post*, May 13, 2014, http://www.washingtonpost.com/politics

/obama-administration-likely-to-refocus-deportation-policy-police-chiefs-say/2014
/05/13/afc298d2-daad-11e3-bda1–9b46b2066796_story.html (retrieved May 19, 2014).

172. Julia Preston, "Young Immigrants Turn Focus to President in Struggle Over Deportations," *New York Times*, April 7, 2014, A11.

173. Micah Uetricht, "Big Business Aims to Crush Worker Centers," *In These Times*, July 30, 2013, http://inthesetimes.com/working/entry/15378/big_business_aims_to_crush _worker_centers/ (retrieved August 18, 2013); Steven Greenhouse, "The Workers Defense Project, a Union in Spirit," *New York Times*, August 10, 2013, B1.

174. Jenny Brown, "Immigrants and Unions Work to Oust Notorious Arizona Sheriff," *Labor Notes*, November 2012, 1.

175. CBS/KPIX, "AP Report: California Immigrant Deportations Plummet After TRUST Act," April 6, 2014, http://sanfrancisco.cbslocal.com/2014/04/06/immigration-deportation -trust-act/ (retrieved September 3, 2014).

176. Shortly after the coalition launched its protests, Pershing Square Capital Management, the New York-based hedge fund, sold its remaining shares in CCA stock. It did not say whether its actions were related to the divestment campaign. In early 2012, the United Methodist Church, which has the largest faith-based pension fund in the country, announced it would be unloading its GEO and CCA stock as a result of the divestment campaign. Joel Handley, "Divesting from Private Prisons," *In These Times*, July 15, 2011, http:// www.inthesetimes.com/article/11623/divesting_from_private_prisons/ (retrieved October 24, 2012); Hannah Rappleye, "Profiting from Prisons," *Crime Report*, February 14, 2012, http://www.thecrimereport.org/news/inside-criminal-justice/2012–02-profiting-from -prisons (retrieved October 24, 2012).

Chapter Eleven
The Prison beyond the Prison

1. Gustave de Beaumont and Alexis de Tocqueville, *On the Penitentiary System in the United States and Its Application in France* (Carbondale: Southern Illinois University Press, 1833/1979), 79.

2. Jeff Manza and Christopher Uggen, *Locked Out: Felon Disenfranchisement and American Democracy* (New York: Oxford University Press, 2006), 9; Jonathan Simon, *Governing Through Crime: How the War on Crime Transformed American Democracy and Created a Culture of Fear* (New York: Oxford University Press, 2007), 164.

3. Bruce Western, *Punishment and Inequality in America* (New York: Russell Sage Foundation, 2006), 191.

4. Michelle Alexander, *The New Jim Crow: Mass Incarceration in the Age of Colorblindness* (New York: New Press, 2010), 12.

5. Craig Haney, "Counting Casualties in the War on Prisoners," *University of San Francisco Law Review* 43.1 (2008), 90.

6. Shawn D. Bushway and Gary Sweeten, "Abolish Lifetime Bans for Ex-Felons," *Criminology & Public Policy* 6.4 (2007), 700; Alfred Blumstein and Kiminori Nakamura, "Redemption in the Presence of Widespread Criminal Background Checks," *Criminology & Public Policy* 47.2 (2009): 327–59.

7. American Bar Association, "ABA Standards for Criminal Justice: Collateral Sanctions and Discretionary Disqualification of Convicted Persons," 3rd ed., 2004, http://www .americanbar.org/content/dam/aba/publishing/criminal_justice_section_newsletter/crimjust

_standards_collateralsanctionwithcommentary.authcheckdam.pdf (retrieved August 31, 2013), 29.

8. American Bar Association Criminal Justice Section, "Adult Collateral Consequences Project News," November 20, 2011, http://isrweb.isr.temple.edu/projects/accproject/blog.cfm?RecordID=1 (retrieved June 26, 2012). See also Margaret Colgate Love, "Restoration of Rights Project," National Association of Criminal Defense Lawyers, n.d., http://www.nacdl.org/rightsrestoration/ (retrieved January 29, 2014).

9. "Holder Urges States to Review Laws Imposing Curbs on Ex-Prisoners," *Crime and Justice News*, April 2011, http://www.thecrimereport.org/news/crime-and-justice-news/2011-04-holder-urges-states-to-review-laws-that-impose-restr (retrieved May 12, 2012).

10. Simon, *Governing Through Crime*, 194–98; Alexander, *The New Jim Crow*, ch. 4.

11. Mireya Navarro, "Ban on Former Inmates in Public Housing Is Eased," *New York Times*, November 15, 2013, A25; Marc Mauer and Virginia McCalmont, "A Lifetime of Punishment: The Impact of the Felony Drug Ban on Welfare Benefits" (Washington, DC: The Sentencing Project, 2013).

12. U.S. GAO, "Drug Offenders: Various Factors May Impede the Impacts of Federal Laws That Provide for Denial of Selected Benefits" (Washington, DC: GAO, 2005), 57, table 14.

13. Brian C. Kalt, "The Exclusion of Felons from Jury Service," *American University Law Review* 53.1 (2003), 67. In one county in Georgia, about 70 percent of the African American men are ineligible for jury service due to a felony conviction. Darren Wheelock, "A Jury of 'Peers': Felon Jury Exclusion, Racial Threat, and Racial Inequality in United States Criminal Courts," University of Minnesota, PhD dissertation, 2006, in Darren Wheelock and Christopher Uggen, "Punishment, Crime, and Poverty," in Ann Chih Lin and David R. Harris, eds., *The Colors of Poverty: Why Racial and Ethnic Disparities Persist* (New York: Russell Sage Foundation, 2008), 278.

14. A 2010 study of racial discrimination in jury selection in eight Southern states concluded that in many instances "people of color not only have been illegally excluded but also denigrated and insulted with pretexual reasons intended to conceal racial bias." Equal Justice Initiative, "Illegal Racial Discrimination in Jury Selection" (Montgomery, AL: Equal Justice Initiative, August 2010).

15. Michael B. Katz, *The Price of Citizenship: Redefining the American Welfare State*, updated ed. (Philadelphia: University of Pennsylvania Press, 2008), 347. See also Judith N. Shklar, *American Citizenship: The Quest for Inclusion* (Cambridge, MA: Harvard University Press, 1991).

16. Michelle Natividad Rodriguez and Maurice Emsellem, "65 Million 'Need Not Apply': The Case for Reforming Criminal Background Checks for Employment" (New York: National Employment Law Project, 2011), 27, n. 2.

17. Robert Brame et al., "Demographic Patterns of Cumulative Arrest Prevalence by Ages 18 and 23," *Criminology & Penology* online version, January 6, 2014, http://cad.sagepub.com/content/early/2013/12/18/0011128713514801.full.pdf+html (retrieved January 30, 2014).

18. Gerard F. Ramker, "Improving Criminal History Records for Background Checks, 2005," Bureau of Justice Statistics Program Report, July 2006, http://www.bjs.gov/content/pub/pdf/ichrbc05.pdf (retrieved September 8, 2013), 1. See also Blumstein and Nakamura, "Redemption."

19. James B. Jacobs and Elena Larrauri, "Are Criminal Convictions a Public Matter? The USA and Spain," *Punishment & Society* 14.1 (2012): 3–28.

20. Alexander, *The New Jim Crow*, 13; Paul Street, "The Vicious Circle: Race, Prison, Jobs, and Community in Chicago, Illinois, and the Nation" (Chicago: Chicago Urban League, Department of Research and Planning, 2002).

21. Devah Pager, *Marked: Race, Crime, and Finding Work in an Era of Mass Incarceration* (Chicago: University of Chicago Press, 2007), 67.

22. Pager, *Marked*, 192.

23. Steven Greenhouse, "Equal Opportunity Panel Updates Hiring Policy," *New York Times*, April 26, 2012, B23; Duane Marsteller, "Dollar General Sued Over Background Check Policy," *Tennessean*, June 12, 2013, http://www.wbir.com/news/article/277221/2/Dollar-General-sued-over-background-check-policy (retrieved August 31, 2013).

24. This paragraph is based on Madeline Neighly and Maurice Emsellem, "Wanted: Accurate FBI Checks for Employment" (New York: National Employment Law Project, 2013), 1–4.

25. Neighly and Emsellem, "Wanted," 1.

26. James Kilgore, "The Myth of Prison Slave Labor Camps in the U.S.," *Counterpunch*, August 9–11, 2013, http://www.counterpunch.org/2013/08/09/the-myth-of-prison-slave-labor-camps-in-the-u-s/ (retrieved January 30, 2014).

27. Alec C. Ewald, "'Civil Death': The Ideological Paradox of Criminal Disenfranchisement Law in the United States," *Wisconsin Law Review* 2002.5 (2002): 1045–1132.

28. *Reynolds v. Sims* 377 U. S. 533 (1964), 555. This decision declared that legislative districts within a state that were not of comparable population sizes were unconstitutional.

29. At least 18 European countries place no restrictions on the right to vote for imprisoned offenders. About half a dozen, including England, do not allow prisoners to vote. Some European countries restrict prisoners' right to vote based on the crime committed or their length of sentence. Isobel White, "Prisoners' Voting Rights," U.K. Parliament, January 15, 2014, http://www.google.com/#q=Isobel+White%2C+"Prisoners'+Voting+Rights%2C"+U.K.+Parliament%2C+May+15%2C+2013+ (retrieved February 24, 2014), 8–9, 48–58.

30. Thirty-five states prohibit parolees from voting, and 30 of those states also bar probationers. Christopher Uggen, Sarah Shannon, and Jeff Manza, "State-Level Estimates of Felon Disenfranchisement in the United States, 2010" (Washington, DC: The Sentencing Project, 2012), 3, table 1.

31. Christopher Uggen, Jeff Manza, and Melissa Thompson, "Citizenship, Democracy, and the Civic Reintegration of Criminal Offenders," *ANNALS of the American Academy of Political & Social Science* 605 (May 2006): 281–310; Khalilah L. Brown-Dean, "One Lens, Multiple Views: Felon Disenfranchisement Laws and American Political Inequality," Ohio State University, PhD dissertation, 2004; Elizabeth A. Hull, *The Disenfranchisement of Ex-Felons* (Philadelphia: Temple University Press, 2006); Manza and Uggen, *Locked Out*, ch. 2; Katherine I. Pettus, *Felony Disenfranchisement in America: Historical Origins, Institutional Racism, and Modern Consequences* (New York: LFB Scholarly Publishing, 2005), chs. 3–5.

32. Uggen et al., "State-Level Estimates," 1.

33. In the 2004 election, this amounted to 600,000 people. Manza and Uggen, *Locked Out*, 76–77, 81.

34. The prevalence of such lifetime bans may be greater than previously thought. New research suggests that administrative practices sometimes turn what are technically temporary voting bans into de facto bans for life on voting. Jessie Allen, "Documentary Disenfranchisement," *Tulane Law Review* 86.2 (2011): 389–464.

35. Uggen et al., "State-Level Estimates," 16, table 3.

36. Uggen et al., "State-Level Estimates," 1–2.

37. Marisa J. Demeo and Steven A. Ochoa, "Diminished Voting Power in the Latino Community: The Impact of Felony Disenfranchisement Laws in Ten Targeted States" (Los Angeles: MALDEF, December 2003), 6, 8.

38. Cartagena, "Lost Votes, Body Counts and Joblessness," 194–95.

39. Manza and Uggen, Locked Out, 192. Traci R. Burch disputes this claim. See "Did Disenfranchisement Laws Help Elect President Bush? New Evidence on the Turnout Rates and Candidate Preferences of Florida's Ex-Felons," Political Behavior 34.1 (2012): 1–26.

40. Manza and Uggen, Locked Out, 192–96.

41. Michael C. Campbell, "Criminal Disenfranchisement Reform in California: A Deviant Case Study," Punishment & Society 9.2 (2007), 195.

42. Writing for the majority in Richardson v. Ramirez, Justice William Rehnquist argued that felon disenfranchisement laws were constitutional under Section 2 of the Fourteenth Amendment of the Constitution. This provision calls for reducing a state's representation in Congress if the state has denied the right to vote for any reason "except for participation in rebellion, or other crime." In his ruling, Rehnquist converted a "provision meant to politically penalize those states that came into the Union after the Civil War and insisted on disqualifying former slaves, into a sword against full Black and Latino political empowerment." Cartagena, "Lost Votes, Body Counts and Joblessness," 194.

43. Khalilah L. Brown-Dean, "Once Convicted, Forever Doomed: Race, Ex-Felon Disenfranchisement, and Fractured Citizenship," mimeo, n.d., 202. These groups included People for the American Way, Demos, the American Federation of Labor-Congress of Industrial Organizations (AFL-CIO), and the Brennan Center for Justice.

44. Nicole Porter, "Expanding the Vote: State Felony Disenfranchisement Reform, 1997–2010" (Washington, DC: The Sentencing Project, 2010).

45. Brandon Sample, "Voting Rights Must Be 'Earned' Back, Says Iowa Governor," Prison Legal News, August 2011, 37.

46. Porter, "Expanding the Vote," 12.

47. Ari Berman, "The GOP's New Southern Strategy," Nation, February 20, 2012, 12–15, 17; Jennifer Stein Auer, "After Fiery Speech, Voting Rights Amendment Is Pulled," The Caucus, May 10, 2012, http://thecaucus.blogs.nytimes.com/2012/05/10/after-fiery-speech-voting-rights-amendment-is-pulled/ (retrieved September 10, 2014).

48. An inaccurate voter registration list that mistakenly identified many eligible voters as felons or former felons who were ineligible to vote was a major source of controversy in the 2000 election in Florida, which was decided by 537 votes in Florida and five votes on the U.S. Supreme Court.

49. David Reutter, "Florida Reenacts Reconstruction-Era Felon Disenfranchisement Rule," Prison Legal News, September 2011, 28–29.

50. Amy Goodnough, "Disenfranchised Florida Felons Struggle to Regain Their Rights," New York Times, March 28, 2004, 1.

51. "115,000 Florida Ex-Felons Have Civil Rights Restored Under New Rules," Prison Legal News, January 2009, 26; Ion Sancho, Supervisor of Elections, Leon County, Florida, "H.R. 3335: Democracy Restoration Act of 2009," testimony, March 16, 2010, U.S. House, Committee on the Judiciary, Subcommittee on the Constitution, Civil Rights and Civil Liberties, http://judiciary.house.gov/_files/hearings/printers/111th/111-84_55480.PDF (retrieved May 24, 2014), 65–67.

52. David Reutter, "Florida Reenacts Reconstruction-Era Felon Disenfranchisement Rule," Prison Legal News, September 2011, 28–29.

53. For a succinct overview of key court decisions on felon disenfranchisement, see Manza and Uggen, *Locked Out*, 28–34.

54. Most lower courts have determined that the VRA is not applicable to the felon disenfranchisement issue. In a dissenting opinion in a 2006 New York federal district court case, Sonia Sotomayor argued that felon disenfranchisement laws fell under the purview of the VRA and could be considered an unlawful bar to voting. Her view caused consternation in conservative circles when she was nominated for the Supreme Court three years later. Linda Greenhouse, "Voting Behind Bars," opinionator.blogs.nytimes.com, July 29, 2010, http://www.google.com/#q=Linda+Greenhouse%2C+"Voting+Behind+Bars%2C"+New +York+Times%2C+July+29%2C+2010 (retrieved May 24, 2014); Ryan P. Haygood, "Disregarding the Results: Examining the Ninth Circuit's Heightened Section 2 'Intentional Discrimination' Standard in *Farrakhan v. Gregoire*," *Columbia Law Review*, May 17, 2011, http://www.columbialawreview.org/articles/disregarding-the-results-examining-the -ninth-circuit-s-heightened-section-2-intentional-discrimination-standard-in-farrakhan-v -gregoire (retrieved May 3, 2012); Warren Richey, "Supreme Court Rejects Massachusetts' Felons Voting Rights Challenge," *Christian Science Monitor*, October 18, 2010.

55. Brennan Center for Justice, "Eric Holder, Rand Paul Unite on Restoring Voting Rights," press release, February 19, 2014, http://www.brennancenter.org/press-release /eric-holder-rand-paul-unite-restoring-voting-rights (retrieved February 24, 2014).

56. Traci R. Burch, *Trading Democracy for Justice: Criminal Convictions and the Decline of Neighborhood Political Participation* (Chicago: University of Chicago Press, 2013); Randi Hjalmarsson and Mark Lopez, "The Voting Behavior of Young Disenfranchised Felons: Would They Vote if They Could?," *American Law and Economics Review* 12.2 (2010): 265–79.

57. Vesla Weaver and Amy E. Lerman, "Political Consequences of the Carceral State," *American Political Science Review* 104.4 (2010), 827; Mark Peffley and Jon Hurwitz, *Justice in America: The Separate Realities of Blacks and Whites* (New York: Cambridge University Press, 2010), 189. See also Cathy J. Cohen, *Democracy Remixed: Black Youth and the Future of American Politics* (New York: Oxford University Press, 2010); Lawrence D. Bobo and Victor Thompson, "Unfair by Design: The War on Drugs, Race, and the Legitimacy of the Criminal Justice System," *Social Research* 73.2 (2006): 445–72.

58. Jason Schnittker and Valerio Bacak, "A Mark of Disgrace or a Badge of Honor?: Subjective Status among Former Inmates," *Social Problems* 60.2 (2013): 234–54.

59. Ian Loader and Richard Sparks, "Beyond Lamentation: Democratic Egalitarian Politics of Crime and Justice," in Tim Newburn and Jill Peay, eds., *Policing: Politics, Culture and Control* (Oxford: Hart, 2012), 30.

60. Traci Burch, "Effects of Imprisonment and Community Supervision on Neighborhood Political Participation in North Carolina," *ANNALS of the American Academy of Political and Social Science* 651 (January 2014): 184–201.

61. Burch, *Trading Democracy for Justice*, 2013.

62. Naomi F. Sugie, "Chilling Effects: Diminished Political Participation Among Partners of Ex-Felons," mimeo, March 2012; Hedwig Lee, Lauren C. Porter, and Megan Comfort, "The Consequences of Family Member Incarceration: Impacts on Civic Participation and Perceptions of the Legitimacy and Fairness of Government," *ANNALS of the American Academy of Political and Social Science* 651 (January 2014): 44–73.

63. Traci R. Burch, "Punishment and Participation: How Criminal Convictions Threaten American Democracy," Harvard University, PhD dissertation, 2007, chs. 5 and 6.

64. Shayla C. Nunnally, *Trust in Black America: Race, Discrimination and Politics* (New

York: NYU Press, 2012). Dozens of state legislatures have debated measures that would permit judges to inform juries in criminal cases of their right to nullify the law. A growing number of attorneys are encouraging wider discussion of jury nullification as a way to correct perceived injustices in the criminal justice system. Peffley and Hurwitz, *Justice in America*, 15; Paul Butler, "Jury Nullification: Power to the People," *Prison Legal News*, June 2009, 14–15.

65. "West Virginia Court-Supervised Parole and Condition Barring Association with Spouse Upheld," *Prison Legal News*, August 2013, 19.

66. Alice Goffman, "On the Run: Wanted Men in a Philadelphia Ghetto," *American Sociological Review* 74.3 (2009), 353. See also Alice Goffman, *On the Run: Fugitive Life in an American City* (Chicago: University of Chicago Press, 2014).

67. Most of these men are wanted for trivial infractions, like a missed court date or a technical violation of probation or parole. Few are on the run for failure to turn themselves in for a major crime. Goffman. "On the Run," 353.

68. Goffman, "On the Run," 353.

69. Edward E. Rhine, "The Present Status and Future Prospects of Parole Boards and Parole Supervision," in Joan Petersilia and Kevin Reitz, eds., *The Oxford Handbook of Sentencing and Corrections* (New York: Oxford University Press, 2012), 637. By one calculation, the average probationer in the United States can expect to have 13 conditions of supervision compared to just 1.5 for probationers in Scotland. Edward E. Rhine and Faye S. Taxman, "American Exceptionalism in Community Supervision: A Comparative Analysis of Probation in the United States, Scotland and Sweden," paper presented at University of Minnesota Law School, Robina Conference, April 26, 2013, 22.

70. Katherine Beckett and Steve Herbert, *Banished: The New Social Control in Urban America* (New York: Oxford University Press, 2010), 52–53, 94. For example, the high-tech license readers mounted on 87 police cruisers statewide in Massachusetts scan literally millions of plates a year. They check out not only the car and owner's legal history, but also create "a precise record of where each vehicle was at a given moment." Shawn Musgrave, "Big Brother or Better Police Work? New Technology Automatically Runs License Plates . . . of Everyone," boston.com, April 8, 2013, http://www.boston.com/news/local/massachusetts/2013/04/08 /big-brother-better-police-work-new-technology-automatically-runs-license-plates-every one/jpEEIHEY9StG44NWqOurbO/story.html (retrieved September 23, 2013).

71. Joan Petersilia, *When Prisoners Come Home: Parole and Prisoner Reentry* (New York: Oxford University Press, 2003), 82.

72. This discussion of modern-day forms of banishment is based primarily on Beckett and Herbert, *Banished*; and Katherine Beckett and Steve Herbert, "Penal Boundaries: Banishment and the Expansion of Punishment," *Law & Social Inquiry* 35.1 (2010): 1–38.

73. Beckett and Herbert, "Penal Boundaries," 3.

74. Amnesty International, "Stonewalled: Police Abuse and Misconduct Against Lesbian, Gay, Bisexual, and Transgender People in the United States," September 2005, http:// www.amnesty.org/en/library/asset/AMR51/122/2005/en/2200113d-d4bd-11dd-8a23 -d58a49c0d652/amr511222005en.pdf (retrieved February 15, 2014); Joey L. Mogul, Andrea J. Ritchie, and Kay Whitlock, *Queer (In)Justice: The Criminalization of LGBT People in the United States* (Boston: Beacon Press, 2011), ch. 3.

75. Beckett and Herbert, "Penal Boundaries," 7.

76. Becket and Herbert, *Banished*, 93–95.

77. Beckett and Herbert, "Penal Boundaries," 9.

78. Beckett and Herbert, *Banished*, 11.

79. Beckett and Herbert, "Penal Boundaries," 30.

80. Western, *Punishment and Inequality*, ch. 5.

81. Western, *Punishment and Inequality*, ch. 6.

82. Becky Pettit and Bryan Sykes, "The Demographic Implications of the Prison Boom: Evidence of a 'Third Demographic Transition'?," mimeo, July 2008.

83. Western, *Punishment and Inequality*, 7.

84. Becky Pettit, *Invisible Men: Mass Incarceration and the Myth of Black Progress* (New York: Russell Sage Foundation, 2012), xii.

85. Pettit, *Invisible Men*, 27, table 2.1.

86. Pettit, *Invisible Men*, 30–31.

87. Pettit, *Invisible Men*, 31.

88. Pettit, *Invisible Men*, 32.

89. These include the National Health Interview Survey (NHIS), the National Health and Nutrition Examination Survey (NHANES), and the National Survey of Family Growth (NSFG).

90. Pettit, *Invisible Men*, 8, 94–96.

91. Bruce Western and Katherine Beckett, "How Unregulated Is the U.S. Labor Market? The Penal System as a Labor Market Institution," *American Journal of Sociology* 104.4 (1999), 1052; and Western, *Punishment and Inequality*, 90.

92. Western, *Punishment and Inequality*, 104.

93. Western, *Punishment and Inequality*, 105; Loïc Wacquant, *Punishing the Poor: The Neoliberal Government of Social Insecurity* (Durham, NC: Duke University Press, 2009).

94. Pettit, *Invisible Men*, 50–64.

95. Stephanie Ewert, Bryan L. Sykes, and Becky Pettit, "The Degree of Disadvantage: Incarceration and Inequality in Education," *ANNALS of the American Academy of Political and Social Science* 651 (January 2014): 24–43; Pettit, *Invisible Men*, 64–67.

96. Manza and Uggen, *Locked Out*, 176–77. Manza and Uggen build on earlier work by Michael P. McDonald and Samuel Popkin. See "The Myth of the Vanishing Voter," *American Political Science Review* 95.4 (2001): 963–74.

97. Thom File "The Diversifying Electorate—Voting Rates by Race and Hispanic Origin in 2012 (and Other Recent Elections)," U.S. Census Bureau, Current Population Survey, May 2013, http://www.census.gov/prod/2013pubs/p20-568.pdf (retrieved August 31, 2013), 3.

98. Bryan Sykes et al., "Mass Incarceration and Racial Inequality in Political Participation," mimeo, 2014. See also Pettit, *Invisible Men*, ch. 5.

99. Kenneth Prewitt, "Foreword," in Patricia Allard and Kirsten D. Levingston, "Accuracy Counts: Incarcerated People and the Census," Prison Policy Initiative, 2004, http://www.prisonpolicy.org/scans/RV4_AccuracyCounts.pdf (retrieved February 27, 2014), i.

100. Rose Heyer and Peter Wagner, "Too Big to Ignore: How Counting People in Prisons Distorted 2000 Census," Prison Policy Initiative, April 2004, www.prisonersofthecensus.org/toobig/toobig.html (retrieved May 5, 2011).

101. Prisoners of the Census, "Too Big to Ignore Interactive Tables: Union County," 2006, http://www.prisonersofthecensus.org/toobig/countydetail.php?geo_id=05000US42119 (retrieved May 12, 2012).

102. Dale E. Ho, "Captive Constituents: Prison-Based Gerrymandering and the Current Redistricting Cycle," *Stanford Law & Policy Review* 22.2 (2011), 356.

103. Peter Wagner and Elena Lavarreda, "Importing Constituents: Prisoners and Political Clout in Pennsylvania," Prison Policy Initiative, June 26, 2009, http://www.prisonersofthecensus.org/pennsylvania/importing.html (retrieved May 24, 2014).

104. Rural communities compose only about 20 percent of the U.S. population but an estimated 40 percent of all prisoners are held in rural penal facilities. Allard and Levingston, "Accuracy Counts," 6.

105. Eric Lotke and Peter Wagner, "Prisoners of the Census: Electoral and Financial Consequences of Counting Prisoners Where They Go, Not Where They Come From," *Pace Law Review* 24.2 (2004): 587–608; Peter Wagner, "Prison Expansion Made 56 Counties With Declining Populations Appear to Be Growing in Census 2000," Prisoners of the Census, April 26, 2004, http://www.prisonersofthecensus.org/news/2004/04/26/fiftysix/ (retrieved May 14, 2012).

106. Peter Wagner, "Wisconsin Sees Dramatic Prison-Based Gerrymandering in New State, County, City Districts," Prisoners of the Census News, July 18, 2011, http://www.prisonersofthecensus.org/news/2011/07/18/wi-districts/ (retrieved May 12, 2012).

107. National Research Council, Panel on Residence Rules in the Decennial Census, *Once, Only Once, and in the Right Place: Residence Rules in the Decennial Census*, 2006, http://newton.nap.edu/execsumm_pdf/11727 (retrieved February 24, 2014), 9.

108. Grits for Breakfast, "Houston Loses State Rep Over Prison Count," April 28, 2011, http://gritsforbreakfast.blogspot.com/2011/04/houston-loses-state-rep-over-prisoner.html (retrieved May 12, 2012).

109. Peter Wagner, "Importing Constituents: Prisoners and Political Clout in New York," Prison Policy Initiative, April 22, 2002, http://www.prisonpolicy.org/importing/importing.html (retrieved February 24, 2014).

110. Peter Wagner, "Momentum Builds to End Prison-Based Gerrymandering," Prison Legal News, December 2012, 1–10.

111. Ho, "Captive Constituents," 394.

112. U.S. GAO, "Formula Grants: Funding for the Largest Federal Assistance Programs Is Based on Census-Related Data and Other Factors" (Washington, DC: GAO, December 2009).

113. Aleks Kajstura, "Census Bureau's Prison Count Won't Mean Funding Windfall," Prisoners of the Census, April 2, 2010, http://www.prisonersofthecensus.org/news/2010/04/02/census-bureaus-prison-count-wont-mean-funding-windfall/ (retrieved April 17, 2010).

114. Peter Wagner, "Breaking the Census: Redistricting in an Era of Mass Incarceration," *William Mitchell Law Review* 38.4 (2012), 1248.

115. Wagner, "Momentum Builds," 5.

116. Pettit, *Invisible Men*, 26–28.

117. Catherine Rampell, "The Beginning of the End of the Census," *New York Times*, May 20, 2012, SR5.

118. On "condemnation scripts" and the connection between desistance from crime and the development of coherent, prosocial identities, see Shadd Maruna, *Making Good: How Ex-Convicts Reform and Rebuild Their Lives* (Washington, DC: American Psychological Association, 2001).

Chapter Twelve
Bring It On

1. Robert Saleem Holbrook, "From Public Enemy to Enemy of the State," in Doran Larson, ed., *Fourth City: Essays from the Prison in America* (East Lansing: Michigan State University Press, 2013), 242. Holbrook has been serving a life sentence without the possibility of parole in Pennsylvania for a conviction of felony murder when he was sixteen.

2. Adam Gopnick, "The Caging of America: Why Do We Lock Up So Many People?", *New Yorker*, January 30, 2012, 77.

3. See Jeremy Travis, Bruce Western, and Steve Redburn, eds., *The Growth of Incarceration in the United States: Exploring Causes and Consequences* (Washington, DC: National Academies Press, 2014), especially chs. 3–5.

4. Rosemary Gartner, Anthony N. Doob, and Franklin E. Zimring, "The Past as Prologue? Decarceration in California Then and Now," *Criminology & Public Policy* 10.2 (2011): 291–2; Tapio Lappi-Seppälä, "Sentencing and Punishment in Finland: The Decline of the Repressive Ideal," in Michael Tonry and Richard Frase, eds., *Punishment and Penal Systems in Western Countries* (New York: Oxford University Press, 2001): 92–150; Claudius Messner and Vincenzo Ruggiero, "Germany: The Penal System Between Past and Future," in Vincenzo Ruggiero, Mick Ryan, and Joe Sim, eds. *Western European Penal Systems: A Critical Anatomy* (London: Sage, 1995): 128–48; John Graham, "Decarceration in the Federal Republic of Germany: How Practitioners are Succeeding Where Policy-Makers Failed," *British Journal of Criminology* 30.3 (1990): 150–70.

5. For detailed analyses of the need for comprehensive sentencing reform, see Michael Tonry, *Punishing Race: A Continuing American Dilemma* (New York: Oxford University Press, 2011); James Austin, "Reducing America's Correctional Populations: A Strategic Plan," *Justice Research and Policy* 12.1 (2010): 9–40.

6. Todd R. Clear and James Austin, "Reducing Mass Incarceration: Implications of the Iron Law of Prison Populations," *Harvard Law & Policy Review* 3.2 (2009), 313. See also Todd R. Clear and Natasha A. Frost, *The Punishment Imperative: The Rise and Failure of Mass Incarceration in America* (New York: NYU Press, 2014), ch. 7.

7. Compare, for example, the comments of Marc Levin of the Texas Public Policy Foundation in Terry Carter, "Prison Break: Budget Crises Drive Reform, But Private Jails Press On," *ABA Journal*, October 2012, http://www.abajournal.com/magazine/article /prison_break_budget_crises_drive_reform_but_private_jails_press_on/ (retrieved December 31, 2013) with his testimony a year later criticizing mandatory minimums. Marc Levin, "Reevaluating the Effectiveness of Federal Mandatory Minimum Sentences," testimony, U.S. Senate Judiciary Committee, September 18, 2013, http://www.judiciary.senate.gov/pdf /9–18–13LevinTestimony.pdf (retrieved February 15, 2014).

8. See, for example, Cara Sullivan, "ALEC Passes Model Policy to Encourage Smarter Sentencing," American Legislator, October 1, 2013, http://www.americanlegislator.org /alec-passes-model-policy-encourage-smarter-sentencing/ (retrieved February 15, 2014).

9. Jonathan Simon, remarks at "The Coming Decarceration," panel, Annual Meeting of the American Association of Law Schools, New York City, January 4, 2014.

10. Glenn C. Loury and Bruce Western, "The Challenge of Mass Incarceration in America," *Daedalus* 139.3 (2010), 5.

11. Ian Loader and Richard Sparks, *Public Criminology* (London: Routledge, 2011), 108.

12. I am borrowing here from Strolovitch's description of what constitutes a utopian vision. Dara Z. Strolovitch, *Affirmative Advocacy: Race, Class, and Gender in Interest Group Politics* (Chicago: University of Chicago Press, 2007), 234–36.

13. Cheryl Marie Webster and Anthony N. Doob, "America in a Larger World: The Future of the Penal Harm Movement," *Criminology & Public Policy* 7.3 (2008), 483.

14. Philip Smith, *Punishment and Culture* (Chicago: University of Chicago Press, 2008), 29, 37.

15. Mosi Secret, "States Prosecute Fewer Teenagers in Adult Courts," *New York Times*, March 6, 2011, A1.

16. Michael Tonry and David A. Green, "Criminology and Public Policy," in Lucia Zedner and Andrew Ashworth, eds., *The Criminological Foundations of Penal Policy: Essays in Honour of Roger Hood* (Oxford: Oxford University Press, 2003): 485–525; Roger Hood, "Criminology and Penal Policy: The Vital Role of Empirical Research," in Anthony Bottoms and Michael Tonry, eds., *Ideology, Crime and Criminal Justice: A Symposium in Honor of Sir Leon Radzinowicz* (Portland, OR: Willan, 2002), 153–57.

17. Adrian Cherney, "Beyond Technicism: Broadening the 'What Works' Paradigm in Crime Prevention," *Crime Prevention and Community Safety: An International Journal* 4.3 (2002), 53.

18. Todd R. Clear, "Policy and Evidence: The Challenge to the American Society of Criminology," *Criminology* 48.1 (2010), 6–7.

19. Tonry, *Punishing Race*, 145.

20. Tonry, *Punishing Race*, 16–17.

21. There is a precedent for this. The leading opponents of the death penalty made an important strategic decision in the mid-1960s. They shifted from challenging capital punishment primarily on a case-by-case basis on procedural grounds, many of them related to race, to launching a broad challenge to the constitutionality of the death penalty even though black defendants bore a disproportionate burden of the death penalty. See Marie Gottschalk, *The Prison and the Gallows: The Politics of Mass Incarceration in America* (New York: Cambridge University Press, 2006), 208–12.

22. Steven Raphael and Michael A. Stoll, *Why Are So Many Americans in Prison?* (New York: Russell Sage Foundation, 2013), 80–81.

23. Michael Tonry, "The Mostly Unintended Effects of Mandatory Penalties: Two Centuries of Consistent Findings," in Michael Tonry, ed., *Crime and Justice: A Review of Research*, v. 38 (Chicago: University of Chicago Press, 2009): 65–114; Traci Schlesinger, "The Failure of Race Neutral Policies: How Mandatory Terms and Sentencing Enhancements Contribute to Mass Racialized Incarceration," *Crime & Delinquency* 57.1 (2011): 56–81.

24. For more on bail reform, see Melissa Neal, "Bail Fail: Why the U.S. Should End the Practice of Using Money for Bail" (Washington, DC: Justice Policy Institute, 2012); Spike Bradford, "For Better or for Profit: How the Bail Bonding Industry Stands in the Way of Fair and Effective Pretrial Justice" (Washington, DC: Justice Policy Institute, September 2012).

25. According to the Pew report, offenders released from state prison in 2009 served on average three years, which is 9 months or 36 percent longer than offenders released in 1990. These average figures mask great variations between the states. The Pew Center on the States, "Time Served: The High Cost, Low Return of Longer Prison Terms," June 2012, http://www.pewtrusts.org/uploadedFiles/wwwpewtrustsorg/Reports/sentencing_and_corrections/Prison_Time_Served.pdf (retrieved February 15, 2013), 3.

26. Jacob Sullum, "Rand Paul: 'I Am Here to Ask That We Begin the End of Mandatory Minimum Sentencing,'" *Forbes*, September 18, 2013, http://www.forbes.com/sites/jacobsullum/2013/09/18/rand-paul-i-am-here-to-ask-that-we-begin-the-end-of-mandatory-minimum-sentencing/ (retrieved February 15, 2014).

27. USSC, "U.S. Sentencing Commission Seeks Comment on Potential Reductions to Drug Trafficking Sentences," January 9, 2014, http://www.ussc.gov/Legislative_and_Public_Affairs/Newsroom/Press_Releases/20140109_Press_Release.pdf 9 (retrieved February 15, 2014).

28. Steven Nelson, "New Mandatory Minimums Added to Bill Seeking to Reduce Stiff Drug Penalties," *U.S. News & World Report*, January 30, 2014, http://www.usnews.com/news/articles/2014/01/30/new-mandatory-minimums-added-to-bill-seeking-to-reduce-stiff-drug-penalties (retrieved February 15, 2014).

29. Robert Gay Guthrie, president, NAAUSA, "Re: Mandatory Minimum Legislation," letter to Senators Patrick Leahy (D-VT) and Charles Grassley (R-IA), January 31, 2014, https://www.naausa.org/news/146.pdf (retrieved February 27, 2014); and letter to Reynaldo Tariche, president, FBI Agents Association, "Re: Save Federal Mandatory Minimum Sentences," January 2, 2014, http://www.naausa.org/news/133.pdf (retrieved February 27, 2014); See also Jerry Markon and Rachel Weiner, "Thousands of Felons Could Have Drug Sentences Lessened," *Washington Post*, July 18, 2014, http://www.washingtonpost.com /politics/thousands-of-felons-could-have-drug-sentences-lessened/2014/07/18/4876209e -0eb1-11e4-8341-b8072b1e7384_story.html (retrieved September 10, 2014).

30. William P. Barr et al., letter to Senators Harry Reid and Mitch McConnell, May 12, 2014, http://www.crimeandconsequences.com/crimblog/2014/05/former-top-doj-leaders -oppose-.html (retrieved May 17, 2014).

31. Rick Raemisch, "My Night in Solitary," *New York Times*, February 20, 2014, A25. See also Aviva Stahl, "New York City's New Corrections Chief, Known for Solitary Confinement Reforms, Faces Steep Challenge on Rikers Island," Solitary Watch, April 22, 2014, http://solitarywatch.com/2014/04/22/new-corrections-chief-new-york-city-known -solitary-confinement-reforms-faces-steep-challenges-rikers-island/ (retrieved May 16, 2014).

32. For example, Charles Hynes, the longtime district attorney of Brooklyn's Kings County in Brooklyn, New York, pioneered programs that offer defendants drug treatment as an alternative to prison, expand services for victims of domestic violence, and help former inmates re-enter society. His initiatives were a model for broader state-level reform in New York and nationally. Charles Hynes, "ComALERT: A Prosecutor's Collaborative Model for Ensuring a Successful Transition from Prison to the Community," *Journal of Court Innovation* 1.1 (2008): 123–49.

33. This discussion of the Rockefeller laws is based on David F. Weiman and Christopher Weiss, "The Origins of Mass Incarceration in New York State: The Rockefeller Drug Laws and the Local War on Drugs," in Steven Raphael and Michael A. Stoll, eds., *Do Prisons Make Us Safer? The Benefits and Costs of the Prison Boom* (New York: Russell Sage Foundation): 73–116.

34. Mona Lynch, "Theorizing the Role of the 'War on Drugs' in American Punishment," *Theoretical Criminology* 16.2 (2012), 180.

35. Anne R. Traum, "Mass Incarceration at Sentencing," *Hastings Law Journal* 64.2 (2013), 448–49.

36. Quoted in Traum, "Mass Incarceration at Sentencing," 448. Traum persuasively argues that sentencing courts are permitted to consider—and should consider—relevant information about the harmful collateral consequences of mass incarceration not only for individual defendants but also for their families and communities when determining what punishment is suitable and fair.

37. Stephen R. Sady and Lynn Deffebach, ABA Commission on Effective Criminal Sanctions, "Second Look Resentencing Under 18 U.S.C. §3582(c) as an Example of Bureau of Prisons' Policies That Result in Over-Incarceration," December 2008, http://or.fd.org /ReferenceFiles/ABACommission.pdf (retrieved January 13, 2014), 1.

38. Charlie Savage, "More Releases of Ailing Prisoners Are Urged," *New York Times*, May 2, 2013, A17; Josh Gerstein, "DOJ Pulls Bush-era Early Release Rules," *Politico*, December 14, 2013, http://www.politico.com/blogs/under-the-radar/2013/12/doj-pulls-bushera -early-release-rules-178834.html (retrieved February 15, 2014).

39. With nearly 200,000 inmates in the federal system, the BOP approved on average less than two dozen motions each year between 2000 and 2008. Sady and Deffeback, "Second Look," 2.

40. Sady and Deffeback, "Second Look," 2.

41. These include underutilization of the Residential Drug Abuse Program (RDAP), enacted by Congress in 1994, and of community corrections options; and stingy and arguably incorrect formulas for calculating "good time" credits and computing release dates. Sady and Deffeback, "Second Look," 2; and Advocare et al., "Organizations Oppose FY 2013 Funding for Federal Prison Expansion," letter to Senators Barbara Mikulski and Kay Bailey Hutchison, April 17, 2012, http://sentencingproject.org/doc/publications/inc_Senate _appropriations_%20ltr_FY2013.pdf (retrieved January 6, 2014); Brandon Sample and Derek Gilna, "BOP's RDAP Program Unevenly Administered and Unnecessarily Costly," *Prison Legal News*, August 2012, 28.

42. William Stuntz, "The Pathological Politics of Criminal Law," *Michigan Law Review* 100.3 (2001), 506; Stephanos Bibas, "Transparency and Participation in Criminal Procedure," *N.Y.U. Law Review* 81.3 (2006), 932-33; and William Sabol, "Implications of Criminal Justice System Adaptation for Prison Population Growth and Corrections Policy," paper presented at the Symposium on Crime and Justice: The Past and Future of Empirical Sentencing Research, SUNY at Albany, School of Criminal Justice, September 23-24, 2010, 20.

43. Angela J. Davis, *Arbitrary Justice: The Power of the American Prosecutor* (New York: Oxford University Press, 2007), 97.

44. Shawn D. Bushway and Brian Forst, "Discretion, Rule of Law, and Rationality," paper presented at Symposium on Crime and Justice, 17. For recommendations on how to improve prosecutorial accountability, see Davis, *Arbitrary Justice*, ch. 10; and John Wesley Hall, "A Fairer and More Democratic Federal Grand Jury System," *Federal Sentencing Reporter* 20.5 (2008), 334-36.

45. Robert J. Sampson and Charles Loeffler, "Punishment's Place: The Local Concentration of Mass Incarceration," *Daedalus* 139.3 (2010), 20.

46. Davis, *Arbitrary Justice*, 5; Brian Forst, "Prosecution," in James Q. Wilson and Joan Petersilia, eds., *Crime and Public Policy* (New York: Oxford University Press, 2011), 437.

47. Joan E. Jacoby, *The American Prosecutor: A Search for Identity* (Lexington, MA: Lexington Books, 1980); Abraham S. Goldstein, "Prosecution: History of the Public Prosecutor," in Sanford H. Kadish, ed., *Encyclopedia of Criminal Justice* (New York: New Press, 1983); Gottschalk, *The Prison and the Gallows*, 91-98.

48. In late 2013, Human Rights Watch released a scorching report on how federal prosecutors coerce defendants to plead guilty in federal drug cases by charging or threatening to charge them with offenses that carry stiff mandatory minimums. Human Rights Watch, "An Offer You Can't Refuse: How Federal Prosecutors Force Drug Defendants to Plead Guilty," December 2013, http://www.hrw.org/sites/default/files/reports/us1213_ForUpload_0_0.pdf (retrieved February 14, 2014).

49. These decisions, among other things, upheld prosecutors' immunity from civil lawsuits, their wide latitude in jury selection, and the "nearly impossible standards for obtaining the necessary discovery to seek judicial review of some forms of prosecutorial misconduct." Davis, *Arbitrary Justice*, 127-29.

50. For example, the Texas District and County Attorneys Association was a critical player in propelling the Texas prison boom, and many of its officers have been influential in the National Association of Prosecutor Coordinators. Michael C. Campbell, "Politics,

Prisons, and Law Enforcement: An Examination of 'Law and Order' Politics in Texas," *Law & Society Review* 45.3 (2011): 177–99.

51. Gottschalk, *The Prison and the Gallows*, chs. 4–6.

52. See, for example, Associated Press, "Alabama DAs, Victims Group Oppose New Sentencing Guidelines," August 10, 2013, http://www.wkrg.com/story/23100067/das-victims-group-oppose-sentencing-guidelines (retrieved December 31, 2013). In the case of penal reform in Illinois, see Steve Bogira, "Pat Quinn, Political Prisoner: A Case Study in How Electoral Politics Stymies Real Reform," *Chicago Reader*, October 28, 2010, http://www.chicagoreader.com/chicago/pat-quinn-rich-whitney-illinois-governor-election/Content?oid=2625950 (retrieved February 15, 2014).

53. Davis, *Arbitrary Justice*, 15.

54. For example, in the early 1990s, the Bureau of Justice Statistics stopped collecting and reporting "aggregate information about arrest rejections and case dismissals, pleas and trials" in jurisdictions across the United States. Shawn D. Bushway and Brian Forst, "Studying Discretion in the Processes that Generate Criminal Justice Sanctions, *Justice Quarterly* 30.2 (2013), 31.

55. Davis, *Arbitrary Justice*, 5.

56. Tanya E. Coke, "Criminal Justice in the 21st Century: Eliminating Racial and Ethnic Disparities in the Criminal Justice System: Conference Report," National Association of Criminal Defense Lawyers (NADCL), n.d., https://www.nacdl.org/reports/eliminate disparity/ (retrieved February 15, 2014), 12.

57. Sonja B. Starr and M. Marit Rehavi, "Mandatory Sentencing and Racial Disparity: Assessing the Role of Prosecutors and the Effects of *Booker*," *Yale Law Journal* 123.1 (2013), 28. For a rebuttal from the U.S. Sentencing Commission, see Glenn R. Schmitt, Louis Reedt, and Kevin Blackwell, "Why Judges Matter at Sentencing: A Reply to Starr and Rehavi," *Yale Law Journal Online* 251 (2013), http://yalelawjournal.org/2013/10/23/schmitt .html (retrieved February 14, 2014).

58. Angela J. Davis, "In Search of Racial Justice: The Role of the Prosecutor," *N.Y.U. Journal of Legislation and Public Policy* 16.4 (2013): 821–51.

59. Adam Serwer, "The Other Black President; The NAACP Confronts a New Political—and Racial—Era," February 16, 2009, *American Prospect*, http://www.prospect .org/cs/articles?article=the_other_black_president (retrieved September 8, 2010).

60. Judith Greene and Marc Mauer, "Downscaling Prisons: Lessons from Four States" (Washington, DC: The Sentencing Project, 2010).

61. Tina Rosenberg, "The Deadliest D.A.," *New York Times Magazine*, July 16, 1995.

62. Upon assuming office, Williams endorsed some laudable reforms, like the decriminalization of marijuana. But he has since proven to be a strong supporter of capital punishment, controversial stop-and-frisk policies, tougher penalties for people caught carrying a gun, and the imposition of sky-high bails in gun-related cases, which has contributed to a big increase in the number of inmates clogging Philadelphia's jails.

63. It included only "certain low-level, nonviolent drug offenders who have no ties to large-scale organizations, gangs, or cartels." U.S. DOJ, "Attorney General Eric Holder Delivers Remarks at the Annual Meeting of the American Bar Association's House of Delegates," press release, August 12, 2013, http://www.justice.gov/iso/opa/ag/speeches/2013 /ag-speech-130812.html (retrieved September 4, 2013).

64. Some criminal defense lawyers and prosecutors commented that remarkably few people would be affected by the change. See, for example, Scott H. Greenfield, "Reality Check: Barely a Ripple, But a Ripple," Simple Justice, August 14, 2013, blog, http://blog

.simplejustice.us/2013/08/14/reality-check-barely-a-ripple-but-a-ripple/ (retrieved February 17, 2014).

65. U.S. DOJ, "Attorney General Eric Holder Delivers Remarks."

66. In his dissent, Justice Antonin Scalia called the decision a "judicial travesty" and "perhaps the most radical injunction issued by a court in our Nation's history." *Brown v. Plata*, 131 S. Ct. 1949–51 (Scalia, J., dissenting) (2011).

67. Margo Schlanger, "*Plata v. Brown* and Realignment: Jails, Prisons, Courts, and Politics," *Harvard Civil Rights-Civil Liberties Law Review* 48.1 (2013), 184.

68. ACLU, "California Prison Realignment One-Year Anniversary: An American Civil Liberties Assessment," September 27, 2012, https://www.aclunc.org/docs/criminal_justice /realignment_packet.pdf (retrieved February 22, 2014); Joan Petersilia and Joan Greenlick Snyder, "Looking Past the Hype: 10 Questions Everyone Should Ask About California's Realignment," *California Journal of Politics and Policy* 5.2 (2013): 266–306.

69. The legislation required each county to establish a Community Corrections Partnership headed by the chief probation officer and including the district attorney, the police chief, the sheriff, a representative from the superior court, the public defender, and social services. Petersilia and Snyder, "Looking Past the Hype," 274.

70. Heather Schoenfeld, "Mass Incarceration and the Paradox of Prison Conditions Litigation," *Law & Society Review* 44.3–4 (2010): 731–68.

71. Pamela A. MacLean, "Prison Realignment: Now What?," *California Lawyer*, August 2012, https://www.callawyer.com/Clstory.cfm?eid=923950 (retrieved February 22, 2014).

72. Raphael and Stoll, *Why Are So Many Americans in Prison?*, 253.

73. Lauren E. Glaze and Erinn J. Herberman, "Correctional Populations in the United States, 2012," *Bureau of Justice Statistics Bulletin*, December 2013, 4.

74. Margo Schlanger, "Inmate Litigation," *Harvard Law Review* 116 (April 2003), 1686, n. 434. Jails tend to be more chaotic and dangerous places than prisons due to more transient populations, inadequate resources to separate prisoners by security risk, fewer programs, and more inmate idleness.

75. In some Los Angeles jails, inmates were allowed only three hours per week outside of their cells—even less than inmates confined to supermax facilities. As of September 2013, county jails in California housed nearly 1,300 inmates sentenced to five years or more. Paige St. John, "Long-term Inmates—and Prison Culture—Move Into County Jails," *Los Angeles Times*, September 8, 2013, http://articles.latimes.com/2013/sep/08/local/la-me-ff-long-haul -inmates-20130909 (retrieved February 23, 2014).

76. Paige St. John, "Population of Prisons to Increase," *Los Angeles Times*, January 10, 2014, http://articles.latimes.com/2014/jan/10/local/la-me-ff-prisons-20140110 (retrieved February 23, 2014); Associated Press, "California Prisoners Could Be Moved Out of State Due to Overcrowding," January 8, 2014, http://www.kpbs.org/news/2014/jan/08/california -prisoners-could-be-moved-out-state-due-/ (retrieved February 24, 2014).

77. The jail population is projected to increase by more than 50 percent between 2011, when realignment began, and 2017. See Petersilia and Snyder, "Looking Past the Hype," 305, fig. 4.

78. Phillip Smith, "Jerry Brown Vetoes California 'Defelonization' Bill," *Drug War Chronicle* no. 805, October 17, 2013, http://stopthedrugwar.org/chronicle/805 (retrieved February 16, 2014).

79. Associated Press, "Prison 'Lifers' Being Released at Record Pace," February 25, 2014, http://losangeles.cbslocal.com/2014/02/25/prison-lifers-being-released-at-record-pace/ (retrieved March 1, 2014).

80. Joan Petersilia et al., "Voices from the Field: How California Stakeholders View Public Safety Realignment" (Palo Alto: Stanford Criminal Justice Center, January 2014).

81. Petersilia and Snyder, "Looking Past the Hype," 1.

82. Dean Miscznski, "Corrections Realignment: One Year Later," Public Policy Institute of California, August 2012, http://www.ppic.org/content/pubs/report/R_812DMR.pdf (retrieved February 24, 2014).

83. Phil Willon, "Abel Maldonado Takes on Jerry Brown, Prison Realignment," *Los Angeles Times*, May 25, 2013, http://articles.latimes.com/2013/may/25/local/la-me-maldonado -prisons-20130526 (retrieved May 25, 2013); Dan Walters, "Can Crime Again Be Big Issue in California?," *Sacramento Bee*, May 10, 2013, http://www.sacbee.com/2013/05/10/5409465 /dan-walters-can-crime-again-be.html (retrieved February 24, 2014).

84. Joshua Page, "Prison Officers, Crime Victims, and the Prospects of Sentencing Reform," March 22, 2011, California Progress Report, http://www.californiaprogressreport .com/site/prison-officers-crime-victims-and-prospects-sentencing-reform (retrieved February 23, 2014).

85. Maura Dolan, "3 Former California Governors Back Proposed Death Penalty Initiative," *Los Angeles Times*, February 12, 2014, http://www.latimes.com/local/lanow/la-me-ln -california-death-penalty-initiative-20140212,0,7551552.story#axzz2uAavEbVc (retrieved February 22, 2014).

86. Robert Perkinson, *Texas Tough: The Rise of America's Prison Empire* (New York: Metropolitan Books, 2010); David M. Oshinsky, *"Worse Than Slavery": Parchman Farm and the Ordeal of Jim Crow Justice"* (New York: Free Press, 1996).

87. Rebecca M. McLennan, *The Crisis of Imprisonment: Protest, Politics, and the Making of the American Penal State, 1776–1941* (New York: Cambridge University Press, 2008).

88. Robert Chase, "Civil Rights on the Cell Block: Race, Reform, and Violence in Texas Prisons and the Nation, 1945–1990," University of Maryland, PhD dissertation, 2009; Gottschalk, *The Prison and the Gallows*, ch. 7.

89. For more on the deinstitutionalization case and decarceration, see Marie Gottschalk, "The Great Recession and the Great Confinement: The Economic Crisis and the Future of Penal Reform," in Richard Rosenfeld, Kenna Quinet, and Crystal Garcia, eds., *Contemporary Issues in Criminological Theory and Research: The Role of Social Institutions* (Belmont, CA: Wadsworth/Cengage, 2011), 356–60.

90. Gerald N. Grob, *The Mad Among Us: A History of the Care of America's Mentally Ill* (New York: Free Press, 1994); David J. Rothman, *The Discovery of the Asylum: Social Order and Disorder in the New Republic* (Boston: Little, Brown, and Co., 1990); Steven M. Gillon, *"That's Not What We Meant to Do": Reform and Its Unintended Consequences in Twentieth Century America* (New York: Norton, 2000); E. Fuller Torrey, *Out of the Shadows: Confronting America's Mental Illness Crisis* (New York: Wiley, 1997).

91. Chris Koyanagi, "Learning from History: Deinstitutionalization of People with Mental Illness as Precursor to Long-Term Care Reform" (Menlo Park, CA: The Henry J. Kaiser Family Foundation, Kaiser Commission on Medicaid and the Uninsured, August 2007).

92. Grob, *The Mad Among Us*.

93. Michelle Brown, "Penal Spectatorship and the Culture of Punishment," in David Scott, ed., *Why Prison?* (Cambridge, UK: Cambridge University Press, 2013), 108, 122–23. See also Michelle Brown, *The Culture of Punishment: Prison, Society, and Spectacle* (New York: NYU Press, 2009).

94. Perkinson, *Texas Tough*; Oshinsky, *"Worse Than Slavery."*

95. McLennan, *The Crisis of Imprisonment*.

96. Convicts would cut off a limb or pack a self-inflicted wound with lye or inject themselves with kerosene to get some relief from backbreaking field labor and to protest their horrid living and working conditions. After 21 prisoners maimed themselves in 1935 at one penal farm in Texas by chopping off their lower legs, the top administrator told the guards, "As long as they want to . . . chop themselves, I say give them more axes." Perkinson, *Texas Tough*, 214.

97. Alan Eladio Gómez, "Resisting Living Death at Marion Federal Penitentiary, 1972," *Radical History Review* 96 (Fall 2006): 58–86. See also McLennan, *The Crisis of Imprisonment*, ch. 10.

98. The Marshall Project, n.d., http://www.themarshallproject.org/ (retrieved February 15, 2014).

99. With the strong support of the state's correctional officers' union, Governor Pete Wilson of California pushed through trendsetting legislation in 1995 to ban all journalists from interviewing any prisoners. Geri Lynn Green, "The Quixotic Dilemma: California's Immutable Culture of Incarceration," *Pace Law Review* 30.5 (2010), 1470. See also Jessica Pupovac, "Will Prisons Ever Open Up to Journalists?," *Crime Report*, January 2, 2013, https://www.salon.com/2013/01/02/will_prisons_ever_open_up_to_journalists/ (retrieved December 21, 2013).

100. Leah Caldwell, "The Decline and Fall of the Prison Press," *Prison Legal News*, June 2006, 20; James McGrath Morris, *Jailhouse Journalism: The Fourth Estate Behind Bars* (New Brunswick, NJ: Transaction Publishers, 2002): 179–86.

101. Ed Pilkington, "Supermax Prison Blocked Obama Books Requested by Detainee," *Guardian*, July 10, 2009, http://www.guardian.co.uk/world/2009/jul/10/barack-obama-books-blocked-prison (retrieved July 16, 2012). Contrary to claims made in court papers, a BOP spokesperson contends the bureau reversed course and permitted the inmate to read the books. Associated Press, "Al-Qaida Inmate Gets Access to Obama's Books," NBCNEWS.com, July 10, 2009, http://www.msnbc.msn.com/id/31854575/ns/us_news-security/t/al-qaida-inmate-gets-access-obamas-books/#.UAQvNa6ttFo (retrieved July 16, 2012).

102. Between 1950 and 1980, 80 to nearly 90 percent of the patients in state asylums were white and nearly half of them were women. Steven Raphael and Michael A. Stoll conclude that deinstitutionalization of the mentally ill contributed to the rise in incarceration rates but was not the major engine. Raphael and Stoll, *Why Are So Many Americans in Prison?*, 156 and 134, table 5.5.

103. Elizabeth B. Clark, "'The Sacred Rights of the Weak': Pain, Sympathy, and the Culture of Individual Rights in Antebellum America," *Journal of American History* 82.2 (1995), 463–65, 470–71.

104. James D. Unnever, "Race, Crime, and Public Opinion," in Sandra M. Bucerius and Michael Tonry, eds., *The Oxford Handbook of Ethnicity, Crime, and Immigration* (New York: Oxford University Press, 2014): 70–106.

105. Kenneth E. Fernandez, "Crime Policy in the New Millennium: The End of the 'Tough on Crime' Era?," paper presented at the State Politics and Policy Conference, Dartmouth College, Hanover, NH, June 2–4, 2011; Pew Research Center for the People & the Press, "Deficit Reduction Rises on Public's Agenda for Obama's Second Term," January 24, 2013, http://www.people-press.org/2013/01/24/deficit-reduction-rises-on-publics-agenda-for-obamas-second-term/ (retrieved December 10, 2013).

106. For example, national surveys seldom include questions to gauge the "relative support for progressive crime policies" and "rarely allow respondents to prioritize which method of crime control they most prefer"—such as greater investment in the police or in early childhood education. Unnever, "Race, Crime, and Public Opinion," 84. For a brief

overview of research on the relationship between early childhood education and crime reduction and the crime-reducing impact of other tailored social programs and policies, see Mark A. R. Kleiman, *When Brute Force Fails: How to Have Less Crime and Less Punishment* (Princeton, NJ: Princeton University Press, 2009), 121–35.

107. See, for example, Mark A. Cohen, Roland T. Rust, and Sara Steen, "Prevention, Crime Control or Cash? Public Preferences Towards Criminal Justice Spending Priorities," *Justice Quarterly* 23.3 (2006): 317–35; Harris Sokoloff and Chris Satullo, "The City Budget: Tight Times, Tough Choices"(Philadelphia: Penn Project for Civic Engagement, March 2, 2009); Mark DiCamillo and Mervin Field, "Paradoxical Views About the State Deficit," Field Research Corporation, press release no. 2275, June 10, 2008, http://field.com /fieldpollonline/subscribers/Rls2275.pdf (retrieved February 15, 2014); Tulchin Research, "New California Statewide Poll Finds Strong Support for Alternatives to Jail for Non-Violent Offenders, Strong Opposition to Building More Jails," September 28, 2012, http:// www.tulchinresearch.com/2012/09/28/new-ca-statewide-poll-results-on-criminal-justice -issues/#more-1632 (retrieved February 25, 2014).

108. As director of the Division of Mental Health of the U.S. Public Health Service in the 1940s, Robert Felix shrewdly maneuvered to end federal passivity on mental health. He was an indispensable catalyst for the development of a succession of pieces of federal legislation that deinstitutionalized much of the mentally ill population.

109. Michael C. Dawson, *Not in Our Lifetimes: The Future of Black Politics* (Chicago: University of Chicago Press, 2011).

110. Cathy J. Cohen and Michael C. Dawson, "Neighborhood Poverty and African-American Politics," *American Political Science Review* 87.2 (1993), 291.

111. Strolovitch, *Affirmative Advocacy*, 10.

112. Strolovitch, *Affirmative Advocacy*, 227.

113. Dawson, *Not in Our Lifetimes*, 166.

114. See, for example, Joey L. Mogul, Andrea J. Ritchie, and Kay Whitlock, *Queer (In)Justice: The Criminalization of LGBT People in the United States* (Boston: Beacon Press, 2011).

115. Toshio Meronek and Martha Wallner, "No Longer a Prisoner of the Past," *In These Times*, September 2013, 12–13; Toshio Meronek, "Trans Prisoners Fight Abuse," *In These Times*, November 2012, 10–11; Derek Gilna, "Transgender Prisoner's Lawsuit Sparks BOP Policy Change," *Prison Legal News*, December 2012, 18; Victoria Law and Tina Reynolds, "Birthing Behind Bars: A Campaign for Reproductive Justice in Prisons," *Prison Legal News*, September 2012, 14–15.

116. Michelle Alexander, "Breaking My Silence," *Nation*, September 23, 2013.

117. Karen F. Parker, *Unequal Crime Decline: Theorizing Race, Urban Inequality, and Criminal Violence* (New York: NYU Press, 2008).

118. The rate for Los Angeles is about 8 per 100,000. FBI, "Crime in the United States, 2011," "Offenses Known to Law Enforcement by State by City, 2011," n.d., http://www.fbi .gov/about-us/cjis/ucr/crime-in-the-u.s/2011/crime-in-the-u.s.-2011/tables/table_8 _offenses_known_to_law_enforcement_by_state_by_city_2011.xls/view (retrieved February 25, 2014), table 8.

119. At the top of the list are small cities like East St. Louis (92 per 100,000), Camden (61 per 100,000), and New Orleans (58 per 100,000). FBI, "Offenses Known to Law Enforcement," table 8.

120. The homicide rate for African Americans fell from about 42 per 100,000 in 1990 to 17 per 100,000 in 2011. Erica L. Smith and Alexia Cooper, "Homicide in the U.S. Known to Law Enforcement, 2011," Bureau of Justice Statistics, December 2013, http://www.bjs

.gov/content/pub/pdf/hus11.pdf (retrieved January 8, 2014), 4–5; Randolph Roth, *American Homicide* (Cambridge, MA: Belknap Press of Harvard University Press, 2012), 441, fig. 9.1.

121. David A. Weiner, Byron F. Lutz, and Jens Ludwig, "The Effects of School Desegregation on Crime," NBER Working Paper no. 1530, September 2009, 1.

122. Andrew V. Papachristos, "The Small World of Murder," *Chicago Sun-Times*, January 17, 2011 (updated April 15, 2011), http://www.suntimes.com/news/otherviews/2877760 -452/homicide-network-social-risk-victims.html (retrieved February 16, 2014).

123. Ruth D. Peterson and Lauren J. Krivo, *Neighborhood Crime and the Racial-Spatial Divide* (New York: Russell Sage Foundation, 2010), 17.

124. Smith and Cooper, "Homicide in the U.S.," 1.

125. Ruth D. Peterson, "The Central Place of Race in Crime and Justice: The American Society of Criminology's Sutherland Address," *Criminology* 50.2 (2012), 306–7.

126. Calculated from "Murder in America," n.d., *Wall Street Journal*, http://projects.wsj .com/murderdata/?mg=inert-wsj#view=all&vr=B (retrieved December 14, 2013); and "Statistical Information about Fatal Casualties of the Vietnam War: Casualty Category," National Archives, http://www.archives.gov/research/military/vietnam-war/casualty-statistics .html#category (retrieved December 14, 2013).

127. Nearly 54,000 black males died by firearms between 2000 and 2010. Calculated from "Murder in America," *Wall Street Journal*; and U.S. Department of Health and Human Services, Centers for Disease Control and Prevention, "Nonfatal Injury Reports," Web-based Injury Statistics Inquiry and Reporting System (WISQARS), http://www.cdc.gov/injury /wisqars/nonfal.html, cited in Rhonda Bryant, "Taking Aim at Gun Violence," CLASP, April 2013, http://www.clasp.org/admin/site/publications/files/Taking-Aim-at-Gun-Violence.pdf (retrieved December 14, 2013).

128. Jody Miller, *Getting Played: African American Girls, Urban Inequality, and Gendered Violence* (New York: NYU Press, 2008), 8; Janet L. Lauritsen, "How Families and Communities Influence Victimization," *OJJDP Juvenile Justice Bulletin*, November 2003, https://www .ncjrs.gov/pdffiles1/ojjdp/201629.pdf (retrieved February 27, 2014).

129. For an overview of this work see Patricia L. McCall, Kenneth C. Land, and Karen F. Parker, "An Empirical Assessment of What We Know About Structural Covariates of Homicide Rates: A Return to a Classic 20 Years Later," *Homicide Studies* 14.3 (2010), 226–28; and Matthew R. Lee, "Concentrated Poverty, Race, and Homicide," *Sociological Quarterly* 41.2 (2000): 189–206.

130. As Robert J. Sampson and William Julius Wilson explain, "regardless of whether a black juvenile is raised in an intact or single-parent family, or a rich or poor home, he or she will not likely grow up in a community context similar to that of whites with regard to family structure and income. Reductionist interpretations of race and social class camouflage this key point." See "Toward a Theory of Race, Crime, and Urban Inequality," in John Hagan and Ruth Peterson, eds., *Crime and Inequality* (Stanford, CA: Stanford University Press, 1995), 44.

131. In not one city over 100,000 people do blacks reside in conditions equal to whites on key economic and social indicators, like rates of poverty, joblessness, and family disruption. Robert J. Sampson, "Urban Black Violence: The Effect of Male Joblessness and Family Disruption," *American Journal of Sociology* 93.2 (1987), 354. Peterson and Krivo found that a mere 31 of more than 3,000 white neighborhoods in their sample could be classified as extremely disadvantaged compared to more than half of African American, Latino, and other minority neighborhoods. Only 3 percent of black and Latino areas and 6 percent of minority areas "are privileged enough that they have no extreme disadvantages" compared to 89 percent of white areas. Peterson and Krivo, *Divergent Social Worlds*, 62.

132. Steven F. Messner, "Economic Discrimination and Societal Homicide Rates: Further Evidence on the Cost of Inequality," *American Sociological Review* 54.4 (1989): 597–611; Parker, *Unequal Crime Decline*, 117–18.

133. McCall et al., "An Empirical Assessment."

134. See Steven N. Durlauf and Daniel S. Nagin, "Imprisonment and Crime: Can Both Be Reduced, *Criminology & Public Policy* 10.1 (2011): 13–54, and responses to this article in the same volume; also, Franklin E. Zimring, *The City That Became Safe: New York's Lessons for Urban Crime and Its Control* (New York: Oxford University Press, 2012).

135. Krivo and Peterson, *Divergent Social Worlds*, 123; Lawrence D. Bobo and Victor Thompson, "Racialized Mass Incarceration: Poverty, Prejudice, and Punishment," in Hazel R. Markus and Paula M.L. Moya, eds., *Doing Race: 21 Essays for the 21st Century* (New York: W. W. Norton, 2010): 322–55. On the importance of residential lending in particular in alleviating violence and property crime, see Darlene F. Saporu et al., "Differential Benefits? Crime and Community Investments in Racially Distinct Neighborhoods," *Race and Justice* 1.1 (2011): 70–102; and Gregory D. Squires and Charis E. Kubrin, *Privileged Places: Race, Residence, and the Structure of Opportunity* (Boulder, CO: Lynne Rienner, 2006).

136. Notably, by the mid-1990s, states with less generous social welfare programs had considerably higher incarceration rates. Katherine Beckett and Bruce Western, "Governing Social Marginality: Welfare, Incarceration, and the Transformation of State Policy, *Punishment & Society* 3.1 (2001): 43–59.

137. Cherney, "Beyond Technicism," 52.

138. See Durlauf and Nagin, "Imprisonment and Crime," and the responses to this article in the same volume.

139. Elliott Currie, "On the Pitfalls of Spurious Prudence," *Criminology & Public Policy* 10.1 (2011), 113–14.

140. Between 1980 and 2006, spending per capita on police quadrupled, a rise that was well above the inflation rate. However, with the Great Recession, some cities, especially smaller ones, have slashed their police forces. Bureau of Justice Statistics, *Sourcebook of Criminal Justice Statistics 2003*, "Justice System Per Capita Expenditures, 2003," n.d., http://www.albany .edu/sourcebook/pdf/t17.pdf (retrieved October 5, 2010), 11, table 1.7; Bureau of Justice Statistics, *Sourcebook of Criminal Justice Statistics Online, 2006*, "State and Local Justice System Per Capita Expenditures, 2006," n.d., http://www.albany.edu/sourcebook/csv/t182006 .csv (retrieved October 5, 2010), table 1.8.

141. Cherney, "Beyond Technicism," 52.

142. Elliott Currie, *The Roots of Danger: Violent Crime in Global Perspective* (Englewood Cliffs, NJ: Prentice Hall 2009), 80–85.

143. Ryan S. Johnson, Shawn Kantor, and Price V. Fishback, "Striking at the Roots of Crime: The Impact of Social Welfare Spending on Crime During the Great Depression," National Bureau of Economic Research Working Paper no. 12825 (January 2007), 4.

144. Johnson, Kantor and Fishback, "Striking at the Roots of Crime," 20–21, n. 4.

145. John R. Sutton, "The Political Economy of Imprisonment in Affluent Western Democracies, 1960–1990," *American Sociological Review* 69.2 (2004): 170–89; David Downes and Kirstine Hansen, "Welfare and Punishment in Comparative Context," in Sarah Armstrong and Lesley McAra, eds., *Perspectives on Punishment: The Contours of Control* (Oxford: Oxford University Press, 2006): 33–54; Tapio Lappi-Seppälä, "Trust, Welfare, and Political Culture: Explaining Differences in National Penal Policies," in Michael Tonry, ed., *Crime and Justice: A Review of Research*, v. 37 (2008): 313–87.

146. Alice O'Connor, "The Privatized City: The Manhattan Institute, the Urban Crisis, and the Conservative Counterrevolution in New York," *Journal of Urban History* 34.2

(2008), 334. The reference to "drop dead" urban policy is a takeoff on the infamous New York *Daily News* headline in October 1975 after President Gerald Ford nixed a bailout plan for the city: "Ford to City: Drop Dead."

147. See, for example, Michelle Goldberg, "The Rise of the Progressive City," *Nation*, April 21, 2014.

148. Michael Kazin, "Whatever Happened to the American Left?," *New York Times*, September 25, 2011, SR4; Michael Kazin, *American Dreamers: How the Left Changed a Nation* (New York: Knopf, 2011). On the importance of community-based organizations in the recent political mobilization of Latino immigrants and the incomplete incorporation of immigrants and African Americans into party politics, see Janelle Wong, "Two Steps Forward: The Slow and Steady March toward Political Mobilization," *Du Bois Review* 4.2 (2007): 457–67; and Zoltan L. Hajnal and Taeku Lee, *Why Americans Don't Join the Party: Race, Immigration, and the Failure (of Political Parties) to Engage the Electorate* (Princeton, NJ: Princeton University Press, 2011).

149. Francis T. Cullen and Karen E. Gilbert, *Reaffirming Rehabilitation*, 2nd ed. (Waltham, MA: Anderson Publishing, 2013), 110.

150. For the classic statement about presidents and exceptional moments in political time, see Stephen Skowronek, *The Politics Presidents Make: Leadership From John Adams to Bill Clinton* (Cambridge, MA: The Belknap Press of Harvard University Press, 1997).

151. John Hagan, *Who Are the Criminals? The Politics of Crime Policy from the Age of Roosevelt to the Age of Reagan* (Princeton, NJ: Princeton University Press, 2011), 176–80, 212.

152. Hagan, *Who Are the Criminals?*, 135.

153. Ben Stein, "In Class Warfare, Guess Which Class Is Winning," *New York Times*, November 26, 2006, http://www.nytimes.com/2006/11/26/business/yourmoney/26every.html (retrieved May 24, 2014).

154. For the top 1 percent, incomes grew by nearly 12 percent in 2010—compared to just 0.2 percent for the bottom 99 percent. Emmanuel Saez, "Striking It Richer: The Evolution of Top Incomes in the United States (updated with 2009 and 2010 estimates)," March 2, 2012, http://elsa.berkeley.edu/~saez/saez-UStopincomes-2010.pdf (retrieved May 1, 2013).

155. Wages now make up 44 percent of GDP, down from 53 percent in 1970 and their lowest share of GDP since World War II. Reductions in wages and benefits were responsible for about three-quarters of the increase in corporate profits between 2000 and 2007, according to the calculations of Michael Cembalest, JPMorgan's chief investment officer. Harold Meyerson, "If Labor Dies, What's Next?," *American Prospect*, September/October 2012, 21.

156. The top 1 percent in the United States now owns 35 percent of the country's wealth. Economic Policy Institute, *The State of Working America*, 12th ed. (Ithaca, NY: Cornell University Press), 380.

157. Low-wage workers are those who receive less than two-thirds of the median wage. One-quarter of all U.S. workers fall into that category, earning no more than about $17,600 a year. Meyerson, "If Labor Dies," 22.

158. After declining in the 1990s, the number of people living in neighborhoods of extreme poverty in which at least 40 percent of their residents are below the federal poverty line rose by about one-third in the first decade of the twenty-first century. Elizabeth Kneebone, Carey Nadeau, and Alan Berube, "The Re-Emergence of Concentrated Poverty: Metropolitan Trends in the 2000s" (Washington, DC: Brookings, 2011); "Deep Poverty on the Rise," Center on Budget and Policy Priorities, September 22, 2011, http://www.offthechartsblog.org/deep-poverty-on-the-rise/ (retrieved June 2, 2013); Carmen DeNavas-Walt, Bernadette D. Proctor, and Jessica C. Smith, "Income, Poverty, and Health Insurance Coverage

in the United States: 2011," U.S. Census Bureau, Current Population Reports, September 2012, 13, fig. 4; "50 Years of Poverty," *New York Times*, January 4, 2014, http://www.nytimes .com/interactive/2014/01/04/business/50-years-of-poverty.html?_r=0 (retrieved January 9, 2014).

159. E. E. Schattschneider, *The Semi-Sovereign People: A Realist's View of Democracy in America* (New York: Holt, Rinehart, and Winston, 1960), 68.

160. Some claim that the vituperation directed at President Obama today is no more intense than what arch conservatives directed at John F. Kennedy and Lyndon Johnson. See Rick Perlstein, "The Grand Old Tea Party: Why Today's Wacko Birds Are Just Like Yesterday's Wingnuts," *Nation*, November 25, 2013, 14–15, 17–19.

161. For a succinct analysis of just how narrow that debate was in the 2012 presidential campaign, see Sherle R. Schwenninger, "The Missing Economic Debate: Instead of Addressing Real Problems, Obama and Romney Are Focusing on Deficit Reduction," *Nation*, October 29, 2012, 29–31. On the death by 10,000 cuts of the Dodd-Frank Wall Street Reform and Consumer Protection Act after Obama signed it in July 2010, see Gary Rivaling, "Wall Street Fires Back," *Nation*, May 20, 2013, 11–22.

162. "Remarks by the President on Unveiling of the Budget in Baltimore, Maryland," The White House, Office of the Press Secretary, February 14, 2011, http://www.whitehouse.gov /the-press-office/2011/02/14/remarks-president-unveiling-budget-baltimore-maryland (retrieved May 1, 2013).

163. Interview with Sean Hannity of Fox TV, December 1, 2011, http://www.realclear politics.com/video/2011/12/01/gingrich_dont_go_to_the_middle_bring_the_middle_to _you.html (retrieved May 1, 2013).

164. This is a view widely promulgated by ALEC and other conservative groups. Contrary to these claims, state and local spending as a proportion of total personal income "has remained remarkably stable for decades without having ever produced anything close to the severe budget crisis tied to the 2008–09 recession." Robert Pollin and Jeff Thompson, "State and Municipal Alternatives to Austerity," *New Labor Forum* 20.3 (2011), 23–24.

165. At the same time, government expenses were growing because more people were losing their jobs and were forced to turn to the state for unemployment, Medicaid, and other benefits to tide them over. Pollin and Thompson, "State and Municipal Alternatives to Austerity," 24.

166. William Mitchell, "Beyond Austerity: Deficit Mania Is Built on a Series of Destructive Myths," *Nation*, April 4, 2011, 11–17.

167. Richard Kim, "Ted Cruz, Role Model?," *Nation*, November 11, 2013, 10.

Select Bibliography

Aas, Katja Franko, and Mary Bosworth, eds., *The Borders of Punishment: Migration, Citizenship, and Social Exclusion* (Oxford: Oxford University Press, 2013).

Alexander, Elizabeth, "Prison Health Care, Political Choice, and the Accidental Death Penalty," *University of Pennsylvania Journal of Constitutional Law* 11.1 (2008): 1–22.

Alexander, Michelle, *The New Jim Crow: Mass Incarceration in the Age of Colorblindness* (New York: New Press, 2010).

Allen, Jessie, "Documentary Disenfranchisement," *Tulane Law Review* 86.2 (2011): 389–464.

Aman, Alfred C., Jr., "Privatisation, Prisons, Democracy, and Human Rights: The Need to Extend the Province of Administrative Law," *Indiana Journal of Global Legal Studies* 12.2 (2005): 511–550.

Appleton, Catherine A., *Life after Life Imprisonment* (Oxford: Oxford University Press, 2010).

Appleton, Catherine and Bent Grøver, "The Pros and Cons of Life Without Parole," *British Journal of Criminology* 47.4 (2007): 597–615.

Armstrong, Sarah and Lesley McAra, "Audiences, Borders, Architecture: The Contours of Control," in Sarah Armstrong and Lesley McAra, eds., *Perspectives on Punishment: The Contours of Control* (Oxford: Oxford University Press, 2006): 1–38.

Austin, James, "Reducing America's Correctional Populations: A Strategic Plan," *Justice Research and Policy* 12.1 (2010): 9–40.

Bair, Asatar P., *Prison Labor in the United States: An Economic Analysis* (New York: Routledge, 2008).

Baldus, David C. et al., "Racial Discrimination and the Death Penalty in the Post-*Furman* Era: An Empirical and Legal Overview, With Recent Findings from Philadelphia," *Cornell Law Review* 83.6 (1998): 1643–1770.

Baldus, David C., Charles Pulaski, and George Woodworth, "Comparative Review of Death Sentences: An Empirical Study of the Georgia Experience," *Journal of Criminal Law & Criminology* 74.3 (1983): 661–753.

Balko, Rodney, *Rise of the Warrior Cop: The Militarization of America's Police Forces* (New York: Public Affairs, 2013).

Barker, Vanessa, *The Politics of Imprisonment: How the Democratic Process Shapes the Way America Punishes Offenders* (New York: Oxford University Press, 2009).

Barkow, Rachel E., "The Court of Life and Death: The Two Tracks of Constitutional Sentencing Law and the Case for Uniformity," *Michigan Law Review* 107.7 (2009): 1145–1206.

Barkow, Rachel E., "Life Without Parole and the Hope for Real Sentencing Reform," in Charles J. Ogletree, Jr., and Austin Sarat, eds., *Life Without Parole: America's New Death Penalty?* (New York: NYU Press, 2012): 190–226.

Baumgartner, Frank R., Suzanna L. De Boef, and Amber E. Boydstun, *The Decline of the Death Penalty and the Discovery of Innocence* (New York: Cambridge University Press, 2008).

Beaumont, Gustave de and Alexis de Tocqueville, *On the Penitentiary System in the United States and Its Application in France* (Carbondale: Southern Illinois University Press, 1833/1979).

Beauregard, Eric and Roxanne Lieb, "Sex Offenders and Sex Offender Policy" in James Q. Wilson and Joan Petersilia, eds., *Crime and Public Policy* (New York: Oxford University Press, 2011): 345–67.

Beckett, Katherine, *Making Crime Pay: Law and Order in Contemporary American Politics* (New York: Oxford University Press, 1997).

Beckett, Katherine and Alexes Harris, "On Cash and Conviction: Monetary Sanctions as Misguided Policy," *Criminology & Public Policy* 10.3 (2011): 505–37.

Beckett, Katherine and Steve Herbert, *Banished: The New Social Control in Urban America* (New York: Oxford University Press, 2010).

Beckett, Katherine, and Steve Herbert, "Penal Boundaries: Banishment and the Expansion of Punishment," *Law & Social Inquiry* 35.1 (2010): 1–38.

Beckett, Katherine and Naomi Murakawa, "Mapping the Shadow Carceral State: Toward an Institutionally Capacious Approach to Punishment," *Theoretical Criminology* 16.2 (2012): 221–44.

Beckett, Katherine and Bruce Western, "How Unregulated Is the U.S. Labor Market? The Dynamics of Jobs and Jails, 1980–1995," *American Journal of Sociology* 104.4 (1999): 1030–60.

Beckett, Katherine and Bruce Western, "Governing Social Marginality: Welfare, Incarceration, and the Transformation of State Policy," *Punishment & Society*, 3.1 (2001): 43–59.

Bedau, Hugo Adam, "Recidivism, Parole, and Deterrence," in Hugo Adam Bedau, ed., *The Death Penalty in America*, 3rd ed. (New York: Oxford University Press, 1982): 173–80.

Bedau, Hugo Adam, "Imprisonment vs. Death: Does Avoiding Schwarzchild's Paradox Lead to Sheleff's Dilemma?," *Albany Law Review* 54 (1989–90): 481–95.

Berk, Christopher D., "Investment Talk: Comments on the Use of the Language of Investment in Prison Reform Advocacy," *Carceral Notebooks* 6 (2010): 115–29.

Bertram, Eva, *Building the Workfare State: The New Politics of Public Assistance* (Philadelphia: University of Pennsylvania Press, forthcoming).

Besser, Terry L. and Margaret M. Hanson, "Development of Last Resort: The Impact of New State Prisons on Small Town Economies in the United States," *Journal of the Community Development Society* 35.2 (2004): 1–16.

Bhui, Hindpal Singh, "Introduction: Humanizing Migration Control and Detention," in Katja Franko Aas and Mary Bosworth, eds., *The Borders of Punishment: Migration, Citizenship, and Social Exclusion* (Oxford: Oxford University Press, 2013): 1–17.

Bibas, Stephanos, "Transparency and Participation in Criminal Procedure," *N.Y.U. Law Review* 81.3 (2006): 911–966.

Binder, Guyora, *Felony Murder* (Stanford, CA: Stanford University Press, 2012).

Binswanger, Ingrid A. et al., "Release from Prison—A High Risk of Death for Former Inmates," *New England Journal of Medicine* 356.2 (January 11, 2007): 157–65.

Bivens, Josh, "Marching Backwards: The Consequences of Bipartisan Budget Cutting," *New Labor Forum* 20.3 (2011): 15–21.

Blackmon, Douglas A., *Slavery by Another Name: The Re-Enslavement of Black Americans from the Civil War to World War II* (New York: Anchor Books, 2009).

Blakely, Curtis R., *America's Prisons: The Movement Toward Profit and Privatization* (Boca Raton, FL: Brown Walker Press, 2005).

Blakely, Curtis R. and Vic W. Bumphus, "Private and Public Sector Prisons: A Comparison of Selected Characteristics," *Federal Probation* 68.1 (2004): 27–31.

Blumstein, Alfred, "On the Racial Disproportionality of the United States' Prison Populations," *Journal of Criminal Law and Criminology* 73.3 (1982): 1259–81.

Blumstein, Alfred, "Racial Disproportionality of U.S. Prison Populations Revisited," *University of Colorado Law Review* 64.3 (1993): 743–60.

Blumstein, Alfred, Jacqueline Cohen, Susan E. Martin, and Michael H. Tonry, eds., *Research on Sentencing: The Search for Reform*, v. 1 (Washington, DC: National Academies Press, 1983).

Blumstein, Alfred and Kiminori Nakamura, "Redemption in the Presence of Widespread Criminal Background Checks," *Criminology & Public Policy* 47.2 (2009): 327–59.

Blyth, Mark, *Austerity: The History of a Dangerous Idea* (New York: Oxford University Press, 2013).

Bobo, Lawrence D., "Racial Attitudes and Relations at the Close of the Twentieth Century," in Neil J. Smelser, William J. Wilson, and Faith Mitchell. eds., *America Becoming: Racial Trends and Their Consequences*, v. 1 (Washington, DC: National Academies Press, 2001): 264–301.

Bobo, Lawrence D., "Inequalities That Endure? Racial Ideology, American Politics, and the Peculiar Role of the Social Sciences," in Maria Krysan and Amanda E. Lewis, eds., *The Changing Terrain of Race and Ethnicity* (New York: Russell Sage Foundation, 2004): 13–42.

Bobo, Lawrence D., "Somewhere between Jim Crow & Post-Racialism: Reflections on the Racial Divide in America Today," *Daedalus* 140.2 (2011): 11–36.

Bobo, Lawrence D. and Devon Johnson, "A Taste for Punishment: Black and White Americans' Views on the Death Penalty and the War on Drugs," *Du Bois Review* 1.1 (2004): 151–80.

Bobo, Lawrence D. and Victor Thompson, "Unfair by Design: The War on Drugs, Race, and the Legitimacy of the Criminal Justice System," *Social Research* 73.2 (2006): 445–72.

Bobo, Lawrence D. and Victor Thompson, "Racialized Mass Incarceration: Poverty, Prejudice, and Punishment" in Hazel R. Markus and Paula M. L. Moya, eds., *Doing Race: 21 Essays for the 21st Century* (New York: W.W. Norton, 2010): 322–55.

Bonilla-Silva, Eduardo, *Racism without Racists: Color-Blind Racism and the Persistence of Racial Inequality in the United States*, 3rd ed. (Lanham, MD: Rowman & Littlefield, 2010).

Bosworth, Mary, "Creating the Responsible Prisoner: Federal Admission and Orientation Packets," *Punishment & Society* 9 (2007): 67–85.

Bosworth, Mary, *Explaining U.S. Imprisonment* (Thousand Oaks, CA: Sage, 2010).

Bosworth, Mary and Emma Kaufman, "Foreigners in a Carceral Age: Immigration and Imprisonment in the United States," *Stanford Law & Policy Review* 22.2 (2011): 429–54.

Bowers, Josh, "Mandatory Life and Death of Equitable Discretion," in Charles J. Ogletree, Jr., and Austin Sarat, eds., *Life Without Parole: America's New Death Penalty?* (New York: NYU Press, 2012): 25–65.

Bowman, Frank O., III, "The Sounds of Silence: American Criminal Justice Policy in Election Year 2008," *Federal Sentencing Reporter* 20.5 (2008): 289–94.

Bright, Stephen B, "Discrimination, Death, and Denial: Race and the Death Penalty," in David R. Dow and Mark Dow, eds., *Machinery of Death: The Reality of America's Death Penalty Regime* (New York and London: Routledge, 2002): 45–78.

Brodeur, Jean-Paul, "Comparative Penology in Perspective," in Michael Tonry, ed., *Crime, Punishment, and Politics in Comparative Perspective—Crime and Justice: A Review of Research*, v. 36 (Chicago: University of Chicago Press, 2007): 49–91.

Bronstein, Alvin J., "Reform Without Change: The Future of Prisoners' Rights," *Civil Liberties Review* 4.3 (1977): 27–45.

Brown, Michelle, *The Culture of Punishment: Prison, Society, and Spectacle* (New York: NYU Press, 2009).

Brown, Michelle, "Penal Spectatorship and the Culture of Punishment," in David Scott, ed., *Why Prison?* (Cambridge, UK: Cambridge University Press, 2013): 108–24.

Brown-Dean, Khalilah L., "One Lens, Multiple Views: Felon Disenfranchisement Laws and American Political Inequality," Ohio State University, PhD dissertation, 2004.

Buchanan, Kim Shayo, "Impunity: Sexual Abuse in Women's Prisons," *Harvard Civil Rights-Civil Liberties Law Review* 42.1 (2007): 45–87.

Bumiller, Kristin, *In an Abusive State: How Neoliberalism Appropriated the Feminist Movement Against Sexual Violence* (Durham, NC: Duke University Press, 2008).

Burch, James H., II, "Encouraging Innovation on the Foundation of Evidence: On the Path to the 'Adjacent Possible'?," *Criminology & Public Policy* 10.3 (2011): 609–16.

Burch, Traci R., "Punishment and Participation: How Criminal Convictions Threaten American Democracy," Harvard University, PhD dissertation, 2007.

Burch, Traci R., "Did Disenfranchisement Laws Help Elect President Bush? New Evidence on the Turnout Rates and Candidate Preferences of Florida's Ex-Felons," *Political Behavior* 34.1 (2012): 1–26.

Burch, Traci, *Trading Democracy for Justice: Criminal Convictions and the Decline of Neighborhood Political Participation* (Chicago: University of Chicago Press, 2013).

Burch, Traci, "Effects of Imprisonment and Community Supervision on Neighborhood Political Participation in North Carolina," *ANNALS of the American Academy of Political and Social Science* 651 (January 2014): 184–201.

Bush-Baskette, Stephanie, *Misguided Justice: The War on Drugs and the Incarceration of Black Women* (New York: iUniverse, Inc., 2010).

Bushway, Shawn D., "Labor Markets and Crime," in James Q. Wilson and Joan Petersilia, eds., *Crime and Public Policy* (New York: Oxford University Press, 2011): 183–209.

Bushway, Shawn D. and Robert Apel, "A Signaling Perspective on Employment-Based Reentry Programming: Training Completion as a Desistance Signal," *Criminology & Public Policy* 11.1 (2012): 21–50.

Bushway, Shawn D. and Brian Forst, "Studying Discretion in the Processes that Generate Criminal Justice Sanctions," *Justice Quarterly* 30.2 (2013): 199–22.

Bushway, Shawn D., Michael A. Stoll, and David F. Weiman, eds., *Barriers to Reentry? The Labor Market for Released Prisoners in Post-Industrial America* (New York: Russell Sage Foundation, 2007).

Bushway, Shawn D. and Gary Sweeten, "Abolish Lifetime Bans for Ex-Felons," *Criminology & Public Policy* 6.4 (2007): 697–706.

Campbell, Michael C., "Criminal Disenfranchisement Reform in California: A Deviant Case Study," *Punishment & Society* 9.2 (2007): 177–99.

Campbell, Michael C., "Ornery Alligators and Soap on a Rope: Texas Prosecutors and Punishment Reform in the Lone Star State," *Theoretical Criminology* 16.3 (2011): 1–23.

Campbell, Michael C., "Politics, Prisons, and Law Enforcement: An Examination of 'Law and Order' Politics in Texas," *Law & Society Review* 45.3 (2011): 177–99.

Campbell, Michael C., "Homicide and Punishment in Europe: Examining National Variation," in Marieke C.A. Liem and William A. Pridemore, eds., *Handbook of European Homicide Research: Patterns, Explanations, and Country Studies* (New York: Springer, 2012): 273–84.

Carlen, Pat, "Carceral Clawback: The Case of Women's Imprisonment in Canada," *Punishment & Society* 4.1 (2002): 115–21.

Carlen, Pat, "Imaginary Penalties: Risk-Crazed Governance," in Pat Carlen, ed., *Imaginary Penalties* (Devon, UK: Willan, 2008): 1–25.

Cartagena, Juan, "Lost Votes, Body Counts and Joblessness: The Effects of Felon Disenfranchisement on Latino Civic Engagement," *Latino Studies* 6.1–2 (2008): 192–200.

Casale, Silvia, "The Importance of Dialogue and Cooperation in Prison Oversight," *Pace Law Review* 30.5 (2011): 1490–1502.

Cavadino, Michael and James Dignan, *Penal Systems: A Comparative Approach*, 4th ed. (London: Sage, 2006).

Chacón, Jennifer M., "Managing Migration Through Crime," *Columbia Law Review Sidebar* 109 (December 12, 2009): 135–48.

Chacón, Jennifer M., "Whose Community Shield?: Examining the Removal of the 'Criminal Street Gang Member,'" *University of Chicago Legal Forum* (2007): 1–41.

Chase, Robert, "Civil Rights on the Cell Block: Race, Reform, and Violence in Texas Prisons and the Nation, 1945–1990," PhD dissertation, University of Maryland, 2009.

Cheever, Joan M., *Back from the Dead: One Woman's Search for the Men Who Walked Off Death Row* (New York: Wiley, 2006).

Cheliotis, Leonidas K., "How Iron Is the Iron Cage of the New Penology? The Role of Human Agency in the Implementation of Criminal Justice Policy," *Punishment & Society* 8.3 (2006): 313–40.

Chen, Elsa Y., "Impact of 'Three Strikes and You're Out' on Crime Trends in California and Throughout the United States," *Journal of Contemporary Criminal Justice* 24.4 (2008): 345–70.

Cherney, Adrian, "Beyond Technicism: Broadening the 'What Works' Paradigm in Crime Prevention," *Crime Prevention and Community Safety: An International Journal*, 4.3 (2002): 49–59.

Chesney-Lind, Meda, "Imprisoning Women: The Unintended Victims of Mass Imprisonment," in Marc Mauer and Meda Chesney-Lind., eds., *Invisible Punishment: The Collateral Consequences of Mass Imprisonment* (New York: New Press, 2004): 79–94.

Chiricos, Theodore G. and Miriam A. Delone, "Labor Surplus and Punishment: A Review and Assessment of Theory and Evidence," *Social Problems* 39.4 (1992): 421–46.

Clark, Elizabeth B., "'The Sacred Rights of the Weak': Pain, Sympathy, and the Culture of Individual Rights in Antebellum America," *Journal of American History* 82.2 (1995): 463–93.

Clear, Todd R., *Imprisoning Communities: How Mass Incarceration Makes Disadvantaged Neighborhoods Worse* (New York: Oxford University Press, 2007).

Clear, Todd R., "Policy and Evidence: The Challenge to the American Society of Criminology," *Criminology* 48.1 (2010): 1–26.

Clear, Todd R., "A Private-Sector, Incentives-Based Model for Justice Reinvestment," *Criminology & Public Policy* 10.3 (2011): 585–608.

Clear, Todd R. and James Austin, "Reducing Mass Incarceration: Implications of the Iron Law of Prison Populations," *Harvard Law & Policy Review* 3.2 (2009): 307–24.

Clear, Todd R. and Natasha A. Frost, *The Punishment Imperative: The Rise and Failure of Mass Incarceration in America* (New York: NYU Press, 2014).

Cohen, Cathy J., *Democracy Remixed: Black Youth and the Future of American Politics* (New York: Oxford University Press, 2010).

Cohen, Cathy J. and Michael C. Dawson, "Neighborhood Poverty and African-American Politics," *American Political Science Review* 87.2 (1993): 286–302.

Cohen, Mark A., Roland T. Rust, and Sara Steen, "Prevention, Crime Control or Cash?

Public Preferences Towards Criminal Justice Spending Priorities," *Justice Quarterly* 23.3 (2006): 317–35.

Cole, David, *No Equal Justice: Race and Class in the American Criminal Justice System* (New York: New Press, 1999).

Coleman, Mathew, "The 'Local' Migration State: The Site-Specific Devolution of Immigration Enforcement in the U.S. South," *Law & Policy* 34.2 (2012): 159–90.

Comfort, Megan, "'The Best Seven Years I Could'a Done': The Reconstruction of Imprisonment and Rehabilitation," in Pat Carlen, ed., *Imaginary Penalties* (Devon, UK: Willan, 2008): 252–74.

Cook, Carrie and Jodi Lane, "Legislator Ideology and Sentencing Policy in Florida: A Research Note," *Criminal Justice Policy Review* 20.2 (2009): 209–35.

Costelloe, Michael T., Ted Chiricos, and Marc Gertz, "Public Attitudes Toward Criminals: Exploring the Relevance of Crime Salience and Economic Insecurity," *Punishment & Society* 11.1 (2009): 25–49.

Coyle, Andrew, "Replacing the Death Penalty: The Vexed Issue of Alterative Sanctions," in Peter Hodgkinson and William A. Schabas, eds., *Capital Punishment: Strategies for Abolition* (Cambridge, UK: Cambridge University Press, 2004): 92–115.

Craun, Sarah W., Poco D. Kernsmith, and N.K. Butler, "'Anything That Can Be a Danger to the Public': Desire to Extend Registries Beyond Sex Offenses," *Criminal Justice Policy Review* 22.3 (2011): 375–91.

Craun, Sarah W., Catherine A. Simmons, and Kristen Reeves, "Percentage of Named Offenders on the Registry at Time of the Assault: Reports from Sexual Assault Survivors," *Violence Against Women* 17.11 (2011): 1374–82.

Crew, Robert E. and Belinda Creel Davis, "Substance Abuse as a Barrier to Employment of Welfare Recipients," *Journal of Policy Practice* 5.4 (2006): 69–82.

Crutchfield, Robert D., George S. Bridges, and Susan R. Pitchford, "Analytical and Aggregation Biases in Analyses of Imprisonment: Reconciling Discrepancies in Studies of Racial Disparity," *Journal of Research in Crime & Delinquency* 31.2 (1994): 66–82.

Crutchfield, Robert D., April Fernandes, and Jorge Martinez, "Racial and Ethnic Disparity and Criminal Justice: How Much Is Too Much?," *Journal of Criminal Law & Criminology* 100.3 (2010): 903–32.

Cucolo, Heather and Michael L. Perlin, "Preventing Sex-Offender Recidivism Through Therapeutic Jurisprudence Approaches and Specialized Community Integration," *Temple Political & Civil Rights Law Review*, Fall 2012, http://papers.ssrn.com/sol3/papers .cfm?abstract_id=2116424 (retrieved October 22, 2013).

Cullen, Francis T., "Assessing the Penal Harm Movement," *Journal of Research in Crime and Delinquency* 32.3 (1995): 338–58.

Cullen, Francis T., "Taking Rehabilitation Seriously: Creativity, Science, and the Challenge of Offender Change," *Punishment & Society* 14.1 (2012): 94–114.

Cullen, Francis T. and Karen E. Gilbert, *Reaffirming Rehabilitaiton*, 2nd ed. (Waltham, MA: Anderson Publishing, 2013).

Cullen, Francis T. and Cheryl Lero Jonson, "Rehabilitation and Treatment Programs," in James Q. Wilson and Joan Petersilia, eds., *Crime and Public Policy* (New York: Oxford University Press, 2011): 293–344.

Currie, Elliott, *The Roots of Danger: Violent Crime in Global Perspective* (Englewood Cliffs, NJ: Prentice Hall, 2009).

Currie, Elliott, "On the Pitfalls of Spurious Prudence," *Criminology & Public Policy* 10.1 (2011): 109–14.

Curtin, Mary Ellen, *Black Prisoners and Their World, Alabama, 1865–1900* (Charlottesville: University of Virginia Press, 2000).

Curtin, Mary Ellen, "'Please Hear Our Cries': The Hidden History of Black Prisoners in America," in Debra E. McDowell, Claudrena N. Harold, and Juan Battle, eds., *The Punitive Turn: New Approaches to Race and Incarceration* (Charlottesville: University of Virginia Press, 2013): 29–44.

Cusac, Anne-Marie, *Cruel and Unusual: The Culture of Punishment in America* (New Haven, CT: Yale University Press, 2009).

Davies, Garth and Jeffrey Fagan, "Crime and Enforcement in Immigrant Neighborhoods: Evidence from New York City," *ANNALS of the American Academy of Political and Social Science* 641 (May 2012): 99–124.

Davis, Angela J., *Arbitrary Justice: The Power of the American Prosecutor* (New York: Oxford University Press, 2007).

Davis, Angela J., "In Search of Racial Justice: The Role of the Prosecutor," *N.Y.U. Journal of Legislation and Public Policy* 16.4 (2013): 821–51.

Davis, Kenneth Culp, *Discretionary Justice: A Preliminary Inquiry* (Baton Rouge: Louisiana State University Press, 1969).

Dawson, Michael C., "3 of 10 Theses on Neoliberalism in the U.S. During the Early 21st Century," *Carceral Notebooks* 6 (2010): 11–20.

Dawson, Michael C., *Not in Our Lifetimes: The Future of Black Politics* (Chicago: University of Chicago Press, 2011).

De Giorgi, Alessandro, *Re-Thinking the Political Economy of Punishment: Perspectives on Post-Fordism and Penal Politics* (Aldershot, UK: Ashgate, 2006).

de la Vega, Connie and Michelle Leighton, "Sentencing Our Children to Die in Prison: Global Law and Practice," *University of San Francisco Law Review* 42.4 (2008): 983–1044.

Deitch, Michele, "Independent Correctional Oversight Mechanisms Across the County: A 50-State Inventory," *Pace Law Review* 30.5 (2010): 1754–1930.

Deitch, Michele, "The Need for Independent Prison Oversight in a Post-PLRA World," *Federal Sentencing Reporter* 24.4 (2012): 236–44.

Dolovich, Sharon, "State Punishment and Private Prisons," *Duke Law Journal* 55.3 (2005): 439–546.

Dolovich, Sharon, "Creating the Permanent Prisoner," in Charles J. Ogletree, Jr., and Austin Sarat, eds., *Life Without Parole: America's New Death Penalty?* (New York: NYU Press, 2012): 96–137.

Dolovich, Sharon, "Two Models of the Prison: Accidental Humanity and Hypermasculinity in the L.A. County Jail," *Journal of Criminal Law and Criminology* 102.4 (2012): 965–1118.

Dow, Mark, *American Gulag: Inside U.S. Immigration Prisons* (Berkeley: University of California Press, 2004).

Downes, David, "The *Macho* Penal Economy: Mass Incarceration in the United States—A European Perspective," *Punishment & Society* 3.1 (2001): 61–80.

Downes, David and Kirstine Hansen, "Welfare and Punishment in Comparative Context," in Sarah Armstrong and Lesley McAra, eds., *Perspectives on Punishment: The Contours of Control* (Oxford: Oxford University Press, 2006): 33–54.

Dünkel, Frieder and Ineke Pruin, "Germany," in Nicola Padfield, Dirk van Zyl Smit, and Frieder Dünkel, eds., *Release from Prison: European Policy and Practice* (Devon, UK: Willan, 2010): 185–212.

Earley, Mark L. and Kathryn Wiley, "The New Frontier of Public Safety," *Stanford Law & Policy Review* 22.2 (2011): 343–54.

Eisner, Manuel, "Modernization, Self-Control and Lethal Violence: The Long-Term Dynamics of European Homicide Rates in Theoretical Perspective," *British Journal of Criminology* 41.4 (2001): 618–38.

Engen, Rodney L., "Assessing Determinate and Presumptive Sentencing—Making Research Relevant," *Criminology & Public Policy* 8.2 (2009): 323–36.

Ewald, Alec C., " 'Civil Death': The Ideological Paradox of Criminal Disenfranchisement Law in the United States," *Wisconsin Law Review* 2002.5 (2002): 1045–1138.

Ewert, Stephanie, Bryan L. Sykes, and Becky Pettit, "The Degree of Disadvantage: Incarceration and Inequality in Education," *ANNALS of the American Academy of Political and Social Science* 651 (January 2014): 24–43.

Fabelo, Tony, "Texas Justice Reinvestment: Be More Like Texas?," *Justice Research and Policy* 12.1 (2010): 113–31.

Fairbanks, Robert P., II, "The Illinois Reentry Imperative: Sheridan Correctional Center as National Model," *Carceral Notebooks* 6 (2011): 175–200.

Feeley, Malcolm, "Origins of Actuarial Justice," in Sarah Armstrong and Lesley McAra, eds., *Perspectives on Punishment: The Contours of Control* (Oxford: Oxford University Press, 2006): 217–32.

Feeley, Malcolm and Jonathan Simon, "The New Penology: Notes on the Emerging Strategy of Corrections and Its Implications," *Criminology* 30.4 (1992): 449–74.

Fernandez, Luiz A., *Policing Dissent: Social Control and the Anti-Globalization Movement* (New Brunswick, NJ: Rutgers University Press, 2008).

Filindra, Alexandra and Melinda Kovács, "Analysing U.S. State Legislative Resolutions on Immigrants and Immigration: The Role of Immigration Federalism," *International Migration* 50.4 (2012): 33–50.

Flamm, Michael W., *Law and Order: Street Crime, Civil Unrest, and the Crisis of Liberalism in the 1960s* (New York: Columbia University Press, 2005).

Flanagan, Timothy J., ed., *Long-Term Imprisonment: Policy, Science, and Correctional Practice* (Thousand Oaks, CA: Sage, 1995).

Fluery-Stein, Benjamin with Carla Crowder, *Dying Inside: The HIV/AIDS Ward at Limestone Prison* (Ann Arbor: University of Michigan Press, 2008).

Forman, James, Jr., "Exporting Harshness: How the War on Crime Helped Make the War on Terror Possible," *N.Y.U. Review of Law & Social Change* 33.3 (2009): 331–74.

Forman, James, Jr., "Racial Critiques of Mass Incarceration: Beyond the New Jim Crow," *N.Y.U. Law Review* 87.1 (2012): 21–69.

Forst, Brian, "Prosecution," in James Q. Wilson and Joan Petersilia, eds., *Crime and Public Policy* (New York: Oxford University Press, 2011): 437–66.

Fortner, Michael Javen, "The Carceral State and the Crucible of Black Politics: An Urban History of the Rockefeller Drug Laws," *Studies in American Political Development* 27.1 (2013): 14–35.

Frase, Richard S., "Excessive Prison Sentences, Punishment Goals, and the Eighth Amendment: 'Proportionality' Relative to What?," *Minnesota Law Review* 89.3 (2005): 571–651.

Frase, Richard S., "What Explains Persistent Racial Disproportionality in Minnesota's Prison and Jail Populations?," in Michael Tonry, ed., *Crime and Justice: A Review of Research*, v. 38 (Chicago: University of Chicago, 2009): 201–80.

Garland, David, *The Culture of Control: Crime and Social Order in Contemporary Society* (Chicago: University of Chicago Press, 2001).

Garland, David, *Peculiar Institution: America's Death Penalty in an Age of Abolition* (Cambridge, MA: Belknap Press of Harvard University Press, 2010).

Gartner, Rosemary, Anthony N. Doob, and Franklin E. Zimring, "The Past as Prologue? Decarceration in California Then and Now," *Criminology & Public Policy* 10.2 (2011): 291–25.

Geraghty, Sarah and Melanie Velez, "Bringing Transparency and Accountability to Criminal Justice Institutions in the South," *Stanford Law & Policy Review* 22.2 (2011): 455–88.

Gertner, Nancy, "Supporting Advisory Guidelines," *Harvard Law & Policy Review* 3.2 (2009): 261–81.

Gillon, Steven M., *"That's Not What We Meant to Do": Reform and Its Unintended Consequences in Twentieth Century America* (New York: W.W. Norton, 2000).

Gilmore, Ruth Wilson, *The Golden Gulag: Prisons, Surplus, Crisis, and Opposition in Globalizing California* (Berkeley: University of California Press, 2007).

Glasmeier, Amy K. and Tracey Farrigan, "The Economic Impacts of the Prison Development Boom on Persistently Poor Rural Places," *International Regional Science Review* 30.3 (2007): 274–99.

Goffman, Alice, "On the Run: Wanted Men in a Philadelphia Ghetto," *American Sociological Review* 74.3 (2009): 339–57.

Goffman, Alice, *On the Run: Fugitive Life in an American City* (Chicago: University of Chicago Press, 2014).

Goldfield, Michael, "Worker Insurgency, Radical Organization, and New Deal Labor Legislation," *American Political Science Review* 83.4 (1989): 1257–82.

Goldstein, Abraham S., "Prosecution: History of the Public Prosecutor," in Sanford H. Kadish, ed., *Encyclopedia of Criminal Justice* (New York: New Press, 1983): 1242–46.

Gómez, Alan Eladio, "Resisting Living Death at Marion Federal Penitentiary, 1972," *Radical History Review* 96 (Fall 2006): 58–86.

Gordon, Avery F., "The United States Military Prison: The Normalcy of Exceptional Brutality," in Phil Scraton and Jude McCulloch, eds., *The Violence of Incarceration* (New York: Routledge, 2009): 164–86.

Gottfredson, Stephen D. and Ralph B. Taylor, "Attitudes of Correctional Policymakers and the Public," in Stephen D. Gottfredson and Sean McConville, eds., *America's Correctional Crisis: Prison Populations and Public Policy* (New York: Greenwood Press, 1987): 57–75.

Gottschalk, Marie, *The Shadow Welfare State: Labor, Business, and the Politics of Health Care in the United States* (Ithaca, NY: Cornell University Press, 2000).

Gottschalk, Marie, *The Prison and the Gallows: The Politics of Mass Incarceration in America* (New York: Cambridge University Press, 2006).

Gottschalk, Marie, "U.S. Health Reform and the Stockholm Syndrome," in Leo Panitch and Colin Leys, eds., *Socialist Register 2010: Morbid Symptoms; Health Under Capitalism* (Pontypool, Wales: Merlin Press, 2009): 103–24.

Gottschalk, Marie, "The Great Recession and the Great Confinement: The Economic Crisis and the Future of Penal Reform," in Richard Rosenfeld, Kenna Quinet, and Crystal Garcia, eds., *Contemporary Issues in Criminological Theory and Research: The Role of Social Institutions* (Belmont, CA: Wadsworth/Cengage, 2011): 343–70.

Gottschalk, Marie, "Lengthy Sentences: The Police Surge and the Forgotten Men, Women, and Communities," *Criminology & Public Policy* 10.1 (2011): 123–36.

Gottschalk, Marie, "They're Back: The Public Plan, the Reincarnation of Harry and Louise, and the Limits of Obamacare," *Journal of Health Politics, Policy, and Law* 36.3 (2011): 393–401.

Gould, Eric D., Bruce A. Weinberg, and David B. Mustard, "Crime Rates and Local Labor Market Opportunities in the United States: 1979–1997," *Review of Economics and Statistics* 84.1 (2002): 45–61.

Graham, John, "Decarceration in the Federal Republic of Germany: How Practitioners are Succeeding Where Policy-Makers Failed," *British Journal of Criminology* 30.3 (1990): 150–70.

Green, David, "Public Opinion Versus Public Judgment About Crime: Correcting the Comedy of Errors," *British Journal of Criminology* 46.1 (2006): 131–54.

Green, Geri Lynn, "The Quixotic Dilemma, California's Immutable Culture of Incarceration," *Pace Law Review* 30.5 (2010): 1453–75.

Greider, William, *The Education of David Stockman and Other Americans* (New York: Dutton, 1982).

Grob, Gerald N., *The Mad Among Us: A History of the Care of America's Mentally Ill* (New York: Free Press, 1994).

Gross, Rebecca, "The 'Spirit' of Three Strikes Law: From the *Romero* Myth to the Hopeful Implications of *Andrade*," *Golden Gate University Law Review* 32.2 (2002): 169–205.

Guetzkow, Joshua and Bruce Western, "The Political Consequences of Mass Imprisonment," in Joe Soss, Jacob S. Hacker, and Suzanne Mettler, eds., *Remaking America: Democracy and Public Policy in an Age of Inequality* (New York: Russell Sage Foundation, 2007): 228–42.

Habes, Heather, "Paying for the Graying: How California Can More Effectively Manage Its Growing Elderly Inmate Population," *Southern California Interdisciplinary Law Journal* 20.2 (2011): 395–423.

Hagan, Jacqueline and Scott Phillips, "Border Blunders: The Unanticipated Human and Economic Costs of the U.S. Approach to Immigration Control, 1986–2007," *Criminology & Public Policy* 7.1 (2008): 83–94.

Hagan, John, *Who Are the Criminals? The Politics of Crime Policy from the Age of Roosevelt to the Age of Reagan* (Princeton, NJ: Princeton University Press, 2011).

Hagan, John, Ron Levi, and Ronit Dinovitzer, "The Symbolic Violence of the Crime-Immigration Nexus: Migrant Mythologies in the Americas," *Criminology & Public Policy* 7.1 (2008): 95–112.

Haines, Herbert H., *Against Capital Punishment: The Anti-Death Penalty Movement in America, 1972–1994* (New York: Oxford University Press, 1996).

Hajnal, Zoltan L. and Taeku Lee, *Why Americans Don't Join the Party: Race, Immigration, and the Failure (of Political Parties) to Engage the Electorate* (Princeton, NJ: Princeton University Press, 2011.

Hallett, Michael A., *Private Prisons in America: A Critical Race Perspective* (Urbana and Chicago: University of Illinois Press, 2006).

Hallett, Michael A., "Reentry to What? Theorizing Prisoner Reentry in the Jobless Future," *Critical Criminology* 20.3 (2012): 213–28.

Haney, Craig, "Riding the Punishment Wave: On the Origins of Our Devolving Standards of Decency," *Hastings Women's Law Journal* 9.1 (1998): 27–79.

Haney, Craig, "The Wages of Prison Overcrowding: Harmful Psychological Consequences and Dysfunctional Correctional Reactions," *Washington University Journal of Law & Policy* 22 (2006): 265–93.

Haney, Craig, "Counting Casualties in the War on Prisoners," *University of San Francisco Law Review* 43.1 (2008): 87–138.

Hannah-Moffat, Kelly, *Punishment in Disguise: Penal Governance and Federal Imprisonment of Women in Canada* (Toronto: University of Toronto Press, 2001).

Harcourt, Bernard E., "From the Asylum to the Prison: Rethinking the Incarceration Revolution," *Texas Law Review* 84.7 (2006): 1751–86.

Harcourt, Bernard E., *The Illusion of Free Markets: Punishment and the Myth of Natural Order* (Cambridge, MA: Harvard University Press, 2011).

Harding, Richard, "Private Prisons," in Michael Tonry, ed., *Crime and Justice: A Review of Research*, v. 28 (Chicago: University of Chicago Press, 2001): 265–346.

Harris, Andrew J. and Arthur J. Lurigio, "Introduction to Special Issue on Sex Offenses and Offenders: Toward Evidence-Based Public Policy," *Criminal Justice and Behavior* 37.5 (2010): 477–81.

Harris, Andrew J., Jill S. Levenson, and Alissa R. Ackerman, "Registered Sex Offenders in the United States: Behind the Numbers," *Crime & Delinquency* 60.1 (2014): 3–33.

Harris, Andrew J., Christopher Lobanov-Rostovsky, and Jill S. Levenson, "Widening the Net: The Effects of Transitioning to the Adam Walsh Act's Federally Mandated Sex Offender Classification System," *Criminal Justice and Behavior* 37.5 (2010): 503–19.

Harris, Fredrick C., *The Price of the Ticket: Barack Obama and the Rise and Decline of Black Politics* (New York: Oxford University Press, 2012).

Hartman, Kenneth E., ed., *Too Cruel, Not Unusual Enough* (Lancaster, CA: Steering Committee Press, 2013).

Henry, Jessica S., "Death-in-Prison Sentences: Overutilized and Underscrutinized," in Charles J. Ogletree, Jr., and Austin Sarat, eds., *Life Without Parole: America's New Death Penalty?* (New York: NYU Press, 2012): 66–95.

Herivel, Tara, "Introduction," in Tara Herivel and Paul Wright, eds., *Prison Profiteers: Who Makes Money from Mass Incarceration* (New York: New Press, 2007): ix–xviii.

Hernández, David Manuel, "Pursuant to Deportation: Latinos and Immigrant Detention," *Latino Studies* 6.1 (2008): 35–63.

Hessick, Carissa Byrne, "Disentangling Child Pornography from Child Sex Abuse," *Washington University Law Review* 88.4 (2010–11): 853–902.

Hicks, Cheryl D., "'Bright and Good Looking Colored Girl': Black Women's Sexuality and 'Harmful Intimacy' in Early-Twentieth Century New York," in Deborah E. McDowell, Claudrena N. Harold, and Juan Battle, eds., *The Punitive Turn: New Approaches to Race and Incarceration* (Charlottesville: University of Virginia Press, 2013): 73–107.

Hipp, John R. and Daniel K. Yates, "Do Returning Parolees Affect Neighborhood Crime? A Case Study of Sacramento," *Criminology* 47.3 (2009): 619–54.

Hjalmarsson, Randi and Mark Lopez, "The Voting Behavior of Young Disenfranchised Felons: Would They Vote If They Could?," *American Law and Economics Review* 12.2 (2010): 356–93.

Ho, Dale E., "Captive Constituents: Prison-Based Gerrymandering and the Current Redistricting Cycle," *Stanford Law & Policy Review* 22.2 (2011): 355–94.

Hochschild, Jennifer L., *Facing Up to the American Dream: Race, Class, and the Soul of the Nation* (Princeton, NJ: Princeton University Press, 1995).

Hochschild, Jennifer L. and Vesla Weaver, "The Skin Color Paradox and the American Racial Order," *Social Forces* 86.2 (2007): 643–70.

Hohler-Hausmann, Julilly, "'The Attila the Hun Law': New York's Rockefeller Drug Laws and the Making of a Punitive State," *Journal of Social History* 44.1 (2010): 71–95.

Hood, Roger, "Criminology and Penal Policy: The Vital Role of Empirical Research," in

Anthony Bottoms and Michael Tonry, eds., *Ideology, Crime and Criminal Justice: A Symposium in Honor of Sir Leon Radzinowicz* (Portland, OR: Willan, 2002): 153–72.

Hooks, Gregory, Clayton Mosher, Shaun Genter et al., "Revisiting the Impact of Prison Building on Job Growth, Education, Incarceration, and County-Level Employment, 1976–2004," *Social Science Quarterly* 91.1 (2010): 228–44.

Hörnquist, Magnus, "The Imaginary Constitution of Wage Labourers," in Pat Carlen, ed., *Imaginary Penalties* (Devon, UK: Willan, 2008): 172–92.

Houppert, Karen, *Chasing Gideon: The Elusive Quest for Poor People's Justice* (New York: New Press, 2013).

Hout, Michael, "Occupational Mobility of Black Men: 1962 to 1973," *American Sociological Review* 49.3 (1984): 308–22.

Hull, Elizabeth A., *The Disenfranchisement of Ex-Felons* (Philadelphia: Temple University Press, 2006).

Irwin, John, *Lifers: Seeking Redemption in Prison* (New York: Routledge, 2009).

Jacobs, James B. and Elena Larrauri, "Are Criminal Convictions a Public Matter? The USA and Spain," *Punishment & Society* 14.1 (2012): 3–28.

Jacobson, Michael, *Downsizing Prisons: How to Reduce Crime and End Mass Incarceration* (New York: NYU Press, 2005).

Jacoby, Joan E., *The American Prosecutor: A Search for Identity* (Lexington, MA: Lexington Books, 1980).

Janus, Eric S., *Failure to Protect: America's Sexual Predator Laws and the Rise of the Preventive State* (Ithaca, NY: Cornell University Press, 2006).

Jeglic, Elizabeth L., Cynthia Calkins Mercado, and Jill S. Levenson, "The Prevalence and Correlates of Depression and Hopelessness among Sex Offenders Subject to Community Notification and Residence Restriction Legislation," *American Journal of Criminal Justice* 37.1 (2012): 46–59.

Jenkins, Philip, *Moral Panic: Changing Concepts of the Child Molester in Modern America* (New Haven, CT: Yale University Press, 1998).

Jenness, Valerie and Michael Smyth, "The Passage and Implementation of the Prison Rape Elimination Act: Legal Endogeneity and the Uncertain Road from Symbolic Law to Instrumental Effects," *Stanford Law & Policy Review* 22.2 (2011): 489–527.

Jensen, Christen, *The Pardoning Power in the American States* (Chicago: University of Chicago Press, 1922).

Johnson, Devon, "Racial Prejudice, Perceived Injustice, and the Black-White Gap in Punitive Attitudes," *Journal of Criminal Justice* 36.2 (2008): 198–206.

Johnson, Robert and Sandra McGunigall-Smith, "Life Without Parole, America's Other Death Penalty: Notes on Life Under Sentence of Death by Incarceration," *Prison Journal* 88.2 (2008): 328–46.

Johnson, Ryan S., Shawn Kantor, and Price V. Fishback, "Striking at the Roots of Crime: The Impact of Social Welfare Spending on Crime During the Great Depression," National Bureau of Economic Research Working Paper no. 12825 (January 2007).

Kalhan, Anil, "Rethinking Immigration Detention," *Columbia Law Review Sidebar* 110 (July 21, 2010): 42–58.

Kalt, Brian C., "The Exclusion of Felons from Jury Service," *American University Law Review* 53.1 (2003): 65–189.

Kanstroom, Daniel, *Aftermath: Deportation Law and the New American Diaspora* (New York: Oxford University Press, 2012).

Katz, Michael B., *The Price of Citizenship: Redefining the American Welfare State*, updated ed. (Philadelphia: University of Pennsylvania Press, 2008).

Katz, Michael B., "Why Don't American Cities Burn Very Often?," *Journal of Urban History* 34.2 (2008): 185–208.

Katz, Michael B., Mark J. Stern, and Jamie J. Fader, "The New African American Inequality," *Journal of American History* 92.1 (2005): 75–108.

Katzenstein, Mary Fainsod and Mitali Nagrecha, "A New Punishment Regime," *Criminology & Public Policy* 10.3 (2011): 55–68.

Katz-Schiavone, Stacey, Jill S. Levenson, and Alissa R. Ackerman, "Myths and Facts About Sexual Violence: Public Perceptions and Implications for Prevention," *Journal of Criminal Justice and Popular Culture* 15.3 (2008): 291–311.

Kennedy, Randall, *Race, Crime, and the Law* (New York: Pantheon, 1997).

King, Desmond S. and Rogers M. Smith, *Still a House Divided: Race and Politics in Obama's America* (Princeton, NJ: Princeton University Press, 2011).

Kjellstrand, Jean M. and J. Mark Eddy, "Parental Incarceration During Childhood, Family Context, and Youth Problem Behavior Across Adolescence," *Journal of Offender Rehabilitation* 50.1 (2011): 18–36.

Kleiman, Mark A. R., *When Brute Force Fails: How to Have Less Crime and Less Punishment* (Princeton, NJ: Princeton University Press, 2009).

Kleiman, Mark A. R., "Toward Fewer Prisoners and Less Crime," *Daedalus* 139.3 (2010): 115–23.

Kleiman, Mark A. R., "Justice Reinvestment in Community Supervision," *Criminology & Public Policy* 10.3 (2011): 651–59.

Kleiman, Mark A. R., Jonathan P. Caulkins, and Angela Hawken, *Drugs and Drug Policy: What Everyone Needs to Know* (New York: Oxford University Press, 2011).

Kobil, Daniel T., "Should Mercy Have a Place in Clemency Decisions?," in Austin Sarat and Nasser Hussain, eds., *Forgiveness, Mercy, and Clemency* (Stanford, CA: Stanford University Press): 36–63.

Kraska, Peter B., ed., *Militarizing the American Criminal Justice System: The Changing Roles of the Armed Forces and Police* (Boston: Northeastern University Press, 2001).

Kruttschnitt, Candace, "The Paradox of Women's Imprisonment," *Daedalus* 139.3 (2010): 32–42.

Kubrin, Charis E. and Eric A. Stewart, "Predicting Who Reoffends: The Neglected Role of Neighborhood Context in Recidivism Studies," *Criminology* 44.1 (2006): 165–97.

Kubrin, Charis E., Marjorie S. Zatz, and Ramiro Martínez, Jr., eds., *Punishing Immigrants: Policy, Politics, and Injustice* (New York: NYU Press, 2012).

Kupers, Terry A. et al., "Beyond Supermax Administrative Segregation: Mississippi's Experience Rethinking Prison Classification and Creating Alternative Mental Health Programs," *Criminal Justice and Behavior* 36.10 (2009): 1037–50.

Kutateladze, Besiki, *Is America Really So Punitive? Exploring a Continuum of U.S. State Criminal Justice Policies* (El Paso, TX: LFB Scholarly Publishing, 2009).

Lacey, Nicola, *The Prisoners' Dilemma: Political Economy and Punishment in Contemporary Democracies* (Cambridge, UK: Cambridge University Press, 2008).

Lacey, Nicola, "Political Systems and Criminal Justice: The Prisoners' Dilemma After the Coalition," *Current Legal Problems* 65.1 (2012): 203–39.

Lacey, Nicola and David Soskice, "Why Are the Truly Disadvantaged American, When the UK Is Bad Enough? A Political Economy Analysis of Local Autonomy in Criminal Justice,

Education, Residential Zoning," London School of Economics, Law, Society, and Economy Working Papers, November 2013.

Lafer, Gordon, *The Job Training Charade* (Ithaca, NY: Cornell University Press, 2002).

Lane, J. Mark, " 'Is There Life Without Parole?' A Capital Defendant's Right to a Meaningful Alternative Sentence," *Loyola of Los Angeles Law Review* 26.2 (1992–93): 165–97.

Langan, Patrick, "Racism on Trial: New Evidence to Explain the Racial Composition of Prisons in the United States," *Journal of Criminal Law and Criminology* 76.3 (1985): 666–83.

Lappi-Seppälä, Tapio, "Sentencing and Punishment in Finland: The Decline of the Repressive Ideal," in Michael Tonry and Richard Frase, eds., *Punishment and Penal Systems in Western Countries* (New York: Oxford University Press, 2001): 92–150.

Larson, Doran, ed. *Fourth City: Essays from the Prison in America* (East Lansing: Michigan State University Press, 2013).

Lasher, Michael P. and Robert J. McGrath, "The Impact of Community Notification on Sex Offender Reintegration: A Quantitative Review of the Research Literature," *International Journal of Offender Therapy and Comparative Criminology* 56.1 (2012): 6–28.

Laub, John H. and Robert J. Sampson, *Shared Beginnings, Divergent Lives: Delinquent Boys to Age 70* (Cambridge, MA: Harvard University Press, 2003).

Lauritsen, Janet L., Karen Heimer, and James P. Lynch, "Trends in the Gender Gap in Violent Offending: New Evidence from the National Crime Victimization Survey," *Criminology* 47.2 (2009): 361–99.

Lawston, Jodie Michelle, *Sisters Outside: Radical Activists Working for Women Prisoners* (Albany: State University of New York Press, 2009).

Lee, Hedwig, Lauren C. Porter, and Megan Comfort, "The Consequences of Family Member Incarceration: Impacts on Civic Participation and Perceptions of the Legitimacy and Fairness of Government," *ANNALS of the American Academy of Political and Social Science* 651 (January 2014): 44–73.

Lee, Matthew R., "Concentrated Poverty, Race, and Homicide," *Sociological Quarterly* 41.2 (2000): 189–206.

Lee, Youngjae, "The Constitutional Right against Excessive Punishment," *Virginia Law Review* 91.3 (2005): 677–745.

Leigey, Margaret E., "For the Longest Time: The Adjustment of Inmates to a Sentence of Life Without Parole," *Prison Journal* 90.3 (2010): 247–68.

Leon, Chrysanthi S., *Sex Fiends, Perverts, and Pedophiles: Understanding Sex Crime Policy in America* (New York: NYU Press, 2011).

Lerman, Amy E., *The Modern Prison Paradox: Politics, Punishment, and Social Community* (New York: Cambridge University Press, 2013).

Lerman, Amy E. and Vesla M. Weaver, "Staying Out of Sight? Concentrated Policing and Local Political Action," *ANNALS of the American Academy of Political and Social Science* 651 (January 2014): 202–19.

Letourneau, Elizabeth J. et al., "Do Sex Offender Registration and Notification Requirements Deter Juvenile Sex Crimes?," *Criminal Justice and Behavior* 37.5 (2010): 553–69.

Letourneau, Elizabeth J. et al., "Effects of South Carolina's Sex Offender Registration and Notification Policy on Deterrence and Adult Sex Crimes," *Criminal Justice and Behavior* 37.5 (2010): 537–52.

Levenson, Jill S. et al., "Public Perceptions About Sex Offenders and Community Protection Policies," *Analyses of Social Issues and Public Policy* 7.1 (2007): 137–61.

Lichtenstein, Alex, *Twice the Work of Free Labor: The Political Economy of Convict Labor in the New South* (London: Verso, 1996).

Liebling, Alison, "Moral Performance, Inhuman and Degrading Treatment and Prison Pain," *Punishment & Society* 13.5 (2011): 530–50.

Lin, Ann Chih, *Reform in the Making: The Implementation of Social Policy in Prison* (Princeton, NJ: Princeton University Press, 2000).

Loader, Ian and Richard Sparks, *Public Criminology?* (London: Routledge, 2011).

Loader, Ian and Richard Sparks, "Beyond Lamentation: Democratic Egalitarian Politics of Crime and Justice," in Tim Newburn and Jill Peay, eds., *Policing: Politics, Culture and Control* (Oxford: Hart, 2012): 11–42.

Logan, Wayne A., *Knowledge as Power: Criminal Registration and Community Notification Laws in America* (Stanford, CA: Stanford University Press, 2009).

López, Ian Haney, "Post-Racial Racism: Racial Stratification and Mass Incarceration in the Age of Obama" *California Law Review* 98.3 (2010): 1023–74.

Lotke, Eric and Peter Wagner, "Prisoners of the Census: Electoral and Financial Consequences of Counting Prisoners Where They Go, Not Where They Come From," *Pace Law Review* 24.2 (2004): 587–608.

Loury, Glenn C., *Race, Incarceration, and American Values* (Cambridge, MA: MIT Press, 2008).

Lovell, Jarret S., *Crimes of Dissent: Civil Disobedience, Criminal Justice, and the Politics of Conscience* (New York: NYU Press, 2009).

Lundahl, Brad W. et al., "Prison Privatization: A Meta-analysis of Cost and Quality of Confinement Indicators," *Research on Social Work Practice* 19.4 (2009): 383–94.

Lynch, Michael J., *Big Prisons, Big Dreams: Crime and the Failure of America's Penal System* (New Brunswick, NJ: Rutgers University Press, 2007).

Lynch, Mona, "Rehabilitation as Rhetoric," *Punishment & Society* 2.1 (2000): 40–65.

Lynch, Mona, *Sunbelt Justice: Arizona and the Transformation of American Punishment* (Stanford, CA: Stanford University Press, 2010).

Lynch, Mona, "Theorizing the Role of the 'War on Drugs' in American Punishment," *Theoretical Criminology* 16.2 (2012): 175–99.

MacDonald, John and Robert J. Sampson, "The World in a City: Immigration and America's Changing Social Fabric," *ANNALS of the American Academy of Political and Social Science* 641 (May 2012): 6–15.

MacDonald, John and Jessica Saunders, "Are Immigrant Youth Less Violent? Specifying the Reasons and Mechanisms," *ANNALS of the American Academy of Political and Social Science* 641 (May 2012): 125–47.

Manza, Jeff and Christopher Uggen, *Locked Out: Felon Disenfranchisement and American Democracy* (New York: Oxford University Press, 2006).

Marion, Samara, "Justice by Geography? A Study of San Diego County's Three Strikes Sentencing Practices from July–Dec. 1996," *Stanford Law and Policy Review* 11.1 (1999–2000): 29–57.

Markel, Dan, "Against Mercy," *Minnesota Law Review* 88.6 (2004): 1421–80.

Markel, Dan, "State, Be Not Proud: A Retributivist Defense of the Commutation of Death Row and the Abolition of the Death Penalty," *Harvard Civil Rights-Civil Liberties Law Review* 40.2 (2005): 407–80.

Marquart, James W. and Jonathan R. Sorensen, "A National Study of the *Furman*-Commuted Inmates: Assessing the Threat to Society from Capital Offenders," *Loyola of Los Angeles Law Review* 23.1 (1989): 5–28.

Martinez, Ramiro, Jr. and Jacob I. Stowell, "Extending Immigration and Crime Studies: National Implications and Local Settings," *ANNALS of the American Academy of Political and Social Science* 641 (May 2012): 174–91.

Maruna, Shadd, *Making Good: How Ex-Convicts Reform and Rebuild Their Lives* (Washington, DC: American Psychological Association, 2001).

Maruna, Shadd and Hans Toch, "The Impact of Imprisonment on the Desistance Process," in Jeremy Travis and Christy Visher, eds., *Prisoner Reentry and Crime in America* (New York: Cambridge University Press, 2005): 139–78.

Matravers, Amanda and Shadd Maruna, "Modern Penalty and Psychoanalysis," in Matt Matravers, ed., *Managing Modernity: Politics and the Culture of Control* (London: Routledge, 2005): 128–44.

Mauer, Marc, *Race to Incarcerate* (New York: New Press, 1999).

Mauer, Marc, "Sentencing Reform Amid Mass Incarceration—Guarded Optimism," *Criminal Justice* 26.1 (2011), n.p.

McBride, Keally, "California Penalty: The End/Price of the Neoliberal Exception," *Carceral Notebooks* 6 (2010): 131–49.

McCall, Patrica L., Kenneth C. Land, and Karen F. Parker, "An Empirical Assessment of What We Know About Structural Covariates of Homicide Rates: A Return to a Classic 20 Years Later," *Homicide Studies* 14.3 (2010): 219–43.

McCarthy, John D. and Mayer N. Zald, "Resource Mobilization and Social Movements: A Partial Theory," *American Journal of Sociology* 82.6 (1977): 1212–41.

McDowell, Deborah E., Claudrena N. Harold, and Juan Battle, eds., *The Punitive Turn: New Approaches to Race and Incarceration* (Charlottesville: University of Virginia Press, 2013).

McLennan, Rebecca M., *The Crisis of Imprisonment: Protest, Politics, and the Making of the American Penal State, 1776–1941* (New York: Cambridge University Press, 2008).

Meares, Tracey L., Neal Katyal, and Dan M. Kahan, "Updating the Study of Punishment," *Stanford Law Review* 56.5 (2004): 1171–1210.

Meirick, Jacquelyn M., "Through the Tier: Are Iowa's New Sex-Offender Laws Unconstitutional?," *Iowa Law Review* 96.3 (2011): 1013–35.

Mendelberg, Tali, *The Race Card: Campaign Strategy, Implicit Messages, and the Norm of Equality* (Princeton, NJ: Princeton University Press, 2001).

Messner, Claudius, and Vincenzo Ruggiero, "Germany: The Penal System Between Past and Future," in Vincenzo Ruggiero, Mick Ryan, and Joe Sim, eds., *Western European Penal Systems: A Critical Anatomy* (London: Sage, 1995): 128–48.

Messner, Steven F., "Economic Discrimination and Societal Homicide Rates: Further Evidence on the Cost of Inequality," *American Sociological Review* 54.4 (1989): 597–611.

Meyer, Walter J., III, and Collier M. Cole, "Physical and Chemical Castration of Sex Offenders: A Review," *Journal of Offender Rehabilitation* 25.3/4 (1997): 1–18.

Miller, Jody, *Getting Played: African American Girls, Urban Inequality, and Gendered Violence* (New York: NYU Press, 2008).

Miller, Lisa L., "The Local and the Legal: American Federalism and the Carceral State," *Criminology & Public Policy* 10.3 (2011): 725–32.

Miller, Lisa L., *The Perils of Federalism: Race, Poverty and the Politics of Crime Control* (New York: Oxford University Press, 2008).

Miller, Susan L., *Victims as Offenders: The Paradox of Women's Violence in Relationships* (New Brunswick, NJ: Rutgers University Press, 2005).

Miller, Teresa A., "Lessons Learned, Lessons Lost: Immigration Enforcement's Failed Experiment with Penal Severity," *Fordham Urban Law Journal* 38.1 (2010): 217–46.

Mitchell, Barry and Julian V. Roberts, *Exploring the Mandatory Life Sentence for Murder* (Oxford, UK and Portland, OR: Hart Publishing, 2012).

Mitchell, Ojmarrh, "A Meta-analysis of Race and Sentencing Research: Explaining the Inconsistencies," *Journal of Quantitative Criminology* 21.4 (2005): 439–66.

Mogul, Joey L., Andrea J. Ritchie, and Kay Whitlock, *Queer (In)Justice: The Criminalization of LGBT People in the United States* (Boston: Beacon Press, 2011).

Morín, José Luis, "Latinas/os and U.S. Prisons: Trends and Challenges," *Latino Studies* 6.1–2 (2008): 11–34.

Morris, James McGrath, *Jailhouse Journalism: The Fourth Estate Behind Bars* (New Brunswick, NJ: Transaction Publishers, 2002).

Mosher, Clayton, Gregory Hooks, and Peter B. Wood, "Don't Build It Here: The Hype Versus the Reality of Prisons and Local Employment," in Tara Herivel and Paul Wright, eds., *Prison Profiteers: Who Makes Money from Mass Incarceration* (New York: New Press, 2007): 90–97.

Muhammad, Khalil Gibran, *The Condemnation of Blackness: Race, Crime, and the Making of Modern Urban America* (Cambridge, MA: Harvard University Press, 2010).

Muller, Christopher, "Northward Migration and the Rise of Racial Disparity in American Incarceration, 1880–1950," *American Journal of Sociology* 118.2 (2012): 281–326.

Muller, Christopher and Daniel Schrage, "Mass Imprisonment and Trust in the Law," *ANNALS of the American Academy of Political and Social Science* 651 (January 2014): 139–58.

Murakawa, Naomi, "Toothless: The Methamphetamine 'Epidemic,' 'Meth Mouth,' and the Racial Construction of Drug Scares," *Du Bois Review* 8.1 (2011): 219–28.

Murakawa, Naomi, *The First Civil Right: How Liberals Built Prison America* (New York: Oxford University Press, 2014).

Murch, Donna, *Living for the City: Migration, Education, and the Rise of the Black Panther Party in Oakland, California* (Chapel Hill: University of North Carolina Press, 2010).

Nagin, Daniel S., Francis T. Cullen, and Cheryl Lero Jonson, "Imprisonment and Reoffending," in Michael Tonry, ed., *Crime and Justice: A Review of Research*, v. 38 (Chicago: University of Chicago Press, 2009): 115–200.

Nazarian, Edith, "Crossing Over: Assessing Operation Streamline and the Rights of Immigrant Criminal Defendants at the Border," *Loyola of Los Angeles Law Review* 44 (2011): 1399–1430.

Nellis, Ashley, "Tinkering with Life: A Look at the Inappropriateness of Life Without Parole as an Alternative to the Death Penalty," *University of Miami Law Review* 67.2 (2013): 439–58.

Nobles, Matt R., Jill S. Levenson, and Tasha J. Youstin, "Effectiveness of Residence Restrictions in Preventing Sex Offense Recidivism," *Crime & Delinquency* 58.4 (2012): 491–51.

Nugent, Christopher, "Towards Balancing a New Immigration and Nationality Act: Enhanced Immigration Enforcement and Fair, Humane and Cost-Effective Treatment of Aliens," *University of Maryland Law Journal of Race, Religion, Gender, & Class* 5.2 (2005): 243–60.

Nunnally, Shayla C., *Trust in Black America: Race, Discrimination and Politics* (New York: NYU Press, 2012).

O'Connor, Alice, "The Privatized City: The Manhattan Institute, the Urban Crisis, and the Conservative Counterrevolution in New York," *Journal of Urban History* 34.2 (2008): 333–53.

Ogletree, Charles J., Jr., and Austin Sarat, eds., *Life Without Parole: America's New Death Penalty?* (New York: NYU Press, 2012).

O'Hear, Michael M., "The Beginning of the End for Life Without Parole?," *Federal Sentencing Reporter* 23.1 (2010): 1–9.

Oliver, Brian E., "My Sentence Is Over But Will My Punishment Ever End?," *Dialectical Anthropology* 34.4 (2010): 447–51.

Olshansky, S. Jay et al., "Differences in Life Expectancy Due to Race and Educational Differences Are Widening, and Many May Not Catch Up," *Health Affairs* 31.8 (2012): 1803–13.

Oshinsky, David M., *"Worse Than Slavery": Parchman Farm and the Ordeal of Jim Crow Justice* (New York: Free Press, 1996).

Owens, Michael Lee, "Ex-Felons' Organization-Based Political Work for Carceral Reforms," *ANNALS of the American Academy of Political and Social Science* 651 (January 2014): 256–65.

Paden, Catherine M., *Civil Rights Advocacy on Behalf of the Poor* (Philadelphia: University of Pennsylvania Press, 2011).

Padfield, Nicola, Dirk van Zyl Smit, and Frieder Dünkel, eds., *Release from Prison: European Policy and Practice* (Devon, UK: Willan, 2010).

Page, Joshua, "Eliminating the Enemy: The Import of Denying Prisoners Access to Higher Education in Clinton's America," *Punishment & Society* 6.4 (2004): 357–78.

Page, Joshua, "Fear of Change: Prisoner Officer Unions and the Perpetuation of the Penal Status Quo," *Criminology & Public Policy* 10.3 (2011): 735–70.

Page, Joshua, *The Toughest Beat: Politics, Punishment, and the Prison Officers Union in California* (New York: Oxford University Press, 2011).

Pager, Devah, *Marked: Race, Crime, and Finding Work in an Era of Mass Incarceration* (Chicago: University of Chicago Press, 2007).

Parker, Karen F., *Unequal Crime Decline: Theorizing Race, Urban Inequality, and Criminal Violence* (New York: NYU Press, 2008).

Patterson, Evelyn J., "The Dose-Response of Time Served in Prison on Mortality: New York State, 1989–2003," *American Journal of Public Health* 103.3 (2013): 523–28.

Peffley, Mark and Jon Hurwitz, *Justice in America: The Separate Realities of Blacks and Whites* (New York: Cambridge University Press).

Perkinson, Robert, *Texas Tough: The Rise of America's Prison Empire* (New York: Metropolitan Books, 2010).

Perrone, Dina and Travis C. Pratt, "Comparing the Quality of Confinement and Cost-Effectiveness of Public Versus Private Prisons: What We Know, Why We Do Not Know More, and Where to Go from Here," *Prison Journal* 833 (2003): 301–22.

Petersilia, Joan, *When Prisoners Come Home: Parole and Prisoner Reentry* (New York: Oxford University Press, 2003).

Petersilia, Joan, "From Cell to Society: Who Is Returning Home?," in Jeremy Travis and Christy Visher, eds., *Prisoner Reentry and Crime in America* (New York: Cambridge University Press, 2005): 15–49.

Petersilia, Joan, "Community Corrections: Probation, Parole, and Prisoner Reentry," in James Q. Wilson and Joan Petersilia, eds., *Crime and Public Policy* (New York: Oxford University Press, 2011): 499–531.

Petersilia, Joan and Joan Greenlick Snyder, "Looking Past the Hype: 10 Questions Everyone Should Ask About California's Realignment," *California Journal of Politics and Policy* 5.2 (2013): 266–306.

Petersilia, Joan and Susan Tucker, "Intensive Probation and Parole," in Michael Tonry, ed., *Crime and Justice: A Review of Research*, v. 17 (Chicago: University of Chicago Press, 1993): 281–335.

Peterson, Ruth D., "The Central Place of Race in Crime and Justice: The American Society of Criminology's Sutherland Address," *Criminology* 50.2 (2012): 303–27.

Peterson, Ruth D. and Lauren J. Krivo, *Neighborhood Crime and the Racial-Spatial Divide* (New York: Russell Sage Foundation, 2010).

Pettit, Becky, *Invisible Men: Mass Incarceration and the Myth of Black Progress* (New York: Russell Sage Foundation, 2012).

Pettus, Katherine I., *Felony Disenfranchisement in America: Historical Origins, Institutional Racism, and Modern Consequences* (New York: LFB Scholarly Publishing, 2005).

Pfaff, John F., "The Empirics of Prison Growth: A Critical Review and Path Forward," *Criminology* 98.2 (2008): 547–619.

Phelps, Michelle S., "Rehabilitation in the Punitive Era: The Gap Between Rhetoric and Reality," *Law & Society Review* 45.1 (2011): 33–68.

Pinard, Michael, "Collateral Consequences of Criminal Convictions: Confronting Issues of Race and Dignity," *N.Y.U. Law Review* 85 (2010): 457–534.

Pollack, Harold A. et al., "Substance Use among Welfare Recipients: Trends and Policy Responses," *Social Service Review* 76.2 (2002): 256–74.

Pollin, Robert and Jeff Thompson, "State and Municipal Alternatives to Austerity," *New Labor Forum* 20.3 (2011): 22–30.

Pomer, Marshall I., "Labor Market Structure, Intragenerational Mobility, and Discrimination: Black Male Advancement Out of Low-Paying Occupations, 1962–1973," *American Sociological Review* 51.54 (1986): 650–59.

Pranis, Kevin, "Doing Borrowed Time: The High Cost of Backdoor Prison Finance," in Tara Herivel and Paul Wright, eds., *Prison Profiteers: Who Makes Money from Mass Incarceration* (New York: New Press, 2007): 36–51.

Pratt, Daniel et al., "Suicide in Recently Released Prisoners: A Case-Control Study," *Psychological Medicine* 40.5 (2010): 827–35.

Prescott, J. J. and Jonah E. Rockoff, "Do Sex Offender Registration and Notification Laws Affect Criminal Behavior?," *Journal of Law & Economics* 54.1 (2011): 161–206.

Provine, Doris Marie, *Unequal Under the Law: Racism in the War on Drugs* (Chicago: University of Chicago Press, 2007).

Provine, Doris Marie and Roxanne Lynn Doty, "The Criminalization of Immigrants as a Racial Project," *Journal of Contemporary Criminal Justice* 27.3 (2011): 261–77.

Provine, Doris Marie et al., "Growing Tensions between Civic Membership and Enforcement in the Devolution of Immigration Control," in Charis E. Kubrin, Marjorie S. Zatz, and Ramiro Martínez, Jr., eds., *Punishing Immigrants: Policy, Politics, and Injustice* (New York: NYU Press, 2012): 42–61.

Raghunath, Raja, "A Promise the Nation Cannot Keep: What Prevents the Application of the Thirteenth Amendment in Prison?," *William & Mary Bill of Rights Journal* 18.2 (2009): 1–43.

Raphael, Steven and Michael A. Stoll, "Why Are So Many Americans in Prison?," in Steven Raphael and Michael A. Stoll, eds., *Do Prisons Make Us Safer? The Benefits and Costs of the Prison Boom* (New York: Russell Sage Foundation, 2009): 27–71.

Raphael, Steven and Michael A. Stoll, *Why Are So Many Americans in Prison?* (New York: Russell Sage Foundation, 2013).

Raphael, Steven and David F. Weiman, "The Impact of Local Labor-Market Conditions on the Likelihood that Parolees Are Returned to Custody," in Shawn Bushway, Michael A. Stoll, and David F. Weiman, eds., *Barriers to Reentry? The Labor Market for Released Prisoners in Post-Industrial America* (New York: Russell Sage Foundation, 2007): 304–32.

Reed, Adolph, Jr., "The 'Color Line' Then and Now: *The Souls of Black Folk* and the Changing Context of Black American Politics," in Adolph Reed, Jr. and Kenneth W. Warren, eds., *Renewing Black Intellectual History: The Ideological and Material Foundations of African American Thought* (Boulder, CO: Paradigm, 2010): 252–303.

Reed, Adolph, Jr., and Merlin Chowkwanyun, "Race, Class, Crisis: The Discourse of Racial Disparity and Its Analytical Discontents," in Leo Panitch, Gregory Albo, and Vivek Chibber, eds., *Socialist Register 2012: The Crisis and the Left* (New York: Monthly Review Press, 2011): 149–75.

Reed, Little Rock and Ivan Denisovich, "The American Correctional Association: A Conspiracy of Silence," in Bob Gaucher, ed., *Writing as Resistance: The Journal of Prisoners on Prisons Anthology, 1988-2002* (Toronto: Canadian Scholars' Press, 2002): 447–70.

Reiner, Robert, "Beyond Risk: A Lament for Social Democratic Criminology," in Tim Newburn and Paul Rock, eds., *The Politics of Crime Control: Essays in Honour of David Downes* (Oxford: Oxford University Press, 2006): 7–49.

Reiner, Robert, Sonia Livingstone, and Jessica Allen, "Casino Culture: Media and Crime in a Winner-Loser Society," in Kevin Stenson and Robert R. Sullivan, eds., *Crime, Risk and Justice: The Politics of Crime in Liberal Democracies* (Devon, UK: Willan, 2001): 174–94.

Reiter, Keramet A., "Parole, Snitch, or Die: California's Supermax Prisons and Prisoners, 1997-2007," *Punishment & Society* 14.5 (2012): 530–63.

Reitz, Kevin R., "Don't Blame Determinacy: U.S. Incarceration Growth Has Been Driven by Other Forces," *Texas Law Review* 84.7 (2006): 1787–97.

Rhine, Edward E., "The Present Status and Future Prospects of Parole Boards and Parole Supervision," in Joan Petersilia and Kevin Reitz, eds., *The Oxford Handbook of Sentencing and Corrections* (New York: Oxford University Press, 2012): 627–56.

Rhine, Edward E. and Anthony C. Thompson, "The Reentry Movement in Corrections: Resiliency, Fragility and Prospects," *Criminal Law Bulletin* 47.2 (2011): 177–209.

Rhodes, Lorna A., *Total Confinement: Madness and Reason in the Maximum Security Prison* (Berkeley: University of California Press, 2004).

Rikard, R.V. and Ed Rosenberg, "Aging Inmates: A Convergence of Trends in the American Criminal Justice System," *Journal of Correctional Health Care* 13.3 (2007): 150–62.

Riley, Russell, *The Presidency and the Politics of Racial Inequality* (New York: Columbia University Press, 1999).

Ritchie, Beth, *Arrested Justice: Black Women, Violence, and America's Prison Nation* (New York: NYU Press, 2012).

Roberts, Dorothy, "Constructing a Criminal Justice System Free of Racial Bias: An Abolitionist Framework, *Columbia Human Rights Law Review* 39.1 (2007): 261–85.

Robinson, Laurie O., "Exploring Certainty and Severity: Perspectives from a Federal Perch," *Criminology & Public Policy* 10.1 (2011): 85–92.

Rose, Nikolas, "The Death of the Social? Re-figuring the Territory of Government," *Economy and Society* 25.3 (1996): 327–56.

Rosen, David L., Victor J. Schoenbach, and David A. Wohl, "All-Cause and Cause-Specific Mortality Among Men Released from State Prison, 1980-2005," *American Journal of Public Health* 98.12 (2008): 2278–84.

Rosenfeld, Richard, "Crime Is the Problem: Homicide, Acquisitive Crime, and Economic Conditions," *Journal of Quantitative Criminology* 25.3 (2009): 287–306.

Rosenfeld, Richard, "Changing Crime Rates," in James Q. Wilson and Joan Petersilia, eds., *Crime and Public Policy* (New York: Oxford University Press, 2011): 559–88.

Rosenfeld, Richard and Robert Fornango, "The Impact of Economic Conditions on Robbery and Property Crime: The Role of Consumer Sentiment," *Criminology* 45.4 (2007): 735–69.

Rosenfeld, Richard and Steven F. Messner, "The Crime Drop in Comparative Perspective: The Impact of the Economy and Imprisonment on American and European Burglary Rates," *British Journal of Sociology* 60.3 (2009): 445–71.

Rosenfeld, Richard, Joel Wallman, and Robert Fornango, "The Contribution of Ex-Prisoners to Crime Rates," in Jeremy Travis and Christy Visher, eds., *Prisoner Reentry and Crime in America* (New York: Cambridge University Press, 2005): 80–104.

Roth, Randolph, *American Homicide* (Cambridge, MA: Belknap Press of Harvard University Press, 2012).

Rothman, David J., *The Discovery of the Asylum: Social Order and Disorder in the New Republic* (Boston: Little, Brown, and Co., 1990).

Rowan, Mark and Brian S. Kane, "Life Means Life, Maybe? An Analysis of Pennsylvania's Policy Toward Lifers," *Duquesne Law Review* 30.3 (1992): 661–80.

Ruckman, P. S., "Executive Clemency in the United States: Origins, Development, and Analysis (1900–93)," *Presidential Studies Quarterly* 27.2 (1997): 261.

Ruth, Henry and Kevin R. Reitz, *The Challenge of Crime: Rethinking Our Response* (Cambridge, MA: Harvard University Press, 2003).

Sabol, William J., "Local Labor-Market Conditions and Post-Prison Employment Experiences of Offenders Released from Ohio State Prisons," in Shawn Bushway, Michael A. Stoll, and David F. Weiman, eds., *Barriers to Reentry? The Labor Market for Released Prisoners in Post-Industrial America* (New York: Russell Sage Foundation, 2007): 257–303.

Sample, Lisa L., "Sexual Violence," in Michael Tonry, ed., *The Oxford Handbook of Crime and Public Policy* (New York: Oxford University Press, 2009): 51–70.

Sample, Lisa L. and Colleen Kadleck, "Sex Offender Laws: Legislators' Accounts of the Need for Policy," *Criminal Justice Policy Review* 19.1 (2008): 40–62.

Sampson, Robert J., "Urban Black Violence: The Effect of Male Joblessness and Family Disruption," *American Journal of Sociology* 93.2 (1987): 348–82.

Sampson, Robert J., "Rethinking Crime and Immigration," *Contexts* 7.1 (2008): 28–33.

Sampson, Robert J., "The Incarceration Ledger: Toward a New Era in Assessing Societal Consequences," *Criminology & Public Policy* 10.3 (2011): 819–28.

Sampson, Robert J. and Janet Lauritsen, "Racial and Ethnic Disparities in Crime and Criminal Justice in the United States," in Michael Tonry, ed., *Ethnicity, Crime, and Immigration: Comparative and Cross-National Perspectives* (Chicago: University of Chicago Press, 1997): 311–74.

Sampson, Robert J. and Charles Loeffler, "Punishment's Place: The Local Concentration of Mass Incarceration," *Daedalus* 139.3 (2010): 20–31.

Sampson, Robert J. and William Julius Wilson, "Toward a Theory of Race, Crime, and Urban Inequality," in John Hagan and Ruth Peterson, eds., *Crime and Inequality* (Stanford, CA: Stanford University Press, 1995): 37–54.

Sandler, Jeffrey C., Naomi Freeman, and Kelly M. Socia, "Does a Watched Pot Boil? A Time-Series Analysis of New York's Sex Offender Registration and Notification Law," *Psychology, Public Policy, and Law* 14.4 (2008): 284–302.

Saporu, Darlene F. et al., "Differential Benefits? Crime and Community Investments in Racially Distinct Neighborhoods," *Race and Justice* 1.1 (2011): 70–102.

Sarat, Austin, *Mercy on Trial: What It Means to Stop an Execution* (Princeton, NJ: Princeton University Press, 2005).

Sarat, Austin and Nasser Hussain, eds., *Forgiveness, Mercy, and Clemency* (Stanford, CA: Stanford University Press, 2006).

Sayed, Faiza W., "Challenging Detention: Why Immigrant Detainees Receive Less Process Than 'Enemy Combatants' and Why They Deserve More," *Columbia Law Review* 111 (2011): 1833–77.

Schartmueller, Doris, "Too Dangerous to Get Out? The Use of Individualized Release Mechanims for Lifetime Incarcerated Offenders in Sweden," *Criminal Justice Policy Review* 25.2 (2013): 1–25.

Scheingold, Stuart A., "Constructing the New Political Criminology: Power, Authority, and the Post-Liberal State," *Law and Social Inquiry* 23.4 (1998): 857–95.

Schlanger, Margo, "Inmate Litigation," *Harvard Law Review* 116.6 (2003): 1557–1706.

Schlanger, Margo, "*Plata v. Brown* and Realignment: Jails, Prisons, Courts, and Politics," *Harvard Civil Rights-Civil Liberties Law Review* 48.1 (2013): 165–215.

Schlanger, Margo, "Prison Segregation: Symposium Introduction and Preliminary Data on Racial Disparities," *Michigan Journal of Race & Law* 18.2 (2013): 241–50.

Schlanger, Margo and Giovanna Shay, "Preserving the Rule of Law in America's Jails and Prisons: The Case for Amending the Prison Litigation Reform Act," *University of Pennsylvania Journal of Constitutional Law* 11.1 (2008): 139–54.

Schlesinger, Traci, "The Failure of Race Neutral Policies: How Mandatory Terms and Sentencing Enhancements Contribute to Mass Racialized Incarceration," *Crime & Delinquency* 57.1 (2011): 56–81.

Schmitt, John and Janelle Jones, "America's 'New Class': A Profile of the Long-Term Unemployed," *New Labor Forum* 21.2 (2012): 57–65, 130–31.

Schnittker, Jason and Valerio Bacak, "A Mark of Disgrace or a Badge of Honor?: Subjective Status among Former Inmates," *Social Problems* 60.2 (2013): 234–54.

Schoenfeld, Heather, "The Politics of Prison Growth: From Chain Gangs to Work Release Centers and Supermax Prisons, Florida, 1955–2000," Northwestern University, PhD dissertation, 2009.

Schoenfeld, Heather, "Mass Incarceration and the Paradox of Prison Conditions Litigation," *Law & Society Review* 44.3–4 (2010): 731–68.

Schoenfeld, Heather, "Putting Politics in Penal Policy Reform," *Criminology & Public Policy* 10.3 (2011): 715–24.

Schuman, Howard, Charlotte Steeh, Lawrence Bobo, and Maria Krysan, *Racial Attitudes in America* (Cambridge, MA: Harvard University Press, 1997).

Sevigny, Eric L. and Jonathan P. Caulkins, "Kingpins or Mules: An Analysis of Drug Offenders Incarcerated in Federal and State Prisons," *Criminology & Public Policy* 3.3 (2004): 401–34.

Shalev, Sharon, *Controlling Risk Through Solitary Confinement* (Devon, UK: Willan, 2009)

Shichor, David and Michael J. Gilbert, eds., *Privatization in Criminal Justice: Past, Present, and Future* (Cincinnati, OH: Anderson Publishing, 2000).

Shklar, Judith N., *American Citizenship: The Quest for Inclusion* (Cambridge, MA: Harvard University Press, 1991).

Sigler, Mary, "Private Prisons, Public Functions, and the Meaning of Punishment," *Florida State University Law Review* 35.1 (2010): 1–29.

Simon, Jonathan, "Refugees in a Carceral Age: The Rebirth of Immigration Prisons in the United States," *Public Culture* 10.3 (1998): 577–607.

Simon, Jonathan, *Governing Through Crime: How the War on Crime Transformed American Democracy and Created a Culture of Fear* (New York: Oxford University Press, 2007).

Simon, Jonathan, "Dignity and Risk: The Long Road from *Graham v. Florida* to Abolition of Life without Parole," in Charles Ogletree, Jr., and Austin Sarat, eds., *Life Without Parole: America's New Death Penalty?* (New York: NYU Press, 2012): 282–310.

Simon, Jonathan, "The 'Hard Back' of Mass Incarceration: Fear, Structural Racism, and the Overpunishment of Violent Crime," in Deborah E. McDowell, Claudrena N. Harold, and Juan Battle, eds., *The Punitive Turn: New Approaches to Race and Incarceration* (Charlottesville: University of Virginia Press, 2013): 192–209.

Simon, Jonathan and Chrysanthi Leon, "The Third Wave: American Sex Offender Policies Since the 1990s," in Shlomo Giora Shoham, Ori Beck, and Martin Kett, eds., *The International Handbook of Penology and Criminal Justice* (Boca Raton, FL: CRC Press, 2008): 733–54.

Skocpol, Theda, *Diminished Democracy: From Membership to Management in American Civic Life* (Norman: University of Oklahoma Press, 2003).

Skowronek, Stephen, *The Politics Presidents Make: Leadership from John Adams to Bill Clinton* (Cambridge, MA: The Belknap Press of Harvard University Press, 1997).

Smith, Philip, *Punishment and Culture* (Chicago: University of Chicago Press, 2008).

Snodgrass, G. Matthew et al., "Does the Time Cause the Crime? An Examination of the Relationship Between Time Served and Reoffending in the Netherlands," *Criminology* 49.4 (2011): 1149–86.

Socia, Kelly M., "The Efficacy of County-Level Sex Offender Residence Restrictions in New York," *Crime & Delinquency* 58.4 (2012): 612–42.

Soothill, Keith, "Sex Offender Recidivism," in Michael Tonry, ed., *Crime and Justice: A Review of Research*, v. 39 (Chicago: University of Chicago Press, 2010): 145–211.

Soss, Joe, Richard C. Fording, and Sanford F. Schram, *Disciplining the Poor: Neoliberal Paternalism and the Persistent Power of Race* (Chicago: University of Chicago Press, 2011).

Sowle, Stephen D., "A Regime of Social Death: Criminal Punishment in the Age of Prisons," *NYU Review of Law and Social Change* 21.3 (1994–95): 497–565.

Spencer, Dale, "Sex Offender as Homo Sacer," *Punishment & Society* 11.2 (2009): 219–40.

Spohn, Cassia C., "Thirty Years of Sentencing Reform: The Quest for a Racially Neutral Sentencing Process," U.S. National Institute of Justice, ed., *Criminal Justice 2000*, v. 3 (Washington, DC: National Institute of Justice, 2000): 427–501.

Stabenow, Troy, "A Method for Careful Study: A Proposal for Reforming the Child Pornography Guidelines," *Federal Sentencing Reporter* 24.2 (2011): 108–36.

Stageman, Daniel, "Entry, Revisited," *Dialectical Anthropology* 34.4 (2010): 441–46.

Starr, Sonja B. and M. Marit Rehavi, "Mandatory Sentencing and Racial Disparity: Assessing the Role of Prosecutors and the Effects of *Booker*," *Yale Law Journal* 123.1 (2013): 2–80.

Steen, Sara, Traci Lacock, and Shelby McKinzey, "Unsettling the Discourse of Punishment? Competing Narratives of Reentry and the Possibilities for Change," *Punishment & Society* 14.1 (2012): 29–50.

Steiker, Carol S. and Jordan M. Steiker, "Should Abolitionists Support Legislative 'Reform' of the Death Penalty," *Ohio State Law Journal* 63.1 (2002) 417–32.

Stenson, Kevin, "Beyond Histories of the Present," *Economy and Society* 27.4 (1998): 333–52.

Stith, Kate, "The Arc of the Pendulum: Judges, Prosecutors, and the Exercise of Discretion," *Yale Law Journal* 117.7 (2008): 1420–97.

Stith, Kate, and José A. Cabranes, *Fear of Judging: Sentencing Guidelines in the Federal Courts* (Chicago: University of Chicago Press, 1998).

Stith, Kate and Steve Y. Koh, "The Politics of Sentencing Reform: The Legislative History of the Federal Sentencing Guidelines," *Wake Forest Law Review* 28 (1993): 223–90.

Strolovitch, Dara Z., *Affirmative Advocacy: Race, Class, and Gender in Interest Group Politics* (Chicago: University of Chicago Press, 2007).

Stumpf, Juliet, "The Crimmigration Crisis: Immigrants, Crime, and Sovereign Power," *American University Law Review* 56 (2006): 367–419.

Stuntz, William J., "Unequal Justice," *Harvard Law Review* 121.8 (2010): 1969–2040.

Stuntz, William J., *The Collapse of American Criminal Justice* (Cambridge, MA: Belknap Press of Harvard University Press, 2011).

Sutton, John R., "The Political Economy of Imprisonment in Affluent Western Democracies, 1960–1990," *American Sociological Review* 69.2 (2004): 170–89.

Sweeney, Maureen A., "Fact or Fiction: The Legal Construction of Immigration Removal for Crimes," *Yale Journal on Regulation* 27.1 (2010): 47–89.

Talvi, Silja J.A., *Women Behind Bars: The Crisis of Women in the U.S. Prison System* (Emeryville, CA: Seal Press, 2007).

Tate, Katherine, *What's Going On? Political Incorporation and the Transformation of Black Public Opinion* (Washington, DC: Georgetown University Press, 2010).

Tewksbury, Richard, "Collateral Consequences of Sex Offender Registration," *Journal of Contemporary Criminal Justice Research* 21.1 (2005): 67–81.

Tewksbury, Richard, "Exile at Home: The Unintended Collateral Consequences of Sex Offender Residency Restrictions," *Harvard Civil Rights-Civil Liberties Law Review* 42.2 (2007): 531–40.

Thompson, Heather Ann, "Why Mass Incarceration Matters: Rethinking Crisis, Decline, and Transformation in Postwar American History," *Journal of American History* 97.3 (2010): 703–34.

Thompson, Heather Ann, "Downsizing the Carceral State: The Policy Implications of Prison Guard Unions," *Criminology & Public Policy* 10.3 (2011): 771–79.

Thompson, Victor R. and Lawrence D. Bobo, "Thinking About Crime: Race and Lay Accounts of Lawbreaking Behavior," *ANNALS of the American Academy of Political and Social Science* 634.1 (2011): 16–38.

Tonry, Michael, "Racial Disparities Getting Worse in U.S. Prisons and Jails," in Michael Tonry and Kathleen Hatlestad, eds., *Sentencing Reform in Overcrowded Times: A Comparative Perspective* (New York: Oxford University Press, 1997): 220–27.

Tonry, Michael, "Determinants of Penal Policy," in Michael Tonry, ed., *Crime, Punishment, and Politics in Comparative Perspective—Crime and Justice: A Review of Research*, v. 36 (Chicago: University of Chicago Press, 2007): 1–48.

Tonry, Michael, "The Mostly Unintended Effects of Mandatory Penalties: Two Centuries of Consistent Findings," in Michael Tonry, ed., *Crime and Justice: A Review of Research*, v. 38 (Chicago: University of Chicago Press, 2009): 65–114.

Tonry, Michael, "Less Imprisonment Is No Doubt a Good Thing; More Policing Is Not," *Criminology & Public Policy* 10.1 (2011): 137–52.

Tonry, Michael, *Punishing Race: A Continuing American Dilemma* (New York: Oxford University Press, 2011).

Tonry, Michael and David A. Green, "Criminology and Public Policy," in Lucia Zedner and Andrew Ashworth, eds., *The Criminological Foundations of Penal Policy: Essays in Honour of Roger Hood* (Oxford: Oxford University Press, 2003): 485–525.

Tonry, Michael and Matthew Melewski, "The Malign Effects of Drug and Crime Control on Black Americans," in Michael Tonry, ed., *Crime and Justice: A Review of Research*, v. 37 (2008): 1–44.

Torrey, E. Fuller, *Out of the Shadows: Confronting America's Mental Illness Crisis* (New York: Wiley, 1997).

Traum, Anne R., "Mass Incarceration at Sentencing," *Hastings Law Journal* 64.2 (2013): 423–68.

Travis, Jeremy, *But They All Come Back: Facing the Challenges of Prisoner Reentry* (Washington, DC: Urban Institute, 2005).

Travis, Jeremy and Christy Visher, *Prisoner Reentry and Crime in America* (New York: Cambridge University Press, 2005).

Travis, Jeremy, Bruce Western, and Steve Redburn, eds., *The Growth of Incarceration in the United States: Exploring Causes and Consequences* (Washington, DC: National Academies Press, 2014).

Tucker, Susan B. and Eric Cadora, "Justice Reinvestment," *Ideas for an Open Society* 3.3 (2003): 2–5.

Tyler, John H. and Jeffrey R. Kling, "Prison-Based Education and Reentry in the Mainstream Labor Market," in Shawn Bushway, Michael A. Stoll, and David F. Weiman, eds., *Barriers to Reentry? The Labor Market for Released Prisoners in Post-Industrial America* (New York: Russell Sage Foundation, 2007): 227–56.

Uggen, Christopher, Jeff Manza, and Melissa Thompson, "Citizenship, Democracy, and the Civic Reintegration of Criminal Offenders," *ANNALS of the American Academy of Political & Social Science* 605 (May 2006): 281–310.

Uggen, Christopher, Sara Wakefield, and Bruce Western, "Work and Family Perspectives in Reentry," in Jeremy Travis and Christy Visher, eds., *Prisoner Reentry and Crime in America* (New York: Cambridge University Press, 2005): 209–37.

Unnever, James D., "Two Worlds Far Apart: Black-White Differences in Beliefs About Why African American Men Are Disproportionately Imprisoned," *Criminology* 46.2 (2008): 511–38.

Unnever, James D., "Race, Crime, and Public Opinion," in Sandra M. Bucerius and Michael Tonry, eds., *The Oxford Handbook of Ethnicity, Crime, and Immigration* (New York: Oxford University Press, 2014): 70–106.

Unnever, James D. and Francis T. Cullen, "The Social Sources of Americans' Punitiveness: A Test of Three Competing Models," *Criminology* 48.1 (2010): 99–129.

Unnever, James D., Francis T. Cullen, and Cheryl Lero Jonson, "Race, Racism, and Support for Capital Punishment" in Michael Tonry, ed., *Crime and Justice: A Review of Research*, v. 37 (Chicago: University of Chicago Press, 2008): 45–96.

Unnever, James D. and Shaun L. Gabbidon, *A Theory of African American Offending: Race, Racism, and Crime* (New York: Routledge, 2011).

Useem, Bert and Anne Morrison Piehl, *Prison State: The Challenge of Mass Incarceration* (New York: Cambridge University Press, 2008).

van Zyl Smit, Dirk, "Outlawing Irreducible Life Sentences: Europe on the Brink?," *Federal Sentencing Reporter* 23.1 (2010): 39–48.

van Zyl Smit, Dirk, "Regulation of Prison Conditions," in Michael Tonry, ed., *Crime and Justice: A Review of Research*, v. 39 (Chicago: University of Chicago Press, 2010): 501–63.

van Zyl Smit, Dirk and John R. Spencer, "The European Dimension to the Release of Sentenced Prisoners," in Nicola Padfield, Dirk van Zyl Smit, and Frieder Dünkel, eds., *Release from Prison: European Policy and Practice* (Devon, UK: Willan, 2010): 9–46.

Vásquez, Bob Edward, Sean Maddan, and Jeffrey T. Walker, "The Influence of Sex Offender Registration and Notification Laws in the United States," *Crime & Delinquency* 54.2 (2008): 175–92.

Vélez, María B. and Christopher J. Lyons, "Situating the Immigration and Neighborhood Crime Relationship Across Multiple Cities," in Charis E. Kubrin, Marjorie S. Zatz, and Ramiro Martínez, Jr., eds., *Punishing Immigrants: Policy, Politics, and Injustice* (New York: NYU Press, 2012): 159–77.

Visher, Christy A., "Returning Home: Emerging Findings and Policy Lessons about Prisoner Reentry," *Federal Sentencing Reporter* 20.2 (2007): 93–102.

Visher, Christy A. and Vera Kachnowski, "Finding Work on the Outside: Results from the 'Returning Home' Project in Chicago," in Shawn Bushway, Michael A. Stoll, and David F. Weiman, eds., *Barriers to Reentry? The Labor Market for Released Prisoners in Post-Industrial America* (New York: Russell Sage Foundation, 2007): 80–114.

von Hirsch, Andrew, *Doing Justice: The Choice of Punishments: Report of the Committee for the Study of Incarceration* (New York: Hill and Wang, 1976).

Wacquant, Loïc, "The New 'Peculiar Institution': On the Prison as Surrogate Ghetto," *Theoretical Criminology* 4.3 (2000): 377–89.

Wacquant, Loïc, *Punishing the Poor: The Neoliberal Government of Social Insecurity* (Durham, NC: Duke University Press, 2009).

Wacquant, Loïc, "Prisoner Reentry as Myth and Ceremony," *Dialectical Anthropology* 34.4 (2010): 605–20.

Wadhia, Shoba Sivaprasad, "The Policy and Politics of Immigrant Rights," *Temple Political & Civil Rights Law Review* 16.2 (2006–07): 387–421.

Wadsworth, Tim, "Is Immigration Responsible for the Crime Drop? An Assessment of Immigration on Changes in Violent Crime Between 1990 and 2000," *Social Science Quarterly* 91.2 (2010): 531–53.

Wagner, Peter, "Breaking the Census: Redistricting in an Era of Mass Incarceration," *William Mitchell Law Review* 38.4 (2012): 1241–60.

Walker, Samuel, *A Critical History of Police Reform* (Lexington, MA: Lexington Books, 1977).

Wang, Xia, Daniel P. Mears, and William D. Bales, "Race-Specific Employment Contexts and Recidivism," *Criminology* 48.4 (2010): 1171–1211.

Weaver, Timothy, "Neoliberalism in the Trenches: Urban Policy and Politics in the United States and the United Kingdom," University of Pennsylvania, PhD dissertation, 2012.

Weaver, Vesla M., "Frontlash: Race and the Development of Punitive Crime Policy," *Studies in American Political Development* 21.2 (2007): 230–65.

Weaver, Vesla M. and Amy E. Lerman, "Political Consequences of the Carceral State," *American Political Science Review* 104.4 (2010): 817–33.

Webster, Cheryl Marie and Anthony N. Doob, "America in a Larger World: The Future of the Penal Harm Movement," *Criminology & Public Policy* 7.3 (2008): 473–87.

Weiman, David F. and Christopher Weiss, "The Origins of Mass Incarceration in New York State: The Rockefeller Drug Laws and the Local War on Drugs," in Steven Raphael and Michael A. Stoll, eds., *Do Prisons Make Us Safer? The Benefits and Costs of the Prison Boom* (New York: Russell Sage Foundation): 73–116

Weisberg, Robert, "Deregulating Death," *Supreme Court Review* (1983): 305–95.

Werth, Robert, "The Construction and Stewardship of Responsible yet Precarious Subjects: Punitive Ideology, Rehabilitation, and 'Tough Love' Among Parole Personnel," *Punishment & Society* 15.3 (2013): 219–46.

Western, Bruce, *Punishment and Inequality in America* (New York: Russell Sage Foundation, 2006).

Western, Bruce and Katherine Beckett, "How Unregulated Is the U.S. Labor Market? The Penal System as a Labor Market Institution," *American Journal of Sociology* 104.4 (1999): 1030–60.

Western, Bruce, Meredith Kleykamp, and Jake Rosenfeld, "Crime, Punishment, and American Inequality" in Katherine Neckerman, ed., *Social Inequality* (New York: Russell Sage Foundation, 2004): 771–96.

Western, Bruce and Becky Pettit, "Incarceration and Social Inequality," *Daedalus* 139.3 (2010): 8–19.

Whitman, James Q., *Harsh Justice: Criminal Punishment and the Widening Divide between America and Europe* (New York: Oxford University Press, 2003).

Whittier, Nancy, *The Politics of Child Sexual Abuse: Emotion, Social Movements, and the State* (New York: Oxford University Press, 2009).

Williams, Linda Faye, "Race and the Politics of Social Policy," in Margaret Weir, ed., *The Social Divide: Political Parties and the Future of Activist Government* (Washington, DC and New York: Brookings Institution and Russell Sage Foundation, 1998): 417–63.

Wilson, David, *Inventing Black-on-Black Violence: Discourse, Space, and Representation* (New York: Syracuse University Press, 2005).

Wilson, William Julius, "The Declining Significance of Race: Revisited and Revised," *Daedalus* 140.2 (2011): 55–69.

Wong, Janelle, "Two Steps Forward: The Slow and Steady March toward Political Mobilization," *Du Bois Review* 4.2 (2007): 457–67.

Wong, Tom K., "287(g) and the Politics of Interior Immigration Control in the United States: Explaining Local Cooperation with Federal Immigration Authorities," *Journal of Ethnic and Migration Studies* 38.5 (2012): 737–56.

Wright, Julian H., Jr., "Life-without-Parole: An Alternative to Death or Not Much of a Life At All?," *Vanderbilt Law Review* 43 (March 1990): 529–68.

Young, Vernetta D. and Rebecca Reviere, *Women Behind Bars: Gender and Race in U.S. Prisons* (Boulder, CO: Lynne Rienner, 2006).

Yung, Corey Rayburn, "Banishment by a Thousand Laws: Residency Restrictions on Sex Offenders," *Washington University Law Review* 85.1 (2007): 101–60.

Yung, Corey Rayburn, "The Emerging Criminal War on Sex Offenders," *Harvard Civil Rights-Civil Liberties Law Review* 45.2 (2010): 435–81.

Yung, Corey Rayburn, "Sex Offender Exceptionalism and Preventive Detention," *Journal of Criminal Law & Criminology* 101.3 (2011): 969–1004.

Zandbergen, Paul A., Jill S. Levenson, and Timothy C. Hart, "Residential Proximity to Schools and Daycares: An Empirical Analysis of Sex Offense Recidivism," *Criminal Justice and Behavior* 37.5 (2010): 482–502.

Zatz, Marjorie S. and Hilary Smith, "Immigration, Crime, and Victimization: Rhetoric and Reality," *Annual Review of Law and Social Science* 8 (2012): 141–59.

Zilney, Laura J. and Lisa Anne Zilney, *Perverts and Predators: The Making of Sexual Offending Laws* (Lanham, MD: Rowman & Littlefield, 2009).

Zimring, Franklin E., "Imprisonment Rates and the New Politics of Criminal Punishment," *Punishment & Society* 3.1 (2001): 161–66.

Zimring, Franklin E., *The City That Became Safe: New York's Lessons for Urban Crime and Its Control* (New York: Oxford University Press, 2012).

Zimring, Franklin E. and Gordon Hawkins, *Incapacitation: Penal Confinement and the Restraint of Crime* (New York: Oxford University Press, 1995).

Zimring, Franklin E., Gordon Hawkins, and Sam Kamin, *Punishment and Democracy: Three Strikes and You're Out in California* (New York: Oxford University Press, 2001).

Zimring, Franklin E., Alex R. Piquero, and Wesley G. Jennings, "Sexual Delinquency in Racine," *Criminology & Public Policy* 6.3 (2007): 507–34.

Index

287(g) program, 226–27, 237, 238
2000 election, 245, 393n48
2008 election, 254, 280
"650-lifer law," 355n3
7UP, 348n165
9/11, 35
10–20–LIFE law, 135
10/6 law, 171, 178

abolition of capital punishment. *See* capital punishment
abolition of slavery, 274
Abraham, Lynne, 268
abortion, 112
Abu Ghraib prison, 135
ACA. *See* American Correctional Association or Affordable Care Act
ACLU (American Civil Liberties Union): and Byrne Grants, 33–34; and correctional health care, 74; and deaths of detained immigrants, 232; and felon disenfranchisement, 246; and Hutto Residential Center, 386n122; and Idaho Correctional Center, 337n9; and indigent defense, 289n53; and marijuana arrests, 127, 342n69; and prison-based gerrymandering, 256; and shackling of pregnant prisoners, 346n148
Adam Walsh Protection and Safety Act (2006), 203, 205–7, 368n5. *See also* SORNA
administrative procedure acts, 50, 72, 307n6, 318n175
administrative segregation. *See* supermax prisons
adoption, 285n8
Adoption and Safe Families Act of 1997, 285n8
ADX Florence (CO), 39, 273
affirmative advocacy, 275

Affordable Care Act (ACA) (2010), 113–15, 280, 335n115–16, 336n123
Afghanistan, 277
AFL-CIO, 393n43
Africa, 134
African Americans: and capital punishment, 124, 134, 153, 399n21; and carceral state, 4–7, 11, 14, 137–40, 142, 149–51, 153, 156–61, 242; and census, 141, 252; and crack–powder cocaine, 127–28, 130, 134–35, 153–54; 159, 170, 342n70; and crime, 126, 141–45, 156–58, 260, 275–79, 406n120; and criminal records, 243–44; and decline of civil society, 275–76, 409n148; and deindustrialization, 85–87; depoliticization of, 31; and deracialization strategies, 156; and drug offenses, 126–30, 134–35, 159, 170, 342n70 (*see also* war on drugs); and education, 86–87, 101, 146, 151, 155, 159, 242, 253; and employment, 85–86, 243–44, 253, 276, 323n49, 355n118, 407n131 (*see also* unemployment); and executive clemency, 187; and felon disenfranchisement, 245–46; and genocide, 151; growing cleavages among, 14, 15, 97, 150–51, 155, 157; and gun fatalities, 407n127; and homicide offenses, 125–26; as homicide victims, 276–77, 406n120; incarceration rates of, 4–5, 121–22; and inequality, 85–87, 155, 242, 251–55, 262, 275; and jury duty, 243, 391n13; and law-and-order politics, 137–61, 274; leadership of, 15, 152–59, 262; life expectancy of, 251, 339n34; and managing marginalization, 31; and organized labor, 275; and political incorporation of, 275–76, 409n148; and "politics of invisibility," 157; and "politics of respectability," 157,